W9-ASR-038

AMERICA'S TROUBLES

a casebook on social conflict

edited by

HOWARD E. FREEMAN

Brandeis University and Russell Sage Foundation

NORMAN R. KURTZ

Brandeis University

Prentice-Hall, Inc., Englewood Cliffs, New Jersey

13-032540-6
Library of Congress Catalog Card Number: 72-77300

Printed in the United States of America

Current Printing (last digit):
10   9   8   7   6   5   4   3   2

Prentice-Hall International, Inc., *London*
Prentice-Hall of Australia, Pty. Ltd., *Sydney*
Prentice-Hall of Canada, Ltd., *Toronto*
Prentice-Hall of India Private Ltd., *New Delhi*
Prentice-Hall of Japan, Inc., *Tokyo*

about the editors

HOWARD E. FREEMAN

Howard E. Freeman is Professor of Social Research at the Florence Heller Graduate School for Advanced Studies in Social Welfare of Brandeis University. He also holds an appointment as Sociologist with the Russell Sage Foundation of New York City.

Professor Freeman is editor of the *Journal of Health and Social Behavior* and is an advisory editor of the *Community Mental Health Journal.* In the past he was associate editor of *Social Problems* and of the *American Sociological Review.* He is a past chairman of the Medical Sociology Section of the American Sociological Association. In 1963, Dr. Freeman was co-winner of the Hofheimer Prize of the American Psychiatric Association for his book, *The Mental Patient Comes Home.* He also is co-author of *The Clinic Habit* and co-editor of *The Handbook of Medical Sociology.* His articles on deviant behavior, medical care, and mental health have appeared in a number of sociological, psychological, and health journals and handbooks.

NORMAN R. KURTZ

Norman R. Kurtz is Assistant Professor of Social Research at the Florence Heller Graduate School for Advanced Studies in Social Welfare, Brandeis University. He received his Ph.D. from the University of Colorado in 1966. Professor Kurtz's publications concern social processes and the problems of urbanization among minority groups.

contents

introduction

One of the most penetrating critics of community life in the United States, the late C. Wright Mills, characterized the decade of the fifties as an era of indifference and social restraint.[1] In contrast, current times are characterized by overt conflict and intense activity; it is a period of protest, of open hostility, and of explicit questioning of our basic social values.

Of course, some community members remain complacent about the current scheme of things. The self-interests of others cause them to resist any imaginative efforts at social change. Still others are dissatisfied with community conditions, but fail to exercise their privilege to critically evaluate the current social scene, and shirk their responsibility to advocate modifications in the existing social order. Policy makers, moral leaders, and social commentators quite properly are distressed by the large number of citizens who fail to participate in remedying the social problems confronting us. Nevertheless, the increased expressions of concern among political leaders, clergymen, business executives, educators, and representatives of other major social institutions, as well as the challenging activity of university students, black Americans, and other minorities, testify to the widespread and intense interest that exists in the social problems of today. Many persons in the community are outspoken and insist that the time has come to correct the injustices and inequities that pervade our society and the social problems that afflict its members.

Whether current concern with the problems of the social order is related to a worsening of social conditions is a matter of debate, and perhaps can be answered only in the future, in historical perspective. But the existence of widespread dissatisfaction is evident certainly in the violence, the riots, and the strikes that have occurred and that apparently will continue to erupt. It is indeed an era of open social conflict and a time for testing the values held inviolable by past generations.

Since the fifties the stance of sociologists also has changed markedly. Debates about so-called "objectivity" in the work of the social scientists have almost ceased.[2] Most sociologists have concluded that while it is possible to operate as scientists and to present social happenings objectively, what is studied and the actions taken in the face of research findings represent a commitment that cannot be value-free. Today the controversial question is: How far can the social scientist go in his efforts as an advocate of policies and programs and still remain identified with "the scientific community" and "intellectualism"; how much of his time and energy can he devote to his involvement in policy-making and practioner roles and still continue to produce the theoretical and analytical work of his scientific discipline?

Some social scientists exercise considerable restraint about participating in policy and program development directed at modification of the social order and amelioration of social problems. They do so on the grounds that such activity will minimize their opportunities to make long-range scientific contributions.

[1] C. Wright Mills, *The Sociological Imagination* (New York: Oxford University Press, 1959), pp. 8-13.

[2] See, for example, such recent discussions as Alvin W. Gouldner, "The Sociologist as Partisan: Sociology and the Welfare State," *The American Sociologist,* Vol. 3, No. 2 (May 1968), 103-17.

But it is increasingly difficult for the social scientist to adhere to admonitions that he should not overextend himself by taking on too many immediate-action oriented assignments.[3] Day-to-day engagements with individuals who occupy political and practitioner roles, and the major social conflicts that the social scientist sees everywhere in sharp focus demand his attention. In research and writing he deals increasingly with the immediate social concerns of the community. In these times, programs of restoration and rehabilitation are derived in a number of cases from his theories and from findings of investigations of the determinants of social ills. Increasingly, the orientations of some practioners and policy-makers today are rooted directly in the conceptual views and empirical research of the discipline of sociology.[4] While the cogency of the conceptual ideas and the craftsmanship of empirical studies in sociology are open to serious criticism and limitations as far as scientific endeavors go, this era of open social conflict has markedly influenced and hastened the application and use of whatever sociologists have available. The general acceptance of the sociologist and his tools and theories by persons searching for answers to community problems has further implicated the sociologist in the practical concerns of current social issues.

It remains to be seen whether the ideological and operational commitments necessary for such close involvement in the practical aspects of community problems are detrimental or beneficial to the development of a body of scientific knowledge about the community and its activities. Indeed, the moral and ethical concerns of the sociologist about problems of community life are not necessarily relevant to objective scientific inquiry and endeavor. The commitment to one side or another of the issue that often accompanies involvement in problem areas may complicate the process of developing systematic accounts of the social arena. Many sociologists today feel, and perhaps justly so, however that ethical and moral issues are imperative and that cold scientific concerns must take second place. It is felt by numerous sociologists that involvement in social action will not fatally hamper the progress of science.

Regardless of the position taken, it is clear that the function of a sociologist is to look at the social order, describe what is going on, and, if possible, offer some explanation of what is observed. Part of his responsibility as a student of social life is to provide a better understanding and to give a clear meaning to particular events in society. The sociologists' intense concern with contemporary issues has resulted in a wide variety of books, monographs, and journal articles expounding new or increasingly sophisticated explanations, providing more precise or additional empirical information, and offering innovative or new-sounding suggestions for social amelioration. Not only do colleagues direct documents to one another and at policy-makers and practitioners, there is also an increased emphasis on communicating the knowledge of sociology to students in

[3]Melvin M. Tumin, "In Dispraise of Loyalty," *Social Problems,* XV (Winter 1968), 267-79.

[4]Howard E. Freeman, "The Strategy of Social Policy Research," in *The Social Welfare Forum, 1963* (New York: Columbia University Press, 1963), pp. 143-56.

universities and to concerned community members.[5] A vast library of scholarly and technical works and a number of textbooks are concerned with current social problems, and there is a growing emphasis on popular reports and sociological explanations in the mass media.

Despite interest in the sociological enterprise among the general public, despite the closer contact of sociologists with the community, and despite an awareness of the need to put forth their knowledge, an examination of the problems of social conflict remains incomplete for most people. There is insufficient descriptive material available in an organized fashion about the social issues that are of major concern. It is simply not possible in the existing sociological literature to easily locate adequate descriptive accounts that permit an appreciation of the social problems confronting us.

The purpose of presenting this collection of cases on contemporary social conflict is modest. It is an attempt to provide a description of what is going on, an effort to provide a feeling for the social conflicts that currently occupy the attention of sociologists and community members alike. The notion that it is important to be in touch with the phenomena that one wishes to study is not a novel one. For instance, survey investigators almost invariably counsel each other to engage, at least in passing, in the collection of data themselves, and rarely do community researchers recommend analyzing information about a place they have never been.

Many investigators seek to become a part of the environment in which they are interested. For instance, one sociologist interested in mental illness became a "patient" in order to understand some of the problems of hospitalization.[6] Another sociologist, interested in gambling, felt it important to spend some time as a dealer in a Nevada casino. Of course, one can develop the principle of participation into an absurdity. The researcher cannot, or should not, always engage firsthand in the sociological events he is interested in studying. Students of marital conflict cannot marry every informant, and investigators of organized crime ordinarily do not join the underworld. Participating actively in everything studied is unusual, but many serious students of social phenomena attempt to understand "the action" by taking a semi-participant role and spending considerable time and energy in the hospitals, the slums, and the prisons they are studying, and by affiliating themselves with the delinquents, minority groups, and other "problem persons" that they are concerned about. Others seek to accomplish the same purposes by use of informants or experts who have been close to phenomena in which they are interested. Ideally, perhaps, all students of social conflict and of problems of deviance and disorganization in contemporary American society should be required to have an array of firsthand experience. But this sort of educational program is impractical because of the demands of time on the student, the difficulty of gaining access to many groups and

---

[5] *Trans-Action*, for example, now provides reports of social research in a manner easily digested by a broad audience.

[6] William Caudill, *The Mental Hospital as a Small Society* (Cambridge, Mass: Harvard University Press, 1958).

situations, and the problems of supervision during such experiences. An alternative is to provide, via the written word, accounts of various arenas of social conflict in contemporary society with as much of the tone, the emotion, and the feeling of the social events and processes as possible. The cases provided here, although secondhand accounts of what is going on, were selected to do just this, to provide a general background for understanding the nature and content of conflict in our society.

THE SELECTION OF CASES

In seeking to organize a series of cases which might serve as a means for appreciating contemporary social conditions and processes, it soon became clear that such cases were not likely to appear in scholarly sociological literature. Engaging descriptions of social conflicts by sociologists are scarce, suggesting, perhaps, how distant many in the discipline really are from their subject matter. Even more, this scarcity is a commentary on the style of sociologists, who rarely provide the data. Instead, they devote most of the pages they publish to interpretations of data that are stored in their files. It seemed useful, then, to have a set of descriptive reports. In presenting these cases, the concern is not to interpret the events; this task is the enterprise of the student and the professor.

Popular magazines, much more frequently than the sociological journals, have been the source of cases contained in this volume. Many of the accounts represent the work of newspaper and magazine reporters, some are autobiographical in nature. No pretense is made that the cases contained here represent unbiased and entirely objective reports. Working members of the communication media seek to interpret events according to their particular social and political orientations, and even when they are consciously attempting to provide an objective account, their social blinders remain at least partly intact. Sometimes in reading the various cases, it becomes obvious that the writers have sympathy or contempt for one or more of the parties involved. Moreover, the selection of the particular material included here naturally reflects the social and political concerns of the editors of this volume.

Although the goal of organizing this volume is simply that of providing an appreciation of contemporary social conflicts, an amount of conceptual development was required. Without it, the end result would have been a chaotic hodgepodge of more or less interesting tales. One of the issues confronted was the choice of the areas of social conflict to be represented in the volume.

The sociological literature presents a number of discussions of the characteristics of social problems and areas the student should concern himself with from an educational and research standpoint.[7] In seeking to identify social problems,

---

[7]Robert A. Nisbet, "The Study of Social Problems," in Robert K. Merton and Robert A. Nisbet, eds., *Contemporary Social Problems* (2nd ed.), (New York: Harcourt, Brace & World, Inc., 1966), pp. 1-26. Also, Howard S. Becker, ed., "Introduction," in *Social Problems: A Modern Approach* (New York: John Wiley & Sons, Inc., 1966), pp. 1-35.

analysts of social conditions and social relations emphasize different criteria in making their judgments. Some pay more attention than others to the extent to which behavior and conditions contradict traditions of our Judeo-Christian value system; some more than others are concerned with the degree to which behavior or conditions vary from the ways the majority of community members behave or from the conditions under which they live; still others use as criteria the actions and situations which provoke responses from social control agents, police, health and welfare agents, and so on.

In estimating the importance of one area of concern over another, the sociologist almost always, implicitly or explicitly, includes an evaluation of the extent to which the problem either challenges the stability of the social order, or minimizes the realization of the full potential for social development of community members, or results in rigidities in social life which stifle communal and personal opportunities for innovation and orderly social change.[8] A trend in sociology today is the explicit acknowledgment of the legitimacy of such value assessments by the sociologist. While there is hardly complete consensus among mature students of social problems on the conditions and behavior that are of most concern and that merit the most intensive scrutiny, there is a remarkable degree of congruence on what areas are included from one orderly analysis to the next.

Naturally, knowledge of the problems of social disorganization and deviance commonly considered in various textbooks has influenced the contents of this volume. But within the confines which come with a commitment to a discipline, the selection of cases in the volume also represents an empirical process. Once aware that it would be necessary to move out from the sociological literature in order to find the needed material, a relatively systematic review of a large body of popular literature was undertaken. It was possible to take into account, in selecting topics, the frequency that various behaviors and social conditions manifest themselves in magazines and other media widely circulated in the community.

Undoubtedly some readers will feel that problems of serious concern to the community and to social scientists have been omitted; we make no claim of comprehensiveness. The selections contained in this volume, however, are on topics that repeatedly occupy current concern, as reflected their appearance in periodicals responsive to the interests of persons in the general community. We do not want to be put in the position of arguing that what appears on the newsstand should be allowed to channel the activities of persons interested in social conflict, or of maintaining that the convergence between popular interests and topics typically covered in systematic reviews of social problems represents a definitive means of identifying the most relevant areas of social conflict. Nevertheless, the repeated discussions of these topics in the popular media and in the social problem texts provide some support for the notion that they are among today's most important issues.

[8] Robert K. Merton, "Social Problems and Sociological Theory," in Robert K. Merton and Robert A. Nisbet, *Contemporary Social Problems,* pp. 775-825.

THE CHARACTER OF SOCIAL CONFLICT

Sociologists and other social scientists who devote themselves to studying social processes and interpersonal relationships are constantly frustrated by the complex and often seemingly illusive causes of deviance and disorganization in contemporary America. Moreover, easy solutions to current social troubles in the United States are readily apparent only to those who stand back and avoid serious confrontations with the society's problems. Although efforts to unravel the determinants of conflicts in the social order have resulted in relatively sophisticated statements of possible domains of factors involved, their relative influence as causes of specific problems are not understood very well and can rarely be specified with precision. It is also difficult to identify those determinants of America's problems that are most vulnerable to modifications which might lead to the amelioration of social stresses.

Analysts of social life who undertake detailed empirical investigations and scholars who develop theories of social behavior have presented a large body of writings on the determinants or causes of social troubles. A continuing task of sociologists, and a major one, of course, is the development of theories of causation which take into account the total range of factors impinging upon the behavior of individuals and groups of individuals. Nevertheless, it should be emphasized that only limited inroads have been made in developing explanations for the various social problems in contemporary communities.

It is generally assumed that social conflicts stem from the interaction of what may be referred to as qualities of individuals and qualities of the social structure. The actions of community members, either in the various social roles they occupy or as represented by the collective behavior of organized groups, come into conflict with the behavior of other persons or organizations when there is a lack of congruence in the objectives of the parties or when one individual or organization regards certain acts or potential acts as detrimental to its place in the social order.

Although genetic, biological, and temperamental characteristics of single individuals are important, potential conflict stemming from these individual characteristics are mediated by the ways in which social life is structured. Most areas of social conflict represent interactions in which an individual's social characteristics, such as economic status, ethnic affiliation, or social prestige, are directly involved. Similar characteristics, while usually more ambiguously defined, also are involved in conflicts between organizations or between individual and organization. Interpersonal and interorganizational relationships are guided and sustained by a series of norms and values that reflect the commitments of individuals and groups; in the continuity of social life they become pervasive determinants of the behavior of community members. An individual internalizes them; they determine his actions as a member of the community. Groups in the community and the community in general regard these norms and values as being important to the maintenance of society and often do not question them. Consequently, both individuals in social roles and organized groups in collective behavior are deeply involved in safeguarding the norms and values that have endured and are held critical to the meaning and conduct of social life. Norms and values can be seen as the frameworks within which social realities are defined for individuals and organizations.

Social conflict is rooted in acts which violate norms and values regarded as important, often sacred, by individuals or organizations. Conflict may be provoked by individual or organizational actions which violate the informally expressed norms of aggregates of individuals or the formally stated ones of organization. Violations, whether perceived or real, are usually met with resistance. For example, an individual may risk life and limb to save his home from the threats of an organizational decision to renew the neighborhood in which he lives. An organization may invest great energy in fighting discrimination practiced by a powerful individual, even if that discrimination is only a potential threat. Often organizations devote their time to counteracting the influence of other organizations, such as the effort of dental groups interested in fluoridation and political groups ideologically opposed to such a measure. An individual may perceive that his welfare is threatened by another individual, as in the case of the victim of an aggressively deranged person. Conflict between such parties may arise not only when violations of norms and values actually occur, but also when they appear as a threat or when they occur to others in similar circumstances.

Our interest is not in what might be described as idiosyncratic social events, but in events which occur with some regularity and which are publicly defined as problematic for society. Thus, the focus on individuals in relation to a social problem may be in terms of the qualities they have in common, or the way they perform social roles, or the particular behavior roles they adopt, or the association they engage in which identifies them with the particular problem. Individuals may be a party to a social conflict because of the behavior they display in their day-to-day social roles as workers, students, parents, children, and the like. Others are identified with a problem because of ideas which community members hold about qualities they possess, qualities which may or may not be relevant to their place in the community, as in the case of being black, an adolescent, old, lower class, or physically handicapped. Still other individuals are regarded as parties to conflicts because of particularly unusual or abhorrent behavior they exhibit, such as homosexuality, mental illness, or prostitution.

It is possible, then, to focus on individuals, or more precisely, on individuals with identifiable qualities, behaviors, or roles. But it is also possible to look at organizational structures — the large number of communal groups in the community — and their involvement in social conflicts. All of us are familiar with the vast number of voluntary groups, fraternal societies, and corporate bodies that exist in the United States. Some of these structures represent aggregates of individuals who have organized themselves for a particular task or are interested in a common goal or set of goals. Another type of organizational structure exists at a more abstract level, a structure that sociologists refer to as the major institution or system in the community. The concept of social institutions or social systems represents efforts to delineate the various social aggregates which are generally acknowledged to be engaged in a set of common communal activities. The economic, political, educational, religious, and familial arrangements in the contemporary community, for example, may be thought of as organizations. Maintenance of social life and stability of the social order is predicated on a reasonable degree of implicit recognition of the legitimacy of the functions of such organizations. While all sociologists do not agree on the extent to which different communal tasks are the assignments of particular institutions, there is widespread acceptance of the idea that, as diffuse as such systems often appear, they constitute an essential part of the workings of the social order.

The community itself may also be conceptualized in the same structural terms. The community, as an organization, may refer to individuals living within a common political boundary who have loyalties and responsibilities to a particular political and social life. When the notion of the community as an organization is used here, however, it refers to more than the town we live or work in or the state we pay our taxes in or even the country as a whole. The concept of the community as an organization here refers to collectivities of persons who have a common place of residence, certain formal or defined sets of relationships with one another, and a psychological identification which is reinforced by adherence to such common elements as tradition, language, and the like.

It is perhaps obvious that, as in the use of the concept *individual,* the concept of an *organizational entity* defies a definition precise enough so that it is accessible across conceptual frameworks which rise out of different special interests. The concept can be defined only in terms of empirical observation that is relevant to specific concerns. Thus, some cases in this volume describe social conflict resulting from encounters individuals have with various voluntary, fraternal, or political groups, while others portray conflict between individuals and traditional societal institutions, and still others deal with their relations to community as a whole. Our interest is not with a particular organization, be it the American Rifle Association, Harvard University, or the city of Boise, Idaho. In a sociological sense, it is not important to concern oneself with organizations when they represent interesting social units; they are important because social conflict often stems from ways in which individuals engage with different types or organizations, and because social conflict can result from the discrepancies in means and goals between one organizational entity and another. Just as individuals are related to social conflicts because of certain qualities, their performance in social roles, and their unusual conduct, so too do aggregates of individuals—organizations—also become involved.

In many instances of social conflict the nature of the interaction is such that it is unclear who is the villain and who the victim or injured party, at least from the perspective of the pervasive norms of the American community. The paid killer of the Mafia who takes the life of a respectable businessman is an instance of social conflict in which most analysts would agree on the labels to be given to the parties involved. More often, however, conflicting norms are present, and the identification of the parties becomes much more shaky and dependent, to a considerable degree, on the perspectives of the analysts involved. How does one decide who is scoundrel and who the abused in the case of students who destroy university property while demonstrating against their educational conditions? Then too, there are instances in which protagonist and victim shift roles during the course of an event of social conflict, such as cases of ghetto residents who begin demonstrating in an orderly manner, are impeded by overzealous police, and end up looting and destroying the dwellings and businesses of apparently uninvolved parties. Nevertheless, looking at social conflicts as interactions in which one of the parties is more or less the initiator, the provocateur, the protagonist, while another is seen as the respondent, the party struck out against, the victim, makes it possible to organize case material in a way that insures some range of systematically selective material.

Thus, in each of the social problem areas considered in this volume, an effort is made to present four cases: a conflict in which an individual is the protagonist and another individual is the victim; a conflict in which the individual is protagonist and the organization the victim; a conflict in which the organization is the protagonist and the individual the victim; a conflict in which an organization is the protagonist and another organization is the victim.

A brief discussion will precede each social problem and will seek to identify the protagonists and victims in each case. It should be emphasized, however, that not all analysts of social conflict may agree with the identification of the particular party in each case as protagonist and the other as victim. Indeed, the reader must judge the matter for himself.

I

the
impoverished

The lack of economic wherewithal plays a critical role in a host of social problems, particularly in this age in which man's livelihood is no longer primarily dependent on his ability to produce the food and fiber necessary for existence, but on his ability to compete for the rewards of a technologically-oriented society. The concept of poverty refers to more than being at the bottom rung of the economic ladder; it includes other handicaps such as the lack of skills and know-how for survival in modern society. The reward system has produced sharp discrepancies between those who are "in" and enjoy the benefits of an affluent society, and the poor who are "out" and are often completely cut off from any opportunities to participate in activities which lead to needed goods and services.

Efforts to ameliorate poverty or to intervene in the processes which produce new generations of poverty seem restricted, perhaps because the most obvious solutions threaten the very structures and societal arrangements which promote the well-being of those members of society who are successful. Poverty is a structural and institutional problem, and it can be affected only by establishing new means by which members of society can qualify and compete for available rewards. This means that resources and wealth must be redistributed and allocation of rewards changed, and this, at the very least, will inconvenience those who have geared their industry and habits to traditional methods for success. But the increase of persons in nonproductive roles, the increase of costs of supporting them, and the increase of active dissatisfaction among the poor themselves presses for radical changes. The steps which society takes or fails to take are crucial. The decisions which are made will be a reflection of the willingness, the reluctance of the willingness, or the reluctance of affluent members of society to disrupt their lives with new ideas and personal sacrifices.

MAKING IT: THE BRUTAL BARGAIN

Although the view that it is possible for anyone in the United States to succeed is exaggerated, channels of upward mobility do exist for many. The struggling aspirant often experiences a wide variety of frustration, shame, and discomfort in the course of making it. In this case, the author reports on his experience of making it and the nature of a relationship with an individual whose interest in helping him may have been genuine, but could well be regarded as thoughtless and cruel. The experience, with its stress and strain, describes the often torturous personal relationships which are part of the process of moving out of poverty and lower-class status. How frequently must the poor who succeed stand ready to be the victims of the thoughtless criticism of those who would help them?

EVEN THE SAINTS CRY

The lives of the poor are often subjected to radical shifts in physical and social environments by well-meaning agencies. The young Puerto Rican mother that Oscar Lewis wrote about was moved from a disreputable slum to a much better housing project. The step upward, however, brought her into contact with a community which had norms and expectations strange and unfamiliar to her. The consequences of her engagement with the new community were, at the very least, unpleasant. Social skills acceptable and used in the slum antagonized persons in the new community. Her failure to fit in the new social milieu greatly deprived her in terms of social relationships; she was aware, however, of the material benefits of the new environ if she modified her behavior to conform with the community.

Organization	Organization
↓	↓
Individual	Organization

THE *WRONG* WAY TO FIND JOBS FOR NEGROES

While the lack of job skills is a central problem of the poor, they also suffer because they are unable to compete successfully on the job market in terms of the skills they do have. Although the case presented portrays the plight of a specific group of Negroes and a particular organization, the problems discussed relate more generally to all poor people. Organizational efforts to enter the life space of the poor are all too often derogatory and simply irrelevant to the world of social experience of the poor. They assume the presence of middle-class attributes and conduct often not found among the poverty class. In the end, many originally well-meaning persons become antagonistic toward the poor, as though this problem were one of individual failing rather than of social structure.

LAREDO LEARNS ABOUT THE WAR ON POVERTY

Accusations of inefficiency which are heaped on federal programs for intervention often represent efforts of conservative members of the community to disparage attempts at social change. It must be realized, however, that large-scale programs for altering the lives of individuals are often characterized by chaotic and inefficient organization. Gilmore's account of what went on in a "demonstration city" reveals the types of conflict generated between organizations engaged in the war on poverty. Such efforts can get bogged down in struggles between different community organizations which are interested in power and resources, while the poor people who provide justification for the activity remain relatively unaffected, without benefit and with additional shattered expectations.

making it:

the brutal

bargain

NORMAN PODHORETZ

One of the longest journeys in the world is the journey from Brooklyn to Manhattan— or at least from certain neighborhoods in Brooklyn to certain parts of Manhattan. I have made that journey, but it is not from the experience of having made it that I know how very great the distance is, for I started on the road many years before I realized what I was doing, and by the time I did realize it I was for all practical purposes already there. At so imperceptible a pace did I travel, and with so little awareness, that I never felt footsore or out of breath or weary at the thought of how far I still had to go. Yet whenever anyone who has remained back there where I started—remained not physically but socially and culturally, for the neighborhood is now a Negro ghetto and the Jews who have "remained" in it mostly reside in the less affluent areas of Long Island—whenever anyone like that happens into the world in which I now live with such perfect ease, I can see that in his eyes I have become a fully acculturated citizen of a country as foreign to him as China and infinitely more frightening.

That country is sometimes called the upper middle class; and indeed I am a member of that class, less by virtue of my income than by virtue of the way my speech is accented, the way I dress, the way I furnish my home, the way I entertain and am entertained, the way I educate my children—the way, quite simply, I look and I live. It appalls me to think what an immense transformation I had to work on myself in order to become what I have become: If I had known what I was doing I would surely not have been able to do it, I would surely not have wanted to. No wonder the choice had to be blind; there was a kind of treason in it—treason toward my family, treason toward my friends. In choosing the road I chose, I was pronouncing a judgment upon them, and the fact that they themselves concurred in the judgment makes the whole thing sadder but no less cruel.

When I say that the choice was blind, I mean that I was never aware—obviously not as a small child, certainly not as an adolescent, and not even as a young man already writing for publication and working on the staff of an important intellectual magazine in New York—how inextricably my "noblest" ambitions were tied to the vulgar desire to rise above the class into which I was born; nor did I understand to what an astonishing extent these ambitions were shaped and defined by the standards and values and tastes of the class into which I did not know I wanted to move. It is not that I was or am a social climber as that term is commonly used. High society interests me, if at all, only as a curiosity; I do not wish to be a member of it; and in any case, it is not, as I have learned from a small experience of contact with the very rich and fashionable, my "scene." Yet precisely because social climbing is not one of my vices (unless what might be called celebrity climbing, which very definitely *is* one of my vices, can be considered the contemporary variant of social climbing), I think there may be more than a merely personal significance in the fact that class has played so large a part both in my life and in my career.

But whether or not the significance is there, I feel certain that my long-time blindness to the part class was playing in my life was not altogether idiosyncratic. "Privilege," Robert L. Heilbroner has shrewdly observed in *The Limits of American Capitalism,* "is not an attribute we are accustomed to stress when we consider the construction of *our* social order." For a variety of reasons, says Heilbroner, "privilege under capitalism is much less 'visible,' especially to the favored groups, than privilege under other systems" like feudalism. This "invisibility" extends in America to class as well.

No one, of course, is so naïve as to believe that America is a classless society or that the force of egalitarianism—powerful as it has been in some respects—has ever been powerful enough to wipe out class distinctions altogether. There was a moment during the 1950s, to be sure, when social thought hovered on the brink of saying that the country had to all intents and purposes become a wholly middle-class society. But the emergence of the civil-rights movement in the 1960s and the concomitant discovery of the poor—to whom, in helping to discover them, Michael Harrington interestingly enough applied, in *The Other America,* the very word ("invisible") that Heilbroner later used with reference to the rich—has put at least a temporary end

to that kind of talk. And yet if class has become visible again, it is only in its grossest outlines—mainly, that is, in terms of income levels—and to the degree that manners and style of life are perceived as relevant at all, it is generally in the crudest of terms. There is something in us, it would seem, which resists the idea of class. Even our novelists, working in a genre for which class has traditionally been a supreme reality, are largely indifferent to it—which is to say, blind to its importance as a factor in the life of the individual.

In my own case, the blindness to class always expressed itself in an outright and very often belligerent refusal to believe that it had anything to do with me at all. I no longer remember when or in what form I first discovered that there was such a thing as class, but whenever it was and whatever form the discovery took, it could only have coincided with the recognition that criteria existed by which I and everyone I knew were stamped as inferior: we were in the *lower* class. This was not a proposition I was willing to accept, and my way of not accepting it was to dismiss the whole idea of class as a prissy triviality.

Given the fact that I had literary ambitions even as a small boy, it was inevitable that the issue of class would sooner or later arise for me with a sharpness it would never acquire for most of my friends. But given the fact also that I was on the whole very happy to be growing up where I was, that I was fiercely patriotic about Brownsville (the spawning ground of so many famous athletes and gangsters), and that I felt genuinely patronizing toward other neighborhoods (especially the "better" ones like Crown Heights and East Flatbush which seemed by comparison colorless and unexciting)—given the fact, in other words, that I was not, for all that I wrote poetry and read books, an "alienated" boy dreaming of escape, my confrontation with the issue of class would probably have come later rather than sooner if not for an English teacher in high school who decided that I was a gem in the rough and took it upon herself to polish me to as high a sheen as she could manage and I would permit.

I resisted—far less effectively, I can see now, than I then thought, though even then I knew that she was wearing me down far more than I would ever give her the satisfaction of admitting. Famous throughout the school for her altogether outspoken snobbery, which stopped short by only a hair (and sometimes did not stop short at all) of an old-fashioned kind of patrician anti-Semitism, Mrs. K. was also famous for being an extremely good teacher; indeed, I am sure that she saw no distinction between the hopeless task of teaching the proper use of English to the young Jewish barbarians whom fate had so unkindly deposited into her charge and the equally hopeless task of teaching them the proper "manners." (There were as many young Negro barbarians in her charge as Jewish ones, but I doubt that she could ever bring herself to pay very much attention to them. As she never hesitated to make clear, it was punishment enough for a woman of her background—her family was old-Brooklyn and, she would have us understand, extremely distinguished—to have fallen among the sons of East European immigrant Jews.)

For three years, from the age of thirteen to the age of sixteen, I was her special pet, though that word is scarcely adequate to suggest the intensity of the relationship which developed between us. It was a relationship right out of *The Corn Is Green,* which may, for all I know, have served as her model; at any rate, her objective was much the same as the Welsh teacher's in that play: she was determined that I should win a scholarship to Harvard. But whereas (an irony much to the point here) the problem the teacher had in *The Corn Is Green* with her coal-miner pupil in the traditional class society of Edwardian England was strictly academic, Mrs. K.'s problem with me in the putatively egalitarian society of New Deal America was strictly social. My grades were very high and would obviously remain so, but what would they avail me if I continued to go about looking and sounding like a "filthy little slum child" (the epithet she would invariably hurl at me whenever we had an argument about "manners")?

Childless herself, she worked on me like a dementedly ambitious mother with a somewhat recalcitrant son; married to a solemn and elderly man (she was then in her early forties or thereabouts), she treated me like a cruelly ungrateful adolescent lover on whom she had humiliatingly bestowed her favors. She flirted with me and flattered me, she scolded me and insulted me. Slum child, filthy little slum child, so beautiful a mind and so vulgar a personality, so exquisite in sensibility and so coarse in manner. What would she do with me, what would become of me if I persisted out of stubbornness and perversity in the disgusting ways they had taught me at home and on the streets?

To her the most offensive of these ways was the style in which I dressed: a T-shirt, tightly pegged pants and a red satin jacket with the legend "Cherokees, S.A.C." (social-athletic club) stitched in large white letters across the back. This was bad enough, but when on certain days I would appear in school wearing, as a particular ceremonial occasion required, a suit and tie, the sight of those immense padded shoulders and my white-on-white shirt would drive her to even greater heights of contempt and even lower depths of loving despair than usual. *Slum child, filthy little slum child.* I was beyond saving; I deserved no better than to wind up with all the other horrible little Jewboys in the gutter (by which she meant Brooklyn College). If only I would listen to her, the whole world could be mine: I could win a scholarship to Harvard, I could get to know the best people, I could grow up into a life of elegance and refinement and taste. Why was I so stupid as not to understand?

II

In those days it was very unusual, and possibly even against the rules, for teachers in public high schools to associate with their students after hours. Nevertheless, Mrs. K sometimes invited me to her home, a beautiful old brownstone located in what was perhaps the only section in the whole of Brooklyn fashionable enough to be intimidating. I would read her my poems and she would tell me about her family, about the schools she had gone to, about Vassar, about writers she had met, while her husband, of whom I was frightened to death and who to my utter astonishment turned out to be Jewish (but not, as Mrs. K. quite unnecessarily hastened to inform me, *my* kind of Jewish), sat stiffy and silent in an armchair across the room squinting at his newspaper through the first pince-nez I had ever seen outside the movies. He spoke to me but once, and that was after I had read Mrs. K. my tearful editorial for the school newspaper on the death of Roosevelt—an effusion which provoked him into a full five-minute harangue whose blasphemous contents would certainly have shocked me into insensibility if I had not been even more shocked to discover that he actually had a voice.

But Mrs. K. not only had me to her house; she also—what was even more unusual—took me out a few times, to the Frick Gallery and the Metropolitan Museum, and once to the theater, where we saw a dramatization of *The Late George Apley,* a play I imagine she deliberately chose with the not wholly mistaken idea that it would impress upon me the glories of aristocratic Boston.

One of our excursions into Manhattan I remember with particular vividness because she used it to bring the struggle between us to rather a dramatic head. The familiar argument began this time on the subway. Why, knowing that we would be spending the afternoon together "in public," had I come to school that morning improperly dressed? (I was, as usual, wearing my red satin club jacket over a white T-shirt.) She realized, of course, that I owned only one suit (this said not in compassion but in derision) and that my poor parents had, God only knew where, picked up the idea that it was too precious to be worn except at one of those bar mitzvahs I was always going to. Though why, if my parents were so worried about clothes, they had permitted me to buy a suit which made me look like a young hoodlum, she found it very difficult to imagine. Still, much as she would have been embarrassed to be seen in public with a boy whose parents allowed him to wear a zoot suit, she would have been somewhat less embarrassed than she was now by the ridiculous costume I had on. Had I no consideration for her? Had I no consideration for myself? Did I want everyone who laid eyes on me to think that I was nothing but an ill-bred little slum child?

My standard ploy in these arguments was to take the position that such things were of no concern to me: I was a poet and I had more important matters to think about than clothes. Besides, I would feel silly coming to school on an ordinary day dressed in a suit. Did Mrs. K want me to look like one of those "creeps" from Crown Heights who were all going to become doctors? This was usually an effective counter, since Mrs. K. despised her middle-class Jewish students even more than she did the "slum children," but probably because she was growing desperate at the thought of how I would strike a Harvard interviewer (it was my senior year), she did not respond according to form on that particular occasion.

"At least," she snapped, "they reflect well on their parents."

I was accustomed to her bantering gibes at my parents, and sensing, probably, that they arose out of jealousy, I was rarely troubled by them. But this one bothered me; it went beyond banter and I did not know how to deal with it. I remember flushing, but I cannot remember what if anything I said in protest. It was the beginning of a very bad afternoon for both of us.

We had been heading for the Museum of Modern Art, but as we got off the subway, Mrs. K. announced that she had changed her mind about the museum. She was going to show me something else instead, just down the street on Fifth Avenue. This mysterious "something else" to which we proceeded in silence turned out to be the college department of an expensive clothing store, De Pinna. I do not exaggerate when I say that an actual physical dread seized me as I followed her into the store. I had never been inside such a store; it was not a store, it was enemy territory, every inch of it mined with humiliations. "I am," Mrs. K. declared in the coldest human voice I hope I shall ever hear, "going to buy you a suit that you will be able to wear at your Harvard interview." I had guessed, of course, that this was what she had in mind, and even at fifteen I understood what a fantastic act of aggression she was planning to commit against my parents and asking me to participate in. Oh no, I said in a panic (suddenly realizing that I *wanted* her to buy me that suit), I can't, my mother wouldn't like it. "You can tell her it's a birthday present. Or else I will tell her. If I tell her, I'm sure she won't object." The idea of Mrs. K. meeting my mother was more than I could bear: my mother, who spoke with a Yiddish accent and whom, until that sickening moment, I had never known I was so ready to betray.

To my immense relief and my equally immense disappointment, we left the store, finally, without buying a suit, but it was not to be the end of clothing or "manners" for me that day—not yet. There was still the ordeal of a restaurant to go through. Where I came from, people rarely ate in restaurants, not so much because most of them were too poor to afford such a luxury—although most of them certainly were—as because eating in restaurants was not regarded as a luxury at all; it was, rather, a necessity to which bachelors were pitiably condemned. A home-cooked meal was assumed to be better than anything one could possibly get in a restaurant, and considering the class of restaurants in question (they were really diners or luncheonettes), the assumption was probably correct. In the case of my own family, myself included until my late teens, the business of going to restaurants was complicated by the fact that we observed the Jewish dietary laws, and except in certain neighborhoods, few places could be found which served kosher food; in midtown Manhattan in the 1940s, I believe there were only two and both were relatively expensive. All this is by way of explaining why I had had so little experience of restaurants up to the age of fifteen and why I grew apprehensive once more when Mrs. K. decided after we left De Pinna that we should have something to eat.

The restaurant she chose was not at all

an elegant one—I have, like a criminal, revisited it since—but it seemed very elegant indeed to me: enemy territory again, and this time a mine exploded in my face the minute I set foot through the door. The hostess was very sorry, but she could not seat the young gentleman without a coat and tie. If the lady wished, however, something could be arranged. The lady (visibly pleased by this unexpected—or was it expected?—object lesson) did wish, and the so recently defiant but by now utterly docile young gentleman was forthwith divested of his so recently beloved but by now thoroughly loathsome red satin jacket and provided with a much oversized white waiter's coat and a tie—which, there being no collar to a T-shirt, had to be worn around his bare neck. Thus attired, and with his face supplying the touch of red which had moments earlier been supplied by his jacket, he was led into the dinning room, there to be taught the importance of proper table manners through the same pedagogic instrumentality that had worked so well in impressing him with the importance of proper dress.

Like any other pedagogic technique, however, humiliation has its limits, and Mrs. K. was to make no further progress with it that day. For I had had enough, and I was not about to risk stepping on another mine. Knowing she would subject me to still more ridicule if I made a point of my revulsion at the prospect of eating non-kosher food, I resolved to let her order for me and then to feign lack of appetite or possibly even illness when the meal was served. She did order—duck for both of us, undoubtedly because it would be a hard dish for me to manage without using my fingers.

The two portions came in deep oval-shaped dishes, swimming in a brown sauce and each with a sprig of parsley sitting on top. I had not the faintest idea of what to do—should the food be eaten directly from the oval dish or not?—nor which of the many implements on the table to do it with. But remembering that Mrs. K. herself had once advised me to watch my hostess in such a situation and then to do exactly as she did, I sat perfectly still and waited for her to make the first move. Unfortunately, Mrs. K. also remembered having taught me that trick, and determined as she was that I should be given a lesson that would force me to mend my ways, she waited too. And so we both waited, chatting amiably, pretending not to notice the food while it sat there getting colder and colder by the minute. Thanks partly to the fact that I would probably have gagged on the duck if I had tried to eat it—dietary taboos are very powerful if one has been conditioned to them—I was prepared to wait forever. And, indeed, it was Mrs. K. who broke first.

"Why aren't you eating?" she suddenly said after something like fifteen minutes had passed. "Aren't you hungry?" Not very, I answered. "Well," she said, "I think we'd better eat. The food is getting cold." Whereupon, as I watched with great fascination, she deftly captured the sprig of parsley between the prongs of her serving fork, set it aside, took up her serving spoon and delicately used those two esoteric implements to transfer a piece of duck from the oval dish to her plate. I imitated the whole operation as best as I could, but not well enough to avoid splattering some partly congealed sauce onto my borrowed coat in the process. Still, things could have been worse, and having more or less successfully negotiated my way around that particular mine, I now had to cope with the problem of how to get out of eating the duck. But I need not have worried. Mrs. K. took one bite, pronounced it inedible (it must have been frozen by then), and called in quiet fury for the check.

Several months later, wearing an altered but respectably conservative suit which had been handed down to me in good condition by a bachelor uncle, I presented myself on two different occasions before interviewers from Harvard and from the Pulitizer Scholarship Committee. Some months after that, Mrs. K had her triumph: I won the Harvard scholarship on which her heart had been so passionately set. It was not, however, large enough to cover all expenses, and since my parents could not afford to make up the difference, I was unable to accept it. My parents felt wretched but not, I think, quite as wretched as Mrs. K. For a while it looked as though I would wind up in the "gutter" of Brooklyn College after all, but then the news arrived that I had also won a Pulitzer Scholarship which paid full tuition if used at Columbia, and a small stipend besides. Everyone was consoled, even Mrs. K. Columbia was at least in the Ivy League.

The last time I saw her was shortly before my graduation from Columbia and just after a story had appeared in the *Times* announcing that I had been awarded a fellowship which was to send me to Cambridge University. Mrs. K. had passionately wanted to see me in Cambridge, Massachusetts, but Cambridge, England, was even better. We met somewhere near Columbia for a drink, and her happiness over my fellowship, it seemed to me, was if anything exceeded by her delight at discovering that I now knew enough to know that the right thing to order in a cocktail lounge was a very dry martini with lemon peel, please.

III

Looking back now at the story of my relationship with Mrs. K. strictly in the context of the issue of class, what strikes me most sharply is the astonishing rudeness of this woman to whom "manners" were of such overriding concern. (This, as I have since had some occasion to notice is a fairly common characteristic among members of the class to which she belonged.) Though she would not have admitted it, good manners to Mrs. K. meant only one thing: conformity to a highly stylized set of surface habits and fashions which she took, quite as a matter of course, to be superior to all other styles of social behavior. But in what did their superiority consist? Were her "good" manners derived from or conducive to a greater moral sensitivity than the "bad" manners I had learned at home and on the streets of Brownsville? I rather doubt it. The "crude" behavior of my own parents, for example, was then and is still marked by a tactfulness and a delicacy that Mrs. K. simply could not have approached. It is not that she was incapable of tact and delicacy; in certain moods she was (and manners apart, she was an extraordinarily loving and generous woman). But such qualities were neither built into nor expressed by the system of manners under which she lived. She was fond of quoting Cardinal Newman's definition of a gentleman as a person who could be at ease in any company, yet if anything was clear about the manners she was trying to teach me, it was that they operated—not inadvertently but by deliberate design—to set one at ease *only* with others similarly trained and to cut off altogether from those who were not.

While I would have been unable to formulate it in those terms at the time, I think I must have understood perfectly well what Mrs. K. was attempting to communicate with all her talk about manners; if I had not understood it so well, I would not have resisted so fiercely. She was saying that because I was a talented boy, a better class of people stood ready to admit me into their ranks. But only on one condition: I had to signify by my general deportment that I acknowledged them as *superior* to the class of people among whom I happened to have been born. That was the bargain —take it or leave it. In resisting Mrs. K. where "manners" were concerned—just as I was later to resist many others—I was expressing my refusal to have any part of so brutal a bargain.

But the joke was on me, for what I did not understand—not in the least then and not for a long time afterward—was that in matters having to do with "art" and "culture" (the "life of the mind," as I learned to call it at Columbia), I was being offered the very same brutal bargain and accepting it with the wildest enthusiasm.

I have said that I did not, for all my bookishness, feel alienated as a boy, and this is certainly true. Far from dreaming of escape from Brownsville, I dreaded the thought of living anywhere else, and whenever my older sister, who hated the neighborhood, began begging my parents to move, it was invariably my howls of protest that kept them from giving in. For by the age of thirteen I had made it into the neighborhood big time, otherwise known as the Cherokees, S.A.C. It had by no means been easy for me, as a mediocre athlete and a notoriously good student, to win acceptance from a gang which prided itself mainly on its masculinity and its contempt for authority, but once this had been accomplished, down the drain went any reason I might earlier have had for thinking that life could be better in any other place. Not for nothing, then, did I wear that red satin jacket to school every day. It was my proudest possession, a badge of manly status, proving that I was not to be classified with the Crown Heights "creeps," even though my grades, like theirs, were high.

And yet, despite the Cherokees, it cannot be that I felt quite so securely at home in Brownsville as I remember thinking. The reason is that something extremely significant in this connection had happened to me by the time I first met Mrs. K.: without any conscious effort on my part, my speech had largely lost the characteristic neighborhood accent and was well on its way to becoming as neutrally American as I gather it now is.

Now whatever else may be involved in a nondeliberate change of accent, one thing is clear: it bespeaks a very high degree of detachment from the ethos of one's immediate surroundings. It is not a good ear alone, and perhaps not even a good ear at all, which enables a child to hear the difference between the way he and everyone else around him sound when they talk, and the way teachers and radio announcers—as it must have been in my case—sound. Most people, and especially most children, are entirely insensitive to such differences, which is why anyone who pays attention to these matters can, on the basis of a man's accent alone, often draw a reasonably accurate picture of his regional, social, and ethnic background. People who feel that they belong in their familiar surroundings—whether it be a place, a class, or a group—will invariably speak in the accent of those surroundings; in all likelihood, indeed, they will never have imagined any other possibility for themselves. Conversely, it is safe to assume that a person whose accent has undergone a radical change from childhood is a person who once had fantasies of escaping to some other world, whether or not they were ever realized.

But accent in America has more than a psychological or spiritual significance. "Her kerbstone English," said Henry

Higgins of Eliza Doolittle, "will keep her in the gutter to the end of her days." Most Americans probably respond with a sense of amused democractic superiority to the idea of a society in which so trivial a thing as accent can keep a man down, and it is a good measure of our blindness to the pervasive operations of class that there has been so little consciousness of the fact that America itself is such a society. While the broadly regional accents—New England, Midwestern, Southern—enjoy more or less equal status and will not affect the economic or social chances of those who speak in them, the opposite is still surely true of any accent identifiably influenced by Yiddish, Italian, Polish, Spanish—that is, the languages of the major post-Civil War immigrant groups (among which may be included American-Irish). A man with such an accent will no longer be confined, as once he would almost automatically have been, to the working class, but unless his life, both occupational and social, is lived strictly within the milieu in whose tone of voice he speaks, his accent will at the least operate as an obstacle to be overcome (if, for example, he is a school-teacher aspiring to be a principal), and at the most as an effective barrier to advancement (if, say, he is an engineer), let alone to entry into the governing elite of the country. (For better or worse, incidentally, these accents are not a temporary phenomenon destined to disappear with the passage of the generations, no more than ethnic consciousness itself is. I have heard third-generation American Jews of East European stock speaking with thicker accents than their parents.)

Clearly, then, while fancying myself altogether at home in the world into which I was born, I was not only more detached from it than I realized; I was also taking action—and of very fundamental kind—which would even-

tually make it possible for me to move into some other world. Yet I still did not recognize what I was doing—not in any such terms. My ambition was to be a great and famous poet, not to live in a different community, a different class, a different "world." If I had a concrete image of what greatness would mean socially, it was probably based on the famous professional boxer from our block who had moved to a more prosperous neighborhood but still spent his leisure time hanging around the corner candy store and the local poolroom with his old friends (among whom he could, of course, experience his fame far more sharply than he could have done among his newly acquired peers).

But to each career its own sociology. Boxers, unlike poets, do not undergo a cultural change in the process of becoming boxers, and if I was not brave enough or clever enough as a boy to see the distinction, others who knew me then were. "Ten years from now, you won't even want to talk to me, you won't even recognize me if you pass me on the street," was the kind of comment I frequently heard in my teens from women in the neighborhood, friends of my mother who were fond of me and nearly as proud as she was of the high grades I was getting in school and the prizes I was always winning. "That's crazy, you must be kidding," I would answer. They were not crazy and they were not kidding. They were simply better sociologists than I.

As, indeed, my mother herself was, for often in later years—after I had become a writer and an editor and was living only a subway ride away but in a style that was foreign to her and among people by whom she was intimidated—she would gaze wistfully at this strange creature, her son, and murmur, "I should have made him for a dentist," registering thereby her perception that whereas Jewish sons who grow up to be successes in certain occupations usually remain fixed in an accessible cultural ethos, sons, who grow up into literary success are transformed almost beyond recognition and distanced almost beyond a mother's reach. My mother wanted nothing so much as for me to be a success, to be respected and admired. But she did not imagine, I think, that she would only purchase the realization of her ambition at the price of my progressive estrangement from her and her ways. Perhaps it was my guilt at the first glimmerings of this knowledge which accounted for my repression of it and for the obstinacy of the struggle I waged over "manners" with Mrs. K.

For what seemed most of all to puzzle Mrs. K., who saw no distinction between taste in poetry and taste in clothes, was that I could see no connection between the two. Mrs. K. knew that a boy from Brownsville with a taste for Keats was not long for Brownsville, and moreover would in all probability end up in the social class to which she herself belonged. How could I have explained to her that I would only be able to leave Brownsville if I could maintain the illusion that my destination was a place in some mystical country of the spirit and not a place in the upper reaches of the American class structure?

Saint Paul, who was a Jew, conceived of salvation as a world in which there would be neither Jew nor Greek, and though he may well have been the first, he was very far from the last Jew to dream such a dream of transcendence—transcendence of the actual alternative categories with which reality so stingily presents us. Not to be Jewish, but not to be Christian either; not to be a worker, but not to be a boss either; not—if I may be forgiven for injecting this banality out of my own soul into so formidable a series of fantasies—to be a slum child but not to be a snob either. How could I have explained to Mrs. K. that wearing a suit from De Pinna would for me have been something like the social equivalent of a conversion to Christianity? And how could she have explained to me that there was no socially neutral ground to be found in the United States of America, and that a distaste for the surroundings in which I was bred, and ultimately (God forgive me) even for many of the people I loved—and so a new taste for other kinds of people—how could she have explained that all this was inexorably entailed in the logic of a taste for the poetry of Keats and the painting of Cézanne and the music of Mozart?

even the

saints cry

OSCAR LEWIS

This article describes the experiences of a young Puerto Rican mother, Cruz Rios, who moved from La Esmeralda— one of the oldest slums in San Juan only a short distance from the governor's palace—about four miles east to Villa Hermosa, a new government housing project in a middle-class section of Rio Piedras. Cruz' story illustrates the difficult problems of adjustment in her new environment and helps us understand why, in spite of the efforts of well-intentioned governments and the spending of huge sums of money on public housing, the positive effects hoped for by social planners are not always forthcoming.

When I began my study of Cruz in 1963, she was just 17 and living alone on relief with her two children. She lived in a small, dark, one-room apartment for which she paid a rental of eight dollars a month. Her kitchen was a tiny corner alcove equipped with a three-burner kerosene stove and a water faucet jutting out from the wall. She shared a run-down hall toilet with two other families and paid a neighbor $1.50 a month for the privilege of an extension cord which supplied her with electricity.

Cruz, a crippled, mulatto girl with reddish brown kinky hair and a pretty face, was lame since early childhood. She left school after the fifth grade, set up house with her sweetheart at 14 and gave birth to her first child at 15. Two years later, before the birth of her second child, she separated from her husband, Emilio, who refused to recognize the baby as his own.

Part I gives the reader a glimpse of living conditions in the slum; part II, recorded five months after Cruz had moved, gives her reactions to the housing projects. (Names of all places and people in this tape-recorded narrative have been changed to guarantee the anonymity of the narrator.)

I

Here is La Esmeralda, the only thing that disturbs me are the rats. Lice, bedbugs, and rats have always been a problem in my room. When I moved in here a year ago, the first thing I found were little baby rats. "Kill them!" my friend Gloria said. "Ay Bendito! I can't do it. Poor little things—they look like children," I said, and I left them there in a hole. The next day they were gone. I didn't kill them, they just disappeared. I cleaned up the house and about a month later they were going back and forth through the room from one hole to another, with me just looking at them.

When Alejandro was living with me, more rats came because there was a hen with eggs under the house. A rat had given birth and had eaten some of the chicks. The owner took the hen and 29 chicks out of there because there were baby rats underneath the hen too. The man threw them out but a week later they came back and were all over the place, even getting into the pan with the baby's milk and eating up whatever I left around.

One Sunday my *mamá* said, "Let's buy a rat trap and see if we can't get rid of some of them." Well, we tried it and that day between us and the next-door neighbor we caught 29 little rats. After a while, more came. Anita used to chase them across the room to see if she could catch them, and the boys who came to the house would say, "Look, a rat."

I would tell them, "Let it be, it's one of the family. They keep me company, now that I'm all by myself. I'm raising them for soup."

So I left them alone, but before I knew it, there were great big rats here. One Sunday I said to Catin, who had just eaten a breaded cutlet, "Catin, you'd better go bathe or the rats will eat you up." Then I forgot about it and she lay down. Later I took a bath and went to bed. About midnight, Catin screamed, *Ay, ay, ay,* it bit me!" The first thing that came to my mind was that it was a snake or a scorpion. "What bit you?" I asked and when I turned on the light, she said, "Look, look!" and I could see a rat running away.

She had been bitten on the arm and I could see the little teeth marks. I squeezed out the blood and smeared urine and bay rum on it.

Then I said, "Catin, you'd better come into my bed with me. God knows whether it was because the crib is dirty or you are dirty." I was wearing only panties, Chuito and Anita were naked, but Catin was wearing a jacket and pants. Well, later that same rat came and bit her again on the other arm. I sprinkled bay rum all over the bed where she was sleeping and rubbed it on her and nothing else happened that night.

The next day I went to the church and told the Sister that the girl had been bitten by a rat. She told me that if Catin didn't start running a fever, to leave her alone, and if she did, to take her to the hospital. Then I said to Catin, "You see? That's what happens when you don't bathe." She took a bath every day after that.

At the end of the year, Anita got a rat bite on the lip. I squeezed it out for her and it dried up and she didn't get a fever or anything. A few days after that, I was sitting in a chair with my arm hanging down when a rat came and *pra!* it tried to take off my finger. It wanted human flesh. I lifted my hand, and the rat ran to a hole and disappeared.

Then I said to myself, "These rats have to be finished off. I can't live like this with so many blessed rats. There are more rats than people." And I bought a trap from the man next door. I fixed the bacon myself and put it in the trap. First I caught a real big rat, then another, and another. Three in all that same night. But there were still more left.

The next morning, I heard screams coming from Rosa Maria's room up above. I said, "Rosa, what's wrong?" Her little boy was crying and shaking his hand, with a rat hanging from it. "Kill it," I said, but he answered, "I can't. Its teeth are stuck in my finger." Finally he got if off by dragging it along the floor.

Rosa Maria attended him but the next day the child had a fever which kept going up. The doctor said that the boy was getting tetanus and had to go to the hospital.

The people upstairs leave a lot of rotting clothes piled there, and cans of food and rice. If they don't get rid of that filth, the rats won't leave. I asked the landlord to cover the holes because the rats keep coming in and out as if they were in a bus terminal. He said he didn't live here and I should do it myself.

There are lots of cockroaches in my room too. And new fleas have come in, I don't know from where, except probably from the rats themselves. There are also crickets and lizards. These houses are hollow underneath, and below the floor there's a lot of old boards and filth and all kinds of garbage that has accumulated, and at night the animals come crawling up.

I've noticed that it's on Thursday nights that the rats give us the most trouble. Every other Thursday, before the social worker comes, I clean my house from top to bottom so there are no crumbs on the floor for the rats to eat and no dirty dishes for them to clean. I've learned that unless I leave something for them, the rats come closer and closer to us. When the house is clean, we are in more danger of getting bitten.

II

The social worker told me it would be a good idea to get the children out of La Esmeralda because there's so much delinquency there. My moving to the housing project was practically her idea; she insisted and insisted. Finally one day she came to me and said, "Tomorrow you have to move to the *caserio* in Villa Hermosa." I didn't want to upset her because she's been good to me, so I said okay.

You should have seen this place when I moved in. It was bursting with garbage and smelling of shit, pure shit. Imagine, when the social worker opened the door that first day, a breeze happened to blow her way. She stepped back and said, "Wait, I can't go in. This is barbarous." I had to go outside with her. I tell you, the people who lived here before me were dirtier than the dirtiest pig. When I moved out of my little room in La Esmeralda, I scrubbed it so clean you could have eaten off the floor. Whoever moved in could see that a decent person had lived there. And then I came here and found this pig-sty, and the place looked so big I felt too little and weak to get it clean. So, fool that I am, instead of sending out for a mop and getting right down to work, I just stood in a corner and cried. I locked the door and stayed in all day, weeping. I cried floods.

And this place isn't like La Esmeralda, you know, where there's so much liveliness and noise and something is always going on. Here you never see any movement on the street, not one little domino or card game or anything. The place is dead. People act as if they're angry or in mourning. Either they don't know how to live or they're afraid to. And yet it's full of shameless good-for-nothings. It's true what the proverb says, "May God deliver me from quiet places; I can defend myself in the wild ones."

Everything was so strange to me when I first moved here that I was scared to death. I hated to go out because it's hard to find your way back to this place even if you know the address. The first couple of times I got lost, and I didn't dare ask anybody the way for fear they would fall on me and beat me. If anyone knocked on my door I thought four times before deciding to open it. Then when I did, I took a knife along. But I'm not like that any more. I've made my decision: if someone wants to kill me, let him. I can't live shut in like that. And if anybody interferes with me it will be the worse for them. I have a couple of tricks up my sleeve and can really fuck things up for anybody when I want to.

After a few days, I finally started cleaning up the place. I scrubbed the floors and put everything in order. I even painted the whole apartment, although I had to fight tooth and nail with the man in charge of the buildings in order to get the paint. That old man wanted to get something from me in return, but I wouldn't give it to him. I never have been attracted to old men.

The apartment is a good one. I have a living room, bedroom, kitchen, porch and my own private bathroom. That's something I never had in La Esmeralda. I clean it every morning and when the children use it I go and pull the chain right away.

I never had a kitchen sink in La Esmeralda either, and here I have a brand new one. It's easy to wash the dishes in these double sinks because they're so wide and comfortable. The only trouble is the water, because sometimes it goes off and the electricity, too—three times since I've been here.

I still don't have an ice-box or refrigerator but the stove here is the first electric one I've ever had in my life. I didn't know how to light it the day I moved in. I tried everything I could think of, backward and forward. Luckily, the social worker came and she lit it for me, but even so I didn't learn and Nanda had to show me again that afternoon. She has worked for rich people so long that she knows all those things. I really miss my own little kerosene stove, but Nanda wanted it, so what could I do? She's my *mamá* and if she hankered after a star I would climb up to heaven to get it for her if I could.

The main advantage of the electric

stove is that when I have a lot of work to do and it gets to be ten or eleven o'clock, I just connect the stove and have lunch ready in no time. In La Esmeralda I had to wait for the kerosene to light up well before I could even start to cook. And this stove doesn't smoke and leave soot all over the place, either. Still, if the power fails again or is cut off because I don't pay my bill, the kids will just have to go hungry. I won't even be able to heat a cup of milk for them. In La Esmeralda, whenever I didn't have a quarter to buy a full gallon of kerosene, I got ten cents worth. But who's going to sell you five or ten cents worth of electricity?

I haven't seen any rats here, just one tiny little mouse. It doesn't bother me much because it lives down below, in a hole at the bottom of the stairs. There's no lack of company anywhere, I guess—rats in La Esmeralda and lots of little cockroaches here.

This apartment is so big that I don't have to knock myself out keeping it in order. There's plenty of room for my junk. I even have closets here, and lots of shelves. I have so many shelves and so few dishes that I have to put a dish here and a dish there just to keep each shelf from being completely empty. All the counters and things are no use at all to me, because I just cook a bit of oatmeal for the children and let them sit anywhere to eat it since I have no dishes with which to set a table. Half of my plates broke on the way from La Esmeralda. I guess they wanted to stay back there where they weren't so lonely.

Here even my saints cry! They look so sad. They think I am punishing them. This house is so big I had to separate the saints and hang them up in different places just to cover the empty walls. In La Esmeralda I kept them all together to form a little altar, and I lit candles for them. In La Esmeralda they helped me, but here I ask until I'm tired of asking

and they don't help me at all. They are punishing me.

In La Esmeralda I never seemed to need as many things as here. I think it is because we all had about the same, so we didn't need any more. But here, when you go to other people's apartment and see all their things . . . It's not that I'm jealous. God forbid! I don't want anyone to have less than they have. It's only that I would like to have things of my own too.

What does bother me is the way people here come into my apartment and furnish the place with their mouths. They start saying, "Oh, here's where the set of furniture should go; you need a TV set in that corner and this one is just right for a record-player." And so on. I bite my tongue to keep from swearing at them because, damn it, I have good taste too. I know a TV set would look fine in that corner, but if I don't have the money to buy one, how can I put it there? That's what I like about La Esmeralda—if people there could help someone, they did; if not, they kept their mouths shut.

I really would like a TV though, because they don't have public sets here, the way they do in La Esmeralda. I filled in some blanks for that program, Queen for a Day, to see if I can get one as a gift. It was Nanda's idea and she's so lucky that maybe I will get it. If I do, then at least I could spend the holidays looking at TV. And the children might stay home instead of wandering around the neighborhood so much.

The traffic here really scares me. That's the main reason I don't like this place. Cars scud by like clouds in a high wind and, I'm telling you, I'm always afraid a car will hit the children. If something should happen to my little penguins, I'd go mad, I swear I would. My kids are little devils, and when I bring them in through the front door, they slip out again by climbing over the porch railing. Back in La Esmeralda, where our house was so small, they had to play out in the street whenever people came over, but here there is plenty of room to run around indoors.

Maybe I was better off in La Esmeralda. You certainly have to pay for the comforts you have here! Listen, I'm jittery, really nervous, because if you fail to pay the rent even once here, the following month you're thrown out. I hardly ever got behind on my payments in La Esmeralda, but if I did, I knew that they wouldn't put me out on the street. It's true that my rent is only $6.50 a month here while I paid $11.50 in La Esmeralda, but there I didn't have a water bill and I paid only $1.50 a month for electricity. Here I have already had to pay $3.50 for electricity and if I use more than the minimum they allow in water, I'll have to pay for that too. And I do so much washing!

It's a fact that as long as I lived in La Esmeralda I could always scare up some money, but here I'm always broke. I've gone as much as two days without eating. I don't play the races at El Comandante any more. I can't afford to. And I can't sell *bolita* numbers here because several cops live in this *caserio* and the place is full of detectives. Only the other day I almost sold a number to one of them, but luckily I was warned in time. I don't want to be arrested for anything in the world, not because I'm scared of being in jail but because of the children.

Since I can't sell numbers here, I sell Avon cosmetics, I like the pretty sets of china they give away, and I'm trying to sell a lot so that they'll give me one. But there's hardly any profit in it for me.

In La Esmeralda I could get an old man now and then to give me five dollars for sleeping with him. But here I haven't found anything like that at all. The truth is, if a man comes here and tries to strike up a conversation I usually slam the door in his face. So, well, I have this beautiful, clean apartment, but what good does it do me? Where am I to get money? I can't dig for it.

In La Esmeralda we used to buy things cheap from thieves. They stole from people who lived far away and then they came to La Esmeralda through one of the side entrances to sell. And who the hell is going to go looking for his things down there? Not a chance! You hardly ever saw a rich person in La Esmeralda. We didn't like them, and we scared them off. But so far as I can tell, these dopes around here always steal from the *blanquitos,* the rich people, nearby. Suppose one of them took it into his head to come here to look for the missing stuff? What then?

Since I've moved I'm worse off than I have ever been before, because now I realize all the things I lack and, besides, the rich people around here are always wanting everything for themselves. In La Esmeralda you can bum a nickel from anyone. But with these people, the more they have, the more they want. It's everything for themselves. If you ask them for work, they'll find something for you to do fast enough, but when it's time to pay you'd think it hurt them to pull a dollar out of their pocket.

Listen, to get a few beans from some people who live in a house near here I had to help pick and shell them. People here are real hard and stingy. What's worse, they take advantage of you. The other day I ironed all day long for a woman and all I got for it was two dollars and my dinner. I felt like throwing the money in her face but I just calmly took it. I would have been paid six dollars at the very least for a whole day's ironing in La Esmeralda. At another lady's house near here I cooked, washed the dishes, even scrubbed the floor, and for all that she just gave me one of her old dresses, which I can't even wear because it's too big for me.

Right now, I don't have a cent. The lady next door lets me charge the food for breakfast at her husband's *kiosko*. She's become so fond of me, you can't imagine. Her husband won't sell on credit to anybody, but there's nothing impossible for the person who is really interested in helping you out. She trusts me, so she lets me write down what I take and keep the account myself.

I buy most of my food at the Villa Hermosa grocery. It's a long way from here and I have to walk it on foot every time I need something, like rice or tomato sauce. It's a supermarket, so they don't give credit, but everything is cheaper there, much cheaper. A can of tomato sauce costs seven cents there and 10 cents in La Esmeralda. Ten pounds of rice costs $1.25 in La Esmeralda and 99 cents here. The small bottles of King Pine that cost 15 cents each in La Esmeralda are two for a quarter here.

Sometimes Public Welfare gives me food, but not always, and I don't like most of the things they give. That long-grained rice doesn't taste like anything. It's like eating hay. The meat they give has fat on top and it comes in a can and it's real dark. They say it's corned beef but I don't know. The same goes for that powdered milk. Who could drink the stuff? In La Esmeralda I saved it until I was really hard up and then I sold it to anybody who was willing to shell out a quarter for it to feed it to their animals or something. But I don't dare do that here because it's federal government food, and it's against the law to sell it. I could get into trouble that way in a place like this, where I don't know anybody. I might try to sell that stuff to a detective without realizing who he was and I'd land in jail.

I haven't been to La Esmeralda often since I moved here, because I can't afford it. Every trip costs 40 cents, 20 cents each way. I want to pay off all my debts in La Esmeralda so that I can hold my head high and proud when I go there. I want people to think I've bettered myself because one can't be screwed all one's life. Even now when I visit, still owing money as I do, I put on my best clothes and always try to carry a little cash. I do this so Minerva, Emilio's aunt, won't get the idea I'm starving or anything like that. She really suffers when she sees me in La Esmeralda, and I do all that just to bother her. I dress up the kids real nice and take them to call on everybody except her.

When I first moved out of La Esmeralda, nobody knew that I was leaving, in the first place because it made me sad and in the second place because that old Minerva had gone around telling everybody she hoped I'd clear out. She even said it to my face. I'd yell back at her, "What right do you have to say that? Did you buy La Esmeralda or something?"

Another reason why I hardly ever go to La Esmeralda is because Emilio spies on me. He has come after me in the *caserio* just the way he did in La Esmeralda, though not as often. He likes to use the shower in my new apartment when he comes. When I start home after visiting La Esmeralda, he gets into his car and drives along behind me, offering to give me a lift. But, listen, I wouldn't get into that car even if I had to walk all the way from San Juan to Villa Hermosa. I put a curse on that car, such a tremendous curse that I'm just waiting to see it strike. I did it one day when Anita had asthma and I had no money to take her to the hospital. I happened to glance out of the window and I saw Emilio stretched out in his car, relaxed as could be, as if he deserved nothing but the best. I let go and yelled with all the breath in my chest, "I hope to God someday you'll wear that car as a hat. I hope it turns to dust with you all fucked up inside it."

Now I can't ride in the car, because I'm afraid the curse will come true some time when both of us are in it.

You can't imagine how lonely I feel here. I have friends, but they're sort of artificial, pasted-on friends. I couldn't confide in them at all. For example, I got pregnant a little while ago, and I had to have an abortion. I nearly went crazy thinking about it. Having a baby is nothing, it's the burden you have to take on afterwards, especially with a cowardly husband like mine who takes the easiest way out, denying that the child is his. So there I was, pregnant and, you know, I was ashamed. I was already out of La Esmeralda, see? Well, I know that my womb is weak, so I took two doses of Epsom salts with quinine and out came the kid. You can't imagine how unpleasant that is. In La Esmeralda you can tell everbody about it, and that sort of eases your heart. But here I didn't tell anybody. These girls I know here are *señoritas,* mere children, and something like that . . . *ay, bendito!*

But, to tell you the truth, I don't know what they call a *señorita* here in Villa Hermosa. The way it is in La Esmeralda, a girl and boy fall in love. For a few months they control themselves. Then they can't any more, and the boy does what he has to do to the girl. The hole is bigger than the full moon and that's that. They tell everybody and become husband and wife in the eyes of all the world. There's no trying to hide it. But here you see girls, who by rights should already have had a couple of kids, trying to keep from being found out. They'll go to a hotel with their sweethearts and let them stick their pricks into every hole in their body except the right one. And then they're so brazen as to come out of that hotel claiming they're still *señoritas.* It's plain shameless.

There are some policemen here who make love like this to some girls I know. Well, the policeman who did it to my friend Mimi came and told me that if I loaned him my bed for a little while he would give me three pesos. As that money wouldn't be bad at all and as he wasn't going to do it to me, I rented him the bed and grabbed the three pesos. Let them go screw! They locked themselves in the bedroom for a little while and then they went away. It was none of my business. If they didn't do it here, they would go do it somewhere else. And she didn't lose her virginity or anything here. So my hands are clean.

Sometimes I want to go back to La Esmeralda to live and other times I don't. It's not that I miss my family so much. On the contrary, relatives can be very bothersome. But you do need them in case you get sick because then you can dump the children on them. Sometimes I cry for loneliness here. Sometimes I'm bored to death. There's more neighborliness in La Esmeralda. I was used to having good friends stop by my house all the time. I haven't seen much of this neighborhood because I never go out. There's a Catholic church nearby but I've never been there. And I haven't been to the movies once since I've been living here. In La Esmeralda I used to go now and then. And in La Esmeralda, when nothing else was going on, you could at least hear the sea.

In La Esmeralda nobody ever made fun of my lameness. On the contrary, it was an advantage because everyone went out of his way to help me: "Let me help the lame girl. Let me buy *bolita* numbers from Lame Crucita, because cripples bring luck." But it isn't like that here, where people just laugh. That's why I'd like to live in La Esmeralda again or have Nanda move in here with me.

The social worker told me that I could go to the hospital and have an operation to fix my back. But who could I leave my little baby crows with? And suppose what they do is take my guts out in order to make me look right? Still, now that I live in a place like Villa Hermosa, I would like to have an operation to make me straight.

the wrong way

to find

jobs for negroes

DAVID WELLMAN

In the summer of 1966 I studied a Federal government program designed to help lower-class youths find jobs. The program was known as TIDE. It was run by the California Department of Employment, and classes were held five days a week in the Youth Opportunities Center of West Oakland.

The TIDE program was anything but a success. "I guess these kids just don't want jobs," one of the teacher-counselors told me. "The clothes they wear are loud. They won't talk decent English. They're boisterous. And they constantly fool around. They refuse to take the program seriously."

"But isn't there a job shortage in Oakland?" I asked. "Does it really *matter* how the kids act?"

"There's plenty of jobs. They're just not interested."

The students were 25 young men and 25 young women selected by poverty-program workers in the Bay Area. Their ages ranged from 16 to 22, and

most were Negroes. The government paid them $5 a day to participate. Men and women usually met separately. I sat in on the men's classes.

The young men who took part in TIDE had a distinctive style. They were "cool." Their hair was "processed." All sported sunglasses—very lightly tinted, with small frames. They called them "pimp's glasses." Their clothes, while usually inexpensive, were loud and ingeniously altered to express style and individuality. They spoke in a "hip" vernacular. Their vocabularies were small but very expressive. These young men, as part of the "cool world" of the ghetto, represent a distinctively black working-class culture.

To most liberals these young men are "culturally deprived" or "social dropouts." Most had flunked or been kicked out of school. Few had any intention of getting a high school degree. They seemed uninterested in "making it." They had long and serious arrest and prison records. They were skeptical and critical of both the TIDE program and white society in general.

The TIDE workers were liberals. They assumed that if the young men would only act a little less "cool" and learn to smooth over some of their encounters with white authorities, they too could become full-fledged, working members of society. The aim of TIDE was not to train them for jobs, but to train them how to *apply* for jobs—how to take tests, how to make a good impression during a job interview, how to speak well, how to fill out an application form properly. They would play games, like dominoes, to ease the pain associated with numbers and arithmetic; they would conduct mock interviews, take mock tests, meet with management representatives, and tour places where jobs might be available. They were told to consider the TIDE

Reprinted from TRANS-ACTION Magazine, April 1968, pp. 9-18. Copyright © 1968 by Washington University, St. Louis, Mo.

program itself as a job—to be at the Youth Opportunities Center office on time, dressed as if they were at work. If they were late or made trouble, they would be docked. But if they took the program seriously and did well, they were told, they stood a pretty good chance of getting a job at the end of four weeks. The unexpressed aim of TIDE, then, was to prepare Negro youngsters for white society. The government would serve as an employment agency for white, private enterprise.

The program aimed to change the youngsters by making them more acceptable to employers. Their grammar and pronunciation were constantly corrected. They were indirectly told that, in order to get a job, their appearance would have to be altered: For example, "Don't you think you could shine your shoes?" Promptness, a virtue few of the youngsters possessed, was lauded. The penalty for tardiness was being put on a clean-up committee, or being docked.

For the TIDE workers, the program was a four-week exercise in futility. They felt they weren't asking very much of youngsters—just that they learn to make a good impression on white society. And yet the young men were uncooperative. The only conclusion the TIDE workers could arrive at was: "They just don't want jobs."

Yet most of the youngsters took *actual* job possibilities very seriously. Every day they would pump the Youth Opportunities Center staff about job openings. When told there was a job at such-and-such a factory and that a particular test was required, the young men studied hard and applied for the job in earnest. The TIDE program *itself,* however, seemed to be viewed as only distantly related to getting a job. The youngsters wanted jobs, but to them their inability to take tests and fill out forms was not the problem. Instead they talked about the shortage of jobs available to people without skills.

Their desire for work was not the problem. The real problem was what the program demanded of the young men. It asked that they change their manner of speech and dress, that they ignore their lack of skills and society's lack of jobs, and that they act as if their arrest records were of no consequence in obtaining a job. It asked, most important, that they pretend *they*, and not society, bore the responsibility for their being unemployed. TIDE didn't demand much of the men: Only that they become white.

PUTTING ON THE PROGRAM

What took place during the four-week program was a daily struggle between white, middle-class ideals of conduct and behavior and the mores and folkways of the black community. The men handled TIDE the way the black community in America has always treated white threats to Negro self-respect. They used subtle forms of subversion and deception. Historians and sociologists have pointed to slave subversion, to the content and ritual of Negro spirituals, and to the blues as forms of covert black resistance to white mores.

Today, "putting someone on," "putting the hype on someone," or "running a game on a cat" seem to be important devices used by Negroes to maintain their integrity. "Putting someone on," which is used as much with black people as with whites, allows a person to maintain his integrity in a hostile or threatening situation. To put someone on is to publicly lead him to believe that you are going along with what he has to offer to say, while privately rejecting the offer and subtly subverting it. The tactic fails if the other person recognizes what is happening. For one aim of putting someone on is to take pride in feeling that you have put something over on him, often at his expense. (Putting someone on differs from "putting someone down," which means active defiance and public confrontation.)

TIDE was evidently interpreted by the men as a threat to their self-respect, and this was the way they responded to it. Sometimes TIDE was put on. Sometimes it was put down. It was taken seriously only when it met the men's own needs.

There was almost no open hostility toward those in charge of TIDE, but two things quickly led me to believe that if the men accepted the program, they did so only on their own terms.

First, all of them appeared to have a "tuning-out" mechanism. They just didn't hear certain things. One young man was a constant joker and talked incessantly, even if someone else was speaking or if the group was supposed to be working. When told to knock it off, he never heard the command. Yet when he was interested in a program, he could hear perfectly.

Tuning-out was often a collective phenomenon. For instance, there was a radio in the room where the youngsters worked, and they would play it during lunch and coffee breaks. When the instructor would enter and tell them to begin work, they would continue listening and dancing to the music as if there were no one else in the room. When *they* were finished listening, the radio went off and the session began. The youngsters were going along with the program—in a way. They weren't challenging it. But they were undermining its effectiveness.

A second way in which the young men undermined the program was by playing dumb. Much of the program consisted of teaching the youngsters how to fill out employment applications. They were given lengthy lectures on the importance

of neatness and lettering. After having filled out such forms a number of times, however, some students suddenly didn't know their mother's name, the school they last attended, or their telephone number.

This "stupidity" was sometimes duplicated during the mock job interviews. Five or more of the students would interview their fellow trainees for an imaginary job. These interviewers usually took their job seriously. But after it became apparent that the interview was a game, many of the interviewees suddenly became incredibly incompetent. They didn't have social-security numbers, they couldn't remember their last job, they didn't know what school they went to, they didn't know if they really wanted the job—to the absolute frustration of interviewers and instructors alike. Interestingly enough, when an instructor told them one morning that *this* time those who did well on the interview would actually be sent out on a real job interview with a real firm, the stupid and incompetent were suddenly transformed into model job applicants.

The same thing happened when the youngsters were given job-preference tests, intelligence tests, aptitude tests, and tests for driver's licenses. The first few times the youngsters took these tests, most worked hard to master them. But after they had gotten the knack, and still found themselves without jobs and taking the same tests, their response changed. Some of them no longer knew how to do the test. Others found it necessary to cheat by looking over someone's shoulder. Still others flunked tests they had passed the day before. Yet when they were informed of actual job possibilities at the naval ship yard or with the post office, they insisted on giving and taking the tests themselves. In one instance, some of them read up on which tests were relevant for a particular job, then practiced that test for a couple of hours by themselves.

Tuning-out and playing stupid were only two of the many ways the TIDE program was "put-on." Still another way: Insisting on work "breaks." The young men "employed" by TIDE were well-acquainted with this ritual, and demanded that it be included as part of their job. Since they had been given a voice in deciding the content of the program, they insisted that breaks become part of their daily routine. And no matter what the activity, or who was addressing them, the young men religiously adhered to the breaks.

The program started at 9:30 A.M. The youngsters decided that their first break would be for coffee at 10:30. This break was to last until 11. And while work was never allowed to proceed a minute past 10:30, it was usually 11:15 or so before the young men actually got back to work. Lunch began exactly at 12. Theoretically, work resumed at 1. This usually meant 1:15, since they had to listen to "one more song" on the radio. The next break was to last from 2:30 to 3. However, because they were finished at 3:30 and because it took another 10 minutes to get them back to work the fellows could often talk their way out of the remaining half hour. Considering they were being paid $5 a day for five hours' work, of which almost half were regularly devoted to breaks, they didn't have a bad hustle.

TRIPS AND GAMES

Games were another part of the TIDE program subverted by the put-on. Early in the program an instructor told the students that it might be helpful if they mastered arithmetic and language by playing games—dominoes, Scrabble, and various card games. The students considered this a fine idea. But what their instructor had intended for a pastime during the breaks, involving at most an hour a day, they rapidly turned into a major part of the instruction. They set aside 45 minutes in the morning and 45 minutes in the afternoon for games. But they participated in these games during their breaks as well, so that the games soon became a stumbling block to getting sessions back in order after breaks. When the instructor would say, "Okay, let's get back to work," the men would sometimes reply, "But we're already working on our math—we're playing dominoes, and you said that would help us with our math."

To familiarize the students with the kinds of jobs potentially available, the TIDE instructors took them on excursions to various work situations. These excursions were another opportunity for a put-on. It hardly seemed to matter what kind of company they visited so long as the visit took all day. On a trip to the Oakland Supply Naval Station, the men spent most of their time putting the make on a cute young WAVE who was their guide. One thing this tour did produce, however, was a great deal of discussion about the war in Vietnam. Almost none of the men wanted to serve in the armed forces. Through the bus windows some of them would yell at passing sailors: "Vietnam, baby!" or "Have a good time in Vietnam, man!"

The men would agree to half-day trips only if there was no alternative, or if the company would give away samples. Although they knew that the Coca-Cola Company was not hiring, they wanted to go anyway, for the free Cokes. They also wanted to go to many candy and cookie factories. Yet they turned down a trip to a local steel mill that they knew was hiring. TIDE, after all, was not designed to get them an interview—its purpose was to show them what sorts of jobs might be available. Given the circumstances, they reasoned, why not see what was *enjoyable* as well?

When the men were not putting-on the TIDE program and staff, they might be putting them down. When someone is put-down, he knows it. The tactic's success *depends* on his knowing it, whereas a put-on is successful only when its victim is unaware of it.

THE INTERVIEW TECHNIQUE

Among the fiercest put-downs I witnessed were those aimed at jobs the students were learning to apply for. These jobs were usually for unskilled labor: post-office, assembly-line, warehouse, and longshore workers, truck drivers, chauffeurs, janitors, bus boys, and so on. The reaction of most of the students was best expressed by a question I heard one young man ask an instructor: "How about some tests for I.B.M.?" The room broke into an uproar of hysterical laughter. The instructor's response was typically bureaucratic, yet disarming: "Say, that's a good suggestion. Why don't you put it in the suggestion box?" The students didn't seem able to cope with that retort, so things got back to normal.

Actual employers, usually those representing companies that hired people only for unskilled labor, came to TIDE to demonstrate to the men what a good interview would be like. They did *not* come to interview men for real jobs, It was sort of a helpful-hints-for-successful-interviews session. Usually one of the more socially mobile youths was chosen to play the role of job applicant. The entire interview situation was played through. Some employers even went so far as to have the "applicant" go outside and knock on the door to begin the interview. The students thought this was both odd and funny, and one said to the employer:

"Man, you've already *seen* the cat. How come you making him walk out and then walk back in?"

With a look of incredulity, the employer replied: "But that's how you get a job. You have to sell yourself from the moment you walk in that door."

The employer put on a real act, beginning the interview with the usual small talk.

"I see from you application that you played football in high school."

"Yeah."

"Did you like it?"

"Yeah."

"Football really makes men and teaches you teamwork."

"Yeah."

At this point, the men got impatient: "Man, the cat's here to get a job, not talk about football!"

A wisecracker chimed in: "Maybe he's interviewing for a job with the Oakland Raiders."

Usually the employer got the point. He would then ask about the "applicant's" job experience, draft status, school record, interests, skills, and so on. The young man being interviewed usually took the questions seriously and answered frankly. But after a while the rest of the group would tire of the game and (unrecognized, from the floor) begin to ask about the specifics of a real job:

"Say man, how much does this job pay?"

"What kind of experience do you need?"

"What if you got a record?"

It didn't take long to completely rattle an interviewer. The instructor might intervene and tell the students that the gentleman was there to help them, but this would stifle revolt for only a short while. During one interview, several of the fellows began loudly playing dominoes. That got the response they were looking for.

"Look!" shouted the employer. "If you're not interested in learning how to sell yourself, why don't you just leave the room so that others who are interested can benefit from this?"

"Oh no!" responded the ringleaders, "We work here. If you don't dig us, then *you* leave!"

Not much later, he did.

Sometimes during these mock interviews, the very nature of the work being considered was put-down. During one mock interview for a truck-driving job, some of the men asked the employer about openings for salesmen. Others asked him about executive positions. At one point the employer himself was asked point-blank how much he was paid, and what his experience was. They had turned the tables and were enjoying the opportunity to interview the interviewer. Regardless of a potential employer's status, the young men treated him as they would their peers. On one tour of a factory, the students were escorted by the vice-president in charge of hiring. To the TIDE participants, he was just another guide. After he had informed the students of the large number of unskilled positions available, they asked him if he would hire some of them, on the spot. He replied that this was just a tour and that he was in no position to hire anyone immediately. One youth looked at him and said: "Then you're just wasting our time, aren't you?"

Although shaken, the executive persisted. Throughout his talk, however, he innocently referred to his audience as "boys," which obviously bothered the students. Finally one of the more articulate men spoke up firmly: "We are young *men,* not boys!"

The vice-president blushed and apologized. He made a brave attempt to avoid repeating the phrase. But habit was victorious, and the word slipped in again and again. Each time he said "you boys"

he was corrected, loudly, and with increasing hostility.

The students treated State Assemblyman Byron Rumford, a Negro, the same way. The meeting with Rumford was an opportunity for them to speak with an elected official about a job situation in the state. The meeting was also meant to air differences and to propose solutions. At the time, in fact, the men were quite angry about their rate of pay at TIDE. An instructor had suggested that they take the matter up with Rumford.

The meeting was attended by both the young men and women in the TIDE program. The young women were very well-dressed and well-groomed. Their clothes were not expensive, but were well cared for and in "good taste." Their hair was done in high-fashion styles. They looked, in short, like aspiring career women. The young men wore their usual dungarees or tight trousers, brightly colored shirts and sweaters, pointed shoes, and sunglasses.

The women sat quietly and listened politely. The men spoke loudly whenever they felt like it, and constantly talked among themselves.

Rumford, instead of speaking about the job situation in the Bay Area, chose to talk about his own career. It was a Negro Horatio Alger story. The moral was that if you work hard, you too can put yourself through college, become a successful druggist, then run for public office.

The moment Rumford finished speaking and asked for questions, one of the men jumped up and asked, "Hey man, how do we get a raise?" A male chorus of "Yeah!" followed. Before Rumford could complete a garbled answer (something like, "Well, I don't really know much about the procedures of a federally sponsored program"), the battle of the sexes had been joined. The women scolded the men for their "disrespectful behavior" toward an elected official. One said:"Here he is trying to help us and you-all acting a fool. You talking and laughing and carrying on while he talking, and then when he finishes you want to know about a raise. Damn!"

"Shit," was a male response. "You don't know what you talking about. We got a *right* to ask the cat about a raise. We elected him."

"We supposed to be talking about jobs," said another. "And we're talking about *our* job. If y'all like the pay, that's your business. We want more!"

The debate was heated. Neither group paid any attention to Rumford, who wisely slipped out of the room.

BATTLE OF SEXES— OR CLASS CONFLICT?

During the exchange it became clear to me that the differences in clothing and style between the sexes reflected their different orientations toward the dominant society and its values. In the minds of the young women, respect and respectability seemed paramount. At one point, a young woman said to the men, "You acting just like a bunch of *niggers.*" She seemed to identify herself as a Negro, not as a "nigger." For the men, on the other hand, becoming a Negro (as opposed to a "nigger") meant giving up much that they considered positive. As one young man said in answer to the above, "You just ain't got no soul, bitch."

The women's identification with the values of white society became even clearer when the debate moved from what constituted respect and respectability to a direct attack on a personal level: "Do you all expect to get a job looking the way you do?" "Shit, I wouldn't wear clothes like that if I was on welfare."

The direction of the female attack corresponded closely with the basic assumptions of the TIDE program: People are without jobs because of themselves. This barrage hit the young men pretty hard. Their response was typical of any outraged male whose manhood has been threatened. In fact, when one young woman gibed, "You ain't no kinda man," some of the fellows had to be physically restrained from hitting her.

One of the men explained that "maybe the reason cats dress the way they do is because they can't afford anything else. Did you ever think of that?"

The woman's response was one I had not heard since the third or fourth grade: "Well, it doesn't matter what you wear as long as it's clean, pressed, and tucked-in. But hell, you guys don't even shine your shoes."

The battle of the sexes in the black community seems to be almost a class conflict. Many observers have noted that the black woman succeeds more readily in school than the black man. Women are also favored by parents, especially mothers. Moreover, the black woman has been for some time the most stable force and the major breadwinner of the Negro family. All these things put Negro women in harmony with the major values attached to work and success in our society. Black men, however, have been estranged from society, and a culture has developed around this estrangement—a male Negro culture often antagonistic to the dominant white society. The black woman stands in much the same relation to black men as white society does.

Even including Rumford, no group of officials was put down quite so hard as the Oakland police. Police brutality was constantly on the youngsters' minds. A day didn't pass without at least one being absent because he was in jail, or one coming in with a story about mistreatment by the police. A meeting was arranged with a sergeant from the Community Relations Bureau of the Oakland police. The students seemed excited about meeting the officer on their own turf and with the protection provided by the program.

In anticipation of his arrival, the fellows rearranged the room, placing all the separate tables together. Then they sat down in a group at one end of the table, waiting for the officer.

PUTTING DOWN THE POLICE

Sergeant McCormack was an older man. And while obviously a cop, he could also pass for a middle-aged businessman or a young grandfather.

"Hi boys," he said as he sat down. His first mistake. He began with the five-minute speech he must give to every community group. The talk was factual, uninteresting, and noncontroversial: how the department is run, what the qualifications for policemen are, and how difficult it is for police to do their work and still please everyone. His talk was greeted with complete silence.

"I understand you have some questions," McCormack finally said.

"What about police brutality?" asked one man.

"What is your definition of police brutality?" the sergeant countered.

"How long you been a cop?" someone shouted.

"Over 20 years."

"And you got the nerve to come on sounding like you don't know what we talking about. Don't be jiving us. Shit, if you've been a cop *that* long, you *got* to know what we talking about."

"Righteous on that, brother!" someone chimed in.

"Well, I've been around a while, all

right, but I've never seen any brutality. But what about it?"

"What *about* it?" There was a tone of disbelief mixed with anger in the young man's voice. "Shit man, we want to know why you cats always kicking other cats' asses."

The officer tried to draw a distinction between necessary and unnecessary police violence. The fellows weren't buying that. They claimed the police systematically beat the hell out of them for no reason. The officer asked for examples and the fellows obliged with long, involved, and detailed personal experiences with the Oakland Police Department. The sergeant listened patiently, periodically interrupting to check details and inconsistencies. He tried to offer a police interpretation of the incident. But the fellows were simply not in a mood to listen. In desperation the sergeant finally said, "Don't you want to hear *our* side of the story?"

"Hell no, motherfucker, we *see* your side of the story every night on 14th Street."

One young man stood up, his back to the officer, and addressed his contemporaries: "We *tired* of talking! We want some action! There's a new generation now. We ain't like the old folks who took all this shit off the cops." He turned to the sergeant and said, "You take that back to your goddamn Chief Preston and tell him."

McCormack had a silly smile on his face.

Another youngster jumped up and hollered, "You all ain't going to be smiling when we put dynamite in your police station!"

The officer said simply, "You guys don't want to talk."

"You see," someone yelled, "the cat's trying to be slick, trying to run a game on us. First he comes in here all nice-talking, all that shit about how they run the police and the police is to protect us. And then when we tell him how they treat us he wants to say we don't want to talk. Shit! We want to talk, he don't want to listen."

From this point on, they ran over him mercilessly. I, with all my biases against the police, could not help feeling compassion for the sergeant. If the police are an authority figure in the black community, then this episode must be viewed as a revolt against authority—*all* authority. There was nothing about the man's life, both private and public, that wasn't attacked.

"How much money you get paid?"

"About $12,000 a year."

"For being a cop? Wow!"

"What do you do?"

"I work in the Community Relations Department."

"Naw, stupid, what *kind* of work?"

"I answer the telephone, speak to groups, and try to see if the police treat the citizens wrong."

"Shit, we could do that and we don't even have a high-school education. Is that all you do? And get that much money for it?"

"Where do you live?"

"I'll bet he lives up in the hills."

"I live in the east side of Oakland. And I want you to know that my next-door neighbor is a colored man. I've got nothing against colored people."

"You got any kids?"

"Yeah, two boys and a girl."

"Shit, bet they all went to college and got good jobs. Any of your kids been in trouble?"

"No, not really."

"What do they do?"

"My oldest boy is a fighter pilot in Vietnam."

"What the hell is he doing over there? That's pretty stupid."

"Yeah man, what are we fighting in Vietnam for? Is that your way of getting rid of us?"

"Well, the government says we have to be there and it's the duty of every citizen to do what his country tells him to do."

"We don't want to hear all that old bullshit, man."

"Hey, how come you wear such funny clothes? You even look like a goddam cop."

"Yeah baby, and he smells like one too!"

The barrage continued for almost half an hour. The instructor finally called a halt: "Sergeant McCormack has to get back, fellows. Is there anything specific that you'd like to ask him?"

"Yeah. How come Chief Preston ain't here? He's always talking to other people all over the country about how good the Oakland cops are and how there ain't going to be no riot here. Why don't he come and tell us that? We want to talk with the chief."

The next day, Deputy Chief Gain came—accompanied by the captain of the Youth Division, the lieutenant of that division, and a Negro sergeant. It was a formidable display of police authority. The youngsters were noticeably taken aback.

Chief Gain is a no-nonsense, businesslike cop. He takes no static from anyone, vigorously defends what he thinks is correct, and makes no apologies for what he considers incorrect. He is an honest man in the sense that he makes no attempt to cover up or smooth over unpleasant things. He immediately got down to business: "All right now, I understand you guys have some beefs with the department. What's the story?"

The fellows started right in talking about the ways they had been mistreated by the police. The chief began asking specific questions: where it happened, when it happened, what the officer looked like, and so on. He never denied the existence of brutality. That almost seemed to be assumed. He did want details, however. He always asked whether the youth had filed a complaint with the department. The response was always No. He then lectured them about the need to file such complaints if the situation was to be changed.

He explained the situation as he saw it: "Look fellows, we run a police force of 654 men. Most of them are good men, but there's bound to be a few rotten apples in the basket. I know that there's a couple of men who mistreat people, but it's only a few and we're trying our best to change that."

"Shit, I know of a case where a cop killed a cat and now he's back on the beat."

"Now wait a minute—"

"No more waiting a minute!" someone interrupted. "You had two cops got caught taking bribes. One was black and the other Caucasian. The black cat was kicked off the force and the white cat is back on."

"Yeah, and what about that cat who killed somebody off-duty, what about him?"

"Hold on," Gain said firmly. "Let's take these things one at a time." He didn't get very far before he was back to the "few rotten apples" argument.

"If it's only a few cops, how come it happens all the time?"

The deputy chief told them that he thought it was the same few cops who were causing all the problems. "Unless you file complaints each time you feel you've been mistreated, we can't do anything about it. So it's up to you as much as it is up to us."

For the first time in weeks, I intruded into the discussion. I pointed out to Gain that he was asking citizens to police their own police force. He had argued that in most situations the department had a good deal of control over its own men—the same argument the police had

used against a civilian-review board. Now he was saying the opposite: that it was up to the citizens. This seemed to break the impasse, and the students howled with delight.

"What happens if a cop beats my ass and I file a complaint?" demanded one. "Whose word does the judge take?"

"The judge takes the evidence and evaluates it objectively and comes to a decision."

"Yeah, but it's usually two cops against one of us, and if both testify against me, what happens? Do you think the juge is going to listen to me?"

"Bring some witnesses."

"That ain't going to do anything."

"That's your problem. If you don't like the legal system in this country, work to change it."

"Okay man," one fellow said to Gain, "You pretty smart. If I smack my buddy here upside the head and he files a complaint, what you gonna do?"

"Arrest you."

"Cool. Now let's say one of your ugly cops smacks *me* upside the head and I file a complaint—what you gonna do?"

"Investigate the complaint, and if there's anything to it, why we'll take action—probably suspend him."

"Why do *we* get arrested and *you* investigated?"

The deputy chief's response was that most private companies with internal difficulties don't want to be investigated by outside agencies. The fellows retorted: "Police are *not* a private business. You're supposed to work for the people!"

"And shit, you cats get to carry guns. No businessman carries guns. It's a different scene, man,"

"How come you got all kinds of squad cars in this neighborhood every night? And have two and three cops in each of them?"

"The crime rate is high in this area," replied Gain, "and we get a lot of calls and complaints about it."

"Yeah, and you smart enough to know that when you come around here, you better be wearing helmets and carrying shotguns. If you that clever, you got to be smart enough to handle your own goddamn cops.

At this point the fellows all jumped on the deputy chief the same way they had jumped on the sergeant the day before:

"Why don't you just let us run our own damn community?"

"Yeah. There should be people on the force who've been in jail because they the only people who know what it means to be busted. People in West Oakland should be police because they know their community; you don't."

"Why do we get all the speeding tickets?"

"How come we got to fight in Vietnam?"

"Why the judges so hard on us? They don't treat white cats—I mean dudes—the way they do us."

The chief began assembling his papers and stood up. "You guys aren't interested in talking. You want to yell. When you want to talk, come down to my office and if I'm free we'll talk."

But the fellows had the last word. While he was leaving they peppered him with gibes about how *they* were tired of talking; promised to dynamite his office; and called the police chief a coward for not coming down to speak with them.

When the deputy chief had gone, the instructor asked the fellows why they insisted on ganging up on people like the police. The answer provides a lot of insight into the young men's actions toward the police, businessmen, and public officials:

"These people just trying to run a game on us. If we give them time to think about answers, they gonna put us in a trick. We've *got* to gang up on them because they gang up on us. Did you dig the way that cat brought three other cats with him? Besides, how else could we put them down?"

A SUBTLE FORM OF RACISM

In effect, the young men had inverted the meaning and aims of the TIDE program. It was supposed to be an opportunity for them to plan careers and prepare themselves for their life's work. The immediate goal was to help them get started by showing them how to get a job. The youngsters had a different view. The program was a way to play some games and take some outings—an interesting diversion from the boredom and frustration of ghetto life in the summer. In some respects it was also a means of confronting, on equal terms, high-status people normally unavailable to them—and of venting on them their anger and hostility. But primarily they saw it as a $5-a-day job.

The program simply did not meet the needs of these young men. In fact, it was not really meant to. The Great Society was trying to "run a game on" black youth. TIDE asked them to stop being what they are. It tried to lead them into white middle-class America by showing that America was interested in getting them jobs. But America does not provide many jobs—let alone attractive jobs—for those with police records, with few skills, with black skins. The youths knew that; TIDE workers knew that, too. They did not train youths for work, but tried to make them believe that if they knew *how* to get a job, they could. The young men saw through the sham.

Ironically, the view that Negro youths, rather than society, are responsible for the employment problem is very similar to the familiar line of white racism. Negroes will not work because they are lazy and shiftless, the old Southern bigot would say. The Northern liberal today would put it a little differently: Negroes cannot get jobs because of their psychological and cultural impediments; what they need is cultural improvement, a proper attitude, the ability to sell themselves. Both views suggest that inequities in the job and opportunity structure of America are minor compared to the deficiencies of Negroes themselves. In the end, Northern liberals and Southern racists agree: The problem is mainly with Negroes, not with our society. This fallacy underlies much of the war on poverty's approach and is indicative of the subtle forms racism is taking in American today.

laredo learns

about the war

on poverty

KENNETH O. GILMORE

"Boondoggle!" "Failure!" "Scandal!" "Hoax!" These charges are hurled almost daily at the federal government's billion-dollar War on Poverty. Unfair, reply its proponents. They maintain that such a vast, controversial undertaking is bound to include a few mistakes. Surely, they argue, the program deserves to be shown at its best.

So, come down to the dusty, wind-swept streets of Laredo, Texas, billed

by Office of Economic Opportunity boss Sargeant Shriver as a "showcase of success." Just 230 miles from the Texas White House, Laredo (population 65,000) has been declared a "demonstration city"—the only one of its kind in the War on Poverty. As one OEO official has said, "We hope to spotlight national attention on Laredo as a model project."

So be it.

Laredo, just across the Rio Grande from Mexico's Nuevo Laredo, is called the "Gateway City." It is a place of paradoxes: a border town of booming commerce and wretched slums, of leather-faced ranchers and barefoot children, of Kiwanis luncheons and welfare lines. In the poverty-blighted *barrios,* sun-weathered wood shacks huddle in decrepit shame on weed-infested dirt streets while, just blocks away, sprinklers spin cool droplets on the green lawns of fine homes.

Although Laredo has the lowest per-capita income among U.S. cities, according to the last census, its retail sales climbed close to $90 million in 1965, and tourist traffic has broken all records. Bank deposits shot up $5 million during a recent 12-month period to $58,452,000, while 165 miles of streets remain unpaved. Inside the county courthouse, an expensive brass plaque commemorates officeholders for installing an air-conditioning system. Outside, within a two-minute drive, children play beside a stinking, trash-infested creek.

"It Doesn't Make Sense." In recent years, Laredo has been handed some pretty large pieces of federal pie—from $630,000 for a shiny civic and convention center with swimming pool to $1,600,000 for a handsome senior citizens' home. But these have done the hard-core poverty-stricken little good.

Some months, up to 11,000 persons get surplus food. More than 400 families collect aid-to-dependent children payments. Approximately 2500 able-bodied persons are normally unemployed.

What creates these conditions? Isolated from other major cities by miles of sand and scrub, and low on natural resources, especially water, Laredo has attracted little new industry. But what has caused economic havoc is the "commuter problem." Every morning, 3500 Mexicans from Nuevo Laredo walk across the International Bridge spanning the Rio Grande to work as clerks, maids, bellhops, typists, factory hands. U. S. immigration laws allow these Mexicans to take jobs desperately needed by Laredo men and women. "It just doesn't make sense," say many poor and unemployed. Concerned citizens declare, "If Washington would stop the commuter influx, we could save millions of federal dollars."

Political Peons. But something far more dramatic was available in Washington—the Great Society's War on Poverty. Laredo got its first real taste of this war in June 1965, when Major J. C. "Pepe" Martin, Jr., returned from the nation's capital and announced the go-ahead for a long-awaited Neighborhood Youth Corps (NYC) project. Expectations were a mile high. Youngsters 16 to 21 from low-income families flocked to sign up for jobs paying $1 an hour for 30 hours a week. "You'll get experience and skills for today's world of work," promised an administrator. Skills? The children of Laredo's poor found themselves assigned to painting street curbstones, washing police cars, collecting garbage.

"There was a lot of talk about improving skills," says one disgusted anti-poverty worker. "And, sure, a few kids benefited. But most became peons for various political subdivisions."

As the NYC payroll built up to 1000 youngsters, it became a bookkeeper's nightmare. Instead of organizing one central operation, Washington doled out dollars to the city, to the local school system, and finally to Webb County, which encompasses Laredo. Each ran a separate little kingdom with its own personnel, resulting in a pile-up of over 50 supervisors, administrators and clerks.

These were several popular children's activity that first year, ranging from Headstart preschool classes to tutoring of backward children to free hot lunches. But the critical need was for jobs—and, as a local radio editorial declared, "Practically nothing was accomplished except a lot of window dressing."

Then, early in January 1966, the Office of Economic Opportunity's southwest regional director, Dr. William Crook, arrived from his Austin headquarters for what a press release heroically described as a "battlefront" inspection. He let it be known that OEO chieftain Shriver himself had requested a comprehensive evaluation of the community's social and economic needs. Soon specialists from Washington and Austin arrived for a three-day "field survey." In early March, the big news was announced: Laredo would become a "multimillion-dollar demonstration city in the War on Poverty." The idea was to show what the full impact of federal aid could do.

The Great Job Rush. Dr. Crook promised that "within the current fiscal year" Washington was prepared to grant the city $2,050,000. That figured out to half a million dollars a month—and now the program shifted into high gear. Within weeks the OEO disclosed that $132,975 had been granted Laredo's Community Action agency for "conduct and administration." This sparkling bureaucratese fooled no one. In a flash, word was out that nine "poverty" staff posts were up for grabs at salaries ranging from $450 to $1167 a month. When the dust from the stampede of applicants settled, five teachers, badly needed in the Laredo schools, had been picked to become paper shufflers in the war on poverty. The nephew of a county commissioner snared one opening.

As "poverty" grants were announced —always first by telegrams from Washington to the local newspapers and radio stations—everyone from secretaries to car salesmen started leapfrogging into this suddenly lucrative field. The child-welfare unit lost its only case worker-registered nurse; she received a $2000 salary boost, thanks to OEO. By August, "poverty" was a huge new industry in town, with more full-and part-time people on its rolls than any single business!

Lassoing the Pork. As a "demonstration city" Laredo started swallowing all types of pills from the anti-poverty medicine chest. There was $39,000 for a medical rehabilitation center and $62,000 for free legal services. A $400,000 *first-year* administrative allotment was approved mainly for salaries at a multi-service center and three outposts—an apparatus headquartered at a refurbished orphanage in the poverty-stricken Azteca neighborhood and designed in part to give the poor a place to discuss their difficulties.

Anti-poverty grants put heavy emphasis on welfare rather than "economic opportunity." The OEO paid out $6000 for recruiters to sign up older citizens for Medicare. Another $21,000 went into citizenship classes for older Mexican immigrants. Why? So they could become Americans and be eligible for old-age assistance.

To line up as many federal-aid projects as possible, Laredo retained a planning consultant in January 1966. He is Paul Garza, Jr., an engineer-city planner and former urban-renewal official who has mastered the art of writing proposals for Washington officials. "You can't just fill out the forms," he explains. "You must learn to think like they do, and give them the detailed information they want."

Garza is helping Laredo lasso a whole new herd of "poverty" grants, a number of them pure pork barrel. They include $1,500,000 to help boost water production and extend lines; $752,000 for a building to house all the county and city welfare agencies; $635,000 for airport improvements. To bring home all this bacon and more (total: $4,274,500) the area will have to fork up $2,466,500 in "local contributions." A worried chamber of commerce official told me, "We may well go broke just trying to take advantage of federal generosity."

Confusion and Competition. But digging up local funds to qualify for Washington's riches wasn't Laredo's only worry. As one program piled upon another, red-tape tangles and stupefying confusion inevitably followed. The government's cure-all catalogue offers a choice of 115 different items, and Laredo figures it's eligible for 113. Part of OEO's money funnels through other federal agencies, such as the Department of Health, Education and Welfare, which also disburses aid-to-education funds for poverty areas. HEW has put so much into Laredo ($2,700,000) that a "coördinator of federal projects" for the public schools had to be hired with his own separate staff and an extensive network of full-and part-time teachers and field supervisors.

Before the poverty war came to Laredo, another federal program, started in 1962, had been successfully training people for specific available jobs. In spite of this proven approach, anti-poverty planners have stumbled over one another in a frantic race to launch three job-training schemes, each with separate, competing staffs. Funds for one $733,000 project under HEW's protectorate sifted through five federal-state echelons before reaching the first group of 146 welfare recipients signed up for "work experience" schooling. Community Action Program (CAP) executive director Luis Diaz de Leon and his staff spent untold hours working up a detailed proposal for training migrants, only to discover, after it was sent to Washington, that HEW's local federal coordinator for poverty had beaten them to it with a $294,000 venture!

In truth, the war between the bureaucracies in Laredo has often been hotter than the poverty war. The local "poverty" office has battled furiously with agencies such as the Texas Employment Commission and Department of Public Welfare. The infighting got so bad that Laredo's poverty-war chief recently complained about "bureaucratic stumbling blocks," and charged that the "influence of political elements" has jeopardized the success of programs. A spokesman for one religious group collecting federal money has openly labeled the Community Action agency as inefficent." Meanwhile, the poor watch in wonder as bureaucrats and politicians squabble over just who is supposed to be "helping" whom.

Federal-Dollar Fever. Something else is happening in Laredo: many people are learning to lean on the federal crutch and like it. The area's representative in the state legislature has said he wished "we had more hands to stick out for federal aid."

The degree to which this philosophy has seeped into the community is illustrated by a $249,208 OEO grant glowingly described in a Washington press release as a "beautification" project for a recreational site that would also give training to jobless workers. Late last summer I drove out to the edge of town

to see this project. I found a large construction crew working on new stables for the local racetrack—housing for horses which was far superior to scores of shacks in poor Laredo *barrios* that I had visited.

Nearby loomed a large grandstand, also slated for "beautification." The track is run by a nonprofit, tax-exempt organization of ranchers, horse owners and other prosperous citizens, called the Laredo International Fair and Exposition (LIFE).

Originally, LIFE had not planned to tap the federal till. But with plenty of anti-poverty cash flowing into this "demonstration city," the temptation to get in on the gravy was irresistible. Why not use "poverty" trainees to build stables at the track, and to make other improvements such as extending the grandstand roof? Federal officials bought the scheme—with a warning to "play down" the racetrack aspects.

The infection that is working its way into Laredo's bloodstream is called federal-dollar fever. Not long ago, the Boy Scouts received a large private donation to increase Scouting in Laredo's poor section, with the provision that matching funds be raised. Bill Harrell, co-owner and manager of radio station KVOZ, who headed this voluntary effort, reported that time and again people shook their heads. "Why should I give you anything," they said, "when the War on Poverty will take care of everything?"

Such warning signals have been lost, however, in the tumult over the "demonstration city." It reached a peak when Shriver visited Laredo last summer. His first stop was at the multi-service center in the Azteca neighborhood. Surrounded by politicians and "poverty" workers, he spoke to a cheering crowd, many from nearby wood shacks. "It's a treat for me to be here in this showcase of the success in the war against poverty," declared Shriver.

The next day, he left and proceeded to President Johnson's ranch, reported that the war was going great guns in Texas, and described the cheering crowds in Laredo.

Poor as Ever. By last fall the cheering had ceased. One evening, 150 residents of the poverty-stricken Azteca neighborhood collected outside their run-down homes to complain that distribution of "poverty" jobs had been unfair. Bitterly they expressed their dissatisfaction at the way administrators had been treating them. "They never keep their promises," cried one. The group was forced to gather in the middle of a dirt road because officials, fearing trouble, had locked them out of the center designed expressly for their benefit.

Policemen were on hand, and a paddy wagon stood by, but there was no trouble, only disillusionment and anger.

It wasn't exactly the stuff that goes into press releases. It was simply people awakening to the harsh reality that prosperity had not suddenly descended upon them just because they were in a "showcase." For, while some poor have received anti-poverty aspirin, Laredo still suffers the same splitting economic headaches—despite the dispensing of over $5,500,000 to date in all types of aid. Commuters still surge across the bridge from Mexico; unemployment remains high; squalid *barrios* still reek with the smells of impoverishment. And the town's poverty problems are as acute as ever—except, of course, for an array of wealthier poverty-war jobholders.

"We are a demonstration city, all right," says Bill Harrell. "We're a demonstration of how to shatter high expectations and pass our problems over to a new federal hierarchy."

If this is the War on Poverty at its best, surely its's time for drastic improvement.

II

black
people

Racial and ethnic discrimination is not a new phenomenon in American society. Each successive wave of immigrants has encountered various negative reactions from the dominant white Anglo-Saxon Protestant group, or as sociologists refer to them, WASPS. Immigrants found in their new habitats, that such differentiating characteristics as language, religion, and customs were used to identify them and to limit their participation and opportunities in society in both obvious and subtle ways. Nevertheless, most minority groups in the United States experience overwhelming discrimination only temporarily.

The case of the Negro, or black man (as he seems to prefer to identify himself today), is held by some to be qualitatively different from the discrimination suffered by non-black groups. The persistence and pervasiveness of discrimination against black people is unique. No other group of any size in the United States has been subjected to inequities so comprehensive and intense as those faced by the black man. Moreover, no other group has either challenged the existing social order or provoked the animosity and hostility of the larger community to so marked a degree. Many aspects of social life, such as movement away from the core city, *de facto* segregation in education, and the rise of new groups of extreme political reactionaries, are in part expressions of the race issue. Furthermore, contrary to other immigrant groups, the black man cannot fade into the dominant society without radical changes in the values of the white community member and in the structural arrangements of the social order, which implicitly discriminate against non-white people. Today the plight of the black man and the consequences of his efforts and the efforts of sympathetic whites to remedy the pervasive discrimination represent perhaps the most pressing problem confronting the United States.

Individual	Individual
↓	↓
Individual	Organization

PORTRAIT OF A KLANSMAN

No single set of social or psychological characteristics can be drawn up to identify the bigot. Alsop's article provides a portrait of a man who appears as a unique example of the racial discriminator. Raymond Crawford's determination to keep the black man in his place is rooted in his emotional makeup, his life experiences, and the gratification he receives as leader of a ruthless organization. It is not possible to separate the activities of the Klan from the individual behavior of Raymond Crawford. As an individual, he rallies the energies and talents of others to persecute black people. The Klan simply provides a convenient structure in which such nefarious individual ambitions can be realized.

THE BRILLIANCY OF BLACK

While Stokely Carmichael may not be identified by name in tomorrow's history books, he is one of a type which is currently responsible for many of the confrontations between black men themselves. He represents a provocateur *vis-à-vis* the white community; he also challenges the more conservative and legally conforming leaders and groups among the black community. While Weinraub's portrait of Carmichael is a sympathetic one, other analysts of the Negro movement view him in a less favorable light. In the midst of the current racial scene, it is impossible to judge the extent to which such people represent a positive or negative force in the amelioration of discrimination against the black man.

Organization
↓
Individual

Organization
↓
Organization

NIGHTMARE JOURNEY

Reactions of the larger community to the riots and violence of the ghetto have been bizarre and extreme. Bob Clark, a Negro news photographer, describes what happened to him in the Detroit riots. Although Clark was injured while legitimately photographing the racial distrubance, the police dealt with him only in terms of his color. Few individuals would argue against police intervention efforts in the face of arson and looting, no matter how sympathetic they are to the cause of the black man. Yet Clark's account reveals how inappropriately an organization may respond to crises. It is likely that such unsympathetic and cruel conduct by agents of social control in the community will have an irrevocable impact on the black man and will serve to exasperate a commitment to violence.

THE CALL OF THE BLACK PANTHERS

Large-scale and violent eruptions in the black community have lead to accusations of conspiracies and organized agitation. While many analysts of the Negro situation maintain that these charges are exaggerated, the Black Panthers do exemplify a well-organized, armed band who believe that force, or threats of force, are essential to the achievement of a better way of life for black people. Stern traces the roots of the black organization with generous understanding of the plight of Negro. He points out that though their numbers may be small, the Panthers do represent an organized effort to resist the community organized against the black man. While the radical behavior of such organizations may concern us, we must remember that they are a response to the discriminatory behavior of the white community.

portrait

of a klansman

STEWART ALSOP

Raymond Cranford, an Exalted Cyclops of the Ku Klux Klan in North Carolina, is a bullet-headed man with expressionless, black-rimmed eyes, who wears his hair close cropped, military fashion. Cranford fully expects to be framed by the Federal Bureau of Investigation, or killed by Negroes or Communists, and he always has a rifle or pistol within easy reach. He talks a good deal about the last war, in which he was wounded, and about the Communists, who are, he believes, getting ready to assume power, and about guns, which he loves. But wherever a conversation with Cranford starts, it always comes back to the same subject—what Cranford calls "niggers."

"The word Negro," he explained, within five minute of our meeting, "that's not in my vocabulary. There's colored folks and there's niggers, there ain't no Negroes."

I first met Raymond Cranford at the airport in Raleigh N. C., where we had lunch. That lunch was my first exposure to his way of talking, which is a kind of brutal monologue. The Raleigh airport restaurant is desegregated, and I pointed to a Negro who was eating next to a white man at one end of the lunch counter. I asked Cranford if the Negro's presence bothered him.

"If that man sitting next to him wants to eat like a nigger," said Cranford, "that's his business. But if that nigger was to come to this table, I'd know how to handle him. I'd say I'd got some alligators I'd like to feed." He looked around the table with a small, closed-mouth grin—he does not show his teeth when he smiles, and he hardly ever laughs. Then the monologue started. A few excerpts will suggest its flavor.

"A white nigger, that's worse than a nigger. A white nigger's a man's got a white skin, and a heart that's pumpin' nigger blood through his veins. If it comes to a fight, the white nigger's gonna get killed before the nigger."

"You come from Washington? I call Washington Hersheytown—ninety percent chocolate and ten percent nuts."

"We believe a white man's got his civil rights too. I'll lay down my life for those rights, if I have to. These nigger civil rights, they're gonna end in the white man's bedroom."

"We don't believe in burning crosses on a man's lawn. If I'm gonna burn a cross, I ram it through the man and burn it." This with a small grin.

"When the Communists take over, they're gonna kill me quick. Well, you only got one time to die."

"I got a daughter, she's nineteen years old. I love my daughter, but I find her with a nigger, I'll take my gun and I'll blow her brains right out of her head."

These observations are not very pretty or enlightening, and in the time I spent with Raymond Cranford, I heard them repeated almost literally *ad nauseam.* And

Reprinted with permission of the author from Saturday Evening Post, *April 9, 1966, pp. 23-27.*

yet it is worth trying to understand Raymond Cranford, for he is one of a very large number of Americans who are wholly alienated from the comfortable American society that most of us know. In the Klan oath, the world outside the Klan is called "the alien world," and in the eyes of a Klansman like Raymond Cranford, that world is heavily populated by "Communists," "white niggers," and other enemies.

North Carolina has an old and well-earned reputation for moderation in race relations. Nevertheless, as the recent investigation by the House Un-American Activities Committee established, North Carolina's Ku Klux Klan, nonexistent three years ago, is now bigger and better organized than the Klan in any other state. Its membership has been estimated as high as 20,000. The hard core of the Klan is in the flat, sandy, cotton-and-tobacco country in the eastern part of the state, where Negroes make up more than 40 percent of the population. The hard core of this hard core is in Greene County, where Exalted Cyclops Raymond Cranford presides over his klavern.

I owe my introduction to Raymond Cranford to a 33-year-old reporter called Pete Young. Young has spent the last two years covering the mushroom growth of North Carolina's Klan, and he has become a close friend of Exalted Cyclops Cranford, Grand Dragon Robert Jones, and dozens of assorted Klaliffs, Kleagles, Klokkards, Kludds, and just plain Knights. Young had invited me to have a look at the Klan, and offered to act as my guide. I had accepted, and asked Ted Ellsworth, an old friend, and *Post* photographer Ollie Atkins to go with me.

Cranford was in the marines in World War II, he told us at lunch, and had been wounded and decorated. "A psychiatrist told me I got backward reflexes," he said. "I got no sense of fear. Till I was twelve years old, I couldn't get to sleep at night without a light in the room. But when I'm in danger, I'm *cool*."

Cranford smokes constantly—upwards of four packs a day, he says. His nails are chewed to the quick, and he has bleeding ulcers. He used to drink a lot, but no longer. "When I was in the marines, I used to go out snipin' Japs with one canteen of water and one of alcohol. In the Klan, you can't get drunk, and you can't swear."

Cranford is deeply proud of being a Klansman. "My daddy and my granddaddy were in the Klan," he says. "I was born in the Klan." He is, he says, "a Klansman full time and a farmer part time." He owns a 200-acre farm with a 22-acre tobacco allotment. In most years his tobacco crop alone brings him a net profit of around $11,000. But Raymond Cranford does not think of himself as a prosperous citizen.

"They wouldn't let a pore white like me past the door of the Waldorf-Astoria in New York," he said, as we walked to the parking lot. "So why should a nigger go anywhere he wants?"

Between the bucket seats of Cranford's red late-model car there was a bone-handled pistol and cartridge belt, and a rifle hung in a halter arrangement by the left front door. Cranford demonstrated how he would react if a "nigger or Communist" threatened him in the car. When he opened the door, he could fire his rifle without taking it out of its halter. The hollow-pointed bullets, he explained, would catch a man in the legs or stomach. "Mister, with this little gun," he said, "you can blow a hole through a man, you could walk right through it."

"I can outrun any FBI car in the state—I got a supercharged engine," he said, as we started on the drive to Greene County. "Course, the FBI taps my phone. I got an alibi for every cotton-pickin' minute, but they'll find a way to frame me." To the relief of his passengers, he turned out to be a cautious driver, careful about passing, and stopping at all stop signs.

Cranford is very proud of being Exalted Cyclops, or No. 1 man, of his klavern. A klavern is the basic Klan unit, with membership ranging from a dozen or so to a couple of hundred—Cranford said he had about 60 men in his klavern.

He was also, he said proudly, a major in the "V.I.P. Security Guard" of the Klan. As such, he wears a major's oak leaves, and a helmet liner, uniform, and regulation paratroop boots at the Klan's cross-burning rallies. His job is to guard the Grand Dragon, the Imperial Wizard, and other Very Important Persons.

"Fren, you better keep your hands away from your pockets at a rally. You lay a hand on the Grand Dragon or the Imperial Wizard, and fren, you're *daid*."

As an Exalted Cyclops, Cranford said, he had direct access at any time of the day or night to the Imperial Wizard himself, Robert Shelton of Alabama, to whom he always referred respectfully as "Mr. Shelton."

"I can't get to see 'Light Bulb' Johnson," Cranford said. "I can't get to see the governor. They wouldn't give me the time of day. But I can call *Mr.* Shelton any time of the day or night. There's the number one man in the nation, and he'll take his time and money to talk to me, or come and see me any time."

A man could identify himself as a Klansman if he wanted to, Cranford said, but no other Klansman would identify him, on pain of death. "In some places," he explained, "you got white niggers, they'll fire Klan people—they won't say it's because they're in the Klan, but they'll always find some excuse."

Then there are anti-Klan people in Greene County? "Some, but everybody knows they're just after the nigger dollar."

By this time we had arrived at the motel where we were to stay. When Grand Dragon Jones was in the neighborhood some months earlier, Cranford said, the manager refused to give him a room. Cranford gleefully explained how he dealt with this insult to the Grand Dragon:

"I went to the manager, and I said, 'Now, fren, I'm not threatenin' anybody. But I got twenty niggers working at my place, and they're *real* dirty niggers, why I bet they haven't washed for weeks, and they sure *do* stink. Now I want a public apology to the Grand Dragon, and if I don't get it, I'm gonna register those twenty niggers right here. If you take them you'll have to fumigate the place, maybe burn it down. If you don't take them, I'm gonna prosecute you under the Civil Rights Act.' So he apologized."

That evening we drove over to Raymond Cranford's house for supper and found that quite a little party had been laid on for us. We were introduced to Mrs. Cranford, a strong-faced woman with reddish hair, and to Bob Littleton, the Exalted Cyclops of a klavern in neighboring Pitt County, and his wife. A Kleagle, or recruiter for the Klan, who didn't want to be identified, was there, and so was the Night Hawk of Cranford's klavern. The Night Hawk, whose job it is to organize the Klan's cross-burning rallies, is a sad-faced, monosyllabic farmer called Bennie Earle Oates. Also at the party were Cranford's 19-year-old daughter and nine-year-old son, as well as various in-laws and other children.

The Cranfords live in a small brick house, close to a village street. The furniture is the kind that is meant to be used, not just looked at. There is an old-fashioned front parlor, a dining room and a "family room" at the back. The party moved into the family room. No liquor was served. Somebody put a record on the phonograph. The song's endlessly repeated refrain was: *Move those niggers north, if they don't like our southern ways, move those niggers north.* Cranford pointed to his young son's school book—there was a big KKK scrawled in ink across its cover. "He's born into the Klan too," Cranford said proudly.

When the record stopped, the male members of the party moved into the dining room and were served a good meal of barbecued chicken by the ladies, who ate afterward. The conversation was dominated, as always, by Raymond Cranford. There were a couple of units of the Deacons for Defense, the armed Negro organization in the area, he said, "But we're not scared of them. You start poppin' bullets around a nigger, and their feet's gotta go."

One of the other Klansmen interrupted to say that the Klan was "against violence, except in self-defense," which is the official Klan line. "That's right," said Cranford. "We believe in ballots, not bullets—a Klansman gets out of line, and the Grand Dragon will clobber him." But the bullets keep creeping into the conversation.

"I'm not here to shoot a nigger, but if trouble starts, the white nigger's first on my list."

"Sure, the white niggers'll get it first. Say there's a bird on the fence and another bird scrunched down behind the fence. Which one's gonna get shot first?"

How much danger, I asked, was there of some sort of Negro uprising in the area—something like Watts?

"Not a chance," said Cranford, and the others nodded in agreement. "Look, I can have a thousand men in one hour, with air-cooled machine guns and two cases of grenades. There are more combat men in the Klan than in any other organization except the V.F.W. We didn't fight in World War Two just to let the niggers take over the country. That's not a threat. That's a promise.

In the living room, after supper, the guns came out. Everybody seemed to have a gun—all the children had toy guns. Cranford showed the shotgun he had won for recruiting members into the Klan, and Littleton passed around his new high-powered rifle. Then Cranford put on his Exalted Cyclops robes, white with a crimson hood. "They call these robes bedsheets," he said indignantly. "Bedsheets! You just feel that satin. That's the finest quality there is."

We got up to go, and I thanked Mrs. Cranford for the delicious chicken dinner. "Now, when you come to write that article," she said, in a sweet-southern voice, "you be fair, You're not fair, I'm coming to Washington with a machine gun."

All the men piled into cars to inspect Cranford's newly built klavern—permission to show these previously secret Klan meeting halls had apparently come from higher authority. The klavern turned out to be a long, windowless cinderblock hut with a cement floor. In the middle of the floor was the "altar"—a wooden table with a bayonet and a Bible on it, flanked by the U.S. and Confederate flags, backed by a cross lit by bulbs. On the wall behind the "altar" were two signs: FIGHT FOR THE RIGHT, DIE IF WE MUST, BUT ALWAYS REMEMBER, IN GOD WE TRUST, and A MAN NEVER STOOD SO TALL AS WHEN HE STOOPED TO HELP A CHILD. The first is the official Klan motto. Putting up the second, Cranford said proudly, was his own idea.

On a mantelpiece were two long strips of rubber tire, attached to wooden handles. These were used, said the Kleagle who didn't want to be identified, to "teach informers a lesson." The Klan, Cranford explained, has its own system of discipline. A Klansman who "gets out of line"—drinks too much, or "cheats on his wife," or disgraces the Klan in some way—may be tried by a Klan court, and punished appropriately. The Klan is, in fact, a kind of inner government—a Klansman swears allegiance to the Klan above any allegiance to the "alien world."

To us outsiders, the visit to Cranford's klavern was a bit anticlimactic—we had expected something more sinister. Perhaps sensing our disappointment, Cranford seized the bayonet and began demonstrating his "karate," showing how, if a nigger or a Communist" made a grab for the bayonet, he would plunge it into his adversary's stomach—"I'll just shove it in, by instinct."

We piled into cars again, to have a look at Bob Littleton's klavern. It is bigger than Cranford's, with seats for more than 100 people. There is also an open coffin—to scare the initiates—and a lot of Klan propaganda tacked up on a post, including a picture of the murdered civil-rights worker, Mrs. Liuzzo, walking with two Negroes. Littleton and the Kleagle both pointed out the damning fact that she was walking barefoot.

There was, we "aliens" agreed at the motel, something very sad about the dreary little klaverns with their kitchen tables masquerading as "altars," and their coffee cans filled with old cigarette butts and their hand-lettered, misspelled signs; and something very sad about the Klan.

The next day, Cranford showed up bright and early with his Klaliff, or No. 2 man. The Klaliff (who didn't want to be identified) turned out to be a pleasant-mannered, freckle-faced young man. He had been in the Korean war, and like most Klansmen we met, he had been a combat soldier.

Cranford took us to the "nigger school" which was, he said, bigger, newer, and more expensive than the white school. I asked if integration of the school had started.

"It started," Cranford said, "but it stopped."

We "aliens" got out to talk to the principal of the Negro school while the Klansmen stayed in the car outside. The principal is a soft-voiced, articulate Negro called Raymond Morris. Yes, he said, it is quite true—the Negro school was newer and better equipped than the white school. Had integration started? Yes, it had started—three specially chosen Negro children had been sent to the white school, in September. They had got along well for a month.

"But then an unfortunate thing happened," Morris said, in his quiet, singsong voice. "One night, someone shot into the homes of the children who had gone to the white school. No one was hurt, but the parents had a natural reluctance to keep the children in that school." Later we asked Cranford about the shooting incident. He grunted, but for once he said nothing.

That afternoon, we went to the town of Ayden, where, Cranford said, "the niggers are stirring up trouble." Outside a store, a line of Negro children were carrying signs reading NO HIRING NO BUYING or WE'RE TIRED OF BEING BAGBOYS AND MAIDS. This trouble, Cranford said, had been "stirred up" by the local head of the N.A.A.C.P., an undertaker called Gratz Norcott.

"He stirs up the trouble, and him being an undertaker, if the trouble gets bad, he stands to get all the business. I tole him, if one of my guys gets hurt, I'm not gonna horse around, I'm comin' right after you."

Norcott, it turned out, had his office in a small house across the street from the store. Ted Ellsworth suggested that we call on Norcott, and get his side of the story. The idea of a confrontation with Norcott had clearly never occurred to Cranford. But he interpreted the suggestion as a challenge to his courage. So he squared his shoulders and strode into the little house, followed by the Klaliff, the Night Hawk, and us "aliens."

Norcott's office is tiny, and by the time I elbowed my way into it, whatever greetings had been exchanged between Cranford and Norcott had already. occurred, and an uncomfortable silence reigned. Norcott, a middle-aged Negro with an expressionless face, was at his desk, with a telephone held against an ear. Occasionally he would mutter something into the telephone, but there were long stretches when he said nothing at all. I shook his hand, and it was wet with sweat, and when he lit a cigarette, the match wavered. But if Norcott was scared by this surprise visit from the Klan, his self-control was remarkable.

For a while, as Norcott held the telephone up to his ear, we white men stood around rather sheepishly—there were only two chairs in the office. Then Norcott held the telephone away from his ear and addressed Cranford in a polite but authoritative tone:

"Mr. Cranford, there are some chairs right across the hall there. Will you fetch a few so these gentlemen can sit down?"

Cranford hesitated a moment, and glared at Norcott, then got the chairs. We all sat down.

At last Norcott put the telephone in its cradle. While he was explaining his side of the "trouble"—the store did most of its business with Negroes, he said, and the Negroes wanted one of the three cashiers' jobs—two young, tough-looking Negroes came into the office, followed by an elderly Negro minister and a Negro doctor. Obviously news of the confrontation had spread rapidly.

The two young men were field workers for Martin Luther King's Southern Christian Leadership Conference. One was a native North Carolinian, the other came from the Bronx. Norcott introduced them, and then introduced Cranford:

"Mr. Cranford here is the Cyclops—is that right, Mr. Cranford? Yes, the *Exalted* Cyclops of the Ku Klux Klan." There was no hint of a smile, only the faint emphasis on the ridiculous adjective.

Cranford, sensing a challenge, glared at the Negro from the Bronx, then addressed Norcott:

"Now, fren, I'm not threatenin' you, I'm just givin' you a bit of advice. You and me, we don't see things the same way, but we'll get along all right, just so long as you don't bring in outsiders to make trouble. If you're gonna bring in outsiders, you could be asking for real *bad* trouble. Now, is that a gamble you want to take?"

"Well, now, Mr. Cranford," said Norcott, his tone polite, almost soothing, "when you had your rallies here last summer, I think I'm right, you brought in Mr. Shelton, the *Imperial* Wizard, I think you call him, from Alabama. And I heard you bring in some *Grand* Dragons, or what is it you call them, from as far away as Ohio. Isn't that right?"

"Well, let me tell you something," said Cranford, "I don't believe in threatenin' a man, or burning crosses to scare him. If I got something I don't like about you, I just walk right up to you in the street and bust you right in the nose."

"Well, now, Mr. Cranford," said Norcott, more soothingly than ever, "I wouldn't walk right up to you and punch *you* in the nose. I'd *discuss* the matter with you. And if we couldn't agree, then I'd put the matter in the hands of the law, because we in the N.A.A.C.P., we believe in the law, we obey the laws of the land."

By this time Cranford was both angry and a little confused, like a bull after the picadors had worked him over.

"I'm against violence," he said, his voice rising, "but I'm gonna protect my rights, and if anybody wants a fight, he can get what he wants. Why, few weeks ago, three niggers pulled up beside my car, I seen they had guns, and I put a clip in my gun, and by God. . . ."

"SHUT UP, RAYMOND," Pete Young said, suddenly and loudly. Cranford subsided. There was some further sparring. Then Cranford said, rather plaintively, "You nigras talk about discrimination. Why, right here, some cops will give a Klansman a ticket just because he's a Klansman."

At this point, Dr. Andrew Best, a Negro physician with a round, good-humored face, intervened for the first time. He spoke with quiet passion:

"But can't you see, that's just what they've been doing to us as long as we've lived, giving us a ticket just because we're Negroes."

"The word 'Negro'," Cranford said, in a Pavlovian reaction, "that's not in my vocabulary. There's colored folk and there's niggers. There ain't no Negroes."

"Mr. Cranford," said Dr. Best, in a tone of infinite earnestness, "I want to ask you to try to imagine something. I want to ask you to try to imagine what your life would be like if my color was your color and your color was my color. Can you imagine what that would be like?"

"Listen, fren," said Cranford, "do you think life's easy for the pore white man in the South?" Cranford got up suddenly and strode out to his car, followed by the Klaliff and the Night Hawk, while we outsiders shook hands with the Negroes and muttered good-byes.

That evening the Exalted Cyclops, the Klaliff, the Night Hawk, and a couple of local Knights joined us "aliens" in a motel room, and we drank a few bourbons and talked. I asked the Klansmen why they hated Negroes. They seemed genuinely surprised. "We don't hate the niggers," the Klaliff said, and others agreed. Cranford told how he supported a family of "no-count niggers" on

his place. "We don't hate niggers, long's they behave like colored people," said a Knight. Somebody added that "Northerners don't understand niggers. A nigger's like a dog, he can smell it when you're scared of him."

There was a silence. Raymond Cranford looked musingly at his big hands. "These hands of mine," he said. "They're my secret weapon. By rights they ought to be locked up as a deadly weapon. My hands are like knives—they'll cut a man right across. I can kill a man with the open hand. The tougher the man is, the better I like it."

Cranford had had nothing to drink. He began talking then about a poor white family we had visited that afternoon. The wife and children had come to the door for groceries supplied by the Klan. The man had been lurking somewhere in the house. He was drunk, and he had left his fields untended, and could not hold a job.

"I'm going out there again, maybe tomorrow," Cranford said, "and I'll straighten him out. I'll tell him, 'You straighten out, or I'll bust your tail.' Then maybe I'll shove him up against the wall, and slap him up against the side of a truck, and maybe turn him upside down and shake his brains up a bit. Then I'll tell him, 'Fren, you straighten yourself out, and then we'll go out and get you a job so you can support your family. Course now, I'm not goin' to hurt him, not unless he fights back. If man don't fight back I can't *stand* to whup him. But if he just puts his fists up, man I *love* that. I'll just tear his tail *up*."

There was another silence, as we contemplated Cranford's cure for alcoholism. Then the Klansmen began talking about the rallies the Klan had held every night in the summer—the burning crosses made of big trees dragged out of the forests, the "nigger speeches," the crowds of robed Klansmen. Someone said that the sight of the burning cross gave him a "real religious feeling." Pete Young described a rally at which Collie Leroy Wilkins and the other Alabama Klansmen accused of killing Mrs. Liuzzo had been introduced to the crowd. They were greeted, Young said, with a wild roar of enthusiasm, and the other Klansmen who had been present at the rally nodded happily at the recollection.

It is a reporter's job to listen, to ask questions, to try to understand, to avoid emotional involvement. But suddenly I felt involved, and angry.

"Look," I said to the freckle-faced Klaliff, "you're proud of having fought for your country, and you're right to be proud. But a young man shooting an unarmed woman through the head at a range of ten feet—I don't care what she did, that's a cowardly thing to do, and I just don't see how a brave man like you can shout and clap for a man who did it."

There was a sudden silence in the room. The Klaliff was genuinely shocked —he blushed beet red, as though I had said something obscene.

"Well, now," he said, "I'm not saying I approve of what was done there, but you've gotta remember what she was doing. . . .Anyway, let's face it—this is a war."

There was another silence. Cranford said nothing, but he stared sullenly with his black-rimmed eyes at his big hands, his "secret weapon." For the first and only time, I smelled danger. Then Pete Young changed the subject, and the smell passed. One by one we drifted off to bed. As I was saying good night, the young Klaliff stopped me, and said earnestly, as though trying hard to explain something to me:

"Maybe there's something you don't understand, coming from the North. When it comes to a woman, in the South, why, there's nothing that's respected any more than that."

The next morning Raymond Cranford

greeted us bright and early, as usual. The Klaliff was with him, and the Night Hawk. So was a high Klan official, the Grand Klokkard of the Realm, a youngish man with a very thin face, quiet manners, and hard eyes, called Sonny Fischer.

The Grand Klokkard insisted on showing us his klavern. Like Littleton's, Fischer's klavern boasted an open coffin. There were two hand-lettered signs in the coffin—A NIGGER TRIDE A NIGGER DIED, and THIS BOX IS RESERVED FOR MR. BIG MOUTH. Hanging from a wall nearby were two of the long five-cell flashlights which Klansmen carry at rallies—they make very effective clubs, and to make them more effective, they are sometimes lined with lead. One of these flashlights had a deep dent in it. I asked how the dent was made.

"On a burrhead," someone said, and the Klansmen laughed.

Behind the coffin there were two signs which read: OUR GOVERNMENT IS DEAD. There was the now familiar picture of Mrs. Liuzzo, walking with two Negroes—again, a Klansman pointed out that she was walking with her shoes in her hand. And hanging from a knob was a little plastic doll of a Negro child.

The doll—it was a girl, in a cotton dress—had a hangman's noose tied around its neck. I asked about this, too, and was told it was "just a joke." I remembered the sign Raymond Cranford had posted in his klavern, and of which he was so proud. A MAN NEVER STOOD SO TALL AS WHEN HE STOOPED TO HELP A CHILD.

Later that day, we said good-bye to Raymond Cranford and his fellow Klansmen. Cranford passed around stickers which read: THE KNIGHTS OF THE KU KLUX KLAN IS WATCHING YOU and BE A MAN JOIN THE KLAN and YOU HAVE BEEN VISITED BY THE KU KLUX KLAN.

"Now, you just stick those on

Light-Bulb Johnson's desk when you get up there to Hersheytown," he said, and laughed out loud, for the first time, at his own joke.

Have I been fair to Raymond Cranford? Or would Mrs. Cranford be justified in bringing her machine gun to Washington?

The Kleagle, the Klokkhard, the Night Hawk, Exalted Cyclops Littleton and their wives and children seemed polite, pleasant-mannered people. Raymond Cranford and the other Klansmen were no doubt brave men and patriots by their own lights. And they were all people who wanted very badly, almost desperately, to be understood. Yet, I never did really understand them.

"Maybe there's something you don't understand coming from the North," the young Klaliff said. Maybe there is. But how *do* you understand people who seem to be moral people, and who feel quite sincerely that a picture of a woman walking with Negroes, with her shoes off justifies her murder?

the brilliancy

of black

BERNARD WEINRAUB

Jesus Christ, His arms outstretched and pleading, is painted in lush blues and pinks in the lobby. Inside the church, the aisles are filling with teen-agers, curiously quiet and solemn, who grip programs (Harlem Youth Unlimited presents... 'The Role of Negro Youth in Shaping Their Destinies' "). Stepping through a crowd a slight woman with a lost, desperate smile hands out a "Come Ye Disconsolate" leaflet and cries out that Brothers and Sisters you are all invited to view the Southern Baptist Stars on their twenty-second anniversary at Mount Moriah Baptist Church.

Outside, bare-chested little boys in sneakers watch the white television men set up their cameras. A white cop, a pudgy man with roly-poly fingers and a hard, blue-eyed Irish face, removes a handkerchief from his rear pocket, scrubs off his forehead sweat and gazes up, up, up at the church — a De Mille Corinthian setting that was once a movie theatre, the Alhambra. The Black Muslims are distributing Muhammad Speaks, and the televison men are nervous and the teen-agers keep surging into the sweltering lobby past the mural of Jesus. It is dusk on Seventh Avenue and 116th Street in Harlem and it is warm and they are waiting for Stokely Carmichael.

Three months earlier, Stokely had taken over the Student Nonviolent Coordinating Committee and had coined those two words "Black Power" that aroused all the white folks and dismayed some of the powerful black folks. He had been on Meet The Press television and on the front page of *The New York Times* and had visited Mississippi and Washington, D. C. and Boston and now, finally, he was in Harlem.

The kids waited. They were fifteen, sixteen and seventeen, the boys in pressed olive-drab suits and seersucker jackets, the girls in sandals, dangling earrings, A-line skirts, and kerchiefs, quite chic, on their African cropped hair. They carried paperbacks and chatted quietly. For the

Reprinted by permission of Bernard Weinraub, c/o Marvin Josephson Associates, Inc., from Esquire, *January, 1967, pp. 130-35. Copyright © 1967 Esquire, Inc.*

past few months they had been in the Haryou-Act anti-poverty program where they worked with the community, and baby-sat for working mothers, and were taught what to wear when they took the A train downtown to apply for a job on Fifth Avenue. And they had read — and discussed — James Baldwin and Chester Himes and explored in heated talks The Role of Negro Youth and The Problems of Negro Youth and What's Ahead for Negro Youth. And now Stokely, who used to play stickball on 137th Street, comes onstage with a half-dozen other speakers and the curious tenseness among the teenagers bursts. They break into wild applause.

Stokely is surrounded by friends. "Hey, baby, how ya' doin'?" he cries. . . . "Hey Thomas, why the hell aren't you back in Alabama doin' some work. . . .Hey, boy, you lookin' good." Stokely looks good too. He wears black Italian boots, a tight blue suit, white shirt, striped tie, a name chain on his wrist. He is six-feet-one and has the build of a basketball guard: a solid chest, slender waist, powerful legs. His smile dazzles—an open unguarded, innocent smile.

The first speaker is seventeen-year-old Clarissa Williams, a striking girl in a loose green dress. She has a gentle voice: *Newsweek* and *Life* have conducted their own surveys of black people. Well, baby, no one has to tell us what the black community is like because we know it, we live it. We intend to be the generation which will make black youth to be unlimited. We intend to be the generation that says, Friends, we do not have a dream, we do *not* have a dream, we have a plan. So, TV men, do not be prepared to record our actions indoors, but be prepared to record our actions *on the streets*. . . ." The audience, and Stokely, applaud and cry, "Hit'em hard, sister."

Clarissa hits them harder and by the time she winds up her tough little speech the audience is electric. And then Stokely rises. His style dazzles. He shakes his head as he begins speaking and his body appears to tremble. His voice, at least in the North, is lilting and Jamaican. His hands move effortlessly. His tone—and the audience loves it—is cool and very hip. No Martin Luther King We Shall Overcome oratory. No preacher harangue. No screaming. He speaks one tone above a whisper, but a very taut, suppressed whisper. His speech—he has made it dozens of times before—varies with the audience, the area, the news that day, his mood. Stokely's words flow musically and build and Stokely pounds into the microphone and stops and the music starts again. The audience is rapt.

"Brothers and Sisters, we have been living with The Man too long. Brothers and Sisters, we have been *in a bag* too long. *We have got to move to a position where we will be proud, be proud of our blackness.* From here on in we've got to stick together, Brothers and Sisters, we've got to join together and move to a new spirit and make of our community a community of love . . . LOVE. There's no time for shuckin' and jivin'. We've got to move fast and we've got to come together and we've got. . .we've got to realize. . .that this country was conceived in racism and dedicated to racism. And understand that we've got to move. . .WE HAVE GOT TO MOVE. . . .We've got to build to a position so that when L.B.J. says, 'Come, heah, boy, I'm gonna send you to Vietnam,' we will say, 'Hell, no.' " ("Preach, boy, preach. . . .Tell'em, Stokely. . . .")

"Brothers and Sisters, a hell of a lot of us are gonna be shot and it ain't just gonna be in South Vietnam. We've got to move to a position *in this country* where we're not afraid to say that any man who has been selling us rotten meat for high prices should have had his store bombed fifteen years ago. We have got to move to a position where we will control our *own* destiny. We have got to move to a position where we will have black people represent us to achieve *our* needs. This country don't run on love, Brothers, it's run on power and we ain't got none. Brothers and Sisters, don't let them separate you from other black people. Don't ever in your life apologize for your black brothers. Don't be ashamed of your culture because if you don't have culture that means you don't exist and, Brothers and Sisters, we do exist. Don't ever, don't ever, don't *ever* be ashamed of being black because you. . .you are black, little girl with your nappy hair and your broad lips, and *you are beautiful*. Brothers and Sisters, I know this theatre we're in—it used to be the Alhambra. Well I used to come here on Saturday afternoon when I was a little boy and we used to see Tarzan here and all of us would yell like crazy when Tarzan beat up our black brothers. Well, you know Tarzan is on television now and from here on in I'm rooting for that black man to beat the hell out of Tarzan. . . ."

The audience roars and is on its feet and Stokely grins and waves. The audience keeps applauding. . . .

Stokely is in the East to build up support, to meet with S.N.C.C. workers in New York, Newark, Boston and Philadelphia. He will make speeches and hold private meetings and endure just a few interviews (he turns down many of them now because of "distortions"). At twenty-five, the most charismatic figure in the Negro movement, Stokely Carmichael rushes from ghetto to ghetto with the drive of a political candidate one week before Election Day. He sleeps just a few hours a night. He eats on the run and drinks milk to keep up his energy. In Mississippi and Alabama, during those five summers of unbearable heat, of prison, of beatings, of death threats, of

rifle shots fired at him through car windows, Stokely smoked three packs of cigaretts a day. He doesn't smoke now and doesn't drink.

His base now—and S.N.C.C.'s headquarters—is in Atlanta and his itinerary in other cities is set up by the local S.N.C.C. office, mostly by twenty- and twenty-one-year-old Negroes whom Stokely led in the South. There are, inevitably, the fund-raising parties—S.N.C.C.'s funds have dropped—but mostly just meetings and speeches.

He spends the next day in Newark, a dismal, grey city which has more Negroes than whites. The highlight of the visit is a speech that evening at the anti-poverty board on Springfield Avenue, in the heart of the ghetto, and then a cocktail party at ten-fifteen across town. The anti-poverty board is packed with an older audience than in Harlem. There are mothers with children on their lap and grandmothers with grandchildren on their bosom; old men in overalls, janitors, civil-service workers, LeRoi Jones, high-school students, tough-looking nineteen-year-olds, leaning against the green stucco walls, and several white poverty workers.

Stokely instinctively knows the audience. He stares quickly across the room and then scribbles down notes on the back of an envelope. He rises to warm applause. He smiles.

"Is it okay if ah take off mah jacket?" he says in a too-Southern drawl.

The speech goes well. Stokely begins by warming up the elderly women in the audience and ends with a cry to the students. The themes are the same. "You gotta understand about white power. It's white power that brought us here in chains, it's white power that kept us here in chains and it's white power that wants to keep us here in chains. . . .What they've been able to do is make us ashamed of being black. . . .ashamed. I used to come home from school and say, 'Hey, Momma.' And she used to say, 'Sssshh, you know how loud we are.' I wouldn't go outside eating watermelon, no sir. They say we're lazy, so we work from sunup to sundown to prove that we're not lazy. We are tired of working for them, of being the maids of the liberal white folks who consider us part of their families. . . .My mother was a maid for a lady in Long Island and this lady wanted me to go to college and she told my mother, 'Your boy is a bright colored boy and we want to help send him to college.' Well, I hated that woman. She gave my mother $30 a week and all the old clothes her kids didn't want. Well, I didn't want her old clothes. I didn't want her to help send me to college. I wanted my Momma." ("Tell it, Stokely. . . .")

"There is a system in this country that locks black people in, but lets one or two get out every year. And they all say, 'Well, look at that one or two. He's helping his race.' Well, Ralph Bunche hasn't done a damn thing for me. If he's helping his race, then he should come *home.* Brothers and Sisters, there's nothing wrong about being all white or all black. It's only when you use one to exploit the other—and we have been exploited. You gotta understand what they do. They say, 'Let's integrate.' Well integration means going to a white school because that school is good and the black school is bad. It means moving from a black neighborhood to a white neighborhood because one neighborhood, they tell you, is bad and the other is good. Well, if integration means moving to something white, moving to something good, then integration is just a cover for white supremacy. . . .

"Brothers and Sisters, we have to view ourselves as a community and not a ghetto and that's the only way to make it. The political control of every ghetto is outside the ghetto. We want political control to be *inside* the ghetto. Like the workers in the Thirties, like the Irish in Boston, we demand the right to organize the way we want to organize. Black power is the demand to organize around the question of blackness. We are oppressed for only one reason: because we are black. We must organize. Brothers and Sisters, the only way they'll stop me from organizing is if they kill me or put me in jail. And once they put me in jail I'll organize my brothers in prison. *Organize!*"

The back of Stokely's white shirt is drenched with sweat. As soon as he finishes the speech, the crowd rises and surrounds him and shakes his hand and Stokely seeks out the old ladies who cry, "My, my, *my,* you are somethin' " and gives the younger kids that special handshake reserved only for a black brother or sister—a handshake in which he clasps a hand with his right hand and places his left hand over the linked hands. (When a white man shakes his hand, the smile is guarded, the handclasp unsure, the left hand remains limp.)

Thirty minutes later the cocktail party on Porter Avenue awaits Stokely, who has stopped off in several Negro bars—not to drink, but to meet and talk with some of the customers. The party is given by a short, burly chemist and his wife in the yard in back of their twelve-room stucco house. At least forty people have paid $5 to see Stokely, with about a half-dozen S.N.C.C. workers admitted free. Weak Martinis and Whiskey Sours are ladled out and, curiously, the middle-aged white and Negro couples stand and drink together near the small swimming pool in the center of the yard. The younger white kids stand alone. The young Negroes stand beneath the Rose of Sharon, uncomfortable, hostile, waiting for Stokely.

He arrives late and in a bitter mood. In the car coming to the party Stokely has been told that David Frost, a candidate running in the upcoming Democratic Senatorial primary on an anti-Vietnam ticket, will also speak at the party. Stokely immediately feels that his name is being used to attract people for a political candidate, a *white* political candidate. The money isn't even going to S.N.C.C., as he had been told in New York, but to a local liberal group. Stokely is furious. He walks to the edge of the backyard and has a five-minute talk with Bob Fullilove, the local S.N.C.C. leader. Across the lawn, the young Negroes glower. . . .This is a real put-down, says one girl who is attending Rutgers Law School. Why the hell are they holding this in the backyard? Can't they hold it inside as if it were a regular, *formal* cocktail party? These people are not my kind of people. . . .I don't like this scene, man. . . .This is bad news. . . .

Stokely and Fullilove end their talk and Stokely walks beneath the Rose of Sharon with the woman who accompanied him to the party, a six-foot-tall, very cool, very black-skinned woman with piled-high Nefertiti hair. She wears a tight white dress and is, she knows and Stokely knows and the entire party knows, the most stunning woman there. Stokely sips a Coke and the girl glowers at the crowd, which tries very hard to be casual, and not stare at her. A white man walks over, smiling, gripping his Martini.

"I just want to tell you, Mr. Carmichael, I saw you on TV and I really agreed with you on, uh, Vietnam and—"

Stokely cuts him off. "Thank you." Stokely gives him the white man's handshake.

"Attention, attention," cries the hostess, a short chubby woman in a knit dress. "Our guests are all here and our program is beginning."

The young Negroes appear startled. "What program?" Stokely frowns.

"I just want to say a few words," the woman goes on. "We have always been an integrated community. . . ." The Negroes begin shifting uncomfortably. "And we've never cared at all here about money or status, whatever that means."

"Shit," says Stokely in a loud whisper. "She don't know about status? Look at that swimming pool."

As soon as Frost begins speaking, Stokely leaves the backyard and walks toward the front of the house with his date. He leans against an elm, his left hand gently on the young woman's shoulder. They chat in a whisper. A Negro girl, slightly drunk, and a white man come out of the house and Stokely glares at the girl. She walks over. "I like what you said about being proud of our blackness," she says.

"That means everyone," says Stokely in an angry whisper.

"Let's get out of here," says Stokely's date.

The girl looks at the white man and says, "Be proud of my blackness, my black womanness." She starts laughing and they walk away to a car.

Stokely watches them drive off.

"Let's leave," says Stokely's date.

They return to the backyard and within minutes Stokely—who had been scheduled to speak—and most of the young Negroes are gone; the whites and middle-aged Negroes are left alone.

Stokely is scheduled to take an eight o'clock flight the next morning to Glens Falls, New York, and then be driven to Benson, Vermont, for a speech at a camp—he's not quite sure what type of camp or who will be there. At two minutes after eight Stokely's cab pulls up to the Mohawk Airlines terminal at La-Guardia Airport and Stokely leaps out and runs toward the ticket desk.

"I'm sorry," the ticket agent behind the desk says with a smile. "The flight just left."

"Oh no, oh no, oh *no*." Stokely pounds his fist on the desk.

"There *is* a flight leaving from Kennedy at eight-forty-five with a stop-off at Albany. And there's another at ten-thirty." The ticket agent smiles again.

Stokely walks away and shakes his head. "I took a cab from the Bronx [his mother's house]. It should have taken twenty minutes to get here. I kept saying, 'Use the bridge, use the bridge, man.' But that son of a bitch kept saying that Bruckner Boulevard was faster. Faster! It took an hour. Oh. . .oh that son of a bitch."

Stokely wears dark glasses, a black shirt with small-flowered print, dungarees and black shoes. He hails a cab for Kennedy Airport and once the cab starts Stokely lifts up the glasses and rubs his eyes—he had gone to bed at five that morning.

"They always do that in Atlanta," he says. "They always give us a hard time with flights down there."

He shakes his head again. The cab glides out of LaGuardia toward the Van Wyck Expressway. The traffic toward Manhattan is heavy; toward Kennedy Airport there are few cars. When Stokely is in New York, he generally spends the night in his mother's South Bronx home (the only Negro family on the block). He had not seen her on this trip, though, since she is working as a maid on a maritime line.

"She's a hard worker and a sharp gal," says Stokely, staring at the cars crawling toward New York. He turns. "She knew, she knows, that if you want to make it you got to hustle, and she hustled from the word go. She took no shit from no one. I got that from my mother. She used to tell me, 'You take nothing from no one, no matter who they are.' She knows the realities of life and she demanded, made sure, that I knew them too."

He smiles. "My old man was just the opposite." Stokely shakes his head and sighs. "He believed genuinely in the great American dream. And because he believed in it he was just squashed. Squashed! He worked himself to death in this country and he died the same way he started: poor and black."

"We came here in '52 from Port-of-Spain. That was a place that was mostly black. It was run by black people and everyone—the cops, the teachers, the civil servants—was black. We came here thinking that this was the promised land. Ha. We went up to the Bronx—I was eleven years old—and I saw this big apartment house we were going to and I said, 'Wow, Daddy, you own that whole thing?' And then eight of us climbed up to a three-room apartment."

"My old man. . . ." Stokely takes off his glasses. . . ."my old man would Tom. He was such a good old Joe, but he would *Tom*. And was a very religious cat too—he was head deacon of the church and he was so honest, so very, very honest. He never realized people lied or cheated or were bad. He couldn't conceive of it. He just prayed and worked. Man, did he work. He worked as a cabdriver at night and went to school to study electricity and during the day he worked as a carpenter. He just thought that if you worked hard and prayed hard this country would take care of you. Well, I remember he tried to get into the carpenter's union—and this is a very racist thing. And the only way for him to get into the union was to bribe the business representative. Well, he would have none of that. So one day when my father is out, my mother calls up the business representative and tells him to come to the house and she gives him $50 and a bottle of perfume and my father gets into the union. And when my father comes home and finds out that he's in the union he says, 'You see. You work hard and pray hard and this country takes care.' And my mother and I. . .laughed. Wow. My old man was like the Man with the Hoe. He just felt that there were millions to be made in this country and he died at forty-two—just a poor black man."

The cab pulls up at the Eastern Airlines terminal in Kennedy Airport. Stokely walks in and within seconds a porter walks up and smiles broadly. "I usually hang out with the porters at the airports," he says, walking quickly through the terminal. "A lot of times I don't have money and they just pass the hat. They're good people. In Memphis last week they bought me a steak dinner."

He walks to Gate 2 where a Mohawk flight is taking off at eight-forty-five. He waits ten minutes on standby but the flight is filled. He trudges back to the ticket desk and makes a reservation for the ten-thirty flight and then phones S.N.C.C. to tell them to notify the camp. By now Stokely is hungry and he walks into the cocktail lounge and restaurant in the heart of the terminal. The alcoholics, the hangers-on, the bored travelers, the women catching the nine o'clock flight to Mexico City line the bar, sipping Bloody Marys and beer and Scotch, straight. A waiter hustles over and says, no, the restaurant is not open at this hour, but there's another restaurant at the end of the corridor. A woman at the bar, blonde, tall, tanned, in her late forties, carrying a large white pillbox, turns and stares through dark glasses at Stokely—this hulking, dungareed figure in dark glasses too. Their eyes meet. The woman smiles, just slightly, and Stokely stares at her for a moment and then turns away and walks out.

"Man, this place says something. You can get a drink at nine o'clock, but you can't get food."

At a table in the restaurant Stokely calls the waitress "M'am" and orders orange juice, bacon and eggs, English muffins and two glasses of milk.

"I used to drink," he says with a smile. "I used to like wine. I used to know a hell of a lot of guys who drank wine all day."

The waitress brings his orange juice and he sips it. "In Harlem I used to know a lot of guys like that. I used to know a lot of guys who were addicts and they were some beautiful cats. I'm not kidding. They had this ability, this profound ability to understand life."

While Stokely's father struggled and his mother worked as a maid to help support the family—Stokely has four sisters—he often spent days and weeks with his aunts on Lenox Avenue and 142nd Street in Harlem. "I like Harlem," says Stokely. "It's a very exciting place. It represents life, real life. On one block you have a church and right next door is a bar and they're both packed. On Saturday night people are always in constant motion. You get all of life's contradictions right there in one community: all the wild violence and all the love can be found in Harlem. You get the smells of human sweat and all sorts of bright colors and bright clothes and people in motion. You get preachers on one side of a street and nationalists on the other."

The waitress brings the rest of the order.

Stokely Carmichael grew up in the Bronx and Harlem, a bright, wild, aggressive boy. He attended P.S. 39, P.S. 34, and P.S. 83 and was involved, almost as soon as the family moved to New York, in fistfights and gang intrigues. In the Bronx, he was the only Negro member of the Morris Park Avenue Dukes and was, he admits, a specialist in stealing hubcaps and car radios.

In 1956 quite suddenly Stokely broke with the past. He was admitted to the Bronx High School of Science, a school for some of the brightest children in New

York. "My freshman year I wanted to leave," Stokely recalls. "I couldn't intellectually compete with those cats. They were doctors' sons and lawyers' sons and read everything from Einstein to *The Grapes of Wrath.* The only book I knew was *Huckleberry Finn.* It was clear to me I couldn't compete. My mother wouldn't accept it though. She wanted me to go to Science and she would have it no other way. No questions asked. 'Remember one thing,' she would say, 'they're white, they'll make it. You won't unless you're on the top.' "

Stokely began reading—Marx, Darwin, Camus, anything he was given. "I began to read as quickly as I could; anything that anybody mentioned. It was naïve at the time, but it was sincere." For the first time, his friends were upper middle-class whites, wealthy kids who would go on to Harvard, Columbia, Brandeis. He began going out with white girls and making the Greenwich Village scene. He was invited to parties on Park Avenue.

Even as he persisted in friendships with white men and women, however, Stokely realized that the white and black worlds he knew were not linking; in fact they were splitting, irrevocably, apart. "I learned at Science that white people, liberal white people, could be intellectually committed but emotionally racist. They couldn't see *through.* I was everybody's best friend. They would say to me, 'Oh, you're so different.' And they didn't know any other black people. What they meant was I didn't meet their image of black people. And their image, their responses, are governed by the thought that Negroes *are* inferior. I was an exception. I was the accepted Negro. But other Negroes weren't like me. They were bums, lazy, unambitious, inhuman, and that attitude was extended to me. They would say to me, 'Oh you dance so well,' when I couldn't dance so well. Or they would say to me, 'Oh, you're so

sensitive.' Well the only thing I was sensitive to was the fact that they all had maids and they saw no inconsistency between being my friend and exploiting a black maid—paying her $30 a week while they went off and made a damned good living. I went to parties on Park Avenue and they called their maids by their first name and the maids were smiling and serving and I knew full well what was going on in their minds and I knew they didn't want to take all that shit. All these kids—these filthy rich kids—they all had maids and my mother was a maid."

When Stokely was a high-school senior, he began reading about the first sit-ins in the South. His first reaction was negative. "What I said was, 'Niggers always looking to get themselves in the paper, no matter how they did it.' My opinion was that they didn't know what they were doing."

Within months, though, he met several students involved in the sit-ins. As the civil-rights movement spread quickly across the South, Stokely's commitment —and fascination—grew. First, he picketed Woolworth's in New York and then sat-in in Virginia and North Carolina. He turned down scholarships to several white schools and enrolled at Howard University, mostly because he could keep working in the movement while at a Negro School. At Howard, he met other civil-rights activists and immediately engaged in sit-ins and the early freedom rides through Mississippi, Georgia, and Alabama. The first ride and the first arrest was in Jackson, Mississippi in 1961. . . .

By now Stokely had finished breakfast at the airport and walked to Gate 2 to board the plane. Almost as soon as he took his seat he began shivering—he is always cold—and he grabbed a blanket off the rack. The plane started and Stokely peered through the window at the rows of A-frame houses below, the cars, the Manhattan skyline. "I went down South when I was nineteen. I was a kid who took nothing from no one. And, man, I took it." He smiled. "In Mississippi, the beatings are by the cops, not by mobs. The mobs, they throw wild punches and if you're cool you can miss them. But the cops are out to get your ass and you get three cops in a back room who are out to get your ass and. . . ." He shook his head. "In Jackson, before they put me in jail, the cops rode me up and down in an elevator; they kept kicking and using billy clubs and pressing the buttons using their fist. I wanted. . . .I just wanted to get my hands on one of them. But like you had to cover your head and. . . .and. . . .you keep thinking why don't you leave me alone. Why don't you beat your wives instead and just leave me alone?"

Stokely then spent time in jail. "Fifty-three days. Oh, lord, fifty-three days in a six-by-nine cell. Twice a week to shower. No books, nothing to do. They would isolate us. Maximum security. And those guards were out of sight. They did not play, *they did not play.* The sheriff acted like he was scared of black folks and he came up with some beautiful things. One night he opened up all the windows, put on ten big fans and an air conditioner and dropped the temperature to 38 degrees. All we had on was T-shirts and shorts. And it was so cold, so *cold,* all you could do was walk around for two nights and three days, your teeth chattering, going out of your mind, and it getting so cold that when you touch the bedspring you feel your skin is gonna come right off.

"I don't go along with this garbage that you can't hate, you gotta love. I don't go along with that at all. Man you *can,* you *do* hate. You don't forget that Mississippi experience. You don't get arrested twenty-seven times. You don't smile at that and say love thy white brother. You don't forget those beatings and, man, they were rough. You don't forget. You don't forget those funerals. I knew Medgar Evers, I knew Willie Moore, I knew Mickey Schwerner, I knew Jonathan Daniels, I met Mrs. Liuzzo just before she was killed. You don't forget those funerals."

The worst experience was what Stokely calls a two-day nervous breakdown just before the Selma-to-Montgomery march. "I was in the Ben Moore Hotel in Montgomery, getting ready to go downstairs, when they locked the doors. I couldn't get out. And downstairs were the marchers and the cops began beating and using hoses. I couldn't stand it. I was by my window and I looked down and saw the cops beating and I couldn't get out. I was completely helpless. There was no release. I kept watching and then I began screaming and I didn't stop screaming. Some guys took me to the airport later and I kept screaming and I tried to kick in a couple of windows at the airport. Oh, Man."

He shakes his head slowly. "There have been people in the movement who have cracked. Like you can't help it. You always work on the assumption that the worst things will happen, you always work on the assumption that you're going to die. I used to say that the only way they'll stop me is if they kill me. I still think that's true. What bothers me now is if I live through all this I just hope I don't get tired or give up or sell out. That's what bothers me. We all have weaknesses. I don't know what mine are. But if they find out they'll try to destroy me. It's a question of them finding out what my weaknesses are—money, power, publicity, I don't know. And sometimes. . .sometimes. . . you just get so tired too."

Stokely peers out the window at the clean, azure sky and shivers beneath the blanket. Within seconds, he is asleep.

Twenty minutes later the plane is landing at Albany Airport where Stokely will catch a plane for Glens Falls. He steps down the ramp and begins singing: "The empty-handed painter on your street is drawing crazy patterns on your sheet."

He grins and walks into the terminal. "Man, that Dylan is a wild guy."

With thirty minutes free before the next plane leaves, Stokely steps into the airport luncheonette and orders a vanilla ice cream soda. The waitress leaves and Stokely turns toward several persons at the counter reading newspapers. "Look at that, look at *that*," he says, laughing, pointing to the sports page headline of The New York *Daily News:* "Operate on Whitey's Arm."

"If they flipped that over and put it on the front page they'd sell a million copies," he laughs.

Within the hour Stokely arrives in the small Glens Falls airport—three hours late. As soon as he climbs off the plane, a smiling, crew-cut youth waves and walks over and introduces himself. He is Frank Levy, a Ph.D. candidate in economics at Yale and a member of the camp's staff.

Stokely struggles into Levy's red MG and they drive off to the camp. about fifty miles away. Stokely asks Levy about the camp and is told that it's called the Shawnee Leadership Institute, an annual two-week summer camp for teen-agers who hold discussions on "issues" and listen to invited guest speakers. (The next day, Lord Caradon, the British Ambassador to the United Nations, was coming up.) There are about seventy campers and a staff of thirty, mostly college and graduate students.

Stokely likes Levy and they begin kidding about Vermont: "I wonder if everyone up here smokes pot." The car crosses New York into Vermont on Route 4 and passes Deak's grocery and

Frank's Taxidermist. "I've never been to Vermont before," says Stokely.

The elms and pines are just starting to blaze with autumn colors and Stokely settles back and gazes silently at the countryside. He waves at farm boys—who wave back—and laughs as they ride past Crumley's grocery in Fort Ann. "A town like this and you go out of your mind," he exclaims. "I read someplace that suicide rates are very high in Vermont— they must be sick of cutting all that grass."

Just outside of Fort Ann, the car breaks down. Stokely moans and shakes his head and begins laughing. "This is my day," he says. The fan belt is broken and Stokely and Levy struggle with the new belt. After twenty minutes they are off again.

As soon as Stokely arrives at the camp he appears startled, then amused. "Wow," he says, as a half-dozen teen-age inter-racial couples, their arms around each other, surround the car. "Hey, like I had visions when I heard the name of the camp of old Protestant ladies sitting around campfires talking about love." They shake his hand and escort him to the dining room.

Once inside, Stokely is greeted by an old friend, Julian Houston, who is president of the Student Government at Boston University. Stokely grins and gives Julian the "black" handshake and embraces him. "Man, you should be workin' down in Alabama," cries Stokely.

With Houston and several other camp leaders, Stokely sits down at a wooden table while the campers, awe-struck, watch him. Plates of ham and cheese and rolls are brought out and Stokely eats hungrily while a long-haired girl strums a guitar and sings *Ain't Gonna Study War No More.*

After the plates are cleared away, all the campers are called into the wooden dining room. Stokely removes his shoes and begins speaking quietly. "Black people have not only been told that they are inferior, but the system maintains it. We are faced in this country with whether or not we want to be equal and let white people define equality for us on their terms as they've always done and thus lose our blackness or whether we should maintain our identity and still be equal. This is Black Power. The fight is whether black people should use their slogans without having white people say, 'That's okay.' You have to deal with what white means in this country. When you say black power you mean the opposite of white and it forces this country to deal with its own racism. The 1954 school desegregation decision was handed down for several reasons. It was a political decision—and it was *not* based on humanitarianism, but was based on the fact that this country was going further into nonwhite countries and you could not espouse freedom and have second-class citizens in your own country. The area in which we move now is politics and within a political context. People kept saying that segregation and racism was wrong because it was immoral. But they still didn't come to grips with the two essential things: we are poor and we are black. You can pass 10,000 bills but you still haven't talked about economic security. When someone is poor, it's not because of cultural deprivation, it's not because they need to be uplifted and head-started. When someone is poor, it's because they have no money, that's all. That's all. They say it's our fault, *our fault* that we're poor when in fact it's the system that calculates and perpetuates poverty. They say black people don't know money, that they'll drink it away, they won't work. But we never had money, and it's presumptuous to tell us we won't be thrifty, brave, clean and reverent. You know who the biggest welfare group is in

this country? You know who they are? You think it's the black people? Well, it's not. It's the farmers. They are the biggest welfare group in this country. But the difference between them and us is that they run their own programs, they control their own resources and they get something out of it. We must, *we must* take over and control our resources and our programs. And if we don't, the black people will wake up again tomorrow morning, still poor, still black, and still singing *We Shall Overcome.*"

The audience responds warmly and as soon as Stokely finishes, the questions begin. Stokely calls on a burly Negro youth who speaks in a thick drawl.

"Stokely, do you believe in God?"

Stokely stares at the youth. "That's a personal question."

The youth smiles. "Oh."

"Where you from?" Stokely asks.

"St. Augustine, Florida, Stokely."

"What you do down there?"

"I worked in the field. Cotton, tobacco, you name it. I worked for $2 a day since I was so high. I worked for $2 a day until I heard Dr. King down there and then I knew I had to join the movement."

"Right." Stokely turns from the boy to the audience. "The reason I joined the movement was not out of love. It was out of hate. I hate white supremacy and I'm out to smash it."

A pause. An older woman rises, a white woman. "Stokely," she asks, a tremor in her voice, "What can we do? What can the whites do?"

"You must seek to tear down racism. You must seek to organize poor whites. You must stop crying "Black supremacy" or "Black nationalist" or "racism in reverse" and face certain facts: that this country is racist from top to bottom and one group is exploiting the other. You must face the fact that racism in this country is a white, not a black problem.

And because of this, you, *you* must move into white communities to deal with the problem. We don't need kids from Berkeley to come down to Mississippi. We don't need white kids to come to black communities just because they want to be where the action is.

"Look," says Stokely, leaning forward, speaking in a loud whisper. "Every white man in this country can announce that he is our friend. Every white man can make us his token, symbol, object, what have you. Every white man can say, 'I am your friend.' Well from here on in we're going to decide who is our friend. We don't want to hear any words, we want to see what you're going to do. The price of being the black man's friend has gone up.

"And you must understand," he says, his voice rising, "that as a person oppressed because of my blackness, I have common cause with other blacks who are oppressed because of *their* blackness. It must be to the oppressed that I address myself, not to members—even friends—of the oppression group."

The audience stirs. Stokely suggests they walk outside so he can get some good country air. Within minutes, the teen-agers sit in a semicircle beneath an evergreen, chatting quietly with Stokely who is lying on his side, his elbow dug into the grass, his chin in his hand. . . .

By dusk, with the apricot-colored sky streaked with violet, the campers implore Stokely to stay the night. He'd love to, he says, he needs the rest and this marvelous clean air, but there are meetings and speeches and appointments the next day.

With Julian Houston, Stokely climbs into a car driven by a Roman Catholic priest from Boston who is on the camp's staff.

"Stokely," says the priest, driving quickly down the darkening road, "what should church people do?"

Stokely pauses. "They should start working on destroying the church and building more Christ-like communities. It's obvious, Reverend, that the church doesn't want Christ-like communities. Christ—he taught some revolutionary stuff, right? And the church is a counterrevolutionary force."

The priest drives a moment in silence. "What should the priest's job be?"

"To administer, through his actions, the teachings of Jesus Christ," says Stokely. "I would also make every church a plain building that could be used for other things, a building that will not be embellished."

"What's next for you, Stokely?" asks the priest.

"Next?" Stokely smiles. "How does the victim move to equality with the executioner? That's what's next. We are the victims and we've got to move to equality with our executioners." He pauses. "Camus never answers that question, does he? We are the victims, they are the executioners. Every real relationship is that victim and executioner. Every relationship. Love, marriage, school, everything. This is the way this society sees love. You become a slave to somebody you love. You love me, you don't mess around with anyone else. One is the victim, the other the executioner. . . ."

It is dark now and chilly and Stokely begins shivering. He begins gossiping with Houston about old friends who have been lost to the poverty program, the Peace Corps, graduate schools.

At the airport in Burlington, Stokely is told that the plane to New York has been delayed an hour. He shakes his head—"It's my day"—and walks around with Houston. He then has two sandwiches and two glasses of milk and averts the stares of several men at the bar who recognize him.

The plane finally arrives. Stokely

shakes hands with the priest and Houston and walks wearily up the ramp. He is cold and tired and sleeps listlessly on the trip to New York.

Shortly before eleven the plane lands at Kennedy Airport. Stokely has a date downtown in Manhattan but decides, instead, just to return to the Bronx and go to sleep. By now he is exhausted. The lack of sleep, the missed and delayed flights, the car trips, the questions, sandwiches on the run, the pressures have taken their toll. He walks through the terminal, breathing heavily, peering blankly through his dark glasses. Once outside, he decides to take a taxi and starts walking to the first cab in line. The driver, who is white, stares at Stokely—dungarees, dark glasses, carrying a paper bag of ham sandwiches, looking vaguely ominous— and drives past him to pick up a laughing white couple who carry cardboard cases of tax-free liquor. Stokely tenses, clenches his fist and takes a deep breath and turns toward the second cabdriver in line. This driver, who is a young Negro, has watched Stokely and is now smiling faintly. Stokely walks over, looks at the cabdriver and begins smiling too. He then opens the door and climbs into the cab and returns home for just a brief rest.

nightmare

journey

BOB CLARK

My long day's journey into a nightmare began Monday afternoon when I received a phone call from Howard Chapnick of the Black Star Photo Agency. He asked me if I wanted to go to Detroit to cover the riots. I found myself saying yes. Actually, I was in the mood to involve myself in this kind of experience. I really wanted to know what was going on behind the scenes and I wanted to know it first hand. I had covered a race riot in San Francisco and worked on news stories in the deep South. I once interviewed Stokely Carmichael for a German magazine. I thought I had a feel for the current picture of race relations in America. But Newark and Detroit were a new breed of cat. What was happening in our big city ghettos and how far would it go? Chapnick called me back within an hour and we made final arrangements. Soon I was on an early evening flight to Detroit.

Aboard the plane I kept trying to think of someone I could contact in the city. I knew there wouldn't be time to just roam. Things were happening fast and if I expected to get photographs I would have to be on top of things from the beginning. Being a Negro photographer would present special problems. I could expect rejection and hostility from both whites and blacks. I knew from past experience that black people won't hesitate to attack a "black sellout." I also knew that when violence has taken over a community, police don't always bother to ask questions or check carefully. I told myself I had better move around damn carefully or suffer the consequences.

As the plane banked into Metropolitan Airport I could see clouds of dense smoke drifting up from the city. As I think back now, I realize that even seeing that smoke I did not foresee the massive devastation or the enormous danger ahead of me. I

Reprinted with permission of the publisher from Ebony, *October, 1967, pp. 121-30.*

remember tensing up and promising my-self I would not be gun-shy. I tried to force myself to relax mentally and I vowed to work real loose.

At the Sheraton Cadillac Hotel there were many reporters and photographers in the lobby. The word at the moment was that there were a great many fires around the city but things seemed to have quieted down. I struck up a conversa-tion with a white man who was standing near by. He was short, stockily built and tough-looking and this appearance matched his trade. An ex-boxer turned promoter, Don Elbaum was in town for a boxing show that was canceled after the riots began. Elbaum said he was in the midst of the rioting on Sunday because a lot of his boxers were Negroes from the city's ghetto area. Now he was waiting in the lobby in the hope of meeting some of his boys and he wondered whether I would like to talk with them. I thought this was a good idea so I raced up to my room, changed clothes and returned to the lobby in a few minutes. Elbaum and I waited about half-an-hour but no one came. I began to get edgy about losing time.

I tried calling police headquarters and local television stations to find out where the action was, but either the phones were not answered or no one could offer any precise information.

Don Elbaum is one of those fast-talking, fast-moving sort of people who are in the know about what's going on and always have to be where the action is. When I decided to move on, he came with me. Don knew Detroit very well and guessed that the West side was the hot spot at the moment. We used his car and headed that way. The streets were deserted except for patrols of state troopers and national guardsmen. I was surprised to see that even in the downtown area of the city, buildings were burned and ransacked. I saw cars filled with volunteer sheriffs. These private cars raced about the city, shotguns and rifles protuding from the windows. Just the sight of them made my heart slip into my stomach, because I sensed that these men were my biggest menace.

We arrived somewhere; I don't know exactly where or how we got there. All I know is that all hell broke loose. It was a national guard position and snipers were pouring their fire into it. Guardsmen returned the fire with automatic weapons. They had a cross-fire going and it was impossible to know who was firing at whom. The guardsmen fired flares into the darkness and there were lengthy fusillades. I couldn't imagine anyone liv-ing through all that fire-power. I crawled out of the car and up into a front posi-tion. As I dodged from one point of cover to the next, I yelled out, "I'm press, don't shoot!" It was pitch black. I couldn't shoot pictures without using strobe lights and that would mean blind-ing some of the guardsmen or expos-ing their positions. I just squatted—listening and watching—for what seemed like an eternal 20 minutes and then went back to the car.

Don and I cruised around again. We spotted fire on the West side and drove toward it. A large warehouse or factory building was burning furiously and before the fire trucks could get into position the sniper-fire began. A small, three-storey house across an alley from the factory began to burn also. Women and children streamed out of this building carrying what belongings they could. Some men who lived in the neighborhood ran up to the house carrying small lawn hoses. The whole scene was like an unreal movie. Now the house was almost completely ablaze but the men refused to stop trying to put out the fire with those ridiculous hoses. I thought they were pathetic and comical. I ran into the building and on the second floor I was stopped by heat and smoke. A guardsman raced past me heading out of the building. "There's an old man in there," he yelled. "He won't come out. He says this is his home." Outside, high voltage wires began to fall and whip about, throwing a spray of deadly sparks. A woman screamed, "My baby, my baby! Where is my baby!" A guardsman tried to comfort her. He looked shaken and frustrated. His commander was shouting for the guardsmen to pull out of the area. The fires raged and the flames seemed to cast shadows of despair over these homeless black people. I wondered where they would go now. If they tried walking to find help and shelter they could very well be shot in the dark by a frightened guardsman. I could still hear guardsmen shouting about the man who refused to leave his house and I wondered: how could anyone be willing to die for such a dilapidated old building in such a filthy, hot, stinking neighborhood? I felt helpless and wondered why men are not supposed to cry.

Don and I drove around the burning streets for awhile. We were stopped and searched at almost every block by scared guardsmen with trembling rifles. The rows of burning buildings seemed endless in the night. It struck me at this moment that this was war; that finally America was feeling the destruction and despair of war on her own shores.

I don't know how long we drove around but soon we heard gunfire again and headed for the sound. This time state troopers were being fired upon from a burning building. They returned the fire intensely. A cease-fire was ordered and soon a man emerged from around the corner of the building. He was a tall, dark Negro. His shirt was almost completely ripped off and his body was covered with blood. "Don't shoot! Don't shoot!" he yelled. He was seized and searched. While the troopers frisked him he kept yelling, "Them niggers shot me! Them crazy niggers around the corner, they shot me! Please don't hurt me. I ain't no sniper." I moved in for a photograph and a state trooper stepped in front of me. I moved around him and prepared to shoot again. This time I was shoved by the trooper. "You don't want that picture, do you fella?" he growled. I got the message but I played dumb. "I'm press. I have a right to photograph this situation." I pulled out my press card. "I don't give a god-damned who you are! You get off this f— — — — —street or you'll be treated like the rest," he yelled. I could see he was rattled. As he hollered, he kept slamming me with the shotgun barrel. I moved on. I was trembling inside and I wondered if I should have pushed my argument further. I was upset because I missed the picture. As dawn grew near, police and troopers got tougher to deal with. Don and I were driving around in the dark without lights. Police and guardsmen had shot out all the street lamps and we were fair game for all. It was almost dawn when we returned to the hotel.

The next morning I called Howard Chapnick in New York and gave him a brief run down on my experiences. I asked him to send me a telegram stating that I was an accredited photo-journalist. Later, armed with this telegram, I went to police headquarters and spoke with the lieutenant in charge. I asked him if I would need any special kind of permit to work in the riot area and what, if any, restrictions were being laid on the press. He told me that the only restrictions were at night in the vicinity of 12th Street and on Linwood Avenue. These had been among the worst trouble spots and were now completely blocked off to everyone. He checked my telegram from Chapnick, and my press card, and said that I should have no difficulty with these credentials.

I spent the afternoon photographing sporadic fires and sniper action as well as scenes of homeless families. In the late afternoon I was shooting some street scenes when a young guardsman, who looked as though the violent events of the past few days had mad him half-crazed, raced up to me and demanded to see my press pass. Singling out me, he had ignored at least half-a-dozen other photographers—all white—who were also working the same area. We argued, and this was one of the few times I pushed the issue. He finally backed off and let me alone. A young Negro who was standing nearby and had been watching this incident sympathetically, came up to me and we began talking. He said he was a Muslim. We spoke about the episode and then he asked me where my sympathies lay. How did I feel about what was happening? I convinced him that I was on the side of Negroes no matter what they did. I expressed the attitude that we are all "soul brothers." I told him I was keenly interested in meeting and talking with young men in the community who were out with the action. The young Muslim said I could walk along with him and he would introduce me to whoever was around.

During our walk I met some youngsters who I later learned were snipers. They laughingly told me that they were spreading rumors that they were planning an attack that night on some suburban communities when in actuality they were going to strike at the downtown district. They told me where they were going to meet later that night and said I could come along if I wished. I photographed these men and then returned to the hotel.

Don Elbaum was still in a mood to stay with the action so we left the hotel together about 9 p.m. We were heading for a meeting with the snipers at a Howard Johnson's somewhere in the downtown district. On our way there, we heard heavy gunfire and followed the sound. As we drew near to the scene our car was fired upon. Shotgun pellets rained on the roof and pelted the windshield. We stopped and crawled to the floor of the car. When the firing died down we identified ourselves and pulled up closer. The position was manned by state troopers and police who were battling snipers. I knew that it's difficult to take pictures during a gun battle but figured I might get some dramatic pictures if any snipers were flushed out and arrested. As Don and I edged closer, the firing started again. The troopers and police were pinned down by a deadly crossfire from the rooftops. The snipers were firing automatic weapons with tracer bullets. We must have stayed pinned for an hour before we were able to sneak away from this skirmish.

We headed for the meeting with the snipers. We found the location but they never showed up. I decided to check with the police department again about my credentials in case the lieutenant on duty during the afternoon had made a mistake about night-time regulations. I was again assured my passes were in order and that I could work during the night.

It was about 10:30 when Don and I left the precinct and saw a fire truck racing to a call. We followed. Our car was stopped and searched many times before we finally arrived at the site of the blaze only to find that the fire truck was returning to its engine house at Warren and Lawton streets. Again, we followed. The area around the firehouse was under heavy sniper attack and the firemen were awfully jumpy. We were checked again and I asked a state trooper at a road block if I could get out of the car and look around. Another fire engine started to pull out of the station and we decided to follow it. We were still near the engine house when we were ordered by guardsmen to halt. We were told to spread eagle against the hood. We showed our press cards and waited. A trooper passed by and called out that he had just checked us and that we were press. The guardsmen ignored the trooper and continued frisking us. Don and I were ordered to lay down on the ground. A young National Guard lieutenant was really giving us a going over. I didn't realize what was happening until another car passed by and someone yelled out, "Halt! Shoot that car! Get them niggers!" There were cries like this all over the place and suddenly shotgun blasts were ringing out everywhere. These fellows were really spooked and acting vicious. They had been under sniper attack all evening without being able to see a thing. I guess they had to take it out on somebody and the somebody was anybody black that passed by in a car.

Don and I were ordered to stand up, hands behind our backs. When I looked up, I froze with terror. There, ahead of us, stood a gauntlet of two long rows of blood-hungry firemen. They were screaming at the top of their lungs: "Kill the black bastards! Castrate those coons! Shoot 'em in the nuts!" A young guardsman crouched before me, his rifle bayonet thrust forward menacingly. His face flushed with fear and excitement and I knew that if I so much as stumbled he would blow a hole in me big enough to put a basketball in. "God-dammit, move!" he hollered. I stepped forward and heard someone scream, "What's that nigger smiling at. Wipe the smile off that monkey's face." A big, red face loomed up in mine. It spit and then suddenly, everyone was spitting, punching, kicking. I don't know how many times I was punched in the groin. I just kept thinking that if I fell I would be shot or stomped to death. I felt the blows on the back of my head. I don't know whether they were rifle butts or what. We must have

been far down the gauntlet and near the firehouse door when Don spun around and yelled, "I'll take anyone of you that thinks he's man enough!" I thought they would finish him for sure but a guardsman gave him a crack with a rifle and he was inside the door. We were butted into a small detention room and left with two guardsmen to watch us. The windows were open and the firemen gathered to scream obscenities at us.

My mind was in chaos and couldn't organize what was happening to me. When I had first looked up and seen the gauntlet of firemen standing and screaming before me, I guess a thousand things ran through my mind. I didn't realize I was smiling because certainly I felt a long way from that kind of emotion. I guess I could have been thinking: so this is America! I know that my smug intellectual philosophy about the race problem was destroyed. I kept thinking about the pain, and perhaps even death, on a more real basis than ever before in my life. I knew they wanted me to cringe and beg and cry out: "Please mista boss man, don't hurt me!" And I wanted to. I wanted to run or plead. But I also knew this wouldn't help, that they would still beat me or kill me and that my pleading would only demonstrate to them how tough they were and add to their violent passions. I know that I don't remember most of the pain. What stands out most in my mind is my struggle then to contain my fear.

We were in the room for about ten minutes when the door flew open and two more "niggers" were shoved into the room. They were badly scared; so scared they couldn't follow orders. "Oh, my God, Oh my God! I'm so scared."

There was more gunfire now outside and the guardsmen ordered us to lie down. The firing lasted for about 15 minutes. We sat for over an hour and I tried to find out why we were being held.

No one seemed to know. The guardsmen vaguely said something about a gasoline can and a knife. We did have an empty can of gasoline in the car trunk. It was rusty and I doubt it had ever been used. The knife was of Boy Scout manufacture and I carried it as a tool in my camera bag.

A police wagon arrived and a guardsman escorted each of us out individually. One of them grabbed me by the hair, stuck his 45 caliber automatic in the base of my skull and shoved me out. The firemen were lined up outside the door again and we received more beatings before we were pummeled into the police van. Inside the wagon we waited again. No one seemed to know what to do with us. State troopers brought in another Negro. He was a big, middle-aged man and they said he had a rifle in his car. They kicked and punched him into the wagon and called him all sorts of names. A cop walked up and said, "Is this the black son-of-a-bitch with a rifle? He must be a big man on his block. Let's make him run. The bastard doesn't deserve a cell." They hauled him out of the wagon and three of them beat him without mercy. One just whipped away at his head with a black-jack while two others hammered at him with rifle butts. Someone yelled, "Stop! You'll kill the coon." A shrill voice answered, "I don't give a good f— — —if I do!" They laughed as the blood seemed to gush from every part of the man's head. He pleaded and cried and then they threw him back into the wagon. I saw that his face and nose looked as though they were split in two. I couldn't look at this.

During the ride to the police station, a national guardsman sat over me and kept telling me about what they did to niggers in his neck of the woods. We arrived at a police precinct but there was no room. We drove on to another station. This place apparently didn't have an arresting officer to book us on the charges we were to be held for. To simplify matters, the driver was ordered to make out charges and be photographed with us. We were then lined up in a garage and kicked and punched. After being mugged and fingerprinted I was told to sign a card which bore my fingerprints and a charge reading: VIOLATION OF CURFEW. I said I would not sign it without legal counsel and that I didn't understand the charge against me. I showed an officer my press card and Chapnick's telegram. He took them from me and left the room. When he returned he told me to sign the card or else I sould spend a long time in jail. Both Don Elbaum and I refused to sign. We were then marched downstairs into the basement where there is a room which is normally used as a pistol firing range. It was damn cold and dirty with no place to sit or lay. About six women were down there and we were only separated by a small railing. By the next morning the room was filled beyond capacity. We were not permitted to make any phone calls or do anything about obtaining legal counsel. Practically everyone in the room was bloody or had been beaten. Most of the men and youths were gangsters and hustlers and practically all of them boasted about looting or sniping they had done.

I spoke to Eddie Dinkins, the man who had been so brutally beaten outside the fire house for having a rifle in his car. Dinkins is 51 years old, has five children and works for a Ford steel mill as a cleaner. He said he was on his way to work on the number one shift, which starts at 12 p.m. Because of the riot and fires next to his home, Dinkins thought it would be best to keep all his valuables with him. In addition to the rifle, he put in his car just about everything that meant something to him. He wanted to keep the rifle, even though he had never used it and the barrel was rusty.

One easily loses track of time in jail. There were no windows so we couldn't have a feeling of day or night. Some of us had had watches so I know that we were brought downstairs about 12:30 Wednesday morning. We received no food until almost 18 hours later. That meal was two slices of bread and one thin slice of lunch meat. Our next meal was 4 p.m. the next day, Thursday, and this was a repeat of the first feast. We had nothing to drink and no decent toilet facilities.

On Thursday afternoon a young white boy, who was arrested for violation of curfew at the same time I was, had an epileptic convulsion. It was a bad one and I knew the danger because my younger sister suffered from the same illness. Both Don and myself administered what first aid we could. We yelled for help and two guards came. I explained the boy's illness and the danger. They looked down at the boy who was foaming at the mouth and one of the guards said, "Tough s . . t!" Then they both walked out of the room. I begged for some ice to help pull the youth out of it. Another guard brought me two ice cubes wrapped in a paper towel. I finally managed to force open the boy's mouth and then I massaged him until the convulsions left his body. He just lay there in the filth and fell into a deep sleep. The boy usually takes pills to control convulsions. I told a guard that he needed medical attention badly but like all the rest of our pleas this one also went unheeded.

During the second day our impromptu "cell" stank. We had about 50 men and six women cramped together, some covered with caked blood and everyone dirty from two days of being unable to clean themselves after using the toilet. The guards thought it was a great joke to show off "the Zoo" (as they called it) to national guardsmen. We could hear them eating, drinking and joking about breaking some nigger's ass. They spoke without inhibitions because we were animals and it didn't matter what they did to us or said about us. When some of them were bored, they would come into the cell and shove a shotgun or rifle into someone's face and make them beg. Thursday night a short, slim Negro was brought in. He was there for only about five minutes because he was a known sniper. He was beaten badly. His shirt was torn off and he was covered with blood. There was a deep gash in his head which was so swollen and distorted that the man looked as though he was born with a deformity in which one skull had grown out of the original. He was taken into a corridor and beaten until it was unbearable to listen to his pleas. I saw the same man again on Friday and found it hard to believe that he could have lived through such a beating or even be moving around conscious. His entire body looked like one massive wound.

A white youth was brought in either Wednesday or Thursday. He was suspected of being a sniper and while being booked he received a large gash in his skull from a bayonet-wielding national guardsman. They gave him little peace. Every time a cop came near the basement, the guard at our door would bring him in to see the little white sniper.

On Wednesday, I believe, we received another inmate. Still high from a big night of adventure, he was just popping to brag about his sniping. "Man, I got four of them last night! I sat up there with my bottle of wine and they didn't know what was happening. There was about 35 of us and we waited until a group of five cars came into the block. Nobody fired until they were right in the middle and then our guys in the front opened up. Two cars backed out of it but the rest of them were pinned and so scared they didn't even know what to shoot at. We kept 'em like that until reinforcements got there and then we split. They just didn't know what to do with us. I was having a good time!" He was arrested on his way home, he said, because someone had tipped the police that he was a looter. He just had time to hide his gun.

The "cell" became unbearable. We were starving, dirty and needed desperately to talk with someone about getting out. Everytime a guard showed his face near the door, dozens of inmates would rush to the bars and beg for food. Tempers flared and fights erupted. We were not far from becoming the animals our guards believed us to be. At first I thought all I had to do was be calm until Black Star found me but as the days passed I realized that it might well take the agency weeks to locate me. It hit me that I could well end up in a state prison or perhaps even be shot for trying to escape while being transported from one prison to another. I saw the power these men had and suddenly everything seemed futile. Everything I had believed about this country just didn't seem real anymore.

Thursday afternoon we were moved upstairs into a small cell that was approximately 20-feet square and hot as an oven. We were given another baloney sandwich and told that we would either be released or sent to court on Friday. That was good news and everyone's spirits rose. I didn't care what they did to me any longer. I just wanted to talk with someone who had some intelligence. I had been holding everything inside of me for three days and I felt as though I had reached my limit and was ready to explode.

Elbaum, four other men and myself had been there longer than anyone else in the group. We were so crowded in our new cell that even floor space was at a premium. If you were lucky enough to find space on the floor so you could stretch your legs out, you just didn't move because someone else would grab it. I bought a paper bag from a guy for a dollar so that I could take notes to occupy my mind.

Most of the prisoners knew each other from their neighborhoods. The majority were hustlers and two-bit gangsters. They boasted about how much loot they got. Listening to them I became convinced there was no outside conspiracy or special organization that had welded them together. Their one common point of focus seemed to be a terrific hate for the Detroit police. Their only "organization" was that they would meet and decide to go out and shoot cops.

Friday morning the guard brought us a new inmate. He looked the role of today's young revolutionary. Under his arm he held a recording of the late Malcolm X's speeches. It was apparent that he had been drinking the previous night and the liquor was still talking to him loud and clear: "Hey guard, you stupid white bastards, I want out!" His voice echoed down the corridor and he continued with a long tirade of abuses until we all became quite nervous. Everyone began telling him to shut up and sit down before the guards returned for another head-whipping session. He looked at us scornfully and in the grandest manner possible told us how lowly and whipped we were. He began to expound the glory of Mao Tse-Tung and tried to convince us to overpower the guards and take over the whole damn precinct.

In a quiet moment, a stocky, powerfully built Negro rose from the floor, calmly looked our young revolutionary in the eye and said: "Boy, if you don't sit down and be nice and quiet, and if they don't feed us because of your big mouth, I'm going to break your neck." I called out: "Motion seconded! All in favor say, 'aye'! Everyone grunted approval. The young revolutionary sat.

Friday afternoon they gave us another sandwich, making a grand total of four sandwiches in three days. Now the police were taking greater numbers of people out of cells. When the guard started calling names everyone would run to the door and this would be the only time the cell would be quiet. Soon, there were only a few of us remaining. Most of those who had been arrested for violating the curfew had been released. But Don and I were still there and I was beginning to lose hope. About 5:30 Friday night a detective came to the window and called my name and my heart leaped. He told me that someone was there to see me and opened the cell door. My visitor was Jack Kaufman of Benyas-Kaufman, two free-lance photographers who also work with Black Star. Jack was thoughtful enough to take a picture of me in the cell before I was released.

As I was being led out, the Chief of Detectives for the Second Precinct stopped me and asked why I had not identified myself when I was brought in. I told him that I had said over and over again that I was from the press and that I had showed my credentials to the patrolman who was standing right next to him. The patrolman, of course, denied it. The Chief said he was releasing me because my arrest was a mistake but he added: "If I should hear of or read of anything detrimental being said about the Detroit police department, you will have the biggest kick back you've ever seen."

The next afternoon, at my hotel, Mayor Jerome Cavanagh called on me personally to apologize for my arrest. He said, "I'm sorry. It should not have happened."

The way I feel about it, nothing in Detroit should have happened and I'm sorry, too.

the call of the black panthers

SOL STERN

In early May, front pages across America carried the illustrated story of an "armed invasion" of the California Legislature by a group of black men known as the Black Panther Party for Self Defense. What actually happened that day in Sacramento was something less than the beginning of a Negro insurrection, but it was no less important for all that: The appearance of the gun-bearing Panthers at the white Capitol was a dramatic portent of something that is stirring in the Nothern black ghettos.

By any yardstick used by the civil-rights movement, the Panther organization is not yet very important or effective. The Panthers' political influence in the Negro community remains marginal. The voice of the Panthers is a discordant one, full of the rhetoric of revolutionary violence, and seemingly out of place in affluent America. But it is a voice that ought to be studied. Like it or not it is increasingly the voice of young ghetto blacks who in city after city this summer have been confronting cops with bricks, bottles and bullets.

The Panthers came to Sacramento from their homes in the San Francisco Bay Area not to "invade" or to "take over" the Legislature, but simply to exercise their right to attend a session of the Legislature and to state their opposition to a pending bill. The bill was, and is, intended to impose severe restrictions on the carrying of loaded weapons in public — a practice not prohibited by present law so long as the weapons are unconcealed. Since the Panthers have been in the habit of carrying loaded weapons at rallies and public meetings, they regarded the legislation as aimed at them in particular and at black people in general. The only thing that was unusual about their lobbying junket is that they brought their loaded guns with them.

The Panthers arrived in hot, dry, lifeless Sacramento and descended on the Capitol with M-1 rifles and 12-gauge shotguns cradled in their arms, 45-caliber pistols visible on their hips, cartridge belts around their waists. Up the white steps and between the classic marble pillars they marched, in two columns, young, black and tough-looking in their leather jackets, boots and tight-fitting clothes. As they marched grimly down the immaculate halls, secretaries and tourists gaped and then moved quickly out of the way. By the time they were halfway down the corridor, every reporter and cameraman in the building had gathered; they stayed in front of the Panthers, moving backward, snapping pictures as they went.

The Panthers, though all were experts on firearms legislation, did not know their way around the building; they followed the reporters and cameramen who were backing toward the legislative chamber instead of veering off toward the spectators' galleries, the group flowed right into the Assembly, past guards who were either too startled or simply too slow to stop them. Actually, it was the photographers, moving backward, who were the first to move through the large oak doors at the rear of the chamber. The Speaker, seeing the commotion, asked the guards to "clear those cameramen." By the time the legislators realized what was happening behind them, most of the group of cameramen and Panthers had been moved out of the chamber. Outside in the corridor, the guards took some guns away from the Panthers — but since the Panthers were not breaking any law, they had to return them. The Panthers read their statement of protest to the reporters and television cameramen, and left. That would have been all, except for a car that broke down.

A Sacramento police officer spotted the armed Panthers at the gas station at which they stopped for repairs, and sent out a hurried call for reinforcements. This time, the Panthers were arrested on a variety of charges, including some stemming from obscure fish-and-game laws. After they had been in jail overnight, the Sacramento District Attorney changed all the charges; 18 members of the group, now out on bail, await trial for disrupting the State Legislature — a misdemeanor — and for conspiracy to disrupt the Legislature — a felony.

As lobbyists, the Black Panthers are not very effective; but then, the Panthers did nor really care much whether the gun bill passed or not. Their purpose was to call attention to their claim that black people in the ghetto must rely on armed self-defense and not the white man's courts to protect themselves.

The adventure at the Capitol assured the passage of the gun legislation, however, and it will soon be signed into law — welcome news to Bay Area police chiefs, who have been frustrated ever since the Panthers first started carrying their loaded weapons in public. In Oakland, across the bay from San Francisco, the police have not waited for the new legislation; they regularly arrest armed Panthers, usually on charges of brandishing a weapon in a threatening manner. The Panthers insist that this is merely harassment, but they have tactically retreated and usually now leave their guns at home.

For the Panthers, their guns have had both real and symbolic meaning — real because they believe they will have to use the guns, eventually, against the white power structure that they charge is suppressing them; symbolic because of the important political effects they think that a few blacks, openly carrying guns, can have in the black community.

"Ninety per cent of the reason we carried guns in the first place," says Panther leader Huey P. Newton, "was educational. We set the example. We made black people aware that they have the right to carry guns."

Only seven years ago, when the head of the Monroe, N.C., chapter of the National Association for the Advancement of Colored People proposed that Negroes should shoot back when armed bands of white rednecks start shooting up the Negro section of town, he set off a furor in the national civil-rights movements and turned himself into a pariah. Robert Williams, eventually charged with kidnapping in what his supporters insist was a frame-up, ultimately left America for Cuba and then China, a revolutionary in exile. It was a short time ago; much has happened in black America since the simple proposal of armed self-defense could provoke so much tumult.

The Black Panther Party for Self Defense was organized principally by 25-year-old Huey Newton and 30-year-old Bobby Seale. Newton looks younger than his years, is tall and lithe, with handsome, almost sculptured features. His title is Minister of Defense, while his darker and more mature-looking friend, Seale, is the chairman. The Minister of Defense is pre-eminent because, they say, they are in a condition of war. "Black people realize," Newton says, "that they are already at war with the racist white power structure."

Being at war, they are reluctant to give out strategic information about the internal workings of their organization. As they put it, quoting Malcolm X: "Those who know don't say and those who say don't know." Outside estimates of their membership run anywhere from 75 to 200, organized into small units, in the various black communities in the Bay area. Each unit has a captain; the captains, along with Newton, Seale and a treasurer, make up an executive committee which sets basic policy for the entire organization. The Panthers get out their message of armed self-defense to the black communities through a biweekly newspaper, and on Saturdays there are outdoor street rallies.

On a sunny Saturday at the end of June, two such rallies were scheduled. The first was on San Francisco's Potrero Hill, at a nearly all-black housing project composed of decaying World War II barracks that should have been torn down years ago. Desolate and windy, the project overlooks an industrial section of the city jammed between Potrero Hill and the Bay. It is an ugly and depressing place.

By the time Huey Newton and Bobby Seale arrive from the other side of the Bay, there are about 30 blacks milling around at the rally site, a dead-end street which serves as a parking lot in the middle of the development. Newton and Seale do not seem disappointed at the turnout. Seale turns over a city garbage can, stands on it and announces that the rally will begin. A half-dozen curious children come running over as the bloods gather. Some women poke their heads out of windows overlooking the street. There is not a white face in sight, nor a policeman, unless someone in the crowd is an undercover agent.

Seale explains the Black Panther Party for Self Defense and the significance of its name. It was inspired, he says, by the example of the Lowndes County Freedom Organization in Alabama, which first adopted the black-panther symbol. That symbol, Seale says, is an appropriate one for black people in America today. "It is not in the panther's nature to attack anyone first, but when he is attacked and backed into a corner, he will respond viciously and wipe out the aggressor."

Seale then introduces the Minister of Defense; Huey Newton provides a 15-minute capsule history of the Negro struggle in America, and then begins to relate it to the world revolution and to the example of the people of Vietnam. "There were only 30 million of them," Newton says of the Vietnamese, "but first they threw out the Japanese, then they drove out the French and now they are kicking hell out of the Americans and you better believe it, brothers." Black people can learn lessons from the fight of the Vietnamese, Newton continues; black people in America also must arm themselves for self-defense against the same racist army. "Every time you go execute a white racist Gestapo cop, you are defending yourself," he concludes.

When Seale returns to the garbage-can platform, the crowd is already with him, shouting "That's right" and "You tell it" as he speaks.

"All right, brothers," he tells them, "let's understand what we want. We have to change our tactics. Black people can't just mass on the streets and riot. They'll just shoot us down." Instead, it is necessary to organize in small groups to "take care of business." The "business" includes among other things "executing racist cops."

Graphically, Seale describes how a couple of bloods can surprise cops on their coffee break. The Negroes march up to the cop and then "they shoot him down — voom, voom — with a 12-gauge shotgun." That, says Seale, would be an example of "righteous power." No more "praying and bootlicking." No more singing of "We Shall Overcome." "The only way you're going to overcome is to apply righteous power."

Seale tells the young crowd not to be impressed by the fact that Negroes are only eleven percent minority in America. "We have potential destructive power. Look around at those factories down there. If we don't get what we want, we can make it impossible for the man's system to function. All we got to do is drop some cocktails into those oil tanks and then watch everything go."

No one in the crowd questions the propriety of the Black Panther program. One man says that it sounds O.K. but it's all talk and the trouble is that, when it's time for action, "most of the bloods cut out." Seale says that's true, but "we have to organize."

While a few of the bloods take membership applications and give their names to the local captain, Seale and Newton jump into a car and race across the Bay Bridge to the second rally in Richmond, 20 miles away on the east side of the bay, just north of Berkeley. Only the surroundings are different: It is a ghetto of tiny homes and rundown cottages with green lawns and carports. The rally is held on the lawn of George Dowell, who joined the Panthers after his brother Denzil was shot and killed by the police. Denzil Dowell's body was riddled with six shotgun pellets. The police say he was shot trying to escape after he was caught breaking into a store. The Panthers and many of the people in the neighborhood say simply that he was murdered.

During the rally George Dowell patrols

the fringes of the small group, carrying a loaded 30-30 rifle. Another Panther stands on the Dowell roof, demonstrating the loading of a shotgun with a 20-inch barrel — a gun which Bobby Seale tells the group he recommends highly.

Driving away from the rally, a tired Huey Newton jokes with a pretty girl who is his date that evening. She is a member of the Panthers, and has her hair done African style. She says that Richmond reminds her of Watts, where she grew up; the people in Richmond, she adds, are very warm and friendly. Newton agrees.

Asked whether the talk at rallies about killing cops is serious, Newton replies that it is very serious. Then why, he is asked, stake everything, including the lives of the Panthers, on the killing of a couple of cops?

"It won't be just a couple of cops," he says, "when the time comes, it will be part of a whole national coordinated effort." Is he willing to kill a cop? Yes, he answers, and when the time comes he is willing to die. What does he think is going to happen to him?

"I am going to be killed," he says with a smile on his face. He looks very young.

To Oakland's chief of police, Robert Preston, the Panthers are hardly worth commenting upon. "It's not the police but society that should be concerned with groups such as this," said Preston, displaying a cool response to the Panthers that perhaps masks a deeper concern. On second thought, Preston said: "They have on occasion harassed police and made some efforts to stir up animosity against us, but they are not deserving of any special treatment. They have made pretty ridiculous assertions which don't deserve to be dignified by anyone commenting on them."

Some of Preston's men on the beat were less reluctant to voice their gut reactions to the Panthers. One of them issued a series of unprintable epithets; another, giggling, suggested, "Maybe those guys ought to pick their best gunman and we pick ours and then have an old-fashioned shoot-it-out."

Despite Huey Newton's fatalism, the Panthers are not simply nihilistic terrorists. When confronted by the police and placed under arrest, as they were in Sacramento, the Panthers have so far surrendered their guns and submitted peacefully. If cops are to be shot — and there is no reason to question the Panthers' willingness to do this — it will be part of a general plan of action which they hope will force revolutionary changes in the society. The Panthers see the white cops in the ghetto as a "foreign occupying army" whose job is to prevent that change by force.

Reflecting on the outbreaks in Northern ghettos recently, Huey Newton said, "They were rebellions and a part of the revolutionary struggle, even though incorrect methods were used. But people learn warfare by indulging in warfare. That's the way they learn better tactics. When people go into the streets in large numbers they are more easily contained. We ought to look to historic revolutions such as Vietnam and learn to wear the enemy down. The way to do that is to break up into groups of threes and fours."

The Panther program calls for the black community to become independent and self-governing. The Negro community in which the Panthers held their second rally that Saturday is an unincorporated part of Contra Costa County; the Panthers are organizing a petition drive that would put the question of incorporation on the ballot. If they should succeed, they will accomplish by legal means one of the goals for which they say they are ultimately willing to engage in violence — removal of the white man's government from the black community.

Like most revolutionaries, the leaders of the Black Panthers do not come from the bottom of the economic ladder. Huey Newton could have escaped from the ghetto, if he had wanted to. He went to the integrated and excellent Berkeley High School, and eventually spent a year in law school. Bright but rebellious, he had numerous run-ins with the authorities (he always remembers them as "white authorities") in high school before he finally was graduated, to go on to Merritt College, a small, run-down two-year institution on the fringes of the Oakland ghetto. That was in the early nineteen-sixties, when Merritt had become a kind of incubator of Negro nationalism.

Both Newton and Seale, who also attended Merritt, remember the time as an exciting period of self-discovery for scores of young Oakland blacks. They would cut classes and sit around the nearby coffee shops, arguing about black revolution, and reading the classics of black nationalism together.

Both Seale and Newton joined their first organization during that period: a group called the Afro-American Association, which advocated black nationalism and stresses Negro separateness and self-improvement. Seale and Newton both became disillusioned with the group because they felt it did not offer anything but some innocuous cultural nationalism. (The group still functions, led by a lawyer named Donald Warden, whom Seale and Newton scoffingly refer to as a "hardcore capitalist.")

After they had left the Afro-American Association, there was a period of political uncertainty for both Seale and Newton. At one point, Newton was tempted to become a Black Muslim; he had great respect for Malcolm X, but could not "accept the religious aspect." There was also a period of "hustling on the streets" for Newton and frequent arrests for theft and burglary. "But even then I discriminated between black and white property," he says.

Eventually came a year in the county jail on an assault-with-a-deadly-weapon conviction. In jail, again, there was the confrontation with white authority. Newton led riots and food strikes — for which he was placed in solitary confinement. In Alameda County at the time this constituted a unique and degrading form of punishment. The solitary cells were called "soul breakers" by the Negro prisoners. Each was totally bare, without even a washstand. The prisoner was put into it without any clothes and slept on the cement floor. In the middle of the cement floor was a hole which served as a toilet. The prisoners did their time in blocks of 15 days, after which they were allowed out for a shower and some exercise before going back in again.

Newton took it as a challenge. The "white bulls" were out to break him, and he had to resist. He made sure that when they opened the door to his cell he would be doing push-ups. It was also a time for thinking, since there was nothing else to do.

"I relived my life," he says. "I thought of everything I had done. And I realized some new things in that jail. I viewed the jail as no different from the outside. I thought about the relationship between being outside of a jail and being in, and I saw the great similarities. It was the whites who had the guns who controlled everything, with a few Uncle Tom blacks helping them out."

For Newton, as for Malcolm X, the prison experience only confirmed his hostility to the white world and made him more militant. Outside, Newton and Bobby Seale hooked up again and began to talk about the need for a revolutionary party that would represent the black masses and the ghetto youth unrepresented by other civil-rights groups.

"We began to understand the unwritten law of force," says Bobby Seale. "They, the police, have guns, and what the law actually says ain't worth a damn. We started to think of a program that defines and offsets this physical fact of the ghetto. I view black people in America as a colonial people. Therefore we have to arm ourselves and make the colonial power give us our freedom."

San Francisco's Hunters Point riot of last summer galvanized Newton and Seale into action. They viewed the disorganized half-hearted attempts of the Negroes to fight back against the cops as a waste. A new strategy was needed. After the riots they moved around the Bay Area talking to groups of bloods and gangs from the ghettos. The young bloods would ask Seale and Newton: "Tell us how we are going to do something. Tell us what we are going to do about the cops." The answer was the Black Panthers.

"The dream of the black people in the ghetto is how to stop the police brutality on the street," says Bobby Seale. "Can the people in the ghetto stand up to the cops? The ghetto black isn't afraid because he already lives with violence. He expects to die any day."

To someone who is not black, the issue of police brutality and police malpractice in the ghetto cannot be disposed of by checking a sociologists's statistics or the records of police review boards. It remains, an unrecorded fact that lurks in unlit ghetto streets, in moving police cars, in the privacy of police stations. It is recorded in the eyes of the young Negroes at Black Panther rallies who do not even blink when the speaker talks of "executing a cop"; it is as if every one of them has at least one memory of some long unpunished indignity suffered at the hands of a white cop.

To these young men, the execution of a police officer would be as natural and justifiable as the execution of a German soldier by a member of the French Resistance. This is the grim reality upon which the Panthers build a movement.

To the blood on the street, the black man who can face down the white cop is a hero. One of the early tactics of the Panthers was the "defense patrol." Four Panthers, armed with shotguns, would ride around in a car following a police car in the ghetto. If the police stopped to question a Negro on the street, the Panthers with their guns drawn would get out and observe the behavior of the police. If an arrest was made, the Panthers would try to raise the money to bail the Negro out.

On the basis of such acts, new members were recruited, taught the rudiments of the law on search and seizure, the right to bear arms and arrest procedure, and introduced to the standard works of militant black revolution: Frantz Fanon, Malcolm X, W.E.B. Du Bois, Marcus Garvey. Currently, Panthers are reading and digesting Mao Tse-tung's Little Red Book. Seale and Newton admit that the rank and file of the Panthers, many of whom are members of street gangs, are not sophisticated politically, but insist that they are "wise in the ways of power."

To Newton and Seale the identification with world revolution is a serious business. They see the United States as the center of an imperialist system which suppresses the worldwide revolution of colored people. And, says Newton: "We can stop the machinery. We can stop the imperialists from using it against black people all over the world. We are in a strategic position in this country and we won't be the only group rebelling against the oppressor here."

If the Panthers are no more than a tiny

minority even among militant Negroes, it does not seem to affect their revolutionary fervor. Theirs is a vision of an American apocalypse in which all blacks are forced to unite for survival against the white oppressors. Newton puts it this way: "At the height of the resistance they are going to be slaughtering black people indiscriminately. We are sure that at that time Martin Luther King will be a member of the Black Panthers through necessity. He and others like him will have to band together with us just to save themselves."

In the meantime, all is not smooth among the black militants. The Panthers have had running feuds with other black nationalist groups, one of them a Bay Area group which has also used the name "Black Panthers," and which has been attacked by Newton and Seale for its overly intellectual approach and for its unwillingness to carry guns in the open. "Cultural nationalists" is the epithet that Newton and Seale use for black nationalists who they claim never try to develop grass-roots support in the ghetto community, but are content to live in an intellectual milieu of black nationalism.

In turn, the Panthers have been criticized for their provocative and public actions by other black militants. One Negro leader in the area said privately, "These cats have just been playing cowboys and Indians." But opinions among black leaders are sharply divided on the subject. When asked about the Panthers on a recent trip to the Bay Area, H. Rap Brown, the new national chairman of the Student Nonviolent Coordinating Committee, had only favorable things to say about them. "What they're doing is very important," said Brown. "Black people are just beginning to get over their fear of the police and the Panthers are playing an important role in helping them to surmount that fear." (Eleven days ago, Brown was arrested on charges of inciting Negroes to riot in Cambridge, Md.)

How does the ordinary, nonpolitical Negro respond to the Panthers? Consider, not because he is representative, but for the quality of the reaction, 22-year-old Billy John Carr, once a star athlete at Berkeley High School. Carr lives in Berkeley's Negro ghetto, has a wife and child now, and tries to keep his family together with sporadic work as a laborer. He has never been a member of any political organization and knows the Panthers only by reputation, "As far as I'm concerned it's beautiful that we finally got an organization that don't walk around singing. I'm not for all this talking stuff. When things start happening I'll be ready to die if that's necessary and it's important that we have somebody around to organize us."

The Sacramento incident clearly won the Panthers' grudging respect and put them on the map in the ghetto. Recently, when traditional civil-rights organizations and Negro politicians in California organized what they called a "Black Survival Conference," the Panthers were invited to speak and got an enthusiastic response.

Are the Panthers racists? Both Huey Newton and Bobby Seale deny it. "Black people aren't racists. Racism is primarily a white man's problem," says Seale, perhaps begging the question. Whatever the root causes of American racism, there *are* Negroes in the society who simply hate whites as a matter of principle, and would commit indiscriminate violence against them merely for their color. The violent rhetoric of the Panthers — which pits the black man against the white cop — undoubtedly fans such feelings.

Yet the fact is that the Panthers, unlike certain other black nationalist groups, have not allowed themselves to indulge in baiting the "white devil." They are race-conscious, they are exclusively "pro-black," but they also seem conscious of the dangers of simple-minded anti-white hostility.

Though the Panthers will not allow whites to attend their membership meetings, they have had friendly relations in the area. They participated in a meeting with leaders of the San Francisco "hippie" community, in which problems were discussed. The hippies had been concerned about trouble with young Negroes in the area who were starting fights and harassing the hippies. "We went around and told these guys that the hippies weren't the enemy, that they shouldn't waste their time on them," says Newton.

The Panthers' relations with the local chapter of S.N.C.C., which has a number of whites in it, have been friendly. Terry Cannon, a white member of the editorial board of *The Movement,* a newspaper affiliated with S.N.C.C., and long a Bay Area activist, sees the Panthers' initial action as necessary. "The Panthers have demonstrated something that was very much needed in Northern cities," says Cannon. "They have effectively demonstrated that the black community is willing to defend itself."

Though they claim to have started chapters in Los Angeles, Harlem and elsewhere in the North, the Panthers remain pitifully small in numbers and their organizational resources meager. Frequent arrests have brought severe financial strain in the form of bail money and legal fees — and police harassment is certain to continue. If the Panthers increasingly "go underground" to escape such pressures, they will find it that much more difficult to broaden their contact with the rest of the black community.

But to write off the Panthers as a fringe group of little influence is to miss the point. The group's roots are in the desperation and anger that no civil-rights legislation or poverty program has touched in the ghetto. The fate of the Panthers as an organization is not the issue. What matters is that there are a thousand black people in the ghetto thinking privately what any Panther says out loud.

III

the
miseducated

Education of high quality and in great quantity is a requirement for all if our social life is to flourish. One's economic well-being, social status, and life chances are virtually dependent on academic achievement and technical competence. Every individual has good reason for pouring energy and resources into education for himself and his family members. Our educational enterprise, however, has not been able to keep up with the demands of the community or the aspirations of individuals. The educational system has become a source of much frustration, anxiety, and hostility, and it has clearly failed to meet the needs of many individuals.

The educational institution, like other ones, tends to become a slave to its own traditions or to strong individuals who dominate it. In some ways, the activities of the enterprise are only remotely related to the goal of educating individuals to cope with the demands of contemporary social life. Moreover, the educational system is rightly accused of being oriented toward middle-class values, needs, and experiences; the unique needs of those who are born into deprived or minority group status are frequently ignored. The burden is generally placed on the individual to adjust himself to the needs of the institution rather than devising types of settings which can tolerate and maximize individual differences. Education is also a major industry in our society and, as such, it does not escape from the hands of policy-makers and community leaders who permit economic and other motivations of self-interest to overshadow the need for an effective and equitable system of education for all. The cases presented here illustrate some of the social problems which produce conflict in this arena. The issues involved are many, and their complex interrelations with other community problems inhibit attempts at solutions.

Individual	Individual
↓	↓
Individual	Organization

WHY PROF. EDELWEISS HAS LITTLE TIME FOR JUNIOR

A one-to-one relationship between student and teacher often is held to be the heart of the formal educational process. At all levels of education there is increasing criticism of the limited time that students and teachers have to interact with each other. Langbaum discusses the problem as it relates to the college and university campus. It appears that perhaps both parties involved, the professor and the student, are victims of a more general problem of supply and demand. The demand for publication and research made on professors are in keeping with the intellectual welfare of all concerned. The lack of sufficient capable professors in light of the surging demands of students is a problem of resource allocation. The problem, however, will continue to reflect itself as a conflict between the professor and the student.

LEGACY OF AN ICE AGE

Most large urban schools are faced with crucial problems which are part of rapid growth, unexpected changes, and limited resources. However, individuals also play a key role in determining the adequacy of the educational enterprise. The case presented here illustrates the burden that perverted leadership can place on the educational system. Individuals can attain leadership positions and then use them to satisfy their own personal ambition at the expense of the institution. Such leaders leave a legacy which frustrates the good intentions of successors. The prospects for a new superintendent to change the tarnished image of leadership are dim and frustrating. Even a powerful institution, such as the Chicago school system, can be imposed upon and victimized by an individual who places his own interests above the needs of others.

HALLS OF DARKNESS: IN THE GHETTO SCHOOLS

Although core city schools have a tendency to attract incompetent and undesirable staffs, this is certainly not true in individual cases. Kozol, a man with obvious compassion for children of poverty and creative interest in teaching such children, reports the difficulties he experienced in the Boston public school system. The educational organization clearly felt it important to prevent him, or at least, it offered him no support in his efforts to deal in special ways with children who bring the problems of economic and social deprivation into the schoolroom. The article portrays well the response of the educational system to individuals who fail to satisfy institutionally defined patterns and who instead pursue solutions to problems which the institution has swept under the carpet.

SPIES ON CAMPUS

The college and university occupy a unique place in our educational system, particularly in respect to the idea of academic freedom. The process of advanced education ideally is one of the free exchange of ideas. Institutions of higher learning, however, are not free from those who would prefer to restrict academic freedom and convert the free market place of ideas into a closed system of ideological indoctrination. Most important of all, those who threaten the educational institution may do so with the support of the federal agencies and under the cloak of such clandestine organizations as the FBI and the CIA. In this article, Donner traces the use of such spies on campus, and he describes how university and college organizations become the victims of organizations which are more concerned with "control" than with education.

why prof. edelweiss has little time for junior

ROBERT LANGBAUM

There is indignation these days over the so-called "publish-or-perish" policy by which professors are rated in our universities. The catch phrase is used as if it described a senseless and brutal mechanism for depriving good teachers of their jobs and students of adequate instruction.

This shows how little the public understands about our universities and the changes that have taken place in them since World War II. Protests without an adequate knowledge of the facts could end by swelling the pressures, already so formidable in our democracy, for a kind of genial mediocrity. They could end by defeating their own purpose—to achieve good university teaching.

Editorialists and others who assert that "teaching comes first" wonder why the universities should encourage professors to divert their efforts from their primary job of teaching and why universities should let anyone go who satisfies the students even if he fails to satisfy the publishing requirement. This argument turns on a false set of alternatives. It suggests that some faculty members publish while others are good teachers. The plain fact, however, is that in any university the best and most successful teachers are also the men who are known, or on their way to becoming known, for their publications. There are, of course, exceptions—the famous scholar who is a bore in class, the great teacher who has published little if anything—but they are exceptions.

The notion that there is something incompatible between teacher and scholar probably derives from a mistaken idea of justice that would have the blessings of this world equally distributed. If one man is handsome, another ought to be intelligent; if one is rich, another ought to be virtuous; if one is a good scholar, another ought to be a good teacher. Fortunately for the universities, however, this last division of blessings does not apply. Both qualities are usually found in the same man, because publication and teaching require the same talents—intelligence and articulateness. That is why universities consider successful publication an index of successful teaching. Indeed, the work that goes into publication is often a positive *condition* of good teaching.

The thing that distinguishes university from high-school teaching is not only the subject matter but the professor's attitude toward it. In a good university course, students ought to get from the professor a sense that the subject is a living thing, being continually made and unmade by living men. They learn from this to respect the subject and to be critical of contributions to it—to see it not as academic fiddling but as a bold and hazardous adventure. Some may be inspired to embark for themselves on the adventure of enlarging knowledge.

Reprinted by permission of the publisher and author Robert Langbaum, from " 'Publish or Perish': Why Prof. Edelweiss Has Little Time for Junior," The New York Times, November 4, 1965. Copyright 1965 by The New York Times Company.

In most cases, it is publication and the work which precedes it, that gives a professor intimate engagement with his subject which students sense and from which they catch fire. But the professor's scholarship is not only good for students; it is, in most cases, necessary for the professor if he is to stay alive intellectually. For most men of energy and talent, teaching is not and cannot be a full-time career. The university system is, in fact, predicated on the idea that the kind of man who would be willing to make teaching a full-time career is probably not of university caliber.

Most professors teach only nine hours a week. Senior men may teach six hours or less. Although the hours in class represent only a fraction of the time spent in preparing for classes; in reading examinations, term papers, masters' theses and doctoral dissertations; in sitting on committees and doing routine administrative chores, it remains true that university teaching is still not quite a full-time job. Those professors who make it so have always the uneasy sense that they are stretching the work. Because the universities do not consider teaching a full-time job, they demand evidence of some other activity relevant to their interest – an administrative job often being accepted in lieu of publication.

Why not get rid of the publishing requirement, then, and by increasing the hours in class *make* teaching a full-time job—and thus help solve the teacher shortage? The problem here is that if university teaching were to become, like high school teaching, a full-time job, the universities would no longer attract men capable of giving first-class *university* courses. And without time or energy to grow intellectually, professors already in the universities would lose ground until in time they would know only as much as they needed to teach their courses—which

for undergraduate courses is not very much. They would cease to be effective university teachers because students would no longer sense an extra depth of knowledge or a position in the adult world based on something other than attending to them.

While a small amount of teaching is stimulating and refreshing for a man of intellect, too much teaching can dull the mind and drain energy without giving much in return. Since it keeps a man from his own work, it can lead to a depressing sense of unfulfillment, of doing something less than a man's work.

Original scholarship, on the other hand, seems like a man's work because it is the activity in which a professor competes with, and is judged by, his peers. In teaching, he always has the advantage of age and experience over his students. There plaudits, though gratifying, cannot be a real measure of his intellectual achievement.

While the successful teacher-scholar is the ideal, there are not, and never will be, enough of them to go around. They constitute a majority of the faculty only in the five or six very best universities. Universities farther down the scale are lucky if they can boast one or two such men in each department. Although some critics rail at these academic "big shots" because they are unavailable to most students, especially to undergraduates, the fact is that distinguished professors are unavailable in relation to the demand for them—because so many students want to crowd into their classes. The truth is these men actually teach *more* than their share of students.

The usual complaint is that Junior cannot get a course with the famous Professor Edelweiss; or if he does, that Edelweiss has little time to give him outside class. Now the university ought, as far as possible, to see that Edelweiss gives at least one course open to qualified undergraduates, but Junior must also realize that he gets the benefit of Edelweiss in all his courses because Edelweiss's presence has attracted faculty and students of a higher caliber than would otherwise have been at the university. If conferences with Edelweiss are short, Junior might well reflect that 10 minutes with him may be worth hours with a lesser man.

If Junior does not agree, if he would rather have from his teachers less distinction and more time, then he is the kind of student who ought to have gone to a college rather than a university. The university offers the advantages of size— celebrities, good libraries and laboratories, a cosmopolitan and intellectually vibrant atmosphere—but the prospective undergraduate must be prepared to find it impersonal and hard on the nerves. If he needs a cozier atmosphere, then college is the place for him.

Colleges and universities are often indiscriminately mixed up in criticisms of higher education, by which critics usually mean undergraduate teaching. But while teaching undergraduates is the sole purpose of colleges, it is only one of the three main purposes of universities. As centers for the advancement of learning, universities are also concerned with teaching graduate students and with research.

This does not mean that colleges are inferior places, of course. Many colleges have higher intellectual standards than many universities, and the size of some of our mammoth state universities can cancel out the advantages. There is a laudable trend nowadays, started at Harvard and Yale, to have the undergraduate spend his college years in one residence house with a resident faculty, where he can feel himself a member of a small community while still taking advantage of a university's cosmopolitan stir and bustle.

It is important that prospective undergraduates and their parents clearly understand the differences between colleges and universities. It is important that teaching problems stemming from the brutal overcrowding of our universities not be blamed upon the publication requirement, for even colleges try to get as many professors as they can who publish. The real problems have to do with the university's change of position from the periphery to the center of American life.

In the old days, when university education was considered a luxury for all except the relatively few people entering the professions, the universities served a privileged minority. Now that our highly technological society has made undergraduate and sometimes even graduate education a necessity for most middle-class jobs, more people are trying for a higher education than we have space or qualified teachers for.

Another problem is that university research, which used to be considered academic and remote from public affairs, has in the nuclear and space age become one of the foundations of national power and survival. The result is that teaching and research are becoming harder to reconcile than ever, because the demand on each has increased so enormously. The danger is that these pressures will force some faculty men to become all teacher and others all researcher, when the university system depends for its quality upon the combination within the same man of both functions.

But the underlying reason for all the attention being paid to universities just now is that they are flourishing as never before. Never before has the American public taken university education so seriously. Never before has the university professor, once patronized as an unwordly, ineffectual figure, been taken so seriously. This applies not only to the scientists who make world-shaking discoveries, but also to the scientists and social scientists who are consulted by government and big business and to professors of humanities who run the apparatus of our cultural life, awarding fellowships and prizes and providing much of the copy printed in the book reviews and better magazines. Indeed, the universities today are subsidizing American culture by supporting a large proportion of the people who make it.

Then, too, the universities, especially the state universities, are doing yet another job—one that never gets discussed. They are creating centers of civilization in the remotest reaches of our continent. The university town is a remarkable place where, often amidst hundreds of miles of cornfields or empty ranch lands, one can find a first-rate library and a book store where the best books, periodicals and phonograph records are sold. The university brings in famous concert artists and lecturers, gives plays and even operas, and may provide the town with an art museum.

All these benefits are available to the local population and their generally elevating effect can be seen in a quality of life far superior to that in other towns, and sometimes even cities, of the state. Electronics and other sophisticated industries have begun moving into university towns because they provide a suitable cultural setting for the high-class personnel they need. It is also too little realized in the current racial crisis how much light has radiated from the Southern university towns.

The university student comes not merely to a school, then, but to a center of civilization, where he can participate in a special way of life that derives much of its quality from the personal distinction of the faculty. The increased wealth and prestige of the universities have attracted men into the academic profession who in the old days would not have entered it, because it would have meant renouncing the world—or at least the chance of influencing it. Now that they find the university precisely the platform from which to influence the world, more and more of the intellectual life of the country is centered in the universities. Our students are being taught by some of the biggest names in American intellectual life.

This raises problems, because these high-powered professors are often away, sometimes more than they should be, on research grants and lecture tours. They are also, in the competitive bidding for their services, being offered fewer and fewer hours of teaching and sometimes no teaching at all. These problems could and should be solved, however, by simple agreement among the universities that, barring exceptional cases, anyone who is to be considered a member of the faculty must teach and be in residence for a specified minimum period of time.

What about the great teacher, the rare and exceptional man who publishes little if anything yet pours out his talent in ways that are fruitful for his colleagues as well as his students? There has always been a place for such a man; he can be found in universities with the most exacting standards. The difficulty, however, is to be sure he is an exceptional case. Sympathetic colleagues have a way of discovering, when a man is to be let go for not publishing, that he is the greatest teacher since Socrates—who did not publish either. One of the best features of the university system is the principle that, when bidding for promotion, the professor competes not only with his local colleagues but with his peers in universities all over the country. This prevents professors from turning their departments into societies for promoting each other. It prevents the teaching staff from encouraging each other in mediocrity.

As for the majority of professors, those who are needed to man the classrooms but do not come up to the ideal of the teacher-scholar, their role is to work toward the ideal, for to do so is to support it and to support the proper standards. What the university really wants, or should want, is some sign that the professor is intellectually engaged. With the expansion of the universities, we are going to have to employ many teachers who will publish little, but this is no reason for attacking the principle of publication itself.

We should recognize that if we do not come up to the ideal of the teacher-scholar, then the deficiency is in us, not in the ideal. If we scrap it, we will inevitably substitute one that is derived from the requirements for the man who only teaches. This substitute ideal would, I am afraid, put such a premium on mediocrity as to make the universities suffocating—indeed, uninhabitable—places for first-rate teachers and students.

legacy of an ice age

CHARLES AND BONNIE REMSBERG

Eight months ago James F. Redmond, a lean chain-smoker with leonine head and slow, dry wit, left the quietude of the school's superintendency in Syosset, New York, to assume a post in the field of public service. Yet for all his $48,500 a year . . . Dr. Redmond is among the least envied of public servants. His new job has put him squarely in the biggest hot seat—some say electric chair—in American education. And the future of the nation's second city may be sitting beside him.

His responsibilities as general superintendent of Chicago schools are awesome. Although 30 per cent of Chicago's children attend parochial schools, the public system still enrolls some 600,000 students, employs 23,000 teachers, and occupies more than 600 classroom buildings. In short, Chicago has more population inside its schools than Denver or Minneapolis have within their city limits.

But what is more critical than size to Redmond's—and the city's—future is the state of the system's health. In the words of Robert Havighurst, a University of Chicago educator who exhaustively investigated Chicago schools at the request of the Board of Education, the system "is sick and getting sicker." Adds school board member Warren Bacon, "If this system were an industry dependent upon the quality of its products for survival, it would have gone bankrupt long ago."

For thirteen stormy years before Redmond took over, Chicago schools were in the iron grip of a superintendent whom sociologist Philip Hauser, another of the system's analysts, has characterized as "a giant of inertia, inequity, injustice, intransigence, and trained incapacity." Under this superintendent, Benjamin C. Willis, schools became the most controversial aspect of life in the Windy City.

What critics termed "his defensiveness, belligerence, hostility, and total lack of respect for the dignity of any person who

Reprinted by permission of the publisher and authors from Charles and Bonnie Remsberg, "Chicago: Legacy of an Ice Age," Saturday Review, May 20, 1967, pp. 73-75, 91-92.

dares even to ask him a question" led to the loss of progressive members from the school board at times when they were desperately needed. His consistent refusal to proceed with plans for racial integration gave birth to the nation's first school boycotts and to an increasingly militant civil rights movement which, experience has already demonstrated, is on a collision course with major violence. His contempt for parents' concern about quality of education accelerated the middle class's flight to the suburbs and shattered some racially mixed neighborhoods that were struggling for stability. His insistence that he could run a "problem-free" system stifled creative experimentation and bred among teachers a morale of fear. And his failure to confront mounting classroom crises produced, in the words of former school board member James Clement, "tragic consequences for all our children." It is quite correct to say," Warren Bacon adds, "that Ben Willis virtually sank the Chicago public schools."

Yet, in attempting to salvage the system, Redmond faces not only the Augean stables Willis left behind but the political realities of the city as well. For all the well documented damage Willis wrought before he reached retirement age last fall, he and his policies were loyally supported by the city administration, the influential business community, and the most powerful press, all of which remain in positions to affect the changes Redmond is able to make. What is more, many needed improvements will require big money, and Redmond finds himself in the state that ranks forty-ninth in the percentage of its per capita income allotted to education and a state where the fiscal fate of major metropolitan areas rests in the hands of a rural-dominated legislature.

Says a Chicago teacher: "I look at Dr. Redmond and I get impatient because nothing is different at the classroom level from before he came here. Then I look at the problems and I say, 'God help this man because this city's schools are doomed.' "

Because of an old scandal in which the school system was exposed as a haven for patronage hacks, the running of Chicago schools today, in theory, is buffered from politics. Yet, like everything else in the city that hosts the last great political machine, the schools are, in the final analysis, politically influenced. Understanding the forces that permitted a Ben Willis and will now help shape Redmond's efforts requires some knowledge of the nature of Chicago's political power.

Since its first settler opened a trading post in the 1790s, Chicago has been first and foremost a businessman's town, and no machine mahatma has taken shrewder advantage of this fact than Democratic Mayor Richard J. Daley, who was just overwhelmingly elected to his fourth term. Daley, one City Council member explains, "is essentially a broker," catering to the needs and desires of big business and finance, in trade for their political support. The exchange works so effectively that in this spring's mayoral elections the Republican party had to search for a sacrificial lamb who would finance the bulk of his own campaign while otherwise Republican business brahmins ran full-page ads for Daley and even the right-wing Chicago *Tribune* backed him.

The schools superintendent, like other potential movers-and-shakers in the city's superstructure, must be compatible with both the Daley machine and its business angels, and the mechanics to see that he is compatible have been provided. Members of the Board of Education, which hires the superintendent and is supposed to set policy, are appointed by Mayor Daley. The fact that he draws exclusively from a list of nominees drafted by a twenty-member commission "representing civic and professional organizations and educational institutions" allegedly inoculates against "politics." But the commission, itself appointed by Daley, is chaired by Dr. Eric Oldberg, the Mayor's Health Board president, and remains in existence only at the Mayor's discretion.

Not surprisingly, the school board in composition is almost a Lilliputian reproduction of the Daley-controlled City Council. Token representation is given to minority groups; two of the board's eleven members are Negro (though more than 50 percent of the public school population is colored). Frequently, Negro appointees have been compliant, but currently one, Warren Bacon, an Inland Steel executive, is doubling in another role characteristically provided for on the board, that of vocal liberal dissenter. The majority of the board, which includes the father of a former Democratic alderman, a judge active in Democratic politics, and personal friends of the Mayor, remain, in Bacon's words, "votes the Daley administration can control."

Thus, even though Willis dictatorially usurped the board's powers—effecting pocket vetoes, indulging in acid petulance, resigning briefly at one point to get his way—his four-year contract was three times renewed and then extended until his retirement. The reason, believes James Clement, a respected patent attorney who quit the board in 1965 to protest what was happening to the schools, was simply that Willis served the city's power structure, despite his divisive effect on the populace.

For one thing, the detail-minded Willis loved to build, and was rumored to know the location of every brick in every school building in the city. He acquired the nickname Ben the Builder after launching a multimillion-dollar school construction program soon after his arrival from Buffalo in 1953. Moreover, Willis's phobia about federal aid to education won him the unflagging loyalty of the *Tribune,* still Chicago's most powerful newspaper. Largely because he made himself a symbol of racial segregation, he also was lionized by whites in the city's blue-collar population. This group has traditionally attached the least importance to quality education, and it is perhaps the most valuable grassroots buttress to the Daley machine, particularly in light of the usually lethargic Negro vote.

Finally, and perhaps most important, Clement explains, "He convinced the business community that Chicago could get quality education at bargain-counter rates."

Critics argue that the business interests have never demanded much from Chicago schools. Ringed by some of the best suburban school systems in the nation, home of a dozen major colleges and universities, still a magnet for the talented young of the Midwest and the Great Plains, Chicago has not been threatened by any letup in the steady stream of professionals and aspirants to the executive suite feeding in from the outside. With their own children by and large attending parochial, private, or surburban schools, "the principal concern of influential business leaders for Chicago schools," contends Alderman Leon Despres, a liberal lawyer elected to the City Council from the University of Chicago area of Hyde Park, "has been keeping costs—and taxes—down." In the context of the system's size, Willis's budgets were always relatively appealing.

Daley, a savvy oldtime "pol," said by experts to be the second-most powerful Democrat in the country, has always been careful overtly to keep hands off school matters. Whenever Willis and the system were under attack, he dragged forth his familiar "great-city-of-Chicago" speech but did not tangle openly with the specific issues. Behind the scenes, though, he worked to stifle criticism with time-tested machine tactics, many of them still in operation. Parents planning to keep their children home to protest conditions in inner-city schools have been quickly visited by welfare workers, public housing officials, and Democratic precinct captains and threatened with rent increases or removal from public-aid rolls if they joined the boycott. Boycott leaders suddenly have been offered jobs, reportedly including positions with the federal antipoverty program (a creature of the city administration in Chicago), which they have interpreted as bribes for silence. In the fall of 1965, when HEW froze some $30,000,000 in federal aid to Chicago schools until a "full investigation" could be made of charges that the system is deliberately segregated by race, the funds were thawed within a matter of hours after Daley allegedly telephoned the White House. Interestingly, the Mayor's Commission on Human Relations, established to combat racial injustice in the city, has an "education expert" but will not accept complaints about the Chicago public schools.

In keeping the power structure convinced that he was doing an adequate job for relatively little money, Willis enjoyed a crucial advantage over his critics: The way he ran the school system, they found it virtually impossible to establish statistically that quality in the schools was jeopardized. Willis, in effect, made Chicago the system that could not be tested.

Among other things, he changed the method of recording students' achievement scores, substituting for a system of *national* norms—which has a nine-point stanine scale—one of *intra-city* norms. "As a consequence," complained a statement issued by a group of high school teachers, "we are no longer able to tell how our students rate in comparison to those in other school systems, and neither can their parents or public." In 1965 Willis flatly refused to permit achievement tests and background information quizzes to be administered to Chicago pupils in a nationwide survey by the U. S. Office of Education. A few months later, he ordered Chicago principals not to answer questionnaires from the OE regarding this survey, and successfully urged the school board to decree that all future contacts between the school system and Washington officials "shall emanate from the general superintendent." A local TV station has found that Chicago school children even have been repeatedly forbidden to participate in a televised "quiz bowl!" program which would put them against surburban and parochial students. In this atmosphere, claims James Clement, "The feeling has grown up that it is just not polite to speak the truth about Chicago schools."

The longer Willis is gone from the scene, however, the more the grim realities of what Redmond faces seem to be coming to light.

Besides political and economic pressures and a paralyzingly centralized administrative bureaucracy, he has, for one thing, inherited the effects of Willis's fanatical commitment to the "neighborhood school" policy. Civil rights leaders such as ex-teacher Al Raby charge that this has been nothing more than a professional disguise for perpetrating school segregation, especially since Chicago is residentially one of the most segregated cities extant. Whatever the motive, the policy led Willis to present his building proposals in five-year packages, denying Chicago any long-term city-wide school planning and resulting in such ultimately costly anachronisms as buildings with as few as twelve classrooms.

In public hearings before the school board last month, parents from a number of middle-class white districts complained that their schools are so small that curriculum is weakened. Unlike larger counterparts, for instance, Norwood Park Elementary School on the far Northwest Side offers no foreign language or art instruction. The size of Bret Harte Elementary School on the South Side, parents claim, prevents it from having a music teacher, a full-time gym instructor, a full-time librarian, or an adjustment teacher for counseling and tutoring.

The tone of the recent hearings and other public statements indicates that one of Redmond's biggest problems will be mending a schism of growing cynicism and despair between parents and the schools. Although the new superintendent has stated publicly that he seeks a lively interplay between schools and community, the atmosphere of arrogance and hostility toward anyone outside the four walls of the school that flourished under Willis is still the prevailing one in most schools.

During Willis's reign, the city PTA president for two years was refused an appointment with him to discuss school issues, and many principals still actively discourage PTA activities by banning evening meetings—a death knell, of course, in inner-city areas where many mothers work during the day. At some schools, teachers have been told that they may not, even on their own time, belong to community organizations without their principals' okay. Volunteers willing to come into the schools from the community to relieve teachers of time-consuming lunchroom duty, truancy calls, and routine record-keeping were, until recently, discouraged. Even the telephone numbers of Chicago schools are unlisted, and one West Side kindergarten teacher

recalls that when she mentioned to her principal that a visiting mother had observed that there were fifty-seven children in the class, the principal shouted: "Parents have no business in your room!"

Undoubtedly, Redmond's major challenge, however, is correcting classroom deficiencies that have become an accepted way of life because of what more than one teacher calls "Willis's reign of fear."

Because of conditioning caused by the ex-superintendent's long and vehement insistence that the system suffers no major ills, the premium in Chicago schools, teachers say, is on "not presenting any problems to the person above you." Thus teachers have found that the best way to receive good performance ratings from their principals, many of whom personally visit classes a maximum of once or twice a year, is to bring no discipline cases to their attention. "In many classrooms, kids are in an atmosphere of control only, no teaching whatsoever," says a North Side teacher. At year's end, it is an unwritten rule that a teacher flunk no more than 3 per cent of her students. "You have to keep them moving," explains a first grade teacher at an inner-city school, "or you destroy the image."

Principals, in turn, are often desperately anxious that their schools not be identified by superiors as trouble spots. Parents complain that even sex crimes against their children have not been reported to the police, and many incidents of violence against teachers go unrecorded.

Innovative teaching, which is likely to have rocky moments, has become anathema to many principals. A celebrated case involves Jo Ann Bowser, who during the Willis regime was a sixth-grade teacher at the slum-area, all-Negro Jenner School, largest elementary school in Chicago. Young Miss Bowser developed imaginative techniques to overcome the environmental apathy of her pupils and persuaded them to come to school an hour early each day, to work on science projects, prepare speeches, write plays and operettas—"anything to stimulate them." Their enthusiasm spread to their regular class work to the extent that they even refused recess. IQs increased markedly. Reading levels skyrocketed, with only five of the twenty youngsters scoring below the sixth-grade-seventh-month level. All scored at seventh grade in math. The class swept the district in awards at science and speech contests, although in competition with white schools. "For the first time," Miss Bowser says, "I was producing a middle-class class in a low-income area." Then her principal, highest paid elementary principal in the system (in Chicago principals are salaried according to number of children under their command), ordered her to stop—because the rulebook issued by the superintendent's office says children are forbidden in the building before the regular class hour. Despite vociferous parent protest, the administrative hierarchy backed the principal. Miss Bowser resigned.

Hundreds of her colleagues in recent years have fled to the suburbs, where many consider educational methods to be "thirty years ahead of Chicago's." Indeed, the exodus of seasoned teachers and the increasing reluctance of talented novitiates to accept Chicago assignments, particularly in light of the fact that most must start in hard-core slum schools without benefit of any orientation or in-service training, has left many schools bereft of personnel.

The Chicago Teachers Union has estimated that 300 to 700 classrooms each day have no teachers whatever, with the concentration of teacherless rooms particularly heavy in Negro areas. One survey showed that in a district encompassing seventeen schools 83 per cent of the teacher absences were not covered. In others, as many as 80 per cent of the teachers on any given day are substitutes. In some schools, libraries are closed down weeks at a time because librarians must be drafted for classroom duty. Likewise, gym classes in some schools have been suspended as long as eighteen months.

Dr. B. J. Chandler, dean of Northwestern University's college of education and a member of the Mayor's commission for school board nominations, estimates that twenty-five out of every 100 teachers who *are* in class are not certified. A person may teach in Chicago without certification if he is willing to forego tenure, assignment security, and the normal salary increments. In some slum areas it is not unknown for a school to have but one or two certified teachers, and many of the uncertifieds are Negroes who themselves have been educated in woefully inadequate Southern schools and whose principal alternative to handling classes in teacher-hungry Chicago is domestic work.

Because the system has been unwilling to confront its problems, Chicago is graduating an inordinate and increasing proportion of "miseducated" and "uneducated" youngsters. Talk among high school teachers seems to focus with ever greater frequency on the alarming number of functional illiterates being promoted from the grades — "kids," one teacher put it, "who not only don't know their multiplication tables but can't mix a bowl of Jello by reading the package directions." A survey of records from the Forrestville North Upper Grade Center, which a complaint to the OE claims "may well be indicative of the entire system," shows that the *median* reading level of the eighth grade graduating class in a recent year was fifth grade, with many students ranging as low as second grade.

In a system so large there are, of course, traditional islands of excellence, the most touted probably being the North Side's Von Steuben High School, to which experienced teachers have gravitated and where a predominantly Jewish student population arrives in class strongly motivated. Scattered around the city, too, are individual teachers and principals who have been willing to run the risks of innovation. Experts have observed that tucked away in various sections of Chicago one can find in progress nearly every kind of educational experiment. But these are not widely discussed nor by any means broadly applied. In fact, says Redmond, "I am told some of these efforts are surreptitious."

The difficulty of functioning as an educator in such circumstances are evident to Northwestern University sociologist Raymond Mack, who recently captained a probe of Chicago schools for the OE's Equality of Educational Opportunity report. He notes that a deepening "don't-care" philosophy among personnel seems to be seeping throughout the system. "Wherever they are located, in white neighborhoods or black," confirms James Clement, "most of Chicago's schools today are second- or third-rate."

The third-rate schools are most likely to be Negro, and the color controversy, ignored by the school administration since the 1964 Hauser report proved the existence of de facto segregation, is one of the first Redmond will be forced to tackle. He has been ordered by the OE to answer charges by the Coordinating Council of Community Organizations, Chicago's civil rights federation, that school boundary lines have been deliberately drawn to promote segregation, that Negro teachers by and large are banned from white schools, and that vocational and trade schools and apprentice training programs practice discrimination in their admissions policies.

CCCO's exhaustively documented complaint states that 90 per cent of Chicago's Negro youngsters attend all-Negro schools (97 percent attend majority-Negro) and that, rather than diminishing, segregation has actually intensified in recent years. "Chicago is in the forefront of the segregated systems," says Sanford Sherizen, education researcher for the Chicago Urban League. "It is segregated as solidly as the South."

In response to the school board's excuse that the color of students in Chicago's neighborhood schools merely reflects the city's housing pattern, the CCCO complaint points out that the board historically opposed and has never complied with a 1963 state law forbidding the location of new schools in a way that promotes racial separation. Instead, schools have been constructed in the very hearts of Negro ghettos and white enclaves, and district boundary lines have been obviously gerrymandered to preserve racial imbalance as housing patterns changed. Meyer Weinberg, author of the complaint and editor of *Integrated Education* magazine, charges that it is naïve not to recognize that school board decisions have been strongly influenced by the desires of the city's powerful anti-integration real estate interests.

Since 1961, sporadic and limited transfer and school cluster plans have been in effect, with the presumed potential for increasing integration. But, according to a national report on racial isolation in public schools published this year by the U.S. Commission on Civil Rights, the Chicago plans have been "incapable of facilitating any substantial number of transfers" from Negro to white schools. Most school critics contend that the plans were designed to fail. Some, for example, were not launched until midterm, after students were already settled in their neighborhood schools. Also, transfer permits are temporary, subject to revocation at any time, and some Negro students have been told, incredibly, that credits from courses in their schools in some cases will not be accepted by the white schools to which they wish to transfer.

Residents of some areas see the school system's reluctance to effect strong and permanent transfer plans as a major threat to community stability. For instance, Marynook, a suburb-like settlement of modest new homes on the far South Side, has fought hard—and so far successfully—to maintain residential integration. "But the schools," says Hugh Brodkey, past president of an area community organization, "have been our worst enemy."

In public statements, Redmond has talked of meeting the civil rights crisis "honestly and intelligently" and of building "ahead [of] the movement of people . . . to help stabilize the existing integrated neighborhoods and make possible experiences of multiracial, multicultural education." Refreshingly, he has also conceded that the Chicago system is "staggering under severe educational handicaps," and he has spoken with heretofore heretical candidness about the need to "create effective dialogue with the communities," to "make decentralization work," to "encourage" teaching innovations knowing "that not all tries will be successful," to bring teacher aides into schools, to "give more than lip service" in developing the maximum potential of each child, and to "feel free" professionally at all levels in the system.

As yet, no significant strides have been

made in these directions. According to Redmond's press aide, David Heffernan, the reason is that the superintendent has been devoting full time to budget and collective bargaining problems. Both these matters are indeed critical. Soon after his arrival last October, Redmond discovered there was "not one penny of local or state money to enlarge one single item in our operation. "Indeed, he was heading into the new budget with a multimillion-dollar shortage.

"Over the last two years," Redmond has said, "the school board has known we were going to need money, but did not take this into account in their planning. New York spends about $800 a year per pupil. Suburban areas with acknowledged good schools spend about $1,200 a year. Chicago spends less that $600. Yet not until last November did the board decide to ask for a local tax increase to help the schools. I suggest this is not very good planning."

With the tax increase approved last February and, possibly, with some additional state aid, Redmond hopes at least "to stand still." But, he says, "to do things we know how to do—including reduced class size (which has been rising)—we could use an additional $100 million tomorrow."

Unless the legislature does an abrupt about-face, this is pie-in-the-sky dreaming. Illinois, third among the states in income, supports only 22 per cent of the expenses of the public schools, compared to a national average of about 40 per cent. Some school districts in the state are so strapped that they have begun paying teacher salaries in script.

In Chicago, most school critics still are taking a wait-and-see attitude toward the new superintendent. Optimistic observers expect that Redmond will move to clean out the Willis underlings and progressively reorganize the system's administration in the near future. Massive plans for decentralization are said to be afoot and presumably will be aided by a study in preparation by management consultants Booz-Allen & Hamilton. A recent contract negotiated by the Chicago Teachers Union and the Board of Education, providing grievance procedures, policymaking, and improved communication, is being hailed as a big step in the right direction.

But, says a federal official in Chicago, to judge how much of a revolution in policy can be expected one must measure the concern of the city's business elite. "And education as an issue is not even before these people. It has not challenged the basic power structure the way the threat of open occupancy has. They do not know the facts about the schools, and they certainly are not convinced that anything needs to be done about them."

Increasing militancy within the civil rights movement may quicken the pace. Much of the local support for Dr. Martin Luther King grew up around concern about the quality of the schools—for black and white—and King has said that the reason he chose Chicago as his Northern base of operations is because it possesses the political machinery to effect change if if chooses to do so. That the Establishment has not so chosen since King's arrival, however, is leading rights leaders to predict privately that Watts-like rioting and burning will erupt in Negro districts this summer on a scale that will dwarf last year's bloody West Side eruption.

"Maybe then," says the federal official, "the business-political tandem here will see the connection between quality of education and society and realize that, the way things stand now, guaranteed rioters are being produced by the education factories of Chicago."

halls of darkness: in the ghetto schools

JONATHAN KOZOL

The school was built seventy years ago and rises along the side of an undistinguished hill. Fifty years ago, the neighborhood in which it stands was solidly white Protestant. Twenty years ago, it was Jewish. Today it is 80 per cent Negro and moving quickly toward 100 per cent. In a matter of years, five, six, or seven at most, there will not be ten white faces in a school which holds six hundred children.

From outside, the school seems morbid, desolate, crumbling. Inside, it overpowers one with a sense of heaviness and darkness. Gloom pervades the atmosphere. Children file in lines of silence. Teachers are present in the manner of overseers: watchful, stern-faced, guarded. They stand at corners, at the tops and bottoms of stairways. They laugh to each other sometimes or smile in whispered confidences, but they do not laugh or smile at the children. "Keep your mouth shut"— "Please walk more quietly"—Get back in line where you belong" are the expressions of morning welcome most commonly heard.

Published in Death at an Early Age *(Houghton Mifflin Company, 1967); also, in the* Harvard Educational Review, *XXXVII, Summer, 1967, pp. 379-94. Copyright © 1967, Jonathan Kozol.*

Two years ago, I was a fourth-grade teacher in this school. My class was located on the second floor, on the street side, in the corner of an auditorium. Severe overcrowding and the school system's refusal either to bus or to redistrict had obliged the school for several years to pack two classes into the corners of this auditorium while still using the central portion for other activities. Singing, sewing, conferences, drama, and remedial work of various kinds all took place simultaneously on many mornings. Torn curtains, rotted window-sashes, broken blackboards, and a faded U.S. flag highlight my memories of that classroom: these, and the dirt on the panes, the cardboard covering over broken windows, desks without tops, walls of peeling paint and, over it all, above it all, looking down upon it all in dark and mocking daguerrotype, a portrait of Abe Lincoln.

The atmosphere within the cellar of the school had qualities belonging to a Dickens novel: rank smells, angry shouts, a long grim corridor leading out into the schoolyard. I remember one teacher who used to post himself down there next to the toilets and coal-furnace every morning during the beginning of recess. There, in the gloomy half-light, he would stand watching the lines of herded children, holding a long thin rattan ever at the ready in his hand. If a small boy walked too slowly, took too long peeing, laughed to another child, or did any other little thing that might be wrong, that bamboo rod began to threaten. I've seen him whip it at a boy on several occasions and I've also seen him do this: He would grab a child, one who was *really* little, maybe only three and a half or four feet tall, and, swinging him by the collar, actually bash him up against the wall. Whatever the pretext, the vehemence of the rebuke was always a hundred times too strong. One day I noticed him virtually hurling a first-grade pupil down the length of the long corridor in the general direction of the door.

There were also teachers who forgot themselves occasionally while we were sitting together in the downstairs teachers' smoke-room and let out the forbidden but, evidently, not yet forgotten terms that one might have believed by now to have been banished from the doors of a schoolhouse, if not from the national memory altogether. Suddenly, as if in total oblivion of all around us, as if in a kind of unknowing and unaware reversion to the habits, vocabulary, and practices of another part of the country, or of a generation long past, the teachers would be speaking of the children in their classes in the language of casual hate and satire. The children, their parents, their people, their ministers, became the "jigs," the "niggers," the "bucks," the "black stuff." And, all at once, within the schoolhouse of an American city, the teachers were speaking with the same words, scorning with the same scorn, hating with the same hate, as those who wear the robes and burn the crosses and stand in angry crowds to shout at Negro children in Mississippi and Alabama whose families have somehow had the temerity to want to send them to an integrated school.

Of all the forms that injustice took within that schoolhouse, the most enduring and enveloping seemed to stem from the cruelty and condescension that were engendered within the attitudes of many teachers. This was as true, I felt, for the quietly reserved and gentle older lady who patted the little children on their heads and then withdrew with immense relief to her home in a white suburb as it was for the outright redneck and head-slamming bigot who would not hestitate to call the kids within the classroom jigs and niggers. In a way, I think, those gently smiling older ladies were even more dangerous and more self-compromising, for it is they, after all, who make up the backbone of almost any urban system; and it is they, in the long run, who are most responsible for the perpetuation of its styles and attitudes.

No one teacher can stand for thousands, but sometimes one teacher can represent in her views and ways a great deal that is most familiar and most disturbing in many others. One such teacher, with whom I had a close involvement in my building, was a lady to whom I will refer here as the Reading Teacher. Unlike many others, this woman was seldom consciously malevolent to anyone. She worked hard, gave many signs of warmth to various children, and spoke often of her deep feelings for them. She was precisely the sort of person whom an outside observer would instantly have designated as a "dedicated teacher," if for no other reason than because she herself and dozens of others in the school would tell him that she was. There is no doubt that she was dedicated, if by dedication one means absorption in the job of teaching. She cared deeply about teaching, about the children, their progress, and the things that they were learning. She also cared, in a highly public and self-conscious manner, about the whole area of fair play and equal rights and racial justice. She would go on at great lengths describing and bemoaning the many forms of open or half-suppressed race prejudice which were, according to her confidences, very nearly universal in the building. It came, however, as a shock, or an insult, or perhaps even at moments as a marginal revelation for her to consider the possibility that she herself might share a few fragments of the same feelings.

One morning she came up to see me in my classroom during lunchtime. She was, as I remember, in one of her familiar moods—making fun of the bigotry of others while at the same time, and almost unknowingly, congratulating herself upon her freedom from such attitudes. "Others may be prejudiced," was the content of her message. "So and so downstairs uses the word 'nigger,' I know, I've heard him say it with my own ears. It makes me sick every time I hear him say that. If a person feels that way, I don't know what he's doing teaching at this school. You wouldn't imagine the kinds of things I used to hear. . . .Last year there was a teacher in this school who used to call them 'black stuff.' Can you imagine somebody even thinking up a phrase like that? If people are prejudiced, they should not be teaching here."

Another time, she spoke of the same matter in these words: "Others may be prejudiced. I know that I am not. There are hundreds like me. Thank God for that. Some teachers are prejudiced. The majority are not. We are living in a time when everything is changing. Things are going along, but they must not change too fast."

I felt astonished at her certainty. I told her, for my own part, that I would feel very uneasy in making that kind of absolute statement. I said that on many occasions I had become convinced that my thinking was prejudiced, sometimes in obvious ways and sometimes in ways that lay deeper and would not have been so easy for other people to observe. Furthermore, I said, I also was convinced that I was prejudiced in a manner hardened over so many years that some of that prejudice undoubtedly would always be within me.

"Well I'm not," she replied with much emotion.

I did not try to turn any accusation toward her. Everything I said was directed at "people in general," at "white society," and mainly at myself. I said to the Reading Teacher that, so far as my own feelings were concerned, I had little doubt of what I was saying. I had learned, in much of the work I'd done in ghetto neighborhoods, that more than once I must have hurt somebody's feelings badly by an undercurrent or an unconscious innuendo in my talk or else the people I was talking to just would not have winced the way they had. I said I was certain, from any number of moments like that, that there was plenty of regular old-time prejudice in me, just as in almost every other white man I ever saw.

To this, however, the Reading Teacher snapped back again, and now with an absolute self-confidence: "In me, there is none."

We stood together in the doorway. The children sat in their chairs. It was almost the end of lunchtime. Each child was having his milk except the ones who couldn't afford it. Sometimes white and Negro children chattered with each other, but there were not sufficient white children for this to happen freely enough. The Reading Teacher looked out at the children and said, "Roger over there, I think, is the most unhappy boy in this class." Roger was one of only three white boys in my class. He was sitting behind a boy named Stephen. Stephen, a Negro child who was regularly harassed and punished all year long, was a ward of the state, an orphan who had been placed in a dismal and unfriendly home and who had been having serious psychiatric problems for some time. The difference between his situation and that of the white child was so enormous that I could not imagine a teacher even balancing the difficulties of two such children within a single scale. Yet the Reading Teacher not only threw them both into the same scale, but judged Roger's case to be more serious. She said to me, "When I look at them, I do not see white or black." But I felt really that she saw white much more clearly than she saw black. She saw the somewhat unhappy and rather quiet little white

boy. She did not see Stephen in front of him, his hands welted from rattannings and his face scratched and scarred with scabs. "I see no color difference," she told me. "I see children in front of me, not children who are black. It has never made a difference to me. White skin or black skin, they are all made by God."

Another day she told me about a trip she had made to Europe during the summer before. She told me that one evening a man on the boat had come across the floor to dance with her. But the man's skin was black. "I knew it was wrong but I honestly could not make myself say yes to that man. It was because he was a Negro. I just could not see myself dancing with that man."

I didn't know if anyone could be condemned for being honest. "What if I fell in love with a Negro girl?" I asked her.

She told me the truth: "I would be shocked."

I said I didn't see why she couldn't dance with a Negro passenger.

"I could not do it."

She also said, "If you married a Negro girl, I have to admit that I would feel terribly sad."

I did not have that in my mind, but I found I was still puzzled about what she had been saying. "Would you have Negroes visit you or come and have dinner with you?"

To that, the answer was clear, elucidating, and exact: "They could come and visit if I invited them to come but not as you could come to see me. They could not feel free to just drop in on me. I would have to draw the line at that."

Hearing that, I asked myself what this kind of feeling meant in terms of one teacher and one child. This woman had drawn the line "at that" just as the city had drawn the line of the ghetto. A Negro was acceptable, even lovable, if he came out only when invited and at other times stayed back. What did it do to a Negro student when he recognized that his teacher felt that she had to "draw the line at that"? Did it make him feel grateful for the few scraps that he got, or did it make him feel embittered instead that there ought to be any line at all? The Reading Teacher apparently was confident that the line did not descend, in her feelings, to the level of the children—or that, if it did, it would not be detected by them. I gained the impression, on the contrary, that the line was very much in evidence in the classroom and that many of the children were aware of it.

There were two ways in which I thought the Reading Teacher unknowingly but consistently revealed the existence of that line. One of these ways, certainly the less important, was in the occasional favors that she showed and in the kinds of arrangements that she would make for various children. She gave a really fine and expensive children's book to one of my pupils. I recall that she presented it to the child before the whole class and spoke of how much the little girl deserved it and of how warmly she admired her. For a poor boy from a large family, she tried to arrange a stay at summer camp. In the case of a third child, she made a friendly contact with his parents, invited them on a couple of occasions to come over and visit in her home, and in general took a warm and decent interest in his up-bringing. The point of this account is that all three of these children were white and, while all may well have deserved her help and fondness, nonetheless it is striking that there was a definite minority of whites within that class of thirty-five, and, during the course of the entire year in which I was teaching them, I did not once observe her having offered to do anything of that sort for any child who was black. When I took it on my own

initiative to do something similar for a couple of the Negro children in my class, she heard about it immediately and came up to advise me that it was not at all a good idea.

In November, I began giving one of the children a lift home after class. In December, I also started to make occasional visits to see Stephen on the weekends, and one day I took him over to my old college to visit for an afternoon. On Christmas Eve, I brought him some crayons and some art paper and visited for a while in his home. From all of these trivial actions, but especially from the last, I was seriously discouraged. It was not good practice. It was not in accord with teaching standards. It could not but ruin discipline if a teacher got to know a pupil outside class. Yet the person who offered me this criticism had just done many things of a similar nature for a number of white children. It seemed evident to me, as it must by now be evident also to her, that the rule or the standard or the policy or the pattern that defines the distance between a teacher and his pupil was being understood at our school, and was being explicitly interpreted, in precisely such a way as to maintain a line of color. The rule was there. It was relaxed for white children. It was enforced rigorously for Negroes. In this way, the color line grew firm and strong.

There was another way in which the Reading Teacher showed her preference. It was in the matter of expectations— what you could even hope to look for "in these kinds of children," meaning children who were Negro. Directly hooked onto this, often expressed in the same sentence, was a long and hard-dying panegyric to the past. The last, the panegyric, was one of the most common themes and undercurrents in our conversations all year long. Even at moments when she knew it to be inappropriate almost to the point of cruelty, still she could not suppress it. Several of the other teachers in the school expressed the same idea frequently, but the most vivid conversations of this sort that I remember from the first part of the year were those with the Reading Teacher.

In the early part of winter, I had to ask the Reading Teacher for permission to take my pupils on a trip to the Museum. I spoke to her of the fact that we would soon be studying Egypt and the desert and said I thought a morning's visit to the Museum of Fine Arts to see the Egyptian collection and also to wander around and look at some of the paintings would be a good idea. The Reading Teacher's manner of reacting to this request anticipated the way in which she and certain of the other teachers would respond to many other requests that I was to make later in the year. Her first reaction was to turn me down flatly. Then she paused for a moment—and, finally, feeling suddenly the need to justify her refusal, she added, "With another sort of child, perhaps. The kind of children that we used to have. . . ." The moment of panegyric: "Oh we used to do beautiful work here. Wonderful projects! So many wonderful ideas. . . ." The present tense again: "Not with these children. You'd take a chance with *him*? or *her*? You'd take a group like them to the museum?"

In a similar vein, I made a suggestion for another child—not for Stephen, because I knew in advance that it would have been doomed to her refusal—but for a little girl. "I thought about next summer. She's one of the best in drawing. I wanted to try to get her into an art class somewhere starting in June."

The Reading Teacher grilled me about it skeptically. "Where?"

I told her that I had two places in mind. One was the school attached to the Art Museum. A summer class for young children was conducted there. Another class that sounded more exciting was located near the university. The latter program, situated in a converted loft, was being spoken about with much excitement by many of the people interested in art education, and it had already won a lively reputation for its atmosphere of openness and freedom. The children of some friends of mine were taking classes there.

"How would she get there?"

I answered that I knew someone who would drive her.

"Who'd pay for it?"

I said the same person had offered to pay for the lessons.

The very idea of this little Negro girl bridging the gap between two worlds seemed inconceivable or mechanically unfeasible to the Reading Teacher. To hear her voice, you might well have thought that it was an arrogant proposal. It was as if I were suggesting a major defiance of nature and of all proper relations and proportions. A moment's pause for thinking and then this answer, finally: "I wouldn't do anything for Angelina because I just don't like her. But if you're going to do anything, the Museum School's plenty good enough for a child like her."

Because she respected herself as highly as she did, I wonder if the Reading Teacher would have been astonished if somebody had told her that she sounded rather ungentle? Perhaps she would not have been astonished—because she probably would not have believed it. She was surely one of the most positive persons whom I have ever known, and she also had an amazing capacity to convince herself of the justice of her position on almost any issue at all. At any moment when she was reminded, by herself or someone else, that she was being less than Christian or less than charitable to kids who already did not have very much in life, she was apt to question whether there was really so much suffering here as people liked to say or whether things were really all that bad. With Stephen, for example, there were only rare moments when she would come face to face with his desperate position. Characteristic of her response to him was the attitude expressed the time she pointed to the white boy in the seat in back of him and called him the most unhappy child in the class. I remember that when I said to her, "What about Stephen? He doesn't even have parents!" the Reading Teacher became instantly defensive and irritated with me and replied, "He has a mother. What are you talking about? He has a foster mother and she is paid by the state to look after his care." But I said maybe it wasn't like having a real mother. And also, I said, the state didn't seem to have time to notice that he was being beaten up by his foster mother while being thoroughly pulverized and obliterated in one way or another almost every day at school. "He has plenty," was her answer. "There are many children who are a great deal worse off. Plenty of white people have had a much harder time than that." Harder than he had? How many? I didn't believe it. Besides, when it got to that point, did it very much matter who, out of many suffering people, was suffering a little bit less or a little bit more? But the Reading Teacher became impatient with the direction of my questioning and she ended it at this point by telling me with finality, "He's getting a whole lot more than he deserves."

It was this, her assumption that people don't derseve a great deal in life, and that a little—even a very, very little for a Negro child—is probably a great deal more than he has earned, which seemed the most disturbing thing about her. Yet, at the same time, she enjoyed delineating to me the bigotry of others, attacking certain of her associates ruthlessly when she was not chatting with them, and making hash out of the Principal when she was not making hash out of someone else. I came into that school as a provisional teacher in October, but it was four months before I had the courage to begin to speak to her with honesty.

One of the other fourth grades within our school building was located in a room across the stairs from me. In this room, for almost an entire year, there was a gentle teacher on the apparent verge of mental breakdown. Instead of being retired or given the type of specialized work in which he might have been effective, the man had simply been shunted from one overcrowded ghetto school into another. His assignment in our school was unjust both to him and to the children. The classroom was filled with chaos, screams, and shouting all day long. The man gave his class mixed-up instructions. He was the sort of mild, nervous person who gives instructions in a tone that makes it clear in advance he does not really expect to be obeyed. He screamed often but his screams contained generally not force but fear. Bright children got confused; all children grew exhausted. There was little calm or order. Going in there on an errand during the middle of the morning, you were not always immediately able to find him. You could not see him in the midst of the shouting, jumping class. On rare occasions, the children, having no one else to blame for this except their teacher, would rise up in an angry instant and strike back. I remember one cold day in the middle of January, when the teacher went out onto the fire escape for a moment—perhaps just to regain his composure and try to calm himself down. One of the children jumped up and slammed the door. It locked behind him. "Let me in!" the man started screaming. It was unjust to him but he must have seemed like Rumpelstiltskin, and the children, not ever having had a chance at revenge before, must have been filled with sudden joy. "Let me in! How dare you?" At last they relented and someone opened the door.

After I went into his classroom the first time in November, I began to find my attention drawn repeatedly to two of the children. One of them was a bright, attractive, and impatient Negro girl who showed her hatred for school and teacher by sitting all day with a slow and smouldering look of cynical resentment in her eyes. Not only was she bright but she also worked extremely hard, and she seemed to me remarkably sophisticated, even though she was still very much a little child. I thought that she would easily have been a sure candidate for one of the local girls' schools of distinction had she not been Negro and a victim of this segregated school. For two years, she had had substitute teachers, and this year a permanent teacher in a state of perpetual breakdown. Her eyes, beautiful and sarcastic, told that she understood exactly what was going on. She possessed enough shrewdness and had a sufficient sense of dignity to know where to place the blame. She was one of thousands who gave the lie, merely by her silent eloquence, to all the utterances of those who have defined the limits and capabilities of Negro children. Five years from now, if my guess was correct, she would be out on the picket lines. She would stand there and protest because, after so much wasting of her years, there alone would be the one place where her pride and hope would still have a chance.

The other child whom I noticed in that fourth-grade room was in an obvious way far less fortunate—he was retarded. For Edward there was no chance at all of surviving inwardly within this miserable classroom, still less of figuring out where the blame ought to be applied. The combination of low intelligence with a state of emotional confusion resulted in behavior which, though never violent, was unmistakably peculiar. No one could have missed it—unless he wanted to, or needed to. The boy walked upstairs backward, singing. Many teachers managed not to notice. He walked with his coat pulled up and zippered over his face; inside, he roared with laughter, until a teacher grabbed him and slammed him to the wall. Nobody said, "Something is wrong." He hopped like a frog and made frog-noises. Occasionally, a teacher would not be able to help himself and would come right out and say, "Jesus, that kid's odd." But I never did hear anyone say that maybe also, in regard to the disposition of this one child at least, something in the system of the school itself was wrong or odd.

Edward was designated a "special student," categorized in this way because of his I. Q. and hence, by the expectation of most teachers, not teachable within a normal, crowded room. On the other hand, because of the overcrowding of our school and the lack of special teachers, there was no room for him in our one special class. Because of the refusal of the city either to redistrict or to bus Negro children to white neighborhoods, he could not be sent to any other school which might have room. The consequence of all of this, as it came down through the chancery of the system, was that he was to remain a full year mostly unseen and virtually forgotten, with nothing to do except to vegetate, cause trouble. daydream, or just silently decay. He was unwell. His sickness was obvious, and it was impossible to miss it. He laughed to near crying over unimaginable details. If you didn't look closely, it seemed often that he was laughing over nothing at all. Sometimes he smiled wonderfully with a look of sheer ectasy. Usually it was over something tiny: a little dot on his finger or an imaginary bug upon the floor. The boy had a large head and very glassy, rolling eyes. One day I brought him a book about a little French boy who was followed to school by a red balloon. He sat and swung his head back and forth over it and smiled. More often he was likely to sulk, or whimper, or cry. He cried in reading because he could not learn to read. He cried in writing because he could not be taught to write. He cried because he couldn't pronounce words of many syllables. He didn't know his tables. He didn't know how to subtract. He didn't know how to divide. He was in the fourth-grade class, it seemed to me, by an administrative error so huge that it appeared an administrative joke. The joke of HIM was so obvious it was hard not to find it funny. The children in the class found it funny. They laughed at him all day. Sometimes he laughed with them since it's quite possible, when we have few choices, to look upon even our own misery as some kind of desperate joke. Or else he started to shout. His teacher once turned to me and said quite honestly and openly, "It's just impossible to teach him." And the truth, of course, in this case, is that the teacher *didn't* teach him; nor had he really been taught since the day he came into the school.

In November, I started doing special work in reading with a number of the slowest readers from all the fourth grades. It was not easy to pick them, for few children at our school read near grade-level. Only six or seven in my own class were fourth-grade readers. Many of them were at least a year, frequently two years, behind. Those who had had many substitutes in the previous two years tended to be in the worst shape. In selecting this special group of children, it seemed to me that Edward deserved the extra help as much as anyone. He wanted it too—he made that apparent. For he came along with excitement and with a great and optimistic smile. He began by being attentive to me and seemed very happy for a while. The smiling stopped soon, however, because he could not follow even the extremely moderate pace that we were keeping. The other children, backward as they had been, were too far ahead of him. He soon began to cry. At this point, the Reading Teacher came rushing on the scene. Her reaction was predictable. Rather than getting angry at either the school or the city or the system for this one child's sake, her anger was all for him; and her outrage and her capacity for onslaught all came down upon his head. "I will not have it," she said of him and of his misery and then, virtually seething with her decision-making power, she instructed me that I was not to teach him any longer. Not taught by me and not by his regular teacher. I asked her, in that case, by whom he would be taught from now on, and the answer in effect was, "Nobody." The real decision, spoken or unspoken, was that he would not be taught at all. In this, as in so many of the other things that I have described, I was reluctant at that time to argue forcefully. Instead, I acquiesced to her authority; I quietly did as I was told. For the duration of the fall and for the major portion of the winter, the little boy with the olive smile would ask me, it seemed, almost every morning, "Mr. Kozol, can I come to reading with you?" And almost every morning, I pretended that his exlusion was only temporary; and I lied to him and told him, "I'm sorry, Edward. Just not for today."

There is a tendency in a great many teachers in all kinds of schools to attribute lies to children who in fact did not lie and had not lied and about whom the teacher may know very little. In a ghetto neighborhood especially, the assumption of prior guilt seems at times so overwhelming that even a new teacher with strong affiliations to the Negro community, and sometimes even a teacher who is Negro, will be surprised to discover the extent to which he shares it. It seems at moments to require an almost muscular effort of the imagination to consider the possibility in a particular case that a Negro child might actually *not* have done it, that he might *not* be telling any lie. I remember several incidents of this kind when a pupil whom I knew for certain to be innocent was actually brought around to the point of saying, "Yes, I did it" or, "Yes, I was lying," simply from the force of an adult's accusation.

One morning the Mathematics Teacher—another among the ranks of dedicated and high-powered older teachers—came rushing into the fourth-grade across the stairs from mine when the regular teacher was not present and when I was taking his class while somebody else was filling in with mine. The children had done an arithmetic assignment the day before. All but two had it graded and passed back. The two who didn't get it back insisted to me that they had done it but that the substitute teacher who had been with them the day before must have thrown it aside or lost it. I had been in and out of that room long enough to know those two boys and to believe what they were saying. I also knew that in the chaos of substitute changes there was continual loss and mislaying of homework and of papers of all sorts. Despite this, the Math Teacher came sweeping into the room, delivered a withering denunciation to the whole class on their general performance, then addressed herself to the two boys whose papers had not been given back. She called them to the front and, without questioning or qualification, she *told* them that they were lying and that she knew they were lying, and furthermore, that she did not want contradictions from

them because she knew them too well to be deceived. The truth is that she did not know them at all and probably did not even know their names. What she meant was that she knew "children who are like them"—in this case, "Negro nine-year-old boys who like to tell lies." Knowing them or not, however, she swept down upon them and she told them that they were liars and did it with so much vigor that she virtually compelled them to believe it must be so.

A somewhat different incident of this sort concerned another boy and involved one of the male teachers in our school. One day while I was working, I saw this teacher coming toward me and holding a boy named Anthony rather firmly by the arm. I asked the class to sit still a moment while I went out behind the portable blackboard to find out what was going on. The teacher continued to hold Anthony by the arm. He stood Anthony before me. Anthony looked down at the floor. I knew him only slightly. He was one of the slow readers who met with me for extra work from time to time.

"ANTHONY," said the teacher, "I WANT YOU TO TELL MR. KOZOL NOW THE SAME THING THAT YOU TOLD ME."

It was spaced out like that, exactly, with a caesura of intensity and measured judgment and of persuasive intelligence in between every parceled word: "I WANT YOU TO GO ON NOW AND SAY TO MR. KOZOL WHAT YOU WANT TO TELL HIM, AND I WANT YOU TO SAY IT IN A VOICE WHICH IS LOUD AND CLEAR, AND I WANT YOU TO LOOK UP AT MR. KOZOL."

When he spoke this way, it was as if every child, or every person, in the whole world might be an isolated idiot and that, if the words did not come out so slowly and carefully, nobody in the world might every truly find out what any other person believed.

"ANTHONY," the teacher continued, "MR. KOZOL IS A VERY BUSY MAN. MR. KOZOL HAS A WHOLE CLASS OF CHILDREN WAITING. NOW WE DON'T WANT TO KEEP MR. KOZOL STANDING HERE AND WAITING FOR YOU, ANTHONY, DO WE? AND WE WOULDN'T WANT MR. KOZOL TO THINK THAT WE WERE AFRAID TO SPEAK UP AND APOLOGIZE TO HIM WHEN WE HAVE DONE SOME- THING WRONG. WOULD WE WANT MR. KOZOL TO THINK THAT, ANTHONY?"

Anthony kept his eyes on the floor. My students poked and peered and stared and craned their necks around from behind the broken blackboard. At last I could see that Anthony had decided to give in. With one of the most cynical yet thoroughly repentant looks of confession that I have ever seen in any person's eyes, he looked up first at the teacher, then at me, and said decently, "I'm sorry." And the teacher said to him, "I'm sorry—WHO?" And Anthony said nice- ly, "I'm sorry, Mr. Kozol." And the teacher said, "Good boy, Anthony!" or something of that sort and he touched him in a nice way on the arm. Now the truth is he *had* been a good boy. He had been a very good boy indeed. He had been a good boy in exactly this regard: he had gone along with the assumption of one white man about one Negro; he had done nothing at all to contradict or to topple that conception; and he even had acted out and executed agreeably a quite skillful little confessional vignette to reinforce it. To this day, I haven't the slightest idea of what it was about.

When something as crazy as this happens, it seems important to try to find out how it could be possible. How can an adult so easily, so heedlessly, and so unhesitatingly attribute to a child the blame for a misdemeanor about which the child has so little information and about which, in fact, he may know nothing? I am sure the reasons are mainly the same as those for the use of corporal punishment: haste and hurry, fear on the part of teachers, animosity and re- sentment, and the potentiality for some sort of sudden insurrection by certain children. The atmosphere at times gets to seem so threatening to many teachers that they dare not risk the outbreak of disorder which might occur if they should take time to ascertain gently, carefully, and moderately the nature of what is really going on. It always seems more practical and less risky to pretend to know more than you do and to insist on your omniscience. When you assume a child is lying and tell him so without reservations, he is almost inclined to agree with you, and furthermore it is often to his advantage to do so since, in this way, he is likely to minimize his punishment. A child, of course, who begins by pretending to accept blame may end up *really* accepting it. If one pretends something well, and if that pretense becomes a habit, and if that habit in time becomes the entire style and strategy with which one deals with the white world, then probably it is not surprising if at last it gets into the bloodstream too. Naturally all children don't react in the same way. Among the children at my school there were many different degrees of blame-acceptance or resignation or docility. There were also children who did not give in at all. It was not these—not the defiant ones—but the chil- dren who gave in to their teachers most easily and utterly who seemed the sad- dest.

One day I was out in the auditorium doing reading with some children. Classes were taking place on both sides of us. The glee club and sewing class were taking place at the same time in the middle. There was also a fifth-grade remedial math group, comprising six pupils, and there were several other children whom I did not know simply walking back and forth. Before me were six fourth-graders, most of them from the disorderly fourth grade and several of whom had had substitute teachers during much of the previous two years. It was not their fault; they had done nothing to deserve substitute teachers. And it was not their fault now if they could not hear my words clearly; I could barely hear theirs. Yet the way that they dealt with this dilemma, at least on the level at which I could observe it, was to blame, not the school but themselves. Not one of them would say, "Mr. Kozol, what's going on here? This is a crazy place to learn."

This instead is what I heard:

"Mr. Kozol, I'm trying as hard as I can, but I just can't even hear a word you say."

"Mr. Kozol, please don't be angry. It's so hard—I couldn't hear you."

"Mr. Kozol, please, would you read it to me one more time?"

You could not mistake the absolute assumption that this mess was not only their own fault but something to be ashamed of. It was a triumph of pedagogic brainwashing. The place was ugly, noisy, rotten. Yet the children before me found it natural and automatic to accept as normal the school's structural inadequacies and to incorporate them, as it were, right into themselves: as if the rotting timbers might not be objective calamities but self-condemning configurations of their own making and as if the frenzied noise and overcrowding were a condition and an indictment not of the school building itself but rather of their own inadequate mentalities or of their own incapacitated souls. Other children were defiant, but most of them were not. It was the tension between defiance and docility, and the need of a beleaguered teacher to justify something absolutely unjustifiable, which created the air of unreality, possible danger, intellectual hypocrisy, and fear. The result of this atmosphere was that too many children became believers in their own responsibility for being ruined; and they themselves, like the teachers, began somehow to believe that some human material is just biologically better and some of it worse. A former chairman of the school committee of this city, a man of extreme conservative leanings and well-known segregationist beliefs, has publicly given utterance to this idea in words he might regret by this time. "We have no inferior education in our schools," he has let himself be quoted. "What we have been getting is an inferior type of student." Is it any wonder, with the heads of a school system believing this, that after a while some of the children come to believe they are inferior too?

spies
on campus

FRANK DONNER

In comparison with most student protests held before and since, the one staged on the evening of February 9, 1967, at State University College at Brockport in Upstate New York was singularly uneventful. Instead of a prolonged marathon involving hundreds of students,

Frank Donner, "Spies on Campus," *originally in* Playboy Magazine, *March, 1968, pp. 107-18, 144-45, 147-50. Copyright © 1968 by HMH Publishing Co. Inc.*

the demonstration—in the form of a sit-in, held at the student union—attracted only a handful of students and lasted a scant 15 minutes. Sponsored by members of a group called the Campus Committee of Concern, the sit-in protested nothing so lofty as Vietnam, civil rights or academic freedom. The students involved simply wanted the union to remain open a while longer at night so they could drink Cokes and talk there. Even the local press, knowing a nonstory when it saw one, devoted only a short item to the action the next day.

But before the month was over, it was clear that this minidemonstration had, like the first element in an elaborate Rube Goldberg device, set in motion a series of more complicated events that ended in the exposure of an extensive network of FBI spying and political surveillance on the Brockport campus.

The story of the snooping—perhaps even more alarming because Brockport is hardly known as a hotbed of political activism—was brought to the surface by the widely respected Reverend John Messerschmitt, ecumenical chaplain to the college and a faculty advisor to the group that sponsored the sit-in. Speaking on February 23 to a hushed meeting of the local American Association of University Professors, Messerschmitt revealed that the morning after the sit-in, a member of the Brockport administrative staff, during a conversation with Messerschmitt about the Campus Committee of Concern, began making remarks about Dr. Ernst A. Wiener, then associate professor of sociology and also a faculty advisor to the C. C. O. C. The administrator asked if Messerschmitt was aware of Wiener's involvement with civil rights, the peace movement and various New Left groups that the staff member "knew" to be Communist fronts. When Chaplain Messerschmitt protested that

without evidence such accusations were irresponsible, the administrator confided (according to the chaplain's notes, recorded shortly after the conversation): "John, I know I can trust you with this information. I'm in regular contact with the FBI. There are four or five of us on the campus—two with the FBI and three with the CIA. We've been asked to watch Wiener very closely. Believe me when I tell you he has quite a background. Be careful." Messerschmitt responded by telling the man he could hardly believe he was actually working for the FBI and that if he was, his position "was in contradiction to what the university stood for and extremely dangerous to the civil liberties of all the individuals he was keeping under surveillance."

For a half hour, the two men argued the subject. "Wouldn't you do this FBI work if your country requested it of you?" asked the nameless administrator. "How can you attack the FBI when it's only trying to protect you?. . .This surveillance work is occurring on every campus in the country. . .Those who are being watched shouldn't have anything to hide if what they are doing and saying is aboveboard. . . .Don't think I get paid for this; I don't. I was asked to do this and I agreed as a service to my country."

From the conversation, the surprised chaplain learned not only that such campus spying was common but that both the FBI and CIA were regularly in touch with friendly Brockport faculty members, who were instructed—in the words of the administrator—"to kind of keep an eye on things on a permanent basis."

"Finally," Chaplain Messerschmitt concluded, "I told him our conversation had left me no less shocked at his disclosure. I was sorry he had assumed a confidence of me without first asking, but because this news was absolutely incompatible with what I understood higher education to be, I could not be quiet about it."

Nor was he. With the fuse lit by his subsequent disclosures, reactions exploded in swift succession. Convinced and outraged by what they had heard but prevented from direct legal action by the fact that the conversation was unwitnessed, the Brockport chapter of the American Association of University Professors passed a resolution strongly condemning undercover operations on the campus—as threat of "faculty intimidation and "thought control." Within the next month, the Brockport faculty senate and the State University Federation of Teachers at Brockport passed similar resolutions. The CIA responded by labeling the Brockport charges "nonsense" and stated that it "does not engage in spying in the United States." The FBI's authority is not so circumscribed, however. A few weeks later, FBI Director J. Edgar Hoover, in a letter to Chancellor Samuel Gould, the administrative head of the New York State University system, admitted the charges. "I would never permit the FBI," Hoover wrote, "to shirk its responsibilities. I feel certain that you, as a responsible educator and citizen, would never condone this Bureau's failure to handle its obligations in the internal security field, or that you would have us ignore specific allegations of subversive activity in any segment of our society, including college campuses."

Professor Ernst Wiener—whose activities and views had sparked all the commotion—seemed less surprised at the discovery of a campus spying network than at the fact that it should be concerned with someone as harmless as himself. "I have never attempted to conceal the nature of my political beliefs," he announced. And in what many felt was a moving document, indeed (a letter published March 17 in the Brockport college paper), he described his participation in the 1965 Selma-Montgomery march, his concern for the local problems of integration, his opposition to the Vietnam war and his membership in various groups supporting these and similar beliefs. He closed his letters by quoting Socrates: "For of old I have had many accusers, who have accused me falsely to you during many years. . . . Hardest of all, I do not know and cannot tell the names of my accusers. . .and therefore I must simply fight with shadows in my own defense, and argue when there is no one who answers."

Professor Wiener must have thought a good bit about Socrates in the month that followed; for on April 20, he committed suicide. In a letter found after his death, he had written: "It is too painful to continue living in a world in which freedom is steadily being constricted in the name of freedom and in which peace means war, in which every one of our institutions, our schools, our churches, our newspapers, our industries are being steadily engulfed in a sea of hypocrisy."

The events that grew from the Brockport affair would be tragic enough even if it were an isolated incident, conceived in the overzealous mind of a local FBI agent or his regional chief. But as Director Hoover's letter makes clear, the FBI regards campus spying as a near-sacred obligation. Just about the same time Dr. Wiener killed himself, *Ramparts* magazine—following up its disclosure that President Ngo Dinh Diem's intrigue-ridden regime in South Vietnam had relied heavily on the expertise of CIA-sponsored faculty members from Michigan State University—exposed a labyrinth of CIA front groups, notably the National Student Association. During the same month, a pseudo coed at the Madison campus of Fairleigh

Dickinson made headlines by announcing that she had been planted there by county detectives to spy on a fellow student; and the president of Brigham Young University reluctantly admitted that a group of students had been used to spy on liberal professors.   In the past two years, disclosures such as these have appeared with what the agencies involved must find embarrassing regularity? and they provide a small glimpse through the curtain that up to now has concealed a nationally organized, centrally coordinated, undercover campus intelligence operation.

Apologists for this collegiate spying frequently adopt the position of the nameless Brockport vigilante: "Those who are being watched shouldn't have anything to hide if what they are doing and saying is aboveboard." Because the agencies engaged in snooping have yet to use in a court case the mass of information they have gathered, they can easily be viewed as concerned—and relatively ineffective—voyeurs. We are only trying to find out the facts, say the surveiller-informers; we neither enjoin nor punish political expression or association.

But even if the snooping were as benign and nonrestrictive as the agencies suggest, there would still remain the thorny question of academic freedom. In theory, colleges are supposed to be open market places of ideas, where students and teachers are free to say and think what they please. Government agencies violate this principle simply by listening in on what is said, even if they never use the information. Their presence—or just the possibility of their presence—can stimulate a self-censorship far more damaging to freedom and learning than most of the restraints against individual liberty currently on the statute books. If a student or a teacher has reason to suspect that Big Brother—or anyone,

for that matter—is surreptitiously listening to or recording what he says, he will surely be more circumspect than he would be in complete privacy. Firmly committed students tend to accept political sleuthing as a predictable risk and often use it to support their alienation from society. But it is measurably daunting to the large number of timid, uncommitted but curious students—the samplers, sippers and tasters of the various causes offered on campus. These are the students who most need the opportunity to experiment and examine, an opportunity that our Bill of Rights—and our concept of academic freedom—was designed to protect. As the Brockport student paper asked editorially last March: "How may academic freedom thrive in a classroom in which the instructor may be the patriotic, right-winged informer to the FBI and the CIA? The students are not so naïve as to believe that liberal or left-wing sentiments go unnoticed by the FBI." The result is that snooping yields maximum returns of control for a minimum investment of official power; it drastically curbs dissent and, in so doing, it evades judicial review in an area for which the courts have shown a special and commendable concern.

The surveillance-informing system is marvelously efficient because life in American society—particularly on the campus—makes the average "subject" extremely vulnerable to fear when he learns his politics are under scutiny by the Government, especially by the FBI. The undercover character of the surveillance, the benighted standards of the investigators, the assumed guilt of the subject, the denial of an opportunity to face charges or to offer a defense and the inability to understand the reasons for the investigation can be shatteringly Kafkaesque. Reputations, brittle as glass, are easily smashed beyond repair. "Of what crime was Ernst Wiener guilty," inquired the Brockport campus paper, "to allow the smearing of his name in a local newspaper as 'under investigation'? This is just more evidence of implying guilt by innuendo, while the investigators and smearers are well covered under a muffling cloak of silence."

Critics of campus spying—and they are legion—claim not only that collegiate surveillance is ethically questionable but that there's little legal justification for it as well. Neither the CIA nor any of the state and local vigilante groups described below can cite a single law permitting the sort of political snooping they engage in as a matter of routine. Even the legality of the FBI's activities in this area is suspiciously ambiguous. In 1956, Don Whitehead, J. Edgar Hoover's Boswell, published in *The FBI Story* a private directive—sort of a "Dear Edgar" letter—sent to Hoover by President Roosevelt in 1939. This letter—which was *not* an Executive Order—authorized the FBI to engage in "intelligence activities" incidental to its newly acquired domestic spy-catching authority. This informal and obscure note—at best intended as a stopgap measure in an atmosphere of impending war—has become the tail that wags the enormous dog of a permanent FBI surveillance apparatus. Hoover seems to have expanded the vague terms of the directive to confer upon the FBI the power, in Hoover's language, "to identify individuals working against the United States, determine their objectives and nullify their effectiveness." These "individuals," Hoover would say, are those whose activities involve "subversion and related internal security problems." With this murky justification, the FBI has assumed the power to police not acts but opinions, speech and association—and not for the purpose of preparing evidence for presentation at a trial but merely to keep track of nonconformists.

No act of Congress has ever authorized the FBI to exercise these powers. In fact, an act permitting the FBI to trail campus radicals, take their photographs, open their mail, record their license-plate numbers, bug their conversations, penetrate their meetings and associations through decoys and informers and assemble extensive dossiers that include tips and complaints supplied by private (and frequently anonymous) individuals would be about as constitutional as a law creating a hereditary monarchy.

Only since 1960 or so has the security establishment zoomed in on the college campus. According to the snoopers' logic, this new focus makes eminent sense. In the 1960s, the campus has emerged as the spawning ground of the most vigorous—and the most radical—antiwar and political movements. The campus is where the action is. As a group, college teachers now dominate the New Left intellectual community. In faculties and student bodies alike, the young, the restless and the militant abound, openly activist and publicly disdaining what they see as the hang-ups and the subterfuges of their elders. These activists can provoke the messianic instincts in the snoopers themselves, many of whom believe they have a patriotic obligation to "save" students from "mistakes they might regret later on." This protective reasoning expresses the quasi-Freudian thesis that political preferences and attitudes are irrevocably fixed before the age of 20 and that unless a youthful subject subsequently defects or informs, he'll bear watching the rest of his life. On a more practical level, the university has also moved up in the intelligence peeking order because of its increasing financial involvement with the Federal Government, particularly in the area of security-related research projects.

Since 1960, the House Un-American Activities Committee, at least in its public and semipublic endeavors, has been inordinately preoccupied with youth and the college scene. The California Burns Committee—HUAC's Golden State equivalent—has "protected" California by issuing four extensive reports (the first based on files apparently stolen from the offices of a New Left student group at Berkeley) on the activities of California's young. But the most ambitious campaign to unearth subversion in collegiate militancy has been mounted by Hoover and the FBI. Since 1963, Hoover has vainly tried to ban Communist speakers from college campuses, justifying his concern on grounds that even some FBI sympathizers found offensive: that seductive Communist propaganda is too treacherous for naïve student ears. Hoover's campaign reached a high pitch of passion in his annual report for 1966: "In its cynical bid to gain an image of respectability, the Party is directing an aggressive campaign at American youth, claiming to perceive a new upsurge of 'leftist' thinking among the young people."

So it's not surprising that when an admitted Communist visits a college campus, the FBI photographs not only him but his host—and keeps careful watch over anyone who visits either of them. An avowed Communist is presumed to be a conspirator, so anyone who breaks bread with him bears scutiny, too. All too often, even more tenuous relationships attract the FBI. In 1963, for instance, John McAuliff, then a junior at Carleton College in Northfield, Minnesota, was investigated after he had sent a check to Dan Rubin, a Communist youth leader who had visited Carleton to speak on a program organized by a campus group (organized for the purpose of presenting controversial speakers of every political stripe) that McAuliff happened to head. The path of this investigation led an FBI agent to one of McAuliff's friends in

Indianapolis. The friend was questioned about McAuliff's politics and then urged to keep quiet about the investigation. Nonetheless, *The Minneapolis Tribune* eventually found out about it, published all the facts and wondered editorially how the FBI knew that McAuliff had sent a check to Rubin—unless it had opened Rubin's mail.

In view of the FBI's overpowering obsession with protecting innocent youth from being duped by the wily Communists, it's also not surprising that FBI agents are now familiar figures in the halls of academe. In their legitimate functions—probes to which the student presumably consents, such as to clear him for Federal employment or to support his conscientious objector claim—FBI agents have routine access to student transcripts (which are not always confined to grades) and also to personal files that may contain political or psychological data. Much of the material in these files is quite unrelated to security matters, but increasingly, colleges keep data on a student's political activities, associations and opinions—because administrators have learned in the past few years that they probably will be asked about these matters.

The presumably legitimate FBI investigations of students and former students have institutionalized the relationship between the Bureau and the universities. The intelligence agent who majors in campus spying develops a soft, friendly relationship with the college staff members with whom he works. The deans, registrars and their assistants know that the agent has "chosen policework as his career" because it is so "challenging." They know that the agent is as concerned as the next man with academic freedom. Didn't he attend college himself, sometimes the very college at which he now spends most of his time? Doesn't he have college-bound youngsters of his own? And, after all, isn't he "only doing his job"?

But when the investigating agents are on a sympathetic, first-name basis with those who keep the records, the shadowy line between legitimate and illegitimate surveillance is not always observed. Early in 1967, Berkeley's admissions officer, David Stewart, admitted that in "three or four cases in the last few months," student records were given to the FBI. These were records of students who had not applied for any Government position, students who had manifestly *not* consented to a *sub rosa* examination of their personal histories and political preferences. And even at universities that strive to maintain the distinction between legitimate and illegitimate investigations, the agent's explanation of the reasons for his investigation is almost invariably taken at face value—on trust.

Since the Government itself now keeps dossiers on literally millions of individuals, information from a student's college files frequently finds its way into the Government's master file. Unhappily, the accuracy of the resultant hodgepodge of facts and observations is far from unimpeachable. At a time when the Government is the nation's largest employer and when some sort of security clearance is practically *de rigueur* for many of the most interesting jobs, the dossier system develops a formidable economic influence. An inaccurate or slanted report of an individual's campus activities—political or otherwise—recorded indelibly in a file the Government consults but that the student can never see, can haunt him with preternatural persistence throughout his life.

As a small but perhaps revealing example: Joseph Tieger, who graduated near the top of his class at Duke in 1963, was denied conscientious-objector status by his New Jersey draft board. The

board, it turned out, had referred to a 5000-word biography of Tieger, anonymously written but apparently prepared by the FBI, mostly from information compiled on Tieger while he was at Duke. This revealing document, which Tieger subsequently had the unique good fortune of obtaining from his draft boards, does not record that a Duke religion professor had signed a statement asserting that Tieger deserved C. O. status "beyond question." It does mention, however, that Tieger in high school "failed to participate in extracurricular activities which is required to make a well-rounded personality"; that he once showed up at a tea party at Duke "in shorts with his shirttail out and wearing tennis shoes"; and that the university library once "addressed a postcard to the registrant indicating that a book concerning the writings of Trotsky was overdue." As we go to press, Tieger, now a law student, has just received a deferment for one year.

Although the once-invisible CIA is confined by statute to intelligence operations outside the United States, its activities, too, spill over into the groves of academe. Students and professors who receive grants for foreign travel or study are frequently approached by CIA representatives, who request that the prospective travelers do a little moonlighting as unofficial intelligence agents during their sojourn abroad. Returning students are also interviewed and often invited to report or answer questions of interest to the CIA; if they have taken photographs, they might be asked for copies. The CIA stimulates such voluntary contributions by offering a generous "consultation fee"—as well as the prospect of a new grant. Some veterans of these sessions have taken to voluntarily stopping by the CIA office for a "debriefing" after sojourns to such places as Africa, Indonesia or India.

This might seem harmless enough, as long as the moonlighting scholars don't take their role as spies too seriously. But foreign-study grants are also used more directly, as a cover for regular CIA agents with legitimate or fraudulent academic credentials. While such a gambit is undoubtedly very useful to the CIA, its effects on the academic discipline involved are somewhat less salubrious. A weighty report recently published by the American Anthropological Association states that in many parts of the world American anthropologists are suspected of being spies. "There is some basis for these suspicions and beliefs," the report notes, adding that as a result, legitimate anthropological research has been severely handicapped. Some anthropologists, the report continues, after failing to get research grants for projects they view as worth while, "have been approached by obscure foundations or have been offered supplementary support from such sources, only to discover later that they were expected to provide intelligence information usually to the Central Intelligence Agency."

A rather similar example involved an instructor at an Eastern university, who in 1963 was turned down for a Fulbright grant for study overseas. The CIA, which seems to keep good track not only of those who get such grants but of those who don't, approached the disappointed instructor and asked him if he'd like to study abroad anyway. He'd receive the same stipend as a Fulbright fellow and, in return, he would only have to report details about the host country and about the activities of the actual Fulbright scholars there. The instructor reluctantly agreed; but before the deal was closed, he attended an antiwar demonstration, where a student was seen taking pictures of him. The instructor subsequently learned that the CIA had assigned the student to check on the instructor's feelings about the war in Vietnam. The instructor apparently failed his CIA entrance' exam, because he never did receive his pseudo Fulbright grant.

Others have been luckier, if you want to call it that. A former Ivy League student who is now a journalist parlayed his impeccable credentials in the Young Republican Organization—which the CIA seems to regard as "safe"—into a jaunt to Europe and then into a free trip around the world. He didn't realize the first trip was at the CIA's expense—until after he returned and was quizzed about it. He reported that all was safe overseas, which must have pleased the CIA, because it sent him back again. After his second return, the CIA never contacted him, so he didn't bother to report at all.

This may be nice work if you can get it, but many of those who succumb to the lure of free travel are not quite as cynical as this chap. Junketeers typically feel they ought to report *something,* if only to justify the CIA's expense. Many also feel that the juicier the information they give, the more likely they are to receive another "foundation grant" in the future. There are no facts to support this assumption, but it's not beyond belief that some of these part-time agents have filed fabricated or greatly exaggerated reports—perhaps to the disadvantage of whatever individuals and groups about which they were reporting.

Besides the CIA and the FBI, there is a surprising number of local surveillance agencies. These are called "Red Squads" or "Bomb Squads" and most of them sprang up in the early years of this century to keep track of Bolsheviks, anarchists, wobblies and the like. While these particular foes are nowadays hardly more than names out of the history books, the forces that once engaged them in battle are still emphatically alive. In fact, campus demonstrations, student antiwar activities and big-city racial disturbances have made them more robust than ever. On campuses in Berkeley, Chicago and New York City—to name a few—political-surveillance bureaus, directly or indirectly related to local police bodies, have taken it upon themselves to watch leftist opinions and associations.

As an example: On the eve of the 1966 National Student Association Convention, a St. John's (New York) University coed, Gloria Kuzmyak, was visited by detectives from New York City's Bureau of Special Services, known as BOSS. Miss Kuzmyak, then an officer in the N. S. A., was planning to attend the convention to be held at the University of Illinois, and the BOSS men solicited her help "to keep a check on demonstrations that were going to take place." Her help in this instance would be confined to giving BOSS the names of all New York N. S. A. students and representatives "associated with the liberal caucus." Miss Kuzmyak declined. After she returned from the convention, she was visited twice, first by the same detectives with a similar plea and subsequently by another of their number, with the request that she "forget all about" the earlier attempts to extract names from her.

Some local Red Squad agents are so well known that they inspire an emotion similar to camaraderie among those they're paid to spy on. Not too long ago, a student "undercover" agent at the University of Texas, whose affiliation with the Texas Department of Public Safety was an ill-kept secret, was elected honorary chairman of the local chapter of Students for a Democratic Society—in recognition of his exemplary attendance record and the attentiveness with which he followed the proceedings.

The dean of all campus Red Squad operatives, until his recent retirement, was an inspector at Berkeley who has become something like Mr. Chips to a generation of Berkeley radicals. "This affable, balding gentleman," recalls one nostalgic Berkeley grad, "was so familiar to us that he would come up on the platform ahead of a meeting and ask for a list of speakers." The inspector claimed to have the authority to attend whatever Berkeley meetings he wished, but according to our informant, he usually left when asked to—"in order not to make a scene."

But indulgent sentiment for operatives such as this one, coupled with student notions of the ultimate harmlessness of the activities they engage in, sometimes conceals the fact that the Red Squad wings of local police forces are particularly useful to the higher security establishment, if only because of the ease with which they disregard state curbs on wire tapping and bugging. The authorities have allowed FBI agents to "tune in" only when national security is at stake (though the FBI tends to see national security threatened more frequently than most of us might); but local police tap phones routinely, without recourse to any high-sounding justifications. When discovered engaging in political bugging, they frequently explain their actions in terms of some conventional police function. In recent years, they have magically transformed what objective observers would construe as out-and-out political surveillance into investigations of such nonpolitical offenses as drug or morals violations.

Completing our roster of agencies that engage in campus snooping are the Army and Navy counterintelligence crews (who probe draft-connected security risks) and the R.O.T.C. For years, the Berkeley Navy R.O.T.C. has conducted systematic surveillance of New Left campus groups. Whether such work earns academic credits isn't clear but Berkeley undoubtedly provides enough radicals and anarchists to keep the N. R. O. T. C. busy. Much of their work involves compiling dossiers and maintaining files of leftish handbills, which are kept in folders marked CONFIDENTIAL–NAVAL INTELLIGENCE–TWELFTH NAVAL DISTRICT.

Recently the Army R.O.T.C. tried to extend the intelligence operation to encompass the eight Western states in the Sixth Army area. R.O.T.C. instructors at each school in the area were provided with "confidential" educational training kits, which made it easy for cadets to sniff out the bad guys.   When a group of professors at the University of Washington learned about the kits, R.O.T.C. officials admitted that the kits had been distributed–but denied that cadets were instructed to snoop. Any spying that had occurred, said the officials, had been done by cadets on their own initiative. But the local chapter of the American Association of University Professors, which perhaps has learned the hard way that students don't usually undertake spare-time projects if they don't count toward the final grade, commended the university for its action against "political propagandizing" and charged the Army with "serious intrusions into academic life."

As both the R. O. T. C. groups and the CIA seem to have perceived, the best people to do spying work on campus are students themselves. If the student agent keeps his cool, the risks of exposure are minimal. He has perfect protective coloring, because, unlike the more conventional agent, his background, life style and appearance are just like everyone else's.   And the role is much less demanding than being a decoy for drug pushers or homosexuals, or other after-school jobs for which students have been recruited. Students whose politics lean to the right tend to regard informing as a civic duty, like giving blood to the Red Cross.

Students who cannot be induced to spy on their cohorts by appeals to patriotism or the lure of free travel will often succumb to the more tangible blandishment of hard cash. Not too long ago, testimony in a court trial revealed that Charles Benson Childs, a student at the University of North Carolina, earned $100 a month, plus expenses–and he received a draft deferment as well.

Today the pay is not as niggardly. When the tiny Advance Youth Organization was on trial in 1963 and 1964 (the Government was trying to compel the group to register as a Communist-front organization), 11 youthful informers testified they had received a total of over $45,000 for brief periods of undercover work. The highest-paid was one Aaron Cohen, whose take from the FBI totaled $6571.65. The sum presumably reflected his extra value as an officer of the organization. Officers, especially secretaries, keep the membership lists, and thus are prime targets for intelligence sleuths. During the 1965 passport-violation trial of three young people who were part of a student delegation that had visited Cuba, several informers–recruited from campuses as far-ranging as San Francisco State and Columbia–surfaced long enough to testify for the prosecution. All admitted they were well paid. One student testified the FBI had given him a $300 bonus for going to Cuba. Another of the informers wasn't even Government sponsored: He turned out to be in the employ of anti-Communist lecturer Gordon Hall, who had planted him in the delegation in order to arm himself with fresh material for the luncheon circuit.

Almost as good a recruit as an actual member is a student who joins a target organization and then leaves it for ideological reasons. As soon as the FBI learns of his defection, he is often offered the opportunity to avenge himself, usually at the expense of his former colleagues. A few defectors become chronic Government witnesses, zealously denouncing their former beliefs and associates. Others, who might be less willing witnesses, are induced to inform more out of a feeling of panic. One day they impulsively join an organization and after weeks of sober reflection, they're stricken with profound regrets. A visit from the FBI at the right moment—or a telephone call by the student himself to the local FBI office—results in a get-together. The experienced FBI agent is predictably adept at manipulating hesitant subjects. He overcomes reluctance to inform by a promise that the information will be kept secret, by patriotic appeals ("Don't you want to help your country?"), by the assurance that "all the kids are doing it," by hints that the agent already possesses compromising information and by expressing sympathy for the humanitarian impulses that led the student into his political lapse. The agent scrupulously avoids the term "informer"; his plea is for "cooperation." The usual result is that the hesitant defector finally identifies other members of his group or pledges to stay on as an informer.

If the soft sell fails, agents do not scorn cruder methods—especially if the potential stoolie seems a worthwhile recruit. If the subject has a job, an agent has been known to confront him there—and threaten to report a refusal to cooperate to the subject's employer. With law and prelaw students, a threat to report them to the bar association's character committee—which must approve all admissions to the bar—can sometimes turn the trick. A similar ploy can be used with students who plan teaching careers. And when all else fails, there's always the possibility of appealing to the subject's parents, to warn them that their offspring is associating with the wrong people on campus.

The recruiter's life is no bed of roses, however: Even though he concentrates on likely prospects, he is often indignantly rebuffed. To the continuing dismay of security types, most students regard informing as betrayal and they regard the invitation to engage in it as a personal insult. Furthermore, student groups persistently refuse to react in ways the security agents are most familiar with. Students, for instance, are unwilling to adopt the closed, Communist-cell-like political associations that agents are so adept at penetrating. Openness is the key to the students' political style. Students feel they have nothing to hide and—especially in their political associations—are largely repelled by secrecy. But the security establishment finds this attitude both perplexing and disconcerting, since it expects its targets to be guiltily concealing everything they do. After all, secret political machinations—loosely interpreted as "conspiracies"—are a key justification for surveillance system.

The colleges themselves have responded to snooping activities in a variety of ways. A disturbing number of universities have been tacitly cooperative—in ways that greatly transcend the cozy personal relationships that often grow up between Federal agents and the college administrative staffs. Documented evidence supports the charge that some universities—Duke, Illinois, Indiana, Kansas, Michigan State, Ohio State and Texas, for instance—have actively collaborated with the FBI. In these institutions, a highly security-conscious bureaucracy compiles data about their students' politics from such sources as deans, faculty, staff, faculty advisors of campus organizations, fraternity officers, judicial boards, housemothers, housemasters, maids, the press and the police—both campus and local. Often this information is not only compiled but interpreted. At Duke, for example, Dean Robert Cox keeps an extensive set of dossiers that have been called "potentially the most explosive of all" by a special university committee headed by Professor John Curtiss, president of the Duke chapter of the American Association of University Professors.

Fortunately, most colleges aren't quite this zealous in lending aid and comfort to the surveillance establishment. But even sins of omission can be grievous enough. Two summers ago, the House Un-American Activities Committee sent subpoenas to Michigan and Stanford universities, requesting lists of officers of campus groups that had criticized the U.S. Vietnam policy. (Many universities require organization to file membership lists to qualify for registration as an official campus body.) Both schools complied with these subpoenas—though many critics of HUAC, both within the schools and outside, thought that the HUAC action could be challenged as unconstitutional. Similar attempts to secure membership lists from the NAACP had been rebuffed by the Supreme Court, which had held that such enforced disclosures may "constitute as effective a restraint of freedom of association" as more direct forms of interference. The "inviolability of privacy," the Court had said, is "indispensable to the preservation of the freedom of association, particularly where a group espouses dissident beliefs." Despite what seemed a perfect precedent for refusal, or at least challenge, neither of the universities even protested or in any way questioned HUAC's mandate. And neither of the universities seemed to realize that they were collaborating in what amounted to a punitive exposure of the individuals on

the lists. Whether or not those listed were summoned as witnesses (some were), all the names were permanently dossiered in the Committee's file and reference service"—available to security bloodhounds and even to the constituents of any Congressman who might ask for them.

To be sure, a few colleges have courageously resisted the intrusions of the surveillance establishment. And with several sorry exceptions—such as California until 1963 and North Carolina and Ohio State until 1965—they successfully resisted the snoopers' attempts to bar Communist speakers from campus. The general response to these two challenges left room for hope that painful memory of the abuses done to dissenting professors in the Fifties would quicken a determination not to collaborate in intimidating the burgeoning student protest movements of the Sixties. But only a handful have lived up to this promise. Following an S.D.S. peace demonstration at Wesleyan University (Connecticut) in the spring of 1966, an FBI agent appeared and asked that college authorities hand over the S.D.S. membership list. College Dean Stanley J. Idzerda refused, saying, "We keep no such lists of any organizations." He added, "We consider the student's activity his own affair. At the same time, it's unfortunate that a climate of suspicion can be created by such activities that might lead some students to be more circumspect than the situation requires. Things like this can be a danger to a free and open community if men change their behavior because of it." The resultant furor brought the FBI agent back to the campus, where he told the dean that there had been a "misunderstanding." No probe of the S. D. S. had been contemplated, but only of "possible infiltration of the S. D. S. chapter by Communist influence."

Another agent involved in the case thoughtfully added that the FBI "makes inquiries every day on campuses throughout the country—we investigate 175 types of violations, security as well as criminal." When a Wesleyan student committee subsequently wrote J. Edgar Hoover that the investigation constituted a gross infringement of academic freedom, Hoover replied that the charge was "not only utterly false but also is so irresponsible as to cast serious doubt on the quality of academic reasoning or the motivation behind it.

When the director of the FBI can hint, without too much subtlety, that uncooperative colleges are themselves flirting with subversion or conspiracy, it's not too surprising that the colleges try to avoid such conflicts—even when their vital interests are at stake. Reluctant to act unless absolutely forced to do so, most colleges unwittingly invite the very pressures they seek to avoid—and then respond to these with more evasion and more compromise. Their caution is reinforced by the inbred conformity that seems common to all bureaucracies—collegiate or otherwise—a conformity that assures not only that accommodation to the demands of the security establishment will be mindless and irresponsible but that it will be uniform. As one student correspondent—who must remain anonymous, since he's still in school—puts it:

"Most university administrators operate on the principle of inertia—it's easier to go along with inquiries than to refuse. Why run the risk of being labeled a Commie-hippie school? Most of them cheerfully give out some information, although not all, without ever thinking

they may be creating a serious problem. Once they are made aware that they also have a prerogative to refuse, many agree it would be fine if all universities refused, but why should one university risk being labeled 'oddball'?"

But unless it is willing to take this risk, the university will soon find itself on a collision course with "national security." It will not be enough for the university to make informing or secret political surveillance—by faculty or students alike—grounds for immediate censure, discharge or expulsion, though this would certainly be a good beginning. In the long run, it is fatuous, or at least diversionary, to attempt to reconcile academic freedom with national security. They simply cannot be reconciled. The university must reconstruct, on the foundation of academic freedom, an ethos that—no matter what the risks or temporary costs—rejects surveillance altogether. If the university is disturbed by nonstudent attempts to gain a voice in its affairs (as in the Berkeley outbreak), then it should feel all the more threatened by the actions of Big Brother. At a time when the life and values of the university are being subjected to unprecedented stress by "security" pressures, the university, if it is to survive at all, must simply learn to say no—to the FBI, the CIA, the R.O.T.C., the Red Squads, the Congressional committees and the tribe of spies, spooks, snoops, surveillants and subpoena servers they have spawned. In the last analysis, the only real threat to our national security is the mutilation of academic freedom that will inevitably result if the security establishment continues to flourish on our nation's campuses.

IV

the sick

Medical care and those who render it have traditionally been regarded with both respect and mystery by community members. These perceptions are reinforced by the ways in which doctors relate to patients and the various trappings they use in their work. Racks of test tubes in the laboratory, masked men with their own jargon in the operating room, nurses in white eternally hurrying to attend to a supposedly urgent need, and unfamiliar apparatus plugged into silent patients are scenes that come to mind when we think of the ill and their medical care. Nevertheless, the technology of medical practice is only one aspect of the process of restoring health and managing illness. Medical care also involves complex sets of human relationships between those who render care and those who need it. The nature, scope, and quality of these relationships, and the context of medical practice is critical to the fate of patients. To the outsider, it may seem that the medical practitioner is above the strains which enter other human endeavors, but this simply is not so. Moreover, the norms of the economic market place and the political and social strivings of persons in the health field have resulted in serious inequities in the provision of services. Many Americans receive care of less than the highest quality, care which is inferior to that given in other parts of the world.

This chapter presents examples of the social conflicts that confront us in the treatment and prevention of illness. Some of the problems are related to the demands that sick individuals make on the medical profession, ones that cannot be met or that are not in keeping with "professional" notions of good care. In other instances, the subtle processes which operate in other areas of social life are found in the treatment of the sick; preferential treatment operates in the provision of medical care. Moreover, individual practitioners take advantage of their almost unassailable status and abuse patients for the sake of personal gain. The accounts presented here indicate some of America's troubles in efforts to maintain health, treat illness, and prolong life.

Individual	Individual
↓	↓
Individual	Organization

DIET PILLS

All occupational groups who deal with the public have their share of unscrupulous people. In most consumer-seller contexts, we almost expect disreputable behavior and stand somewhat prepared to deal with it. A mark of the professions, however, is an emphasis on scrupulous behavior. The physician is held up as an epitomy of integrity because of the helplessness of the patient. Yet most medical care is rendered in privacy where the behavior of the doctor depends largely on self-discipline and personal honesty. There are those who are willing to break the trust, who take advantage of community members concerned and worried about their well-being. "Diet Pills" describes charlatans taking advantage of individuals who seek them out and believe in their therapeutics.

WITH A LIFE AT STAKE

Increased specialization of personnel and the development of extensive bureaucratic arrangements in the provision of services are outgrowths of technological advances and increased scientific knowledge in the health field. Most leaders in medicine maintain that it is now impossible for any one person to master enough knowledge to be proficient in all areas of medical care. Continued improvement in medical care is at least partially dependent on even greater specialization, on the recruitment and the training of individuals willing to concentrate their work in narrowly circumscribed areas. The development of the many subspecialties, however, has created organizational problems which may impede the treatment of an individual patient. Edward Brecher describes his attempt to deal with a complex medical organization in order for his wife to receive care.

Organization	Organization
↓	↓
Individual	Organization

DEAD ON ARRIVAL

Considering the variations in treatment accorded persons of different social and environmental classes in other social relationships, it should not be too surprising that similar distinctions hold even for the dying patient. Most community members would like to think that, in the face of death or serious illness, everyone receives the best care, or, at least, that the money and prestige of the patient does not enter into the way he is treated. But persons do not receive similar medical care, even when they stand in the doorway of death. David Sudnow found that the amount of effort physicians extended toward patients near death or actually dead was related strongly to the patient's age, social background, and perceived moral character. Some people in the United States, it seems, are deader than others.

A SACRED TRUST

Despite the seeming affluence, the struggle for bare existence continues for many persons in the United States, including a significant proportion of the aged. Old people who are modestly well off can literally be made into paupers with the heavy expenses of chronic illness or long term hospital care. Consequently, decades after most European countries developed such programs, many policy makers and health planners in America have advocated a system of public medical insurance to protect the elderly. The medical profession, or at least its major spokesman, the American Medical Association, was a major opponent of the recently initiated medical insurance. They fought hard, and some say ruthlessly, to protect their powerful hold on the distribution of medical services and control over who should benefit from the best in health care. Harris describes the AMA battle against the community and its aged citizens.

diet pills

SUSANNA McBEE

No one has ever called me fat. A little on the hippy side perhaps. But never fat. I am a reliable size 10, and my weight, without clothes, is 123 to 125, respectable enough for my 5'5" frame.

By ordinary standards I would flunk out as a candidate for obesity treatments. But in a recent six-week period, traveling to nearly every section of the country, I went to 10 doctors who treat weight problems and instead of bouncing me out of their offices as I had expected, they welcomed me. Although three of them said I had no weight problem and another even congratulated me for catching the problem early (that is, before it developed), they all, every last one of them, gave me diet pills. My "haul" was 1,479 pills.

The pills, analyzed later by a chemist, included amphetamines, barbiturates, sex hormones, diuretics, thyroid and digitalis. They came in various sizes and colors, some of them very pretty and all of them—for me, at least—completely unnecessary. Even though I had undergone an arduous eating program—several buttered rolls with every meal, gobs of sour cream on my baked potatoes and enough cheesecake to supply a White House banquet I had gained only

five or six pounds and was definitely not a "medical overweight problem."

The first doctor I visited was an osteopath. Dr. Edward A. Devins, whose drab suite on the third floor of the Altman Building in Kansas City, Missouri had been raided less than a month earlier. Agents of the Food and Drug Administration's Bureau of Drug Abuse Control and a deputy U.S. marshal had confiscated 2.5 million pills most of them amphetamines and some barbiturates. The pills were seized on the basis of a civil complaint alleging that Dr. Devins had failed to keep accurate records of the pills he received and dispensed.

At Dr. Devins' office, as at the others, I gave my correct name, made up a local address and occupation, and said only that I wanted to lose weight, never asking for pills. The day I appeared, a girl handed me a form with 195 questions, starting out conventionally enough with eyesight, hearing, nose and throat conditions, and progressing to my mental condition, which was hardly improved by the queries: "Do you feel alone and sad at a party?" "Do you often cry?" "Does life look entirely hopeless?" "Do you often wish you were dead and away from it all?"

A girl read over my questionnaire, asked if I were allergic to medicine and if I were nervous. "What is the highest your weight has ever been?" she asked; then she weighed me with my clothes and shoes on. I came to 130½ pounds. Not bad, considering I had just gorged myself at a late lunch.

"You should weigh 120 to 125." she said reprovingly, "and we'll get you down to 120." She took my blood pressure, pulse and measurements. When she got to my waist, which normally is about 25 inches, it measured 28 because I stuck

Life, *January 26, 1968.* © *Time Inc., 1968.*

out my stomach. She seemed not to notice but recorded the statistic. Then she asked who had referred me. I said I'd heard about Dr. Devins at a party from a woman whose name I couldn't remember.

"I've never heard that one before," the girl said cheerfully, "but one lady said she heard about us at a bus stop." Obviously, this girl *wanted* to believe me. She then announced. "I'm going out now and prepare your medication."

Several minutes later Dr. Devins entered, carrying a box of pills which he had picked up before even seeing me. He did not examine me but said I would feel different after taking his pills "because, after all, you're on diet medicine."

Talking rapidly, Dr. Devins said, "We don't advise going on a diet." He then read me the instructions on my pillbox, which contained 140 tablets—pinks, browns, tans and grays. "If you're not nervous (my questionnaire indicated I was not), they won't make any difference." He said I might not sleep too well with the pink pills but not to worry about it.

I asked what was in the pills. He did not tell me but said only that the pinks would suppress the appetite, the browns would keep me from being constipated ("People tend to get constipated when they lose weight") and the others would work with the pinks to reduce me. They contained, it turned out, amphetamines, laxatives and thyroid.

Dr. Devins said he would see me in a month and directed me to the receptionist, who looked at my chart and said, "Ten dollars."

That was easy, I thought, but the Rubel clinic in Decatur, Illinois, which attracts the heavy set from all over the state, might be difficult. Perhaps, if I were rejected as a patient there, a fat man posing as my husband could go through the clinic and tell me about it. A friend in

Decatur said he'd locate one, and while waiting I realized I would need a gold ring, too.

At the local Woolworth's a clerk showed me a large tray of rings. She pointed to some with stones.

"No, I just want a gold ring."

She pointed to gold rings with stones.

"No, no. Just a plain gold ring," I said, trying to smile.

Her eyebrow arched toward her scalp. Her eyes narrowed. She knew exactly what kind of woman she was dealing with. Coldly, she displayed a section of gold bands. I grabbed one, paid $1.05 and started to put it in my purse. "Don't you even want to try it on?" the clerk asked as I hurried out.

I did not find a fat husband and went alone. In the Rubel waiting room a nurse called my name over a microphone and gave me a one-page, 136 questions form to fill out. It asked about my current physical condition, past illnesses and eating habits. I saw several women go beyond the reception desk, presumably for their monthly checkup, and come out again, carrying a little white sack of pills—all in less than five minutes.

The clinic, which is one of three in the Midwest run by Dr. Louis L. Rubel, has an array of tests for new patients: weight, measurements, blood pressure, pulse, urinalysis, blood sample from a finger, an electrocardiogram. There is also the ankle-jerk test, which most internists and endocrinologists regard only as a measure of hypothyroidism, and an inconclusive one at that. I took it sitting on my knees on a cushion beside a machine called an "Achilleometer," and after a technician tapped my Achilles tendon and saw the indicator on the machine jump into the middle range, she told me this meant I could take an average dose of their medicine. Of which medicine? "Of all our medicine."

Dr. William K. Franta, who saw me after my tests, is one of four osteopaths at the clinic working for Dr. Rubel, also an osteopath. "You're not really over-weight," said Dr. Franta, who has a weight problem of his own. He reviewed my tests, which came out normal, and my weight 129½. He asked if I took any med-ication. Just vitamins, I said.

"Well, we'll give you our own vita-mins so you won't have to take the others if you don't want to." He wrote a prescription, and I asked what the pills were. He said one kind was a "gland substance" and the others were vitamins and minerals. He made no effort to examine me, not even to listen to the heart or feel the impulse over the chest both considered part of a complete heart examination.

Instead he gave me a little talk. Weight control, he said, is a matter of glandular balance. Since I was in the normal weight range, which for me he said is 119 to 129, I might not make too much progress. We would try the pills for a few months and see how I did.

Dr. Franta spent three to four minutes with me discussing my diet, handed me the prescription and told me to drop it in the wicker basket at the front desk. When I did, the office manager put it on a dumb-waiter pulley behind her and it was lifted upstairs. Shortly, a white paper bag with three small envelopes inside slid down the pulley, and after I paid $15 and was told that each succeeding visit would cost $10, I was given the bag. It housed 84 pills, 28 each of vermilion vitamins, magenta vitamins and lime-green thyroid. There was also a brochure explaining the Rubel program and beginning with the words that fatties love to hear: "Overweight or obesity is a very common disorder which can be corrected without dieting."

When I telephoned the office of Dr. C. C. Mendenhall in Gardena, California, the first thing the girl said was that visit and medication would cost $15. That's cash; no personal checks, she said. When I arrived, a girl led me to a small room with an ankle-jerk machine, this one called a "Photomotograph." While the machine was warming up, she quizzed me about my physical condition, even about how my liver and spleen were doing, as if a layman could know. She said I looked slim and asked what I wanted to weigh. I had just hit 132½; the cheesecake obviously had gotten to me. I said I wanted to weigh 120 to 125. She tapped my Achilles tendon, measured me and took my pulse and blood pressure. (Later, Dr. Mendenhall's services to new patients were expanded to include a physical exam, electrocardiogram, urinalysis and blood tests.) The girl gave me a brochure which urged patients to follow a high-protein, low-fat diet, and she told me not to eat fried foods, salad oils or soft drinks.

Dr. Mendenhall appeared, looking tired, perhaps because he sees 60 or more patients a day. He reviewed my medical history, put a stethoscope to my heart in two places, felt the front and back of my neck and checked my ankles for possible swelling. I asked how much a person of my height and build should weigh.

"It wouldn't do any good to tell you because you people aren't going to get down to the weight you should weigh anyhow," he said.

You people?

He said he was just trying to get people down to a weight where they would be happy. "I'm not trying to reform the world. Very few fat people get down to their ideal weight and stay there."

I asked about medication, and he told me I would be getting an appetite depressant, a laxative to take if I needed it, some protein, thyroid and something for my hips (which I said I wanted to reduce). I asked what the hip medication was. "My own preparation." It turned out to be prednisone, an anti-inflammation hormone.

I left Dr. Mendenhall with 364 pills to consume in a *month*, and the next day, after a visit with Dr. Myron F. Babcock in the Los Angeles office of Raymond A. Landis, D. O., I had 84 more pills, including amphetamines. After several tests (weight, measurements, ankle jerk, blood), Dr. Babcock said, "You're not overweight, honey," then congratulated me on "catching the problem in time." The pills? "Things to make you lose weight." And, after I persisted: "This one's a thyroid-acting substance—something you could put young children on."

From there I went to San Diego, where Dr. Orville J. Davis' patients receive a 10-page mimeographed notebook which begins, "WELCOME ABOARD!.... FIRST, if you are NOT overweight by average standard I DO NOT WANT YOU TO WASTE YOUR MONEY AND MY TIME WITH EVEN AN INITIAL VISIT" and concludes, "I do not consider you to have ANY medical overweight problem at all unless you are 15% or more over your average weight."

My average standard was 125. That day I was 130 with my clothes on, only 4% over—an honest-to-God test case for Dr. Davis. Technicians first put me through a physical exams procedure—urinalysis, blood drawn from the vein in my left arm, weight, measurements, blood pressure, pulse and electrocardiogram and then I saw Dr. Davis. He said, "You're in great shape, kid. You have no weight problem," then he prescribed progesterone, which is a sex hormone, and 234 pills, including diuretics, thyroid and appetite suppressants. I paid $40 and wondered how many pills Dr. Davis would give someone *with* a medical overweight problem.

In Denver I saw Dr. Charles William Breitenstein, and after being weighed and measured—nothing else—paid $12 for a 28-day supply of appetite suppressants and tablets containing thyroidlike material. Then I went to the office of Chester M. Rasmussen and Duane A. Thompson, D.O.s, in Hillsboro, Oregon, where a brown-haired woman with glasses, a white dress and the sweetest of voices told me she wanted to check my hemoglobin count. She jabbed the side of my third finger, right hand, but couldn't draw enough blood, then rubbed my finger, trying to push something, anything, out of the capillary. She apologized, gave up and tried the third finger, left hand. Only an insignificant drop or two came. As she kept rubbing and apologizing, her hands got sweaty and so did mine. Now very flustered and very contrite, she attacked my middle finger, right hand. Same result. She kept saying, "You just don't know how sorry I am." She had no idea just how sorry *I* was.

Finally, she called in another woman who noted that jabbing should be done at the tip of the finger, not the side. She demonstrated on me, and she was right: there was all kinds of blood.

The first woman, still apologizing, resumed the testing—urinalysis, ankle jerk, pulse, blood pressure, measurements, weight. In a heavy suit and shoes I came to 131¾ pounds.

Then she posed a medical history quiz, replying. "Real good," whenever, I indicated I had no problem. She asked if I had any swollen extremities—hands, feet. I told her I had some swollen fingers.

After she left, Dr. Thompson discussed my diet, said, "We don't want to make you look like Twiggy, Ha, Ha, Ha," but nevertheless prescribed the sex hormone, progesterone, and other pills, including digitalis, thyroid, amphetamine—268 in all for the month.

My next stop was the Manhattan office of Gordon L. Green, M.D., one of the most prosperous "fat doctors" in the country. He has 19 offices and grosses just under a million dollars a year. Here, I encountered machine-age medicine. The receptionist told me to listen to a tape recording, which said that the pills I'd receive would not affect any illness I might get one way or the other. You can lose weight without pills, said the voice, but you came to me for an easy way to reduce.

After listening to the tape, I asked the receptionist where Dr. Green was. She said he was not in any of the 19 offices. "He just runs the business." I asked if that voice on the tape was his. "Oh, no. We got a disc jockey to do that."

She weighed me (129 with clothes on), took measurements and asked about my medical history. She took a plastic box of capsules and tablets off a shelf and directed me to the doctor's office, where she put the pillbox on his desk. Then Dr. Sam Provenzano checked my blood pressure, listened to my heart, asked some questions about my medical history and explained how I should take the pills—46 for the week, including amphetamine-thyroid combinations.

In Falls Church, Virginia, Dr. Julius Seymour Siegel said I weighed 129 pounds and that he could tell, "by the size of your arm." that I ought to weigh 115. "Eat and drink anything you want," he said. "All you have to do is take the pills I'm going to give you" three a day until I got down to 115, then one a day as "maintenance medicine." He took my blood pressure and pulse rate, listened to my heart, said, "Ah, perfect," asked no questions about medical history, current illnesses or allergies to medicine. Then he picked up a wall phone that was a direct line to a pharmacy, said he wanted pills for, uh. "Hey, what's your name?" and,

hanging up, gave me directions to the Falls Church Drug Center. "Can I get the prescription filled at my own pharmacy?" I asked the secretary-nurse. "Oh, no," she answered. "You *must* go to the Drug Center." I paid her $3 and left to pick up 150 amphetamine-barbiturate-thyroid combinations for $7.50. I had spent three minutes with Dr. Siegel.

Dr. Siegel set the record for short office calls, and my next doctor, Harry Needelman, M.D. of Miami Beach, Florida, the record for long ones. Dr. Needelman holds another record. In 1955 he was convicted of illegal sales of narcotics, was later pardoned and is still battling the Dade County Medical Association for reinstatement.

Despite his legal difficulties, Dr. Needelman has a booming weight-control practice, seeing, according to one report, 750 patients a week. When I joined the ranks, I brought along a LIFE photographer who said he was my husband and asked if he could watch. "Sure," said the receptionist, "we'll be glad to let him go through the factory, too."

I was weighed (130¼), measured and tested (blood pressure, temperature, hemoglobin, urine), then directed through a door that said "Doctor's office" and opened into a small auditorium. The room was remarkable. The doctor's elaborate, crescent-shaped desk was on a platform a step higher than where the patients, or audience, sat on 11 large black leatherette chairs arranged in three rows.

The thick carpet was Kelly green, with standing ashtrays sunk into it. The doctor's desk had a camera (for taking before-and-after pictures of patients), a tape recorder and a rotary slide projector.

Three of us "fatties" had settled into the audience chairs by the time Dr. Needelman, a small, overweight man in his mid-fifties, bounced into the room, smiling frequently and talking very much like Eddie Cantor, through with a slight lisp. He took his place onstage, at his desk, and for an opener told us we could, if we wanted, eat six turkey sandwiches a day. "Doesn't that sound like a fairy tale?" All we had to do was to follow his advice on eating the right foods and we would lose five to seven pounds the first week and three to five pounds a week thereafter.

Then, amazingly enough, he called each of us up to his desk, one by one, and discussed our individual cases in front of the other patients. I listened, for example, as he interviewed one woman who loses weight under his program but gains it back when she returns home to New York. She had been going, off and on, to Dr. Needelman for four years. When she first came, her weight was 128; it was now 148. I asked her later about her downhill progress, and with the loyalty fat patients characteristically have for their "fat doctors," she said huffily, "Dr. Needelman can't help it because I'm a pig."

It was my turn. "You're a young woman," he told me. "Would you like to get down to 120?" He promised to get me down to that in two weeks, then put me on a maintenance program of one pill a day for a month. In front of everyone, he reviewed the state of my kidneys, hemoglobin and blood pressure. He listened briefly to my heart and asked about any swelling. But he took no medical history.

He proudly proclaimed that we were about to see "the longest-running show in the world," that he had been giving the same lecture, with variations, for 14 years. "Now," he said, "we'll put our little show on the road." He flicked on the tape recorder and sat silently as his voice came down at us from a loudspeaker in the ceiling.

The tape went on and on and on as the slide projector flashed "before-and-after" pictures of patients. The voice would name the patients and tell where they worked. It mentioned a local lawyer, shoe salesman, grocer, hotel employee, even a local bookie. "You see, I give all the local businesses a little plug," explained the voice. "With my pills, you can eat 3,000 to 4,000 calories a day and lose weight." After an hour or more, Dr. Needelman, in person, allowed questions from the audience, even asked himself questions, answered them and reviewed what he had already said. "Aren't we having fun this afternoon?" he beamed. He kept calling himself the "talkingest doctor in the world."

Finally it was time for our weekly shot, which he explained only by saying it was the first gear in revving up the body machinery. I was reluctant, but he overwhelmed me with, "Try it this time. If you don't like it, you won't have to take it next time." I took it. I also received 26 pills for the week—diuretics, barbiturates and a combination of amphetamine, laxative and thyroid—and paid $15. A sign at the desk advised that after Jan. 1 prices were going up: $20 for the first visit and $10 a week thereafter. Dr. Needelman told us our capsules contained thyroid, adding that he would be able to determine the following week if we were getting the correct dosage. The "show" was over. It had run three hours, 15 minutes.

Among the "fat doctors" I visited, there was no consensus on diet—some said eat anything you want; others offered elaborate programs. They did not agree on exercise, or on liquor consumption. Their physical examinations ranged from several tests to merely a weight and measurement check. There was consensus, though, on one point: pills, pills, pills.

with a life

at stake

EDWARD M. BRECHER

When my wife, Ruth, fell suddenly and seriously ill two years ago, we faced together the same baffling kinds of questions countless other families each year must find some way to answer: Was a major operation really necessary? Could it safely be postponed a few weeks or months? Should it be performed at a small nearby hospital or at a major medical center? Which medical center? Which surgeon?

During the weeks after Ruth's operation, questions multiplied—and so did our doubts concerning the quality of the care she was receiving at the medical center we had selected (reputed to be one of the country's best). Doctors came and went; no one of them was in command. One of them told Ruth one thing, the same doctor or someone else gave me an altogether different report, and there was not one to whom we could turn to tell us which version was true. Like many other patients we came to know during those stress-laden days and nights, we felt as if we were floundering in a quagmire of medical confusion. When things went wrong, as they not infrequently did, there was no one in authority to listen to us. One capable young hospital resident—the friend of a friend of ours—did take a personal interest in Ruth's problems at one point; but because he lacked status in the hospital's rigid hierarchy, no one would listen to *him*, either.

More and more, as the weeks wore on, we felt ourselves aboard a ship in a gale, buffeted and about to capsize—with no captain on board. One bright spring afternoon, when our doubts and anxieties were at a peak, Ruth even dragged herself out of her hospital bed and started to pack the few belongings she had with her into her little satchel. The effort to secure humane, competent care from that chaos of medical disorganization seemed to her at the moment too harrowing to be worth the effort. Why not return home and let nature take its course?

Then, literally overnight, the confusion was resolved. We both relaxed and were comforted, for now we could see for ourselves that all the rich resources of the modern medical sciences were in fact being harnessed, effectively and sensitively, for Ruth's benefit. When she asked a question, she now got a straight answer—and I got the same answer. She knew that someone was thinking about her needs, planning in advance how to meet them, consulting her when important decisions were to be made. Her simple day-to-day preferences, and her deeper beliefs about life and death and truthfulness, were now respected. Though her physical condition remained grave throughout the remaining year and a half of her illness (which was cancer), the real hazards and discomforts were no longer intensified by the struggle to extract good care from an impersonal medical-hospital system in which we felt friendless and powerless.

The change came when we took a step we should have taken at the very beginning and which I fervently urge on other families: *We secured the services of an internist*—a highly trained and fully qualified specialist in the care of patients rather than just of organs or diseases—to supervise Ruth's care and to serve as a

Reprinted by permission of the author from McCalls, *October, 1967, pp. 96-97, 132, 134-35.*

guide for us both. Thus Ruth at last had what every sick human being needs: a personal physician of her own, one she liked and could trust, pledged to fight on her side in the twin battles against physical illness and medical-hospital bureaucracy.

What kinds of thing go wrong when a patient entrusts his care to a busy specialist he doesn't know or to a faceless medical center, instead of to his personal physician? Many families can answer from their own experience; let me review a few examples Ruth and I observed or were ourselves involved in.

One common difficulty arises when you try to get into a hospital in the first place, as a friend of mine learned one Sunday afternoon. His wife had been operated on at the same medical center where Ruth was being cared for, had gone home and had then had three days of almost continuous vomiting; her body was seriously dehydrated from loss of so much fluid. My friend therefore took his wife back to the center, first phoning one of her doctors to make arrangements. But that phone call wasn't enough. For a patient, he learned, can be admitted to a hospital only by a doctor who has "admitting privileges"; and the doctor my friend phoned, though a fully qualified, board-certified specialist employed full time by the medical center, belonged to one of the medical specialities that lacks admitting privileges. The doctor concerned with his wife's care had full privileges, but he wasn't "on call" that Sunday afternoon. So hour after hour my friend's wife waited in the emergency room first sitting miserably on a chair and then stretched out on a table, pleading for a sip of water. Hospital rules, it seemed, prohibited anyone from giving a patient in so critical a condition anything, even water, without her doctor's order. When my friend filled a glass and took it to her the glass was snatched away and

placed in a nurse's desk drawer, to discourage him from trying again.

Uncowed and resourceful, my friend found a paper cup in the men's room, filled it and took it back to her. Then, when a nurse approached to snatch it away, he stood firmly blocking her path until his wife had finished drinking.

This unusual act of defiance apparently jarred the hospital's stalled machinery into action. A chief resident was summoned, and the wife was at last offered admission. Needless to say, the first medical step taken was to get as much water as possible into the patient, both by mouth and intravenously.

Once admitted to a hospital, every patient finds himself low man on the totem pole in the medical hierarchy, but a patient without a personal physician ranks a little lower than the others. His care is often the concern of two or more hospital departments, and he therefore runs the risk of having neither department bother to assume full responsibility.

The case of one of the women who for many days shared Ruth's semiprivate room was typical. Almost continuous diarrhea, day after day, was causing Ruth's neighbor increasing distress. Eventually a young intern from Syria took notice.

"How often are you getting your Lomotil?" he asked her.

"Lomotil? What's that?" Ruth's roommate responded.

The Syrian intern, obviously embarrassed at having spilled the beans, did not answer—but that afternoon the patient received her first dose of Lomotil, and the next day her diarrhea was belatedly under control. Clearly, each of the several physicians concerned with her underlying illnesses had assumed that one of the others was prescribing for her diarrhea. This might have continued indefinitely if an intern from another part of the world, trained in a different medical tradition and not yet fully acclimated to American hospital procedures, had not happened to "make a mistake" and take a personal interest.

Ruth's problem was almost the reverse. Instead of finding herself ignored by several departments, she found herself caught in a tug-of-war between two of them. We first became aware of this when the surgeon who had operated on her recommended immediate radiation therapy.

"Don't worry about it," he told me. "The radiation dose will be small, only twenty-five hundred units, and only to a limited region of Mrs. Brecher's abdomen. Hence she need not fear any subsequent radiation damage. Since the tumor has already spread beyond control, there is no point in adding to her discomfort by too much radiation. The important thing is to get the treatments started as soon as possible—next Monday morning. I will remain in personal charge."

The surgeon's associate underlined some of these points to the two of us a little later. "You're fortunate," he added to Ruth, "to be here where we will give you continuing personal attention. At many medical centers the surgeons would just turn you over to the radiation therapists and forget all about you. We'll get your treatment started Monday morning; every day saved is a day gained."

Bright and early Monday morning, as the surgeon had promised, Ruth was wheeled to the radiation-therapy department. I accompanied her. She was photographed, handed a paper to sign waiving claims against the medical center, asked a few questions about her hospital insurance, then wheeled into a small room dominated by a linear accelerator—an imposing ultramodern device that looked like something out of a science-fiction television show.

Ruth and I were alarmed. So far, she had not been examined by, or even introduced to, a physician specializing in radiation therapy. Was her treatment to be in the hands of one of the nonmedical attendants we saw wandering aimlessly around, apparently none too sure of what they were supposed to be doing?

Our alarm was not relieved when a young woman attendant threw a switch. Soft music began to play. "You'll have to leave the room now," she told me. "We're going to start the treatment." I left and went in search of a radiation therapist. None was in sight. A few minutes later, Ruth was wheeled out of the linear-accelerator room, still untreated, and returned to her own room. Something, apparently, had gone wrong; we never were told what.

Later that day, a radiation therapist examined Ruth, studied her record and gave her a talking to. "I have ascertained," he told her in a voice meant to carry conviction, "that this is a tumor of a kind which can be totally *eradicated* by radiation if we deliver a large enough dose over a large enough portion of your body—your entire abdomen and chest. Hence I propose to eradicate that tumor." He was careful not to say "cure"; that would have been unethical. But the impact on a naïve patient would surely have been the same. "We'll start your treatments," he concluded, "*next* Monday morning." This was precisely the delay the surgeon and his associate had warned against.

The two departments concerned with Ruth's care were thus in basic disagreement about almost everything—the time when treatment should begin, the amount of radiation, the area of her body to be irradiated and the probable outcome. Which was right? There was nobody we trusted to tell us or to explain the reason for the disagreement. We could only wait helplessly to see which department would win the tug-of-war in which Ruth's future was the stake.

"I feel like a character in a novel by Kafka or in a play written by Ionesco for the Theater of the Absurd," Ruth wrote in a note to a physician cousin of hers that evening. She was a Quaker and much more tolerant than I of human and institutional shortcomings.

During the next week of anxious waiting for therapy to begin, Ruth's urgent need for a personal physician to take the helm should have been clear to us both—but it wasn't. Instead, we saw the problem as too many doctors already. Why add an internist to further compound the confusion? We hadn't yet realized that an internist is not just another specialist, but a man whose essential function is to bring order out of chaos.

In addition to such confrontations with specialists, a patient lacking a personal physician can expect difficulties with nurses and other hospital personnel during a prolonged hospital stay. *They* know which patients are the personal concern of an influential physician and which ones have no one to fight their battles for them. Ruth's most distressing encounter with hospital personnel concerned her intravenous (i.v.) feeding.

Because she could not take food by mouth immediately after her operation, she was fed intravenously for many days. A bottle filled with i.v. fluid hung at the head of her bed from a stand on rollers that looked like a chrome-plated hat rack. A tube led from this bottle to a needle implanted in a vein in her wrist. During the day, when she saw that the fluid in the bottle was running low, she would ring for a nurse, and after a while, a fresh bottle would be hung on the stand and hitched to the tube. But the second night, while she was sleeping, the i.v. bottle ran dry.

This, Ruth was told, was too serious a crisis to be remedied by a mere nurse; for if a fresh i.v. bottle were to be attached to the air-filled tube, the fluid might drive the air—in the form of a life-threatening embolism—through her veins to her heart. So a resident physician was wakened. He sleepily performed a series of manipulations, which Ruth found quite painful, designed to empty the equipment of air. Failing in that effort, he none too skillfully inserted a fresh needle into a fresh vein. He had trouble finding one, for most of Ruth's wrist veins had already been used in earlier medical and surgical procedures.

Ruth mentioned the incident without rancor when the doctors made their rounds next morning. (She never did get angry, as I so often did.) The doctors all smiled cheerily. "Accidents will happen, you know," one of them remarked. "You *are* a perfectionist, aren't you?" another added. Their manner left no doubt that to be welcome in a hospital a patient should refrain from complaining. Neither Ruth's inherent gentleness nor my ill-suppressed rage seemed to get through to anyone.

That night all went well. Two mornings later, however, I found Ruth weary, restless and more anxious than ever before. She had not slept very much, she told me, because the i.v. bottle had run dry *twice* during the night. Uncomplainingly, she had run two more risks of air embolism and had endured two more series of tube-needle manipulations.

Ruth was a remarkably stable person, able even in a crisis to see things in clear perspective, but that morning she came close to losing her inner calm. Her whole consciousness seemed narrowed down to a weary concern with the amount of fluid remaining in that accursed i.v. bottle. Her neck was stiff from craning her head to make sure it wasn't running dry a fourth time.

I took the obvious step and rolled the stand forward a foot or two so that she could watch the bottle without twisting her neck; but that, I learned, wasn't permitted. The attendants who neglected to notice when the bottle was running dry were alert enough to notice its change of position and rolled it back to "where it belonged."

Our oldest son and I accordingly solved the problem in another way. We assured Ruth that we would stay with her and keep an eye on the i.v. bottle until 10 p.m. and that we would return at 2 a.m. for another check on it. Ruth trusted us and fell asleep. The hospital doors were locked tight after 10 p.m.; but we found a way to enter through the emergency room, carrying a black briefcase and trying to look as much as possible like a doctor and an intern in a hurry. We bowed to the guard on duty at the emergency door, strode confidently past him to the physicians' all-night elevator and pressed the button for Ruth's floor. After that first night, we took turns. The guard became so accustomed to our 2 a.m. missions that he would tip his hat and sing out, "Good-evening, doctor," when he saw one of us coming. Thus Ruth got the rest she so desperately needed, and on one occasion, my son was able to save her from further vein damage by summoning a nurse to replace the almost-dry i.v. bottle before it was too late.

For more than twenty years preceding her illness, Ruth and I had worked together as writers, of medical articles for McCALL'S and other magazines. We had interviewed hundreds of specialists of many kinds, including internists, had grown to know many of them personally, to like them and to respect their expertise.

As authors of a book on medical and hospital care, we had also learned quite a bit about the way hospitals and medical centers are supposed to be organized (though the need for an internist during hospitalization had escaped us). In addition to these advantages, Ruth was not there alone; our three sons and I had ample time to be with her. If a family as sophisticated as ours in the ways of doctors and medical centers feels so helpless and forlorn, I found myself thinking on one of those 2 a.m. visits, how much worse it must be for a patient far from home and all alone, sick, in pain, surrounded only by strangers, knowing nothing about hospital routines and baffled as well as frightened by the bizarre never-never land in which she finds herself.

During Ruth's subsequent stay at a different hospital under the care of an internist, let me add, the solution to the problem of the i.v. bottle proved absurdly simple. Instead of one small bottle, two large ones were hung on the stand and hitched up in a special tandem harness. When the fluid in one bottle ran low, a valve opened and fluid from the other began to flow automatically. Insist on this simple precaution if you or anyone dear to you require intravenous feeding.

It was a psychiatrist I consulted when I found myself wanting to smash things who first convinced me that an internist might be worth trying. The one Ruth and I turned to was a young specialist I shall call Dr. Jones.

His first step, quite simply, was to get to know Ruth. He asked her about her children, her work, her beliefs, her relationship with me. He treated her like an adult rather than like a child in need of professional smiles and empty reassurances. Moreover, he gave her an opportunity to get to know him—his reasons for becoming a doctor and his reasons for selecting internal medicine rather than some other specialty.

Later, he reviewed her physical condition with her in detail, the nature of her illness, the various courses of treatment still available, the hazards ahead and the probable outcome. He let her talk. He listened. He answered questions. If he didn't know the answer, he said so—and looked it up or consulted another specialist. He was not afraid to call a cancer a cancer—a small point, but one which favorably impressed us both. Ruth had always expected simple common honesty from the people around her, and saw no reason to make an exception merely because she was sick and the liar was a doctor.

I felt the same way about Dr. Jones. Earlier, I had resolved not to let any doctor tell me anthing except with Ruth present; the burden of being told one thing while Ruth was being told another was too heavy on both of us. I recommend this policy to other husbands and wives—but with Dr. Jones, who told the truth to both of us, that precaution wasn't necessary. One incident that particularly buttressed our joint trust in him occurred one morning, when Ruth and I were living at home together between hospital stays.

Fluid was continuing to accumulate in her abdomen, so that it was necessary for her to go back to the hospital once a week or so for what is known as an abdominal tap. On these visits, Dr. Jones would introduce an exploratory needle gently through the anesthetized skin and muscle, trying to avoid puncturing an intestine or other organ. Then he would put in a larger needle and wait patiently at her side for half an hour or longer, while the clear fluid seeped slowly out. On one occasion, however, the exploratory needle did enter an intestine. Dr. Jones immediately withdrew it, gave Ruth an antibiotic injection to ward off infection and then explained frankly what had happened. Would Ruth mind staying in the hospital for the next few days, Dr. Jones asked, so he could keep a close eye on her?

Both Ruth and I felt our confidence in this man grow. He did not resort to subterfuge, or try to cover up the mishap, or lie about it or exude false confidence. We already knew he was truthful; now we knew he could be relied on even in an embarrassing emergency. Throughout Ruth's fifteen months in Dr. Jones' care, he never violated that trust.

Are all internists like Dr. Jones? After Ruth's death, I resolved to find out. McCALL'S sent me to Detroit, where I spent five days living, eating and studying with internists assembled from seventeen states for a postgraduate seminar on patient care at the Lafayette Clinic. Then I went on to San Francisco, where 8,000 internists were gathered for the annual conventions of their two national organizations, the American College of Physicians and the smaller American Society of Internal Medicine. In both cities I not only interviewed internists but sat in on their bull sessions, while they talked about their patients and their attitudes toward their specialty.

I quickly discovered that all internists are *not* like Ruth's Dr. Jones. Some are much more authoritarian; they should do well with patients who want to leave everything in the hands of an expert—and the less he tells them the better. Some were kindly and fatherly—excellent, no doubt, for the kind of patient who needs a father figure. And there were many other variations among them. A few impressed me as inadequate men whom I would hesitate to trust with the care of my car, much less my wife's health or mine; and a few sounded to me like bluffers, specialists in bedside manner rather than in the serious business of caring for sick patients. Some were less truthful than Dr. Jones; they honestly believed that truthfulness must sometimes be dispensed with for the benefit of the sick patient. But the great majority had two essential features in common; they were personally concerned with their patients, and they were prepared to take responsibility for a patient's entire care. I came back home without any illusions that all internists are supermen, but with a strong feeling that a family shopping for a personal physician would do well to look first among the internists in his home community.

A generation or two ago, patients were expected to rely on their general practitioner or family physician for comprehensive, continuing care. The G.P. delivered babies and saw them through their childhood illnesses. When they grew up, he set their broken bones, prescribed medicines, performed minor operations—and advised and counseled. He attended them on their deathbeds, too, easing their passing as best he could and comforting the survivors as a friend. If you needed a surgeon or a specialist of some other kind, the G.P. summoned one or sent you to him; but he remained in charge of your care, in hospital, office or home, year after year. You might even find your G.P. in the hospital operating room to hold your hand or assist the surgeon. Perhaps it wasn't always like that in reality; but that, at least, was the comforting theory. And G.P.s were everywhere, even in small villages; there were seven of them for every one specialist.

Now, times have changed. Today, there are two specialists for every G.P.—and the G.P. is generally too busy seeing 600 or more patients a month in his office to spend more than five or ten minutes with any one of them. The scene of most important medical, as well as surgical, procedures, moreover, has shifted from the doctor's office to the hospitals and medical centers, and the G.P. has been more and more ruthlessly fenced out of these private preserves of specialists.

Many hospitals do not grant G.P.s admitting privileges. Thus the patient who most needs a familiar figure at his side in a time of crisis may find himself, instead, in the hands of total strangers who have devoted themselves to the study of the liver or the pancreas or the bone marrow, but who, in far too many cases, have only a passing interest in patients as sick humans.

And there are so *many* specialists. "I can identify more than fifty different specialties and subspecialties in my own medical center," a University of Minnesota internist remarked at the San Francisco conventions.

That's why the internist is today the key figure for most patients, as Ruth and I learned the hard way.

"We internists drifted almost accidentally into the vacuum left by the decline of the G.P.," I was told by a middle-aged Los Angeles internist, who had lived through the changeover in his own practice. The great internists of the 1920s and 1930s, he went on to explain, were the professors of medicine at the good medical schools. When a doctor himself fell ill, or a member of a doctor's family, he naturally turned to one of these eminent internist-professors for the best possible care and counsel. Thus internists initially became the personal physicians of other doctors and their wives.

Soon millionaires, movie stars and industrialists discovered this way of securing continuous, comprehensive, high-quality care, in the hospital and outside, from a personal physician who was also a qualified specialist. Indeed, having an internist of one's own became a sort of status symbol in select social circles. A woman in mink might gossip about "my limousine" or "my country estate." Middle-ranking business executives and their wives soon caught the message and sought out internists for themselves. The loss of these uppercrust patients of course, contributed further to the decline of the G.P.

The new-style internist referred his patients to other doctors when appropriate, but it was he who was in charge of their care. He was the quarterback calling the signals, the captain of the team. Because he held unquestioned rank as a specialist in his own right, because his patients were wealthy and distinguished and because he controlled their referrals, he was—unlike the G.P.—listened to with respect by other specialists and by hospital personnel. His new central role, however, was never publicized. It was kept almost a secret—as if internists feared that outsiders might grow jealous of the privileged status of their patients. Millions of people today still have no clear notion of just what an internist does.

In recent years, fortunately, a further change has occurred; the internist's practice has become more and more democratized. The big prepayment health plans, like the Kaiser-Permanente Plan in California, Group Health Association in Washington, D.C., and the Health Insurance Plan of Greater New York, were among the first to realize that, in addition to specialists qualified to treat specific illnesses, a properly organized medical system needs doctors concerned with the patient as a whole—someone to provide continuing personal care and to route patients to the specialists and services they need. After World War II, the prepayment plans recruited internists by the hundreds for this role, and people in modest circumstances began benefiting from their care.

Medical students, of course, saw what was happening and flocked into training as internists. Today, despite the three additional years of grueling training required, internal medicine is both the largest and the fastest-growing specialty. And the ranks of the G.P. are continuing to thin out; in a recent survey, only three students among the hundreds graduating from Boston's five large medical schools announced their intention of becoming G.P.s.

Some internists, it is true, are primarily subspecialists concerned with heart disease or glandular disorders or some other narrow subspecialty, and some serve primarily as consultants for the patients of other doctors. But most of these men carry at least a few families on their rolls as personal patients. Another common arrangement is for each of the internists in a community to develop a special interest in a different subspecialty—hematology, toxicology, diseases of the chest, diabetes, arthritis, and so on. They then serve as consultants to their fellows in cases requiring this special knowledge, while continuing to devote most of their time to the general care of their personal patients.

Internists, let me add, are not the only physicians willing and able to play the role of personal physician. Many pediatricians play exactly the same role for the infants, children and teen-agers in their charge. Some individual G.P.s continue to provide high-quality care, keep up with the progress of scientific medicine, hold the respect of their specialist colleagues and have full hospital privileges—though many others are too busy removing splinters and prescribing tranquilizers or "psychic energizers" for a dozen patients an hour.

Some women who have found an obstetrician they trust continue to use him as personal physician long after the last baby is born; there is nothing wrong with that. Some surgeons, psychiatrists and other specialists play the same role for a few of their friends, relatives and neighbors. But more and more, without fanfare, the internist is becoming the personal physician for adults.

Some internists today engage in solo practice, like the traditional G.P. (Ruth's Dr. Jones is one of them.) Many have formed groups of their own. Many more are associated in groups with specialists of other kinds; in such groups, the internists generally serve as personal physician for adults in the family, while the pediatricians provide continuing, comprehensive care for the children.

Entering the charmed circle of patients who can boast a personal internist is fairly easy these days. If you enroll in a well-organized medical group or prepayment plan, you usually get one as your physician automatically and can shift to another if you choose to. If you remain outside such groups, your best approach is to phone an internist's office some day when you are feeling healthy and ask for an appointment for a general checkup. For a list of qualified internists in your community, consult your county medical society or, even better, call the hospital you would prefer to go to in the event of illness and ask for the names of internists who can admit and treat patients there.

When the time for your appointment comes, you will be struck first of all by the tempo of the internist's practice. Most internists, even today, schedule a full hour for the initial appointment. During that hour they take a complete medical and family history, examine you from head to toe and make or arrange to have made a series of diagnostic tests. Of equal importance, they get to know what sort of person you are. That introductory hour may be the most important in your life; for if life-threatening illness later strikes, you will have—from the very beginning—a man who knows you personally to fight your battles for you.

dead
on arrival

DAVID SUDNOW

In County Hospital's emergency ward, the most frequent variety of death is what is known as the "DOA" type. Approximately 40 such cases are processed through this division of the hospital each month. The designation "DOA" is somewhat ambiguous insofar as many persons are not physiologically *dead on arrival*, but are nonetheless classified as having been such. A person who dies within several hours after having been brought to the hospital might, if upon arrival he was initially announced by the ambulance driver to be dead, retain such a classification at the time he is so pronounced by the physician.

When an ambulance driver suspects that the person he is carrying is dead, he signals the emergency ward with a special siren alarm as he approaches the entrance driveway. As he wheels his stretcher past the clerk's desk, he restates his suspicion with the remark, "possible," a shorthand reference for "possible DOA." (The use of the term *possible* is required by law, which insists, primarily for insurance purposes, that any diagnosis unless made by a certified physician be so qualified.) The clerk records the arrival in a log book and pages a physician, informing him in code of the arrival. Often a page is not needed, as physicians on duty hear the siren alarm, expect the arrival, and wait at the entranceway. The patient is rapidly wheeled to the far end of the ward corridor and into the nearest available foyer or room, supposedly out of sight of other patients and possible onlookers

Reprinted by permission of the publisher from David Sudnow, Passing On: The Social Organization of Dying *(Englewood Cliffs, N.J.: Prentice-Hall, Inc., © 1967).*

from the waiting room. The physician arrives, makes his examination, and pronounces the patient dead or not. If the patient is dead, a nurse phones the coroner's office, which is legally responsible for the removal and investigation of all DOA cases.

Neither the hospital nor the physician has medical responsibility in such cases. In many instances of clear death, ambulance drivers use the hospital as a depository because it has the advantages of being both closer and less bureaucratically complicated a place than the downtown coroner's office for disposing of a body. Here, the hospital stands as a temporary holding station, rendering the community service of legitimate and free pronouncements of death for any comers. In circumstances of near-death, it functions more traditionally as a medical institution, mobilizing lifesaving procedures for those for whom they are still of potential value, at least as judged by the emergency room's staff of residents and interns. The boundaries between near-death and sure death are not, however, as we shall shortly see, altogether clearly defined.

In nearly all DOA cases the pronouncing physician (commonly that physician who is the first to answer the clerk's page or spot the incoming ambulance) shows in his general demeanor and approach to the task little more than passing interest in the event's possible occurrence and the patient's biographical and medical circumstances. He responds to the clerk's call, conducts his examination, and leaves the room once he has made the necessary official gesture to an attending nurse. (The term "kaput," murmured in differing degrees of audibility depending upon the hour and his state of awakeness, is a frequently employed announcement.) It happened on numerous occasions, especially during the midnight-to-eight shift, that a

physician was interrupted during a coffee break to pronounce a DOA and returned to his colleagues in the canteen with, as an account of his absence, some version of "Oh, it was nothing but a DOA."

It is interesting to note that, while the special siren alarm is intended to mobilize quick response on the part of the emergency room staff, it occasionally operates in the opposite fashion. Some emergency room staff came to regard the fact of a DOA as decided in advance; they exhibited a degree of nonchalance in answering the siren or page, taking it that the "possible DOA" most likely is "D." In so doing they in effect gave authorization to the ambulance driver to make such assessments. Given that time lapse which sometimes occurs between that point at which the doctor knows of the arrival and the time he gets to the patient's side, it is not inconceivable that in several instances patients who might have been revived died during this interim. This is particularly likely in that, apparently, a matter of moments may differentiate the revivable state from the irreversible one.

WHO ARE THE 'DEAD'?

Two persons in similar physical condition may be differentially designated dead or not. For example, a young child was brought into the emergency room with no registering heartbeat, respirations, or pulse—the standard "signs of death"—and was, through a rather dramatic stimulation procedure involving the coordinated work of a large team of doctors and nurses, revived for a period of eleven hours. On the same evening, shortly after the child's arrival, an elderly person who presented the same physical signs, with—as one physician later stated in conversation—no discernible differences from the child in skin color, warmth, etc., arrived in the emergency room and was almost immediately pronounced dead, with no attempts at stimulation instituted. A nurse remarked, later in the evening: "They (the doctors) would never have done that to the old lady (attempt heart stimulation) even though I've seen it work on them too." During the period when emergency resuscitation equipment was being readied for the child, an intern instituted mouth-to-mouth resuscitation. This same intern was shortly relieved by oxygen machinery, and when the woman arrived, he was the one who pronounced her dead. He reported shortly afterwards that he could never bring himself to put his mouth to "an old lady's like that."

It is therefore important to note that the category DOA is not totally homogeneous with respect to actual physiological condition. The same is generally true of all deaths, the determination of *death* involving, as it does, a critical decision, at least in its earlier stages.

There is currently a movement in progress in some medical and lay circles to undercut the traditional distinction between "biological" and "clinical" death, and procedures are being developed and their use encouraged for treating any "clinically dead" person as potentially revivable. Should such a movement gain widespread momentum (and it, unlike late 19th-century arguments for life after death, is legitimated by modern medical thinking and technology), it would foreseeably have considerable consequence for certain aspects of hospital social structure, requiring perhaps that much more continuous and intensive care be given "dying" and "dead" patients than is presently accorded them, at least at County. (At Cohen

Hospital; where the care of the "tentatively dead" is always very intensive, such developments would more likely be encouraged than at County.)

Currently at County there seems to be a rather strong relationship between the age, social background, and the perceived moral character of patients and the amount of effort that is made to attempt revival when "clinical death signs" are detected (and, for that matter, the amount of effort given to forestalling their appearance in the first place). As one compares practices in this regard at different hospitals, the general relationship seems to hold; although at the private, wealthier institutions like Cohen the overall amount of attention given to "initially dead" patients is greater. At County efforts at revival are admittedly superficial, with the exception of the very young or occasionally wealthier patient who by some accident ends up at County's emergency room. No instances have been witnessed at County where, for example, external heart massage was given a patient whose heart was stethoscopically inaudible, if that patient was over 40 years of age. At Cohen Hospital, on the other hand, heart massage is a normal routine at that point, and more drastic measures, such as the injection of Adrenalin directly into the heart, are not uncommon. While these practices are undertaken for many patients at Cohen if "tentative death" is discovered early (and it typically is because of the attention "dying" patients are given), at County they are reserved for a very special class of cases.

Generally speaking, the older the patient the more likely is his tentative death taken to constitute pronounceable death. Suppose a 20-year-old arrives in the emergency room and is presumed to be dead because of the ambulance driver's assessment. Before that patient will be pronounced dead by a physician, extended listening to his heartbeat will occur, occasionally efforts at stimulation will be made, oxygen administered, and often stimulative medication given. Less time will elapse between initial detection of an inaudible heartbeat and nonpalpitating pulse and the pronouncement of death if the person is 40 years old, and still less if he is 70. As best as can be detected, there appeared to be no obvious difference between men and women in this regard, nor between white and Negro patients. Very old patients who are initially considered to be dead solely on the basis of the ambulance driver's assessment of that possibility were seen to be put in an empty room to wait several moments before a physician arrived. The driver's announcement of a "possible" places a frame of interpretation around the event, so that the physician expects to find a dead person and attends the person under the general auspices of that expectation. When a young person is brought in as a "possible" the driver tries to convey some more alarming sense to his arrival by turning the siren up very loud and keeping it going after he has already stopped, so that by the time he has actually entered the wing, personnel, expecting "something special," act quickly and accordingly. When it is a younger person that the driver is delivering, his general manner is more frantic. The speed with which he wheels his stretcher in and the degree of excitement in his voice as he describes his charge to the desk clerk are generally more heightened than with the typical elderly DOA. One can observe a direct relationship between the loudness and length of the siren alarm and the considered "social value" of the person being transported.

The older the person, the less thorough is the examination he is given;

frequently, elderly people are pronounced dead on the basis of only a stethoscopic examination of the heart. The younger the person, the more likely will an examination preceding an announcement of death entail an inspection of the eyes, attempt to find a pulse, touching of the body for coldness, etc. When a younger person is brought to the hospital and announced by the driver as a "possible" but is nonetheless observed to be breathing slightly, or have an audible heart beat, there is a fast mobilization of effort to stimulate increased breathing and a more rapid heartbeat. If an older person is brought in in a similar condition there will be a rapid mobilization of similar efforts; however, the time which will elapse between that point at which breathing noticeably ceases and the heart audibly stops beating and when the pronouncement of death is made will differ according to his age.

EMERGENCY CARE AND SOCIAL WORTH

One's location in the age structure of the society is not the only factor that will influence the degree of care he gets when his death is considered possibly to have occurred. At County Hospital a notable additional set of considerations relating to the patient's presumed "moral character" is made to apply.

The smell of alcohol on the breath of a "possible" is nearly always noticed by the examining physician, who announces to his fellow workers that the person is a drunk. This seems to constitute a feature he regards as warranting less than strenuous effort to attempt revival. The alcohol patient is treated by hospital physicians, not only when the status of his body as alive or dead is at stake, but throughout the whole course of medical treatment, as one for whom the concern to treat can properly operate somewhat weakly. There is a high proportion of alcoholic patients at County, and their treatment very often involves an earlier admission of "terminality" and a consequently more marked suspension of curative treatment than is observed in the treatment of nonalcoholic patients. In one case, the decision whether or not to administer additional blood needed by an alcoholic man bleeding badly from a stomach ulcer was decided negatively, and that decision was announced as based on the fact of his alcoholism. The intern in charge of treating the patient was asked by a nurse, "Should we order more blood for this afternoon?" and the doctor answered, "I can't see any sense in pumping it into him because even if we can stop the bleeding, he'll turn around and start drinking again and next week he'll be back needing more blood." In the DOA circumstance, alcoholic patients have been known to be pronounced dead on the basis of a stehoscopic examination of the heart alone, even though such persons were of such an age that were they not alcoholics they would likely have received much more intensive consideration before being so decided upon. Among other categories of persons whose deaths will be more quickly adjudged, and whose "dying" more readily noticed and used as a rationale for apathetic care, are the suicide victim, the dope addict, the known prostitute, the assailant in a crime of violence, the vagrant, the known wife-beater, and, generally, those persons whose moral characters are considered reproachable.

Within a limited temporal perspective at least, but one which is not necessarily to be regarded as trivial, the likelihood of "dying" and even of being "dead" can be said to be partially a function of one's place in the social structure, and not simply in the sense that the wealthier get better care, or at least not in the usual

sense of that fact. If one anticipates having a critical heart attack, he had best keep himself well-dressed and his breath clean if there is a likelihood he will be brought into County as a "possible."

The DOA deaths of famous persons are reportedly attended with considerably prolonged and intensive resuscitation efforts. In President Kennedy's death, for example, *The New York Times* (Nov. 23, 1963) quoted an attending physician as saying:

Medically, it was apparent the President was not alive when he was brought in. There was no spontaneous respiration. He had dilated, fixed pupils. It was obviously a lethal head wound. Technically, however, by using vigorous resuscitation, intravenous tubes and all the usual supportive measures, we were able to raise the semblance of a heart beat.

THE USES OF A CORPSE

There are a series of practical consequences of pronouncing a patient dead in the hospital setting. His body may properly be stripped of clothing, jewelry, and the like, wrapped up for discharge, the family notified of the death, and the coroner informed in the case of DOA deaths. In the emergency unit there is a special set of procedures which can be said to be partially definitive of death. DOA cases are very interestingly "used" in many American hospitals. The inflow of dead bodies, or what can properly be taken to be dead bodies, is regarded as a collection of "guinea pigs," in the sense that procedures can be performed upon those bodies for the sake of teaching and research.

In any "teaching hospital" (in the case of County, I use that term in a weak sense, that is, a hospital which employs interns and residents; in other settings a "teaching hospital" may mean systematic, institutionalized instruction) the environment of medical events is regarded not merely as a collection of treatable cases, but as a collection of experience-relevant information. It is a continually enforced way of looking at the cases one treats to regard them under the auspices of a concern for experience with "such cases." That concern can legitimately warrant the institution of a variety of procedures, tests, and inquiries which lie outside and may even on occasion conflict with the strict interests of treatment; they fall within the interests of "learning medicine," gaining experience with such cases, and acquiring technical skills.

A principle for organizing medical care activities in the teaching hospital generally—and perhaps more so in the county hospital, where patients' social value is often not highly regarded—is the relevance of any particular activity to the acquisition of skills of general import. Physicians feel that among the greatest values of such institutions is the ease with which medical attention can be selectively organized to maximize the general benefits to knowledge and technical proficiency which working with a given case expectably affords. The notion of the "interesting case" is, at County, not simply a casual notion but an enforced principle for the allocation of attention. The private physician is in a more committed relation to each and every one of his patients; and while he may regard this or that case as more or less interesting, he ideally cannot legitimate his varying interest in his patients' conditions as a basis for devoting varying amounts of attention to them. (His reward for treating the uninteresting case is, of course, the fee, and physicians are known to give more attention to those of their pa-

tients who shall be paying more.)

At County Hospital a case's degree of interest is a crucial fact, and one which is invoked to legitimate the way a physician does and should allocate his attention. In surgery, for instance, I found many examples. If on a given morning in one operating room a "rare" procedure was scheduled and in another a "usual" procedure planned, there would be no special difficulty in getting personnel to witness and partake in the rare procedure, whereas work in the usual case was considered as merely work, regardless of such considerations as the relative fatality rate of each procedure or the patient's physical condition. It is not uncommon to find interns at County who are scrubbed for an appendectomy taking turns going next door to watch a skin graft or chest surgery. At Cohen such house staff interchanging was not permitted. Interns and residents were assigned to a particular surgical suite and required to stay throughout the course of a procedure. On the medical wards, on the basis of general observation, it seems that one could obtain a high order correlation between the amount of time doctors spent discussing and examining patients and the degree of unusualness of their medical problems.

I introduce this general feature to point to the predominant orientation at County to such matters as "getting practice" and the general organizational principle that provides for the propriety of using cases as the basis for this practice. Not only are live patients objects of practice, so are dead ones.

There is a rule in the emergency unit that with every DOA a doctor should attempt to insert an "endo-tracheal" tube down the throat, but only after the patient is pronounced dead. The reason for this rule (on which new interns are instructed as part of their training in emergency medicine) is that the tube is extremely difficult to insert, requires great yet careful force, and, insofar as it may entail great pain, the procedure cannot be "practiced" on live patients. The body must be positioned with the neck at such an angle that the large tube will go down the proper channel. In some circumstances when it is necessary to establish a rapid "airway" (an open breathing canal), the endo-tracheal tube can apparently be an effective substitute for the tracheotomy incision. The DOA's body in its transit from the scene of the death to the morgue constitutes an ideal captive experimental opportunity. The procedure is not done on all deceased patients, the reason apparently being that it is part of the training one receives in the emergency unit and is to be learned there. Nor is it done on all DOA cases, for some doctors, it seems, are uncomfortable in handling a dead body whose charge as a live one they never had, and handling it in the way such a procedure requires. It is important to note that when it is done, it is done most frequently and most intensively with those persons who are regarded as lowly situated in the moral social structure.

No instances were observed where a young child was used as an object for such a practice nor where a well-dressed, middle-aged, middle-class adult was similarly used. On one occasion a woman supposed to have ingested a fatal amount of laundry bleach was brought to the emergency unit, and after she died, several physicians took turns trying to insert an endo-tracheal tube, after which one of them suggested that the stomach be pumped to examine its contents to try to see what effects the bleach had on the gastric secretions. A lavage was set up and the stomach contents removed. A chief resident left the room and gathered a group of interns with the explanation that they ought to look at this woman because of the apparent results of such

ingestion. In effect, the doctors conducted their own autopsy investigation without making any incisions.

THE INTEREST DOCTORS TAKE

On several similar occasions physicians explained that with these kinds of cases they didn't really feel as if they were prying in handling the body, but that they often did in the case of an ordinary death—a "natural death" of a morally proper person. Suicide victims are frequently the objects of curiosity, and while there is a high degree of distaste in working with such patients and their bodies (particularly among the nursing staff; some nurses will not touch a suicide victim's dead body), "practice" by doctors is apparently not as distasteful. A woman was brought into the emergency unit with a self-inflicted gunshot wound which ran from her sternum downward and backward, passing out through a kidney. She had apparently bent over a rifle and pulled the trigger. Upon her "arrival" in the emergency unit she was quite alive and talkative, and though in great pain and very fearful, was able to conduct something of a conversation. She was told that she would need immediate surgery and was taken off to the operating room; following her were a group of physicians, all of whom were interested in seeing the damage done in the path of the bullet. (One doctor said aloud, quite near her stretcher, "I can't get my heart into saving her, so we might as well have some fun out of it.") During the operation the doctors regarded her body much as they do one during an autopsy. After the critical damage was repaired and they had reason to feel the woman would survive, they engaged in numerous surgical side ventures, exploring muscular tissue in areas of the back through which the bullet had passed but where no damage had been done that required repair other than the tying off of bleeders and suturing. One of the operating surgeons performed a side operation, incising an area of skin surrounding the entry wound on the chest, to examine, he announced to colleagues, the structure of the tissue through which the bullet passed. He explicitly announced his project to be motivated by curiosity; one of the physicians spoke of the procedure as an "autopsy on a live patient," about which there was a little laughter.

In another case, a man was wounded in the forehead by a bullet, and after the damage was repaired in the wound, which resembled a usual frontal lobotomy, an exploration was made of an area adjacent to the path of the bullet, on the forehead proper, below the hair line. During this exploration the operating surgeon asked a nurse to ask Dr. X to come in, and when Dr. X arrived, the two of them, under the gaze of a large group of interns and nurses, made a further incision, which an intern described to me as unnecessary in the treatment of the man, and which left a noticeable scar down the side of the temple. The purpose of this venture was to explore the structure of that part of the face. This area of the skull, that below the hair line, cannot be examined during an autopsy because of a contract between local morticians and the Department of Pathology to leave those areas of the body which will be viewed free of surgical incisions. The doctors justified the additional incision by pointing to the "fact" that since he would have a "nice scar as it was, a little bit more wouldn't be so serious."

During autopsies themselves, bodies are routinely used to gain experience in surgical techniques, and many incisions, explorations, and the like are conducted that are not essential to the key task of uncovering the "cause" of the death. Frequently specialists-in-training come to autopsies though they have no interest in the patient's death; they await the completion of the legal part of the procedure, at which point the body is turned over to them for practice. Mock surgical procedures are staged on the body, often with co-workers simulating actual conditions, tying off blood vessels which obviously need not be tied, and suturing internally.

When a patient died in the emergency unit, whether or not he had been brought in under the designation DOA, there occasionally occurred various mock surgical procedures on his body. In one case a woman was treated for a chicken bone lodged in her throat. Rapidly after her arrival via ambulance a tracheotomy incision was made in the attempt to establish an unobstructed source of air, but the procedure was not successful and she died as the incision was being made. Several interns were called upon to practice their stitching by closing the wound as they would on a live patient. There was a low peak in the activity of the ward, and a chief surgical resident used the occasion to supervise teaching them various techniques for closing such an incision. In another case the body of a man who died after being crushed by an automobile was employed for instruction and practice in the use of various fracture setting techniques. In still another instance several interns and residents attempted to suture a dead man's dangling finger in place on his mangled hand.

THE ROUTINE OF DYING

What has been developed here is a "procedural definition of death," a definition based upon the activities which that phenomenon can be said to *consist of.* While in some respects this was a study of "dying" and "death," might be better summarized as a study of the activities of managing dying and death as meaningful events for hospital staff members. My attention has been exclusively given to the description of staff behavior occurring in the course of doing those things which daily ward routines were felt to require.

It was in the course of these routines—handling bodies, taking demographic information on incoming and outgoing patients, doing diagnosis, prognosis, medical experimentation, and teaching—that certain patients came to be recognized as persons legitimately accorded special treatments—the "dying" and "death" treatments. In the hospital world these treatments—organized to fit institutionalized daily ward routines built up to afford mass treatments on an efficiency basis, to obtain "experience," avoid dirty work, and maximize the possibilities that the intern will manage to get some sleep—give "dying" and "death" their concrete senses for hospital personnel. Whatever else a "dying" or "dead" patient might mean in other contexts, in the hospital I investigated, the sense of such states of affairs was given by the work requirements associated with the patients so described. For a "dying" patient to be on the ward meant that soon there would be a body to be cleansed, wrapped, pronounced dead, and discharged, and a family to be told. These activities and the work requirements they entailed provided the situational frame of interpretation around such states.

At least one question that has not been directly addressed is that which would ask why hospital personnel feel treatments must be organized on a mass basis. Its answer, I believe, is to be found in a historical analysis of the development of the medical ideology toward the nonpaying patient and in the peculiarly impersonal environment of the charity institution I examined. I decided at the outset of my investigation to leave unexplained general matters of ideology about patient care and to proceed from there to learn something about the ways in which existing practices were organized and what these practices entailed as regarded the occurrence of "dying" and "death."

While hospital personnel managed, on the whole, to sustain a detached regard for the event of death, it occurred, on occasion, that routinely employed procedures and attitudes became altered and upset. The successful daily management of "dying" and "dead" bodies seemed to require that patients have a relatively constant character as social types. So long as the patient whose death was anticipated or had occurred was an elderly, poor, and morally proper person, the occasion of his "dying" and "death" was treated with little notice and in accord with ordinarily enforced routines of "death care." On critical occasions, however—when, for example, a child died or a successful, middle-class person was brought into the emergency unit as a DOA—ordinarily employed procedures of treatment were not instituted, and special measures were felt to be necessary. Nowhere was this disruption clearer than with the deaths of children. Nurses have been known to break down in tears when a child died, and in such cases, particularly, "dying" and "death" temporarily cease to have their firmly grounded, organizationally routinized meanings, activities, and consequences. When an intoxicated or suicidal or "criminal" patient was treated, these persons' moral characters intruded as prevalent considerations in the way in which they were regarded, providing a special frame of interpretation around the way care was organized over and above

These theories are invoked on a daily basis to support the patterns of care that which the category "patient" established. In key instances, patients' external attributes operated to alter the institutional routine in significant ways, causing vehemence, disgust, horror, or empathetic dismay, and—particularly in the case of children's deaths—a radical though short-lived movement entirely out of role on the part of staff members. No matter how routinized an institution's methods for handling its daily tasks, those routines remain vulnerable at certain key points. No matter how nonchalantly staff members managed to wrap patients' bodies for discharge to the morgue, taper off in the administration of drugs and care to the "dying," pronounce deaths, and return to other tasks, special circumstances caused these routines to be upset—either made more difficult to carry off, more interestedly attended, or substantially revised.

NONTYPICAL EMOTIONS

In regarding these special cases—those persons deemed particulary obnoxious or particularly worthy—perhaps insight may be gained into the requirements for usual, orderly ward activities. On those occasions when a nontypical death caused staff members to step outside their regularly maintained attitudes of indifference and efficiency, one could glimpse a capacity for emotional involvement which ordinary work activities did not provide proper occasions for displaying. The maintenance of appropriate impersonality in the hospital requires an enforced standardization to the types of events and persons which personnel confront. This work of *affect* management is aided by staff-held theories of proper fate, proper deaths, proper persons, and notions regarding the appropriate role of medicine and surgery in prolonging life and delaying death.

given the dying, the tentatively dead, and the decidedly dead, but they can be employed only as long as the patient in question can be construed to fit the categories for which the theories are relevant. I made every effort to construct classifications of patients so as to provide for the propriety of treating them in organizationally routine ways, but occasionally there was a case which resisted that classification. The death of a child, a young adult, or the deaths of those persons who were regarded as morally imperfect stirred a noticeably atypical degree of moral sentiment.

This class of atypical deaths, those occurring for atypical persons or in atypical ways, became set off as the specially noteworthy events of hospital life, the cases which staff members recounted for long periods of time and built into stories that were frequently retold when death was made a specific topic of conversation. In selecting certain cases to invest with special meaning, staff members demonstrated that despite their work involvements in matters of life and death and their routinely casual attitude toward such events, death nonetheless was an event which could call forth grief and empathy.

"Dying" and "death" are categories that have very broad currency, being variously used in many settings throughout the society. I have examined only one setting, only one locus of meanings and associated activities. The use of the categories in the hospital is to be regarded as hospital specific, although in other domains their usages may share features in common with those found in the hospital. While clinical death occurs, in American society at least, chiefly within the hospital setting, that setting provides only one of a variety of socially organized worlds within which its meaningful character is provided. What "dying" and "death" procedurally entail among staff physicians within the hospital would seem to share little in common with those activities anticipatorily organized by and consequential for the patient himself and members of his family—those for whom doing autopsies, handling the census of a hospital ward, cleaning up dead bodies, and the rest are not relevant considerations. My restricted interest in death in the hospital requires that the formulation of the notions "dying" and "death" given here be clearly confined in generality to this highly instrumental domain of technical activity.

a sacred trust

RICHARD HARRIS

Although a politician who has won an election invariably announces that he has been given a mandate to carry out all the campaign promises he made, it is usually impossible to determine whether the voters' support means that they share all, many, or even some of his views. Maybe they simply couldn't stand the other fellow. During the campaign of 1964, President Johnson repeatedly promised that if he was elected he would see to it that Congress enacted a program of national health insurance for men and women sixty-five or over—a program usually known as Medicare—which during the previous session had been passed in the Senate but not in the House. The supporters of the bill naturally interpreted Mr. Johnson's overwhelming victory at the polls as a complete triumph

for their own cause. "Clearest Mandate for Medicare in Lyndon B. Johnson's Landslide," ran a headline in the *Senior Citizens News,* the monthly newsletter of the National Council of Senior Citizens, whose members—two and a half million of them—had been avidly lobbying for passage of the measure throughout the Kennedy-Johnson administration. And, just as naturally, the opponents of the bill—primarily the American Medical Association—dismissed claims of this sort out of hand. According to Dr. Donovan B. Ward, president of the A.M.A., such statements constituted "an arrogant affront to the dignity and integrity of those who have just been elected." Those who had just been elected to Congress were far less impressed by all the claims and counterclaims about mandates than they were by the fact that most of the sixty-nine freshmen Democrats who had just been elected to the House of Representatives—long a burial ground for all health-insurance legislation—owed, or believed they owed, their victories to the Johnson landslide. Beyond that, a fair number of incumbents who occupied shaky seats were indebted to Mr. Johnson for help during the campaign. Accordingly, as far as most of the Democrats in the House were concerned, if the President said he had a mandate for Medicare, he had a mandate for Medicare.

When President Johnson delivered his State of the Union Address on January 4, 1965, the first day of the Eighty-ninth Congress, and called for action on a Medicare bill as the first order of business, no one in the government doubted that he would get it. In a ceremonious response to his appeal, the Democratic leaders in Congress immediately arranged to let Senator Clinton P. Anderson, of New Mexico, and Representative Cecil R. King, of

California, introduce identical bills, numbered S. 1 and H.R. 1, in the Senate and in the House. In its provisions for hospital and nursing-home care, the measure was much the same as one that Anderson and King had submitted to the previous Congress, but there was one significant change in its financing. Representative Wilbur Mills, of Arkansas, the chairman of the House Committee on Ways and Means, and one of the two or three most powerful men in Congress, had formerly opposed government health insurance; after the election he had come around to accepting the fact that some sort of Medicare bill was inevitable, but he insisted upon protecting the actuarial soundness of the Social Security program, through which funds for Medicare were to be raised, by keeping those funds entirely separate from the program's pension funds, and the administration had acceded to his demand. On the second day of Congress, the membership of the Ways and Means Committee, reflecting the Democrats' new majority in the House, of better than two to one, was changed from fifteen Democrats and ten Republicans to seventeen Democrats and eight Republicans. This gave the bill's supporters a margin of at least three votes on the committee, where all tax legislation must originate in the House, thus assuring that the measure would not be blocked there, as it had been in the past. Moreover, there was a general feeling that the increase in Democratic support for Medicare had been attended by a lessening of Republican opposition. Polls showed that two-thirds of the nation's voters favored the bill, and it was believed that many Republicans were far more sensitive to public opinion on this topic than they had been a few months before. At the beginning of the session, Representative Frank T. Bow, a conservative Republican from Ohio, sent all members of his party in the House a letter in which he said, in part, "Social Security and medical care were primary issues in 1964, and the Republican response on these issues was a major factor in the disaster that befell us." Representative Charles Halleck, of Indiana, who had played a large role in that disaster, was replaced as Minority Leader in the House by Representative Gerald Ford, of Michigan, who promised a program of positive opposition to the Democrats. Rumor had it that one move in this direction would be a Republican alternative to Medicare.

On January 7th, the President sent a special Health Message to Congress, in which he again called for passage of the King-Anderson bill. Afterward, Mills told reporters that he hoped to get it through his committee and onto the floor of the House by March. Although Mills had previously stated in public that he was no longer opposed to Medicare, the A.M.A.'s leaders were stunned by this remark. "They were furious at Mills for what they considered the ultimate in perfidy," Michael J. O'Neill, a Washington correspondent for the New York *Daily News* who had covered A.M.A. activities for many years, reported at the time. "And Mills was furious at them for their blind refusal to accept reality. They couldn't understand that on a great controversial issue like this one Mills wasn't a conservative or a liberal or a moderate. He was a politician. And he has always been a consummately adroit one. If he couldn't stop the bill, he was naturally going to turn it to his own purposes, even if it meant that he ended up sponsoring it."

A couple of days after Mills predicted prompt action on Medicare about two hundred representatives of state medical societies met in Chicago, in accordance with arrangements that the A.M.A. had made the previous November. At the Chicago meeting, the Association's trustees reaffirmed their determination to fight on, and said they hoped to get Mills to reverse himself, or, failing that, to get the pro-Medicare people who had been elected to the House to reverse themselves. Several of those present pointed out that Mills, having finally put himself on record, could not possibly retreat, even if he wanted to. Moreover, they noted, if the new pro-Medicare margin in the House was cut by half—which was more than anyone could reasonably hope—it would still be large enough to put the bill through. "To concede defeat is to invite it," one of the trustees told the rebels sternly. Then, in a surprise move, the trustees informed the gathering that they had devised a new program, which, they stated, "would provide far more to our elderly citizens than is proposed in the administration's Medicare tax program." As the plan was outlined in broad terms by Dr. Ward, it would provide federal and state grants to subsidize private health-insurance policies for old people who wanted them. This would be done through the procedures already established by the Kerr-Mills law, which made federal money available to match state funds for providing medical care for old people who were not on welfare but were too poor to pay their own medical bills. The A.M.A. called its plan the Doctors' Eldercare Program, and Dr. Ward announced that in order to secure support for Eldercare among doctors—whose enthusiasm for the expenditure of their own money was beginning to wane noticeably—and to arrange for still another publicity drive to arouse the lay public, the House of Delegates, which theoretically sets policy for the Association, would meet early in February for a two-day special session.

On January 27th, the day the Ways and Means Committee convened to hold executive-session hearings on the King-Anderson bill, two of its opponents on the committee—A. Sydney Herlong, Democrat of Florida, and Thomas B. Curtis, Republican of Missouri—introduced Eldercare in the House, an event that Dr. Ward called a "breakthrough of historic importance." Apart from its sponsors, no one in Congress took the breakthrough very seriously. "Everyone in the House knows that it's nonsense," Representative Al Ullman, Democrat of Oregon, who was a leading Medicare supporter on the committee, said at the time. "By itself, it would provide little that cannot be done under existing law—that is, if the states agree to do it." He went on to suggest that since few states had been able to participate in the Kerr-Mills program to any appreciable extent, even fewer would be able to participate in the A.M.A.'s far more expensive plan through the same procedures. If all the states did participate, it was estimated, the program would cost them and the federal government a total of something like four billion dollars annually. Another Democrat, Representative Frank Thompson, of New Jersey, expressed his opinion of Eldercare by informally suggesting an alternative to it, which he called Doctorcare. It was to be financed by a two per cent federal tax on applesauce, and the funds were to be used to provide special therapy for any physician who felt himself suffering from an urge to make house calls; if he didn't respond satisfactorily to the arguments of his colleagues over the phone, he was to be rushed to the nearest Cadillac showroom.

The day after Eldercare was dropped into the legislative hopper, Representative John W. Byrnes, of Wisconsin, announced that he had prepared a new bill that would pay just about every kind of medical expense incurred by the elderly. As the ranking Republican on the Ways and Means Committee, Byrnes was understood to be acting on behalf of his party's leadership in the House. His bill, which had actually been prepared by a leading insurance company, provided, like Eldercare, for subsidies to pay for private health-insurance policies. Unlike Eldercare, the disposition of the subsidies was to be in the hands of the federal government rather than of state governments—an arrangement that had always been unacceptable to the A.M.A. Two-thirds of the cost—about three and a half billion dollars a year—was to come out of the general revenues of the Treasury, and one-third out of deductions from the monthly Social Security checks received by those who voluntarily signed up. The A.M.A. pleaded with Byrnes not to submit his bill, arguing that it would drain away support for Eldercare. Since there was no support for Eldercare to speak of anyway, Byrnes went ahead and submitted his bill. The move was generally dismissed as a political grandstand play, and Byrnes himself privately conceded that the bill had no chance.

The A.M.A.'s House of Delegates met on February 6th, in a Chicago hotel called the Pick-Congress. Dr. Milford O. Rouse, the speaker of the house, opened the session by calling for "sober, optimistic, practical, dedicated enthusiasm and action." He refused afterward to tell reporters how much the action was going to cost. "We are not a wealthy organization," he said. "We have a modest reserve for a day just like this." The reserve was $14,735,000. The trustees denied reports that they were ready to spend four million dollars on the campaign, but it was then revealed that the A.M.A. had already distributed that sum to the state societies, which were expected to match it. One figure that was not in dispute was five hundred and fifty thousand dollars, which had been set aside, Dr. Ward announced, for newspaper, magazine, radio, and TV

advertising. Shortly after the meeting, the Illinois Medical Society levied a special assessment on its members that raised a quarter of a million dollars, and a little later the Maryland Medical Society, also through a special assessment, raised a hundred and forty thousand dollars. When a member of the House Ways and Means Committee was told about these efforts, he smiled and said, "If we can rush Medicare through, we should be able to save the doctors several million dollars."

The A.M.A.'s strategy at that time was inspired by two recent events. The first was the publication early in January of a Gallup poll showing that although two-thirds of the people supported Medicare, forty per cent of them thought it covered all medical expenses. During the previous year, the A.M.A. had, more or less in passing, attacked Medicare on the ground that its coverage was inadequate, and now the Association began concentrating on this point, charging that the bill would take care of, variously, only twenty, twenty-three, or twenty-five per cent of the participants' medical expenses. The second event was Goldwater's unintentional success in scaring the wits out of older voters by his attacks on the Social Security system. An A.M.A. advertisement, fairly typical of thousands that soon appeared around the country, showed a pair of hands tearing a Social Security card in two, and warned "DON'T LET THIS HAPPEN TO YOU!" Below were the heading "Federal Medicare," followed by a description of its limited benefits, and, next to it, the heading "Doctors' Eldercare," followed by a description of its "unlimited" benefits, including coverage of all charges for hospitals, physicians, nursing homes, and drugs. The last line of the advertisement read, "A federal Medicare program could jeopardize your future through bankrupting the Social Security system." This particular advertisement appeared widely in the home district of one of the co-sponsors of the Eldercare bill, Representative Herlong. Prompted by the National Council of Senior Citizens, some of the elderly among Herlong's constituents flooded him with angry letters; an old man in Ormond Beach, for example, asked, "Congressman, what aren't you capable of?" The National Council tipped off a reporter for United Press International about these letters, and he called Herlong, who promptly attacked the A.M.A. for making misleading statements. "For them to give the impression that [Eldercare] provides complete coverage is not so," he said. "It just makes it available for the states to provide it if they want to." Shortly after this interview appeared in Washington newspapers, one of the A.M.A.'s top officers and its chief lobbyist called on Herlong at his office. An hour later, Herlong issued a statement modifying what he had said earlier and attacking the Medicare forces for circulating "implied claims" about *their* bill.

On February 8th, the day after the A.M.A.'s House of Delegates wound up its special meeting in Chicago, Dr. Ward and several of his colleagues appeared before an executive-session hearing of the Committee on Ways and Means. In the committee's earlier, public hearings, the chairman had indulged those witnesses, for both sides, who were clearly more interested in scoring debating points than in contributing to the committee's legislative purpose. But executive-session hearings were businesslike affairs. The committee was about to devise a bill, and its members wanted, and needed, all the expert assistance they could get on the complicated technical problems involved. In the invitations that Mills sent out to witnesses he specifically asked them to restrict their testimony to matters within

their competence. All the witnesses complied except Dr. Ward and the A.M.A. officials accompanying him. They talked about economics, sociology, public welfare, and the Social Security system, and repeated, almost verbatim, the allegations made in their advertising. "The A.M.A. people had absolutely *nothing* constructive to offer," one member of the comittee said afterward. "They spouted the usual nonsense, as if we were conducting a propaganda forum rather than a serious meeting. Then, when we indicated that we weren't interested, they got rude and ungentlemanly. Even Herlong and Curtis were annoyed. The behavior of the A.M.A. witnesses was the greatest favor that could have been done for the Medicare cause. Their refusal to cooperate relieved us of any obligation to them."

At one point during Dr. Ward's presentation of his prepared statement, he said:

We have seen a story in the Feburary 1 issue of the St. Louis *Globe-Democrat* which quotes "an unpublished study by top government actuaries" and contains some rather ominous information, to state the matter mildly. According to the *Globe-Democrat,* the government actuaries have estimated that the cost of H.R. 1 would reach $3.8 billion a year by 1975, and, further, that the proposed special health-care fund would be just about broke by then. Let me quote. . .from the news story: "By 1975, according to the still secret study, the fund would be down to about $275 million. By 1976 the fund would be empty. What would happen then, in all probability, is that money would have to be diverted from the regular Social Security retirement fund to meet the Medicare deficits."

Representative Ullman, after saying, "I am only sorry that we must proceed in the writing of this bill without the technical assistance that your organization might have given us," proceeded to take up the *Globe-Democrat* story in some detail. "These are serious charges, and you simply don't bandy them around," he said to Dr. Ward. "Do you know where they came from?" Dr. Ward answered that he could get the reporter's name, since it was a by-line story, and added that he would be "very happy to authenticate that statement." Ullman told him that it wouldn't be necessary. One reason Ullman and other members of the committee didn't feel that any further elaboration by the A.M.A. was necessary was that they already had a pretty good idea how the figures had found their way into print. A week earlier, Robert J. Myers, the chief actuary of the Social Security Administration, had appeared before the committee to answer various technical questions about the funding provisions of the King-Anderson bill. In the course of his testimony, Myers had used the figures that were later cited in the *Globe-Democrat* article, but had used them as a hypothetical demonstration of the fact that health-care funds would be depleted by 1976 unless the taxable wage base was raised periodically—as the bill provided. Having testimony taken by his own committee quoted back to him in a distorted form obviously angered Mills. "This was not secret information," he said to Dr. Ward. "This was information that I understand was obtained directly from Mr. Myers." Myers himself was in the room at the time, and Ullman asked him what had happened. It seemed that while Myers had not discussed the figures in question with any newspaper reporters, he had discussed them in some detail with other individuals. "The figures were obtained from my office by a representative of the American Medical Association, and they were from our worksheets," Myers said. When Dr. Ward

left the witness chair, Mills watched him depart, and then turned to a colleague and said, "It's amazing. They haven't learned a thing."

After the Committee on Ways and Means had heard the six-hundred-and-forty-first witness to appear before it since it opened its first hearings on the King-Anderson bill, in 1961, Mills announced in mid-February that the committee would begin to prepare the bill that would be sent to the floor of the House. Besides Medicare, Eldercare, the Byrnes bill, and a dozen other health-insurance measures that members of the House had submitted, the committee had before it an expanded and liberalized Kerr-Mills bill that Mills had introduced in the House in January and an amendment to the Social Security law providing a cash increase in pension benefits that had been deadlocked in a joint Senate-House conference committee the previous fall. Curtis and Herlong seemed rather embarrassed by Eldercare, and had little to say for it—so little, in fact, that they never brought it up for a vote—but Byrnes went all out for his contribution, which he began calling Bettercare. Byrnes's claim that his bill provided far more comprehensive coverage than any of the other bills made the Democrats uneasy, for although the Republicans might have no hope of getting the measure through Congress, they could be counted on to use it later as an example of how they had been trying to take care of old people when the Democrats betrayed them with a halfway piece of legislation. Mills had long been convinced that many people would be disappointed in Medicare—and angry at the administration that was responsible for it—when they found out how relatively little it gave them. Now, to make matters worse, the A.M.A.'s publicity on this point seemed likely to give organized medicine a we-told-you-so advantage in the consideration of any future legislation. In any event, on the morning of March 2nd Mills called on Wilbur Cohen, an Assistant Secretary of Health, Education, and Welfare, who was the administration's representative at the hearings and its expert on everything pertaining to Social Security, and asked him to give the committee a run-through of the various bills under consideration. At around three o'clock that afternoon, Cohen finished with the last of them—the Byrnes bill—and everyone looked at Mills to see what he would do next. No one was prepared for what happened. Turning to Byrnes, Mills said, "You know, John, I like that idea of yours"—the idea being Byrnes's plan for a voluntary program that the participants would help to pay for by agreeing to have small deductions taken from their monthly Social Security checks. As Mills continued, however, it became apparent that he liked the idea not as an alternative to Medicare but as a supplement to it. This arrangement, he explained, would provide a sort of three-layer cake: the expanded Kerr-Mills program making up the bottom layer, to take care of those close to indigence; Medicare making up the middle layer, to take care of the costs of hospital, nursing-home, and home-health care for the rest of the elderly; and the voluntary supplement making up the top layer, to take care of doctors' fees, in and out of hospitals. Then Mills turned back to Cohen and asked if the supplement could be made a part of the King-Anderson bill. Cohen quickly said that it could, and Mills asked him to draw up an amendment to that effect, along with an analysis of the costs, and adjourned the meeting until the following morning.

"Like everyone else in the room, I was stunned by Mills's strategy," Cohen said afterward. "It was the most brilliant legislative move I'd seen in thirty years. The doctors couldn't complain, because they had been carping about Medicare's shortcomings and about its being compulsory. And the Republicans couldn't complain, because it was their own idea. In effect, Mills had taken the A.M.A.'s ammunition, put it in the Republicans' gun, and blown both of them off the map." Byrnes, too, was stunned. "He just sat there with his mouth open," a member of the committee said later. Byrnes admitted after the meeting that Mill's maneuver had come as "quite a surprise" to him. "But, after all," he added, "the A.M.A. opened the door to all this with those advertisements." President Johnson was also surprised, and amused, when he received a memorandum from Cohen describing the events of that afternoon and concluding, "The effect of this ingenious plan is. . .to make it almost certain that nobody will vote against the bill when it comes on the floor of the House." The President laughed, and said to the aide who had brought the note, "Just tell them to snip off that name 'Republican' and slip that little old amendment into the bill." Early the next morning, a man from the A.M.A. appeared at the office of Representative Charles A. Vanik, a liberal Democrat from Ohio who was a new member of the Ways and Means Committee. Vanik wasn't in, but an assistant came out to the waiting room, and found the A.M.A. man slumped in a chair. The visitor asked if the rumor about Mills's coup was true, and upon being assured that it was he shook his head and got to his feet, with a dazed look. As he left, he said, "I never thought we'd end up spending several million dollars in advertising to expand the bill."

Cohen's presentation of the new plan before the Ways and Means Committee that morning took about half an hour. Myers had estimated that a contribution of three dollars a month by each participant, plus five hundred million dollars a year from the Treasury, would be sufficient to pay for eighty per cent of all the doctors' bills involved after each patient had paid fifty dollars out of his own pocket. "O.K., it sounds fine," Mills said. That was all he said, and it was enough for the other members of the committee, who were used to accepting a casual remark from Mills as a final decision on even the most crucial matters. In effect, Mills had told them that he was adding the amendment to the bill—subject, of course, to the committee's approval in a final vote. Later in the day, Cohen discussed the new measure with the President, who, he feared, might have had second thoughts about its added cost, since he was reported to be worried about the size of the forthcoming budget. Cohen told the President what the amendment would cost and outlined some of the political problems that this might present. When he had finished, the President nodded and asked what he could do to help. Somewhat puzzled, Cohen said that the basic question was whether the President could accept a five-hundred-million-dollar increase in the budget. As Mr. Johnson later recalled the conversation, he replied, "I'm going to run and get my brother." A good deal more puzzled, Cohen said he didn't understand. The President's explanation itself seemed cryptic, at first: "Well, I remember one time they were giving a test to a fellow who was going to be a switchman on the railroad, giving him an intelligence test, and they said, 'What would you do if a train was coming from the east going sixty miles per hour, and you looked over your shoulder and another one was coming from the west going sixty miles an hour, and they were heading for each other at just a mile separate? What would you do?' And the fellow said, 'I'd go get my brother.' And they said, 'Why would you get your

brother?' And he said, 'Because he hasn't ever seen a train wreck.' " With that, the President told Cohen that he could have the five hundred million dollars, and warned him to watch out for trains.

A week later, on March 10th, two hundred members of the New York Council of Golden Ring Clubs, one of the largest affiliates of the National Council of Senior Citizens, went to Washington for a luncheon and rally in behalf of Medicare. When Mills heard about their plans for a gathering, he suggested that it be held in the hearing room of the Ways and Means Committee, and he offered to preside as host. Next to the A.M.A., Mills had long been the chief villain of the Medicare drama in the view of many old people, but when he welcomed the members of the Golden Ring Council, they gave him a standing ovation. And when he told them that, as they had heard, the bill was to be greatly expanded, they gave him another. "Mills is a politician of the first rank," William R. Hutton, of the National Council, said after the luncheon. "He anticipated the inevitable. He cooperated with the inevitable. And then he capitalized on the inevitable." Being a realist, Mills expected the Republicans to accept the inevitable with comparable grace, since they could now turn the bill to their own advantage by claiming credit for a large part of it, but after the Golden Ring lunch he was told that Byrnes was talking about not voting for the bill, either in committee or on the floor. "He's got to," Mills said. "He's painted himself into a corner." But on March 23rd, when the Ways and Means Committee took a final vote on the bill (it was now being jocularly referred to in some quarters as Elder-Medi-Better-Care), Byrnes and all his fellow-Republicans voted against it, in a straight seventeen-to-eight party-line vote. The Democrats were jubilant. "I couldn't believe my ears when they voted no," one of them said. "Of course, Ford, the Minority Leader, had instructed them to. It was incredibly inept, politically. Now we'll get *all* the credit."

Leaving nothing to chance, President Johnson went on television at eleven o'clock on the morning of March 26th to describe the new bill. After giving a brief account of its provisions, he introduced nine other Democrats—from the House there were Mills, King, Speaker John McCormack, Majority Whip Hale Boggs, and Majority Leader Carl Albert, and from the Senate there were Anderson, Assistant Majority Whip George Smathers, Majority Leader Mike Mansfield, and Harry F. Byrd, chairman of the Senate Finance Committee. All but Byrd spoke glowingly of the new measure (even Smathers, long an opponent of Medicare, said, "I'm delighted with the bill"), and then the President turned to Byrd, who had opposed all the earlier, and far more modest, versions of the bill, and who, it was feared, might hold up the present version by postponing hearings on it in the Senate Committee on Finance. In a dialogue that Representative Albert described later as not only an outstanding example of the famous "Johnson treatment" but the first instance of it ever to be shown on a national television hookup, the President smiled at Byrd and said, "I know that you will take an interest in the orderly scheduling of this matter and giving it a thorough hearing." Byrd looked at him blankly, whereupon Mr. Johnson asked, "Would you care to make an observation?"

Byrd, who had engaged in many conversations with Presidents but never before with millions of people watching, shook his head. "There is no observation I can make now, because the bill hasn't come before the Senate," he replied gruffy. "Naturally, I'm not familiar with it."

President Johnson pressed on. "And you have nothing that you know of that would prevent [hearings] coming about in reasonable time, not anything ahead of it in the committee?" he asked.

"Nothing in the committee now," Byrd answered, shifting uneasily.

"So when the House acts and it is referred to the Senate Finance Committee, you will arrange for prompt hearings and thorough hearings?" the President asked, leaning forward intently.

Senator Byrd, in a voice that was barely audible, said, "Yes."

Smiling broadly, Mr. Johnson banged his fist on the desk, stared into the camera lens, and said, "Good!"

In a mood of high expectancy, the House met on April 8th to vote on the first national health-insurance measure ever to come before it. The Ways and Means Committee enjoys such great prestige in the House, in large part because of the thoroughness with which it customarily conducts its business, that the bills it reports out are rarely amended on the floor. Instead, a period is set aside for description of the bill and for debate on it, and then the opposition is permitted to recommend recommittal of the measure and its replacement by a substitute. Mills received a standing ovation from both sides of the aisle when he went to the rostrum in the well of the House to describe what had by now become known as the Mills bill. He quickly justified the reputation he had acquired for always being in command of his material. Speaking without a trace of an accent—it is reported that he has an unusually strong one whenever he talks to a group of his constituents—and only rarely referring to notes, he outlined the provisions of the bill, which was two hundred and ninety-six pages long. The measure, he explained, included a seven per cent increase in pension benefits (thus breaking a tradition of keeping total Social Security taxes below ten per cent), an expanded Kerr-Mills program, a modification of the King-Anderson bill, and the Byrnes voluntary supplement. In all, the layer cake, with its cash frosting, was to cost about six billion dollars the first year—roughly half of it for health insurance. When Mills sat down, Byrnes presented his own original bill as the Republican alternative, and then for several hours members of both factions had their say. (Representative Herlong praised the Mills package.) When the vote on recommittal was taken, it showed that Mill's estimation of the situation the year before—that there wasn't enough support to get a Medicare bill through—had almost certainly been right, for now the margin against the motion to recommit was only forty-five votes, or one more than the number of new Medicare advocates, both Democrats and Republicans, known to have been elected to the House in 1964. Sixty-three Democrats defected to Byrnes (Herlong among them), but only ten Republicans went over to the Medicare side. Once the recommittal vote was out of the way, however, and the Republicans were released from party discipline, the bill was approved by a vote of three hundred and thirteen (including Herlong) to a hundred and fifteen.

The A.M.A.'s diagnosis had always been that once the body politic was infected by government health insurance, the illness would be irreversible. Although the patient was clearly on the point of succumbing by the spring of 1965, the A.M.A. prescribed another dose of its favorite medicine—a massive injection of publicity. Stepping up the campaign for Eldercare, the A.M.A. announced that the results of several polls showed the public to be heartily in favor of what the Association liked to call the Doctors' Program. At about that time, the A.M.A. sent every member of Congress a booklet of a hundred and seventy-one magazine-size pages containing "a cross-section of American editorial opposition to Medicare" and support for Eldercare. Anyone who took the trouble to glance through the compilation discovered that batches of the editorials were identical; for example, the same text appeared in the Birmingham *Post-Herald*, the Denver *Rocky Mountain News*, the Washington, D.C., *Daily News*, the Logansport, Indiana, *Press*, and the New York *World-Telegram & Sun.* Senator Pat McNamara, Democrat of Michigan, who had been an enthusiastic Medicare man from the beginning, pointed out on the Senate floor that two of the editorials had appeared in ten different papers each, that another had appeared in eleven papers, and that six of the editorials had appeared in a total of fifty papers. The Association declared that McNamara had "slanted his remarks to imply editorials were sent out by the A.M.A.," and it denied the implied accusation. Shortly afterward, a Washington *Post* reporter traced some of the editorials in question to a couple of companies that specialized in preparing and distributing canned editorials. Neither of them charged the newspapers that used their services, but both charged those who wanted to have their views distributed; the A.M.A. was a client of both. A little later, Senator Joseph D. Tydings, Democrat of Maryland, told his colleagues that his office, like theirs, had been flooded with mail—mostly form letters and form postcards—attacking Medicare and praising Eldercare. Members of Congress usually ignore mail of this sort, but Tydings, who had been in the Senate only a few months, had conscientiously set about replying to more than ten thousand pieces of anti-Medicare mail with a two-page form letter of his own. He stopped before long, he said, because of the first three hundred and fifty replies mailed out of his office, seventy-two came back marked "No such street," "No such street number," "Addressee unknown," or "Deceased." After Dr. Ward charged, in a speech before the Maryland State Medical Society in the spring of 1965, that Medicare would lead to government control of Medical practice and would deprive patients of the right to choose whatever doctor they wanted, Dr. Walter F. Perkins, who for many years had been the president of the Johns Hopkins Hospital, in Baltimore, told the press, "The American people are getting fed up with that sort of nonsense—and the members of Congress know it only too well."

Senator Byrd, having committed himself on television, scheduled the Finance Committee hearings on health care legislation for late April. In fifteen days, the committee took more than twelve hundred pages of testimony, and heard scores of witnesses, among them the A.M.A.'s Dr. Ward. Apparently chastened by the reaction he had got from the Ways and Means Committee, Dr. Ward stuck quite closely this time to matters that fell within his competence as a physician. It was too late. The deference that was once shown to any representative of the medical profession who appeared before Congress had all but disappeared. In its place was outright derision—most openly displayed on this occasion by Senator Anderson, co-sponsor of the bill, who presided over many of the sessions, including the one at which the A.M.A. representatives appeared. Dr. Ward, in his opening remarks, brought up the Eldercare program, which he said had "aroused enthusiastic public support" and was the only measure providing medical care for the elderly that had been written "in consultation with the medical profession." Senator Anderson broke in to

list the names of a number of eminent physicians who had been consulted on the framing of the Medicare legislation, and then he asked whether the witness considered Dr. Benjamin Spock, whose name was on the list, a member of the medical profession. "If he has a Doctor of Medicine degree, yes," Dr. Ward answered. Sitting forward, Anderson asked sharply whether he meant to imply that Dr. Spock was not a licensed physician. Making amends, Dr. Ward said he was under the impression that Dr. Spock was a baby specialist. Anderson then produced a burst of laughter from the audience in the hearing room by inquiring whether Dr. Ward, a surgeon, was "an elderly specialist." After a few more tart exchanges, Anderson asked whether the A.M.A. objected to all forms of Social Security, including the monthly retirement check. Dr. Ward said that it did not, but Anderson pursued the subject.

SENATOR ANDERSON: If you don't object to providing it for [the pensioner's] rent and other bills, why do you object to it for hospital bills?

DR. WARD: In the first place, it should be based on need.

SENATOR ANDERSON: Well, wait a minute. It isn't in the other case at all. If a man comes to the age of retirement and has a million dollars, he can draw his Social Security whether he needs it or not.

DR. WARD: Yes, sir.

SENATOR ANDERSON: You don't mind it as long as it isn't in your field.

DR. WARD: No sir; I didn't say that.

SENATOR ANDERSON: What *did* you say?

DR. WARD: I object to the inclusion of people who are able to take care of themselves.

SENATOR ANDERSON: These people in Social Security who paid their money over a period of time, they are allowed to draw their Social Security whether they need it or not. Do you object to that?

DR. WARD: We have no argument about that.

SENATOR ANDERSON: You don't object to that?

DR. WARD: We are concerned with health.

SENATOR ANDERSON: It is only when you get to your field that you object to it, isn't that right?

DR. WARD: After a fashion, yes, sir.

SENATOR ANDERSON: Thank you. I have no further questions.

The Finance Committee completed its hearings on May 19th and adjourned until the following week, when it was to go into executive working session to prepare its version of the House bill. The afternoon of the adjournment, Senator Russell Long, of Louisiana, who had won the post of Majority Whip after Hubert Humphrey became Vice-President, and who, after the death of Senator Robert Kerr, of Oklahoma, had become the ranking Democrat on the committee, held a press conference to announce that he intended to submit two amendments to the Mills package. The first of them, he said, would make Medicare's provisions unlimited, in order to take care of what he called "catastrophic illness." (Since a ten-minute illness can be catastrophic for the person suffering it, it was assumed that Long was using the term to describe long-term illnesses that were catastrophically expensive.) The second was designed to pay for this open-end feature by adding, on top of the increase in Social Security taxes, a sliding scale of deductibles, or amounts to be paid by the patients themselves, based on their incomes. While the announcement came as a surprise to many people in Washington, it was clearly no surprise to the A.M.A., for the next issue of the *AMA News,* which had gone to press before Long called in the reporters, carried his description of the amendments. This set off speculation about whether

the A.M.A. had developed the new program, but it turned out that Long had actually been contemplating such a plan for some time. As far back as the spring of 1963, he had mentioned the idea to an official of the Department of Health, Education and Welfare, who was appalled by it for several reasons; namely, because it contained a means test (in the form of the deductibles based on income), because it was certain to be an administrative monstrosity, and because it was impossible to estimate how much it would cost, for, despite Long's assurances, there was no way of determining what would happen if hospitals were open to all comers of indefinite lengths of time.

In any event, Long did nothing further about his amendments during the first few weeks of the Finance Committee's executive-session deliberations. From time to time, he wandered into the room where the committee was meeting, and then, apparently deciding that the lineup of those on hand was unfavorable, explained that his duties as Whip required his presence on the floor, and departed. In the meantime, though, he talked privately with several of the liberal Democrats on the committee, assuring each of them in turn that his amendments, which none of them had yet seen, were nothing more than a reasonable expansion of the administration's bill. Since, as Whip, he was in some measure a representative of the administration, they assumed that he would not propose anything against the wishes of the President. Finally, late on the morning of June 17th, just as the committee was about to recess for lunch, Long appeared, looked around to see who was present and who was absent, and offered his amendments—not in the usual manner, by passing printed copies around, but by describing the details from his own copy. The amendments were far more extensive than he had indicated either in his press conference or in his private conversations with other senators. In explaining his plan, he repeated that it was merely an expansion of the administration's bill, and said that for a quarter of a billion dollars more they could provide unlimited hospital care for everyone sixty-five or over. He went on to warn his colleagues that the bill as it was currently written meant political disaster for all of them. The first time an old lady who had used up her allotted days of hospital care was carried out to die in the street, he said, there would be such a deafening public outcry that no senator who had voted for Medicare would ever be reelected. Hurrying on, he told the committee that the scale of deductibles in his plan would be highly favorable to the poor, and described the breakdown—five per cent of the first thousand dollars of income, six per cent of the second thousand, and seven per cent of all income above that, with a minimum deductible of twenty dollars, and no maximum. After a few minutes' discussion—representing perhaps the most casual treatment of a major piece of legislation in Senate history— Long called for a vote. The tally stood at seven to six for the amendments when Anderson, who had argued futilely against the plan, cast a proxy that had been given to him by Senator J. William Fulbright, of Arkansas. That made it a tie, and a defeat for Long. But Long broke in to say that he had a later proxy from Fulbright, and asked the committee's clerk to verify his claim. The clerk checked the date on Long's note from Fulbright and confirmed that it was more recent than the date on Anderson's. That made the vote eight to six for the amendments, and they were added to the bill. After the committee adjourned, Anderson, who was bewildered because he had been given Fulbright's assurance of support, asked the clerk for the proxy submitted by Long. When he examined it, he saw that it was indeed dated later than his but that it concerned another matter altogether.

In the Senate chamber that afternoon, Anderson told Fulbright about the incident, and together they confronted Long. "I thought this was supposed to be a gentlemen's club," Anderson said angrily. Long shrugged, said that perhaps there had been a misunderstanding, and offered to take another vote. Anderson, though he accepted the offer, did not accept the explanation—nor, it turned out, did many other senators, including Mansfield, who later gave Long a heated lecture on senatorial propriety at a Democratic policy meeting. Another proxy that had been misused—this one unintentionally—was one that Senator Albert Gore, Democrat of Tennessee, had given Senator Abraham Ribicoff, of Connecticut, over the telephone. Since Ribicoff had been a Medicare supporter all along, first as Secretary of the Department of Health, Education and Welfare under President Kennedy and than as a senator, Gore assumed that he would use the proxy in accordance with administration policy. Ribicoff, for his part, assumed that he was free to use it in accordance with his own best judgment, and he cast it for Long's amendments. The two incidents had produced a good deal of uncertainty all around, and, furthermore, Senator Paul Douglas, of Illinois, who had voted for Long's plan, began to have doubts about what he had done almost immediately. After the meeting broke up, he went to his office and sat down to think things over. Douglas, a former professor of economics, had no trouble working out the financial aspects of the bill, and, as he put it later, he realized that the proposal would "turn the nation's hospitals into warehouses for the senile." He added, "I saw that I had made a mistake. I simply hadn't understood the proposal." According to one high administration official, this may have been the first time in American history that a senator admitted he had been wrong.

On the morning of June 18th, the Cabinet met in a special session to discuss the situation in Vietnam. As the meeting got under way, Anthony Celebrezze, Secretary of Health, Education and Welfare, said he was obliged to inform the President that there was a domestic crisis, and he explained what had taken place in the Finance Committee the previous day. The President jumped up and began pacing back and forth. "How could this have happened?" he demanded angrily. As soon as the meeting was over, he took steps to find out not only how it had happened but how it could be changed. Besides making telephone calls to the Democrats on the committee who had voted for the amendments without fully understanding their meaning, President Johnson called Long and appealed to him to withdraw his plan—without success. "I did not ask for this fight, but I do not run from one," Long told reporters. "I know the White House is doing everything in its power to reverse the decision of the committee on my amendments. In my opinion, I will win." Winning was a complicated matter for him, however, in the view of several senators who had worked with him over the years. If he couldn't stop the bill, they said, he intended to put his own stamp on it as clearly as Mills had put his. Moreover, having been compelled to go along with the administration on a civil-rights voting act, which had hurt him back in Louisiana, he was not publicly challenging the President as a way of showing his constituents that he was no Presidential errand boy. Long was warning the White House that he couldn't be taken for granted. Whatever his motives

may have been, he refused to discuss them in public. To one reporter who brought up the matter, he replied by launching into a forty-minute filibuster consisting largely of the A.M.A.'s favorite arguments—that Medicare was socialized medicine, that the British National Health Service was a failure, and that the labor movement supported the bill solely to save on its own welfare outlays. He also refused to explain why the only Republican on the committee who had supported him was Senator Carl Curtis, of Nebraska, an arch-conservative who was generally considered to be the A.M.A.'s most ardent champion in the Senate now that Smathers had defected. All in all, Long appeared to enjoy the attention he was getting. He was reported to be especially amused by attacks on him in Northern newspapers, such as an editorial in the *Times* that took him to task for "acting in sublime disregard of his obligations as Democratic whip" and called his proposal "so disastrous that it is hard to believe it was put forward with any aim except to kill any prospect of Medicare in this session of Congress." In Louisiana, one senator later remarked, an attack by the *Times* hurts about as much as an attack by *Pravda*.

One of the key votes on the committee was that of Senator Ribicoff, and as part of an effort to persuade him to change his vote Nelson Cruikshank, head of the A.F.L.-C.I.O.'s Department of Social Security, asked union members in Connecticut to let Ribicoff know that they strongly opposed the Long amendments. Then, a day or so later, Cruikshank went to see Ribicoff at his office. The Senator jumped up and waved a sheaf of telegrams at Cruikshank. "What's all this?" Ribicoff demanded. "What do you mean by turning your people on me? You know I can't be pressured." Cruikshank heard him out calmly, and then said, "You know, and I know,

Abe, that if I came in here and you *hadn't* got all those wires, you wouldn't pay much attention to me." The issue, as Cruikshank saw it, was that the Long amendments were fiscally irresponsible, and he told Ribicoff that under no circumstances would the unions support any pie-in-the-sky scheme. Blue Cross, welfare assistance, and Social Security had limits, he said, so why shouldn't Medicare? But the issue, as Ribicoff saw it, was humanitarian as well as political. "You don't have to walk along the street in New Britain, say, and have a constituent stop you and get sore because his dying mother was put out of a hospital after sixty days," he said. Besides, he went on, he supported only the open-end amendment, and not the deductible plan. Cruikshank tried to convince Ribicoff that he couldn't support the first without also supporting the second, since the unlimited-care proposal had to be paid for. He got nowhere, and at the end of an hour each man stood where he had at the start.

Meanwhile, the A.M.A.'s lobbyists were busy drumming up support for the bill as it had been amended by Long—not because they approved of it but because they saw in it a way to create a deadlock in the Senate-House conference committee, for everyone was convinced that Mills would never accept such a drastic change in his bill. The A.M.A. people had to move inconspicuously in this matter. For one thing, they could not openly support any legislation that set up a health-insurance program under Social Security, and, for another, they had become such political pariahs by this time that their support for a measure was apt to be a rather heavy burden. Not long before, an A.M.A. lobbyist, having learned that the A.F.L.-C.I.O. opposed the inclusion of chiropractors in the bill, since it felt, as the A.M.A. did, that they were not strictly medical practitioners,

called a union lobbyist on the telephone and asked, "Can I announce that the A.M.A. and the A.F.L.-C.I.O. are shoulder to shoulder on this?"

"No," the union man answered at once, and went on, "It's not a question of vengeance on our part. It's a question of tactics. If you want to get something defeated in Congress, just say that the A.M.A. backs it."

There was a pause, and then the A.M.A. man said, "It's that bad?"

He was assured that it was.

The administration's strategists assumed that Long had originally avoided lining up the Republicans on the Finance Committee (except Curtis, who was believed to be working with him on the plan) because their support would have aroused the suspicions of the liberal Democrats, whom he needed far more. And now that the purpose of the plan had become clear it was also assumed that the rest of the Republicans, who hadn't understood the amendments the first time around any better than the Democrats had, would get behind Long in the hope that they could block Medicare. This assumption proved to be correct. On June 23, when a new vote was called for on the first of Long's amendments—the one adding a graduated deductible to the bill—all six of the Republicans sided with him, and all ten of the other Democrats, acceding to what the *Wall Street Journal* called "the administration's strenuous behest," voted against him. On the amendment providing unlimited care, two Democrats (Ribicoff and Vance Hartke, of Indiana) who liked the idea, behest or no behest, went over to Long, but two Republicans (Thruston B. Morton, of Kentucky, and Frank Carlson, of Kansas) went over to Anderson. That defeated both amendments. The next day, the committee voted out its version of the House bill by a final vote of twelve to five. After the meeting broke up, several of the senators met with a group of reporters to explain the measure. Long had taken his defeat cheerfully, and he seemed to enjoy bantering with the newsmen, telling them that if they held off awhile the committee report would be ready as source material. "The staff is working on it right now," he said, and added, with a smile, "I guess we can dispense with the myth that senators write their own reports." He did not mention that the dissenting report he would submit was being written by a lobbyist for the A.M.A.

After nearly two decades of struggle and controversy, million-dollar advertising drives, rallies, and political-action campaigns, the A.M.A.'s crusade has failed," the *Medical World News* observed that June. "And in the opinion of many knowledgeable people in Washington, the A.M.A.'s own strategy of uncompromising resistance contributed to the dimensions of its defeat." As if those dimensions weren't broad enough already, the A.M.A. now laid out still more money on still another public-relations push. Before June was over, it had placed a large advertisement entitled "An Open Letter to Our Patients" in a hundred major newspapers. A week after that, it put on nationwide television a half-hour show called "Health Care at the Crossroads." And its members continued to pour letters and telegrams by the thousand onto the desks of congressmen, urging them to oppose any interference by the government with what the medical profession had traditionally regarded as its own "sacred trust" of caring for the sick. On June 20th, some twenty-five thousand doctors arrived in New York for an A.M.A. convention, and were met by five hundred elderly pickets who handed out leaflets entitled "An Open Letter to Our Doctors." The opposition that had arisen at the previous convention among doctors

who felt that the A.M.A. was going too far was now drowned out by outcries from doctors who felt that it wasn't going far enough. Six weeks earlier, the Ohio State Medical Association, representing ten thousand doctors, had approved a resolution calling on its members to refuse to take part in any federal health-insurance program. Shortly after that, the Association of American Physicians and Surgeons—an organization whose members, numbering sixteen thousand, were also members of the A. M. A. but which was generally considered to be far to the right of the A.M.A.—sent a letter to every doctor in the country urging that "now is the time for you and every other ethical physician in the United States to individually and voluntarily pledge nonparticipation in. . .the socialized hospitalization and medical care program for the aged." The delegates in New York seemed to be strongly in favor of a boycott. Dr. Ward, in his speech as outgoing president, told them, "One poll after another has demonstrated beyond question that the American people have the most serious misgivings about welfare statism," and he received tumultuous applause. But when Dr. James Z. Appel, the incoming president, warned the assemblage against "unethical tactics such as boycott, strike, or sabotage" and said that doctors should defy neither the letter nor the spirit of any law passed by Congress, he got a very different reaction. He was accused of being responsible for "appeasement," "surrender," and the destruction of "the American dream." In the convention's first session on legislative matters, nine state delegations—from Arizona, Ohio, Florida, Texas, Indiana, South Carolina, Connecticut, Nebraska, and Louisiana—introduced separate resolutions calling for a boycott. When the House of Delegates' Committee on Legislation and Public Relations heard testimony on the boycott resolutions, only a few physicians stood by Dr. Appel. The view of the majority was perhaps expressed most eloquently by a delegate from New Jersey who told the committee. "Force must be used when reason will not prevail."

Actually, a number of A.M.A. members and officials, including most of the trustees, saw danger in the head-long rush toward a boycott. They expected the issue to be resolved by the delegates' designation of a president-elect, to be installed the following summer. The two leading contenders for the post were Dr. Charles L. Hudson, of Ohio, who opposed his state medical society's boycott resolution, and Dr. Durward G. Hall, of Missouri, a Republican member of Congress, who had openly campaigned for a boycott. The trustees had always had their way in the past, and they had it this time, too—after they had rounded up enough votes to elect Dr. Hudson. Though Hudson was an avid Goldwater fan ("I'm still unhappy he didn't win," he said), he was a moderate in the A.M.A. After his election, and the investiture of Dr. Appel, the delegates accepted a recommendation by the trustees that they sidestep the boycott question by reaffirming the Association's previous policy declarations in general terms. By this time, most of the advocates of uncompromising resistance had been calmed down. "Only one doctor rose on the floor in favor of a boycott," the Washington *Post* reported, "but he tried to illustrate his point with a joke about an unwed Negro mother, which did nothing to help his cause."

When the fog of partisan oratory over a controversial measure before Congress finally thins out and the road of political necessity appears ahead, legislators usually find that a bandwagon is the most comfortable vehicle to ride on. The House Medicare bill emerged from the Senate by a vote of sixty-eight to twenty-one and with five hundred and thirteen amendments and a billion and a half dollars in costs added to it. In part, the Senate's access of generosity was due to its members' awareness that they could claim credit for trying—and in a third-of-a-billion-dollar amendment to assist the blind, in which the definition of blindness was broad enough to include poor eyesight—but could confidently rely on the Senate-House conferees to behave responsibly and eliminate the unnecessary embellishments. Byrd had appointed Long to serve as the floor manager of the bill, and by the second day of the three-day debate so many amendments had been loaded on that the administration began to suspect that some of the senators were deliberately trying to make the bill unacceptable to the House conferees. Accordingly, the President asked Long not to consider any but essential amendments from that point on, whereupon Long went to the floor and called for more amendments. To many of those watching the performance, it seemed that Long, having been beaten in the Finance Committee, was carrying his fight to the floor of the Senate. As a matter of fact, he had entered into an agreement not to do that. The news of his initial success in putting his amendments through the committee had irritated one of his more influential and resourceful constituents, a labor leader in Louisiana, to whom Long had previously given his word that he would support Medicare down the line. Moving quickly, the man made arrangements to block action on a tax-write-off on oil holdings that was then being considered by a committee of the state legislature and that had been written expressly for the Longs, whose money was largely in oil. When Long heard about this maneuver, he telephoned the union leader and asked him what he thought he was doing. "What do you think you're doing to Medicare?" the man demanded. In the end, the labor leader agreed to release the tax bill in exchange for Long's agreement to confine his fight against Medicare to the Finance Committee. True to his word, Long did not carry his fight to the floor of the Senate. He let others carry it there for him. When he openly supported the amendments he had originally proposed, and failed to line up votes for the administration's position, Anderson said to Mansfield, "My God, Mike, we've got a floor manager who's against the bill!"

Senator Curtis submitted Long's amendment for graduated deductibles, which was by now almost universally interpreted as a maneuver in behalf of the A.M.A., to create a stalemate when the conference committee met. There were certain ironies in the situation, both for Curtis and for the A.M.A., since the amendment was clearly aimed at soaking the rich. Under its provisions those who paid the most into the Social Security fund during their working years would get the least out of it for medical care after they retired. In large part because Long had failed to explain the administration's policy to the members of his party, the amendment came within ten votes of being passed. An administration official who was asked whether the narrow margin might not encourage Curtis to reintroduce the amendment in another form said, "No, that would be too dirty. It was offered for a vote and beaten fairly." The next day, Curtis did reintroduce it in another form, and again it lost. Long's other amendment—for unlimited hospital care—was offered by Senator Ribicoff, who made an impassioned plea for it, as Long nodded and smiled. Anderson and Douglas had done their best to persuade Ribicoff that he was endangering the entire Medicare program, but Ribicoff had gone ahead anyway. After taking a

head count, Mansfield told his colleagues that they couldn't hope to beat the amendment. The prediction upset Anderson so much that he became ill and was forced to take to his bed. During the debate, several liberal senators who were uncertain about which way they should vote were told that the A.F.L.-C.I.O. was behind the amendment. When the story reached Cohen, who was on hand outside the chamber, he rushed to a telephone and called Cruikshank to ask if it was true. Cruikshank said it wasn't, and hurried over to the Capitol, where he found Douglas and Gore trying to rally the Medicare forces, and told them where the unions stood. Douglas and Gore passed the word around, and then Mansfield arose to deliver a rebuttal to Ribicoff that Anderson had been scheduled to give before he became ill. The speech (which, Anderson himself publicly said later, had been written by Cruikshank) and the authority it bore because of Mansfield's position as the administration's spokesman finally carried the day—but only by four votes.

One of the last issues to be raised before the final vote was taken on the bill was whether doctors should be put under the Social Security system. At that time, they were the only major professional group not covered. Polls conducted by state medical societies showed that a majority of the country's physicians wanted to be included in the program, but the A.M.A., which had refused over the years to poll its members nationally on the question, opposed their inclusion. Just before the vote on the amendment, Gore rose to say, "The A.M.A. has made such a fine contribution to the enactment of Medicare that I think it has earned the right to come under its benefits." Amid general laughter, the proposal was approved, and shortly after that, on July 9th, so was the entire bill.

As had been expected, Mills lopped a

great chunk off the Senate measure when the conference committee met—one and a quarter million dollars, in fact. One of the major differences between the House and Senate bills concerned the way four categories of specialists—pathologists, radiologists, anesthesiologists, and physiatrists (physical therapists)—were to be paid. The measure that Mills reported out of the Ways and Means Committee transferred the arrangements for paying these doctors from the Medicare, or hospital, section of the act of the voluntary—insurance supplement. Most of the specialists in the four categories either worked on salaries at hospitals or billed the hospitals for their work, though some of them did bill patients directly. This last method was the least common and the most costly, but the Mills provision would make it standard for millions of elderly patients, and hospitals would lose control over fees for even the most routine procedures. The A.M.A. backed Mills on this point—it had always opposed the idea of doctors' working on salary—and the specialists themselves insisted that they should be treated like other doctors, not like mere technicians. "Although the arguments have largely revolved around ethics and patient care, the issues have almost inevitably ended up in dollars," Dr. Albert W. Snoke, the executive director of the Grace-New Haven Community Hospital and a former president of the American Hospital Association, wrote Mills in a letter complaining about alterations that had been made in the King-Anderson bill. Dr. Snoke argued that once the four kinds of specialists were free to charge what the traffic would bear, the costs to patients and hospitals would skyrocket, and the ultimate consequence, he said, would be total government control. The President naturally didn't want to be held responsible for supporting a program that was certain to raise medical costs, so he instructed Cohen to see if he could persuade Mills to change his mind. Cohen got together with Mills, McCormack, Albert, and Boggs in the office of the Speaker of the House to try to work something out, but when McCormack picked up the telephone to call the President, Mills—apparently unwilling to be subjected to the Johnson treatment—quickly left the room. His decision, he later told an administration official, was political and was not open to negotiation. After the bill reached the Senate floor, Douglas pointed out that as the bill stood, it interfered with medical practice, and he offered an amendment that would leave it up to the hospitals to decide how the specialists were to be paid. At the urgent request of the President, Secretary Celebrezze, the American Hospital Association, and hundreds of hospitals and doctors around the country, the Senate accepted the Douglas amendment. In the conference, Mills led the administration to believe that he was ready to compromise on the issue, and Cohen thereupon prepared an amendment that excluded from the Medicare section of the law only the anesthesiologists, who often billed patients directly anyway, and the physiatrists, whose bills were not expected to constitute a large financial problem. But when the time came for a vote, Mills held out for the House position, and Boggs, who in the past had always stuck by the administration on Medicare, did, too. After no resistance at all, Long and Smathers joined their Republican colleagues in supporting Mills's position, and the compromise plan was defeated. "It was obviously pre-arranged," one of the other Senate conferees said afterward. "Mills had promised the doctors that he would never put any of them under any compulsory system, and he kept his word. Unfortunately, it's going to cost the

American people hundreds of millions of dollars. It's also going to make a hopeless mess out of normal hospital procedures. The President has asked us to repeal the amendment, so we'll just have to start fighting all over again."

The final form in which Medicare was reported out of conference on July 26th was far more comprehensive than any of the bills that had led up to it. The bill provided every person sixty-five or older—except retired federal employees, who are covered by the Federal Health Benefits Act—with sixty days of free hospital care, after a standard forty-dollar deductible, to avoid unnecessary hospitalization; thirty more days of hospital care at a charge of ten dollars a day; twenty days of free nursing-home care; eighty more days of nursing-home care at a charge of five dollars a day; a hundred home visits by nurses or other health specialists after hospitalization; and eighty per cent of the cost of hospital diagnostic tests, after a twenty-dollar deductible for each series. To pay for this, the taxable wage base of the Social Security system was raised to sixty-six hundred dollars a year, and the tax itself was increased by one-half of one per cent for both employee and employer. (Because of Mills's insistence that the program be actuarially sound, the increase was double the amount originally proposed.) The voluntary supplement provided for payment of eighty per cent of what the bill called "reasonable charges" for all physicians' services, after a fifty-dollar-a-year deductible; another hundred home health visits, whether a patient had been hospitalized or not; and the costs of non-hospital diagnostic tests, surgical dressings, splints, and rented medical equipment. To pay for this coverage, people sixty-five or older who wished to participate were to contribute three dollars a month apiece, and their contributions were to be supplemented by about half a billion dollars a year from the Treasury's general revenues. After more than fifty years of debate on whether the United States should adopt a national health-insurance program and, if so, what form it should take, this complex but somehow typically American solution to the problem was passed, as Public Law 89-97, by the House on July 27th and by the Senate on July 28th.

In order to discuss the application of Medicare, the A.M.A. requested an appointment with the President, and on July 29th he met with eleven of its leaders at the White House. "I'd never seen anything like it," one of the administration officials who attended the meeting said afterward. "The President made a powerful, moving appeal to the doctors to accept the new law, and reminded them that it had been devised after long and thorough consideration by the people's representatives under our constitutional procedures. He went on in that way for some time, and then he began talking about what wonderful men doctors were, and how when his daddy was sick the doctor would come over and sit up all night with him, and charge a pittance. He was getting terribly corny, but he had them on the edge of their seats. Then suddenly, he got up and stretched. Of course, when the President of the United States stands up, everybody stands up. They jumped to their feet, and then he sat down, so they sat down, too. He started off again, with another moving statement about this great nation and its obligation to those who had helped make it great and who were now old and sick and helpless through no fault of their own. Gradually, he moved back to the cornfield, and then he stood up again, and again they jumped to their feet. He did that a couple more times—until they were fully aware of who was President— and then he turned to a memorandum on his desk. He read them the statement in the bill prohibiting any government interference in any kind of medical practice at any time, and also the statement guaranteeing freedom of choice for both doctors and patients, and assured them there would be no government meddling in these matters. Next, he explained that Blue Cross and private insurance carriers, who are the administrative middlemen under the law, would determine the bill's definition of 'reasonable charges' on the basis of what was customary for a given area. Naturally, the doctors went for this, because they have great influence with most of those outfits. Toward the end, he asked for their help in drawing up regulations to implement the law. Then he got up one last time, and said that he had to leave. Before he went, he turned to Cohen, who is the A.M.A.'s idea of an archfiend, and, shaking a huge forefinger in his face, he said, 'Wilbur, I want you to stay here with these gentlemen, and work things out according to my instructions—no matter how long it takes you.' Afterward, I overheard one A.M.A. man say to another, 'Boy, did you hear how he talked to Cohen?' Of course, Wilbur had written the memorandum."

The day after the conference with the doctors, President Johnson flew out to Independence, Missouri, to sign Public Law 89-97 at the Harry S. Truman Memorial Library, in honor of the former President who had been the first chief executive to come out publicly for government health insurance. Although by this time the A.M.A.'s leaders had apparently seen the futility of continued opposition, boycott fever among doctors had reached epidemic proportions. The Association informed its members that while its lawyers had advised it that any concerted boycott might constitute a violation of the Sherman Antitrust Act, individual doctors were free to refuse on their own to participate in the program.

The statement obviously ran counter to Dr. Appel's plea for moderation and for obedience to the laws of the land, but it didn't satisfy the more militant A.M.A. members. The Association of American Physicians and Surgeons accused the A.M.A. of "an indefensible display of collaboration with the complicity in evil," and appealed by mail to all doctors to join it in a boycott, concerted or not. Dr. Edward Annis, one of the Association's most valuble opponents of Medicare, estimated that ninety per cent of all the physicians in the country would refuse to touch a government form. By early fall, the pressure for a strike against the law had become so nearly irresistible that the A.M.A., in response to petitions from its state societies, called a special session of the House of Delegates. At the meeting, which was held in Chicago at the beginning of October, Dr. Annis told the delegates, to resounding cheers, that Medicare had been "passed by every mockery of the Democratic process," and that the nation's physicians had been betrayed by "appeasers," "collaborators with the enemy," "labor bosses," and "power-hungry political leaders." He did not recommend a boycott, however. Instead, he declared that the A.M.A. should cooperate with the government and get "inside the camp of the enemy" in order to "find the vital, the vulnerable spots." Dr. Annis's views carried a good deal of weight, and in the end they prevailed. Still, a number of delegates threatened to conduct personal boycotts, and several of them said they would go to jail before they would cooperate in any way with the government. Actually, there was no way for them to carry out this threat short of forcing their way into jail, for the law provided that if a doctor refused to fill out a Medicare form, the patient could collect from the government by simply sending in the doctor's bill and a record of its having been paid. Dr. Appel was not warmly received when he rose and told his colleagues that they were "expected by the public, the press, and the Congress to act as reasonable and mature men and women." And the response was even cooler when he said in conclusion, "I submit. . . that no political crisis is as deleterious to medicine as one brought about by its members."

Not long afterward, Senator Douglas, who had become Congress's unofficial overseer of the Medicare program, submitted several bills to amend the law—chief among them an amendment that returned the four specialist groups to the hospital-coverage part of the plan. Along with many other members of Congress who had fought for government health insurance over the years, he was increasingly upset by the doctors' threats to boycott or in one way or another sabotage the Medicare program. "We've had a lot of reports about doctors planning to raise their fees so that the 'reasonable charges' prevailing in their area would be higher," the Senator said. "Of course, as soon as the bill was passed, they said it would never work and that the administration would be to blame for its failure. We'll know where the blame lies—and so will the people. The doctors of this country say they have a sacred trust. I hope they keep it."

V

the
emotionally
disturbed

Mental health practitioners and laymen in the community have changed their views considerably in recent times with regard to labeling someone as mentally ill. Today there is much more appreciation of the relationship between one's position in the social structure and social behavior. Also, there is less willingness to identify persons as mentally ill simply because they behave somewhat differently from most of us. In addition, there has been a deepening understanding of the many possible determinants of mental illness, although unfortunately we do not know the causes of most mental disorders. There has been great progress made in the humanization of treatment of the mentally ill; there have been strenuous efforts to decrease custodial care and bring treatment into the community; there has been at least some success in stabilizing the condition of many patients through drug therapy.

The problem of mental illness continues to represent one of the major health concerns. The emotionally disturbed not only suffer themselves, but their conditions are often disruptive to the lives of family members and close intimates. While the behavior of most mental patients is disturbing primarily because of its bizarreness, the occasional person who is destructive (in the sense of harming community members) creates fear and anxiety in many of us about the emotionally disturbed and the illnesses of the mind. Moreover, the broadscale efforts at treatment and prevention, and the participants in these efforts are often opposed by groups and individuals in the community, sometimes because of antagonism toward the mentally ill, and sometimes because they disagree with the political and social views of persons seeking to improve mental health services.

Individual
↓
Individual

Individual
↓
Organization

THE MIND OF A MURDERER

It is possible to understand most crimes of violence in terms of the personal economic and emotional relationships between the protagonist and his victim. Richard Speck received great notoriety and instilled fear in many community members by his apparently unexplainable attack on eight young nursing students who shared an apartment together. Ziporyn, who co-authored this case, was a jail psychiatrist who became intimately acquainted with Speck and was able to arrive at some understanding of the factors which stimulated the attack. Although cases of an individual wantonly striking out against others are exceedingly rare, it is the mental aberrations of a few like Speck that are closely related to the fears we hold about the emotionally troubled.

THE LAST WORD (WE HOPE) ON GEORGE LINCOLN ROCKWELL

At sometime in their careers, almost all persons with overly intense leadership aspirations are accused of manifesting emotional illness. The label "neurotic" or "pathological" has been attached to many political leaders whose stands are antagonistic to the fundamental values of a democratic society. A large number of persons would certainly attach a label of some mental deviation to the recently murdered George Lincoln Rockwell, whose attitudes towards minorities and ways of behavior were patterned after Adolph Hitler. Shapiro describes Rockwell's constant confrontation with the American community. While Rockwell's organization has not achieved a modicum of power in the United States, the case describes well the engagement of a man against his community.

Organization ↓ Individual	Organization ↓ Organization

SIXTY-TWO YEARS FOR VAGRANCY

Hospital care for mental illness has become more humane, if not more effective. There still exist, however, institutions so inadequate and harsh that they bring disgrace to all community members; perhaps the most notorious of these are for the so-called criminally insane. Half jails, half mental hospitals, they have the worst features of both. Persons in these institutions in many cases would have been better off in prison, where most sentences at least have an endpoint; persons committed to criminal hospitals are at the mercy of an inadequate and sometimes incompetent staff. Bridgewater Hospital has been a dumping ground for generations. It is only recently that an enlightened staff has been concerned with remedying the situation. The impact of prolonged commitment on the individuals described in Richard's article is irreversible. The consequences of their hospitalization is a shameful burden to be borne by persons responsible for mental health care and by the entire community.

TARGET: MENTAL HEALTH

A manifestation of progress in the care of the mentally ill is the increased involvement of community members in the problem of mental illness. Indeed, many of the changes and improvements in mental health care stem from the organized activities of citizen groups. Individuals identified closely with conservative right wing organizations, if not the organizations themselves, impede the work of community groups concerned with mental health. While Burrus, in the articles compiled here, is quite careful to identify the conflict with individuals rather than with organizations, it is perhaps no mere coincidence that the opposition to mental health programs comes from individuals strongly identified with groups such as the John Birch Society. It is difficult to provide another interpretation except that of the interorganizational conflict.

the mind

of a

murderer

JACK ALTMAN
AND MARVIN ZIPORYN, M.D.

At 12:30 p.m. on July 29, 1966, a young man was brought to Ward 1 of the hospital at Cook County Jail on Chicago's Southwest Side. A nurse and a doctor helped him into bed No. 11 in a corner of the narrow olive-drab ward. Only 10 of the 20 other beds were occupied. From one of them, four beds away, a Negro prisoner sat up and screamed at the newcomer, "I'll kill you, you bastard! I'll get you, sure as God!" The rest of the patients stared in silence. The young man looked startled at the outburst but said nothing. He turned and faced the brick wall, clenched his eyes and tried to sleep. A guard was posted at the foot of his bed. The young man was Richard Speck, accused of murdering eight nurses.

The jail psychiatrist, Dr. Marvin Ziporyn, was making his regular rounds of the patients, chatting quietly. He stopped by the newcomer's bed to exchange a few words with the guard. The psychiatrist glanced down at Speck, who was propped up on two pillows. The prisoner wore a regulation white hospital smock, loose around the neck and revealing on his upper chest pockmarks like those that pitted the hollow cheeks of his pale, angular face. Beneath a mass of sandy hair slicked back from a high forehead, his watery blue eyes flickered apprehensively. His dry, colorless lips hung half open. Speck looked haggard, tense and considerably older than his 24 years. He had lost a lot of blood from cuts on his right wrist and the inner side of his left elbow—the result of a suicide attempt. During treatment he had also suffered an inflammation of the heart sac. The strength his muscular body once had now seemed to have seeped away.

Ziporyn walked away and was approached by the head nurse as he left the ward.

"Are you going to talk to him?" she asked.

"Speck? No, I don't want to jeopardize his rights," the psychiatrist replied. "He might say things to me that could hurt him." But the decision was not for Ziporyn to make, as he discovered a few minutes later in the office of the chief warden, Jack Johnson. The warden asked:

"Do you think Speck is suicidal?"

"No idea."

"Well, I think you should go down and

see him. See whether he is suicidal and tell us what precautions we should take."

This was the bald assignment, in its way a routine task, but in Speck's case, the horror of the murders had immeasurably raised the stakes. He had already attempted suicide once since the murders. Warden Johnson did not want Speck making another such attempt.

The state's attorney's office had made unusual efforts, following recent Supreme Court decisions on interrogation, to protect the prisoner's rights. The warden was concerned with protecting the prisoner against himself. It was the psychiatrist's job to anticipate the risks.

This was the immediate task, but it did not represent the limit of Ziporyn's responsibility. Johnson had given him the broadest of mandates when he started work at Cook County Jail in 1965.

Ziporyn worked out his own program in the jail, providing group therapy for women prisoners and individual therapeutic counseling for inmates in need of it, advising on whether they could benefit from activity in the prison's workshops for printing, carpentry, baking. He also prescribed medicine and submitted diagnostic reports to the courts on request. He was required to make a report on each interview with a prisoner, but the content of those interviews was left entirely to him.

In the case of Richard Speck, Ziporyn was to calculate the chances that the prisoner might try to commit suicide. Ziporyn would have to probe the thoughts, memories, worries and fears, and also the fancies and whims that made up the man, Richard Speck.

Speck was lying in bed reading a magazine when the psychiatrist returned. It was a sticky July afternoon. A large electric fan whirred from the corner opposite Speck's bed. As Ziporyn approached the prisoner stared fixedly at the magazine. Ziporyn coughed and said quietly, "Mr. Speck, my name is Dr. Ziporyn. I'm the jail psychiatrist, and I've been asked to find out a little bit about you. Mind if we talk?"

Speck shrugged and continued looking at the magazine. He said nothing. The psychiatrist went on, "Do you like to read?"

Without looking up, Speck muttered, "Nope." He paused and added, "I don't read too well. I just like to look at the pictures."

"Can you read at all?" Ziporyn asked. "I'd like you to show me." He took the magazine and asked Speck to read an advertisement. In a Texas drawl, stretching out each word in a halting rhythm that had nothing to do with the sense of what he was reading, Speck stumbled his way through two lines of text. The only words that came without difficulty were familiar brand names.

"You see?" he said blandly. "I just don't read well, do I?"

Speck's manner remained remote. Ziporyn asked Speck to name the year, the month, the day, where he was, who the President was, the Vice President, the mayor of Chicago. The date, the place and Lyndon Baines Johnson he knew, but then he halted. Ziporyn followed up with two tests in which he spoke numbers and words in sequence and asked Speck to repeat them in sequence. Speck did badly at it.

Given the careful warning that he would have to repeat the numbers and the sentence, a normal person could recite them back. Speck's failures of mental status and memory suggested possible brain damage. Ziporyn went on with a subtraction test, at which Speck also did badly.

The psychiatrist asked, "Did you ever get hit on the head?"

"Plenty of times," said Speck, showing more interest in this than in the arithmetic questions. "When I was playing in a sandbox, I hit myself on the head with a claw hammer. Accidentally. I knocked myself out. Then, a few years later—I must have been about ten—I was playing with some kids. They chased me, and I climbed into a tree. I hid there for a while, maybe ten feet from the ground, and lost my hold. I fell on my head. My sister found me. She thought I was dead. They told me I was out for about an hour and a half. About five years after that, I did it again. This time I was running down a street and ran my head straight into a steel awning rod. I was knocked out again. That thing must have gone right into my brain. See that patch of light-colored hairs on my head? That's where the awning rod hit me. On top of that I've been pistol-whipped by cops, and I've been beat up in bar fights. Hundreds of times."

Cause for brain damage seemed sufficient right there. Ziporyn then asked a series of questions that were standard primary tests for indication of schizophrenia. Speck's answers satisfied Ziporyn that he showed no cognitive or perceptive defects indicative of schizophrenia. But the psychiatrist needed evidence of a secondary nature, based on Speck's psychological history.

"Do you ever hear voices?" Ziporyn asked.

Speck blushed and did not seem to want to reply. Ziporyn waited. After a long pause Speck said, "Well, sometimes." He paused again and added, "When I take drugs."

"Whose voices?" Ziporyn asked.

"You'll kind of think I'm silly, I mean it sounds ridiculous, but they're like my conscience talking to me. They warn me, tell me, 'Don't do it,' when I'm thinking of doing something bad." Speck was obviously embarrassed. With great deliberation he added. "But I want you to know, it only happens when I'm on drugs."

"What kind of drugs?"

"Yellow-jackets and red-birds." [Slang names for habituating barbiturates capable of causing hallucinations and bizarre actions.] "And then sometimes I shoot myself with inhalers. You know, glue and stuff."

"And do you drink?"

"Boy, do I drink."

"What?"

"Anything I can lay my hands on—wine, beer, whisky, gin, you name it. I drink from the time I get up till I get drunk and fall back into bed. Sometimes it makes me feel real good. But sometimes it puts me in a real bad temper, and then I get into fights."

Speck talked slowly, quietly, in a monotone. What part his real or apparent involvement in the murders was playing in his behavior was not yet evident. Ziporyn decided it was an appropriate moment to approach the subject. He took a deep breath and said, "Dick, you know that everybody is saying you killed these nurses. What happened?"

"I don't know anything more about it than you do," Speck replied.

"Did you do it?"

Speck sighed deeply and replied in a low voice, with a shrug of resignation: "Everybody says I did it. Must be so. If they say I did it, I did it."

Ziporyn repeated his question.

"Did you do it?"

"Look, I was drinking that day. I told you how I drink. And I had six red-birds. To tell you the truth, I don't know nothing about anything from eight o'clock that night till I came to, about eleven o'clock the next day. All I remember is I met three sailors in a tavern on the South Side in the afternoon. We had some drinks, then we went off some place and had a fix—a shot in the arm. I don't know what it was exactly, but it wasn't heroin. It was something in a blue bottle, I think, I don't remember a thing after that. I couldn't tell you or anybody else what any of those nurses looked like."

"You remember going into the building, the place where they lived?"

Speck smiled quizzically and looked around the room. Then he said, "You know, my lawyer told me not to talk about this to anybody."

"But this is part of the jail routine. You can tell me," said Ziporyn.

"Is it? Well, I guess it's OK then. Nope, I don't remember going into no building."

"What did you do when you came to, the next day?"

Speck snorted self-mockingly and said, "Same thing I always do. Went out and got drunk again."

"Did you hear about the murders when you went out?"

"Yeah, I heard something about it."

"You didn't connect it with yourself?"

Speck considered the question and shook his head with a look of surprise on his face. It seemed to be striking him for the first time that his feeling of detachment was a little odd. "No," he said slowly. "No, I didn't make no connection, not till I heard my name on the radio."

"Were you frightened at all?"

"No. By that time I was too drunk again to feel anything."

"And how do you feel about it now?"

The tired air of resignation deepened in his voice as he drawled, "Well, if I burn, I burn."

There was a pause, and then he spoke again. "When I heard what they said I'd done, on the radio, I just felt there was no point in living. If I was that kind of person, then I was no good to anybody any more, no good to myself neither. First I tried a bottle of sleeping pills, a whole bottle, but that was no good. I had to do something, I had to find some way.

I mean, what's the use of living, somebody like me? So then I tried cutting myself, with a razor blade. But that didn't work either, did it? I'm still here."

Ziporyn nodded. Speck's depression was deepening, and the psychiatrist decided to stop the interview. He left Speck and went to tell Warden Johnson what he wanted to know.

Yes, Speck was suicidal. He was emotionally unstable, impulsive, depressive. Throughout the 65 minutes of the interview his mood had shifted constantly—sometimes bland, then cheerful, then depressed, never the same for more than two or three minutes at a time. Ziporyn recommended standard psychiatric tests. And the usual practical precautions against suicide.

Ziporyn was assigned to see Speck on a regular basis. This meant he would see him whenever he came to the jail, which was usually twice a week.

Ziporyn was able to reconstruct many of the events of mid-July that had brought his new patient to Cook County Jail, but there were gaps. Police investigation had been quick and largely efficient. The surviving nurse, Corazon Amurao, furnished an account of the accused man's arrival on the scene and described the events that led to the murders. There was, however, no eyewitness to the actual killings, of which Speck professed total ignorance. The police had announced that they were satisfied they had the right man.

The scene of the murders was a sedately middle-class neighborhood on the southeast edge of Chicago. On the south side of East 100th Street, between Luella and Crandon avenues, is a block of six simple two-story houses, with pastel-green wooden façades and buff brick walls. Three of the houses were rented by the South Chicago Community Hospital as a residence for 24 of their 115 student nurses. Across Crandon Avenue, on the southeast corner of East 100th, is the red-brick branch office of the National Maritime Union.

As she later told the police, Miss Amurao, a 23-year-old Filipino exchange nurse living at 2319 East 100th, started to get ready for bed at about 10:30 p.m. She and two roommates shared a front bedroom on the second floor. At 11 p.m. the young women heard a knock on the door of the room.

"I opened the door," Miss Amurao said in her statement, "and a man was standing there. The first thing I noticed about him was the strong smell of alcohol."

She described the man as about 25, six feet tall, fair-haired, weighing about 170 pounds. He wore a black jacket, dark trousers and black shoes. According to the police version of her statement, he carried a small black gun in one hand and a knife in the other. He told her, "I'm not goint to hurt you. I'm only going to tie you up. I need your money to go to New Orleans."

Motioning with the gun, he told Miss Amurao and the other two girls to go to a bedroom at the back of the house, where he found three more girls. He made all six lie on the floor. Repeatedly assuring them that he did not want to harm them, he took a sheet from a bunk, methodically tore it into strips and bound each girl.

At 11:30 another nurse, Gloria Davy, returned from a date and was met by the intruder. She was led to the back bedroom and was bound with the others. Half an hour later Suzanne Farris came home with her friend Mary Ann Jordan. They, too, were met by the man and taken to the bedroom. He asked them all where they kept their money, and they gave him what they had.

Of the nine girls lying on the floor, six were senior nursing students and three were exchange nurses from the Phillipines. Only eight of them actually lived in the house. The ninth, Mary Ann Jordan, intended to stay overnight with Suzanne Farris, who was engaged to be married the following spring to Mary Ann's brother, Philip. Mary Ann, 20 years old, lived at home.

Nina Schmale, 24, of Wheaton, Ill., had been a Sunday-school teacher for four years and had worked as a volunteer nurse's aid at the Du Page Convalescent Home before coming to South Chicago Community Hospital. Patricia Matusek, 20, was a local swimming champion and member of a water-ballet team. She was to start work in the Chicago Children's Memorial Hospital when she finished her training in September. Pamela Wilkening, 20, came from Lansing, Ill. Nursing had been her goal since early childhood.

Perhaps the prettiest of the girls was Gloria Davy, a 22-year-old brunette. She had worked for a year as a nurse's aid at Our Lady of Mercy Hospital in her hometown, Dyer, Ind. She was president of the Illinois Student Nurses Association, and planned to join the Peace Corps after finishing her training.

The Filipino girls—Merlita Gargullo, 22, Valentina Pasion, 23, and Corazon Amurao—were all graduates of Manila nursing schools. They had arrived in Chicago two months before for postgraduate training. Now, they and the six American girls lay at the mercy of a stranger, a man who had, as the sole survivor was later to tell the police, "soft eyes, a very gentle appearance."

One by one he took the girls out of the back bedroom. Each gave a muffled cry as she was led from the room, but otherwise, Miss Amurao related, there were no screams, no sounds of violence. At the time, she said, she had no idea of what was happening. During one of his absences from the room, she rolled herself under one of the bunks set against the wall. She lay there, petrified, through the night. At 5 A.M., when the nurses regularly awoke to get ready for the hospital Jeep that picked them up for work, Miss Amurao heard an alarm clock go off in one of the other bedrooms. Apart from that, not a sound. Thinking the man might still be in the house, she lay still for another hour and then wriggled out from under the bed. She freed herself and crept out of the bedroom along the hall to her own room at the front of the house.

As she went from room to room on the second floor she found the bodies of her friends. She smashed the screen of her bedroom window and crawled onto the two-foot-wide ledge that ran along the front of the house, about 10 feet from the ground. There she cowered, screaming for help.

"Help me, help me. Everybody is dead, I am the only one alive on the sampan." In her terror she imagined herself back in the Philippines.

Two houses away, Mrs. Betty Windmiller heard the screaming and rushed to the street where she met a neighbor, Robert Hall, walking his dog. Together they ran to number 2319, where Miss Amurao was crouching on the ledge, screaming, "My friends are all dead, all dead, all dead. I'm the only one alive, oh God, the only one. My friends are all dead." While other neighbors emerged and tried to calm Miss Amurao, Mrs. Windmiller and Mr. Hall called the police.

Daniel Kelly, a policeman who had been cruising through the area in a patrol car, entered the house through the rear door, which he found open. Inside he found Gloria Davy lying naked, face-down on a divan in the downstairs living room. He recognized her as the sister of his former girl friend, Charlene. According to the published portion of Coroner Andrew Toman's autopsy, Miss Davy was strangled by a strip of clothing. She had been sexually assaulted.

The other bodies were upstairs. Patricia Matusek was found in the bathroom, lying on her back. She had been strangled. In the doorway of the front bedroom, through which Miss Amurao had crawled to scream for help, lay Mary Ann Jordan, stabbed in the heart, through her left breast, in the neck and in the left eye. Beside her was Suzanne Farris. She had been stabbed several times in the back, slashed across the neck and chin and finally strangled. Pamela Wilkening was strangled with a strip of sheet and stabbed in the left breast. On the floor of the other front bedroom the body of Valentina Pasion, who had died of stab wounds in the neck, was found lying across that of Merlita Gargullo, who had been strangled and stabbed. Nina Schmale lay on the bed, stabbed in the neck and strangled. Miss Davy was the only one whom police described as having been left completely naked.

More than 30 fingerprints not belonging to the nurses were found by police on the walls, the furniture and the girls' belongings. The only extraneous item reported at the time was a man's sweat-soaked T-shirt, lying on a desk in the living room.

Miss Amurao was taken to a hospital, where she was placed under mild sedation while police interviewed her for two hours. By 8:30 on that Thursday morning the description of the intruder had been circulated to patrol cars touring the neighborhood. Twenty minutes later they learned that a man of that description had left two bags with an attendant at the gas station opposite the National Maritime Union, telling the attendant that he was seeking work there. At the N.M.U. office police learned that a man had been there in the past few days looking for a job aboard a ship to New Orleans. They found his name on an application form: Richard Speck.

Speck had had a number of jobs as a seaman, and his photograph was filed with the U.S. Coast Guard. The police included the picture among 180 others of men with records of sex crimes, to be shown to Miss Amurao at the hospital, but she was in too serious a state of shock to be disturbed. Meanwhile, it was decided to set a trap for Speck by having the N.M.U. offer him a job on a ship going to New Orleans. Detectives combing the area learned from one of his drinking pals that Speck had been staying on the South Side, hopping from tavern to tavern. At 3:10 p.m. Speck telephoned the N.M.U. and was told of the job. The police waited for an hour, but there was no sign of Speck. They traced the telephone call to the Shipyard Inn, a seaman's tavern and lodging house about a mile from the N.M.U. and the nurses' home. When they arrived there, they found that Speck had left just five minutes after making the telephone call, taking a taxi to the North Side.

Speck's trail there led to the skid row section of North Clark Street, where he had danced in a twist lounge with a blonde prostitute named Mary. He paid her three dollars and took her to a room in a cheap Clark Street hotel. Then he moved on.

At 8:15 a.m. Friday, the manager of the Raleigh Hotel on North Dearborn Street telephoned the Near North Side 18th police district to report a Puerto Rican prostitute's complaint that the man she was with had a gun. Two patrolmen went to room 306 and found the man in bed. He said the gun belonged to the girl. He identified himself as Richard Speck and gave as his address the Chicago home of his sister, Mrs. Martha Thornton. The police took the gun and six cartridges,

filed a report, but did not arrest Speck. His description had not yet filtered through to the North Side district stations, and his name was not matched with the man being hunted on the South Side. Speck left the hotel at noon, returned to collect a bundle of laundry and left again at 9:30 p.m., just 15 minutes before the police came rushing back for him.

The police had shown the collection of photographs to Miss Amurao, and she picked out Richard Speck as the man who had invaded the nurses' home. From the files of the Federal Bureau of Investigation in Washington, D.C., it was learned that Speck had a police record in Dallas and that among his identification marks was a tattoo on his left forearm with the words "Born to Raise Hell." His fingerprints arrived from Washington. By 4:30 on Saturday morning the Chicago Police Department's crime laboratory had established to its satisfaction that they matched some of the fingerprints found at 2319 East 100th Street.

At 2:40 p.m. on Saturday, Superintendent Orlando W. Wilson made the following announcement: "The killer of eight nurses from South Chicago Community Hospital on Thursday, July 14, 1966, has been named and a warrant sworn out for his arrest. After a city-wide dragnet· for clues, the murderer was identified as Richard Franklin Speck, white male, twenty-four, a seaman, also known by aliases as Richard Franklin Lindbergh and also Richard Benjamin Speck. Latent fingerprints taken at the scene of the mass killings identified Speck as the killer."

At midnight on Saturday, Richard Speck was lying on an uncovered mattress in room 584 on the fifth floor of the seven-story, 90-cents-a-night Starr Hotel on West Madison Street, in Chicago's sleaziest skid-row area. The room had been booked in the name of "B. Brian." On the bare cement floor beneath the bed lay a newspaper with the headline: POLICE SAY NURSE SURVIVOR CAN IDENTIFY SLAYER OF 8. The paper was soaked with blood that had run from cuts on Speck's wrist and elbow. Weakly, he called out to the man in the next room, George Gregrich, "Come and see me. You got to come and see me. I done something bad."

Gregrich tried to ignore him. "Leave me alone," he said. "You're a hillbilly, you just want to get at me. I don't trust no hillbilly."

Speck persisted. "I'm going to die if you don't come and see me."

Still Gregrich refused, and Speck staggered out of his room, covered with blood, to kick at Gregrich's door. As he did so, two men saw him, and one of them shouted to the elevator operator, "Hey, this guy's bleeding himself to death." The desk clerk was alerted and he called the police.

Suicides are not uncommon on Madison Street, and the two patrolmen who answered the call to this typical flophouse regarded their task as strictly routine. They scarcely glanced at the bleeding man they carried out on a stretcher to Cook County Hospital. At 12:30 a.m. they left him in the hands of Dr. LeRoy Smith, resident physician in the trauma unit of Ward 32.

Dr. Smith looked down at the man thrashing his legs about on the bed. The name tag that the police had put on him read "B. Brian," but Smith thought he saw a resemblance to the picture of Richard Speck that he had seen in the newspapers. Beneath the caked blood on the left forearm the doctor could see the traces of a tattoo. He rubbed away some of the blood to reveal the letter "B." He sent one of the nurses to bring a newspaper. To Smith's eyes the picture seemed to tally, but the nurse saw no resemblance at all. Smith rubbed away some more blood to reveal the letters B O R N. The doctor leaned over the man and asked, "What's your name?"

The man replied faintly: "Richard . . .Richard Speck."

Smith sent for the police.

Speck was weak from loss of blood—Smith estimated one and a half pints—from a nicked brachial artery in the left arm and lacerations of his right wrist. He was given five stitches in the arm and a transfusion of a quart of blood. As he was reviving, Speck looked up at Smith and said, "Do you collect the ten thousand dollar reward?"

After the surgery, the police arrested him and placed him in leg irons. Gasping faintly, "I'm scared. . .I'm scared," Speck was wheeled out of the county hospital and driven in an ambulance to Bridewell prison hospital at four o'clock on Sunday morning.

In his third-floor room at Bridewell, Speck was placed under restraint—held spread-eagled in bed by leather thongs—the normal procedure for potentially suicidal patients. He was too weak on Monday from the loss of blood and prolonged sedation for the police to confront him with Miss Amurao. The next day she stood in the doorway of his room and looked at him. She went out and told a detective: "That is the man." He was kept at Bridewell until he was considered fit, on July 29, to be transferred to Cook County Jail.

From police investigations of Speck's past, Ziporyn knew that his patient was born on the eve of the United States' entry into World War II, December 6, 1941, in Kirkwood, Ill., about 180 miles southwest of Chicago. His father, a potter named Benjamin Speck, moved the family of three sons (one of whom died when Speck was 13) and five daughters to nearby Monmouth shortly after Richard's birth. They stayed in Monmouth until the father died in December, 1947.

Speck then moved with his mother, Mary Margaret, to Dallas, Tex., where she married Carl Lindbergh. Of the time Speck spent at the J.L. Long Junior High School in Dallas, an eighth-grade teacher said, "He seemed sort of lost. It didn't seem like he knew what was going on. I wasn't able to teach him anything. I don't think I ever saw him smile. No one could get through to him. He was a loner. He seemed to be in a fog, sort of sulky. He didn't have any friends in class."

Speck went on to Crozier Technical High School and dropped out after one semester. During his teens in Dallas he ran up a record of 10 arrests for trespassing, burglary and assorted misdemeanors. His police record was a handicap when looking for jobs, and he didn't last long as a laborer, garbage collector, truck driver or carpenter.

In January, 1962, he married a 15-year-old girl, Shirley Malone, when he was 20. They separated in January, 1966, and at their divorce in March she retained custody of their three-year-old daughter, Robbie. His mother told a reporter that the couple had both been hot-tempered and had fought throughout the marriage.

One of his sisters, Mrs. Carolyn Wilson, commented that Speck had been devoted to his daughter. "He took that little girl everywhere with him," she said. "He loved that baby so much—in fact, he loved all little children, but he loved that child."

Just four months before the murders, Speck returned to Monmouth. The local police chief said he was arrested in March on a charge of disorderly conduct after a knife fight in Gulfport, 30 miles from Monmouth. He had stayed with some old friends of the Speck family and spent most of his time bar-hopping around

town. At one of his favorite taverns, a fellow drinker later recalled: "He showed me a picture of a real nice-looking gal. He said she was his wife, and he was going back to Texas and kill her if it was the last thing he ever did."

He left Monmouth and found work in Michigan aboard a Great Lakes ore boat, working the waters of Keweenaw Bay, an inlet of Lake Superior. Stricken with appendicitis, he was rushed to St. Joseph's Hospital in Hancock, Mich., for an emergency operation. In May, while convalescing from his appendectomy, Speck befriended a 28-year-old nurse, Judy Laakaniemi. They went to dances together and took long walks along the beaches. She later described him as "quiet and gentle" at that time, but added that when he returned to see her toward the end of June, "he had a hatred in him." He was fired from an Inland Steel Company ship, the *Randall,* for quarreling with an officer.

He came to Chicago at the beginning of July, seeking the help of his sister, Mrs. Martha Thornton, and her husband. On Sunday, July 10, they drove him to the N.M.U. hiring hall, gave him $25 and left. For three days he tried without success to get work on a ship going to New Orleans.

On Tuesday, July 26, 1966, a grand jury indicted Richard Speck for the eight murders.

Amid tight security arrangements, Speck was arraigned on August 1.

Public Defender Gerald W. Getty was appointed Speck's defense counsel, and on Speck's behalf entered pleas of not guilty to each of the indictments. The case was then assigned to Judge Herbert C. Paschen.

Getty told reporters after the arraignment that his client had been "confused and bewildered."

Speck's attitude of resignation and apathy continued at Ziporyn's second session with him, the afternoon following the court hearing. The only subject on which Speck spoke strongly was his distaste for the hospital ward. Herman Bernette, the prisoner who had vowed to kill Speck when he first arrived in Ward 1, was repeating his threat every day with growing vehemence.

"That guy bugs me," said Speck. "I want out of here. Why don't they put me in the isolation block?"

Ziporyn let him vent his irritation and then brought him back to their conversation of three days ago.

"Do you remember how you said you often got into a real bad temper after a few drinks, a temper that made you violent? Is that what happened on the night the nurses were killed?"

"I don't know," Speck replied. His manner was glum.

"Let's suppose it was," Ziporyn said, probing. "What do you think the girls did to provoke your temper? What do you think made you do it?"

Suddenly Speck flared up angrily. "Me? I like girls—I wouldn't hurt *women*. Anyway, I don't remember a thing about that night. I never knew those girls."

He was becoming more and more morose and hostile, and Ziporyn saw little point in continuing the interview. He cut it short and prepared to leave. Speck leaned forward and gripped his arm as he rose. "Get me out of here, Doc, will you?" he said. "Out of this hospital, I mean, not the jail." For the first time the psychiatrist noticed Speck's hands as they held his arm. They were huge, powerful, with long fingers—a carpenter's hands, the psychiatrist thought.

By the time of his next session with Ziporyn, Speck had recovered sufficiently from his suicide attempt to be moved to the three-cell isolation tier, the maximum-security section of the Cook County Jail. Speck occupied the middle cell, flanked by Louis Stamos, better known as Tony Gambrino, and by Mark Clancy, both in for armed robbery and placed in the isolation tier because of two escape attempts. Next door to the tier was the execution chamber containing an electric chair.

Speck's cell was 10 feet by 10 feet by 12 feet, painted dark green. The only furniture was a low steel-spring bed covered with white sheets, a dark gray blanket and two pillows. An around-the-clock guard insured that Speck would not hang himself.

Despite the grimness of the cell, Speck appeared relieved and cheerful now that he had left the hospital. He greeted Ziporyn amiably from his bed. "Hi, Doc. How're you doing?"

Speck offered Ziporyn a cigarette and part of a candy bar. His sister, Mrs. Thornton, was sending him $10 a week with which he was able to buy coffee—he preferred Sanka—and cigarettes and candy from the jail commissary.

Speck walked over to a pipe-shelf arrangement above a radiator where he had neatly stacked his mail. He was receiving an average of three letters a day, in addition to a lot of "crank" mail which Warden Johnson confiscated. Speck showed the letters, with some pride, to Ziporyn.

"See what I got?" he said, waving them and grinning broadly.

Most of the letters were from religious people who quoted comforting or admonishing passages from the Bible and urged him to turn to Jesus. One of the tenderest notes was anonymous. In spidery printed letters it said:

Dear Richard,

Just a few lines to let you know how I feel about what has happened to you. I wish I could see you in person—but since I live in Connecticut that is pretty impossible. I wish I could let you know face to face that *if* you did what they blame you for—I can't believe you knew what you were doing. I'm with you—I'm not against you, and I hope God is with you. I pray every day and night that things will turn alright and the best for you. *If* you are guilty—it's not you that is to blame—I can't believe it was something you had intentions of doing. . . .

So Long for now,
A friend you don't even know.

Speck complained to Ziporyn of headaches and dizziness, then drifted off into silence, and Ziporyn left.

On the next visit Speck was eager to take a look at his own personality. "I want to know everything you can tell me about myself," Speck told Ziporyn. "I want you to see my family. I want you to learn all you can and explain all this." Tears welled up in his eyes as he told Ziporyn once more, "If they don't pull the switch, I'll find a way to do it myself. I can't live with my conscience—could you?"

For a moment he brightened. "You know, Doc," he said, "I like you. Say, have a cup of coffee.

He called the guard over to the cell to get a cup for the psychiatrist. Carefully he poured out the instant coffee, using hot water from the tap in the cell, and handed it to Ziporyn, grinning through still moist eyes. Speck showed the doctor some religious tracts that had been sent to him.

Ziporyn noticed that Speck was squinting as he tried to read the text and asked him if he needed glasses.

"Yeah," Speck replied, looking at Ziporyn somewhat sheepishly. "I used to have a pair, but I threw 'em away. I don't like wearing glasses."

This note of vanity, which was to become more and more pronounced as Ziporyn probed into Speck's behavior, struck the psychiatrist as entirely in keeping with the prisoner's fastidiousness in tending his cell. (In the hotel room where Speck had tried to commit suicide, police found among his toilet things some Old Spice After Shave and Max Factor eau de cologne.) At the same time, Speck's poor eyesight offered a possible explanation for why he read so badly, since Ziporyn was beginning to suspect that he was considerably more alert than his lack of reading skill would suggest.

On Thursday, August 18, Speck returned to court to hear his attorney, Gerald Getty, ask that eight mental experts be appointed to examine the accused man. The panel of experts would be asked to report, first, on Speck's sanity at the time of the eight killings and, second, on whether he was now mentally fit to cooperate with his counsel and stand trial. (It was not intended that the resident jail psychiatrist, Dr. Ziporyn, be included on the panel.)

Back in his cell the next day, Speck talked to Ziporyn as he had never talked before. He was depressed and pale, but quickly explained that this was because of his headaches.

About the previous day's court hearing, Speck said, "I didn't understand a thing that was happening." When Ziporyn explained Getty's petitions, Speck said dryly, "I ain't gonna plead crazy." When the psychiatrist explained that a successful plea of insanity could save him from the death sentence, Speck said, "I'll never see the chair."

They talked of headaches and head injuries, going over the childhood accidents again. Speck recalled when the headaches began.

"I was fighting this kid," he said. "It was in Dallas. I was sixteen. I had him on the ground, really giving it to him, and a cop came to break it up. He broke it up, OK—cracked my head with his club till he knocked me clean out. A year after that the headaches started. Man, those cops are brutal, real animals. They gave me a real hard time."

He paused a moment, as if waiting for a comment from Ziporyn, but none came and he went on, "I was always getting into fights. Hit my stepfather once, round about when I was eighteen. Man, did I hate him. Lindbergh, his name was. Mine, too, till I got married and changed it back. One of his legs, the right one, was cut off half way, after a car accident. So he had crutches. Thought I'd never hit him 'cause of those crutches. Just went on needling me. He was drunk. I was too, I think. Anyway, he came at me with one of those crutches and I hit him. Then he said he'd had enough and was gonna leave. I told him 'Fine' and threw him out and his clothes and things after him. I think my mother was glad to see him go. He came back a year later, but then left again, for good."

Ziporyn asked him whether he had ever struck his mother.

Speck looked shocked. "No, I would never hit her. I did hit my wife, Shirley, once. She was acting too friendly with some guy. Another time I got hold of a guy in a washroom, in Dallas. I thought he'd been hanging around Shirley. I beat him up. I was mad."

He talked of his rages. "I got mad at just about anything. When I was a kid, just a teen-ager, in East Dallas, I was with some guys and we got some red birds. Whew, they made me wild. We were watching a parade once, and we had some blockbusters [white barbiturate pills with a yellow stripe]. I just passed out, and they took me to a juvenile home. I don't remember exactly what happened after that, but I've been told that when my mother came to get me she says I was talking nice and polite, then suddenly I went wild. Started swinging and kicking at everybody. But I

don't remember a thing about it myself.

"Hey, would you go see my sister Martha for me? Write a note for me to her, and I'll sign it so as she'll talk to you about me."

Ziporyn agreed, then turned the conversation. "Let's go over the murders again," the psychiatrist said, "and what Corazon Amurao said about it. You know, she's the one that survived."

Speck nodded and said in a soft voice, "I'm glad she did." He stared earnestly at Ziporyn.

"Now," Ziporyn continued, "she says you came in the back door, came up to her room and awoke her. Then she says you. . .or rather, let's say 'the killer'. . ."

In the same soft voice, Speck interrupted the psychiatrist: "Let's just say it was me."

Ziporyn resumed the narrative. Then suddenly Speck launched into a monologue. It was the first time Speck had ever given Ziporyn a detailed version of what he remembered of his activities around the time of the murders.

"I'd been on an ore boat, and the hiring hall got me this job on a ship in Indiana. One of the sailors drove out there with me in a truck. I was on board maybe thirty minutes when they told me it was all a mix-up—somebody else had the job. So I came back to Chicago. I didn't have no room, didn't have enough money to get one either—just a few dollars. This was Tuesday. I asked a guy in a filling station if I could leave my bags there. Then I went to a beer joint about a block away and called my sister, I told her what happened, told her I was broke. She said she'd help.

"Near the bar there was an apartment house they were working on. It was raining hard. I went into the basement, wrapped something round my shoes for a pillow, and went to sleep.

"Next morning I went to get my bags,

but the gas station wasn't open yet, so I went across the street and had a Royal Crown. Back at the hiring hall they told me there was a job on an ocean boat. That sounded good, and I told 'em I wanted it. You know, I love being a sailor. That's something makes me feel good. But they told me the job wasn't till the next Monday. I played a game of Hearts at one of the tables there, and my brother-in-law came in and gave me twenty-five dollars.

"I went off and got a room at the Shipyard Inn and started playing some pool. I'm a real good pool player. I won ten, eleven dollars. I had a big knife, really it was a dagger, like a bayonet. Anyway, I made another buck from that, sold it to some guy. I pepped myself up on a few red-birds, six of them, and took a walk by one of the little lakes out there, then went back to the bar for a drink. I had some whiskey and a pint of wine and got talking to these sailors, like I told you before. They took me to their room. It was dark. They had this disposable syringe and took this stuff from a bottle and started 'popping.' I tied a handkerchief around my left arm and stuck it in. All the way. Before I had even got the needle out I could feel, you know, feel— Zzzoommm—a buzzing all over me, and I was feeling real, real good.

"The next thing I know I was back in my own room and it was morning. I had a gun, and I don't know where I got it. I just sat there wondering where the hell I got that gun."

Ziporyn asked whether he had noticed any blood on his clothes that morning.

"No, I had on black Ivy Leagues and a new black shirt with white buttons. Everything was clean."

Speck stopped suddenly, stared at Ziporyn for a moment, and then turned his face to the wall as he lay there on his bed. Softly he said, "I'm going to tell you something."

Not a sound in the cell for another minute. Speck slowly turned around to face the psychiatrist again and said, "There was blood on my right hand that morning. I didn't really see it or know what it was till I put my hand in the water and the water turned red. I thought I'd cut myself."

This observation was parenthetical in the narrative which he then calmly resumed. He did not seem to realize that he had just volunteered the most damning circumstantial evidence, which need never have been revealed to anyone. This revelation, more than anything else, dispelled any doubts Ziporyn might have had about Speck's story.

Speck continued, "I went back to the bar at the Shipyard Inn for some more wine. I still couldn't make out how I got that goddamn gun. It bugged me. While I was there a detective came in and asked the bartender some questions. It didn't bother me. I didn't know why he was there. In the afternoon I heard them talking about the murders on the radio. I remember saying to the guy next to me at the bar, 'I hope they catch the son of a bitch.'

"I moved on to a few other bars in the neighborhood, and all day long the police were coming in and out, asking questions. I was wanted for a burglary in Dallas, and the cops were beginning to worry me. So I beat it up to the North Side. . .I played some more pool. I won a few more bucks. I checked into the Raleigh Hotel and went out again to pick up a prostitute. She stripped to her panties and we just sat in my room drinking. We had a fight about money, and I went to sleep. She called the cops, and they came and took the gun.

"The next day I saw the police picture of the killer in the papers. It didn't look nothing like me so I didn't know it was me, because of that flat top. My hair was never that short.

"It was Saturday afternoon when I first heard that it was me they were looking for. I couldn't believe it at first."

Ziporyn returned to earlier events, before Speck's arrival in Chicago. "When you went back to Monmouth, what did you do there?" Ziporyn asked. "The police there are saying they'd like to talk to you about a rape case."

"I'm no rape-o," Speck said indignantly, adding with a sly smile. "I don't have to be. But I'd sure like to know what made me kill those girls. Why would I do a thing like that?"

"Well," Ziporyn began, hesitantly. "As a psychiatrist I might suggest you were working out some kind of hostility, anger, that you felt at your mother for marrying your stepfather."

"But I love my mother," said Speck.

"That's the whole point. You love her and maybe you're angry at her for betraying that love. At least, that's how you may feel unconsciously, without realizing it, I mean."

"That doesn't make sense," Speck replied. "What's that got to do with those girls? Why should I kill them?"

Ziporyn explained how Speck's attitude toward his mother could work on his unconscious and be transferred to women in general. Speck nodded doubtfully. Ziporyn added that Speck was probably so heavily influenced by the drugs and alcohol he had taken earlier in the day that he could not be held responsible for the acts of that night.

"We could even say you didn't kill them, it was—"

Speck cut in: "It was me, all right."

Ziporyn paid a visit on August 22 to Speck's sister, Mrs. Martha Thornton, living in an apartment building in Chicago. She refused to talk to him.

"That doesn't sound like Martha,"

Speck muttered when Ziporyn told him, later that day, what had happened. "Man, I'm really nothing but trouble. All I've done is hurt my family, shame them. The best thing I could do for them is die. You wanna know something, Doc? That special lock they put on my cell, 'cause Clancy next door is an escape artist? Well, you couldn't chase me out of here. I wouldn't want to be outside—I'm afraid of myself."

The psychiatrist explained that there might be real value in Speck's trying to understand for himself what made him the way he was.

Ziporyn said, "The bumps, beers and red-birds make a different person out of you. Without the alcohol or the drugs, you're Doctor Jekyll, the normal man. With them, you turn into Mr. Hyde, the monster."

"You may be right," Speck replied. "But not beer, though. Beer makes me feel good. Whiskey makes me wild. When I'm on that I can do some terrible things.

"Last year I was in Dallas, and I had a few drinks and some 'drivers,' you know—pep pills. Anyway, I was talking to this guy, I think he was queer. Suddenly everything blacked out. Next thing I knew, the guy was on the ground, covered with blood, and I was battering at him with a tire handle. My buddy pulled me off."

Four days later Ziporyn returned to find Speck cheerful, even lighthearted. Ziporyn had learned not to expect his patient to sustain a mood for any great length of time. He recalled that Miss Amurao had said the intruder had been quite gentle at first.

Speck seemed pleased when Ziporyn told him his attorney would be visiting him before the next court hearing which was to decide whether a panel of psychiatrists and psychologists would be appointed to examine Speck.

Ziporyn recalled the drunken fight Speck had with his stepfather and again asked him whether he had ever hit his mother while he was drunk.

Indignation seized him again as he replied, "I wouldn't lay a finger on my mother. I took good care of that. She'd yell at me if I was drinking. I knew how I got when I was drunk, and I didn't want any trouble with her, so if I drank too much I stayed away from home. It was safer that way. I was always trouble at home, even when I was a little kid.

"By the way," he said, "you didn't see this yet." He handed Ziporyn a letter, smirking with a certain smugness as the psychiatrist read it aloud. It was from a 19-year-old college girl named Susan. "Dear Richard," she wrote. "Ever since I read about you in the paper I've followed the day by day news. When I saw you were sick I nearly died. I want you to know there is someone who cares. . ."

"Ain't that something?" Speck said. Ziporyn grinned appreciatively.

Speck was still in good spirits at the next visit on August 29. Ziporyn explained that the psychiatric panel, if approved, would test Speck's I.Q.

"I know all about I.Q.'s," said Speck, grinning. "I got a low one. They tested it twice when I was in prison, for jobs, and I couldn't pass. So they sent me out in the forest, cutting wood. I wasn't too bad in prison. Only got into one fight—over a game of dominoes.

"While I was in prison I heard my wife was running around. When I got out I got me a sawed-off shotgun and went round to his house—I made Shirley give me the guy's name, told her I'd kill her if she didn't tell. I talked to his wife—he wasn't home. I waited in my car. I watched three or four kids playing around the house. When he came, I shoved the gun in his face, but I couldn't do it, not with that family. Wonder what kind of guy he was. "Once I thought I saw Shirley driving

into a motel. Then another car drove in. I went and got a pistol, then came back and kicked the door down. There was nobody there. Last year she left me for good. She said she had another guy. When she told me that, I went out and got drunk and smashed my car into a tree. Then I saw her in a tavern with a guy. I tried to get her to come home with me, but she wouldn't. I knocked 'em both down and left.

"You know," he added, suddenly weary. "The Bible says not to hate, but if there's anybody I hate in this world—besides that stepfather—it's Shirley, and that's the truth."

On September 2, Ziporyn called on Speck in the afternoon.

Speck told him: "Saw my sister yesterday. In the visiting room. She wants to see you. She wants to talk to you."

"Why?" Ziporyn asked.

Speck shrugged. "Dunno. It was her idea. *She* wants to see you."

Ziporyn told Speck that Getty was talking about having the trial moved out of Chicago.

"I don't see it'll make much difference." Speck said casually.

Speck offered Ziporyn some coffee. He was still obsessed with the idea that his isolation from the rest of the world left him with no reason to go on living. Ziporyn reminded him of the letters he was receiving as proof that some people did care about him.

"Well," said Speck, after a short silence, "maybe not everyone hates me, but I sure hate my old lady."

Ziporyn was a little taken aback by the suddenness of this comment. There was no indication of what had stimulated it. "You mean your wife, Shirley?"

"Right. There's a guard here nights who reminds me of her. His name is Malone, like hers was. I hate that woman, I really do."

The next week Ziporyn paid his

second visit to Speck's sister. The apartment was small and clean, with neatly arranged furniture. The colors in the living room were drab except for a few small religious pictures on the wall. The windows overlooked the tracks of the Chicago & North Western railroad.

Mrs. Martha Thornton, a dark-haired woman in her early 40's, was calm, though her face was drawn. Ziporyn asked her about Speck's childhood.

"Richard was very close to Dad. He was the apple of his father's eye," she said. "He used to follow Dad around like a shadow." She did not see much of him after they moved to Dallas, but, she said, the member of the family he was closest to in Dallas was his sister Carolyn, two years younger than he.

"He was always getting into fights with his stepfather," she added. "Richard couldn't bear that man, but then none of us liked him much. He was always getting drunk. He was supposed to be in the insurance business, but he had a mind like a three-year-old."

She confirmed Speck's long history of headaches. "He was always asking for aspirins when he was here. I think part of the reason for those headaches was because he wouldn't wear glasses. He's a bit of a dandy, a very neat and clean person, used to shower three or four times a day when he visited us this summer."

"Yes," said Ziporyn. "Dick does seem very conscious of his appearance."

"You mustn't call him Dick. He doesn't like that. He prefers Richard," she said with a smile. She went on. "I think he enjoyed visiting us. He liked my two little daughters. He used to play cards with them, talk to them, tell them all sorts of things he would never tell anyone else. For instance, he told them about his bad drinking habits, and the effects it had on him, and the drugs he took. Always liked those kids. Of course,

he adored his own child too. When he was staying with us in July—just before it happened—he was walking around the neighborhood and saw a kid that reminded him of his own little girl. He tried to find her again but couldn't, and came home and told us about it."

Mrs. Thornton smiled for a brief moment, but then added grimly, "At the same time, he was very depressed. He was fed up with not being able to get a job. It depressed him a lot. He kept on saying how the world wasn't worth anything and he'd be better off dead, and that was two weeks before the murders."

Ziporyn nodded. "Yes, what about the murders. Any ideas?"

Mrs. Thornton thought for a moment and said, "Well, we've discussed this thing in the family over and over. We've read all the reports. Carolyn—like I said, she was always the one who was closest to Richard—she won't believe he did it."

On September 9 Judge Paschen approved Getty's request for a panel to examine Speck's mental condition. State and county mental-health experts would interview Speck and report back to the court on his competence to stand trial.

Ziporyn visited Speck the same day to tell him of the conversation with his sister. They discussed her memories of him. Speck protested vehemently at his sister's theory that his headaches came from his not wearing glasses.

"She's wrong," he said. "Sure I get eye headaches, but they come right here behind the eyes. The headaches that really bother me are the ones at the back of my head."

He was in full agreement, however, that his sister Carolyn, now living in Dallas, and he were very close as children. "Remember I told you how I fell out of a tree onto my head? Well, it was Carolyn who found me knocked out. She was hysterical about it."

Ziporyn let the conversation drift on a

while and then stopped to take some papers from his briefcase. "I've got something to show you," he said. "Ever see this before?"

Speck leaned forward and saw that Ziporyn was holding up two pages from *Time* magazine, an account of the murder of the nurses. Speck studied a diagram of the nurses' home that showed the rooms where the murders were committed.

Nodding his head slowly, he said, "Looks like a new type of house. Look at that stairway; it's set right back from the door, the way they have it in modern places."

He turned the page over and looked at a picture of Corazon Amurao. "She sure is beautiful," he said. "What a beautiful girl." At the top of the page the photographs of the dead nurses had been cut out. "How come you cut something out here?" Speck asked.

"I'll show you," Ziporyn replied. He took the eight photographs, each cut out separately, from his briefcase and handed them, one by one, to Speck.

Speck had not seen all the press accounts immediately following the murders. This was the first time he had been confronted with pictures of the girls since he was brought to the jail. He stared at the first one, Mary Ann Jordan, for about half a minute, completely absorbed. He reached for the next, Suzanne Farris, shaking his head slowly, painfully slowly, from side to side and murmuring in a scarcely audible whisper, "They're so young, so pretty. Look at them, real pretty things, aren't they?"

Ziporyn slipped the third into his hand—Patricia Matusek. "Say, she's good-looking," Speck commented with an appreciative nod. "Looks like Elizabeth Taylor."

The psychiatrist made no comment and held out the fourth to him—Gloria Davy. Speck reached for it and suddenly froze. He drew his hand back from the picture as if it might sting him. His eyes opened wide, his lips quivered slightly. He looked terrified. Ziporyn offered the picture to him again. He reached forward and gingerly took the tiny photograph with both hands. He placed it in the palm of one hand, like some poisonous insect, and as he stared at it, a rush of whistled air escaped through his lips.

"You know what?" he said, looking up from the picture to Ziporyn with a stunned, distant gaze. "This is a dead ringer for Shirley."

***

Richard Speck was in an exuberant mood. He greeted Dr. Marvin Ziporyn, the psychiatrist who had been interviewing him for several weeks, with an expansive wave toward the wall of his cell in Cook County Jail in Chicago.

"See my diploma?" Speck said, smiling broadly. "That's the first thing I ever passed."

The diploma certified that Richard Speck had passed the Emmaus Bible School Correspondence Course. Speck muttered over and over again: "First thing I ever passed, first goddam thing I ever passed. Ain't that something? I tell you, I was dumb when I was in school, but dumb. First thing I ever passed."

When Speck had raised his left arm to point to the diploma, the psychiatrist noticed the tattoo just below the elbow—BORN TO RAISE HELL. A description of this tattoo had been used by the police in their bulletins when Speck was being sought for the murder of eight young nurses. The last word of the slogan was barely visible, and Ziporyn asked the prisoner about it.

"To tell you the truth, Doc," said Speck, after some hesitation. "I was trying to burn it out of my arm when I was in jail in Texas."

"Why did you do that?" Ziporyn asked.

"I guess I was ashamed of it or something." Speck replied. "I mean, it's not a nice thing to have on your arm, is it?"

Ziporyn asked him how he got the tattoo.

"I was maybe nineteen, and with this bunch of kids," Speck recalled. "We was in Dallas, and we all went to this tattooer together. We all had something different—a skull, a heart, a girl's name—I couldn't think of nothing to have on my arm, so I asked the tattooer if he had any ideas. He suggested all kinds of things, slogans and stuff, and one of them was 'Born to Raise Hell.' That sounded kinda good, so I let him put that. Didn't mean anything special to me. I mean, what does something like that mean? Not much, does it? Never thought about it."

Speck's arms were a mass of tattoos. He rolled up his sleeve and pointed to one above his right elbow: RICHARD AND SHIRLEY. He had tried to burn that out, too, but without success. Shirley was his former wife, whom he hated.

"I've been trying to wipe her out of my mind," Speck told the psychiatrist. "But it's not easy. I was ready to settle down when I got out of prison in Texas, but Shirley wasn't ready. Hope she's satisfied now."

Speck showed Ziporyn the other tattoos he had acquired during a life as a wandering seaman, in and out of various jails. Etched at the top of his right arm was ROBBIE LYNN, for his daughter. Below that, less distinct, were the initials R.L., which he said stood for Richard Lindbergh. This was his stepfather's surname, which Speck had used until his marriage. This, too, he had tried to erase. Below the right elbow was a long dagger with a snake coiled around it.

On the little finger of his right hand was the solitary letter L. "I started to have 'Love' and 'Hate' on my knuckles," he explained, "but I stopped. See, at least I could hide the others under a long-sleeved shirt, but on the

hands it would show too much."

On the back of his left wrist was the initial R. for Richard. Above that was BORN TO RAISE HELL, and above the left elbow a grinning skull with a World War I aviator's helmet.

Nor was that all. "There's one more tattoo that you haven't seen yet," Speck told Ziporyn as he rolled up the left leg of his trousers. He revealed an obscene picture crudely tattooed on his shin.

"Why did you have all these tattoos put on your arms and leg like this? What's it for?" the psychiatrist asked.

"Aw, nothing special," Speck replied diffidently. "All the guys was doing it, so I went along. Doesn't mean nothing to me. It was just the thing to do."

It was now the fall of 1966. On the night of July 13, an intruder carrying a gun and a knife had entered a nurses' home in a quiet neighborhood in southeast Chicago, gathered nine nurses into a bedroom and bound them, then removed them, one by one, to other parts of the house, where he murdered eight of them, savagely stabbing, cutting and strangling. The nurses made no outcry. One nurse, Corazon Amurao, 23, rolled under a bunk and survived, apparently overlooked.

Chicago police found that Richard Speck, a 24-year-old drifter from Dallas, had been in the neighborhood at the National Maritime Union branch hiring hall, seeking work. Fingerprints found in the nurses' home matched Speck's. The police got a photograph of him, which Miss Amurao identified. Speck, hearing he was being sought, had tried to kill himself in a skid-row hotel, cutting his arms. He was taken into custody in a hospital.

Ziporyn, who had been assigned to determine whether Speck was still suicidal, saw the prisoner on his twice-weekly visits to the Cook County Jail, and slowly a warm relationship developed. Speck traced his life for the psychiatrist, revealing a long history of head injuries, wild drinking and drug-taking which led to violent brawls, about which he said he later remembered nothing.

Of the night of the murders, Speck told Ziporyn, he remembered taking barbiturates, and drinking with some sailors with whom he injected some form of drug, and that his next memory was of waking up the next morning with a gun, wondering where he got it. Speck confided to Ziporyn that he had found blood on one hand when he awoke. Speck accepted the accusation of the surviving nurse, but insisted that he remembered nothing.

Speck was indicted for eight murders. The case was assigned to Judge Herbert C. Paschen. Public Defender Gerald W. Getty, appointed as Speck's defense counsel, obtained the appointment of a panel of six doctors, five of them psychiatrists, to examine Speck and determine whether he was competent to stand trial.

Speck's interviews with the panel had begun in earnest, and Speck was bewildered and at times exasperated by the persistence of their probing into the same areas of his behavior, his past, his activities on the day and night of the murders.

His bitterest complaints were reserved for a doctor whose Freudian orientation was more than Speck could bear. "That guy sure bugs me," he said. "He kept asking me whether I like sex books. That's all he could talk about, sex. I tell you, there's something wrong with him. He should be examined or something."

By contrast, Speck seemed to have enjoyed his interviews with another doctor. "He told me how I got that gun. Remember, I couldn't figure how I got hold of it? Well, he says I got it from some whore. I remember her now. Met

her when I was with the sailors—you know, when I took those shots. Real ugly broad. I sure hope they don't bring her into court as a witness or something. I'd be ashamed for people to know I associated with something like that. I mean, she's real ugly—long hair all over her face."

He now remembered that the woman appeared after the sailors had left him on the night of the murders, but the rest was still blackness.

Returning to the examining panel, Speck said, "I don't bother to tell them much. What's the point?" he said. "But I'll tell you something I haven't told them. I have a split personality. My mother knows all about that. You see, when I'm sober, I'm. . .I'm. . .I'm—well, OK, but when I drink, I'll tell you. Once I smashed my hand through a wall rather than hit her."

The anger on Speck's face, his narrow eyes and his rising voice as he recalled the behavior of the "ugly broad," had reminded Ziporyn of the prisoner's reaction to memories of his wife and stepfather. The psychiatrist sensed that there was a link. As Speck had already said, his stepfather and his wife were the two great hatreds of his life. They were both a manifestation of woman's betrayal: Shirley because he suspected she "ran around" with other men, and the stepfather, Carl Lindbergh, as the cause of his mother's betrayal of him, replacing both his father and him in her affections. From this dual disillusionment Speck seemed to have developed an all-pervading suspicion of women, particularly in his sexual relations with them. It was Speck's experience that women gave their affections to men too easily and too freely. He reacted negatively even when he was the object of those affections.

The psychiatrist left the cell. As the guard closed the cell door, Ziporyn noticed a rolled newspaper emerging through the bars, hovering over the guard's desk and suddenly flicking the guard's cap to the floor. The newspaper disappeared back into the cell, and Speck appeared at the bars, grinning like an impudent schoolboy.

Speck was taken to Bridewell hospital for tests on September 29. Returning to the jail that night in a high state of tension, he assaulted a fellow prisoner. Speck later related the incident to Ziporyn: "We were in the reception area, and I noticed one of the guards had a gray hair on his shoulder. I kidded him about going around with old broads. The guard said old broads are sometimes still good, and I said, 'Yeah, nine to ninety, old ones, young ones, crippled ones.' Then this smart-ass next to me opened his big mouth and said, 'Dead ones?' So I swung at him know what I mean?" Speck waited for some kind of endorsement from the psychiatrist but did not seem perturbed when Ziporyn did not respond.

As Ziporyn approached Speck's cell on his next visit, the sergeant on duty said, "Your boy is getting mean. He threw hot water at me last night."

Ziporyn nodded but made no comment. These incidents of violent behavior were becoming more frequent. "I'm sick of it, Doc," Speck shouted. "I've had it up to here, all this stuff. I wish they'd kill me and get it over with. I'm sick of being a freak. Did you see today's paper? There's another story about me. Every day they write about me. Doc, you know I've got a temper—well, I'm just about cracking and you know what I'm like when I get these tempers. Once, I even kicked my mother in the head—of course, I was on pills, but still. . . ."

His voice tapered off into silence. Ziporyn stared at him, waiting. In every previous interview Speck had reacted violently whenever it was suggested that he might have attacked his mother in one of his tempers. Now, though it was not certain that he was telling the truth, with his defenses suddenly down, he was saying that he had struck her, and violently.

Ziporyn asked him, "Did you know what was happening at the time that you kicked your mother?"

"Nope," Speck replied. He was not interested in pursuing the subject. "Anyway," he went on. "now I'm going after everybody, and the trouble is I know they're right and I'm wrong. I tell you, I'm cracking."

Ziporyn nodded and said he would get him some tranquilizers.

On October 10, Speck seemed more cheerful. He greeted Ziporyn effusively, bustling about the cell to make coffee.

Speck recalled that he had been a carpenter. "Liked it too. I was a good carpenter—till I got fired. I was working as a carpenter, and one of the guys I worked with was jailed for being drunk and disorderly. His wife had to go out of town a ways to raise bail money for him. I went with her. On the road we had us a few beers and a few more beers, and we finished up in this motel. She got me mad, the way she was behaving, it was disgusting, and I told her she was nothing but an old whore. First chance I got I lifted a hundred bucks from her."

The pattern of Speck's contempt for women was now well established. Ziporyn pointed this out to him and suggested a parallel between his anger at his friend's wife and at his own wife.

They talked again of the murders, his moods, his angers, their possible interrelation. Speck was alert and curious about the implications. "Could this mean that if I can't control myself when I'm angry and go wild, that I don't know what I'm doing and that's what happened?" Ziporyn said this was possible and quoted Plato's observation that the wild beast is in all of us.

On October 17, exactly three months after Speck's arrest, Ziporyn brought him a transistor radio. Speck tuned in a station. WJJD, playing the twanging strains of *Silver Dagger*, and slumped into a blissful daze.

They talked of a murderer who had told Speck he had nightmares in which his victim spoke to him. "Do you believe that?" Speck asked Ziporyn.

"It happens. For that matter," the psychiatrist said evenly, "a lot of people don't believe you when you say you don't remember the murders. They say you're lying to me, trying to cop a plea."

"Listen," said Speck in a low, solemn voice, "I didn't kill those girls for fun, I'll tell you that. I don't know why I killed them."

"Do you ever think about that night?"

"Naw, it's all gone. I only think about it when people ask me questions."

Speck was on the defensive. He was constantly reminding himself of the horror of the crimes he was accused of committing. Yet when he was in public—in his court appearances—he appeared cool, even carefree. This defense mechanism is very common in the type of obsessive-compulsive individual that Ziporyn considered Speck to be, and its appearance now tended to confirm the psychiatrist's interpretation.

Assuming convincing evidence of such personality, the murder of the eight nurses—if it was Speck who did it—could be explained as follows:

With the rigid and sadistic tendencies of an anal personality, Speck developed a specific hostility toward women when his mother remarried, and later when he feared that his wife was unfaithful to him. This hostility cannot be controlled when his inhibitions are low. Successive traumas have caused brain damage, which

makes his emotional control difficult at any time. Under the influence of whiskey and drugs— which he takes to relieve the headaches created by the brain damage—his tenuous control breaks completely and his hostility is left raw at the surface. This was his condition on the night of the murders. The hostility might still have been contained had there not been a trigger. This could have been provided by the resemblance between his wife and Gloria Davy, the only one of the murdered nurses who had been sexually assaulted.

On the next visit Speck handed the psychiatrist some coffee already prepared for his arrival. The "sessions" had by now taken on the character of a *Kaffeeklatsch,* though the easygoing atmosphere often belied the tensions underneath.

Speck lit a cigarette, deftly bending a match double and striking it in one movement between the thumb and forefinger of his right hand. Again Ziporyn was struck by the size and grace of Speck's fingers.

"You have great hands," the psychiatrist said. "You could have been a fine craftsman."

Speck stared at Ziporyn, searching his face for signs of irony. "Are you kidding? Still, I guess I could have been a lot of things." He sounded bitter now. "I should have seen a doctor when I was eighteen, when I beat the hell out of my mother."

"When was that?"

"I told you about it—when they took me to that juvenile home, and my mother came to get me. They say I was just sitting there, talking quietly, and then I went wild—beat my mother up. They had to flatten me out." Speck had given Ziporyn one version of this incident, had recounted how, after taking some drugs with his friends, he had gone wild, but he had never mentioned that it was his mother he had attacked. This, then, was the second instance of his having hit his mother. His insistence that he would never do such a thing was now forgotten, his indignation at such a suggestion replaced by the same remorse that he felt every time he acted out his savage impulses. The psychiatrist tried once more to explain that surrendering to impulse was not the same as taking deliberate action.

"Yeah—like those girls. I sure didn't do that for kicks. I don't know why I did it. I still don't remember anything about it, but I sure as hell wonder about it a lot, like *how* it happened. Why didn't one of them yell or scream or something? Seems like one of them would."

A razor blade suddenly flashed between Speck's fingers, Ziporyn had no idea how he had obtained it. Speck leaned toward Ziporyn, holding the blade just a few inches from the psychiatrist's throat, and said, "Look, if I'm such a killer, how come I don't kill you? I've got nothing to lose."

"That's easy to explain, Richard. You don't have whiskey or pills in here."

Speck slipped the blade out of sight again. The psychiatrist was satisfied that Speck had progressed beyond the point where he would be dangerous with a razor blade.

"Somebody asked me the other day if I'd trust you to baby-sit with my kids," Ziporyn said.

Speck looked indignant. "Why not? I like kids."

On October 31, Ziporyn brought Speck a 650-piece jigsaw puzzle depicting the Bangkok floating market, along with some more Western and men's magazines. Speck expressed great delight with the big, boxed puzzle.

"How'd you know I like this kind of stuff? You know what I'll do? I'll get some glue—don't worry, I won't do no sniffing—and when I've finished it, I'll stick it together as a picture."

Speck flicked through one of the men's magazines. He came across some pictures of girls in their underwear. He snorted: "Look at all these nude women. It's disgusting." He turned back to the puzzle and looked at the pieces, planning how to begin it.

"How would you like to try painting by numbers?" Ziporyn asked. "Did you ever try that?"

"Yeah, I did one. I liked it. I did some in Dallas. I was doing it one night while I was baby-sitting with Robbie. Shirley was out, you see. I heard a car pull up and heard the door close. I looked out and some guy was letting Shirley out of his car down the street. I ripped up that painting. Next week I was in the penitentiary. See, I started to drink again. I just didn't care."

The reports of the examing panel were completed by the end of October. Despite a warning from Judge Paschen not to discuss the contents of the reports, one panel member let it be known a few days before the November 4 court hearing that the panel felt Speck was mentally competent to stand trial. Gerald Getty stated that he had decided to abandon his plans for a defense on insanity grounds, but would ask for the trial to be taken out of Chicago because press coverage had been prejudicial to the selection of an impartial jury. On November 2, Assistant State's Attorney William Martin asked Ziporyn to come to his office to discuss the case.

Ziporyn told Martin that he thought Speck was competent to stand trial, but that he had been incapable of distinguishing between right and wrong at the time of the crime. He cited Speck's brain damage.

Ziporyn told Speck he had had a meeting with the assistant state's attorney. "He wanted to know if I thought you could stand trial. I told him I feel you can."

"OK." Speck did not seem to care one way or the other.

"The panel thinks you can too. They think you're in great shape. They also think you're a sociopath."

"What's that?"

Once more, it was important to use the simplest terms. "Well, they think you killed those girls for kicks."

"Hell, they're crazier than I am."

Ziporyn reminded him that it was his own fault, since they did not all know about his head injuries. "Didn't you tell them?"

"Only if they asked me." Speck pouted. He was sulking again. "Some did, some didn't."

"And if they didn't ask you, you didn't tell them?"

"Yeah, that's about it."

"That's a big help. I know that you figure it's hopeless, but it doesn't have to be."

"I want it to be. I want it over with. I'm ready for the chair."

"Don't give me that kind of talk," Ziporyn replied. "You want to live as much as I do. You're just talking, to talk yourself into not being afraid."

As Ziporyn was leaving, Speck stopped him. "Say, Doc, I wanted to tell you something," he said. "You can read my brain like a book. You were right. I am scared."

Speck was evidently reacting to Ziporyn's coldness. He was eager to win back his attention.

"I'm glad you understand," Ziporyn said. "And I think I understand, if it was you, why you did the murders."

"Why did I?"

If Speck was being more receptive now, it was worth Ziporyn's while briefly to reiterate his theory. He might be more ready to understand it.

"I think that Gloria Davy reminded you of Shirley."

"But why did I kill the rest of them,

then? I don't hate nobody—except Shirley."

"That's the point I am making. And that's why you apparently treated Gloria differently."

"What do you mean, differently?"

"Well, you did things to her you didn't do to the others, or at least that's what it seems from the reports."

Speck reached through the bars and his powerful hands gripped Ziporyn by the shoulders. He stared wildly into the psychiatrist's eyes.

"What did I do to her? Tell me the truth. You've got to tell me the truth."

"Look, I won't lie to you. You see, she wasn't there at first. She came in later. You took her to the bedroom with the others. I don't know what happened. Maybe she said something, maybe it was just that she looked like Shirley. Anyway, you stripped her. . . ."

Ziporyn stopped. Speck's head slumped forward between his shoulders. When he raised it again, his eyes were glistening with tears.

"Doc, I'd die eight times over if I could bring them back. I should have been shot the first time I hit my mother. And I choked Shirley once. I'm just no good."

On his next visit, Ziporyn brought a painting set. Speck was grateful. The psychiatrist also had picked up a copy of *Detective Cases*—"All Stories True." The cover of the publication was a color version of the newspaper picture taken of Speck lying in a prison bed after his suicide attempt in July. Beside his expressionless face were pictures of the eight dead nurses surrounding a picture of the survivor, Corazon Amurao. The cover headline read: CHICAGO ATROCITY: THE NINE LIVES OF RICHARD SPECK.

Speck read through the account, taking issue with various points as he went along. He objected particularly to suggestions by the Municipal Court psychiatrist, Dr. Edward Kelleher, that the murders were the work of a "sexual psychopath." "I ain't no sex-killer," said Speck, almost sulkily. For Speck now, guilt was not an issue—it was to be taken for granted—but his motivation was important to him. Kelleher was also quoted as saying the killer had evidently done a certain amount of planning for the crime. Again Speck was indignant. "I never was there before. I never knew anything about the place."

Prompted by the article's report on his past, Speck recalled a fight in which he had been involved as a boy—a public altercation with a woman—which he described in great detail for Ziporyn.

"You know what there was about that?" Speck told the psychiatrist. "That woman was a lezzie—you know what I mean? She was a Lesbian. And there was a queer living with her." His voice had a ring of earnest indignation.

This was the second time Speck had talked of violence directed against homosexuals. He had attacked a homosexual in one of his many bar fights.

Speck did not have a monopoly on the mass-murder headlines. In the second week of November, 1966, an 18-year-old high-school senior, Robert Benjamin Smith, made five women, a three-year-old girl and a baby lie on the floor of a beauty parlor in Mesa, Ariz., and proceeded to shoot all of them. Only the baby and one of the women survived. As usual with the murder cases he read about in the newspapers and magazines, Speck was incensed, but in this case the reasons became more personal.

"Did you read about this guy in Arizona? What a guy! Said he wanted to be famous. Said he was inspired by the Chicago case. Boy, I'd like to take care of him. If I could have a last wish, it would be to kill him. That's all—just kill him and I'll die happy."

"Easy there," said Ziporyn. "Don't you feel sorry for him?"

"Sorry for him? After what he did? He deserves to die."

"Yes. But Richard, don't you think that a person must have something wrong with him to do all that? Don't you think he must be sick?"

Speck stared at Ziporyn, wide-eyed with incredulous amazement. "Are you sure you read about this? Listen." He spoke slowly, deliberately, as if the psychiatrist were a child who needed to have simple facts drummed into his head. "He . . .made. . .them. . .lie. . .in. . .a. . .circle and. . .he. . .shot. . .them."

Ziporyn replied, "That's why we're talking—to learn as much as we can about what makes you tick—maybe it will prevent a killing someday."

Then the interview took a new tack. In a discussion of his family, Speck casually recalled that he had had syphilis and that he was sterile.

"Have you had any sperm studies to find out if you really are sterile?" Ziporyn asked.

"No. I'm finished. I know that much. That girl really fixed me."

"Do you know the girl with whom it happened?"

"Never forget her. Sure would like to get back at her. She was Chinese or Japanese—some kind of Oriental, know what I mean?"

Extending the hypothesis of what might have happened on the night of the nurses' murders, it was possible in the turbulence of Richard Speck's mind that the Filipino girls reminded him of a previous encounter with an "Oriental." This could have increased a wild rage already kindled by the sight of a girl resembling his wife.

At the end of the visit Ziporyn rose to leave.

"You know," said Speck. "That doctor, he really makes me mad."

Ziporyn wondered what could have suddenly reminded him of his interviews with the examiners. "Why?"

"Questions he asked me. Like, did I ever mess with boys? Hell, I'm not that way at all."

Speck was still eager to insist on his masculinity. Ziporyn believed that Speck had been showing many signs of latent homosexuality—positively, in his vanity and his fussiness around the cell, and negatively, in his hostility toward women, his strong reaction against "queers" and his resentment at the questions of the examiner. In his response to these questions he was going to the opposite extreme in his behavior to prove the suspicion false. Ziporyn, however, saw these manifestations of homosexuality as a definite component of Speck's hostility toward women, but by no means the basic problem. The roots of this latent homosexuality could only be guessed at, since Speck had revealed so little about his earliest years. Of his relationship with his father, it was known only that it had been very close. His father died when Richard was six, and there is no indication of how strong a figure he had been. But it was also apparent that Speck had been extremely close to his sister Carolyn and his mother. Whatever contributed to his latent homosexuality in his early years may have been intensified with the arrival of his hated stepfather. Speck had no strong male figure to identify with in his adolescence.

The Speck competency hearings of November 28-30 had a foregone conclusion. Gerald Getty assumed that his client would be found competent to stand trial. He therefore concentrated on a change of venue for the trial (which he obtained). William Martin, assistant state's attorney—with Judge Herbert Paschen's support—insisted on having members of the psychiatric panel heard in open court and their conclusions read

into the record. The report stated:

The panel is in unanimous agreement that Richard Speck is competent to stand trial at this time. . . .The panel is of the further opinion that Richard Speck was responsible for his behavior as of July 13 and 14, 1966.

The diagnosis established by the panel in accordance with the American Psychiatric Association nosological classification [systematic classification of disease] is sociopathic personality, antisocial behavior, with alcoholism. These opinions are in accordance with legislative standards established by Illinois statutes.

The signatures to the report represented an impressive professional lineup against Ziporyn's contention that Speck was not a sociopath. The psychiatrist studied the panel's diagnosis of Speck's mental status: "sociopathic personality, antisocial behavior, with alcoholism." Ziporyn turned for his text to *Modern Clinical Psychiatry* by Noyes and Kolb. Of antisocial personality it states:

Individuals without the capacity to form significant attachments or loyalties to others, to groups, or to codes of living. Thus they are callous. . .convince them[selves] that their actions are reasonable and warranted. . . .[The psychopath] has no critical awareness of his motives. . . .He shows few feelings of anxiety, guilt or remorse.

They are cynical, devoid of a sense of honor or of shame . . . . Many feel pride in their [unlawful] accomplishments. Punishments are considered as expressions of injustice.

Speck was distressed. His trial was to be held in another city. He would have to move from his cozy Cook County cell. He asked to see Warden Jack Johnson. The warden told Ziporyn about their talk.

"I came down there," said Johnson, "and Speck was looking out of the cell door, needling the guard. He said, 'The paper says I got the I.Q. of a ten-year-old. I always told you you were nothing but a baby-sitter for an idiot,' and he started to laugh. Then he saw me and said, 'Here's Big Daddy now.' I'll Big Daddy him." The warden chuckled. "He wanted to talk to me alone, so I took him to my office. He said he wants to burn here with all his friends around him. He's upset at getting moved. I explained the procedure to him."

When Ziporyn saw Speck, the conversation turned to the trial, another forbidding prospect—"more people saying lies about me."

"They're not lies," said Ziporyn. "People just get details confused sometimes. And you know, I might testify too. You're going to be mad at me too, when I testify."

"No, you can say whatever you like."

"Well, remember, it's not a popularity contest. The idea is not to say you're an angel. If I testify, I'll tell the truth as I see it—that you have had severe head injury, that you drank to stop the pain—"

"Getty said I left quite a trail that night. He said they found I was in and out of bars, wild drunk. They say I waved a gun in a boy's face. I told Getty I wasn't hiding anything, so that's why it was easy to trace me. I didn't know anything had happened that should make me hide."

And again, "You don't remember any of this?"

"Nothing."

"Nor the killings?"

"No."

"You're sure you killed them?"

"It's hard to believe, even now. I'm no killer. Guess I am though."

"It's hard to argue with the fingerprints."

"Yeah, but there's one thing I can't understand. What was I doing over there—it's so far away? The nurses' house is about a mile from the Shipyard Inn, where I was staying that night. At least, that's what Getty says. Over a mile."

"That's an easy walk."

"Not if you're against walking, like me. I don't walk nowhere."

On December 5, the day before Speck's 25th birthday, he was in a festive mood. The psychiatrist gave him some birthday presents—another jigsaw puzzle, a new paint set, a model airplane and a magazine entitled *Adventure*. Their talk turned to publicity.

"I've had enough publicity," Speck said. "Why don't they write about that guy in Arizona instead of about me?"

"You've captured the public imagination. The thing is that nobody knows what happened in the nurses' house. Half the people think you raped those girls."

"What?" Speck's voice rose incredulously.

"Sure. They think you're the stud of the century."

Speck laughed in a disbelieving manner, but he gave the distinct impression that the notion pleased him.

"That's impossible," he said to Ziporyn. "I couldn't rape no eight girls."

"You know that and I know that, but the general public doesn't. They think you are some kind of sex symbol. Why do you think women keep writing to you?"

Speck's laughter grew louder, his pleasure at the fantasy growing with it. "I couldn't rape two girls, let alone eight. No man could do that. Truth is, I was probably too messed up to rape anybody. You can't do it when you're on drugs. I'm no rape-o. I never raped a girl in my life—well, maybe one, in Dallas, but it really wasn't rape. She was just shy, so I held her arms while my buddy did her. Then I did. But we all laughed about it afterward. But you don't have to rape women. There's always whores and lots of girls. Buy them a drink and they're yours. We used to call them nymphos in Dallas."

The suggestion that he might be considered "the stud of the century" had made a direct if unintentional appeal to the masculinity he was always so anxious to fortify. Now he was eager to embellish the legend with boasts.

The stories that he told the psychiatrist were a mixture of barracks bragging and matter-of-factness , about compliant girls on dates in Dallas, including one whose favors he shared with three of his friends.

"I've had lots of pleasure from women. I like them." His expansive tone suddenly froze to a cold snarl. "All except one. I've got hate, jealous hate for her. Shirley. She's the only woman I've ever hit sober. Oh, yeah, and her mother. That woman—I wonder what she's thinking of me now. She was always low-rating me. Once I came round to her house, pulled out a Luger and fired four shots. Then, I hit her at a New Year's party. Oh yeah, and one more time when I was sober."

"What about the time you hit your mother?"

"No, I was stoned then. I wouldn't hurt my mother. She's the only girl that knows me. But I could have killed her that time. That's when I should have given up drugs. Wish I had. But outside of Shirley and her mother, I like women. But I'm no sex fiend." Speck thumbed through the men's magazines, snorting in disgust at the pictures of girls in bras and panties, one showing half-naked girls at a party. "Who would get excited about those? I've been to parties like this."

For the psychiatrist, Speck's talk had revealed more of the nature of his ambivalence toward women. This kind of ambivalence, typical of the obsessive-compulsive, is known as the Madonna-Prostitute complex because it assigns every woman to one category or the other.

A week later Ziporyn joined Defense Attorney Getty's assistant, James Gramenos, on a trip to Dallas for an interview with Speck's mother, Mrs. Mary Margaret Lindbergh, and her daughter Carolyn. They met in a hotel lobby, and it was Ziporyn who first saw the women. The mother was of medium height, thin and angular, with gray hair. She wore a black fur-trimmed coat. Her daughter, also very slim, was a pretty brunette, her hair done in bouffant style. She, too, wore a fur-trimmed coat, in blue. Both women had sharp-featured faces, and the psychiatrist could see that his patient strongly resembled them.

"Hello," said Ziporyn, as the two ladies stepped off the Escalator. "We're the people who came to see you."

The daughter stared at Ziporyn suspiciously. Gramenos said, "I'm the man who talked to you on the phone. I'm from Mr. Getty's office. You're Richard's family?"

They nodded, but said nothing. Ziporyn sat down with the two women in the lobby while Gramenos went off to find a vacant conference room.

Carolyn was fiercely indignant. "I don't believe my brother did it," she said, when they got to the room. "I just don't believe it and I never will."

With help from Carolyn in establishing a date or place, Mrs. Lindbergh related six separate incidents in which her son Richard sustained head injuries.

Mrs. Lindbergh recalled Speck's assault on her when she came to collect him from the juvenile home.

In a soft, measured voice, Mrs. Lindbergh said, "He was swinging and kicking; he kicked me in the hip—he was just wild."

"Did he know what he was doing?"

"No, he was just out of his head."

"Did he remember the incident?"

"No, we told him about it the next day. He wouldn't believe it."

Ziporyn then turned to the subject of Speck's drinking, asking specifically whether he drank as much as his anecdotes would indicate.

"Usually just on weekends," the mother said. "He would be all right during the week, but his friends would get him on weekends."

"How did he act when he was drinking?" Ziporyn asked.

"He was hateful and cross," said Carolyn.

"What was he like, then, the rest of the time?"

"What do you mean?" Carolyn asked.

"Was he hard to get along with—when he was not drinking, I mean—selfish, cold?"

"He was very good," the mother said emphatically. "He was always generous with his money, and helpful—used to help old ladies with their packages, and that sort of thing. And he was very responsible at work."

Ziporyn moved on. "Did he ever throw his stepfather out?" Ziporyn asked.

"His stepfather was handicapped," said Carolyn.

"I know, but Richard says they always fought."

"That's true. That's Richard's problem right there. His stepfather hated him—always did—always called him a gutter rat."

"Why?"

"I don't know," she said. "And Richard always wanted a father. I think he really suffered. He used to cry about it sometimes.

"Now let's talk about Shirley," said the psychiatrist. "Richard has told me he disliked her."

"Disliked her?" said the mother, incredulously. "I never knew that."

"Well, he says he was always fighting with her because, as he claims, she stepped out on him."

Carolyn confirmed what her mother did not want to believe. "That's true, they always did fight about that."

Gramenos went alone to talk to Speck's former wife. He and Ziporyn met in the evening.

"Did you see Shirley?" Ziporyn asked. There had been no hope of seeing her himself.

"Yes, she's no help."

"What's she like?"

"Confused—or lying. Of course, her new husband stood right there with her. I asked her if Richard ever got drunk. She said, 'No, he just used to pretend to be drunk."

"Pretend?"

"Yes. He'd come home, fall on the floor, roll out on the porch, pound on the door, cry, carry on. Just pretending, she says. She also says she can't remember where she met him. I said, 'I heard you met at the Texas State Fair,' and she said she didn't remember that. She 'thinks' they got married in 1963, and when I asked her how old Robbie is, she said five. Even her husband tried to straighten her out on that, but she just played stupid, said she couldn't remember anything."

Gramenos shrugged. The smoke screen had grown thicker, but through it, Ziporyn could perceive that the basic, important facts of Speck's story remained true.

Speck was excited about Ziporyn's return from Dallas, and Ziporyn told him about the interviews.

"Are they talking about me all over Dallas?" Speck asked. "I wonder what Shirley thinks. Did you see that witch?"

Ziporyn explained that James Gramenos had visited her. "She said she couldn't remember where she met you."

"Was her husband around?"

"He wouldn't let her out of his sight."

"She was just afraid to talk, then. Anything else?"

"Carolyn said Shirley used to slap you and get upset when you wouldn't pay attention to her."

Speck was solemn now. He stared through the bars of the cell, seeming to retrace the span of his brief, unhappy marriage. "Yeah, she used to say she wanted me to love her more than I did my mom. I told her, 'That will never be.' Then she'd get mad."

Ziporyn recalled an incident of drunken rage that Speck had spoken of, and asked, "Does that happen often when you drink?"

"Yeah, I get to feeling people are trying to push me around. When I'm sober, I let them. It doesn't bother me so much. But when I drink, I won't take it, I won't let them get away with it."

The paranoid core of Speck's personality had been glimpsed at times in the expression of his fears and suspicions of the world around him, but this was the first time that Ziporyn had heard his patient express his paranoia so overtly.

Ziporyn paid a brief call on Gerald Getty on January 13 to review the clinical assessment that he had made of Speck: "chronic brain syndrome associated with cerebral trauma." He also conferred with William Martin, the prosecutor. "Doesn't he have any remorse?" Martin asked.

"Remorse?" said Ziporyn. "Yes, lots of it. He's constantly expressing regret, saying the whole thing was so unnecessary."

"But he still claims not to remember. Do you believe him?"

"I do."

"Why?"

"If he is trying to deceive me, why would he tell me something incriminating like the blood he found on his hand the morning after the murders? Also, he knows how important the head injuries are. Why didn't he tell all the psychiatrists on the panel about them? Some came away knowing nothing about them."

"What would *you* do with Speck?" Martin asked.

"You mean, if I were the judge and knew what I know now?" Ziporyn said. "Well, the chair is out of the question. I guess I'd give him a long prison term, 199 years or so. He's a nice guy when he's sober, but he says himself he can't quit

drinking and he doesn't trust himself. So I guess prison is the solution."

The trial was now scheduled for February 20 in Peoria, 150 miles southwest of Chicago.

Ziporyn's last interview with Speck was on February 13. The cell was in total darkness as the psychiatrist approached, and for a moment he thought Speck had already left. But Speck was still there, lying on his bed. When Speck switched the light on, Ziporyn saw that his face was suffused with fury. The psychiatrist glanced around and saw the reason. The cell had been stripped of all the trimmings with which Speck had made it into a home in the past six months.

"So you're finally moving out?"

"Yeah," said Speck bitterly. "The captain came in at three-thirty today and told me to pack. He said I might go tomorrow. And they lied to me. The Peoria sheriff and the warden, they told me that I could take my radio and my paint stuff. Now they say I can't take nothing." (As it turned out, he was allowed to take his paints and clothing with him.)

It was Ziporyn's last chance to try to impress on Speck the true nature of his responsibility, or lack of it, for the crime he was accused of committing.

"Richard, I believe you did not choose to be a killer. I believe that what happened was not the result of your conscious decision. Like every other human being, you, Richard, are the product of your heredity and your environment. *You* didn't pick either one. I can find what you did terrible. I do, and you do too. But I can't honestly find you responsible for your actions. Do you understand?"

Richard Speck did not answer. He held his head in his hands and sobbed. He looked up and tears were streaming down his face as he shook his head, still unable, unwilling to comprehend his situation.

Ziporyn made one more effort. "As

you've been told many times, you have real brain damage. You just can't control your feelings. It's not your fault that you didn't get real medical care."

"What good would it have done?" Speck answered. "You know what would have happened if I'd been brought to you on the outside. I'd have listened politely, agreed with what you said, and then gone away and laughed at you."

The psychiatrist took his leave, promising to see him again in Peoria.

Speck was watching *Machine Gun Kelly* on television when the sheriff's deputies came to his cell at midnight to take him to Peoria. He had been looking forward to the movie for several days and was annoyed that the deputies had interrupted him in the middle of it. As he left, he asked his friend in the next cell, Mark Clancy, to write and tell him what happened to Machine Gun Kelly.

The date was February 14, 1967, exactly seven months after eight nurses were murdered. The deputies put Speck into the back seat of an unmarked car and drove along Route 55 to Peoria. At 2:45 a.m. they left him in a cell in the county jail.

A few days later Ziporyn talked to Clancy, who laughed at the outcome of the movie Speck had been watching. "Wait till I tell him Machine Gun Kelly turned out to be a fag," Clancy said. "At the end, Kelly was whimpering, crying, begging for mercy, just a punk. Richard'll flip when I write and tell him."

Speck, waiting for the trial to begin, settled into the new cell, quietly painting and sketching.

On the morning of Monday, February 20, he dressed in his "court" suit, with a handerchief, monogrammed "R.S.," tucked in the breast pocket. He wore a slim dark tie and white shirt. Freshly shaved and barbered, and handcuffed, he was ready to go.

It took Judge Paschen 12 minutes to read the indictments.

"The Cook County grand jury of July, 1966, charges that on or about July 14, 1966, in said county, Richard Franklin Speck committed the offense of murder in that he intentionally and knowingly strangled and stabbed and thus killed Suzanne Farris.

"The Cook County grand jury of July, 1966, charges that on or about July 14, 1966, in said county, Richard Franklin Speck committed the offense of murder in that he intentionally and knowingly strangled and killed Nina Jo Schmale . . . ."

The litany, with its eight almost identical verses, told in colorless, horribly simple language, of the savage murders of the eight young women, all aged between 20 and 24—Miss Farris, Miss Schmale, Patricia Ann Matusek, Mary Ann Jordan, Pamela Wilkening, Gloria Davy, Merlita Gargullo, Valentina Pasion. All were student nurses at the South Chicago Community Hospital, and the last two named were—like Corazon Amurao, 23, the only survivor—Filipino exchange students.

Richard Speck sat through it all, holding his chin in his right hand, his eyes staring glassily ahead of him, not at the judge, but through him. His jaws chewed slowly on some gum. He looked neither tense nor relaxed, just numb.

It took six weeks to select a jury. During this period, Ziporyn went to Peoria to see Getty and visited Speck. But Getty and Gramenos were with him, and the talk was inconsequential.

Speck was surpirsed to see Ziporyn and seemed a little shy. His cell was large and well lighted, and the psychiatrist noticed that the change of scene was not having the feared bad effect on him. He looked comfortable and well fed.

"You're getting paunchy," Ziporyn teased him.

"Yeah, the food's better here than in Chicago," said Speck, patting his stomach with an appreciative grin. He saw Ziporyn looking round the room and up at the light in the center of the ceiling. Speck had tied the light cord in the form of a noose.

"That's my appeal," Speck commented.

Getty, in his opening statement, announced that "the theory of the defense is that Speck, this defendant, is not the perpetrator of the crime." He would claim that Speck was not in the nurses' house on the night of the murders, and would fight the evidence, piece by piece.

The prosecution, led by William Martin, introduced witnesses who placed Speck in the neighborhood. Then Martin called the only survivor to the stand—Corazon Amurao.

Miss Amurao told of the events of the evening up to the point at which there was a knock on her door.

"Now, Miss Amurao," the young prosecutor said, "if you see that same man in the courtroom today who came to your bedroom door on Wednesday night, July 13, 1966, would you please step down and point him out."

Corazon Amurao stared intently and unflinchingly at Martin as he asked the time-honored question. Without any word of acknowledgement, she rose slowly, and walked a dozen short steps to the polished oak defense table. Clutching a white handkerchief in her left fist, she held her tiny body erect and steadily raised her right hand to within six inches of Richard Speck's ashen face. "This is the man."

Her small features remained expressionless as her accusing hand hovered by Speck's left cheek. Speck's eyes flickered momentarily toward Miss Amurao and then resumed their glassy stare at the judge's bench behind her.

Miss Amurao's voice faltered as she went on with her story. "I went to the...I went to the door," she said, fighting back tears, "and I unlocked it and started to open it, and at once there's somebody who's pushing the door." She broke down and wept as she added, "I saw a man standing on the center of our door with a gun in his right hand pointed toward me, and I noticed that he had marks on his face, the clothes was dark from the shoulders to the foot, and his hair was blond, hair combed toward the back and some hair in the front."

After she had identified the man in court, Miss Amurao unfailingly referred to the intruder as "Speck" throughout her testimony. The repetition of the name gave it the aura of a proven fact. She recounted how he took the girls to the house's large south bedroom, making them sit on the floor.

"One of the girls," she said, "asked Speck, 'What do you want?' And then Speck answered, 'I want money, I'm going to New Orleans.' "

Her account revealed that he did not have to rummage through the house for the money, since the girls fetched money for him from their purses; that they remained unbound for about an hour after his arrival, and that he carried on conversations with the American girls which she did not understand. She told how he bound each girl, then stood up and walked over to Pamela Wilkening, untied her ankles, and led her from the room. Then, returning, he took the others out of the room, one by one.

"After Speck had taken Miss Wilkening from the south bedroom, did you hear anything?"

"After about one minute, I heard Miss Wilkening say 'Ah.' It was like a sigh."

"Did you hear anything after the noise you just described?"

"Before he came back to the south bedroom, I heard water running in the bathroom, as if Speck was washing his hands."

And the next. "After about one minute, I heard Nina Schmale say 'Ah,' just the same like Miss Wilkening."

A period of 20, 25 or 30 minutes passed between each girl's disappearance from the south bedroom and the man's return. During one of these periods, Miss Amurao stated, she and three other girls tried to hide behind and under beds, but all except Miss Amurao were discovered when the man returned. The story resumed.

"Did you hear anything after Speck had taken Miss Pasion from the south bedroom?"

"After about two minutes, I heard Miss Pasion say 'Ah' more loud than the two other American girls." More water running in the bathroom, another 20 minutes passed.

"What happened after you saw Speck carrying Miss Gargullo from the south bedroom?"

"Then after about five minutes, I heard Miss Gargullo say, 'Masakit.' "

"Could you tell the court and jury what 'Masakit' means in your native language [Tagalog]?"

"It means 'It hurts.' "

Detail was piled upon pathetic detail. Miss Amurao reported Patricia Matusek's last words: "Will you please untie my ankles first?"

At that point, Miss Amurao broke down and wept. Judge Paschen called a brief recess.

After the recess, Miss Amurao resumed her testimony and told the court that it was 45 to 50 minutes before Speck returned after removing Gloria Davy— "the longest time he was out." Everything that followed—the man's departure, her rescue and recuperation in hospital—was necessarily anticlimactic, but the effect of her appearance in court that Wednesday, April 5, was indelible; in Getty's own private words, "devastating."

Getty's cross-examination of Miss Amurao was kindly, persistent and largely unavailing. He sought to weaken her identification of Speck by raising points of discrepancy; her principal, repeated answer was, "I don't recall."

Getty sought, with witnesses, to prove that Speck was elsewhere at the time of the murders. A bartender and his wife both testified that Speck was in Kay's Pilot House, a tavern, at midnight on July 13, at the time Miss Amurao had sworn Speck was preparing to remove the first of eight murder victims from the bedroom, 12 blocks from the tavern. The prosecution could not shake their testimony—but apparently it wasn't necessary to do so.

After only 49 minutes of deliberation, the jury returned with their verdict. On all eight charges they decided: "We, the jury, find the defendant, Richard Franklin Speck, guilty of murder in the manner and form as charged in the indictment, and we fix his punishment at death."

Richard Franklin Speck sat motionless in his chair at the defense table, showing not the slightest emotion. Judge Paschen adjourned the court, preparatory to hearing post-trial motions. Speck stood up between two policemen and left the courtroom. As he was going through the door behind the judge's bench, the courtroom door at the front was opened, and a deputy announced the verdict to a crowd of spectators waiting downstairs. Cheers and applause arose from the crowd, mainly girls and middle-aged women. Speck turned his head at the noise. His mouth dropped open, uncomprehending eyes stared across the courtroom. One of the policemen beside him put his hand on Speck's shoulder, and the boy who was born to raise hell disappeared.

On June 2, Judge Paschen held a hearing in Chicago for presentation of evidence which, under Illinois law, a judge may consider in possible mitigation of a jury-recommended death sentence. Dr. Ner Littner, a psychiatrist, told the court that Speck was mentally ill and not responsible for his actions last July when the murders were committed. The psychiatrist traced Speck's history of head injuries and violent behavior. Speck was living in "a mental pressure cooker" last July, the psychiatrist said.

On June 5, in Peoria, Judge Paschen sentenced Speck to die in the electric chair on September 1. He stayed the death order pending appeal to the Illinois Supreme Court, and assigned Getty to make the appeal. Review by the Illinois Supreme Court is mandatory in death sentences.

the last word (we hope) on george lincoln rockwell

FRED C. SHAPIRO

My queen's knight forked George Lincoln Rockwell's king and castle. The commander of the American Nazi Party accepted the loss of a piece calmly, then, without hesitation, brought his bishop to bear on a pawn my knight had left unguarded, revealing a well-screened queen's attack. While I groped for an answer, I asked Rockwell if he thought he would fare as well in the courts of New York as he appeared to be doing on the chessboard at his Arlington headquarters. "Sure," he said, patiently refilling the corncob pipe that has come to be his trademark. "I've got a smart Jewish lawyer."

As it turned out, both the chess game and the court case worked out to Rockwell's satisfaction. After a good deal of thought, I resigned my game, and a few days later, with equal reluctance, District Attorney Frank S. Hogan resigned his case, moving in Criminal Court for the dismissal of two charges against Rockwell of disorderly conduct, sometimes known as breach of peace. "The abhorrence with which we regard the ideas of this defendant may render our task here particularly onerous, but our duty is no less compelling," the district attorney wrote in his petition. "We can not, and dare not, substitute our personal judgment of the defendant for the requirements of the law." Thus, on June 27, six years and five days after he was nearly overrun by hostile listeners while propounding genocide in the rotunda of New York Supreme Court in Foley Square, Rockwell was free again to ply his trade in New York City. He did not, however, leap at the opportunity. After profusely thanking his New York Civil Liberties Union attorney, Rockwell announced he would hold a press conference within two days to let New York know what he had in store for it. The two days came and went without further notice from the "half-penny Hitler" Mayor Wagner once barred from speaking at Union Square.

It is now more than eight years since Rockwell, a Navy pilot against Germany during World War II, proclaimed himself a

Reprinted by permission of John Cushman Associates, Inc., first published in Esquire *Magazine, February, 1967, pp. 101-5, 137-42, 144. Copyright ©1967 Fred C. Shapiro.*

disciple of Adolf Hitler, particularly in regard to the "Jewish question." Communism, he said, is a Jewish plot to subvert the world, and eighty percent of American Jews are traitors and should be executed. For Negroes he had a milder fate: deportation. And it was to promote these ends that Rockwell founded, in November, 1958, in Arlington, Virginia, the American Nazi Party. It was a few months after that that I first interviewed Rockwell over a six-pack of beer at his first party headquarters. The beer was mine. At his suggestion, I had brought it when I went to interview the man who had become successively the leader of the National Committee to Free America From Jewish Domination, the World Union of Free Enterprise National Socialists, the American Nazi movement and, finally, the American Nazi Party.

On three occasions, I, a Jew, one of those marked by Rockwell for trial and execution, sat in the house of the commander (Rockwell spurns the title of führer; there was only one führer, he insists, Hitler) and listened to him outline the methods with which he would win support and, of course, financial backing for a grandiose and horrific program. I particularly remember one time, while Rockwell was outlining a revolting blueprint for improving on Hitlerian gas ovens as a method of mass murder, he paused to ask: "How does that strike you?"

"I like to talk to Jews," Rockwell told me on my first visit. "They're very fascinating and very literate people. They keep you interested. As a matter of fact, you can quote me on this: I like Jews. I'll be very sorry when we've killed the last of them." If Rockwell likes Jews then, who does he hate? Well, from his own words and history, it would appear that he has, at least, a marked distaste for the men and women he leads and competes with as a professional anti-Semite. "The anti-Jewish movement abounds with cowards, jerks, queers and fanatics," he told me in 1958, and, even as he had gained support, he had never abandoned this position. "Many of the characters who were attracted to us were pretty sorry," Rockwell complained in his self-printed autobiography, *This Time The World*. "One man arrived late at night with a caged bird and some 'sacred' book, to 'join the party.' He told us the 'bolsheviks' were wrecking his sex life and were always keeping him from having a girl friend—and he wanted to 'fight them'; he and the bird, that is." And to a reporter from the Santa Ana, California, *Independent*, Rockwell confirmed a charge that his following was made up largely of criminals, psychotics and social misfits. "That's true," the paper quoted him. "You have to be abnormal to join a party like this."

It was one of these despised supporters—an ex-supporter, to be precise—who directed me to Rockwell in the first place. This was Harold Noel Arrowsmith, Jr., a "fat cat" that Rockwell had brought to national attention by so describing him in a letter to Wallace H. Allen, for whom Rockwell once worked. "I'm going to make these fat cats, these sniveling cowards pay through the nose," Rockwell told me. "They think they can use me—but it's going to cost them." He said this sitting in the house that Arrowsmith had bought for him, his hands stained with ink from the basement press that Arrowsmith had paid for. Already, Rockwell had found that being—or appearing to be—the bravest of the bigots of America was a profitable operation. "Contributions have been coming in. . . .There's not too much in any one envelope; our people don't generally have too much to give at any time, but the money does come in."

But at least no more is coming in from Arrowsmith, a denizen of the *Baltimore Social Register,* who learned from Rockwell that race hatred can be an expensive business. Says Arrowsmith of his former front man: "George Lincoln Rockwell talked me into buying a house in Arlington, Virginia, which was not my intention at any time, which could be used as a place to print certain kinds of historical documentary material. This talking into was done by means of quite a large number of falsehoods, gross misrepresentations . . . . I am the last of a series of . . . persons who have been victimized by Rockwell. I am apparently the only one who has been willing to take him to court."

Retorted Rockwell of Arrowsmith and his ilk: "They're cowards. They want a front man, and I'm him. But they'll have to pay."

Comparatively, George Lincoln Rockwell came to his vocation late in life. To master it, he left behind generally promising careers as Navy pilot, artist and sign painter, advertising-agency executive, magazine publisher, salesman and writer, as well as two marriages and seven children. He is, himself, the son of a man once prominent in America, the vaudeville and radio comedian, Doc Rockwell, who had disassociated himself from his son's method of earning a living. The young Rockwell traveled the vaudeville circuit before his parents were divorced, and he recalls pleasantly his early associations with it, even to being dandled on the knees of eminent—and Jewish—comedians such as Groucho Marx. After a less than notable prep school career at Hebron Academy in Maine, he matriculated at Brown Universary (in *This Time The World* Rockwell claims the lowest grades of anyone admitted to the university up to that time, and the highest College

Aptitude Test score). At college, his most notable achievement was drawing for and art editing the humor magazine, *Sir Brown.* In later years, a psychiatrist studied this early work of Rockwell's with a view toward submitting the conclusions into the record of a 1960 commitment proceeding. (Rockwell's sanity was questioned in connection with a disorderly conduct charge resulting from an arrest at a July 3, 1960, Washington, D.C. fracas.) The psychiatrist found that the drawings showed "the continuing and consistent preoccupation with violence. . .the recurrent themes of death, cannibalism, blood and bombing." Rockwell maintains in his defense that he was merely a contemporary of Charles Addams. As significant as the contents of those early cartoons was the name signed to them, "Link." In his later, race-baiting years, Rockwell dropped the George from his signature in favor of Lincoln, a much more dramatic name, he feels.

Sir Brown lost the services of "Link" prematurely when, in his junior year, Rockwell abruptly enlisted in the Navy. His rise in the service was exceptional. After flight training, he was assigned to bombing patrols over the South Atlantic and later he took part in operations which resulted in the sinking of at least two submarines. "I deeply regret killing those German boys at the behest of the internationalist Zionist Jews," he later reflected.

With victory in World War II, Rockwell returned to civilian life and his interrupted art career. Married now and the father of a daughter, Rockwell entered Pratt Institute in Brooklyn on the G. I. Bill. He left Pratt also without graduating, but did, while there, make his mark at the school by winning, in 1948, a one-thousand-dollar poster contest sponsored by the National Society of Illustrators. Back in Maine, Rockwell set to work expanding a small sign-painting company into a sizable advertising agency. A dispute among partners (a circumstance to be repeated many times in his life) forced Rockwell out of that enterprise at about the time he was recalled by the Navy in the Korean emergency. And it was while serving his second flying hitch that Rockwell discovered anti-Semitism as a way of life. It began after he was assigned to San Diego to teach junior pilots the tactics of supporting ground troops. A woman, whose name he says he has forgotten, gave him a copy of *Common Sense*, a New Jersey hate sheet, and when he responded appropriately, she steered him to an appearance of Gerald L. K. Smith, a senior rabble-rouser who, that year, grossed from anti-semitism $139,640, according to statements filed with Congressional probers. Rockwell was certainly impressed, at first, by Smith. "Old Gerald L. K. sure talked a good game," he recalled. "That was his trouble, though. All he did do was talk. He wouldn't get off the dime." One thing Smith did do, however, was inspire Rockwell to read *Mein Kampf*. "And that," as Rockwell wrote, "was the end of one Lincoln Rockwell, the 'nice guy' . . .and the beginning of an entirely different person. *Mein Kampf* was like finding part of me."

For the time being, however, the Navy had use for all of Rockwell, and he was detailed to Iceland as executive Officer of a Fleet Aircraft Service Squadron with patrol bombers. His first marriage, already torn by domestic turbulence, was unable to withstand the strain of the enforced separation, and it was while living a "monkish existence" in Iceland that he found time to reread *Mein Kampf* a dozen times, and also to fall in love again. After consenting to $400 per month child support for the three daughters of his first marriage (later

reduced to $200, for which he has often been in arrears) Rockwell married Thora Hallgrimsson, herself a divorcée with a child. His new bride was from a prominent family and was, Rockwell says, the niece of both the Icelandic prime minister and the ambassador to the United States. Her father was a director of an international oil combine. For their honeymoon, Rockwell took his bride to Berchtesgaden, Germany.

Matters were going well in Iceland. Rockwell became commander of his squadron and requested, and received, a year's extension of his assignment, but at the year's end he was caught by a Navy reduction in force and released to inactive reserve status. He took his new wife and their firstborn ("after three daughters, at last a *son!*") back to the United States and Washington, D. C., where, in mid-1954, on a capital of $300, he founded *U. S. Lady,* a purportedly nonpolitical, slick magazine aimed at the wives of servicemen. It was his intention, Rockwell says in *This Time The World,* to print in *U. S. Lady* "sickening" examples of brotherhood which, he hoped, would "drive out the filthy ideas of Marxism, 'mass democracy' and racial defilement." He could not fulfill the ambition, however. Shortages of capital, inability to pay salaries and personality differences made him vulnerable to a staff mutiny, and, in the midst of dissension, he sold his interest in the magazine and turned to direct political action, using as a base a group of Washington associates informally known as the Die Hards. He then moved on to form the American Federation of Conservative Organizations, described by Rockwell as" 'an operation for sneaking up on the Jews' without ever mentioning them."

Publicity frightened off the more timid of his backers and ended the usefulness of the federation, and after a short and unsuccessful period of employment as an assistant to Robert B. Snowden, the backer of the conservative "Campaign for the Forty-eight States," Rockwell made his second assault on the magazine field. He sold Russell Maguire, publisher of the right-wing *American Mercury*, an article, *No Wonder Iceland Hates Us!*, which led the January, 1957, issue. The contention of the piece was that the United States had exported socialism to the tiny North Atlantic republic. Author Rockwell noted wryly that "books in the U. S. Legation Library were all that McCarthy said they were." Maguire was impressed enough to hire Rockwell as his. assistant, but the connection was short-lived. Finding Maguire reluctant to provide substantial backing for a "hardcore"—i.e., anti-Semitic—organization, Rockwell soon moved on, leaving the publisher with a final warning of the presence of left-wing sympathizers among his staff. The parting was amicable, however, and Rockwell was, shortly, able to sell to the *Mercury* two more articles, both in defense of Marine Corps training methods. "Above all," he warned in the conclusion of the second piece, "remember the Reds are out to get the Elite Corps."

Rockwell found a nonpolitical job, selling the services of a management-engineering firm. He was as successful at this as he has been, from time to time, at other selling jobs (in one notable venture, Rockwell is said to have tripled the gross sales of a firm manufacturing ball-point pens), but this wasn't the job Rockwell wanted, and in late 1957, he loaded his second family into a trailer and drove South to work for the United White Party, later the National States Rights Party. Concurrently he found himself working for Wallace H. Allen in Atlanta, as he told me, "in the printing and advertising line." The recession cut both his and the party's income, so the Rockwells moved again, this time to Newport News, Virginia, site of the anti-Semitic publication, *The Virginian*. And it was in Newport News, after yet another disagreement, this time with *Virginian* publisher William Stephenson, that Rockwell was recruited by Arrowsmith, the pudgy Baltimorean. Under the aegis of Arrowsmith and his hapless National Committee to Free America From Jewish Domination, Rockwell moved to the modest Arlington home to which he later invited me. Arrowsmith told me he put up a $15,200 down payment on the $23,500 home, and that he also had paid for the press which was installed in the basement. It was this prodigality that inspired Rockwell to write Wallace Allen the "fat cat" letter. The relevant portion of the letter, which was to give Rockwell publicity coming almost up to his dreams, and Arrowsmith publicity beyond his nightmares, read: "Suffice it to say we are finally beginning to do what we have all so long talked about, mostly thanks to one man—the one fat cat—who is putting $$$ where his mouth is, God bless him."

Of course, this honeymoon was not to last either. Arrowsmith says merely that Rockwell "made some remarks in my presence which aroused my suspicions. Then I started to investigate. What that turned up was enough to turn your hair." Rockwell, on the other hand, says that Arrowsmith was constantly agitating for overt action, but that he refused to allow time for organization and was also chary on further financial support. Just before the falling out, Arrowsmith paid $1,000 more to Rockwell to picket the White House with a handful of followers and a sign reading, "Save Ike from the Kikes." President Eisenhower was not in the White House at the time, July, 1958, during the Lebanon crisis, and the picketing was allowed to proceed peacefully. Arrowsmith did not take part in the demonstration, but observed it, Rockwell says, from across Pennsylvania Avenue, peering timidly around the base of a monument in Lafayette Park.

Thus temporarily satiated, Arrowsmith disappeared from the picture. Rockwell says he learned of the defection of his backer when a man showed up with a truck to cart away the press. Rockwell refused to turn over the equipment; instead, he set up shop for himself in Arrowsmith's home, fighting a delaying and eventually unsuccessful battle against eviction. He horrified the quiet, residential neighborhood by at last fulfilling his dream, displaying the swastika in a window, and coming out unreservedly as the commander of the American Nazi movement, later amended to the American Nazi Party. The dirty, ill-kept house where he, so to speak, entertained me was startlingly decorated with the Nazi banner, pictures of his deity, Hitler, and a world map with paste swastikas denoting, he said, his supporters. "Yup, that's where we have movements. We're picking up all the time." Rockwell explains the use of the symbols of the Third Reich quite candidly: "When I was in the advertising game, we used to use nude women. Now I use the swastika and storm troopers. You use what brings them in."

By this time Thora Rockwell had packed up their four children and had gone back to Iceland. Rockwell has given two versions of this move. He told me a bomb was thrown at the house, exploding under the window of their son, Lincoln, and he decided, "for their own safety," it would be better that they leave him. However, later, to another reporter, he charged that "diplomatic pressure" from Thora's family, particularly from her uncle, the ambassador, persuaded her to leave. They were divorced a year later and Rockwell is not supporting the children of his second marriage.

Without the restraining influence of his family, Rockwell was able to set up his drive for publicity, a campaign which soon afforded him the status of the most notorious racist headline grabber in America. He threw open his swastika-decorated home with its huge Nazi banner, particularly encouraging visits from students at nearby schools. Not all his neighbors were favorably impressed. "A lot of people call me up," Rockwell said. "Jews and all. They say they're going to come over and knock hell out of me. I say, 'Fine, I'll wait outside for you.' But they drive by and see me, and they don't stop." This is credible. Even at forty-eight, the six-foot Rockwell is an imposing figure.

When the excitement caused by his public embrace of the Nazi cause began to die down, newspaper space again became hard to come by, and Rockwell discovered the publicity value of libel suits. He drew them up himself, filed them with noticeable fanfare, and rarely bothered to prosecute them. In addition to a $500,000 action against Arrowsmith, newspapers reported suits by Rockwell against Drew Pearson, The Washington *Post*, Arlington Cardozo Lodge of B'nai B'rith and Arlington Commonwealth Attorney Willian J. Hassan. Lawsuits, too, may have been a tactic taught Rockwell by Arrowsmith who sued unsuccessfully the defunct New York *Mirror* and The Providence *Journal*. He won small settlements from the Atlanta *Constitution* and the New York *Daily News*. His only substantial legal victory, however, came over Rockwell. After a year, he was finally able to evict the Nazi Party and its commander from the Arlington house, to the relief of the immediate neighbors.

For months Rockwell made his headquarters in a shack in Fairfax

County, Virginia, but by the end of 1959 he had found another home. Floyd Fleming, a supporter Rockwell had inherited from John Kasper, purchased a house for the party at 928 North Randolph Street, Arlington, and it was here that Rockwell began recruiting storm troopers. With the recruits, Rockwell hoped to be able to satisfy at least some of the demands of his supporters for action and more action. He soon, however, found this an impossible appetite to sate, trapped as he was in the publicist's nightmare. Having already advocated genocide ("the only cure for Jewitis is old Doctor Adolf's *gas cure!*") he found himself unable to come up with a topper. He therefore shifted his sights, reverting to his old John Kasper training, and attempted to stir up anti-Negro and anti-Semitic violence in Washington. He astounded Christmas shoppers in 1959 with leaflets under the imprimatur of the American Nazi Party. One was headlined, "WHITE MAN! ARE YOU GOING TO BE RUN OUT OF YOUR NATION'S CAPITOL (sic) WITHOUT A FIGHT?"

Rockwell has consistently stated that Negroes have no place in his new world. "We've got a generous aid program . . . What we offer is $10,000 per Negro family of five or more, free first-class transportation back. They'll love it back in Africa, they'll live like potentates with all that money." Where "all that money" will come from, he does not state, presumably from the confiscated property of the victims of the proposed genocide.

But even this failed to create the splash Rockwell sought, and so it was with gratification that the commander greeted the announcement that he was being thrown out of the Naval Reserve. A Pentagon spokesman noted that "Mr. Rockwell was discharged from the naval service because of his public and open espousal of race and religious hatred, which reflected upon his judgment as an officer of the Naval Reserve to such an extent as to raise serious questions concerning his mobilization potential. . . ." With this much of a boost, Rockwell found himself ready to ride into the spotlight grudgingly provided by the American press. In April, May and June of 1960 the Nazis, inspired by tourist crowds, set up open-air meetings on the Washington Mall. Guarded by several storm troopers, Rockwell stood on his own speaker's stand and harangued crowds through his loudspeaker. Small scuffles occasionally resulted and were duly reported.

Greatly encouraged, Rockwell looked for new worlds to inflame. He applied for a permit to speak in Union Square, New York City, on July 4, 1960. In short order, the application became a political, as well as a legal issue. The Public Awareness Society went to court to seek an injunction against the Rockwell appearance, and it was to oppose that action that Rockwell came to New York City and the State Supreme Court on June 22, 1960. The proceeding that morning, before Justice Vincent A. Lupiano, was an intricate one, and during the morning a recess was declared. Rockwell stepped into the building rotunda to find a battery of television and radio reporters, as well as a contingent of the Jewish War Veterans, many wearing campaign hats, and a number of survivors of concentration camps, wearing, in symbolic protest, their striped uniforms. Predictably, Rockwell headed for the waiting microphones and cameras. With the first question, the crowd swelled until police estimated that some one hundred fifty spectators were watching the interview. "Do you have any. . .estimate on the percentage of Jews that you would say are traitors?" the commander was asked. "A very loose estimate which I have no backing for except my own guess and that's eighty percent," he replied. "Do you think that if you came to power that eighty percent of the Jews would have to be tried and executed?" "I suspect that," Rockwell said, and there came from the crowd a shout, "Let's get him." "Kill him," somebody else shouted, and the crowd surged forward.

The court security guards got to Rockwell first, however. Then a cordon of sixteen patrolmen arrived and hustled Rockwell into an antechamber, and back into the courtroom. After the hearing was concluded later in the morning, reinforced police escorted Rockwell out of the courthouse and, with difficulty, cleared a path for him to a taxi. As the vehicle drove away, somebody spit through the open window at its occupant.

That afternoon Mayor Wagner rendered the morning's legal proceeding moot. Acting as the city's chief magistrate, he ordered the parks commissioner, the late Newbold Morris, to deny Rockwell's application to speak in Union Square. "Left to their own devices, the people of the city will stone Rockwell out of town," the mayor said. "There is not a decent responsible citizen in the city who would follow him in his preaching. There are millions who have friends and relatives who died because of this race hatred either as unarmed victims or soldiers fighting for freedom. . . .In this case, every fact we have shows Rockwell's presence as a preacher of race hatred will cause a riot the police will have to quell. This is an invitation to riot and disorder from a half-penny Hitler. The invitation is declined. Mr. Rockwell will not speak here on the Fourth of July or any other time in terms of race hatred and race extermination." Several papers supported the mayor, but The New York Times disapproved editorially: ". . . we believe in the First Amendment even when it hurts. . . .Rockwell is not going to shake the foundations of this Republic. If he were left quietly to speak his piece, however revolting and abominable it is, he would create no impact."

The day the editorial appeared, however, a few days after the near riot and the mayor's statement, Lester Fahn, an attorney who held the title of "Anti-Rockwell Co-ordinator" of the local Jewish War Veterans, swore out a warrant for the commander's arrest in the Supreme Court incident. For nearly six years the warrant, charging disorderly conduct, tending to incite riot, kept Rockwell from being heard in New York City, not that he had any immediate desire to return. The mob at the Supreme Court had, he admitted to me, put a fright into him. "Sure, I was scared. Who wouldn't have been? I want police protection and, if necessary, the Army and Navy National Guard troops. I'm going to need it. If they can call out the National Guard and the Army for three Negro girls in Little Rock, they can call out the Army for me." Pending that mobilization, however, the commander had other fish to fry. He returned to the Washington Mall and Judiciary Park and made a nuisance of himself elsewhere in the capital as well. He and perhaps a dozen troopers picketed the appearances of Negro entertainers, particularly Sammy Davis Jr., and there were occasional skirmishes around the Arlington headquarters. "The papers wouldn't give me any publicity," Rockwell boasted to The New York Times. "They can't ignore me any longer." Neither, apparently, could the Washington authorities. After a relatively minor skirmish on the Mall on July 3, 1960, government attorneys, rather than prosecute Rockwell on disorderly-conduct charges, moved to commit him. Assistant Corporation Counsel Clark King said there were adequate grounds "to show this defendant, Rockwell, is of unsound mind. . . . We have prima facie evidence to show that this man may not be competent. We feel he should be sent down for observation."

In a later hearing, Dr. John D. Schultz, medical director of District of Columbia General Hospital, basing his opinion on Rockwell's writings and cartoons, many of them obtained from the files of the Anti-Defamation League, supported the government, and Rockwell was ordered in for a mental examination. The stated period of commitment was thirty days, but within a week Rockwell was freed after psychiatrists found him competent to stand trial. In *This time The World* Rockwell credited his speedy release to his cooperation with a Jewish psychiatrist. "He reasoned correctly that if I really were a paranoid nut, I would be totally hostile to a Jew . . . ."

By this time, however, the tourist season was ending and Rockwell found diminishing returns in the weekend hate rallies. A few tame sessions in Judiciary Park, without the speaker's stand and the loudspeakers, and, significantly, without swastika armbands for the storm troopers, and the speeches were dropped in favor of another program Rockwell had developed to remain in the headlines and keep the envelopes coming in. He determined to picket with advance notice to police and the press, of course, various city premieres of *Exodus,* a motion picture dealing with the escape of Jewish refugees to Israel and with that nation's fight for independence. The most notable of these picketing incidents were the fiascos in Boston and New Orleans.

Rockwell flew to Massachusetts with five supporters, leaving thirteen storm troopers to arrive by truck. When, on January 15, 1961, after advance trumpeting, the leader reached the theatre, he found a crowd of five thousand angry Bostonians waiting. Rockwell roamed through the crowd, a coat covering his uniform, until recognized. The crowd gathered ominously around him and a flying wedge of police plucked him out of the mob and hustled him through the back of the theatre he had come to picket and into a prowl car. The thirteen troopers in the truck had trouble, too. One trooper explained later that Rockwell's reinforcements were delayed because the vehicle had broken down five times. A more palpable cause of the delay was the runaround Boston police had contrived. Each time the brown-shirted, swastika-flaunting troopers stopped to ask directions, they were deliberately misled by well-briefed patrolmen. Finally, as they cruised hopelessly lost in a suburb, word went out over the police radio that Rockwell had been placed in protective custody and a prowl car was dispatched to bring the troopers into a station house. The radio order, not without humor, was: "If the driver has any questions, tell them their leader is there. Take them to their leader." After brief questioning, Rockwell and his troopers, ranging in age from twenty-two to thirty-five, were escorted out of town. The commander went home by air, of course, but thirteen sorry and ineffectual troopers had to crowd back into the breakdown-prone van without having so much as seen the theatre they had come to picket.

It is hard to determine whether the Nazis fared better—or worse—in New Orleans. A since-defected party officer, Schuyler Ferris, who also held a more routine job with the strategic Army Map Service, had provided a Volkswagen Microbus for the nine troopers making the trip, but, for his part, Rockwell still preferred flying. The troopers motored through the South—making sure to pass through racially troubled Montgomery,

Alabama—in the conveyance plainly labeled, "Lincoln Rockwell's 'Hate' Bus...We Hate Jew-Communism...We Hate Race Mixing." Trailed through most of their journey by police cars, both marked and unmarked, the Nazis were stopped just inside the New Orleans city line. "You are not to move a wheel until you cover up every one of those signs," the troopers were told by a police captain who cited a statute prohibiting acts which would "unreasonably disturb or alarm the public." The troopers covered the signs, but they then had trouble finding a place to stay since police had considerately explained to motel owners the significance of the uniforms worn by the would-be guests. The following day the "hate" bus came a cropper as the Nazi driver, attempting to elude a following police car, steered into a railing. He was jailed for reckless driving.

Undaunted, the remaining troopers continued downtown to join Rockwell in picketing *Exodus.* Their signs, reading "America for Whites." "Africa for Blacks" and "Gas Chamber for Traitors," brought them immediate arrest under the statute originally cited to them by New Orleans police. But even the bars of New Orleans Jail weren't to deprive Rockwell of his headlines. He put himself and his men on a hunger strike which lasted five days until Rockwell applied for release on $300 bail. His first stop out of jail was a French Quarter restaurant and a steak dinner. That concluded, he wired his still imprisoned and hungry troopers: "YOUR WILL AND DEDICATION IS INSPIRING WHITE MEN EVERYWHERE TO STAND UP AND FIGHT. START EATING AND GOD BLESS YOU. SIEG HEIL." The Nazis were later sentenced on charges of conspiracy to breach the peace and unduly alarming the public. Rockwell drew a $100 fine and a sixty-day sentence, and the troopers

received lesser terms. (The convictions were reversed on appeal, however. A three-judge panel ruled that "conduct of the defendants, no matter how repugnant to the average mind, did not involve a violation of the law.")

The following month, July, 1961, back in Arlington, two troopers were also successful in finding their ways to jail. Richard Braun, twenty-six, and Robert Garber, thirty-one, drew one-year terms after they dragged a passing thirteen-year-old Jewish boy into the Arlington headquarters, handcuffed him and quizzed him about his religion. The resulting furor inspired the Virginia Legislature, in 1962, to enact a bill rescinding the Nazi Party charter and forbidding the use of the words "Nazi" or "National Socialist" in a state charter. The party is, therefore, now formally incorporated as the George Lincoln Rockwell Party. The State of Virginia was not alone, either, in pondering the question of the legal status of the Nazis. When he was attorney general, Robert F. Kennedy announced that he would not undertake to add the party to the list of subversive organizations, since such a listing would require public hearings and afford Rockwell a forum to spread "obnoxious doctrines."

Denying Rockwell the forum he needs to attract contributions has been, indeed, a persistent topic. In 1965, when the Nazi commander was a candidate for governor of Virginia (he garnered 5,730 votes out of 562,789 cast), the Danville *Register* in an editorial noted that it had not covered a previous night's speech because "Nothing Rockwell has said or done in the past suggested that he might have anything to say or that he might do anything which would be worth printing as information for readers. This newspaper has not ignored Rockwell, nor will it. When he makes news, it will be covered and printed—no matter how much we disagree with what he says or does."

There are, however, editors who would ignore even the wildest stunts of Rockwell. Ben H. Bagdikian, a free-lance reporter, recently charged that there was, in Washington, a "gentle suppresion" of news on the Nazi. "It is," he wrote in the *Columbia Journalism Review,* "a quarantine under the best possible conditions of a subject odious to most Americans, but the quarantine is still pernicious....Who is to decide whether Naziism is an issue in this country? And how is anyone to know if it is quarantined from public study?" An interesting suggestion for freeing Rockwell from such a quarantine and yet minimizing his potential support was put forth in 1965 by William F. Buckley, Jr., the editor of the conservative *National Review.* In a column appearing in the New York *Journal-American* Buckley noted with approval that *The Times* of London was reporting the activities of British Nazi Colin Jordan "with that benign toleration that distinguishes the Englishman's attitude toward eccentrics." The "urbanity" of *The Times* reporting, Buckley maintains "is in refreshing contrast to the battlefront treatment so frequently given to the movements of our own Mr. Rockwell, a man...whose rodomontade happens to take the form of vulgar and brutal pro-Nazi posturing. . . .The British have a great deal to teach the American press on how to deal with such as Rockwell. It is, one supposes, necessary to cover the most conspicuous exploits of Mr. Rockwell. Hardly necessary, I should think, to treat them with that sober-seriousness that encourages the wild exaggerations of his importance, and that of his handful of fellow cretins, that some foreigners attach to them."

It is, perhaps, the "battlefront treatment" cited by Buckley that makes Rockwell a surprisingly effective speaker on American college campuses. Students who have been led to believe they will witness a madman are taken aback by the amicable and scholarly demeanor Rockwell adopts for such appearances. This rational effect is often enhanced by the furious denunciations which rain upon university administrations when it becomes known that Rockwell has been invited to speak, usually by a campus group eager to prove its independence from institutional control. Such an outcry helped Rockwell hold the attention of a student audience in February, 1964, at Hofstra University. Sometimes, also, there are bomb threats and student reactions. When Rockwell spoke to nine hundred students at Antioch College eight months later, for instance, he was met by an organized and planned silence. When he finished his talk, the crowd rose silently and left, although Rockwell had indicated he would be willing to answer questions. He wasn't too nettled, Rockwell maintained later. The student groups pay no actual fees, but the commander of the American Nazi Party demands, and receives, quite adequate "expense" payments. Now and then somebody will choose a less subtle response to Rockwell. In 1962 he yielded his microphone to a San Diego State College student who, instead of asking a question, turned and caught the surprised Nazi with a right hook. The assault brought Rockwell publicity, all right, but it is doubtful that he appreciated it. His picture, flinching away from the punch, appeared in newspapers across the country the next day.

Rockwell is, however, rarely so effectively answered. And not only students are surprised by his ability as a speaker. Early last year executives of Oklahoma City radio station KTOK took newspaper advertising to print a letter of apology for Rockwell's participation in a panel discussion, "We thought long and hard about allowing this man to appear on KTOK," the letter said. "Our conclusion was that it is important to know your enemies, and that exposing Rockwell and his views to honest and open scrutiny would discredit him. We made a serious error in thinking that the speakers we had invited to debate with him could compete equally with a man who disregards the truths of history and known evidence. It was our intention to show this man up for exactly what he is. Our performance did not live up to our intentions. We are sorry."

In essence, however, neither the speeches nor the lawsuits bring in much money. Only action, and outrageous action at that, fills the post-office boxes that Rockwell has scattered in and around Washington. Rockwell and the troopers often picket conventions, particularly political conventions, hoping to incite a scuffle or incident worthy of being reported by the wire services to papers all over the world. They were successful at the August, 1964, Democratic National Convention, and one of those arrested in the melee at Atlantic City, Lon Donaway, outdid even that headline the following month when he physically attacked a witness who was testifying at a House Un-American Activities Committee hearing. The embarrassed committee chairman was forced to apologize to the witness, Morton Slater, who was about to undergo questioning on visits by American students to Cuba.

The Nazis topped even that invasion of the Capitol in 1965 when another trooper, "Captain" Robert A. Lloyd, in blackface and a stovepipe hat, ran onto the floor of the House of Representatives preceding the challenge of the Mississippi Democratic Freedom Party to the credentials of Mississippi Congressmen. "I'se de Mississippi delegation, I want to be seated," Lloyd shouted, and, as he was dragged away, "Long live Rockwell." Considering the publicity that stunt garnered, it was quite inexpensive: Lloyd forfeited $20 disorderly-conduct collateral.

Finally, all other publicity devices failing, Rockwell stands ready to turn on his followers. In August, 1963, after an unsuccessful attempt to protest the civil-rights march on Washington, Rockwell made sure of getting his name in the papers by denouncing, in a short harangue, "the cowardice of the white race—right wingers." Not quite a year later, when Rockwell lent his support to an organization which called itself the Committee of One Million Caucasians to March on Congress, the scheduled rally was hastily called off. Some two hundred thousand demonstrators had been summoned to the Washington Monument Grounds, but only Rockwell and three hundred, many of them curiosity seekers, appeared. "Gazing at the empty space ahead of him," the Washington *Star* reported, "Mr. Rockwell mused: 'Our cause is almost ridiculous,' an admission that drew laughter from the audience. 'We are ridiculous,' he decided." He looked still more ridiculous when he entered the 1964 Presidential primary race in New Hampshire and then found that the single state resident he could persuade to run as a pledged delegate was not a registered voter.

Thus, feeding on scorn and ridicule when all else failed, the party has survived, and, despite three major setbacks, Rockwell has prospered. He and the party were most seriously affected, probably, by the wave of revulsion that swamped extremist movements after the assassination of President Kennedy. "It louses up the political picture for the preservation of the white race," Rockwell correctly predicted at the time. Contributions dropped off almost to nothing, and even Rockwell was forced to remain remarkably silent for some months.

Another obstacle to party expansion has been the frequent mutinies. Rockwell admits to three, but in point of fact the Nazi movement seems to have trouble keeping its officers. For example, during his eight years as "commander," Rockwell has identified four different men as his "deputy." The present one is Mathias Koehl. Not all the mutineers are permanently disaffected. One, John Patler, returned to the party and was promoted to the rank of "captain." He is now in charge of the printing facilities the party maintains in Spotsylvania, Virginia. Another participant in the Patler mutiny, Daniel Burros, was also later restored to party membership, but not to the ranks of the storm troopers. Burros committed suicide in 1965 after The New York Times revealed his Jewish background. "If Burros had come and told me the truth," Rockwell said regretfully, "I believe we could have straightened it out. . . .I would have sent him as infiltrator into Jewish organizations."

Rockwell's biggest setback, at least from a financial point of view, came a year ago December when the Internal Revenue Service padlocked his Arlington headquarters, charging him with nonpayment of $3,429.25 in various taxes over a three-year period. Seized in the building were two small presses and other printing equipment, as well as the Hitlerian memorabilia displayed in the "Shrine Room." Officials proposed to include the Nazi paraphernalia and souvenirs in the auction to satisfy the tax lien until New Jersey Senator Clifford Case pointed out that such an act would put the I.R.S. and therefore the United States "in the position of purveying for profit the same stock in trade as the American Nazi Party." The embarrassed tax men decided eventually that the swastika armbands and the portraits of Hitler were not worth the cost of selling them, and these were restored to the party, along with Rockwell's mailing list and other items which Federal Judge Oren R. Lewis ruled exempt from seizure as "tools of the trade." Sale of the remaining office equipment netted a little more than $700 toward the lien, and Rockwell says he is paying off the balance of the tax "extortion" in installments.

If he is as successful as he claims to be, Rockwell should have no trouble in meeting the payments. The American Nazi Party boasts that it has a roster of five hundred troopers and fifteen hundred members, all of whom are supposed to pay monthly dues of $5. Rockwell maintains he is strict about enforcing these payments (he estimates he expels nine out of ten members, mostly for nonpayment of dues). By his own greatly disputed figures, therefore, he should be grossing, in dues, $10,000 every month. Then there is the mail-order business. The party magazine, The Stormtrooper, offers for sale at least thirty items: photographs of Hitler and Rockwell "suitable for framing," fifty cents; a "Hatenanny Hit Record" featuring singers who call themselves the "3 Bigots," ninety-nine cents; American Nazi stickers, "Bright little hell raisers in black and bright red with Swastika!", twenty-five for a dollar, and that old, discredited forgery, "The Protocols of the Learned Elders of Zion," at a dollar. The mail-order items, Rockwell estimates, account for about half the party's income. There are also contributions to the party and the "expense" payments Rockwell receives for speaking appearances. And finally, as he frankly admits, "in certain cases I get money given to me as a person by certain people." Rockwell's enemies say that two of these "certain people," from Texas and California, pay Rockwell $500 and $400 per month respectively.

Despite all this, Rockwell maintains, for the record, that party income reached a maximum of $30,000 in 1965, "and that's because we had a campaign for governor." Certainly, however, the Nazis are drawing enough money to support several minuscule chapters around the country, and to pay the printing bills in Fredericksburg. In addition to the quarterly *Stormtrooper,* the party also puts out, from time to time, a publication entitled *The Rockwell Report,* and, as of a year ago, a $2.50 pseudo-scholarly offering, *National Socialist World.* Except for the inevitable article by Rockwell and certain of the mail-order items, *National Socialist World* bears little resemblance to the twenty-five cent pocket-sized *Storm-trooper.* Its first issue, in fact, appeared to be devoted almost entirely to a "condensed" article of approximately seventy thousand words, dedicated to Adolf Hitler and devoted to upholding the führer's concepts of a master race.

Even more pleasing to Rockwell is the fact that he no longer has to depend entirely upon his own publications to see his words and pictures in print. The Nazis were subjects of a pictorial study in *Esquire* several years ago, and in April, 1966, *Playboy* published a lengthy interview Rockwell had courteously granted Alex Haley, a Negro reporter.

Matters might seem to be looking up for Rockwell, especially in New York City. For nearly six years the warrant stemming from the Supreme Court rotunda incident had had the effect of sparing the five boroughs his public appearances, this despite the fact that he eventually was granted his speaking permit. Acting in his absence, American Civil Liberties Union attorneys won, on appeal, a reversal of Mayor Wagner's ban. Appellate Division Justice Charles D.

Breitel ruled that Rockwell must be given a platform and that in the lack of actual criminal provocation on the part of the Nazi, "his right, and that of those who wish to listen to him, must be protected, no matter how unpleasant the assignment." The State Court of Appeals upheld the ruling, and after the United States Supreme Court declined to hear a city appeal, the Parks Department grudgingly issued Rockwell a speaking permit, not in Union Square, but in a handkerchief-sized park south of the Fulton Fish Market. The commander never even bothered to pick up the permit. However, possibly acting in the mistaken belief that the civil action nullified the then almost two-year-old warrant, he did accept an invitation to speak at Hunter College in April of 1962. New York City police were quick to warn him of the error. A since-mutinied aide, "Captain" Seth Ryan, made the Hunter speech for him.

For several years thereafter there was an undeclared truce. So long as Rockwell did not publicly announce his presence in New York City, officials here made no move against him. When he spoke at Hofstra College in February, 1964, the warrant was not forwarded to Nassau County. The next year Rockwell came, unannounced, to the city to record a radio panel discussion and found on the other side of the debate Martin Berger, an attorney associated with the New York Civil Liberties Union, the local chapter of the national organization which had appealed successfully for the speaking permit. Rockwell told Berger of the New York stalemate and asked if this wasn't, in effect, a deprivation of his civil liberties. "I told Rockwell the usual civil-liberties position, that we felt he had a right to state his views," Berger recalls. "I said if I were asked to represent you on a civil-liberties matter, I would represent you, regardless of my feelings."

Rockwell professed to see no reason for Berger's revulsion toward him personally. "What are you so excited about?" he asked. "I'm a pro just like you."

Rockwell then proved himself willing to gamble that Berger was, indeed, a "pro." He accepted a bid to speak before Humanitas, a Columbia University student group. The date was set for February 10, and an audience of fifteen hundred—not counting one hundred and fifty pickets—awaited the Nazi speaker at McMillin Auditorium. Rockwell never arrived. He was arrested in the apartment of the president of Humanitas. "Get me Martin Berger," the New York *Post's* Kenneth Gross quotes Rockwell as saying as police took him away. "I was at home getting ready to go out to dinner," Berger said later, "and the phone rang. The caller said he was associated with Commander Rockwell, and would I come down to Night Court on this arrest? I decided I would have to do what I said I would do." For Berger it was an expensive decision. Not only did he miss his dinner, but, after it was reported that he was Rockwell's unpaid, volunteer attorney, several paying clients found other attorneys. "Two I could understand. They had been refugees during the war." In all, Berger estimates, working free for Rockwell cost him $2500.

Before Judge James L. Watson, a Negro, Berger was able to win the release of Rockwell on $100 bail, a sum posted at once by one of the troopers. The commander was ordered to appear the next morning in Criminal Court, and after several postponements a preliminary hearing was scheduled for April 11 before Criminal Court Judge Neal P. Bottiglieri. At that proceeding Berger moved to dismiss the complaint on the grounds that Rockwell's statements, while "noxious and poisonous . . . are privileged statements under the Constitution, statements which the defendant has every

right to make, particularly in response to a question in private conversation, the only response to which was illegal action on the part of bystanders." The lawyer also made the point that the almost six-year delay between the procurement of the warrant and its execution violated the defendant's right to a speedy trial. The reply of Assistant District Attorney Irwin Rochman was that Berger had jumped the gun, that both defenses were issues of constitutional law, and, as such, not within the province of a hearing magistrate. "The defendant is not being tried for suppression of ideas," the prosecutor said, citing the uncontradicted testimony of Fahn, the Jewish War Veterans official, now himself an assistant district attorney in Brooklyn. Fahn had repeated, for the record, Rockwell's rotunda remarks and had described the ensuing near-riot. "It is the people's position," Mr. Rochman said, "that at the time these statements were made, they were being made knowingly and willfully with intent [to cause a riot]."

Judge Bottiglieri set May 16 as the trial date. It soon became apparent, however, that despite Rochman's in-court pleading, the district attorney's staff was giving serious thought to the Constitutional issues raised by Berger. Rockwell's trial was put off six times, all at the request of the district attorney. ("This is holding up my business," the Nazi commander was heard to complain in the court corridor after one of the postponements.) Finally, the prosecution was ordered to proceed on June 27.

In the intervening time I went down to Arlington to revisit George Lincoln Rockwell. Deprived of his former headquarters after the tax raid, Rockwell has moved to his troopers' "barracks" on the outskirts of town. Unlike the former headquarters, easily distinguishable by a second-story sign ("WHITE MAN . . . *FIGHT!* SMASH THE BLACK REVOLU-

TION NOW'') and the notoriety which made it an embarrassment to the neighborhood, the "barracks" is hidden modestly away from passersby. Even though I knew the address, far out Wilson Boulevard, almost to the Fairfax County line, the building's partially concealed driveway was difficult to locate. Having found the driveway, I followed it about two hundred yards, up a steep hill and past a sign which reads "NO TRES-PASSING. Survivors will be prosecuted." At the end of the road I drove between strands of barbed wire and up to a white, two-story house badly in need of paint. I parked next to the building, beside the El Dorado camper which Rockwell uses on trips around the country.

There was no bell so I knocked twice. Inside, I could hear the barking of two dogs (both large and quite friendly, I found later) but no voices. Finally, the door was opened by "Lieutenant Colonel" Welch, then the ever-present deputy, a blond, taciturn Texan. He was wearing khaki pants, a white T-shirt and a holster. Inside the foyer I spotted Rockwell's old red-and-black swastika flag, recovered from the Internal Revenue Service. Beneath it, a portion of the ceiling was falling down. A sign at the foot of the staircase warned that no liquor or beer would be tolerated on the premises. Rockwell's room was at the head of the stairs. Welch knocked, and we entered. Rockwell was already on his feet, his hand extended. I tried to ignore it. "No, sir," the commander said. "If that's the way you feel about it, you go right back out of here."

"Isn't that a little ridiculous," I asked him. "You want to exterminate me, yet you want me to shake hands." Rockwell was adamant. "By shaking your hand, I am not trying to be your friend. It's merely a custom that symbolizes that you come here in peace, and, for my part,

that you're welcome in peace." We shook hands.

Rockwell motioned toward a chair, and, after I sat down, so did Welch, in a chair slightly behind mine. His hand rested on his holster. I was surprised to see the room so clear and uncluttered. Gone were the swastikas, banners and eagles that Rockwell had favored in the first headquarters I had visited seven years before. There was a neatly made bed in this room and several filing cabinets, as well as a desk on which an electric typewriter rested. There were also two bookcases, one partially filled with an *Encylopedia Britannica,* the other containing dozens of reels of recording tapes. I also noticed a small table which bore a board and chessmen. White had won the last game. There was only one picture in the room, identified by Rockwell as that of his oldest daughter Judith. The only two items I could find that indicated the political nature of the occupant were a small bust of Hitler over the desk, and a flag which, at first, I could not identify. "Vietcong," Rockwell enlightened me. "We took it away from some peaceniks in Washington. Now, I suppose you'll go ahead and write that Rockwell is flying a Vietcong flag in his room." I assured him that if I mentioned the flag, I would put it in the proper context. Where was his tape recorder, I asked? In recent years Rockwell has been taping his interviews. He even appeared with a recorder (which he was forbidden to turn on) at a New York State legislative committee hearing to which he was subpoenaed after his arrest in February, 1966. "I gave up," he said. "You guys never print what I say anyway."

Rockwell and I discussed old associates. He and Arrowsmith "have more or less made up," he said (this was later to come as a surprise to Arrowsmith). "Not that I mean to imply he has contributed a penny, which he has not." Weston Weed, a would-be trooper who came to Arlington only to be arrested for a bank robbery in New Jersey, went to jail and has not been heard from since. Ralph Forbes "is now the captain in charge of our Los Angeles operation." Robert Lloyd, who was named party security officer after his blackface demonstration on the floor of the House of Representatives, is on "leave of absence." He was snatched from the party "by a beautiful Texas woman." Seth Ryan, the "captain" who spoke for Rockwell at Hunter College, "joined a mutinous group that tried to take over the party." Matt Koehl "is the third man in the party now, a major." (Koehl as of December, 1966, has moved up to second.) George Lincke, once of the New York group, "is no longer associated with the party. We have nobody officially in New York now. I will not allow a unit there because we have no leadership." Floyd Fleming, who donated the headquarters later padlocked by the I.R.S., "never was a regular party member. He was a friend and supporter, and still is."

The day of my visit happened to be the day after the shooting, in Mississippi, of James Meredith, and, in that perspective, I asked Rockwell if he still believed, as he had once told me, that "arrogance and defiance" would protect him against assassination. "That's true," he said. "You notice Meredith didn't get killed. Much as I despise the S.O.B., he had the balls to go into Mississippi as he did. I think when the man came to shoot him—it is a hell of a thing to get yourself to do—I don't think he could do a good job in view of the arrogance of Mr. Meredith."

In the seven years since we had last talked I told Rockwell I had noticed two variations in the stated policies of the American Nazi Party. The first seemed to be a shift in primary targets. No longer ranting exclusively about Jews, Rockwell now appears to be devoting most of his hate-mongering hours to Negroes. "We still say the Jews are behind the ferment of social decomposition," the commander explained, "but the masses of people can't see Jews. They can see Niggers, who are the ulcers caused by the Jewish virus. Where the patient can't understand medical terms, we talk about the ulcers, which is Niggers."

The other point I asked Rockwell about was the puritanism that seemed to have found its way into party doctrines. I asked if it were true that drinking, smoking and cursing were now discouraged among the troopers. "That's correct," he said. "None of us smoke cigarettes. I still smoke my pipe because my boys felt it was a good public-relations proposition, but I don't drink anymore. I haven't touched a drop in four years. On Hitler's birthday party I got gassed and did something I didn't want to do." I asked what that had been, but it was apparent that Rockwell neither wanted to answer the question nor to offend me by refusing. Several years before, the man I was now interviewing had not, on occasion, hesitated to tell me to keep my "Jewish nose" out of his personal business. Now he appeared to be trying to turn my question away softly. He also seemed anxious for me to leave. He hinted that he had to get back to work, that his article for *Stormtrooper* had to be finished that morning. Yet he did not come out directly and ask me to leave. Somehow, this new, moral Rockwell had, like his corncob pipe, become a "public-relations proposition."

I had had enough, but, rising to leave, I accidentally knocked over a chessman on the table beside my chair. As I replaced it, I asked Rockwell if he were good at the game. "I think I am an unconventional player," he said.

"Everywhere I tackle players around the country I am called a bloody chess player. I play chess like I fight the Jews. I think a man reveals a lot about his nature in a chess game."

I wondered if he had time for a game, and, *Stormtrooper* deadline apparently forgotton, he had. "You'll have to take black, though," he said. "You can have first move, but I have to play with white." I gave him white and first move both.

"Boy, if only some people could see this," Welch said. He had spoken so infrequently I had almost forgotten he was in the room. "You playing chess with a Jew."

Rockwell played a slashing, offensive game for which I had, unfortunately, little defense. When, at last, I tipped over my king to resign, he leaped up, laughing, and abruptly there was a flash of the old Rockwell. "A portent of what is to come," he crowed. "Do you smell the gas?" The flash lasted only a minute. Then, his public relations restored, Rockwell was graciously excusing me from shaking hands as I left.

In New York City, on June 27, Rockwell's Criminal Court trial lasted little longer than the chess game, and it was just about as one-sided. Jerome Cohen, counsel to the Jewish War Veterans, and therefore to Fahn, struggled vainly—and alone—to initiate prosecution before a three-judge panel. Rockwell, he said, had deliberately inflamed the crowd in the rotunda. "If I can incite, I will incite," he quoted from the Nazi's writings. "When I appear in any public area, I will get these people so excited, a riot will break out."

Arrayed against Cohen—in addition to Berger, who really had very little to do in this proceeding—were two assistant district attorneys, Rochman, who had handled the case at the pretrial hearing, and Paul Savoy. In their eighteen-page petition for dismissal of the charge, the district attorneys cited, among other recent Supreme Court precedents, a 1949 decision written by Justice William O. Douglas: "A function of free speech under our system of government is to invite dispute. It may, indeed, best serve its high purpose when it induces a condition of unrest. . .or even stirs people to anger. . . .That is why freedom of speech, though not absolute. . .is nevertheless protected against censorship or punishment, unless shown likely to produce a clear and present danger of a serious substantive evil that rises far above public. . .unrest." Savoy cited four reasons why the case in point failed to meet the "clear and present danger" test. Rockwell, he pointed out, was in Supreme Court not to make a speech, but in connection with a legitimate judicial proceeding; the onlookers who rushed him were not a captive audience, but "appeared and listened voluntarily and with knowledge of the nature of the racist views" held by Rockwell; the statements made by him were not in the form of a speech, but were responses to questions posed by reporters, and, finally, the crowd did not become disorderly until the end of the interview, "and at that time, the police were able to disperse the crowd and protect the defendant from physical injury."

When it, at last, became their turn, the justices on the bench brought out their precedents and citations. Presiding Justice Simon Silver quoted a Supreme Court opinion on a 1966 Louisiana case: "Reaction by critics in disorder cannot be used to prevent the utterances."

I watched Rockwell as the case droned to its foregone conclusion. Judges and prosecutors were vying to uphold his right to speak the unspeakable, and the commander fidgeted in his seat, bored and anxious to leave. The camper was parked somewhere outside, and he had to get out, like any salesman, and make his rounds. There were people to see, prejudices to fan, post-office boxes to fill, and sitting in court while vindication swirled around him wasn't going to bring the money in.

Two months later, the reason for the commander's impatience became apparent. Capitalizing on the white blacklash from open-housing and civil-rights marches in Cicero and Chicago, Rockwell would enlist scores of Illinois recruits and fill a bushel basket full of coins and bills collected from those who marched behind his swastika emblem. Besides the immediate profit— enough to enable Rockwell and Forbes to pay $700 in court fines—there was the larger gain. "I told the New York *Times* I'd make them pay attention to me," Rockwell once said, and, by the time he left Chicago, he had. Stories and a picture of young, white toughs flaunting his swastikas had made The *Times'* front page, as well as those of most American papers. It was the commander's most conspicuous publicity coup.

By his own terms, George Lincoln Rockwell had made it. Through diligence and enterprise and perseverance, he had nurtured Naziism until it paid. And, as he liked to point out, those post-office boxes don't fill themselves. George Lincoln Rockwell had come a long way from the days when he had nothing more profitable to do than plan, at lip-smacking length, my execution. Now it was all business, and there was, at most, time only for a brisk game of chess, an exercise which could be rationalized as a symbolic test of the "nature" of his opponent.

"There'll be time for another beer together before you go to the gas chamber," Rockwell had once promised me. But that was before he gave up drinking and got down to business. And, in that freer and less lucrative era, I'll bet he would have found the time. Of course, I still would have had to buy the beer.

62 years for vagrancy

RAY RICHARD

A weary old man of 83 years sleeps peacefully on a canvas-covered mat in his cell at the State Hospital now, his mind no longer tortured by the sadness of being forgotten for 62 years.

No longer does this man, arrested as a vagrant and committed to the criminal hospital for a two-year sentence in 1905 ask himself, as he probably had done for decades, "Why could this happen to me?"

No longer can his mind try to reason why, since the day he was admitted, July 7, 1905, he has never had a visitor, never had a letter, a package or a message from outside his prison walls.

His mind is gone now. As far as living is concerned, his life is all wrapped up. His reason, his memory can never be regained. Nor can he ever tell his story of being a forgotten man.

Even his identity is almost erased. The officers who care for him know it, and maybe some of the other troubled men who spend their fading years in the same geriatric ward at the hospital have enough

Reprinted with the permission of the Boston Globe from The Boston Sunday Globe, *February 12, 1967, p. 66.*

of senses left to remember his true name, but hospital regulations, set by law, order that the identity of patients cannot be publicized. So we will call him George.

He has spent more years at Bridgewater State Hospital than any other of the 650 inmates now there.

But he's not the only forgotten man.

A man named John has been committed there since November 6, 1909. His crime, the commital papers reveal, was "Breaking and entering a building with intention to steal."

Another patient, named Charles, has been confined as a criminal in Bridgewater since February 2, 1910. His crime was breaking and entering, the maximum penalty for which was two years at the time he was committed.

A fourth patient has been committed to Bridgewater since 1910. His crime was vagrancy.

Still another man, now elderly like these others, has spent 56 years committed to the hospital for the criminally insane because on August 17, 1911, some judge ruled him "a tramp."

These are the men who have felt the back of society's hand. These are the patients for whom help, although late, may be on the way. The superintendent of the hospital, The Massachusetts Medical Society, the Massachusetts Bar Association and a special legislative commission updating our mental health laws all are fighting decades of apathy to help men like George and prevent others like him from being committed as criminals, then forgotten, for more than half a century after their sentences ran out.

Life once was exciting for George. He was 13 years old when he sailed into Boston Harbor, a shouting, waving, exhilarated young Swiss coming to the "promised land."

"He has been most carefully brought up by his grandmother," reads a plaintive, bewildering message written in longhand for hospital records in behalf of George's real mother in 1906.

"I am writing this because she does not know English," a clergyman, apparently from Lausanne, wrote.

"His mother says he drank, but she never knew him to drink to intoxication," reads another aged message in the files at the hospital, records which cast one weak ray of light into the darkened world of George, the forgotten man.

Why was he committed to Bridgewater?

The records tell all—or all that was required in those years to commit a young man of 22 to the institution which was officially known then as "The Massachusetts State Asylum for Insane Criminals."

Carefully preserved within the records are his commitment papers, his medical records, records of any visitors he might have received, a listing of any packages or other mail which may have been sent to him, the findings of psychiatrists and medical doctors who have examined him from time to time.

They all are carefully preserved under his name and his distinguished, unenviable number: Inmate 1304.

Inmate numbers are allocated consecutively as men are admitted as patients.

The last inmate to be admitted Saturday got number 9835.

The commitment papers, all properly signed by two physicians as required by law in these days, tell why this young immigrant who had been in the United States only eight years and in Massachusetts four months, was committed.

"He does not seem to comprehend questions" was the reply of the physicians to "Why was the patient admitted?"

Other reasons for George's being confined also were clearly delineated in the long questionnaire the physicians had to answer to make his commitment legally complete.

The questions included: The patient's appearance and mannerisms?

The doctors replied, "Dull, imbecilic; from appearances he would be unable to take care of himself."

An accurate knowledge of the previous history of the patient?

"At the age of six years," is the penciled reply, "a needle was introduced on his neck and the soul of his foot and produced no pain."

Under the question, facts indicating insanity personally observed by me (the physician) there was no answer, only 16 empty lines.

The answer to the next query was more specific: What the patient did? (Here state what the patient did in the presence of each examiner separately, unless it was done in the presence of both.)

The reply reads "Nothing special."

"Has he ever been insane before?" is the next question on the formal commitment paper.

"No," reads the reply, "except he was never normal."

The most detailed descriptions of George's shortcomings are explained in response to the instruction to the doctors. "Describe any disease, accident or change of circumstances that seem to have caused this attack."

He was sentenced for vagrancy in Somerville, other affidavits show.

Other documents describe the man, then 22, as he was seen at the time by relatives and neighbors, who replied to routine questionnaires sent acquaintances of men committed to Bridgewater in that era.

"At the last meeting with his mother (before being arrested for vagrancy) he offered her a dollar, which the mother wouldn't take," wrote one respondent. "She admonished him to buy clothing with it. This shows he was never angry at his mother. He listened always, silently to advice and to reproach and promised to do better."

But once committed, George was cast aside by our commonwealth. His file at the hospital has, almost mockingly, as its first entry: CRIME: vagrancy. SENTENCE BEGAN: July 1, 1905. SENTENCE EXPIRED: July 7, 1907.

Subsequent medical reports on the man detail almost inexplorably, his mental and emotional decline. A few years later, words like "regression" are noted in doctors' reports.

His downhill plunge is clearly noted by reports, each of which contains the statement: "STATEMENT: CUSTODIAL CARE."

From his mattress on the cold floor of his cell, George sat up Saturday evening in response to a friendly pat from an officer. It was plain that George had had it. His only response was an incoherent mumbling with a hauntingly rhythmic beat while he waved his right hand back and forth, then sideways, first like a trombone player, then as though he were leading a band.

His condition has regressed, the medical reports show. From the man committed because he "did not seem to comprehend questions," George was described recently in a psychiatric report in these terms:

"A mumbling, restless, growling, muttering, chanting, humming, drowsy, incongruous, hyperkinetic, ill-at-ease white male."

Others among the oldtimers at Bridgewater who have been forgotten by the law have similarly distressing records.

A former Brockton shoe worker who

was sentenced in 1910 for a two-year term, and is still there, had his "insanity" blamed, according to his records, on "poor heredity and alcohol."

The plight of these men distresses the staff of officers and medical personnel at the hospital.

"Please don't blame us for keeping them here for so long," one officer pleads. "We've had to. The laws required us to."

"These men cannot be saved now," Charles W. Gaughan, superintendent, says, "but they should not be in a criminal institution. They should be in a civil mental hospital which has many more comforts than we can offer here."

The president of the Massachusetts Bar Association, Attorney Paul Tamburello of Pittsfield, vigorously agrees and is leading his 6000-member organization in an effort to help these forgotten men.

"This man had a life to lead, but our commonwealth took it away from him," Tamburello said. "It's too late now to salvage his life, but we can't let this happen to any more men."

target:

mental health

BILL BURRUS

The volunteer worker's telephone rang for the third time that morning in May.

"You're either a Communist or just naively helping their cause," said the anonymous woman caller. "For your sake, dear, we urge you to get out of this mental health campaign."

Same as the two previous calls. Same as the anonymous letters and the yellow anti-mental health literature. Their terseness, their anonymity, were ominous. This housewife with two children—whose name is available as proof—was shaken. She called the Dallas Association for Mental Health and withdrew from the drive.

One volunteer lost wouldn't hurt much. But Mrs. Eleanore Carney, DAMH executive director, got resignations from more than 500 volunteers during the May drive. All because of pressure from the "anti" groups.

It had been the same during the benefit fashion show sponsored by DAMH three weeks before its Bellringer drive. It is the same now, with most of the new board members getting literature or calls. One new board member has recently resigned because of the pressure.

Jack McLendon, professional producer of the benefit fashion show, got an estimated dozen calls from the "antis."

"One told me I wasn't too healthy, and said I shouldn't do the show," said Mr. McLendon. "He had an exceptionally southern accent. I regarded the call as a threat."

Declared Mr. McLendon: "I've never produced a show that has created this much controversy before."

The orchestra leader was told he might lose future bookings if he played for the show. Volunteer ticket sellers were bluntly advised in anonymous calls that their Communist front was showing.

A fashionable Dallas women's store was threatened with a boycott if it participated. The owner doesn't want to talk about it now.

Reprinted with permission from The Dallas Times Herald from The Dallas Times Herald, *August 2-6, 1964.*

Newspapermen who reported the campaign against the mental health movement were called biased in anonymous letters and telephone calls, and a publisher was called a vile name by an unidentified telephone voice because the stories were run. This writer was warned that he had better watch what he wrote in the future, "for your own sake."

One of the leading volunteers in the benefit show reported her experiences with the "anti" group in an interview, then later declined the use of her name for the sake of her husband's business and her children.

"Until now I couldn't believe there was so much hate," said this active Dallas woman. In more than 10 calls castigating her or mental health, "they tried to talk me out of participating right up to the very end," she said.

"They told me that anyone could be picked up for no reason and carted kicking and screaming to an institution in Alaska," said the woman. The Alaska Mental Health Bill, which the "antis" use as one of their main arguments, will be described later.

Mrs. Rose Mary Hunt was helping to sell tickets for the show, and her two children were in it.

"A woman with a list of volunteer workers called and said flatly that I was working for the Communist conspiracy in helping this benefit," said Mrs. Hunt.

"Several others I contacted to buy tickets, and other persons who called me said similar things," Mrs. Hunt recalled.

When she became ill from a virus infection Mrs. Hunt continued to sell tickets from her bedside, although she couldn't participate in the show itself as originally planned. Because of the "antis" pressure she took her children out of the show, but received an award as one of the top volunteer ticket saleswomen.

"I just believe in the cause that much," said Mrs. Hunt. "There certainly is nothing communistic about the Dallas Association for Mental Health, and there is such a dire need in this field. Why, this is the nation's number one medical problem."

Mrs. Carney came here in January from the job as director of development of the Greater Chicago Association for Mental Health. She was picked by Dallas civic leaders on the DAMH board to fill the Dallas post.

"Callers told volunteers and me that I was sent here by the National Association for Mental Health, and that this organization was communistic and interested primarily in one-worldism," said Mrs. Carney.

With the "antis" still actively fighting the mental health association, Mrs. Carney said: "I have begun to be afraid for myself and my children. I get calls at night and there is only silence when I answer. Are they trying to find out if I am not there? Do they want to ransack my home to see if there are any messages from the Kremlin in it? I am a patriotic citizen and I want to fight this vicious, lying, un-American campaign."

Mrs. Fred Wiedemann, chairman of DAMH's annual fund-raising campaign, got a lot of anonymous calls and mail, but the weirdest was a piece of paper on which someone had drawn a small red circle the size of a dime, with a dot inside it.

Mrs. Wiedemann said she had seen an Alfred Hitchcock mystery show on television a few weeks before that letter came, in which the killer sent a similar cryptic message to his intended victims.

She said she wasn't afraid, but called police any way.

Most of the anonymous letters Mrs. Wiedemann received were printed in red ink on the same typewriter. (So was one subtle threat to this writer).

The anti-mental health movement doesn't limit itself to opposing DAMH or its state and national counterparts. It opposes anything that smacks of the mental health effort or psychiatry on the grounds that these are part of the Communist conspiracy.

It isn't carried out by a few hysterical people, nor is it confined to Dallas. Much of the literature circulated here is printed in cities throughout the country.

The movement is nationwide, although Dallas was the hotspot this year, according to NAMH officials. The opposition criss-crosses many organizations big and small.

The fashion benefit show made some clear money, and the annual fund drive this year collected $32,000—nearly $8,000 more than last year. But before this was accomplished strife fomented by the "antis" caused fears, and internal dissention.

"It follows the same pattern," new DAMH president Jack Gray Johnson said of the "anti" campaign. "Everytime they see anyone's name in the newspaper linked with the mental health association, they start calling, they start writing."

The volunteer who declined to be identified said that the anti-mental health people of which she is aware "often work like the Gestapo. They can imply something and do a lot of damage, for then the listener's imagination is likely to run away."

The hash of people who are indignant over the mental health movement would never be caught at the same social gathering. They range from unwealthy racists to multimillionaires.

The groups and individuals working against the mental health cause have one thing in common. They fervently believe that the mental health programs are Communist-inspired, a threat to liberty and the American way of life.

There are several organizations pushing this point of view with zeal, although some members within them take the alarmist views of their brethren with a shrug.

For instance the Daughters of the American Revolution both nationally and locally are as an organization among the most active anti-mental health groups.

Streams of literature from the DAR's national defense committee oppose the National Association for Mental Health as Red, and express the fears heard from many "antis" that Communists can use incarceration of political prisoners accused of mental illness as a means of taking over the country.

Most of the individuals and groups against mental health think of psychiatry in terms of a potential too for "brainwashing" patriots, and consider psychiatry anti-religious.

A state officer and one of the most prominent Dallas DAR's in terms of posts held and activities, said she hews to the national DAR line on the mental health issue.

"The mental health movement is tied together locally, nationally and worldwide," said the DAR leader. She labeled it as a force toward one-worldism and against democracy.

"We furnish material from our national defense committee on this subject," she said. "This year is not the first time, nor the last time, for it is a continuing program.

The difference of opinion of members within the DAR points up the conclusion that it is individuals, not groups, who are most active against mental health efforts.

In New York Mrs. Russell C. Langdon, a vice regent of the DAR, resigned because she could not endorse its stand—which she called in an interview "subversive to the best interests of our country."

In Dallas, Mrs. Martha Kate Allen—a past vice regent—said:

"I approve of my DAR in most things, and we do have a fear of world government. If fear outruns good judgment we will lose our spot in the sun."

"In reading all of this (DAR) material," said Mrs. Allen, "I can't find facts that justify the attack on the mental health association. If anything is wrong anywhere we should clean up and rebuild, not destroy something that we have such a vital need for in our community."

The John Birch Society through its American Opinion magazine of May, 1958, opposes the "one-world" aspect of the mental health movement it says is exemplified in the United Nations' World Health Organization and the independent World Federation for Mental Health.

The National Association for Mental Health is a member of the latter, as are 27 other American organizations, including the American Medical Association.

Robert Welch, founder of the Birch group, said on another matter in the society's "Blue Book" that even the AMA has been " 'took,' to the extent that we could not count on any direct help there."

But just as there are individual differences within the DAR, there are in the Birch Society, too.

Tom Wunderlick, construction executive and past coodinator of the Birch Society here, said there may be Birch members opposing mental health in Dallas, but the organization as a whole does not.

"The mental health work on the local level has certainly been good, and mental health support is needed here and elsewhere," said Mr. Wunderlick.

The Rev. Carey Daniel, pastor of the First Baptist Church of West Dallas and president of the Citizens Council of America for Segregation, said some of his members also belong to the Birch Society.

He named an Oak Cliff contractor who fights both integration and mental health

movements, a man the Rev. Mr. Daniel identifies as a member of the Birch Society and his council. "Our work often overlaps," said the Rev. Mr. Daniel.

Individual members in both the council and the Birch Society have made telephone calls and sent literature against the mental health movement, said the Rev. Mr. Daniel.

"Mental Health is one of the worst Communist conspiracies in Washington," the segregationist preacher declared emphatically. (He called back a week later and said his comments were not those of an expert, but "what I've heard.")

"Our organization sends out scads of literature against mental health," said the Rev. Mr. Daniel. "But I don't believe we stepped up the program during the mental health drive."

The Rev. Billy James Hargis is a Tulsa evangelist endorsed by the Birch Society. He toured the country with ex-Mayor Gen. Edwin A. Walker expressing their views on patriotism, Christianity and the Communist threat. The Rev. Mr. Hargis has written and spoken many words linking mental health efforts and communism. In Dallas, however, Mr. Walker declined to discuss the mental health issue with a reporter. "Viet Nam is the important thing right now," he said.

The list of smaller organizations opposing mental health is virtually endless. Many are little known, and purposely or not, they follow advice from Robert Welch in his Blue Book of the Birch Society.

He urges the organization of many sub groups with high-sounding titles to further Birch objectives, and on Page 85 he calls for "continuous organized letter writing" by these groups.

Mr. Welch says on Page 96 of the Blue Book that when communism is suspected but can't be proved, innuendo by questions can be devastating.

"The question technique, when skillfully used in this way, is mean and dirty," said Mr. Welch. "But the Communists we are after are meaner and dirtier, and too slippery for you to put your fingers on them in the ordinary way—no matter how much they look and act like prosperous members of the local Rotary Club."

The mass-mailings of anti-mental health literature in Dallas bear the names of many organizations. Many bear stamps from two ultra-right wing outlets, American Bookstore Co. on Snider Plaza and Teacher Publishing Co. at 3815 Bird St.

Unproved charges in anti-mental health literature mailed in Dallas show a score of organizations, unknown and vague in title.

In addition to the well-known Birch Society and the DAR, they include diatribes from such sources as Caxton Printing Co., Liberty Bell Press, Ltd., the Elmore County (Ala.) White Citizens Council, Arizonans for Mental Freedom, Dan Smoot Reports, CIVICS, the Patrick Henry League, Clarence Manion Forum, Aware America Campaign and the National Republic.

Also American Mercury, the Network of Patriotic Letter Writers, Inc., Common Sense, "The Nation's Anti-Communist Newspaper," a book called "Brain-Washing" by Kenneth Goff, an avowed ex-Communist, another on the same subject by the Freedom Builders of America, the American Public Relations Forum, Inc., National Economic Council, a book by American Nazi party leader Lincoln Rockwell, and many others.

The flood of literature is frequently years old, and it has one thing in common.

That is the theme that the mental health movement is out to enslave Americans' minds and de-power by incarceration true American patriots prior to assumptions of control by the communists.

The same words are often used in the literature. The same fears are expressed. Some of the literature still circulated now, is eight or more years old. Even the fresh "anti" literature offers little in the way of new arguments.

VI

the
sexually
unusual

Man's sexual conduct is surrounded with more taboos, rules, and constraints than perhaps any other aspect of his social life. Sexual behavior is rigidly prescribed: The range of persons who are appropriate sex partners is usually narrowly defined, the entry age for sexual activity is restricted, and the context in which it can take place is often specified. While the marriage bed hardly has a monopoly as a place for fun and games, members of the community tend more or less to accept most of the rules on sex behavior that have to do with the characteristics of the partner and exactly what is done. They hold that some sexual encounters are normal or natural, while others are abhorrent and unnatural. The hard impact of these rules is quite evident on our psychological well-being and social adjustment; the sex life of many community members is a compromise between the pressure for expenditure of sexual energies and the constraints of the community.

Man's potential to provide himself with sexual stimulation usually goes far beyond the narrow bounds set forth by norms of the community; in actuality, wide deviations flourish in spite of all the pressures toward conformity. Some females are unable or unwilling to accept males as sex mates, and some males are unable to achieve sexual gratification in heterosexual encounters because of their failure to identify properly with sex objects as they were growing up, the unavailability of persons of the opposite sex, or simply the greater hedonistic pleasure they derive from homosexual experiences. Others may be led to seek or to desire very young sex partners, or they may prey on unwilling and unwitting partners, or find their pleasure in "unnatural" acts. The general liberal tendencies in our times, some hold, have led to greater tolerance of sexual deviance; others maintain that we just talk more openly about what is going on. Even if tolerance for deviance has increased, however, many types of sexual encounters are still regarded as extremely undesirable or are viewed as symptoms of illness.

Individual	Individual
↓	↓
Individual	Organization

ALL THAT GLITTERS IS NOT GUILT

Persons who persist in following different sexual patterns from those of most individuals in the community are often led to develop an "under life" in order to continue in their extraordinary activities. Beyond his sexual behavior, the homosexual described in this case, like others, has a need for a meaningful social life. Donald Webster Cory describes a "gay" Thanksgiving party and provides keen insights to the problems of the sexually deviant. The "drag" which included deviant males and females, provides a place where individuals can meet each other for the purpose of sexual adventure. It also provides a social setting in which deviancy suddenly becomes acceptable, and the straight society can be ignored. Perhaps in this context the individual is the victim of another only in the eyes of some "straight" persons.

THE TRANSSEXUAL OPERATION

The development of a sexual identity, one's self-concept as being male or female, and the learning of appropriate ways of relating to both sexes are major results of early socialization. The importance of parents to the infant in the process of developing a sexual identity is well-accepted. However, the specific causes of failure to be adequately socialized in this respect are largely unknown. Furthermore, the biological process also may fail to endow an individual with the full attributes of either sex. As a result, from a physical standpoint, some persons are sexually marginal. Tom Buckley describes the experiences of such persons and their attempts to change sex roles after attaining maturity. Such individuals are not likely to be accepted or understood. Instead, they frequently may be seen as challenging the community and its attempts to maintain sharp lines between male and female.

Organization	Organization
↓	↓
Individual	Organization

THE LESBIAN IN AMERICA

One of the most difficult problems to remedy is the sexual attractiveness that some have for persons of their own sex. More than just having sexual relations with other women, lesbians tend to focus most of their social relationships about their sexual mates. Members of the straight community are often unwilling to accept such behavior and frequently assume that such persons are purposefully deviant or free agents who elect to become perverted. Extreme pressure is applied in many instances to bring the unusual to conformity. This case of a lesbian describes some of the problems encountered because she insisted on remaining true to her "real nature." She perceives herself as being persecuted by society because others want to force her to live a lie in terms of her personal desires for sexual gratification.

NEW YORK'S "MIDDLE-CLASS" HOMOSEXUALS

The term "pervert," used to describe homosexual individuals, has a pejorative connotation. It, like the slang expressions "fag," "queer," "fairy," and so on, expresses the contempt that the community has for gay people. In part as a response to community pressures, homosexuals develop their own social organizations which support and order the lives of the sexually unusual in their rebellion against the community's norms. Without such a structure it would probably be very difficult for individual homosexuals to endure the implicit and explicit negative sanctions of the larger community. William J. Helmer provides an introduction to the unique network of social organizations in New York City that meet the needs of the sexually unusual.

all that glitters is not guilt

DONALD WEBSTER CORY

The street-corner...the gay bar...and finally the drag. Let us take the reader on a third journey to a homosexual meeting place.

It is Thanksgiving. In one of the larger cities of the United States, tickets and invitations and word-of-mouth information have been circulating in all of the little islands that make up the homosexual fringes of society. The tickets pass around at the bars, and for weeks they have been brought home to lovers at night, discussed at length at many parties.

"Oh, I just don't know what I'm going to wear to the drag!" a youth shouts in a shrill voice.

"Can I get dressed in your house?"

"My sister has a beautiful gown—black velvet. Only I don't know where I'll get a pair of shoes to fit."

"Those high heels; If there's one reason I hate to go in drag, it's on account of the high heels."

"Why don't you go butch? Everybody'll take you for a girl dressed up as a man."

"You mean until they start dancing with me?"

"Don't brag. There she goes, bragging again!"

"Wouldn't she look sweet, masquerading as rough trade?"

The long-awaited Thursday night rolls around. Festivities and fun and carving turkeys in most American homes, and children dressing up in costume in many others. Before one of the largest halls in the city a crowd of neighborhood children gather, with a sprinkling of their elders. They stand on the sidewalks and form a gantlet, and they tease and taunt and, in shrill and obviously imitative voices, they scream like caricatures of women as the visitors arrive. They are, in fact, caricaturing the caricatures.

The hall itself is usually outside one of the more fashionable districts of the city, for it is safer for people to attend this costume ball in a neighborhood where they are not likely to be recognized.

Taxis pull up before the hall, and out come the masqueraders. Automobiles, driven by a man or woman in conventional dress, allow the passengers to alight before the door, then continue to find a parking place so that the driver may return for the evening of fun.

By ten o'clock the hall is beginning to fill; by eleven it is crowded to capacity. The band plays loudly, men are dancing with men, women with women, and men and women dancing with each other, or perhaps not quite sure of either the sex or the sexual temperament of the partner.

There are beauty and grace and grotesqueness all interwoven, sometimes a little of each in a single person, sometimes only the loveliness of the successful female impersonator, or only the horror of an individual who can never be what he was not made to be.

Are they play-acting, these men and women in masquerade, and their friends who are wearing "civies"? Some hardly take themselves seriously. They laugh, giggle, flirt and are coy, and then become engaged in their big affair of the night. Others have come to watch. They feel they are not quite one with these people, and they would not participate in the masquerade, yet they are participants, despite themselves. They are irresistibly attracted, yet they condemn themselves for all that is degraded around them. They are happy to be there, yet sad that such things be; they regret that they are a part of it, and yet envy those who are able to be more a part of it than themselves.

When I last attended a drag, not very long ago, I watched a sailor dancing with a young man. The sailor was in uniform, his companion in a tweed suit. They both talked loudly and vociferously. Their bodies were in exciting contact, their faces close upon one another's. They had no secrets from the world on this night; even their words must be shared. I could not help but be an eavesdropper.

"Ever come here in drag?" the sailor asked.

"Just once, never again," came the reply. "How about you?"

"What do you call this?"

They laughed and danced, and I passed on to another group. A man and a woman, each about twenty, were gracefully gliding along the floor. A man and a woman. . .they were not the only such pair in the hall. They seemed so contented together. Their intimacy seemed to arise from the closeness of knowledge, not of contact. Are they sweethearts, or man and wife, I asked myself. What are they doing at the hall of

the outcasts on this night? Did they arrive by accident, or have they friends or brothers here, or are they among those rare souls who especially enjoy the company of gay folk, although they are not themselves gay? Or, perhaps, are they thrill-seekers and slummers who have merely looked in upon another world?

These are the questions I ask myself. The band stops, and as they walk past my table, I ask them to join me for a drink. They accept and are seated, order drinks as I stare at the man. In this atmosphere the stare has lost its rudeness. Perhaps the face, with its telltale signs of never having been shaven, will betray the true sex, the biological sex, or perhaps the evidence will be found in the figure. Now my stare has trespassed the bounds of good taste even for this hall, but it is greeted only by a mysterious smile from one who is taking a delight in withholding the answer from my probing curiosity. I ask, but I might just as well ask the Sphinx. They leave. I shall never know whether they were. . .but what difference. They look like a happy couple.

Perhaps three-quarters of the people at the drag are males, and perhaps a third are in masquerade. Some can be spotted from afar. They trip over their skirts and their shoes. They are clumsy, gawky, uncomfortable. Others require close scrutiny, and a few can never be identified with certainty.

Everyone seems to be having a good time, even the recreational police, who are present in abundance, particularly in the hallways and the washrooms. No intoxication is tolerated, no exposure, no lewd behavior.

At midnight, the striking of the drum, the flashing of the lights, and the floor is cleared. The parade of the queens will take place. Every male in female attire who so chooses may get in line. The gowns are mainly on the lavish side, with here and there some striking simplicity.

But mostly one sees flowing skirts, flamboyant colors, an ostentatious overdressing. Many wear wigs; while others have scarves skillfully tied around their hair. There are no visible crew-cuts among them.

One by one they march to the platform, each stopping to pose like a model. Each turns around, shows form and figure to the judges and the audience, smiles coyly, listens for applause, and then descends. Perhaps the march continues for an hour. After the first few rounds of applause, the audience gives only a cursory clapping, except for an outstanding costume or an extremely effective impersonation.

Now and then the judges halt the march and examine more closely, seeking conviction that this is impersonation and not fraud. No woman may compete with these men who have faced the competition of women all of their lives.

Then the awards, with the queen being crowned, and second and third prizes given, followed by applause and protest, and by more dancing, drinking, flirting, weeping, long into the hours of the night. The time of departure draws near. Some part, alone and lonely, wishing to remain, although anxious to forget the evening. Others make their way out with the friends or lovers with whom they had come. Some leave in the company of new-found friends. For them, the evening of adventure remains to be explored. The night tis young and does not end even when the sun comes up in the morning.

"An outrage!" exclaim many citizens when they hear of the drag, and their judgments are reflected by many homosexuals. "These drags are a disgrace. That's the sort of thing that gives the gay life such a bad name," one of my friends is fond of saying to me.

"No one compels you to go," I retort. "But I know a lot of people who get a great kick out of them and who look forward to them from year to year."

When I see these men and women in masquerade, and at numerous other places where large crowds of gay people are gathered, as on a special boat-ride and at very large but informal dances, I cannot help but feel that the wearing of the clothes of the opposite sex (or *transvestism*, as this phenomenon is called) is but a very small part of the appeal of such affairs. The gay folk do not go for the thrill and the adventure, nor are they seeking new friends. I do not believe they are primarily motivated by a need to exhibit themselves. In the main, what attracts them to the drag is the feeling that they will be among many of their own kind. Here they are known, liked, and accepted for what they are. It is a masquerade, ironically enough, where one goes to discard the mask.

The drag—if there is anything in the relationship of the homosexual group to the dominant society that is anomalous, it is the drag. That it is desired by the homosexuals is an indication that they find unsatisfactory so many of the ordinary pursuits of entertainment and relaxation. That it is tolerated by a society which condemns so bitterly is an indication that the condemnation is neither whole-hearted nor sincere. If the people congregating at these affairs were the immoral and lecherous types that are depicted in journalism and literature, then it is downright irresponsible, if not immoral, to permit such gatherings, and to send police and detectives to oversee them. The dominant group tacitly admits, by its attitude toward the drag (just as it does by its failure to enforce its own laws) that it is neither willing nor able to carry out the consequences of its own moral judgments. Is it possible, then, that these moral judgments are built on shaky foundations, and are believed in only to a limited extend even by those who sponsor social hostility with the greatest vigor?

For the homosexual minority, most of whom never attend the drags and are little interested in them, and many of whom are indignant at their very mention, these gatherings play a role which is not frequently understood. Anything of a semi-legal nature which aids in breaking down the veils of secrecy and in bringing the homosexual life into the open is desirable. It is necessary to compel recognition of the minority, to insist upon its right of assembly as well as publication and agitation, as a prelude to the struggle for civil rights, judicial rights, and finally for social equality.

But, back to those who have come for the night. For a fleeting moment, this becomes their world. The abnormal is the normal, the straight fellow is a curiosity, and love is synonymous with the attraction of one person to another of the same sex.

I breathe deeply and though the air is stuffy and the hall noisy, it is refreshing and quieting to know that I am where I can feel that I belong. For this brief moment of unreality, many days of sorrow are worth living.

I look around and see the tortured, the grotesque, all of the tragedies of lives not yet lived. In their costumes, and out of them, I am with these people, and I hope that they enjoy this moment of peaceful triumph as much as I do.

It was at one such drag, as I watched a very lovely and graceful person being crowned queen of the night, that a companion muttered to me: "Happy soul for an hour, but what a guilty unhappy person you can be sure she is."

I looked quizzically at my friend: "I am not at all sure," I said. "I have learned one thing in the gay life that people from the outside cannot seem to believe."

"What is that?"

"All that glitters is not guilt."

the transsexual operation

TOM BUCKLEY

Some are secretaries, attentive and efficient, anxious to please; they are matrons in black, with pearls and gloves, in town for a day of shopping with friends from a quiet suburb; they are bar girls whose vulpine smiles light the corners of shady cafés.

They are young and they are middle-aged, beautiful and plain, but their coiffures, the makeup, the manicure, the perfume, the line of the neck, the angle of the wrist, are perfect, nearly perfect. Their voices are dark contralto; their words are carefully chosen; their poise is complete.

Who are they? You will never know. Nor will the lecherous shoe salesman who glances above the matron's stocking tops; the executive who pursues his secretary around the desk; or the John who embraces the bar girl on sheets of satin.

These women must be the happiest people in the world. Childhood dreams have come true. The impossible has happened. "How you pray for it!" says the secretary. "Like a blind man to get his sight back."

Yes, but who are they? Ah, friend, they are the great masqueraders of the world. They live in that umber land where illusion and reality, identity and anonymity, death and rebirth, mingle and diffuse. *They have changed their sex.*

"I was walking on Collins Avenue in

Miami Beach when I passed this women's shop," the secretary is saying. "I admired those clothes tremendously. I can't tell you what kind of feeling I got. It was such a thrill.

"Anyhow, to make a long story short, I bought a complete outfit. No, not there. I couldn't take a chance. I sent away to Sears, Roebuck. As soon as I got the package I locked the door and I went up to my bedroom. I put everything on—panties, padded bra, a garter belt, stockings, the dress. I relaxed completely. My tension disappeared. For the first time in years I was at peace. (I never could take dope or drink. I think it's the weak way out.) 'Oh, boy,' I thought, 'I'm losing my mind. This is wonderful.' So every night after I got home I'd change into my female clothes."

I'll call her Adeline. She is drinking ginger ale in my apartment. She is fifty years old and plain, but her back is arched against the sofa and her knees are together, just so.

"After about a year I took a long chance. I drove back to Miami Beach wearing one of my outfits. When I think back on it, the dress was all right but the wig and makeup were terrible. I went to a restaurant, and while I was there I had to go to the ladies' room. Dressed the way I was I couldn't go to the men's room, could I?"

"When I came out I felt someone looking at me. Anyhow, I paid the check and got into my car. I was driving away when a state trooper pulled me over. He asked to see my driver's license. When I showed him he looked it over very carefully and said: 'It says here that you're a man. Why are you wearing women's clothes?"

"It isn't against the law in Florida to wear women's clothing, but I was arrested for disorderly conduct, for using the ladies' room. When I came to trial it was just my luck that the case ahead of mine was the arraignment of a murderer. There were a lot of reporters in court and I got into the papers, too.

"I was a high-school teacher and when they heard about it in my town I was fired, pronto. But it was worse than that. People threw rocks through my windows. I got telephone calls every hour of the day and night. It got so I had to go twenty miles to do my shopping. I was a Methodist, and they threw me out of the church. 'We don't want any part of you,' they said."

"I couldn't stand it anymore. I felt more and more like a woman. I sold my house and went to Atlanta. Finally I decided to have the operation.

"I hated the idea. I thought I would be making myself a freak. But nobody was able to help me. I had been going to psychiatrists for years. When I came back, I still fought it. I made no progress. I felt like a man dressed like a woman. Then, one day when I was buying some cosmetics at Rich's in Atlanta, the saleswoman who waited on me seemed very sympathetic.

" 'Here is a woman I can tell my problems to,' I said to myself. It was hard to do but I was right. She was just one of those people with lots of empathy. She told me that I didn't know how to make myself up or do my hair. She took me to her beauty parlor.

"I began to perk up, to relax and enjoy living a little bit. A woman at an employment agency, I told her everything, too. She helped me to get a job. A wonder job; I've already had two raises. And I met a man, a wonderful, considerate man, not that sex is so important to me anymore.

"I always used to say to myself that the first time I dream of myself as a woman rather than a man I will know that the conversion is finally done. Well, it finally happened eight months ago."

In California last summer I met a girl

I'll call Suzanne. She was appearing at a "topless" nightclub, sweeping gracefully around the floor to the accompaniment of a rock-and-roll band playing *The Girl From Ipanema*. Suzanne was very pretty, dark-haired and brown-eyed, with long legs and a full figure.

"When I was ten or eleven I used to go to see Maria Montex movies," she said. "You remember her? I'd come home and I'd like to put on a turban like the ones she wore. When I was in junior high school the boys used to call me a fruit, a queer, a fairy. In a crowd with their friends they'd do that, but what I mean about how hypocritical they were, you'd be surprised how many would come up to me when they were alone and want me to do various things for them.

"When I was fifteen I dropped out of school. A couple of months before that I had met a boy who was in the gay life. I was good-looking and, I remember, he said to me, 'I'd bet you'd look wonderful in drag.' I didn't know what he meant. But I found out. I liked to wear women's things. I moved away from home and moved around the state. Let's face it, I was a prostitute. I was busted a couple of times. They don't do anything to stop homosexuality in jails. They had a gay tank where they segregated us, but there were always some guys who'd say they were homosexual so they could get transferred there. They'd become the big daddies of the gay tank.

"I tried to stop lots of times," she said. "I worked as a busboy. I got a crew cut and thought I was very butch. I always worked hard but I found out I could never get a promotion or the respect of my fellow workers. And there was always somebody grabbing me."

Suzanne was sitting in her sunny apartment. She wore a frilly white blouse and close-fitting jeans. Her lover, a dark, muscular man who had known her before her operation, watched her closely.

Always, she said, there was that deperate yearning to be a woman. It went with the certainty that, except in body, she *was* a woman. In her early twenties Suzanne worked as a featured dancer in a touring company of female impersonators and, again, as a prostitute.

"I was a very good hustler," she said dispassionately. "I had sugar daddies." She pulled some dog-eared nightclub photographs out of a trunk. They showed her, in full drag, sitting next to a succession of grinning apes in glittering suits and white-on-white shirts. The ashtrays bore the names of the places where men like that take girls like that. "I would tell them it was my time of the month, something like that," she said, "and offer, you know, to do something else."

Four years ago she met a wealthy man, a European with what one assumes is a taste for the bizarre. He offered to pay for Suzanne's operation.

"I jumped at the chance," she said. "It wasn't any trouble, except when I came through customs on the way back. I wore women's clothes all the time I was away, buy my passport still had my male name. So I had one sort of male outfit that I wore on the plane. I tucked my hair up under a hat. When the customs man opened my bags, though, he saw nothing but women's clothes. He gave me a very funny look but he let me on through."

Six months later, Suzanne told me, she went back to California for a silicone-implant operation to increase the size of her breasts. They had already started to develop, as had her hips, because of the female hormones she had begun taking before her surgery.

"When you realize you're passing, it's a wonderful feeling," she said. "But what gave me as much pleasure was this. . . ." She reached into her pocketbook and produced a birth certificate. It had been issued in 1965, and identified her as

Suzanne----, and gave her sex as female. It also listed a birth date that made her thirty-five. Since she had told me she was twenty-seven I noted that she had become female enough to lie about her age.

Although Suzanne still sees many of her old friends among the female impersonators, a certain distance has developed. They have always taken advantage of her openhandedness, she says; they are mean and hypocritical.

"To your face they'll say you're very brave to have the operation," she said, "but when they're talking to each other they'll say, 'Ooh, honey, is she kidding?'". . . I couldn't be bothered having the sex change. . . .She thinks she's so grand because she had the operation.' It's false friendship. I would say, not to flatter myself, that they're purple with envy. I call them candlelight beauties, those drag queens. They make a wonderful illusion, but they couldn't pass from here to the door."

Wanda lives in a Chicago surburb. She had sex-change surgery in Denmark in 1955. ("I was one of the first," she says.) Five years ago she married an accountant. He didn't know of Wanda's past. After brooding for a couple of years about the possible results of this concealment, she finally told him.

"He didn't mind," she said, "but he asked me not to bring it up ever again, and I haven't."

Wanda is from a small town in Indiana. Like Adeline and Suzanne, she says there was never a time when she can remember not wanting to be a girl. She is now sliding comfortably into middle age, tending a flower garden and canning plum preserves. She goes to church regularly. Her face is plump and powdery. She wears harlequin glasses and behind them her hazel eyes gaze at the world with the unconsciousness of the bishop's wife. Her manner of speech, in the language of the half-world, is very "nellie," that is, affectedly precise.

She doesn't like to talk about her life before she became a woman. "It was twenty-seven wasted years," she said. "That's all. When I see gay men and women now, all I think is, 'How sad it is.' " Wanda wants to be a paragon of virtue. Would she ever be unfaithful to her husband? I asked. "Oh, no," she said. "Never in a million years."

The last of the girls I talked to was Sheila, a ravishing creature with mane-length chorus-girl red hair, peachy clear skin, a magnificent bust, long legs and lots of jewelry. She lives in a Philadelphia apartment with her longtime boyfriend, an interior decorator, and she sees another man regularly, once or twice a week. He is divorced and has money. He doesn't know about her sex change.

"We make it to all the best places," she says. "I'm very accepted in his circle. He's a lawyer and it's very hard for someone like me to get accepted. He really digs me. When I get out of bed he'll say, 'You're the best built broad I've ever seen.' "

"A sex-change has a unique look at life, like no one else. How does a woman have sex? I know, but you'll never know. You'll never know all the little things there are to learn. Like getting in and out of bed. A man will just plop himself down; a woman has to kind of *slink* into bed [she switched her shoulders and hips]. Things like that.

"I was always very effeminate," she went on. "When I was a little boy I used to dress up in my mother's clothes every chance I got." Had she found out? I asked. "Oh, yes, lots of times," she replied. "My mother was very understanding. She used to say, 'Just make sure you get them off before your father gets home.' "

Sheila leaned toward me. She wore a green suede skirt and a jersey blouse that half-exposed those creamy breasts. "You know," she said. "I'm not any different since my, uh, operation. I think the same, do everything the same. Except now I can see through people. I can tell at a look or a glance what's going on when I come into a room. I know what the men are thinking and I know what the women are thinking."

The man she lives with had known her before her operation. He is a real homebody, she said. "What he likes to do when he comes home is eat and get his feet up in front of the television." She denied that he was "queer." "I've never seen him look at a man," she said. "If he did I'd walk out."

How did she feel about her rich lover? I asked. Wasn't she afraid her imposture would be found out?

"Actually, men have no conception," she said with a toss of her head. "Anyhow, how can he be made a fool of? What can anyone prove? Some girls *have* been found out. But what does a man do? Beat them up? No, they just quietly bow out of the picture."

These four women, like perhaps fifteen hundred people in the world, have undergone what is called sex-reassignment surgery. From being physically normal men they have been transformed into women whose femininity will withstand all but the closest gynecological scrutiny. Four hundred, say, live in this country, but the identity of only a third of them is known, even to physicians. The rest have, for practical purposes, vanished. They have taken new identities, found new jobs in places far from their old homes.

I learned these facts from talking over a period of several months with Dr. Harry Benjamin, a New York endocrinologist who in the past thirteen years has made himself the friend, defender and medical consultant of people who yearn for sexual transformation. In fact, it was Dr. Benjamin who coined the generally used term "transsexual" to describe them. He has described his observations in professional journals and last year published *The Transsexual Phenomenon,* which is the only full-length study of the subject.

Dr. Benjamin, who is a hale, rosy-cheeked eighty-two years old, dates his special interest in transsexualism from 1953, when he met Christine Jorgensen, the best-known subject of sex-reassignment surgery, at a party.

"She told me that she had received hundreds of letters from people who wanted the operation and wanted to know what to do," he said. "I urged her to reply to them all and I offered to help her compose a form letter to send out."

Pleasantly surprised to find an interested and sympathetic physician when the medical profession in this country seemed unanimous in regarding her as a particularly repellent sort of carnival attraction, Christine began referring her correspondents to Dr. Benjamin.

The functioning of the glands, Dr. Benjamin's specialty, is of course intimately associated with sexual activity. Beyond that, though, Dr. Benjamin had been a student of the broader field of sexology since his student days at Berlin and Tübingen before the First World War.

In those days a young doctor in Germany could hardly avoid the subject. Research was only just beginning, and Germany and Austria dominated it in much the same way that the United States does now, and perhaps for the same reason. The French and Italians, and the Samoans and the Japanese, for that matter, have always been able to take sex pretty much for granted. Not so the stolid Teuton or the churchgoing, kid-raising Americano. For them it is spiced with guilt and fear, and pursued with all the avidity, and about as much pleasure, as an Eagle Scout collecting merit badges.

As a result, Germany, Austria, the United States and, for that matter, England have always had a lot of raw material for study-devotees of pastimes that would have amazed the Greeks and Romans of antiquity, as well as the Byzantines, Hindus, Chinese and other representatives of erotically imaginative cultures.

In Dr. Benjamin's youth there were red-faced butchers (Adolph H., age forty-two) who cherished hindquarters of veal in their iceboxes, there were tightly corseted teachers (male) who were perhaps a little too fond of applying the corrective rod, noble Hussars at the Kaiser's court who amused their pals with their graceful pirouettes in tutus and toe shoes, and mild-mannered clerks in solemn black who collected ladies' kid gloves or button shoes (for the left foot only) or stole lacy bloomers from Potsdam clotheslines.

The Central Powers not only produced exponents of cannibalism, zoophilia, coprolagnia, tribadism, voyeurism, frottage, fetishism, transvestism, pederasty, pedophilia and the like, but also a host of explorers into these shadowed byways of love. Among the last were Krafft-Ebing, whose *Psychopathia Sexualis,* published in 1886, set the tone for the era that fluttered up to the destruction of 1914, as well as Möbius, Löwenfeld, Eulenberg, Bloch, Moll, Hirshfeld and von Schrenk-Notzing. Freud himself and his colleagues in the infant school of psychoanalysis made many contributions to the chronicles of deviant sexual behavior, although their main interest was theoretical.

Several of these observers have recorded interviews with persons who demonstrated a compulsive and apparently unshakable wish to change their sex. At the time, though, such a fixation was regarded merely as a particularly perverse form of homosexual transvestism. It was called usually psychic hermaphroditism, a diagnosis that could have been applied to the Stone Age man who found he got a funny zing out of slipping into his wife's dogskin negligee or to the Roman Emperor Heliogabalus who offered a province to anyone who could perform an operation on him to change his sex.

"I myself encountered transsexuals—of course I didn't call them that then—from time to time," Dr. Benjamin told me. (His accent make it come out, "zem zat zen.") "But until the late Thirties there was nothing at all to be done for them. After that we had effective female hormones. Injections reduced their libido and made them feel more comfortable, but it was a negative treatment, a kind of chemical castration."

As he interviewed and treated with hormones more and more of the persons referred to him by Miss Jorgensen, Dr. Benjamin became convinced that they represented something new in medicine. Although the men often came in full drag, looking like the hottest of flaming faggots, and the relatively few women in T-shirts and blue jeans, they reported in many cases that they were *not* homosexual. The reason was that they could not bear the thought of being another homosexual's love object. The men wanted to be made love to as women by men who were straight; for the women it was vice versa. Nor were they heterosexual; making love in accordance with their biological sex was physically impossible; indeed after a month or two of hormone treatments it was psychically impossible. Thus they were sexually neuter.

Many of his patients, Dr. Benjamin said, had been treated by psychiatrists or psychoanalysts for up to three years without improvement. Therapists were not anxious to treat them. Both homosexuals and transvestites—often sexually normal men or women who derive a fetish-istic pleasure from wearing the clothing and affecting the manner of the opposite sex—are notoriously resistant to change and consequently difficult to treat.

And simply *knowing* that a conversion operation could be performed increased their reluctance to stop short of a change. Furthermore, the knowledge increased their frustration when they were unable to get the medical approval for the surgery, in some cases to find a man to do the job, or get together the money to pay him.

Dr. Benjamin pities these people who had chased up so many blind alleys. He decided that if their minds could not be changed to adjust to their bodies, it was only sensible and humane to reverse the procedure and adjust the bodies to the minds. He began presenting these views in medical journals in 1953.

"I was well aware," he has written, "that I would meet opposition in various quarters and by no means only the medical. . . .Breaking a taboo always stirs quick emotions. . . .The forces of nature, however, know nothing of this taboo, and facts remain facts. . . .Furthermore, I felt that after fifty years in the practice of medicine, and in the evening of life, I need not be too concerned with a disapproval that touches much more on morals than on science."

Although sex-change surgery seemed to me to be an unpleasant subject, my admiration for Dr. Benjamin never wavered. He has a sophistication that is rare in my experience in domestic medical circles, a good deal of continental charm, a wardrobe of custom-made suits and haberdashery from Sulka. He is, furthermore, a connoisseur of wines, of the food of San Francisco, where he has spent the summer months since 1930, and New York, where he lives in a Murray Hill apartment with his vivacious blonde wife the rest of the year.

"To me it is just a matter of relieving human suffering the best way we can," he told me one afternoon as we gazed across at the Golden Gate Bridge from the Top of the Mark. "For years transsexuals have been in despair. Some commit suicide. Others are put into mental institutions. Still others try to mutilate themselves. Many just have to struggle along at terrible cost to themselves. It is a very sad situation."

I met other experts in the field through Dr. Benjamin. While they differed with him in peripheral matters, I found that there was general agreement on the broad outlines of transsexuals. They are almost invariably physically normal, at least as far as can be ascertained. They are not hermaphro-dites—that is, possessing the physical characteristics of both sexes. (The word, I finally realized, derives from Herma-phroditus, the son of Hermes and Aphro-dite.) In any event, "perfect" herma-phrodites, possessing full sexual equip-ment of both sexes, are all but unheard of; in most cases, only vestiges of the second sex are present that can be easily and routinely removed in in-fancy.

Central to any discussion of trans-sexualism is the distinction that must be made between a person's *sex,* which is biological, and his *gender,* which is social. We are born with a sex but we acquire a gender as we grow up.

In a recent paper included in the collection, *Sexual Inversion,* edited by Dr. Judd Marmor, Dr. Robert Stoller of the Medical Center of the University of California at Los Angeles wrote, "A person's sex is the result of a number of factors: chromosomes, external genitalia, internal genitalia, hormonal status, the secondary sex characteristics produced by estrogens and testosterone, and the gonads. There are biological attributes of both sexes in everyone, but the sum of these attributes falls in most people decidedly toward one or the other pole of the continuum between male or female.

"Gender," he continues, "connotes behavior learned from a tremendous pool of cues present in every culture and from a massive, intricate, though usually subtle, system of rewards and punishments in which every person lives from birth on....It is therefore more precise to talk of 'gender identity' than 'sexual identity.' "

To make matters even more confusing, Dr. Stoller, who is both a psychiatrist and a psychoanalyst, makes a distinction between gender identity, which is the way a person thinks of himself, and gender role, which is the way he actually lives. For example, a transvestite male who thinks of himself as a male is playing a gender role when he is wearing women's clothes; a transsexual male, who thinks of himself only as a woman, has female gender identity.

"When a person's core gender identity has been invaded," Dr. Stoller has written, "he may truly not adequately know to which sex and gender he belongs. To resolve this identity dilemma, such a person may attempt to pass....As with secret members of political undergrounds, spies, Negroes who become white, Jews who become Gentiles, impostors and so forth, there are people who pass from originally ascribed gender roles to the opposite one."

Dr. Stoller believes that this may be the bedeviled mind's last line of defense against the diffusion and loss of identity, which "is probably at the bottom of impending psychosis (panic states) and of the nightmarish quality of the paranoid condition."

As his research continues, Dr. Stoller has become convinced that this gender confusion occurs in infancy. He suggests that it may be partly caused by the

mother's holding the naked infant against her body for long periods of time. "In time the child doesn't know where his body begins and his mother's ends," he told me.

With depth interviews with transsexuals and their parents, Dr. Stoller is also trying to find out the answers to a pair of fascinating questions that move his research almost to the edge of fantasy: How does an infant's imitation of his mother become in time identification with her? What role is played in the development of transsexualism by infant's games and fantasies?

Dr. Benjamin doubts that conditioning is entirely responsible, believing that there is an as yet undiscovered constitutional vulnerability in some infants to transsexualism.

"A great deal has yet to be learned about genetic sex and until more is known," he has written, "it may be well to keep an open mind as to the possible causes of some mental abnormalities and sex deviations. At present, they are mostly ascribed to psychological conditioning; but they may yet find an additional explanation in some still obscure genetic fault, perhaps as a predisposing factor for later environmental influences....The actual cause of sex and gender disorientation, with its transvestite and transsexual syndromes, is still to be discovered."

A similar view is taken by Dr. John Money, a brilliant medical psychologist at Johns Hopkins in Baltimore, who with his associates has done important original research into the psychology of hermaphrodites, the influence of hormones on sexual behavior, and the development of "sissy boys."

Speaking of an infant's "gender neutrality," he said, "the psychosexual differentiation isn't always something that's settled at birth. With some people you cannot predict what the response to life circumstances will be, and this development may take a very stormy course. Some people seem more able to override these stresses than others. There's a question of vulnerability there plus environmental provocation."

This notion of an organic cause or predisposition not only for transsexualism but for homosexuality and transvestism has been around for a long time. Krafft-Ebing argued that there were both male and female centers in the human brain. If the female center was stronger in a man the result would be homosexuality. Magnus Hirschfeld theorized that the brain contained, by inheritance, male and female substances and that a wrong proportion could cause homosexuality. Even Freud believed that there might be a biological predisposition to homosexuality.

This would make a convenient explanation for the four million or so American males who are exclusively or predominantly homosexual. Regrettably, however, no solid evidence of an organic basis for homosexuality has yet been discovered. But believers in an organic theory are not giving up hope. One researcher wrote recently, "The basic experiments to demonstrate the effect of hormones on sexuality have not yet been done. . . .And even if all known hormones were carefully measured, the argument that some important unknown hormone is related to psychosexuality could not be refuted."

Perhaps the best synthesis of the theories was offered by a senior psychiatrist at a prominent New York hospital: "The problem—transsexualism—is such a fundamental one that it's on the dividing line, really, between the organic and the psychological."

As someone who grew up in an era in which nearly magic powers were ascribed to psychotherapy, I was surprised to hear from virtually every psychiatrist and psychoanalyst I talked to that transsexualism was, as far as they were concerned, incurable. For that matter, homosexuality itself is extremely hard to deal with.

Under the circumstances, many psychiatrists feel obliged to give approval for the operation, although they might prefer to have it otherwise. "I'm not convinced that the operation is all that successful over the long term," a New York psychiatrist-psychoanalyst said. "It's an expedient procedure, but that doesn't rule it out. There are many expedients in medicine."

A cautious demurrer was entered, however, by Dr. M. Ralph Kaufman, the director of the department of psychiatry at Mount Sinai Hospital in New York and a president of the American Psychoanalytic Association: "Should the operation be performed? I'd say generally no. I feel you shouldn't interfere with basic biology to that extent. But then again there can't be a general rule. In psychiatry the only general rule is that there are no general rules."

Dr. Daniel Cappon, a British-born psychiatrist-psychoanalyst who is associated with the University of Toronto, took a far stronger stand in his recently published book, *Toward an Understanding of Homosexuality*. He calls sex-transformation surgery "infamous" and absolutely unjustified on medical or psychiatric grounds [except] in some rare cases of physical or somatic intersexuality, when the genes of both sexes and the glands, anatomical organs, and functions of both sexes exist in the same person."

He told me: "A homosexual's saying he wants the operation may be mere willfulness. What they say is one thing; what they really mean is another; and what they want unconsciously still a third. For example, a woman goes to a doctor and says she wants an abortion. The fact of the matter is that she wants to lose her baby less than a woman who is infertile or doesn't get pregnant for one reason or another or who has a series of miscarriages."

As a group, transsexuals, their doctors admit, would win no popularity contests. Even the kindly Dr. Benjamin, who treats many of them without charge, has written: ". . . all kinds of objectionable traits may exist. Unreliability, deceitfulness, ingratitude, together with an annoying, but understandable impatience have probably ruined their chances for help in more than a few instances. Many transsexuals are utterly self-centered, concerned with their own problems only and unable to consider those of anyone else. . . .Still another handicap. . . is their rather frequent immaturity in thinking and acting."

In my conversations with transsexuals who had already undergone surgery I sensed a colossal self-righteousness, a certain godlike detachment in discussing themselves, which, indeed, is the only subject that interests them very much. On my part, I suppose, there was an underlying prejudice against what could be called deserters from the male sex. Furthermore, the effeminate has always been an acceptable subject for robust tavern or locker-room humor, and it was not easy to take them, at all times, as seriously as they would have liked.

Discussing my observations with Dr. Money one day, I found a measure of agreement. He, too, thought that transsexuals had a disagreeable tendency to self-righteousness. No matter how checkered their lives had been, he said, they seldom showed any signs of guilt. All defects were described to their gender ambiguity. "I remember one saying, referring to the opportunity for homosexual contacts, "What a ball you have in jail!' " As he repeated it, he shook his head in dismay.

And yet there is a general agreement among psychiatrists that transsexuals are not psychotic. "Unless," says Dr. Stoller, "you want to say, that someone who wants something that you find bizarre or highly unusual is psychotic. In fact, aside from that one area, it's surprising how healthy many of them are by psychiatric standards."

"It seems to be mainly a question of the terrible frustration they feel in trying to make their bodily image conform to their mental image of themselves," another psychiatrist said. "It's this factor that leads to their chronic depression, their efforts at self-mutilation and suicide and what a lot of people find is their just plain disagreeableness. And many of them have been isolated for so long because of this illness that they've never had the chance to develop interpersonal skills. For this reason they may seem almost schizoid. When the problem is . . . removed, they almost always show a marked improvement all the way around."

For as long as they can remember, since early childhood, transsexuals have thought of little else but getting rid of their hated sexual organs. But the energy they spend in wishing and their confusion in identity often conspire to prevent, or at least delay, the realization of their dreams. They are not, in most cases, people who plan. Their misery lowers their horizons; it becomes difficult for them to look more than a day or two ahead. In fact, the ability to work, to plan and to save money for the surgery is regarded by psychiatrists as an indication that the transsexual is approaching this crucial step with a degree of maturity and insight.

By then, Dr. Money told me, the genitals have been relinquished, rejected, for so long that the operation is hardly more than a technicality. There is seldom any last-minute soul-searching; neither he nor Dr. Benjamin had ever heard of a change of heart.

Indeed, the four women I talked to could not have been more matter-of-fact. The glory of it, or the horror of it, the extraordinariness of it, were absent. And yet, how surprisingly odd this notion that either by birth or conditioning a woman's mind could possess a male body and then order its death and transformation.

Because of the feeling in medical circles that no individual should have this power, similar as it is to suicide, over his own body, sex-transformation surgery has occupied an ambiguous place in medical practice, in part, perhaps, because the term itself is a misnomer. There can be no change of sex. What the surgeons create is an *illusion* of femininity or masculinity. The external signs of sex are made to conform with the subject's dream of himself. When they finish their work the masquerade becomes permanent.

As far as is known, the first transformation operations were performed in Denmark in the early Fifties by a team headed by Dr. Christian Hamburger, who, like Dr. Benjamin, is an endocrinologist. One of Dr. Hamburger's first patients was a twenty-six-year-old Long Islander named George Jorgensen, who returned from Copenhagen as Christine Jorgensen. The story came to the attention of The New York *Daily News*—against her will, Christine says—and it was the tabloid sex sensation of the decade. (Christine decided to cash in on her notoriety. She worked up a nightclub act and a few years ago became an actress. She has just finished an autobiography.)

After Dr. Hamburger reported on his work in the ultraconservative *Journal of the American Medical Association*, a few surgeons in this country performed the operation, perhaps twenty-five times in all. However, the legal and ethical questions were still largely unresolved.

Doctors wondered if they might not be prosecuted under state mayhem laws for doing the surgery or be liable for huge malpractice suits by patients who later changed their minds. Furthermore, hospital boards, which are nothing if not conservative, generally frowned on making their facilities available for an operation they found at best a potential source of trouble, at worst a disgusting interference with nature's plan.

In medicine, as in everything else, a service that people want badly, and are willing to pay well for, somehow becomes available. Before long, the transsexual grapevine told of doctors in Mexico City, Rome, Casablanca and Tokyo who were willing to perform the surgery at prices ranging from $2,500 to $5,000. In the view of surgeons in this country who have seen samples of this work, the most gifted of these foreign practitioners is Dr. Georges Burou, who operates a pleasant private hospital in Casablanca. "He does really excellent work," I was told. Dr. Burou also pioneered in techniques that are being adopted wherever the surgery is done, and so far as is known, he has never had a fatality or an instance of serious complications.

And there matters rested until nearly two years ago, when the missionary work of Dr. Benjamin and Dr. Money began to have an effect. Johns Hopkins agreed to study transsexualism with a view to performing reassignment surgery. It established a nine-member Gender Identity Committee composed of medical specialists. Among the members were Drs. Money and Milton T. Edgerton, a plastic surgeon in charge at the hospital, who performed the operation.

After more than a year of monthly meetings the committee decided that the surgery did not offend the laws of the State of Maryland, medical ethics or public morals, and, most important, that it was clinically justified. "It took us a long time to get the committee off the ground," one of its members said, "but we were determined to do everything in a completely scientific way."

Last July the committee established the Gender Identity Clinic, the first in the world, and began considering applications for surgery. Within a few months it had more than a hundred candidates in addition to those referred to it by Dr. Benjamin, with whom the committee has worked closely since it was set up. Dr. Benjamin, meanwhile, had established the Harry Benjamin Foundation, primarily for the study of transsexualism, and was carrying out an ambitious program of psychological testing, physical examination and the taking of family histories from his patients.

The clinic decided to limit itself to considering only one person a month. It also decided that it would not consider anyone who was not already living transsexually—as a woman in the case of a man or as a man in the case of a woman—and had been regularly receiving hormone injections.

"We wanted to reduce the chances of a poor postoperative adjustment," I was told. "For instance, we had someone down here from the West Coast. He was working as a bank clerk—a male—during the day and as a door-to-door cosmetic saleswoman at night. We told him to come back when he had decided which one he wanted to do on a full-time basis."

In September the first operation was performed by the clinic. The subject was a male in his twenties. The surgery, performed by a two-man team, took nearly four hours and, the committee said, was completely successful. The only complications were postoperative. The patient was happy but the nurses and orderlies gave him some rough kidding. I gave the staff a talking-to and soon straightened that out," one of the physicians said. Another difficulty arose,

though, with the psychiatric residents. Several of them protested against the operation so strongly that a psychiatrist who was a member of the committee spoke to them.

The Johns Hopkins surgical team is using pretty much the technique developed by Dr. Burou in Casablanca, but as it gains experience it hopes to make improvements. Unlike the French surgeon, though, it will publish its findings, thereby improving the quality of the surgery as it is performed, and often botched, elsewhere around the world.

Dr. Hoopes, the thirty-five-year-old chairman of the Gender Identity Committee, called the surgery "one of the last frontiers in medicine." While I would not care to have to do it on a submarine slipping past Japanese destroyers at the entrance to Tokyo Bay, it is not in fact all that difficult or dramatic. In the case of men, the testicles and the penis, except for the skin, which is used to line the vaginal canal that is created, are removed. (Dr. Hoopes is expert at creating a realistic-looking vaginal entrance, molded around a plastic tube that is removed when the incision is healed.) Women transsexuals will have a hysterectomy and breast removal if necessary. A penis-like appendage can be created, but it cannot be made to erect.

For three of my four women the first months after recovery from surgery were a Roman carnival of sexual indulgence. The gorgeous Sheila told me that she had made herself available to anyone who took the trouble to smile at her. And because they are all different, many of these new women will not change; their postoperative lives will be as barren of meaningful human contact as they were before. Then again, they may be perpetually dissatisfied, wanting breast enlargement, a smaller nose, a higher voice. They will clock their lovers, watch them sweat, and laugh inwardly. They will experience, some of them, orgasm, or at least a wonderful warm romantic glow. Perhaps the last cracked laugh will be on them. But their wiser sisters will, as far as they can, obliterate their past, marry—as many of them have already—adopt children and devote themselves to making their families happy.

the lesbian

in america

DONALD WEBSTER CORY

Jeanie, an astute woman of 30 who seems to be on her way to a remarkably successful career in the advertising world, is never at a loss for an invitation to one of the gay parties. Like most of her friends, she prefers the all-female ones, but now and then, "just for kicks," as she says, she goes to one with the boys, as well. That is, with the gay boys. As friends, she finds it difficult to come close to these men; it is almost easier to become friends with a heterosexual male, she finds. But at parties they are a lot of fun, although given her choice of lesbian or mixed (that is, all homosexual, but mixed male and female), she would usually choose the former.

"The more noise, the more music, the more hubbub of voices, the lonelier everyone seems," she says. "And the lonelier they are, the lonelier I am — and the more I feel that this is where I belong."

For Jeanie, the feeling that she must be where she belongs, where she is wanted and accepted, has followed her since early adolescence. "If you were not gay yourself; if I hadn't seen you at parties with men," she said to me, "I couldn't let my hair down with you" — a refrain that I was to hear many times while doing studies for this work.

"You can tell these things to a psychiatrist — if you want to," she said, "and sometimes I do want to. A girl in the office gets married, and we give her a party and I buy her something, and for a minute as I watch her face and she seems so radiant, I envy her. I sort of wish I were in her boots, so respectable, so middle-class, so fulfilled, with the babies coming and a family and a permanent home and all that, but before I know it, I'm not envying her, but her boy friend. I wish I could marry, not him, but her."

"You can, in a sense, can't you?" I asked.

"Yes, sort of, but it's not the same," she quickly answered. "We try to make it the same, we struggle to imitate real marriages, and I have had some success, but things don't quite work out the same. Yet, I couldn't give it up, even if I were able to, even if a psychiatrist could help me. I couldn't live without loving a woman, no matter what it does to me."

If there is a typical member of a society of atypicals, it might be Jeanie, our introduction to the lesbian in American society. She has had experiences that are shared by many of her friends, and by many others whom she has never encountered. And, despite the difficulties that have made her antipathetic to physical contact with men, she did make one brief effort to find a relationship with a man, but in vain.

Reprinted with permission of the publisher from Donald Webster Cory, The Lesbian in America *(New York: The Citadel Press, Inc., 1964), pp. 28-38.*

Physically, Jeanie so closely resembles any heterosexually-oriented girl that one would have to search with all-knowing eyes to find some betrayal of the problem that lies within her. She is neither big-boned nor muscular, does not cut her hair shorter than do other girls, never fails to pluck her eyebrows, or to put on a normal supply of lipstick, powder, perfume, and other make-up. In short, there is nothing in Jeanie that looks masculine; in fact, she might be eyed by a man who likes highly feminine girls. She smokes a good deal, drinks lightly, and avoids swearing: "When one of our girls swears, it's like one of your boys lisping; it's just an act, people trying to be what they are not."

"And isn't that what we are, all of us, you and I, trying to be — what we are not?" I asked.

"No," she quickly replied. "I don't see it that way. I'm not trying to be a man. I'm trying to be a woman, loving another woman."

"If that's what you want, nobody is stopping you," I suggested, to which she quickly gave the rejoinder:

"Except myself."

It was not difficult to draw out Jeanie's story. She reminisced about childhood and youth, family and early friends, innocence followed by revelation, and considerable relish. She seemed at times detached from the story she narrated, as if the Jeanie she was talking about was someone else, and she her observer.

She told about her upper-middle-class home in an almost typical New England town, where she was the oldest of three children, followed by a brother and then a sister, each spaced two years apart. She smiled and commented: "Until I was 19 years old, I couldn't believe my parents had sex, except once every two years."

Jeanie was a favored and protected child, and the atmosphere was sur-rounded with pristine purity.   There would be no contamination of these good children. Her parents lived in the right neighborhoods, saw to it that she had the right friends, allowed her to read only the right books. She went to Sunday school were she was taught the good life.

In recent years, Jeanie has read a good deal about homosexuality, and she intermingled her own story with comments on the theories of others, and how they did or didn't dovetial with her own experiences. "The psychiatrists talk about early seduction of gay boys and girls, as if we became homosexual because someone showed us what it was like before we were old enough to know better. Why, do you know, I still believed in storks when I was 13 years old, and when I finally learned that babies came out of their mothers' bellies, I was 14, and didn't even have the curiosity or the brains to ask how they got there in the first place!

"And, to top it all, I was not only a bright child, I was a precocious one. I was ahead of my age-group in school. I was always at the top of the class, or at least of the girls — sometimes a boy would beat me out. How could I have been so ignorant, so dumb, about sex? I just don't know."

Looking back, Jeanie said that she had a good home life, although there was a great deal of competition with her brother for her parents' affection. Although she was favored, or at least felt that she was, she was willing to relinquish her mother to Jack provided there was no serious threat to her place with her father. "I sort of gravitated toward my father, and Jack toward my mother, while Louise was cuddled by all of us. She was the baby, and even Jack could accept her.

"And that's the way it all started. Now, I understand the whole business when I find my case history written up by an orthodox Freudian analyst. My name was Electra, and I used to sit on Daddy-Agamemnon's lap, and I fell in love with him; while little Jackie-Oedipus was falling in love with Mama-Jocasta. It's all so clear, except that Oedipus grew up to like women, because I was in love with Daddy. So it doesn't explain everything – at least not to me."

In high school, Jeanie gave no thought to the fact that she was not dating. Her parents did not approve of a high-school girl going on dates, and she was more serious, was interested in studies and books, not in good times with boys. When she learned, for the first time, that there was an act of body contact between men and women, indulged in for pleasure, and resulting in the birth of a new life, she was shocked. She looked at the bodies of those she loved, and at her own body, and felt a deep shame. Man was born not only in sin, but in guilt. She resolved to withdraw from the ugly world of sex, and to be good, pure, fine. "I was a perfect candidate for the nunnery," she reminisced, "except I had the wrong religion."

During the latter years of high school, words like *fairy, queer,* and *faggot* sometimes came to her attention; there was an effeminate boy who was ridiculed; there were passages one saw now and then in a novel; there were allusions to strange men who loved men, women who loved women. "It all left me cold and repelled. It never entered my mind that I might be one of them. I just never had a suspicion."

"Until when?" I asked.

"College, naturally. I must have been the purest, most innocent, most asexual kid who ever entered college in America. I had never been kissed by anyone outside of the family – not by a boy – thank God – and not by a girl – though now I'm making up for lost time. I knew people did things they shouldn't do, just

for the fun of it, but I felt my parents were above such evil ways, and I would be, too. And then my world collapsed.

"I was rooming with this girl, I think her name was Lola something or other. Never met her before, we were thrown together by the school. Lola tried to get me to go out with her on double dates, and I always said no. Except one time, we went out together, and I just felt sick when the boy tried to come close to me, and he must have said something to Lola, because she never asked me again. I didn't think there was anything wrong with me. I just felt that a boy who wanted sex with a girl was a beast.

"Then, one day, Lola said to me that there was a scandal brewing in the school. It seems that the dean got wind of the fact that some lesbians were in the dorms.

"I felt very curious. I was excited, and didn't know why. Who were these girls, what were they doing, what kind of people were they? I couldn't get them out of my mind, and yet I never suspected the source of my own curiosity.

"I found out their names, and just slipped into a seat next to one of the girls in the cafeteria, and that's the beginning of the story. The first experiences, the changing of roommates, the feeling first that I had found myself and the elation, and then the letdown, the guilt and depression. And the resolutions, over and over again, to give it all up, that it's only a dead end, that even if it's not immoral it can't lead anywhere, that it's not fulfilling.

"When I came home for my first Christmas, I brought my girl friend with me. That's the wonderful thing about girls together, we can live together, share a room, hold hands, kiss in public – not as passionately as I should like – and everyone thinks it's fine. Mom and Dad were so happy that I had made a close friend in college that they couldn't do enough to make her feel at home. But it does sort of make you feel funny when your parents are doing this for you right in your own home, and then you go up to the bedroom and spend the night having sex with the girl."

Jeanie tasted of the tenderness of love between women, and learned of the strong bonds of friendship among many of these lovers, but found that, for the most part, these loves were ephemeral and fleeting. She sought the faithful friendship of a single partner, but found her own interests wandering to others, and felt guilty with each transgression, or frustrated by suppressing the desire for it. She longed to discover a love that would be as meaningful to her life as she thought her parents' love was to theirs, and so began with increasing frequency to wish that she were not caught in this net, that she could escape, perhaps with a young man.

Her experience with David came in her senior year at college. He, too, was a senior. They had sat together in several classes; they had collaborated on a project for the college magazine. When Jeanie was with David, she longed to tell him that she was a lesbian, to warn him to stay away, because she was in love with her roommate. And yet, she thought that he might save her, if only he knew the difficulties with which she was struggling — but this was a part of her life she had learned must remain muted and unspoken before all but the intimate few.

Perhaps he, too, was gay, she sometimes thought, not because of any outward suspicious signs, but because of his lack of forwardness in approaching her, and his seeming disinterest in the romantic and dating patterns in the school. Once, the subject came up — a tennis player on the varsity squad had been the butt of frequent rumors.

"Poor kid," David said. "I sort of feel sorry for him."

"Sorry?" Jeanie asked. "Why sorry? He's got his life, and you've got yours."

"But what a life he's got. It's sick."

"May be it's only society that makes it so. Society says it's sick, so it's sick. And if we said it was normal and healthy, then he could have his boy friends, and he'd be normal and healthy."

"I don't believe it," David replied.

"Why don't you just stop persecuting him, and give him a chance?"

"Persecuting him? Me? Why, I wouldn't touch a fly, much less a fairy."

"There you go. That's just what I mean."

And then she stopped. You only go so far in discussing this subject with straight people, unless you have decided that there is no mask, or no need for one.

During the last semester at college, she and David began to date, and she grew fond of him. She didn't discourage him when he put his arm around her, or when he kissed her. But she went back to her roommate, happy for the soft and lovely arms and the scented body. David's companionship and the friendship that was developing between them was stimulating, but as soon as she left him, her whole being ached for the embraces of her girl friend.

As Easter vacation approached, David suggested that they spend a few days together in New York. "We can stay in separate places, or together — if you're ready," he said.

"I don't know if I'm ready," she said, and then added: "David, I'm a virgin."

"I looked straight in his eyes when I told him," Jeanie said to me, "but he just couldn't look back at me. I thought I had him caught in his own middle-class trap of virtue and goodness. He looked away from me, as if he could not face the implication that I was accusing him of stealing my virginity.

"But that wasn't why he couldn't face me. He had something else to say, and it's easier to say it when you're not looking directly into the person's eye. 'I don't call that being a virgin,' he said, hesitating on every word as if he didn't know if he should go any further, 'not with all the girls they say you've been with.'

"I think he would have liked me to slap his face, but I simply looked down, and found myself saying that if he wanted to go with me, then I wanted to go with him."

They went to New York together. They carefully counted their money and took in plays and chose not-too-expensive restaurants, went to museums until their tired legs could no longer carry them, and then went home, she exhausted and ready for sleep, he exhilarated and ready for love. She did not participate, she submitted. She felt cold and helpless, anxious to have the experience over with, while he assured her that she must become accustomed to it, that it was always painful at first, but it would become fulfilling. She waited until they returned to school before telling him it was all over between them.

"David, I would like to love you, but a person can't go on pretending all her life. Every time I was with you, I closed my eyes and tried to imagine that I was with a girl." He winced. "I'm not going to get married that way," she added. "I can't live a lie all my life."

"No, but that's exactly what you've decided to do. All your life you'll live a lie. Are you going to tell your parents every time you're making love with a girl? Are you going to tell the bosses you'll work for, or the kids who'll come and work for you if you're the boss? Are you going to tell the world that you're this way and you're proud of it? Tell me, are you — or are you going to live a lie?"

"It's the world's fault if I can't tell them, not mine. And besides, it's none of their business. If I live with a man or a woman, and I'm in love and that person loves me, then it's my business and the other person's not to live the lie."

This was Jeanie's first sexual experience with a man, and it was her last. A few years later, during a short try at therapy, the therapist reviewed the episode, and told her that she had refused to give it a chance, breaking it off precipitately after a one-week stay in New York, as if she were frightened that she might come to like and accept it. "Maybe so," Jeanie admitted, "but that was me — even the need to break it up before it became anything — that was me."

Now and then, she makes a resolution to try again with a man, but the resolution is half-hearted, and has behind it no effort or conviction. Her resolve today is to find self-acceptance, peace with herself, and this, she feels, she will accomplish only as she is, a woman with a woman.

new york's "middle-class" homosexuals

WILLIAM J. HELMER

As might be expected, the common view of homosexuality we find in recent

William J. Helmer, "New York's 'Middle-Class' Homosexuals," Harper's Magazine *(March, 1963), pp. 85-92.*

novels, plays, and films is often very limited. Even the more "understanding" studies of the problem seem to consider homosexuals as a definable group—distinct from heterosexuals—whose chief concern in life is to satisfy their sexual desires while shamefully concealing them from friends and associates.

In fact, homosexuality is a condition which takes so many forms that the word is of little use in describing any single group of people. And many homosexuals insulate themselves from hostile heterosexual society, taking refuge in a separate homosexual community which possesses its own customs, social structure, ethics, argot, organizations and even business establishments.

To the extent that police or anonymity permit, every large city in America contains a homosexual community. It has no physical dimensions, and it certainly does not include everyone who would legally, psychiatrically, or otherwise qualify as a homosexual. But for some it offers a virtually complete personal world where one can pursue a busy and varied "gay" life, socially as well as sexually, practically independent of "straight" society.

Like most heterosexuals I was barely aware of the gay community in New York when I first came to work in the city. A friend who knew it well offered to introduce me to his friends, with the understanding that I would try to write an objective study of their way of life. I spent several months talking chiefly to homosexuals who participate in gay life more or less exclusively, sometimes to the extent of working in a so-called "gay trade" (such as hairdressing) or in an office where other employees are homosexual. This article thus concerns itself with what might be called the

homosexual bourgeoisie—people who are community-oriented, provincial, critical of undesirables. They are themselves frequently disdained by other homosexuals, some of whom are less preoccupied with their deviancy and participate freely in both gay and "straight" society. Still other homosexuals live more private and self-sufficient lives and have little or nothing at all to do with gay society.

But the homosexuals who confine themselves to their own "middle-class" community seem to me the appropriate group from which to gain some insight into the social aspects of homosexuality. Because they are much concerned with their own position in the community, they draw many distinctions among themselves which are too subtle to be reflected in police records or psychiatric studies of the isolated individual. In introducing some of the habits and styles of their life, I must however emphasize that the varieties of actual behavior among homosexuals are endless and I have undoubtedly oversimplified them here. Furthermore, the homosexuals who described themselves and their friends to me could be expected to generalize in defensive and self-interested ways—even unintentionally—when talking to a "square" reporter.

New York probably has the country's largest homosexual community if only because of its size, but few reliable statistics are available. The late Dr. Robert Lindner, drawing selectively on the statistics of several psychologists, psychiatrists, and sexual researchers (including Kinsey), arrived at an estimate of 4 to 6 per cent of "the total male population over age sixteen" who are homosexual in the gay sense of the word. Applied to New York City's population, this estimate would indicate a homosexual population of about 100,000. The number may be much higher, since any large city, and especially New York, attracts deviants seeking a degree of privacy, anonymity, and gay life not available in smaller communities. It would be impossible to estimate the number who participate in New York's homosexual society more or less exclusively, since many persons are socially or sexually disqualified for various reasons and others take part in it only to a limited degree.

GAY BARS AND BEACHES

In New York, as in other cities, bars are an important part of gay life, especially for young men who have just discovered homosexual society and for those new to the city who want to get acquainted. In Manhattan, about twenty bars cater to homosexuals exclusively and about twice that number are "mixed." They are scattered around the city with concentrations in the Greenwich Village area and the Upper East Side. In most cases they are located away from main business districts, and about the only thing which might distinguish them from any other neighborhood tavern is that their customers tend to be young, well-groomed, and well-dressed, and therefore not quite typical of New York neighborhood bar clientele. Lesbians have their own bars, but they are fewer in number and somewhat more obvious because all the customers are female, and at least some of them are "butch" lesbians, made conspicuous by their short hair, manly clothes, and generally tomboyish appearance.

A few gay bars have private back rooms where homosexuals can dance with one another. These, more than the other bars, seem to be dominated by a young crowd of regular patrons whom my guide referred to as "bar society," and the first one we visited proved to be fairly typical.

It was an inconspicuous but very busy street-corner tavern near the Hudson River in West Greenwich Village. Although we went on a Thursday night, the back room was so crowded that many were standing, and the atmosphere was that of a speakeasy: dim lights, loud noise, cigarette smoke, music, and, I was told, a signal to stop dancing in the event of a police raid.

My reaction to the unusual sight of men embracing each other on the dance floor was one more of curiosity than aversion, probably because the dancers appeared so casual and others in the room so indifferent. I was far more surprised to see no one who "looked" homosexual. A few were a little too well groomed or elegant in their behavior, and a few were dressed younger than their age (though all looked to be under thirty), but otherwise the only noticeable difference was that everyone resembled the dashing young men in college sportswear advertisements. At other bars I did see a few obviously effeminate persons, but they were not flamboyant, and I was told that the better class of gay bar usually discourages conspicuous homosexuals in order to avoid police crackdowns.

Word spreads quickly once a bar becomes gay, and many are opened with the intention of catering to homosexuals who will keep a place busy until closing every night of the week. A new bar will sometimes raid another, hiring away a popular bartender who will bring with him a large personal following.

New York's gay bars are periodically closed by the police, but no serious effort has been made to eliminate them—either because the owners pay off the police (as customers widely assume, and as bartenders sometimes intimate in justifying their dollar-a-bottle price for beer in the back rooms), or because the police believe they can be more easily watched and controlled if a few are permitted to operate in the open. A police cruiser was parked in front of one of the dancing bars I visited and its driver was standing inside the door talking to the proprietor as I entered, but no one in the back room, where about twenty-five male couples were dancing, paid any notice to this.

Bar owners are not the only businessmen who cater to the gay trade. A number of smart men's shops in the Village and on the Upper East Side feature slim-cut and youthfully styled clothing designed to appeal to homosexuals. Some stores carry bikini-type underwear and swimsuits for men, and fancy silk supporters. Swimsuits of this sort cannot be worn on public beaches, but certain parts of Fire Island (and sometimes other beaches) have become the more or less exclusive domain of the gay crowd, and there they have more freedom to dress and behave as they please, and generally "camp it up," i.e., act "homosexually" without inhibition.

A number of restaurants, barber shops, tailors, gyms, athletic clubs, and Turkish baths also cater to homosexuals. Some stationers even carry a line of greeting cards for "gay occasions," and sometimes an apartment or rooming house becomes predominantly homosexual. Some homosexuals feel enough group loyalty to patronize mainly those establishments considered gay, usually because of their employees, but others are indifferent to the point of calling them "fruitstands."

"DRAG BALLS" AND "SICK" BEHAVIOR

Gay social life takes many forms. Some men spend practically every evening in bars, drinking beer and exchanging news and gossip; others are continually holding or attending parties, which may range from sedate evenings of drinking, talking, and listening to music, to wild nights of orgy. Hundreds of gay parties take place during a New York weekend and the homosexual can usually find one open to him. The genuine orgy, however, is less common and regarded by some as rather jading and degrading, but still "okay if you like that sort of thing." A colorful—but not necessarily sexual—event in the gay world is the "drag party" to which guests may come dressed as women. Unlike genuine transvestitism, however, such masquerading is often done as a titillating joke, the idea being to dress like a ridiculous parody of the female in order to humorously exaggerate one's "perversion."

The term gay, which often strikes a heterosexual as inappropriate if not ironic, becomes meaningful at parties and dancing bars. Any private gathering is an opportunity to relax and "drop the mask" one wears in public, and there is usually an air of conspiracy and intrigue which is not without its appeal. Such conditions tend to promote a spirit of good-fellowship, and everyone tries to outdo each other in being friendly, sociable, and "gay." Part of this is artificial—the same sort of attempt at jolly behavior that may go on between males and females after a few drinks at a dull cocktail party. But no doubt homosexuals do feel a genuine exuberance in temporarily escaping the sense of rejection implicit in their frequent need to conceal their nature from employer, acquaintances, and family. The "gaiety" of many homosexuals is also expressed in a sense of humor, perhaps defensive, which often makes fun of themselves. ("Sorry I'm so late, dearie, but I kept tripping in my high heels.") Gay homosexuals I talked to frequently used such terms as fag, fairy, swish, pansy, screaming queen (but rarely queer) to describe persons they did not like; however, they used the same terms often (plus the plain *queer*) in referring humorously to gay friends. One person introduced me to his roommate as a "queen for a day who is writing a fairy tale."

What I saw and heard of party life and bar life left with me the impression that the homosexuals, at least in those circles, are often quite lonely people who need to surround themselves with friends and stay continually amused. Some have virtually no heterosexual friends, serious interests or outside diversions, or long-range goals. They are content to support themselves through low-paying white-collar jobs, and otherwise are preoccupied with the intricacies of cliquish, competitive gay society.

About the only social event staged publicly for homosexuals is the "drag ball," at which so-called "drag queens" can legally impersonate women, these are held regularly in commercial halls and may draw a thousand or more persons, including a sizable number of heterosexual curiosity seekers. At the Exotic Ball and Carnival held in Manhattan Center last October, forty-four men were arrested for masquerading as women when New York Police Commissioner Michael J. Murphy saw the group as he arrived to attend a policeman's ball on another floor of the same building. The charges later were dismissed since the affair was a bona fide masquerade party, but one man was booked for indecent exposure.

Some New York nightclubs feature female impersonators and other "gay entertainment," but these are strictly off beat tourist attractions for hertero-sexuals.

Drag balls, and especially the nightclub entertainment, are objected to by some homosexuals who say that they oppose any type of public behavior or appearance that sustains the stereotype of a freak who minces, wears cosmetics, and speaks with a lisp. In fact, appearance and behavior, to a large extent, determine whether or not an individual will find acceptance in gay society.

By far the majority of homosexuals have no obvious mannerisms and can pass easily in heterosexual society, and many claim to regard the "flaming faggot" with contempt. Similarly excluded from polite gay society are the hoodlums who engage in male prostitution, shake-downs, muggings, or other antisocial behavior, as well as the "degenerate fag" who regularly risks arrest by openly soliciting in public restrooms and parks. Generally speaking, any behavior which attracts heterosexual attention is disapproved, if for no other reason than that it is considered bad public relations.

Many psychiatrists trace effeminism to a deepseated identification with the female sex, pointing out that effeminate mannerisms are not necessarily an indication of homosexuality. Effeminate homosexuals often believe they are "just born that way," but I heard other theories advanced. One was that mannerisms sometimes are acquired, perhaps unconsciously, by young men who try to find acceptance in gay life by adopting what they believe to be its conventions. Another held that the ostentatious queen was simply a "sick and neurotic" person who cannot adjust to his condition, and who compensates by "thumbing his powdered nose" at the society which rejects him. Blatant effeminism seems to be more prevalent among homosexuals of the lower socio-economic classes; if so, it may be that such men are more distressed by their loss of masculinity and less able to reach an intelligent understanding of it, and thus are more inclined to exhibit abnormal behavior.

Some sexual tendencies are unacceptable in gay society. The more flagrant homosexual sadists and masochists have formed their own little outcast groups on the fringes of gay life and are characterized by their penchant for leather, denim, or rubber clothing, and by their interest in matters of "bondage" and "discipline." Some cultivate a tough, masculine appearance—black leather jacket, motorcycle boots, tight denims, sometimes a symbolic piece of chain dangling from the belt or hooked around the upper arm. Some wear a Band-Aid on the hand to indicate masochistic inclinations. The two types are lumped together and referred to as S-Ms or "sadie-masies" by other homosexuals who seem to know little about them and say they do not associate with them.

Transvestitism and fetishism, too, are generally regarded as "sick" behavior. The ordinary gay person tends to think of himself as an otherwise normal individual whose sexual inclinations are merely reversed; but he will say that he considers other forms of deviancy to be genuine "perversions," insisting that such inclinations are not "normal" to either the male or female. This is especially true with regard to violent sex crimes, and child molesting.

If anything, the gay person is even more scandalized by violent psychopathic behavior than other people, since the police, the public, and newspapers tend to use the term "homosexual" in describing any crimes involving members of the same sex, thereby implying that homosexuals are inherently depraved. Ordinarily, criminal psychopaths who are homosexual have no wish to participate in gay life, even if they could find acceptance. Most of the people I talked to believed that homosexual child molesters and other "sex maniacs" were secretive and tortured men who were incapable of openly acknowledging their deviancy; hence they had no desire to fraternize with other homosexuals. I was told that many male prostitutes were homosexuals who refused to acknowledge their inclinations but used prostitution as an excuse to indulge in homosexual relations. Some, known as "rough trade," then beat and rob the "dirty queer" to preserve their own heterosexual illusions.

The bisexual—defined here only as a person who describes himself as one—is a kind of mulatto in gay life. He is rejected by conventional heterosexual society and sometimes by gay homosexuals who argue that there is no such thing as true bisexuality and that those who claim to be attracted equally to men and women are only trying to prove their masculinity to themselves. Bisexuals disagree vigorously, and criticize other homosexuals for being too narrow in their interests.

It should be kept in mind that homosexuals, like heterosexuals, do not always practice what they preach. Engaging a prostitute, extreme effeminism, associating with various "undesirables," accepting money, indiscreet "cruising" in public, and so on, are practices generally frowned upon in polite gay society, although an individual may well indulge in them when his friends aren't looking.

Sexual satisfaction is usually seen as a matter of personal preference, and homosexuals tend to be liberal in what they consider respectable sex. A person may specialize in the active or the passive role, or in partners who are very masculine, very effeminate, younger, older, or blond and blue-eyed. Sexual eccentricities, even when socially unacceptable by gay standards, rarely are condemned as wrong or immoral. To some extent, attitudes toward sex divide along familiar heterosexual lines— one person being casually promiscuous, another insisting on only one "boyfriend" at a time and exhibiting jealousy in the event of competition. A few seek to elevate their relationships to an idealized level—the ultimate spiritual union between two faithful lovers in what they conceive to be the classic Greek tradition. (Some homosexuals manage to establish lengthy or even permanent relationships, but successful "marriages" seem rare. One obvious reason is the lack of legal and social sanctions; family disputes are easily settled by separation.)

FREUD'S REASSURANCE

The homosexual's position in society is often precarious. Discovery can cost him his reputation and perhaps his career. He is aware that, according to New York law, every sexual act could cost him years in prison (though it rarely happens). He feels society hates him, and unjustly. Frequently he is guilt-ridden, aware or not, and lacks the self-acceptance he needs in order to live comfortably with his condition, which itself is thought to be closely related to an unhealthy early psychological environment. These factors, rather than homosexuality alone, are what some believe to be the main causes of emotional instability, effeminism, violence, and other problems commonly blamed on sexual deviation. Homosexuals themselves argue that while these problems are indeed widespread, they tend to be exaggerated by psychiatrists, the police, and other authorities whose work brings them into contact only with disturbed individuals; they insist that many homosexuals can be reasonably happy and productive people, capable of leading quite as fulfilled lives as heterosexuals.

Although psychologists are far from agreement on the causes and remedies for homosexuality, there is considerable support for this claim. In a letter to a despairing mother, written in 1935, Freud himself expressed a general view of the problem which many analysts would no doubt affirm today:

Homosexuality is assuredly no advantage, but it is nothing to be ashamed of, no vice, no degradation, it cannot be classified as an illness; we consider it to be a variation of the sexual function produced by a certain arrest of sexual development. Many highly respectable individuals of ancient and modern times have been homosexuals, several of the greatest men among them. . . . It is a great injustice to persecute homosexuality as a crime, and cruelty too.

[You ask if we can] abolish homosexuality and make normal heterosexuality take its place. The answer is in a general way, we cannot promise to achieve it. In a certain number of cases we succeed in developing the blighted germs of heterosexual tendencies which are present in every homosexual; in the majority of cases it is no more possible.

What analysis can do for your son runs in a different line. If he is unhappy, neurotic, torn by conflicts, inhibited in his social life, analysis may bring him harmony, peace of mind, full efficiency, whether he remains a homosexual or gets changed.

Some psychiatrists do consider homosexuality a severe emotional disorder that both can and should be corrected —if the individual sincerely wants to change. The relatively few instances of successful treatment would seem to indicate most do not. Another view which seems to be gaining wider acceptance is that homosexuality may arise out of faulty differentiation of the male and female components in the "psychosexual" development of the individual, and thus should be considered a character or personality problem rather than a deep-seated neurosis. Such broad hypotheses subdivide into numerous and often conflicting theories. Some experts are now reconsidering the possibility that hereditary factors, which were once dismissed, may indeed play a role. There is however a fairly wide consensus that adjustment to homosexuality is sometimes preferable to attempts at cure.

Evidence that there may be no inherent connection between homosexuality and pathology has been gathered in a study conducted by Dr. Evelyn Hooker of the University of California and published in 1957 as a preliminary report on "The Adjustment of the Male Overt Homosexual." For the study, thirty apparently well-adjusted homosexuals were matched for age, IQ, and education against thirty apparently well-adjusted heterosexuals. The teams then were given a battery of psychological tests, the results of which were analyzed blind by two of Dr. Hooker's colleagues who found themselves unable to pick out which of the subjects were homosexuals. Nor was there any significant difference between the groups in overall adjustment ratings. Dr. Hooker does not present her results as at all conclusive, but she considers them ground for reviewing the theory that homosexuality and pathology are inherently related.

Many homosexuals have always contended they were no different from anyone else—just sexually left-handed. A few even argue that homosexuality would be an altogether superior way of life were it not for society's square attitudes. However, such militancy is more characteristic of the few "organized" homosexuals than of the rank and file. The New York Homosexual League conducted an informal poll among three hundred deviates, asking each, among other things, if he would want to become heterosexual if a safe, easy means were available. Ninety-six percent answered no, but only three percent said they would want to see a child of theirs homosexual. The attitude which seems to be most commonly held is that homosexuality is not the preferable condition, but there's nothing morally wrong with it, it even has some things to recommend it, and in any case one has to make the best of the situation. Out of this desire to make the best of it grows a gay community with a social structure specially adapted to homosexual needs.

THE EASY WAYS TO STATUS

Still, the term *gay society* must be used very cautiously. If a fairly self-conscious and recognizable gay community can be observed in New York, it should be clear that its habits and standards do not apply to thousands of homosexuals who have little or nothing to do with it. Generalizations about gay "social structure" thus must be even more tentative than those about heterosexual society. Nevertheless, gay society does seem to deal with such questions as status and money in roughly consistent ways.

For obvious reasons, personal attractiveness and age seem the most important qualifications for getting ahead socially in the gay world. A premium is placed on appearing neat, fashionably dressed, young, and handsome, and anyone who is slovenly or physically unattractive is severely handicapped. Fashionable dress currently means slim-cut Continental or extreme Ivy League styles in suits, and well-tailored, collegiate-looking casual wear. The perfect dresser is extremely up-to-date, but careful to avoid styles so radical or grooming so fastidious as to be termed "faggoty-elegant." Homosexuals commonly dress younger and try to look younger than their years, but those who overdo it are often ridiculed. Although one finds quite a few exceptions, young homosexuals generally prefer their own age group socially as well as sexually, and an older person who insists on a youthful sexual partner may have to turn to male prostitutes.

Wealth and family background themselves usually are not sources of status within the homosexual community, though their manifestations—possessions, manners, etc.—may be. Since most homosexuals have no dependents and only personal expenses, a modest income will usually provide the obvious luxuries of "sophisticated" city life, reducing the importance of real wealth. Most homosexuals who participate exclusively in gay social life have a relatively low income, so there exists no real moneyed class within the community toward which to aspire. A prominent family background brings little status since few homosexuals can afford to mix their gay life with their straight life.

A college education, as such, confers relatively little status within the community, but in many circles it is important to display cultural interests and a degree of cool sophistication or "hipness." The folklore of the gay world has it that homosexuals tend to be specially gifted in the creative arts. There is not much evidence to support this notion, although living in an "enemy" society of heterosexuals may well increase one's sensitivity and perception. Quite naturally, however, homosexuals tend to be attracted to creative fields, which are traditionally tolerant, rather than to occupations like law, engineering, or business management where disclosure could be ruinous. A young single man, moreover, can better afford the risks and financial insecurity of an artistic career. A few occupations such as clothes designing, window dressing, decorating,

modeling, and hairdressing are considered gay trades and carry more prestige than office work and clerking. So do some types of performing (ice-skating, chorus dancing, etc.). For the most part, however, the homosexuals of the gay community are not notably successful people by the standards of the outer world. If they are gifted professionals or artists, for example, they will usually find their way to more complex and interesting homosexual, and mixed, milieus, and their lives will seldom center in gay society.

The gay social climber (like any other) considers address and neighborhood important, but he sometimes goes to extremes that would strike the status-seeking heterosexual as too obvious. Some will sacrifice every other luxury to live in a plush apartment in Sutton Place on a clerk's salary, or pay high rent for a cramped room because it has an East Fifties address.

In gay society an individual is often typed (not always accurately) according to his neighborhood. The "East Side Snob" is described as an elegant, high-class dandy, or a bland, pseudo-sophisticated "organization man with a flair," and both tend to confine themselves to their own more private social circles. The West Sider is thought to be a lower-class, sometimes bizarre person, and the two extremes seem to meet in the Village where stereotypes mix. To some homosexuals, Forty-second Street between Sixth and Eighth Avenues is practically a taboo area because of the hustlers, hoodlums, and generally undesirable types who often congregate there. The West Seventies are said to be a "pansy patch" because of the number of obviously effeminate homosexuals, often Puerto Rican, who live there; and some areas of the Upper East Side are called "fairy flats" because they are supposedly inhabited by "conspicuously elegant types usually walking poodles," as one informant put it. Brooklyn Heights, just across the East River from Lower Manhattan, is thought of as a kind of homosexual suburbia popular with "young marrieds."

Despite the social discrimination and class distinctions operating at most levels of the gay community, upward social mobility is not only possible but fairly easy. The superficial nature of many status symbols makes them simple to acquire, and the most humble and unsophisticated rural bumpkin arriving cold in the big city can advance socially by adopting the right conventions and cultivating the right interests. A homosexual illustrator, complaining about fashion consciousness in gay life, told me that a friend of his considered Vance Packard's *The Status Seekers* a valuable "get-ahead book," full of good tips.

Race is less often a deciding factor of acceptability in homosexual circles. Attractive Negroes and Puerto Ricans can sometimes use their homosexuality to enter various elite gay circles, particularly in the Village, and even many white homosexuals who will not accept Negroes socially nonetheless are "quite democratic in bed." Talking of racial as well as other distinctions, one man told me: "Homosexuals are terrible snobs, you know; but not sexually, at least when no one's looking."

Homosexuals who are not deeply involved in the gay community often criticize the conformity, phoniness, and lack of individuality they believe characterizes much of this society. There are few interesting eccentrics or bohemians; most of the men seem preoccupied with "belonging" or getting ahead, and one is not aware of much depth of personality. These qualities may reflect the strong sense of rejection and insecurity, which creates a compelling need in some homosexuals to find personal acceptance. Responding to this need are a community and a value system which seem to diminish the homosexual's social handicaps by attaching status to objects well within his reach. Furthermore there are sexual considerations: homosexuals are reluctant to erect insurmountable social restrictions that would severely limit their sexual activities by excluding many personally desirable partners.

THE NEW PRESSURE GROUPS

Some of the people I talked to believe the homosexual's lot is gradually improving. More and more novels, plays, and even movies are venturing into the subject, usually treating it with some understanding. Since the late 1950s a number of radio and television programs have explored sexual deviation, and talks on the subject are increasingly common, both by professional persons and by homosexuals themselves. In 1961, Illinois became the first state to exclude from its criminal code private homosexual relations between consenting adults, a revision now advocated by many legal, medical, and psychiatric societies. One conspicuous step toward toleration took place in 1950 when homosexuals first were able to form organizations, hold meetings and conventions, and publish their own books and magazines. Earlier attempts had failed, usually in the face of extra-legal and social pressures.

The most prominent homosexual organization, the Mattachine Society (so named after medieval court jesters who dared to speak the truth in the face of stern authority) originated in California in 1950 and later opened chapters in other cities. It was followed by One, Inc., and by the Daughters of Bilitis, a national organization for female homosexuals. Today there are more than a dozen national and local organizations for "homophiles," publishing *One Magazine, One Quarterly, The Ladder* (Daughters of Bilitis), *The Mattachine Review,* The League for Civil Education *News* (a biweekly newspaper published in San Francisco), and numerous local newsletters.

In New York, the local Mattachine Society (now independent of the California group) has around two hundred members and holds regular meetings and study groups at which psychiatrists, lawyers, and other professionals speak. A new group called the Homosexual League was founded last year and is chiefly the work of Randolfe Wicker, a young man in his twenties whose main objective is to "bring the subject of homosexuality into the open" by speaking before interested groups and arranging for others to lecture on the subject.

Despite the increase in organizational activities, very few homosexuals belong to groups or subscribe to publications. Some are afraid to join or subscribe, and others oppose organizing on the grounds that it only attracts attention which will make things worse. The majority simply are not interested in crusading and want only to be left alone. Judging from the readers' letters published, the magazines are of greater interest to homosexuals in smaller cities who tend to feel more isolated.

Even though the organizations and magazines are not widely supported, they have exerted a subtle influence on both heterosexual and homosexual thinking. To city, state, medical, and other authorities they are tangible evidence that homosexuals are not altogether the either dangerous or laughable perverts that police arrests or locker-room jokes imply. Moreover, they document many aspects of homosexuality and examine its problems, and no doubt provide a welcome source of information and understanding to many young persons suddenly confronted with the realization they are "queer."

Some authorities who hold that homosexuality is a neurotic symptom might warn against increasing its social acceptance, in the belief that this would invite latent deviants to become overt, and discourage the overt from seeking therapy. But those who consider it to be a type of personality disorder in which adjustment is often preferable to attempts at cure, believe that increased tolerance of homosexuality may help reduce the intense guilt that sometimes leads to seriously neurotic or antisocial behavior.

In any case, even a superficial inquiry into the community life of homosexuals should make two things clear. First, the term *homosexual* itself means little unless it is carefully qualified. The latent homosexual, the transvestite, the child molester, the lone wolf, the gay person, and so on, may all have very different problems and social roles, deriving from radically different causes. Secondly, the isolated life of the gay community may be seen as a reflection of the dominant social order itself. Our society has been quick to adopt defensive and mocking attitudes toward homosexuals and painfully slow to acquire a humane and mature understanding of their condition.

VII

the
stigmatized

Social relationships are regulated by systems of norms which define appropriate behaviors and attributes for various sets of social activities. It is possible for individuals and groups to deviate from the norms to some degree without provoking negative responses from community members. Some deviations, however, are not tolerated. Certain types of extreme behavior or unusual attributes may result in denial of access to normal social relationships or in interpersonal responses which make the deviant feel uncomfortable and uneasy. The phenomenon of stigma is an effective mechanism of social control and, although the use of it is not always subject to rational explanation, it can shut out the stigmatized both socially and psychologically.

The feelings of stigma on the part of the afflicted individual or group have important consequences for their social behavior. In fact, the stigma itself may be a greater problem than the deviation from societal expectations that lead to it. Thus, those who are concerned with deviant groups must not only deal with their non-normative behavior, but they must also seek to change the attitudes of both those who are disapproved and those who do the disapproving. The cases here include accounts of individuals and groups who have faced personal deprecation and social limitations because of an unusual status that they occupy. It becomes apparent that the actual event or characteristic which provides the object of focus for the process of stigma need not necessarily be unusual of itself; it only appears unusual because of the way it is viewed. The social weapon of stigma is useful for controlling the behavior of others. Such control may be justified and necessary in many areas of social conduct, but often it does little to ameliorate the effects of deviant status or change the lot of the stigmatized.

Individual
↓
Individual

Individual
↓
Organization

QUESTION OF CUSTODY

An area in which society is loathe to interfere is that of family relationships. In general, society will tolerate a wide range of behavior within the family setting. Nevertheless, if a family situation is different in a significant way and if attention is called to it, the community's response may be one of righteous indignation. Mitford's article discusses a lengthy legal battle for custody of a child between a father and his deceased wife's parents. The father originally lost the case because his bohemian style of life made him unacceptable in the eyes of some as a parent. Even though the child's grandparents had an especially friendly court, it is doubtful that they would have been able to victimize the father if it had not been for the unusual style of his personal life. The reader may be interested to know that in 1968 the child was returned by the grandparents to the father, after further legal action.

STRANGE COURTSHIP CUSTOMS OF THE FORMERLY MARRIED

Values on matters of family break-up and divorce have changed considerably over the last few decades. Today, divorce is not likely to affect the individual's job status, or opportunities for participation in community affairs. In fact, it may not present even a serious barrier to one's chances for being elected President. The divorced person, however, bears a stigma in the community in regard to certain activities. Communities do not generally prescribe ways or places for divorced persons to develop heterosexual relationships, and consequently the means by which they meet dates and prospective mates are very special ones. Hunt describes the unique relationship which develops between divorced persons who pursue courtship and romance. The behavior is at least somewhat a result of the individual's unusual marital status.

Organization	Organization
↓	↓
Individual	Organization

ABORTION: ONE GIRL'S STORY

Although views on sexual conduct have become more liberal, it is still viewed as inappropriate for any woman not to want to give birth to a child once she has conceived it. The community does not provide opportunities, except in rare cases, for married or unmarried women to prevent the birth of a child. The article by Yudkin describes in a rather factual way the meaning of these community restrictions in terms of one girl's effort to avoid bringing an unwanted child into the world. In many instances, a woman who seeks abortion is protrayed as a victim of unscrupulous medical practitioners who assist her. This account presents the community as the protagonist, while the medical personnel involved are only intermediaries in the conflict which exists between the community and the pregnant girl.

WHEN CHILDREN CAN'T LEARN

Numerous intervention efforts have been attempted with the retarded or the presumed retarded even though the results are discouraging. In the face of limited alternatives for efficacious treatment, new ones are often grasped at without adequate evaluation of their utility by intimates of the field. At the same time, the professional establishment of medical researchers and practitioners is sometimes too skeptical of new theories of treatment and techniques. Bird describes the development of an organization dedicated to a new approach for treating a particular mental syndrome. The antagonism and barriers placed in the path of the proponents of the new method by the organized medical and research establishment indicate the types of organizational tensions which can develop in dealing with a stigmatized group.

question of custody

JESSICA MITFORD

Mark Painter was almost five years old when his mother, Jeanne Bannister Painter, and his little sister, Janet, were killed in a car crash in the winter of 1962. A few months after this tragedy, Mark's maternal grandparents, Mr. and Mrs. Dwight Bannister, of Ames, Iowa, offered to take Mark to stay with them temporarily, until the father, Harold Painter, could make satisfactory arrangements for his care. Harold Painter gratefully accepted. In 1964, he remarried and settled in Walnut Creek, California. When he and his new wife, Marylyn, sought to bring Mark home, the Bannisters refused to relinquish him. Harold Painter took the case to court and was awarded custody of his son by the trial judge. The Bannisters appealed the decision and won custody of Mark in the Iowa Supreme Court.

Why the passionate nationwide reaction touched off by the case of seven-year-old Mark Painter? Not, surely, just because it is painful to think of a child being caught up in a family tug-of-war. Literally thousands of custody cases are heard in the courts every day, each one no doubt a microcosm of human misery and a searing experience for those involved. Generally, these cases merit not even a line in the local paper.

The Iowa judges themselves, flooded with angry letters about their decision, have expressed surprise that what they considered "a routine child-custody case" should have caused such a stir. A routine child-custody case, or "a judicial kidnapping," as many observers have charged?

The reasoning unfolded in the Iowa Supreme Court's written opinion supplies the clue, setting the stage as it does for a contest between the California way of life of the father and the Iowa way of the grandparents. The sixty-year-old Bannisters, says the court, are "highly respected members of the community. Mr. Bannister has served on the school board and regularly teaches Sunday school." Their home would provide Mark "a stable, dependable, conventional, middle-class, Middle West background." And here are the Painters: "Unstable, unconventional, arty, bohemian, and probably intellectually stimulating." Furthermore, Harold Painter is "either an agnostic or atheist, has read a lot of Zen Buddhism, and is a political liberal. Mrs. Painter is a Roman Catholic." Painter has a "bohemian approach to finances . . . his main ambition is to be a free-lance writer and photographer." Worse yet, "He was contemplating a move to Berkeley at the time of trial." True, said the court, "in the Painter home, Mark would have more

Reprinted from McCalls, *May, 1966, pp. 97-110.* © *1966 by The McCall Corporation.*

freedom of conduct and thought, with an opportunity to develop his individual talents. It would be more exciting and challenging in many respects, but romantic, impractical and unstable."

Having stated the issue in this way, the nine Iowa judges (whose average age, by coincidence, is sixty), gave the nod to the stable, conventional Bannisters.

The court decision, while seeming to uphold staid respectability against unconventional modernity, upset all traditional notions—old-fashioned, nineteenth-century notions, if you will—and all existing legal concepts of parental rights. The court specifically found that Painter is not an unfit parent. The legal rights of grandparents in child-custody cases are held in most states to be no greater than those of strangers. The U.S. Supreme Court has said, "The right of a parent to the care and custody of a child cannot be taken away merely because the Court may believe that some third person can give the child better care and greater protection. This right can only be forfeited by a parent on proof that the parent is unfit to have such care and custody."

The Iowa judges in effect took a look at two environments, two sets of values, two financial standards of living—and decided the father's home was less to their liking than that of the grandparents.

Thus the chilling implication underlying the decision: that any time, anywhere a court may decide to step in and play Big Brother, may arbitrarily remove a child from his real parents because it happens to disapprove of their ideas or dislike the way they choose to live. . . .

Harold Painter gave me directions to his home in Walnut Creek. "It's at the end of Locust Street. To the right, there's a dirt road leading up to a sort of Charles Addams house—that's ours."

I should describe it as a quite nice old house on a grassy hill. But I will stipulate (as lawyers say) to the description given in the opinion of the Iowa State Supreme Court: "The house in which Mr. Painter and his present wife live, compared with the well-kept Bannister home, exemplifies the contrasting ways of life. In his words 'it is very old and beat up and lovely.' The interior is inexpensively but tastefully decorated. They live in the rear part. The large yard on a hill in the business district of Walnut Creek, Calif., is of uncut weeds and wild oats. The house is not painted on the outside."

Harold Painter and Marylyn, a graphic designer, to whom he has been married for a little over a year, came out to meet me among the wild oats ("I don't know who sowed them," Harold commented wryly) and led me into their brightly painted living room.

Although the Painters are a warm, attractive couple, frank and friendly, and easy talkers, somehow our first meeting started off on an awkward note. Marylyn nervously apologized for the untidiness of the house (which seemed quite neat and ordinary to me), saying she hadn't had time to do much housekeeping. (Did she fear I would run a surreptitious finger over the coffee table, checking for dust?) She showed me the curtains she had sewed for Mark's room, the large poster she had hung, depicting soliders' uniforms throughout the ages. She described their quiet, homey way of life—chess, music, television, lots of friends who drop in.

As Hal related the background, I began to see why he and Marylyn felt defensive. They have been through some very grubby experiences in connection with the case, particularly Hal, whose entire past life was resurrected, scrutinized and denounced by the Bannister lawyers in the course of the five-day trial. They have been trailed by private investigators and have felt the malaise these indistinct persons can produce by their furtive presence. They resent being labeled as "unstable, arty, bohemian," and they do not relish having suddenly become a *cause célèbre.*

At the center of their concern is the effect that all this may have on Mark. Hal tried to explain to him, in perhaps the only terms a seven-year-old could be expected to grasp, what this case is all about. "I told him that his grandparents are pulling for him, and we are pulling, too, just because we all love him so much, and because we all want him to live with us."

Mark has obviously been exposed to his grandparents' arguments. In a recent telephone conversation, he said to his father, "I won't be coming there, maybe not for twenty years. I don't like the way you spend your money. Anyway, Grandfather says you can't go to the Supreme Court about me. He says it would cost twelve thousand dollars, and you don't have that much money."

The smell of money hangs pervasively over this case. In the first place, the well-off Bannisters were able to retain two lawyers, partners in a leading Des Moines law firm, and to fly them to Washington and California for the taking of depositions. They were able to obtain the services of a child psychologist, whose testimony proved to be of decisive importance. The Painters managed as best they could; they found the name of a lawyer in the Ames phone book who agreed to represent them. But they could not afford to fly their witnesses to Iowa for the trial or to hire a psychologist to testify for them.

Harold Painter's preference for the intellectual life over the pursuit of tangible assets was, he told me, a constant source of irritation to his in-laws and in fact constituted the backbone of their case against him in court. Illustrative of the allegations made against him during the trial: Once, long before his marriage to Jeanne Bannister, he bought $200 worth of books. He read some, kept some, gave some away and sold the rest, "realizing only fifteen dollars." He bought photographic equipment and "sold it at a loss." He and Jeanne made a bad bargain over the purchase of their first home. For a short time, he quit work to try free-lance writing, and "realized but seventy-five dollars" for an article that took him a whole month to write. After Jeanne's death, he spent part of her estate on a boat on which he could take Mark sailing—he hoped it might help both of them begin to recover from the tragedy that had overtaken them. He sold the boat "at a loss." He quit good, steady, well-paying jobs, and turned down others, because he did not find the work stimulating.

Hal readily admits that he cannot work up much enthusiasm for the accumulation of money as a primary goal in life. (He is employed as a photographer in the Job Corps at a salary of $167 a week.) "I wasn't brought up to think that money is God," he said. "And I know I'm not much of a businessman, probably never will be. My values and those of the Bannisters are totally different."

Other charges developed in the course of the trial, and given due consideration by the Iowa Supreme Court, pointed to unorthodoxy of belief and behavior: Hal does not attend any church. He reads Zen Buddhism ("I think the Bannisters once spotted a book by Alan Watts in my house," he told me). He got into difficulty in his job at the University of Washington for his support of the American Civil Liberties Union in the university news bulletin. He wore a sports shirt and sweater at his wife's funeral. He permits Mark to call him by his first name. Hal does not dispute any of this—in fact, he is proud of much of it. He does not intend to mend his ways, because he does not think they need mending.

The implicit standards by which the Iowa Supreme Court judged Harold Painter could have come right out of the famous study *Middletown,* by Robert and Helen Lynd, which describes just such a Middle Western city as Ames: "Middletown is against anything that curtails moneymaking, any striking innovations in art, ideas, literature, people engaged in thinking about or working for change, anybody who knows too much." To win approval in Middletown a man "must be active in trying to get on in the world. The quality of his life is measured in terms of tangible success, achievement, 'something to show for it,' ability to 'produce the goods,' but this success is mistrusted unless it is won by hard work, common sense, and careful planning."

Middletown, and Ames, and the Iowa Supreme Court judges have every right to prefer these standards. Do they have the right to impose them on others?

Since their fitness as parents was called into question by the Bannisters, the Painters' presentation of their case was necessarily defensive. They applied to the Social Welfare Department of the county in which they live for an investigation of their home. The social worker who visited them reported that it is a "pleasant, warm, 'homey' setting, comfortable and pleasant for a boy of Mark's age. This family should be able to offer deep affection and excellent understanding, consistent, intelligent care and nurturance to Mr. Painter's son."

Friends and former coworkers of Harold and Jeanne's came forward to testify in depositions to the quality of their marriage and of Mark's upbringing in the first years of his life.

The composite picture from this testimony, and from Hal's own description of his first marriage, is of two pleasant, intelligent young people, very much devoted to each other and to their children.

They met and married in Anchorage, Alaska, where both were working as journalists for the Anchorage *Times.* Later they moved to Pullman, Washington, where Jeanne met her death.

Jeanne's own opinion of Harold's fitness as a father also came to light in the trial. Shortly before the fatal accident, she had taken the step, unusual for a young woman, of making a will consigning the children to their father, "as I am confident that he will faithfully provide for their care and I wish him to have unfettered power to do so."

The trial judge, the Honorable Ed Kelley, of Ames, had a long private interview with Mark. In his written opinion, he says that "for obvious reasons" he did not ask Mark which home he preferred. Judge Kelley found Mark to be "considerably above average in mental abilities, pleasant, courteous and well-behaved. It is apparent that Mark has many of his father's characteristics and exhibits a great deal of the good early training given him by his beloved mother." In awarding custody to the father, Judge Kelley found that Painter "is a proper and fit person to have the care and custody of his own minor son, and that it is for the best interests of the son to be reared and educated in his own father's home; that the father is the person to properly maintain his son and to properly educate him."

The judge also had praise for the Bannisters. He noted that they have "provided a very fine home for their grandson" and that they have shown they can give him "certain advantages, material and spiritual. They have done a great deal for, and have been a good influence on, their grandson. They have shown him great love and affection, even to excess."

I have never met the Bannisters. They declined to see me and referred all inquiries to their lawyers, which I thought a perfectly understandable attitude under the circumstances.

They are apparently "good people," a term that occurs over and over with all those who have had to do with this case. The trial judge, while awarding Mark away from them, said they are good people. The Iowa Supreme Court, reversing Judge Kelley, says they are good people. Harold Painter thinks they are in some ways good people. He told me they were aloof and unfriendly when he first married Jeanne (a familiar tale; after all, who is good enough for Our Daughter? Hardly anyone), but he said that after Jeanne's death, they were for the first time really warm and cordial to him. "I began to have the feeling we could at last be friends."

The Bannisters may indeed be good people according to their lights. They are also long-range planners.

There is evidence that almost from the moment of their daughter's death the Bannisters started to lay the foundation for obtaining custody of Mark. If their attempts to build a case against Harold Painter as an unfit father were signally unsuccessful, it was not for lack of trying.

Two months after Jeanne's fatal accident, the Bannisters wrote to Hal's former employers asking for a confidential report on him. "It was imperative to find out what connections he had and what moneys he might owe," Mr. Bannister testified at the trial. These many inquiries drew but one reply, from a former supervisor who, although he had asked for Painter's resignation because of disagreements about editorial style, gave on the whole a favorable picture of him: "He was an energetic worker, and I think he possesses above-average competence in many of the areas associated with publishing."

Shortly before the custody trial, private detectives posing as government investigators began appearing at the homes of Hal's friends, in California, and at the newspaper offices where he had worked. They asked how good a worker Hal was, what were his political leanings, if he is pro-Communist. Evidently they drew a blank on all counts, for their testimony was not called for at the trial.

The Bannisters, through their lawyer, demanded that Hal should submit to a psychiatric examination. Hal agreed. The examination was administered by Dr. Adrienne Applegarth, a San Francisco psychiatrist selected by the Bannisters. Her report must have been a disappointment: "It is my impression that Mr. Painter falls quite squarely within the range of normal," she wrote. "It is evident that there exists a large difference in ways of life and value systems between the Bannisters and Mr. Painter, but in this case, there is no evidence that psychiatric instability is involved. Rather, these divergent life patterns seem to represent alternative normal adaptations."

The Bannister lawyers paid for this report, but did not offer it in evidence. It was eventually incorporated into the record by Painter's counsel.

The painstaking and expensive quest for evidence to prove that Harold Painter is an unfit parent was unsuccessful. As it turned out, the decisive testimony was given by a person who had neither set foot in the Painter home nor set eyes on Harold and Marylyn.

Despite their evident disapproval of Painter and his way of life, the Iowa Supreme Court justices might have found it awkward to disregard traditional parental rights by arbitrarily depriving a father of a child—had they not been supplied with a rationale admirably tailored to lend substance to their own sentiments. "We do not believe it is for Mark's best interest," they declared, "to take him out of this stable atmosphere in the face of warnings of dire consequences from an eminent child psychologist and send him to an uncertain future in his father's home."

The oracle who presaged these dire consequences is Dr. Glenn R. Hawkes, child psychologist at Iowa State University, at Ames (where Mr. Dwight Bannister was also employed), who was retained by the Bannisters to testify for them at the trial.

The trial judge, not impressed, had made short work of Dr. Hawkes: "The Court has given full consideration to the good doctor's testimony but cannot accept it at full face value because of exaggerated statements and the witness' attitude on the stand."

Dr. Hawkes' testimony, which runs to some seventy pages of transcript, is phrased in the dreary jargon of his calling. "I think Mark is working very extensively at an identification and ego development." "He is at a restless point in his life, at latency, which is prior to pre-adolescence." "He is developing a strong sub-ego."

While Dr. Hawkes spent a total of twenty-five hours interviewing Mark and his grandparents, he did not see the Painters. Asked why not, he said: "In order to make a determination of where Mark's welfare lies, I do not think it is essential to know the type of father, the type of home, and the type of life he is going to lead if moved. When a child has constructed his life around these parent-substitutes [the Bannisters], I think this is the most critical factor and I think the other—knowing about his natural father and wife—is relatively unimportant."

His findings, translated into ordinary English, are these: Mark is an unusually intelligent child. He was upset when he first went to the Bannisters shortly after the death of his mother and little sister, he had bad dreams about being killed, he was quarrelsome with other children.

Over the past two years at the Bannisters' home, he has improved greatly and is now a much happier, calmer little boy, who gets on well with his schoolmates. He has come to look on Mr. Bannister as a substitute father.

To the layman, none of this seems at all surprising. One would expect a five-year-old to be terribly upset at the loss of his mother and at being suddenly moved away from his father; one would expect him to improve as time goes by, as he grows older and the tragedy begins to fade. It would be odd if he did not love and obey a doting grandfather, with whom he lives, as he might a real father.

The conclusion that Dr. Hawkes draws from his observations are, however, enough to boggle the mind.

He says that should Mark be returned to his father, there is "a ninety per cent chance that he will go bad" and a strong likelihood that he will become a juvenile delinquent. Worse still would be the effect on Mark if the Painters should have a baby: "I think siblings coming into the home at the present time would dilute his own strength about himself. I think this would not be healthy for him unless it were very skillfully handled. It causes some intense rivalry, which would be repressing." And what of the fact that Harold Painter is, after all, the boy's own father? "The biological father of a child is only necessary obviously at the time of conception. . . . The biological father is an accident of conception in many cases. . . . Disruption at this point, I think, would be detrimental to the child even though Mr. Painter might well be a paragon of virtue."

According to Dr. Hawkes, the age difference of the two couples—the fact that the Painters are in their early thirties and the Bannisters in their sixties—is, far from being detrimental to the Bannisters' case, rather in their favor: "When mothers of children are past forty-five, they tend to be more accepting of their children.... I think our statistics can allow us to say that older people tend to be more accepting of young children."

Are these pronouncements really representative of the thinking of professionals in the mental-health and child-development fields? Apparently not.

Dr. Benjamin Spock told me he was appalled when he read newspaper accounts of the Iowa decision. He felt the whole line of Dr. Hawkes' reasoning was "preposterous, ridiculous." He said the most upsetting thing that can happen to a child is to feel that his real father does not want him: "It is absolutely crucial to a child to know his parents love him and want him with them. It would be most harmful to Mark if his father did *not* press for custody. To say the father is only a 'biological necessity' for purposes of conception is completely off base. The tie is *not* only biological, but is also of overwhelming importance from a psychological point of view."

I showed the transcript of Dr. Hawkes' testimony to Dr. Paul Mussen, professor of psychology at the University of California. He expressed amazement and profound disagreements with Dr. Hawkes' conclusions.

His major criticism was that all Dr. Hawkes' findings about Mark could equally well be used as arguments in favor of returning Mark to his father. "Hawkes says Mark is a relatively healthy child from a psychological point of view. If he is relatively healthy, then he can adjust to change.

"There is something peculiar about Hawkes' reasoning. He feels any move is traumatic to a child—yet a fairly well-adjusted child, as he says Mark is, thanks to the good job the Bannisters have done with him, can adjust to change. What is so disturbing about Hawkes' testimony is the underlying feeling that

children do not have much flexibility. That is absolutely incorrect; they have a great deal of flexibility."

Dr. Mussen said he was amazed that Dr. Hawkes should fear for Mark's mental health if other children should be born to the Painters. "What evidence is there that the birth of siblings dilutes a child's own strength about himself? On the one hand, Hawkes talks about the strength of this boy; on the other, he gives that strength no weight—he maintains that all outcomes of a change to his father's house must be bad." As to the testimony that there is a 90 per cent chance that Mark will go bad if returned to his father, Dr. Mussen said it is ludicrous: "It assumes far more knowledge than we have about children."

The most disturbing portions of the testimony, said Dr. Mussen, are those dealing with Painter himself, whom Dr. Hawkes has never seen. "There is a tacit disapproval of Painter throughout. He makes inferences about him without any knowledge of him. He says, 'One has to earn the right to be a father.... I think it would be very difficult under the present circumstances for Mr. Painter to earn that.' Yet he knows nothing about Painter, who may have very great strengths."

A move to the Painter home, Dr. Mussen emphasized, could be a rich, new opportunity for Mark. "The notion that a solid middle-class home is the best kind for kids is without foundation; there's no evidence that this is so. The kind of stimulation a bright boy like Mark could get from the Painters could be extraordinarily valuable. The implication that the Bannisters represent stability and the Painters instability is not justified. Hawkes says that Mark's IQ is 120 on the test, and that he feels his real IQ is higher than this. Perhaps if he were in the more stimulating environment of the Painters' home, his score on the

IQ tests would rise in a very short time."

The assistant chief of psychiatry at a San Francisco hospital, to whom I showed the transcript (and who for professional reasons prefers not to be quoted by name), termed Dr. Hawkes' testimony "a terribly presumptuous use of pseudo-scientific psychological knowledge, replete with value judgments. Just about every point is open to challenge." As to Dr. Hawkes' contention that the Bannisters' age was not against them, he said, "It is an outrageous statement, a gross mistake. The Bannisters' age would become of critical importance by the time the child is a teen-ager." Like Dr. Mussen, he thought the statement that there is "a 90 per cent chance he will go bad" if returned to his father is "completely unjustified and unwarranted." The inferences about Painter's instability are "based on the most dubious technique; I feel extremely strongly that a person should not give an opinion about another's personality without examination."

What about opinion in Iowa? The Des Moines *Register* has vigorously upheld the Supreme Court ruling in editorials and lengthy news stories. Yet, surprisingly, the people in Ames seem on the whole to side with the Painters.

Two Episcopalian ministers of that region who hold diametrically opposed views on the Painter case agreed nevertheless that sentiment in their parishes is running about 80 per cent against the court decision.

Father Paul Goodland, of Ames, said, "I feel in my own mind that from every point of view—legal, moral, social—the opinion is bad." On the Sunday after the opinion was published, he discussed it from the pulpit. "I said that it has vast and far-reaching implications, that it deserves meditation and prayer whether you are pro or con. Then I read the prayer for Independence Day." Father Goodland feels that in Ames "the reaction depends on how old you are. If you are a grandfather, you are likely to side with the Bannisters. The younger generation is siding with Painter, on the whole. They see the decision as an effort to stifle individualism—a decision by nine grandfathers, as one put it." Father Goodland observed that, in his experience, the ideal way of child upbringing favored by the Iowa Supreme Court is no guarantee of success: "The high-school and college dropouts I know in Ames come from just such middle-class homes."

For another view of the case, Father Goodland referred me to a colleague in Des Moines, Father Richard Walter, who is strongly in favor of the court decision. "I'm smack up against popular opinion," said Father Walter. "But I feel this child will surely benefit from the upbringing of concerned grandparents." He believes the court acted in an enlightened way and that most of the criticism of the opinion is shallow and emotional. "The court had courage to go against all precedent in taking the child away from his natural father, and this shows forward thinking." Intellectual stimulation might benefit Mark later on, Father Walter said; but at his present age, the secure atmosphere and stable background of a solid Middle West home are more important.

A man-in-the-street interview survey conducted by some Ames college students turned up roughly the same percentage of pro-and-con views as reported by the ministers.

Typical comments of those who supported Painter's right to custody: "Just because you don't like the way a guy lives you can't take his kid away. An awful lot of fathers would lose their children." "It was sloppy, fuzzy thinking. If the court honestly felt Painter was incompetent, they should have said so." "If people were punished for unwise spending, fifty per cent of people's children could be taken away."

Those who felt Mark should remain with his grandparents were more taciturn: "I feel the little boy is safe with his grandparents." "The grandmother has the child and he's accustomed to her. Stepmothers are not as good."

And there were those who thought it wrong even to question the voice of authority: "The court was just, one should follow the law and not make a fuss." "The decision surprised me, but the court must have had its good reasons." "The court had all the information. Should we question people of high caliber?"

The Painters have received eloquent expressions of support in hundreds of letters from all over the country, from lawyers offering their services, from parents, students, even from children not much older than Mark. While the letters comment on many aspects of the case, one theme emerges over and over again: There, but for the grace of God, go I.

"As a teacher and an educated human being struggling to provide just such an 'intellectually stimulating' atmosphere for my own children," wrote one, "I shudder to think of the consequences of the court's action." And another: "The decision would seem to be a dangerously arbitrary determination of what one's behavior should be. If intellectual stimulation is not a good thing, we are ALL in trouble."

Parents like these feel directly threatened. Before accepting that exciting invitation for the children to spend the summer with Grandma and Grandpa on the ranch, prudence might suggest they first consult their lawyer. How stands the law of Wyoming, of Indiana, of Kansas, of South Dakota? How many judges in these states are over sixty?

The Painters are appealing their case to the U. S. Supreme Court. They will be represented by one of the nation's leading constitutional-law firms, which has volunteered its services. The American Civil Liberties Union has agreed to support their cause. They face a long and costly struggle, for although they will not have to pay lawyers' fees, court costs can run high. Formidable legal obstacles lie ahead; the U. S. Supreme Court is by no means obliged to review the case, and instances where the high court has overturned the ruling of a State Supreme Court in matters of family law are rare. Yet the Painters are determined to see it through.

Even their well-wishers, and possibly the Painters themselves, may begin to wonder if, should they eventually win the case, it will be possible for Mark to settle down happily with them after all the turmoil. They might take comfort from the sage words of the Honorable Roger Traynor, present Chief Justice of the Supreme Court of California. In reviewing another child-custody case, some years ago, he wrote:

"Even if the child is required to make some sacrifice to be with his natural parent or adjust to a new environment, it does not necessarily follow that his welfare will be correspondingly impaired. It may not be to the best interest of the child to have every advantage. He may derive benefits by subordinating his immediate interest to the development of a new family relationship with his own parent, by giving as well as receiving. Thus, although a change in custody from an outsider to a parent may involve the disruption of a satisfactory status quo, it may lead to a more desirable relationship in the long run."

strange courtship customs of the formerly married

MORTON M. HUNT

What on earth is ailing Raymond Hartwell, Esq.? Three times today, his secretary entered his office and found him staring out of the window, lost in thought, a pile of briefs still unread in front of him. Two of those times, she asked him questions about documents he had dictated yesterday and was met with a blank look that yielded to comprehension only after some effort; the third time, he sharply told her to use the head God gave her and sent her off with eyes brimming over. This past hour, he has been thumbing through a little guidebook of some sort and making phone calls; betweentimes, he has played with paper clips, paced the floor in thought and stared at his reflection in the glass doors of the law-reports bookcase, frowning at the gray in his temples and the slight bulge at his waist. His twenty-four-year-old secretary assumes there is some weighty legal problem on his mind; but if she knew what was troubling him, her tears would give way to a fit of derisive giggles: Raymond Hartwell, Esq. (the name is fictitious), is going out tonight on his first date as a formerly married man and, quite simply, he is nervous.

Yet it is nothing to laugh about. This momentous occasion was preceded by a great deal of anxiety, fear, hope and just plain effort, much of which centered about the problem of finding a suitable woman for his first postmarital adventure. Where did Raymond Hartwell find her?

A resident of the World of the Formerly Married (an "FM") is not likely, as we have seen, to find a prospective new partner through the good offices of his married friends, helpful as they may try to be. But the World of the Formerly Married offers the newcomer a number of other, and often more efficient, ways of finding and appraising potential partners. These range from the slightly unconventional to those that ignore middle-class proprieties. The majority of FMs are torn between their desire to use more effective ways of finding partners and a contrary desire to respect the rules of middle-class society; as a result, they favor methods with an acceptable façade concealing the fact that what they offer is a chance to shop around among strangers for new partners.

One such informal, pseudoconventional mechanism is the grapevine. This is an invisible, spontaneous network of communication along which passes the news that such and such a desirable person is now available; the message results in phone calls and other approaches from persons not known to the FM being called but known to a mutual friend. This mention of a mutually known name is the nod to convention; when the man phones the woman, it reassures her and makes it acceptable for her to talk to a stranger; and when she phones the man, it gives her some flimsy pretext for phoning (she may say, for instance, that she is having open house the following week and had heard from their mutual friend So-and-So that he might be available).

At first, newcomers are astonished by the grapevine, and some view it sourly: "The men just seemed to appear like vultures. I couldn't get over it. It never occurred to me that men would give my name to other men all over the place, and I resented it." Other women either have no objection or learn to make the most of the situation. Men, though they are less apprehensive about such phone calls, are astonished to find women taking the initiative, even under the guise of legitimate business: "Somehow, the word got around that I was separated, and they just came zooming in on me. And this in a Southern town, too! I was amazed, but I soon got to like it. I've met quite a few women that way."

The grapevine is not only accepted as a windfall by some, but diligently cultivated. The newly separated person sometimes starts back in circulation by calling friends, both married and unmarried, and asking them to pass his or her name around. One is not usually this blunt with the married (though it is easy to be so with fellow FMs), but mentions in passing that he or she is starting to get around; or one may say something like, "Know anyone just right for me?" —adding a little chuckle as though it were only a joke, although none but a clod could misinterpret the message. But these obeisances to convention are being abandoned more and more. One veteran man of seven years' standing says that half a dozen years ago a middle-class FM woman would ask her friends if they knew a man for her and suggest that perhaps she could meet him at their place some evening, while nowadays many such women say merely, "If you know anyone I might like, please give him my name."

Such boldness and willingness to try new methods are increasingly common among FMs hunting for partners, even though they still cling to some shred of semiconcealing convention. How tiny that shred can become—and yet be retained—is indicated by an unusual communique from a divorcée in Scarsdale, New York: "The latest thing is for a girl to make up a list of men she's heard about or seen and send them invitations to a cocktail party she has no intention of giving. Then she phones each one a few days later to apologize and gives some reason for canceling. And if she's a good conversationalist, she can wind up with half a dozen different dates with new guys." Even if this particular contrivance is a local idiosyncrasy, it expresses the general need of FM women to take unusual and daring action because they are so much less free to initiate contacts openly.

A more familiar pseudoconventional mechanism is the club or association that has some unimpeachable stated purpose but also, and more importantly, happens to serve as a marketplace for FMs.

Parents Without Partners is a fast-growing national organization, which now has 166 chapters and 18,500 members, with the stated purpose of enabling single parents "to learn better ways of helping themselves and their children cope with life in the one-parent or divided family."

Chapter presidents and membership directors of Parents Without Partners continually make public avowals such as this: "Now, bear in mind that we are *not* a marriage bureau and not basically a social club. It happens that we do socialize, but that's only incidental. We're here to help you adjust to life as single parents; we're here to make you better and stronger than when you walked in that door." Privately, however, the very officer who makes that pious statement concedes that the primary motive of nine tenths of the incoming members is to look for eligible partners.

The disinterested observer can recognize this at any monthly meeting. Before the meeting starts, men and women—most of them secretaries, teachers and housewives or salesmen, businessmen and lower-echelon executives—drift into the rented auditorium in somewhat of a party mood: they mill about, talking, laughing, searching, speculating, maneuvering themselves a little closer to someone who looks interesting. The chairman raps for order, but has great difficulty in getting everyone to sit down and be silent.

At last the meeting begins; there are the usual committee reports, announcements of activities, followed by the speaker of the evening; but during all this, scores of eyes roam the room, necks crane, whispers rustle in the background. When the speech is over, applause is duly rendered and the meeting is adjourned for coffee and cookies. Now the real business of the meeting begins. Female faces don the bright, welcoming look, and male faces a studied indifference or an equally studied air of appraisal. Little groups form, disintegrate and re-form; wallflowers stand immobilized around the margins or wander slowly about, trying to look as though they were going somewhere; the more daring men cut through the throng to speak to some woman they have spotted; the more daring women openly smile at some man they hope to interest; and those who are neither wallflowers nor daring talk to someone of their own sex, protecting each other against isolation but keeping a lookout on all sides for any better possibility.

Yet perhaps that is only how it looks to one who has no personal stake in the goings-on. To those who do, the meetings, parties and dances may be a trifle bleak and somewhat competitive, but at least they do bring together large numbers of men and women who have the same basic problem.

Numerous other organizations and groupings exist whose stated aims have nothing to do with being a marketplace for unattached adults; they thrive, nevertheless, because this is what they are. They run the gamut of literary discussion clubs, bowling leagues, bridge circles, skiing associations, summer-home groups (cooperative renters), tennis leagues, and the like. Any excuse for gathering the unmarried together will do; often the excuse itself is something worthwhile—an art-appreciation course, a health club, dancing instruction—but newcomers seldom return for a second or third visit if the people present are not eminently suitable as potential dates. Many such groups are ephemeral and last only very briefly; but others go on year after year, with a membership that changes continually except for a small, hard core of the intractably unmarriageable.

The pretext of some of these pseudo conventional devices often becomes thin to the point of transparency—and still they are retained in order to save face. But the thinner the pretext and the more evident the real motive, the harder it is for some users to stomach, as one young divorcée makes plain: "I tried a Caribbean cruise last winter. It was a total waste of time and money—seventy-eight girls and eleven men. And what men, at that! My God, they were impossible! Either real drips or attractive enough but insufferably egotistical—as they could well afford to be. It was awful. We girls were just there to be picked over, and most of us ended up on the scrap heap."

The same situation prevails at those large resort hotels that attract mobs of unattached hopefuls on weekends, especially on advertised "singles weekends." Most women who go to such hotels seeking to meet men cannot help feeling almost naked under constant scrutiny; if they are continually passed by, their embarrassment is superseded by shame and depression. But it is not altogether a lark for the men, either; aside from a minority who are cheerfully predatory, many men are made uncomfortable by the continual appraisal or hopeful signaling of so many eyes and by their own fear of entrapment by some undesirable woman.

All this is probably true to a greater degree for FMs than for never-married people. The Formerly Married have lived for years in social tranquility, away from the turmoil and stress of open competition; it is unsettling to be thrust back into it and to see one's own needs so transparently mirrored on so many hopeful, overeager faces. Most of the formerly married men and women who go to such resorts candidly say that they detest doing so, even though it sometimes proves useful.

A 53-year-old man is a case in point: "I avoided going to resort hotels for a long while, and when I finally tried, in a desperate period of my life, I found it very unpleasant. The congregation of women—the hungry, eager, slightly shopworn women—at those places seem to me terribly sad. It was a freak bit of luck that I found Audrey [his present wife] there."

A 34-year-old divorcée is even more vehement: "I hate being on the open market. It isn't fear of competition—I think I'm more attractive than most of the women at those places—but the men are so *awful* in their manner. They're all looking for something quick and easy and they think all the women are, too. It's really disgusting. But I go because how many legitimate ways are there to meet men anyhow? You have to try."

This willingness to take a chance is a key feature of the emergent philosophy of the Formerly Married. Though most are unable at first to tolerate any but the conventional means of seeking new partners, the inadequacy of those means and the permissiveness of the subculture cause many of them to adopt new and more venturesome methods and take chances they had not imagined they ever would.

The outstanding case is that familiar way of meeting new partners known as the pickup. Although it has long been casually accepted at the lower levels of society as a legitimate and natural way for male and female to meet, the middle class has always frowned on it. The "nice" girl is taught to shun it altogether; the "nice" boy, uneasy about it, is more likely to use it to seek a quick sexual encounter with a lower-class girl than to make the acquaintance of a girl he would like to date regularly.

This remains more or less true among unmarried adults; most pickups in public places are intended to result in a quick and uninvolved sexual connection rather than a serious relationship. But nowadays many middle-class FMs are borrowing the pickup technique in their search for suitable dates and potential love-partners.

"I've learned to keep my eyes open wherever I am," a 37-year-old woman says. "I now have no prejudice against any avenue of meeting. I even met a very fine man on a subway platform one time. You have a number of disappointments that way, and sometimes I am even frightened, but I feel I must take every chance. You never know when or where you'll meet someone."

More promising than the subway platform are the sites where the pickup is common procedure. Just as a favorite locus of the pickup among the lower class is the corner saloon, so among the middle class it is the cocktail lounge or bar, or at least those that have spontaneously become known as rendezvous for unattached adults.

Many a newly separated person, on first hearing about this, is startled at the thought of openly searching for a pickup date in public places. The first time he visits one of the pickup bars or watches the commerce on a busy beach, he may find the whole scene vulgar and cheap—a reaction which helps combat the alarming thought that maybe he ought to try it, too. But time, need and exposure to the customs of the subculture gradually make the pickup seem a less crass and distasteful procedure, even to female FMs, and fear of it diminishes with increasing experience of unconventional methods until the pickup is only the next and not very giant step.

The bar or restaurant, as a pickup site, is not totally outside the conventions; the very woman who will allow a strange man to talk to her in such a place might rebuff him if he tried to talk to her on the street. Even so, the bar or restaurant is used by only about one out of ten women and one out of six men, and then rather infrequently. For some reason, about twice as many of each sex feel that a pickup in a plane or train is acceptable. Like planes or trains, beaches, museums, libraries and business or professional conventions have their own small coteries of adherents.

Nevertheless, even some who grow accustomed to the pickup continue to dislike it and feel nervous about it. A slim, debonair, 40-year-old actor from Los Angeles explained his feelings: "During my years as a divorced man, I found that a much more productive way for me to meet new girls than through friends or at parties was to pick them up on the beach. I did so for years, but I always hated it. I always feared the possibility of being rejected and looking like a jackass. I had to force myself to do it."

Most women seem to accept the method grudgingly, out of sheer necessity. Says an attractive 32-year-old legal secretary from a medium-size city in the Southwest: "I thought it wouldn't be too easy to meet men. It turned out to be completely impossible. The people I know don't give parties with single people present, and I couldn't afford to go alone to public events. After nearly a year, I still have found no way other than going to a 'joint' alone where I can meet anyone. Pretty shocking for a girl raised as a good Baptist, isn't it?"

But surprisingly enough, some middle-class women actually come to accept the practice of pickups without misgivings. A successful writer of children's books, 37 years old and quite pretty, says: "One of the main surprises was pickups—conversations begun while walking, traveling, shopping, et cetera, which often turned out to produce some delightful dates. I think it's just a myth that this is not a 'nice' way of meeting people. One just has to be careful, that's all."

Basic to all the genuinely unconventional methods is their lack of pretense. There is, for example, a species of unconventional get-together that might be called the "open party"; there is no guest list, but by word of mouth all kinds of friends, acquaintances and strangers hear of it and come—the only requirement being that each man bring a bottle, the only purpose being to prospect for new partners.

Open parties vary greatly, but most are given by people with bohemian or shabbily furnished apartments (none with decent furnishings would risk it). While sometimes the guests may be well dressed and well-bred, more often they are either flashily or ill dressed, and most of them are manifestly undesirable in one way or another—physically, psychologically or socially. They are, by and large, the leftovers and discards of the dating-and-mating process.

Some open parties are run by individual proprietors, "friendship clubs" or nonprofit social organizations; they are open in the sense that the only impediments to entrance are a door fee and, sometimes, a suggested age bracket.

Such open parties—which usually take the form of dances, to make meeting and breaking away easier—have recently proliferated like Mayflies. In New York City on a typical winter weekend, roughly 150 public parties and dances are held, some being advertised in the papers and others by direct mail to "members" (anyone who pays a door admission, at most of these so-called clubs, becomes a mailing-list member). Here are excerpts from listings in one New York newspaper:

THE DIVORCED SET
Call _____
Sundays at 6 p.m.

Dance: The Second Quarter Club—a co-ed group of select singles, 25-40. Total contribution $1.25.

Lecture & Ladies Nite Dance, for singles 25-40. "Communication between the Sexes." by Dr. Irving Delugatch. Stan Kaye & His Orchestra. Adm. $1.75.

DOCTORS & TEACHERS, you are cordially invited to_____'s exclusive HOUSE PARTY, Friday 9 p.m., ages 21-36, Saturday 9 p.m., ages 23-37. Call _____ for invit.

Previously Married People.
4 Select Socials.
Saturday   8 p.m.   ages 27-37
Sunday   3 p.m.   ages 25-40
Sunday   6 p.m.   ages 28-45
Sunday   9 p.m.   ages 30-50
Call _____

One can pick and choose, according to his own age, pocketbook and interests and according to his preference for dancing or talking, crowds or small groups, the intelligentsia or the hoi polloi.

But the idea is far from being special to New York; indeed, it originated in Milwaukee in the early 1930s with the first so-called "friendship club"—a public dance, with a modest admission charge (50 cents at that time; $1.50 to $3 today), where unattached people could meet. Public dance halls were nothing new, as far as lower-class people were concerned; what was new was the application of the idea on a lower-middle- and middle-class level in the guise of a "club." It quickly met a need of FMs and other unattached adults and spread from the Midwest to the West and the East.

If it is rather unconventional to pay a small fee to make an introduction unnecessary, it is far more unconventional to pay a larger fee to somebody to select a partner for one and arrange a meeting. Such an intermediary may call himself a marriage adviser, a matrimonial consultant or a social adviser, or label his business a date bureau, introduction service, friendship service or matrimonial agency; but no matter what euphemism he uses, he is practicing the ancient profession of the marriage broker or matchmaker. No one knows how many matchmakers there are in the United States; the most recent published figure dates back to 1951, when Dr. Clyde Vedder, a sociologist at the University of Florida, reported that there were 800 marriage brokers in this country. They have an active clientele of several hundred thousand, and probably about a quarter to a third of these are FMs.

Some matrimonial agencies are highly ethical, service-minded and devoted to the often substantiated proposition that widely dissimilar backgrounds in marriage partners spell trouble. The Scientific Marriage Foundation, a nonprofit organization based in Mellott, Indiana, was started by George W. Crane, a

Chicago physician, and uses electronic sorting techniques to match prospective partners according to such things as age, education, race, religion, marital status, hobbies and habits.

According to Dr. Crane, it works beautifully. With an active clientele of about 50,000—each of whom pays $25 for the service—the foundation manages about 20,000 introductions each year, and Dr. Crane guesses that about a quarter of all the clients eventually marry as a result. It is too bad that there has been no study of the ratio of success to failure in these marriages; one would like to know whether the use of the machine produces more happiness than human beings have managed to achieve on their own.

Quite different in its approach but equally dedicated is a small agency in Los Angeles called Friends Finders Institute. Two sisters, Mrs. Marjorie Richmond and Miss Alice Thornton, both with some training in counseling, founded and operate the organization; they give their clients a good deal of individual personal attention and therefore restrict themselves to a total case load of some 350. Each applicant is interviewed for one or two hours, fills out detailed biographical-data sheets and takes a set of sociometric tests of tastes and attitudes. Mrs. Richmond and Miss Thornton then weigh the results, and having found two people seemingly compatible in most of their habits, likings and experiences, the sisters introduce them at one of the institute's socials and later do some premarital counseling with them if they become serious about each other.

Over a ten-year period, the institute has married off about ten per cent of the enrolled clients. Recently, however, the rate has gone far higher, due to a new policy of requiring a one-year enrollment, which costs $102; with this much time to work on a case, Mrs. Richmond and Miss Thornton married off nearly eighteen per cent of their enrollees in 1964. Forty-two per cent of all the clients who have gotten married through their services were divorced persons.

Marriage brokers or introduction services are looked on askance by most middle-class FMs and are thus a very small part of the present marketplace; but as the unconventional aspects of FM life become more and more acceptable and commonplace, it is quite possible that matchmakers or their modern equivalents will become a more important part of it. The subculture tolerates and even encourages a great deal of unconventionality in the search for partners, because any avenue by which the FM can hasten on the way to dating, courtship and remarriage is assumed to be the right road.

The resumption of dating is as difficult and filled with anxiety for the FM as are the first shaky steps a patient takes after a serious illness and prolonged confinement to bed. The very word "date" may make him wince: it sounds so juvenile, and so artificial. Dating implies behavior he thinks would look silly in him—dancing to records in the living room, going to the movies and a hamburger joint, necking in a parked car, grappling on a couch. Even getting dressed up, going out for a drink and dinner with someone new and making conversation for a couple of hours may, in advance, seem awkward, unnatural and mechanical.

Among other uncertainties, the man is unsure what sort of evening to offer the woman. He may think that dinner, dancing and a round of drinks are almost obligatory; but what with alimony and child support, he is reluctant to spend forty or fifty dollars merely to get acquainted. He may want to invite her just for a drink, as the veteran FM suggested, but is embarrassed to propose it, rightly feeling that his motives would be transparent and wrongly fearing that such an invitation would be unacceptable. He may want to suggest that they spend the evening quietly at her home, talking and playing music, but fears she would think him cheap. He may think of inviting her to come help him make dinner at his place, but wonders if she would take it to mean that he intended to play the wolf.

The woman as a beginner, is uncertain whether to accept a date for cocktails only or to be offended and refuse. But if she is invited to dinner, should she let him spend freely or show a kindly—and perhaps belittling—regard for his wallet? If she invites him to spend the evening at her place, will he assume he needn't ever take her anywhere? And if he wants her to go to his place, would her acceptance be construed as agreeing to seduction?

Once the FM actually starts dating, he rapidly finds there is great flexibility among the Formerly Married and that he can arrange the details of his dating in whatever way best suits his own personality, age, means and taste. The prevailing philosophy of the subculture, as he soon realizes, is thoroughly permissive. No one need consent to any suggestion he or she dislikes, but it is not impermissible for the other to have made it. If a man wants to invite a woman just for cocktails, it is not improper for him to do so. If he wants to have dinner with her and then go dancing, she, as the early-rising mother of schoolchildren, is perfectly within her rights to suggest a shorter evening. An invitation to his apartment is allowable and is possibly, but not necessarily, an advance notice of an attempt at seduction; an acceptance on her part is no guarantee that she will comply—although she well might. But in either case, there is nothing dreadful about his attempt or her refusal. The emotional needs of FMs are so imperious

and their haste is so great that, short of misusing or damaging another person, almost nothing is disallowed.

If the FM woman has children, she has still other problems to solve when she begins to date. She must wrestle with the complexities of finding a reliable baby-sitter (she worries more about a sitter's reliability than she did when married), feeding the children, issuing instructions about homework and lights-out time, and getting herself ready in time. The children, if they are not infants, are bound to see her going out with a man, and she will have to explain it to them—but how? If they are very young, she may get away with saying almost nothing ("A friend of ours is coming here tonight"); if they are a bit older, she may try a plea for sympathy ("Mommy needs to have some fun, too") or even appeal to their self-interest ("I'm going out with a gentleman because I'm trying to find a new daddy for you"); and if they are teen-agers, she may make no explanation at all, but merely announce it casually at the breakfast table, hoping not to be questioned.

The reactions, especially from small children, can be disconcerting. One correspondent writes that although she had explained about her dating to her five-year-old son, he waited until the man arrived before firing off this barrage of questions: "Won't Daddy be angry? Can I go with you? Are you going to marry him? Is he sleeping here tonight?" Small children also sometimes stage last-minute rebellions, after Mother's date arrives, in the form of temper tantrums, throwing up or crying spells; older ones suddenly fight with each other or announce a crisis over a missing homework assignment that is due the next day; teenagers may unsettle their mother's nerves by acting sullen and churlish toward the new competitor for her attention or, conversely, competing with her for his attention. (One woman says that her buxom teen-age daughter put on her tightest sweater and openly flirted with the caller, thereby making the mother feel at the very outset like an old crone.)

If men do not have the special problem of resident children, they nevertheless share with women one other problem—stage fright, like that afflicting Raymond Hartwell, Esq. The anxiety before a first date is so strong as to produce diarrhea, hives and other disorders in some FMs and to make others phone at the last moment and cancel the date on some pretext. But the great majority, despite their deep discomfort, go through with it because they must—and because, too, they have a feeling of anticipation and hope. Three out of four FMs do begin dating within the first year, and over nine out of ten do so before the end of the second.

A minority of FMs have only indifferent or even distressing experiences when they first begin dating; but most FMs are surprised and pleased to find how communicative and outgoing they can be on a date.

They freely dwell on their own and the others' feelings with the unabashed self-absorption of adolescents. They may discuss neutral topics now and again, but gravitate automatically toward themselves and toward a comparison of attitudes and emotions about their state. After a while, perhaps, feeling perilously exposed, they veer off to some other topic—only to return soon, as if hypnotized, to the incomparably fascinating subject of themselves. Within the first half dozen dates, therefore, most FMs begin to see themselves as relatively open, communicative and responsive persons with social skills.

A 37-year-old woman was surprised at herself: "I realized, after dating awhile, that I am much more outgoing and warm than I had thought. I seem to inspire confidence. Men really open up to me, maybe because I offer so much of myself without guile."

A 40-year-old man who had avoided dating for a long while says: "I found it very exciting that I could seem to interest almost any woman—that I could talk about myself in a way that almost always got through to them. At the same time, I found that I could draw almost any woman out and get her to open up and reveal herself. It was a revelation to me that I could do this. I'd hate to think of the total amount of money I spent in bars that first year charming the bejeezus out of dozens of different girls."

The exchange of biography between two people on a first date has a special fascination that most conversations between husband and wife cannot have. It is also true that what seems so fascinating and exciting at first may become burdensome and tedious after many a repetition.

A tart-tongued young advertising woman puts it this way: "I'm sick of the whole business of 'explaining myself' to each new man on the first date or two. Sometimes I think I ought to make a résumé for them, listing my college, major subject, degree, favorite composers, favorite books, how long married, reasons for breaking up, favorite foods, attitudes toward sports, religion and sex. I could mimeo the whole thing and just shove it across the cocktail table. It would be a funny bit, but I don't really have the guts to do it."

But for most FMs the process of mutual exploration and discovery remains fascinating for a long while, and there is nothing they more urgently need to tell about than their own broken marriages. Sometimes they offer a superficial formula, but more often FMs are likely to talk about their experience in some depth—not necessarily with insight, but with bits and scraps of reminiscence that evoke sympathy and tenderness and convey the nature of their fears and what they hope to avoid in a new relationship.

A recently divorced man tells a new friend: "It's so good talking to you—after eleven years of living with someone I could hardly talk to. All that interested her was clothes and money and possessions. Every time I wanted to invite people over who were interested in books and ideas, she'd find some way to cancel the party, or she'd say she had a headache and stay upstairs the whole evening, and then be so furious that she wouldn't talk to me for a week."

A young divorcée says: "My parents can't understand why I left him, and I can't tell them. . . . Well, you tell me—you're a man. Do you think a man should insist on it even when his wife isn't in the mood? I mean, insist that she let him *use* her? I think sex is a beautiful thing—but when it was like that, it was so ugly I wanted to scream."

Such disclosures concerning the broken marriages can be viewed as a special form of courtship; they are nearly always meant to show the speaker as a fine, decent, wounded human being who deserves to be loved and has been wronged.

Behind all these complaints and confessions of one's recent agony is a plea: "Listen to my story and pity me, and that will make us love each other."

Among the Formerly Married, all this happens at a greatly accelerated pace; the result is what we might call "instant intimacy." Since instant intimacy requires a sense of kinship and a fund of common experience, many of the Formerly Married find that dating never-married or widowed people is far less satisfactory than dating other FMs. Among the people I queried, fellow FMs were preferred as dates about two to one over the other two categories of unattached people combined; this preference was particularly marked among people in their upper thirties and older.

The formerly married man suspects that the never-married girl of thirty or more has deep emotional problems—fear of men, fear of sex, and so on. Even if this is not the case, or if she is younger, he finds that many of his most significant recent experiences are not particularly meaningful or interesting to her. He may talk about his children, or about married life, or about the strangeness of returning to single ways; but instead of responding with complete understanding, as a formerly married woman would, she listens and replies with obvious effort, as though he were speaking in a foreign tongue she had studied but was not fluent in. She does, of course, have the great advantage of being a more convenient date—there are no baby-sitting or scheduling problems, and she can easily go with him, stay out late, even remain at his place without advance planning. Yet even these advantages are outweighed by the sense of fellowship and understanding he finds in women who have been married before.

And FM women, in their turn, have equally strong suspicions and reservations about unmarried men in their thirties or older. Most of these men, even if attractive, agreeable and well-off, seem incomplete or unreachable to FM women who date them. As one 32-year-old woman of considerable experience summed them up: "Bachelors in their thirties and forties talk and act supervirile, but most of them are Mama's boys and sexually very feeble. Sometimes they think they're very passionate, and I never have the heart to tell them that they're really nothing. They're so self-centered you can't make real contact on any level."

Widows and widowers, though they have been married, seem to most FMs even less satisfactory as dates than do the never-married. The formerly married man going on a date with a widow is aware in a matter of minutes that it is a distinctly different experience from dating a formerly married woman. The widow may be friendly and talkative on the surface, but she wears her loyalty to the dead man like a mask over her face; it is as though any show of interest or warmth would be a betrayal of her own love—especially if directed toward a man who had broken up his marriage instead of having it broken up, as hers was, by fate. At best, her attitude seems to be: "See if you can possibly make me like you. I doubt that you can, but I dare you to try."

Similarly, many an FM woman, on meeting or dating a widower, finds him condescending toward her, emotionally chilly, passive rather than outgoing. This is a sample comment: "Widowers seem to think there is something lacking, or something wrong, with the divorcée, or else she would have been able to work it out. They have no understanding and no sympathy. They sit in judgment on you, rather than try to make you feel desirable."

Undoubtedly, many widows and widowers do not act like this, and it is true that the Formerly Married and the widowed do mingle, date and enter into affairs. But the fact remains that, by and large, they are somewhat antagonistic toward one another and prefer to date their own kind. The preference is neither temporary not superficial; much later on the Formerly Married and the widowed will show the same inclinations when they come to select partners for remarriage.

The Formerly Married, in their initial dating experiences, gain new skills, a sense of identity and a comforting familiarity with the practices of the world they now live in. But even more important than these are the aid and stimulus they get in their task of revaluing themselves and repairing their egos. In a collapsing marriage, a man or woman may feel worthless, unsexed, prematurely old; out of that marriage and beginning to date, the same person may perceive himself or herself as valuable, sexual and youthful.

This is how two of them have expressed it: A woman of 37 who manages a perfume store: "Dating as an ex-married person was a whole new experience. I learned to enjoy the fact of being a woman—a condition I think I had never really appreciated until I met men who really *liked* women." A 41-year-old psychologist, male: "I discovered that I had drastically underestimated my own appeal to woman and my ability to be both tender and manly at the same time."

This regained respect and liking for oneself, though it may seem somewhat superficial and vain, is a prerequisite for more profound experiences that are to follow, and a significant advance toward the recapture of emotional health. Dating, though it may sometimes look like an adolescent and contrived form of heterosexual interaction, is an effective way for the FM to reappraise and reconstruct himself, even while exploring and testing the qualities that he needs in a potential love-partner.

Postmarital dating differs in various respects from premarital dating, and nowhere more sharply than in the area of the sexual overture. The main differences lie in the far greater speed and frankness with which such overtures are made and in their permissibility very early in the acquaintance of the dating couple. "Permissibility" does not mean that the woman routinely acquiesces, but that, in the World of the Formerly Married, it is within the bounds of convention for the man to try. It is common, almost standard, for the man to make an overture—verbal or physical, jestingly or seriously—within the first few dates and, in many cases, on the first or second date. Over half the women I queried said that all or most of the men do so on the first or second date, and the men confirm it.

Second, though it is not standard, it is fairly common for women to acquiesce to propositions made so early in an acquaintance; possibly half of these very early propositions are accepted, without there being any need for the intermediate stages of necking, petting and emotional attachment. Of those women who refuse, moreover, the majority do so pleasantly and conditionally, indicating a possibility that they will change their minds in the future.

Women new to the World of the Formerly Married find the prevalence of these attitudes and practices not only startling, but frightening and degrading. Even some of those who think of themselves as sophisticates are not emotionally prepared for the sexual expectations and unabashed approaches of many of the men.

A woman copywriter in an advertising agency, who had always considered herself knowledgeable and emancipated, felt like this when first thrown into the arena: "It's kind of horrible. They're a bunch of nuts, all trying to prove something. After my first few dates, I wouldn't go out with anyone new for a long while—I just didn't want to have to face that inevitable try, and the inevitable anger that my refusal produced."

A Midwestern homemaker in her early thirties had this to say: "I was so shocked the first time that I cried. The second time, I got mad. The third time, I was waiting for it, and I got the giggles. That was the worst—it made him absolutely livid with rage."

Only after a while does such a woman adjust to the climate of opinion in the world she now lives in. She may still choose to be chary of awarding her favors, but she is no longer upset or angry at the frequency or seeming casualness of solicitation.

Men are less likely to be sharply taken aback; the initiative, after all, is theirs most of the time, and they are therefore not often taken unawares or propositioned against their will. Yet this does happen more frequently than it did in their younger years, and a man new to the World of the Formerly Married may well be surprised and rather uneasy when certain looks or a gentle pressure of the hand seem to indicate that it is high time for him to make a move. Even more surprising to him may be the broad hints dropped by the somewhat bolder female who senses that she is dealing with a slow-moving novice and seeks to arouse him, in order to reassure herself of her feminine appeal.

He may be skittish the first time this happens; but unless he is one of the very badly damaged, he will soon get used to the milieu and feel freer to act according to his own wishes and needs, without undue fear of offending or creating an unpleasant scene. Whether he becomes a fast operator or chooses to hold back until he knows a woman well and genuinely desires her, he will cease being overly anxious about the subject; he will learn to handle the come-on with equanimity, even if he continues to prefer a woman who allows him to be in charge.

The veteran FM man, if he is sensitive to a woman's mood, can usually tell in advance whether or not a degree of rapport exists between himself and the woman that will make an overture welcome, and if it does exist, he hardly need put the suggestion in words. One man of savoir faire explains: "I never suggest sex verbally or try to see how far I can get with a girl. Only boors and bores make passes of that sort. When I am with a woman who appeals to me sexually, I indicate to her by my whole manner how I feel—but only if I really feel that way. And she sends signals back in kind—a glint in the eye, a *moue* at the corner of the mouth, a little pressure of her hand on mine or of her thigh against mine while dancing. Sometimes it's even subtler than that, and I just know from her overall attitude toward me. If I don't see or feel it in her, I don't try. But if I do see or feel it, I don't have to 'ask'—it happens with hardly a word."

The FM woman just beginning to date is lucky if she goes out with such a man; he will sense her unreadiness and will take her home and bid her good-night with a kiss. But to judge from what women have to say about it, such refinement is not the general rule. The fault is only partly that of the men.

Though FMs communicate most marvelously about many things, many women—especially newcomers—hide or disguise their sexual feelings; they are as likely to act falsely flirtatious as falsely reluctant. This makes it difficult for the man to read the message correctly; besides, he is either in the process of rebuilding his self-confidence or anxious to keep it rebuilt by achieving continued conquests. Many FM men therefore fall into the habit of making a routine suggestion on a first or second date, whether or not they have been getting positive signals.

Whatever form of approach he uses, the man justifies it to himself: "She needs, I need, we're both adults, so why beat around the bush?" "She feels flattered as hell, even if she doesn't want to give in." "I'm not lying when I speak of love on a first or second date—I do feel a kind of love at the time." Still other men say they try to bed their dates on little acquaintance because sex is intensely pleasurable, or necessary to the soul, or the only way a man and woman can really get to know each other. Of all their reasons, this last one touches closest to home; most FM men, whatever they think they want, are desperately anxious to find the temporary reassurance of a few hours of intimacy, to replace the lost intimacy of their shattered marriages.

abortion:
one girl's story

VIVIAN YUDKIN

Don gave her the $500 in brand-new $20 bills, and the woman's phone number.

"How far along are you?" the brisk phone voice asked her.

How far along? It must be no bigger than a thumbnail. Two months along, she said.

"Bring the money," said the voice. "In cash. No check. And wait outside 'X' Hotel at eight o'clock Thursday night. And be sure to wear a pink dress. You'll know me by the red rose in my lapel."

This was July, the Washington kind. Everything damp and stale. No air to breathe. She was to wait in a pink dress? This was making it really cloak-and-dagger, really wicked.

Reprinted with permission of The Washington Post from Potomac, *February 26, 1967.*

Thursday, the voice had said. So on Thursday she had to cross that lonesome valley by herself. How did she ever get into this? A "mistake," as her mother would say. Didn't know enough, obviously. Nobody unmarried got pregnant anymore. No more plays and movies and stories about how He Done Her Wrong.

She found the pink dress. She hadn't wanted to wear it again. Was keeping it for Remembrance of Something Special.

The voice—that befriender of girls—met her outside the hotel wearing a red, red rose stuck into the lapel of her expensive navy-blue silk suit. Her hair was upswept and the color of wet tobacco. "Good evening. Are you Miss Rose?"

Give another name, Don had said—you never know.

"There'll be a car along in a few minutes, Miss Rose—a long black car. There'll be other girls in back, and the driver will be wearing a white carnation. Got the money? Hold on to it. You'll be asked for it when you get there."

The woman left. What a job! She must be going all over Washington. Outside each hotel there's someone standing and waiting with the sweat trickling down between her shoulder blades. The whole town smelled of gasoline and sweat, and nothing moved. When this was over she'd go to Colorado, where it was cool—or to Maine.

There was the long black limousine. She felt such relief that she rushed toward it, almost with a shout of Hi!

Sitting in the back with five others— girls, women, all ages—and seeing their faces in the streetlights as they passed, she felt the false relief seep away. She sat still and quiet; nobody said a word. All the Miss Roses were in their summer dresses, all pastels—blue, yellow, mauve, mint-green. A bunch of blossoms all tied together and going out for a nice evening ride.

The loneliness came suddenly. It wasn't that she was scared or tired or angry or embarrassed or tough. No, it was loneliness; and she knew by the silence that they were all feeling it—the kind of loneliness people feel when they are on their own, really on their own.

"Where are we going?" someone whispered.

The driver said without turning around, "Tie these around your eyes"—and moved a handful of black blindfolds over the back of the seat. "Go on now. It's· for your own protection. Just in case." She tied hers tightly around her head, and closed her eyes inside the blackness.

They were away from D.C. now, out in the country. The windows were rolled down, the warm air flowed in, and she smelled the scent of honeysuckle. They must be almost there; she could tell by the way the driver shifted around in his seat.

The car slowed. Crunch. They were all thrown forward. The driver's voice said, "You can take off the blindfolds now, girls."

Girls. Her palms were sweating; her belly crawled nervously. Blinking, the blindfolds off, they all tumbled out of the car onto a wide gravel driveway. The House was big, four stories at least, lit up as if for a party. And no other light from any other house in sight.

Up the white painted steps. The driver unlocked the door. A woman was waiting. The chandelier light showed rows and rows of platinum curls, a vast and endless smile, heavy arms stretched out in welcome. "Oh, hello, everyone! Isn't it *warm*? Come right in!" Then the door was closed, and the smile dropped to the floor.

Just ahead and everywhere she looked, she saw stairs winding up to other parts of the enormous house, room after room, doors painted white, and closed. Going into a room at the left of the foyer was like stepping into *Arabian Nights*. Oriental rug, a black grand piano, yellow-velvet armchairs, a turquoise divan. "Make yourselves comfortable, girls."

They had been in a cluster until now, not talking, but staying very close. In this room they spread like a fan opening, flopped on the yellow armchairs, ran to the locked terrace doors to exclaim over the fountain outside. One girl lay down on the divan with her shoes on.

The woman passed out pills. Nobody knew what for, and nobody was told. Against the pain, probably. They wouldn't let you feel pain after paying all that money.

Six of them in the room, and the door was opening now on six more. That made 12. Twelve times $500!

The insides of her mouth ran; sickness flooded her body. Funny sickness, funny taste in her mouth. Pregnancy sickness. She bent forward suddenly and vomited all over the Oriental rug.

"Now, get hold of yourself, honey," said the woman with the platinum curls. "Ruby, get something and clean up this mess, will you? Come on, honey. Let's clean you up and get you started."

Grasped by the arm, taken to the bathroom, she was sponged with an orchid sponge and dried with an orchid towel and sprayed with cologne. "Nervous? Well, that's natural enough, though you don't have cause. Got the best doctor there is. Been doing it for over 15 years. Got the money?"

She took Don's $500 from her pocketbook, all those brand-new $20 bills. The woman counted to herself, carefully, very slowly—four-sixty, four-eighty, five. Music played very dimly from the walls.

She took off her clothes and put on the peach-colored hospital gown. The woman tied it at the neck for her as if she were going to have her hair done, then

took her toward another room down the hall. Through the door and into a blazingly white, bare hospital room.

A nurse with a mask was bending over a table of instruments. There was the obstetrical table, high as a mountain. "Hop up," said the nurse with a grin in her voice. "Come on, sweetie. Relax. There, all set?" Something contemptuous in her bright blue eyes, and in the touch of her fingers as they deftly did their job. Something which said, Stupid, how stupid can you get?

"Now, don't make any noise," Blue Eyes said. "Hold my hand tight all you want, but don't cry out or anything. Best thing to do is keep talking, anything at all, and take your mind off it. The pill you had is to take the edge off. Anyway, you won't feel much."

The doctor appeared. Above the mask, icy gray eyes, clear as lakes. "Hello, hello." He gave an old man's coarse, amused chuckle. Put in the levers, bent down, grunting. Handled her body like a baker molding dough, swift, sure, certain, absolutely in command. "Kick over that bucket, Nurse."

Oh, that made her feel sick, that noise, and the sound of her blood running into the bucket. The noise was the worst. It filled the entire air, the whole wide world. Leave me alone, get away from me, she wanted to scream. She arched her back, and the nurse pressed her down with a disapproving hand. "Now it doesn't hurt, honey," she said sharply. "I told you to think of something else."

"Hold *still*," the doctor commanded. "There it is."

She lay still, her eyelids slack. Silence chimed in her ears.

The nurse was busy with her. Now she helped her from the table into another room, ready for the next one, happy as a lark. "Two pills against infection now and one every half hour, and rest for two days, and in two weeks you'll be out dancing again, right as rain." Righto. Fixed formula of farewell. Bet she said that to all the girls.

The room she was in now was like a sorority house—pretty little cots, pink and blue blankets, organdy frills around the dressing tables, lamps with satin bows. All the beds occupied and the maid serving cups of Sanka and Bovril and tea from a heavy silver tray. "Cream and sugar?" asked the maid politely.

There must be another doctor in the house. This was a different set of women, flushed in the face, all talking a mile a minute, laughing.

"I would have had mine, but his mother woudn't hear of it. 'He's only 17,' she kept saying. She gave me the money. . . ."

"Am I glad that's over. . . ."

"I was so scared. Ridiculous to be so scared. Lord, I was scared. . . ."

Then they sobbed, some of them, in the middle of a sentence, or with the cup of Bovril at their lips. Suddenly the face crumpled into bits, the eyes poured, they dug their faces into the pretty pillows and cried like animals.

She put on her clothes slowly and hobbled out into the hall to the car and the waiting driver.

"Good-by, girls," said Platinum Curls. "Glad you could come. So happy to have you visit." The little tableau at the door, staged for any possible passerby. You never knew; you had to be safe.

The blindfolds again. Sagged against the back of the car. He let them all out again, at one hotel after another. Everything smooth as clockwork. Almost midnight. A little less than four hours.

She stood on the sidewalk and watched all the people crawling home. She ought to call Don, let him know. But he was probably asleep. And it didn't matter all that much whether he knew or not.

when children can't learn

JOHN BIRD

At six, when Richie Bergman started school, his I.Q. was far below normal. He walked with an awkward, shuffling gait. His eye-hand coordination was so poor that he couldn't tie his shoes. Doctors advised his broken-hearted parents, both of them highly educated, to accept the fact that Richie was retarded, to realize that with special education he might be trained for a workshop life.

The only hopeful signs were Richie's sparkling-bright hazel eyes, his seeming eagerness to learn—and his terrible frustration when he couldn't. The first-grade teacher told the Bergmans that "Richie *looks* so bright, but there seems to be some barrier that he just can't get through."

Now Richie Bergman has broken through that barrier. At the age of 11½ he is headed for the sixth grade, is a spelling champion, a Boy Scout. He reads such books as *Please Don't Eat the Daisies* for fun. He also is an energetic, well-coordinated boy who likes baseball, football, playing in the school band, camping and fishing. When I went to see his parents, Richie insisted that I interview him first. He told me about a trip he had taken to Valley Forge, concluding with an oratorical flourish: "I stood on a hill and could imagine George Washington and his men there, ragged, no shoes on their feet, planning a surprise attack on Trenton. George Washington

Reprinted with permission from The Saturday Evening Post *from* Saturday Evening Post, *July 29, 1967, pp. 27-30, 72-74.* © *1967 The Curtis Publishing Company.*

won all of his battles . . . well, most of them, and that's why we are free and independent."

Richie is just one of the dozens of retarded or once-retarded youngsters I saw while gathering information on an unorthodox method of treating children who have learning disabilities. Usually the system is known as the Doman-Delacato, method, after the team of Glenn Doman, a physiotherapist, his brother, Robert J. Doman, M.D., and Carl H. Delacato, Ed.D., a psychologist and educator specializing in remedial reading. To put it in an oversimplified way, their system seeks to bypass or remove the barriers to learning which exist in the brains of some children. They "treat the brain, not the symptons," they say, with highly formalized, concentrated patterns of exercises—including creeping and crawling—designed to stimulate and to build up a child's "neurological organization," that is, the step-by-step development of his central nervous system.

The Doman-Delacato system is highly controversial as well as unconventional. Some medics and teachers see the concept of neurological organization as a possible break-through, a means of improving the minds and bodies of many neurologically handicapped children. Some physicians have had their own retarded or brain-injured children treated by Doman-Delacato methods. A number of doctors refer patients to Doman-Delacato institutes for treatment.

At the same time the Doman-Delacato concept has met with skepticism, criticism and outright hostility from certain branches of the medical profession and from some educators and organizations dealing with retarded children. The principle criticisms are that: (1) the system oversimplified the problems of retardation and their solu-

tion; (2) the theory of neurological organization has not been scientifically proven; and (3) the Doman-Delacato treatments have not been subjected to large-scale, impartially conducted tests—that case histories of recoveries don't, of themselves, constitute ironclad proof.

Certain neurologists, listing the wide variety of possible brain dysfunctions, express doubt that any one type of treatment can be helpful for many of them. "There is always danger in pat solutions," I was told by Dr. Richard L. Masland, director of the National Institutes of Neurological Diseases and Blindness, U.S. Department of Health, Education and Welfare.

And, the American Academy of Pediatrics has pointed out in an official statement: "To the Academy's knowledge, no controlled studies are available to support the greater value claimed for the [Doman-Delacato] program as compared with conventional treatment of the neurologically handicapped child. Without such studies, a medically acceptable evaluation is not thought possible." (Since the statement was issued, at least one small-scale, controlled test recently completed by Pennsylvania's Department of Public Instruction does give evidence that Doman-Delacato methods may improve the physical and mental functioning of certain retarded children.)

Richie Bergman is just one of the millions of neurologically handicapped children in our society. The severity of their afflictions ranges from hopeless to mild. Some, such as the Mongoloids, are obviously defective. Others appear to be quite normal but simply and mysteriously are "slow learners." In total, perhaps *one child in five* has some sort of learning disability.

Fortunately, children at the lower end of the scale are relatively few, only one out of 1,000 births. Here are those who are profoundly defective because of genetic flaws or extensive brain damage. A step up are the moderately retarded who may have an I.Q. of 50, reach a mental age of seven years, and can be trained to take care of themselves, but are not "educable." About three children out of every 1,000 fall into this category.

But where there are thousands of deeply blighted children, there are millions of the mildly retarded. The President's Panel on Mental Retardation estimated in 1962 that 2.6 children per *100* born would reach I.Q.'s no higher than 70. These youngsters seem relatively normal as babies, but when they enter school they can't compete with their classmates and may develop serious emotional problems. Richie Bergman once fell into the lower part of this group.

And beyond this category—or perhaps part of it in some ways—are the children whose brains seem to work well enough except in reading or writing. It is estimated by educators that at least *12 million children* in our elementary schools are two or more years behind their grade in reading and writing skills. Some may be inherently stupid or culturally deprived or emotionally upset. But a good many have some kink or flaw in their perceptual process which hampers them in transferring printed or written words to their minds. We have been hearing for at least 30 years that "Johnny can't read." Dozens of different teaching methods have been developed, advocated and applied with indifferent success.

And, despite all of our scientific, educational and social progress, most experts readily admit that we can clearly identify the causes of neurological handicaps in only about one out of five cases. Further, only a small fraction of such ailments, when diagnosed, can be

effectively treated by conventional means. A children's neurologist told me, "I don't even say that I am treating. I am providing medical measures which may support any natural recovery."

In view of all this it is no wonder that Dan and Dorothy Bergman regard the transformation of their Richie as a miracle and are firmly convinced that the Doman-Delacato treatments unlocked their Richie's bright mind.

It is easy to see why. When Richie was born he seemed normal, but when he wasn't trying to sit up at 8½ months his parents became worried. The family pediatrician suspected brain injury. Richie was taken to a neurosurgeon who, after extensive tests indicated brain damage, performed operations to remove two hematomas—blood-filled tumors—which perhaps were the aftermath of a birth injury.

Richie then improved, to a point. "He began sitting up," Mrs. Bergman told me. "At two he was learning to walk. Not well, but he was on his feet. We began feeling better. At three we put him in a nursery school and he seemed to get along all right."

Then new trouble started. "When Richie was four, the other kids were getting older in behavior, he wasn't," said his mother. "He couldn't play their games. He became withdrawn." Tests of Richie's I.Q. placed him at 58 to 60.

Mrs. Bergman, a slender, energetic, highly organized woman, joined the local Retarded Children's Association to help her accept the fact that she had a retarded child. People in the association suggested she undergo psychotherapy to get rid of her guilt complex. A pediatrician to whom she spoke at a lecture told her, "Mother, be complacent. You've got to accept the fact that you can't do anything about the situation."

Hotly, Mrs. Bergman replied, "I'm sure Richie is aware of things. I can't sit back and not even try to help him."

When Richie reached school age he went into a class for the retarded. The teachers worked hard but just couldn't get through to him. He would try to trace letters, but they came out a mass of scribbles. He was given a little board with a shoe on it so he could learn to tie his laces, but he couldn't master the skill. "He would become terribly frustrated and angry," says his mother.

When Richie was seven, the Bergmans took him for an annual checkup by the doctor who had operated on him. The neurosurgeon found the boy making progress physically but, hearing of Richie's troubles in school, he told the Bergmans of the new therapy developed by Dr. Carl Delacato for treating children with reading and writing problems. He suggested that the Bergmans get an appointment.

Two weeks later the Bergmans, with Richie in tow, found themselves at the entrance to an old estate in the Chestnut Hill section of Philadelphia. Over the stone gatepost hung a signboard: THE INSTITUTES FOR THE ACHIEVEMENT OF HUMAN POTENTIAL. Inside the gate, the grounds of the institutes looked something like a small college campus, with several new buildings clustered around a faded mansion. The Bergmans were directed to the Institute of Reading Disability. There they met Dr. Carl Delacato, a short, bristle-haired, snappy-eyed man who seemed to jump with energy. Before long Delacato had Richie sitting on his knee while he explained to the parents the theory of "neurological organization" behind his treatments.

Although modern science has deeply probed the incredible complexities of the human brain, charting its structure, chemistry and functions, the fact is that as yet nobody knows exactly how the brain works, how it "learns." However,

the Doman-Delacato team believes that the stages by which a child's whole nervous system normally develops—how it "organizes" itself for increasingly complex functions—provide a key for diagnosis and treatment of certain kinds of brain injury, arrested development and associated learning problems. As Delacato explained the theory to the Bergmans, the main idea is that the nervous system of each new human being must go through a definite series of developmental stages before his brain can operate at its full potential. In effect, these repeat in telescoped time man's evolution from lower forms to the unique human achievements of speech, abstract thought, reading and writing. As college students learn, "ontogeny recapitulates phylogeny"—the life history of the individual repeats that of the race. At birth, according to the theory, only the lower part of the brain has been organized; the baby has only reflex actions controlled by the spinal cord and medulla. As the baby develops, the higher parts of the brain come into operation—the pons, midbrain and last, the cortex. The process is something like programming a blank computer: The baby "programs" his motor-perceptual equipment, his nerves and brain cells, by trial and error, using his whole body and all of his senses. He "learns" by stages, trying motions, feeling things, tasting them, hearing them, looking at them.

A vital part of the Doman-Delacato rationale holds that if a child skips or skimps any phase in this developmental sequence because of brain injury or lack of opportunity, there is likely to be inadequate development at higher levels. They find, for example, that many of the "slow" children they see never had an opportunity to learn to crawl or creep well; they were imprisoned in playpens or play chairs until they could walk. Glenn

Doman says, "You know, we buy playpens for ourselves, not our babies. Babies belong on the floor where they can crawl, creep and learn."

The last, highest step in a child's neurological programming, according to the theory, is the development of laterality, or one-sidedness, which is unique to human creatures, thought to have evolved as we became users of tools and weapons. This occurs when a child, usually at three to six years, begins to use one hand in preference to the other for finely controlled movements. For a majority of us this means that the left side of the cortex, which governs the right side of the body, becomes the dominant, or leading, part of the brain. The dominant side also governs speech, while the other, sub-dominant, cortical hemisphere supposedly governs tonality and music.

An article of faith in the Doman-Delacato concept is that a child cannot realize his full potential in receptive and expressive abilities until he develops complete one-sidedness—that is, when his leading hand, eye, ear and foot are all on the same side, be it right or left. This is not a new idea, of course. There long has been evidence that speech and reading and visual difficulties may be associated somehow with mixed-sidedness or lack of definite-sidedness.

Richie Bergman was put through a battery of tests at the institutes. The results were clear: Richie wasn't neurologically well organized. After two years of special education his reading and writing were like a beginner's. He couldn't tell the difference between simple shapes, such as diamonds, circles and squares. He couldn't walk in normal cross pattern, swinging his arms to counterbalance opposite foot movements. When put down to creep, he didn't know how. He kept his hands fisted, knuckles down, as does a chimpanzee, and his legs went

in all directions. The various tests for laterality showed that he was mixed-sided: Right-handed, left-eyed and left-footed.

The Bergmans went home with a prescription for Richie that seemed peculiar, to say the least. The emphasis appeared to be physical, not mental, and the exercises were laborious. Each day he was to creep in cross pattern for at least 15 minutes. He was to practice cross-pattern walking for 10. He was to sleep in a certain pattern—on his stomach, with the right side of his head down, in much the same position used in crawling.

Richie also was to be trained to be completely right-sided. He was given a toy gun with the holster on the right side. When any object was given to him, it was placed in his right hand. For an hour a day he wore a red filter over his left eye while drawing or writing with a red pencil. Thus, only his right eye could see the pencil strokes and was stimulated to become his "lead" eye. For reading, he uses two-color glasses and a corresponding one-color transparent overlay on printed matter, which forces him to read with him to read with one eye.

Over the months Richie's coordination gradually improved. He became able to crawl and creep in proper patterns without guidance. Four months after the treatment started, he tied his own shoelaces. He learned to ride a bicycle. His performance in school began to pick up. He was able to go into the regular second grade, where he became champion speller of the class. At the end of the term he was promoted to third grade.

Richie has been doing well ever since, making A's and B's and reading well beyond his grade level. Last fall he scored 116 on an I.Q. test. His astonished parents didn't believe the figure and arranged another test with a different psychologist. This time the score was 119.

Such dazzling recoveries may not

convince the more conventional medics and teachers that the Domans and Delacato have found a touchstone for a wide assortment of neurological handicaps, but it does the Bergmans. They and other grateful parents have become ardent crusaders for the Doman-Delacato system, and this has helped the institutes in Philadelphia to become one of the largest rehabilitation centers in the world, now treating more than 2,400 children.

Because of the founders' fondness for the word "institute," singular and plural, The Institutes' organization table seems somewhat confusing at first glance. Basically, though, The Institutes for the Achievement of Human Potential, with Glenn Doman as its director, is a nonprofit, tax-exempt administrative body. It guides and finances eight special-purpose institutes which under a hospital setup might be called departments. The Children's Evaluation Institute, for example, determines the status of a child's neurological organization and the feasibility of treatment. The Institute for Neurological Organization supervises the programs of therapy for neurologically handicapped children on an outpatient basis. The Rehabilitation Center takes a limited number of inpatients for intensive treatment when home therapy is not practical or doesn't seem to be producing results. The Institute of Reading Disability treats children with problems of speech, reading and writing on an outpatient basis, as does the Institute of Learning Disability, which deals with general learning problems. In addition there are individual institutes for clinical investigation, analytical research, and postgraduate training in Doman-Delacato concepts and procedures.

Satellite institutes based on the same plan have been springing up in a number of U.S. cities, 10 at last count. The system also has spread to Latin America; 9 institutes now are operating in Brazil alone. Dozens of schools in the U.S. have established special classes in which children with learning problems crawl, creep and practice visual exercises for certain periods of the day. The Roman Catholic Archdiocese of Baltimore is experimenting with neurological organization as part of an extensive remedial-reading program in parochial schools. And near Dallas, Tex., a new university, established to rescue dropouts, has a required course in neurological organization—that is, patterned crawling and creeping.

To reach the men responsible for this movement, one has to wade through swarms of children. The route to the office of either Glenn Doman or Carl Delacato at the Philadelphia Institutes is beset by children of all sizes and conditions, waiting with their parents, being examined by teams of doctors and psychologists, or demonstrating to graduate students their proficiency in crawling, creeping, walking, hearing and seeing. Creepers still in diapers are likely to patter uncertainly into conferences. It is a place where a reporter may find his tape recorder jammed with the remains of a peanut-butter sandwich.

"Let's face it," said Carl Delacato, 43, director of the Institute of Reading Disability. "The bare idea that you can improve the way a kid's brain works by making him crawl and creep *does* seem ridiculous at first. We didn't discover that technique all by ourselves. We kept watching kids over the years and they forced the truth on us."

Glenn Doman, founder and director of the institutes, is a powerfully built 47-year-old man whose gentle manner doesn't quite conceal his drive and outspokenness. "The problem of brain-injured kids was being swept under the rug when our team started working with them twenty years ago," he told me. "They still were being hidden in attics. Medicine didn't know how to help them. At that time we had never heard of a single one that had been made completely well.

"Since then we have worked with more than five thousand hurt kids," he added. "Now we *know* that one third of them can be made well, brought up to normal. Another third can be made better-functioning human beings. Tragically, there is another third that can't be helped, or very little."

There was a time when Glenn Doman and Carl Delacato didn't speak out so bravely. They first met in 1946. Doman, a physical therapist just back from military service, then was working with Temple Fay, M.D., a famed neurosurgeon at the Temple University School of Medicine, on a project for intensive care of brain-injured children. Delacato, a young teacher and psychologist, was called in to help with the testing. He and Doman clicked immediately, becoming close friends and partners in a number of projects.

Both young researchers became acolytes of Doctor Fay, a man of far-ranging scientific curiosity, a bold innovator. Among other things, Fay pioneered the use of hypothermia, human refrigeration, originally to slow down the growth rate of malignant cells, now widely used for a number of medical purposes. At this time Fay was pursuing a theory that ways could be found to stimulate the brains of neurologically injured children. He reasoned that even an injured brain had billions of "spare" cells and that these might be activated to take over functions of the dead ones, enabling the child to move arms and legs that had been paralyzed. He recruited Doman and Delacato for a study involving a combination of all the known treatments, such as massage, electrical stimulation and whirling baths, applied intensively.

The experiment was a failure. Over several years a few of the children improved a bit, some stayed the same, others went downhill. A control group which received no treatment made just as much progress.

After much soul-searching the team reached the air-clearing conclusions that: (1) The treatments they used had been aimed at symptoms, not causes, and were ineffective; (2) the cause of the trouble was in the brain, and (3) some way must be found to stimulate the brain for better functioning.

The big question was: How?

One of Fay's theories had to do with basic patterns of movement in relationship to evolutionary development. Gradually the idea evolved: Why not put brain-injured infants through the normal sequence of patterns by which normal babies "organize" themselves, from wiggling to crawling to creeping to walking? Perhaps the stimulation could impose the patterns on the undamaged parts of the brain, awaken its levels in proper sequence.

In 1955, when the family of a brain-injured child made an old estate available in Chestnut Hill, Philadelphia, the team established a nonprofit rehabilitation center, surrounded itself with children, took movies of them sleeping, crawling, walking, eating, playing. The researchers were impressed by the amount of development that takes place on the floor and the way one pattern builds on another.

At first the team worked out what seemed to be a suitable crawling pattern, then spent hours putting paralyzed children through these motions. The work was slow and tedious and at times seemed futile. Then one day the first patterned child was put on the floor and began crawling under his own power.

Soon some other once-immobile children began learning to crawl.

The experimenters moved on to the next stages, devising patterns for creeping. They practiced on each other. (Today, when lecturing to groups of parents or classes of students, Glenn Doman and Carl Delacato are likely to get down on their hands and knees on a big table or on the floor to demonstrate.) They found that a number of patterned children learned to creep and eventually to walk.

At times, say Doman and Delacato, they failed to grasp fully their own concept that neurological organization affects the whole child. "Time after time we kicked the truth away," says Delacato, "because of some standard preconception."

There was, for example, the matter of eyes. Brain-injured children often have eyes so badly crossed that they seem to be looking right into the nose.

As Delacato tells it, he didn't really pay attention when an enthusiastic new nurse said to him, "Isn't it wonderful the way these youngsters' eyes straighten out when they are creeping?"

"I thought she was imagining things, so I told her to mind her own business," he says. "But later she came back and said she had been watching carefully and she knew she was right. So we told her to make a study of it, and damned if she wasn't right." A number of ophthalmologists now are using body-coordination exercises, including creeping, in treating children whose eyes aren't well organized for reading.

Fay turned to other things not long after the rehabilitation center was established. He died in 1963. Meanwhile, as their research progressed, Doman and Delacato built up what they call a profile of neurological organization. This charts the upward steps of brain development and indicates the capabilities a child should display at each stage. The institutes use the profile as a diagnostic tool. By comparing a retarded child's actual development—physical, visual, auditory—with the chart, they believe they can determine where the brain damage may be, or where neurological organization is weak. They then prescribe treatments designed to stimulate the appropriate level by patterning visual exercises, stepping-up the blood flow to the brain by increasing carbon-dioxide intake (using a rebreathing mask), and by use of sound, heat and cold as stimulants. As a last step, they seek to establish clear-cut laterality, or sidedness.

It is understandable that Delacato, a teacher, became highly excited when some of the brain-injured children at the center not only learned to creep, walk and talk, but even to read after they got "organized." He also observed that there were similarities between brain-injured youngsters at certain levels and non-readers who apparently were quite normal. The non-readers often lacked smooth coordination, tended to twist words and often were mixed in sidedness. Even more puzzling, children with reading problems often could learn through their ears, but not their eyes, Delacato recalled.

"That nailed me," he says. "Why should the *same* brain be smart through its ears but not through its eyes?"

Delacato came to the conclusion that reading was not, as many teachers believed, an intellectual act, but a perceptual one. He reasoned that if a child's brain circuits aren't properly developed to handle perception through his eyes, the child will have difficulty in reading and, of course, in writing. He wondered: *Could this be the reason for millions of poor-reading children?*

Long before Delacato asked this, there had been considerable theorizing that poorly developed sidedness and reading problems go together. Back in the 1930's, Dr. Samuel T. Orton, a neuropsychiatrist of some note, tested thousands of children with reading and writing disorders. He found that most of them either had mixed laterality or lacked strong laterality. He suggested that such youngsters simply did not see letters and words in the same way normal people do. They might perceive such symbols backward, as in a mirror, or even upside down. They confused such letters as "b" and "d," or "n" and "u." They might see "c-a-t" as "t-a-c," "s-a-w" as "w-a-s."

Delacato reasoned that methods used to organize brain-injured kids could also be used to organize children with reading difficulties.

He began trying his theory on a number of children. He tested them, diagnosed weaknesses which showed up in their performance against the profile of neurological organization, and gave them programs to follow under their parents' supervision. The treatment included reading practice as well as patterning.

"This was one of the most exciting times in my life," Delacato told me. "The treatment showed results in most cases. It failed completely about ten percent of the time. We had some tough cases. Remember, our system sounded crazy and people came here after trying everything else."

One day I sat in Delacato's office while he conferred with parents and children. The staff had tested the children; Delacato went over the results with the parents.

A small 12-year-old girl we'll call Nancy is here for her first visit, and her parents are nervous. The tests show her reading at second-grade level. The girl seems poorly coordinated, her movements being jerky and her eyes wavering out of focus at times. Delacato looks at the test reports, calls the girl over and has her sight at objects, follow his pencil with her eyes as he moves it in various patterns, and checks the way she turns her hands, grips with them, how she holds a pencil while writing.

Then he explains to the parents that Nancy, a brain-injured child, probably needs more therapy than is usual for reading problems. Among other things, the auditory tests reveal that she is slightly deaf in one ear, which they should have checked by a specialist. She probably should go into the Institute of Learning Disability, which treats more seriously involved children, but there is a long waiting list. However, he will prescribe a heavy program. If it helps her, fine. If it doesn't, she will have to go on the waiting list.

Then there was Ken—not his real name—the 15-year-old son of a square-jawed, pipe-smoking government official and a pretty, smartly dressed mother. The handsome youth is polite and co-operative—but edgy. He is a "slow-learner," so frustrated that he wants to drop out of school when he reaches 16. He is repeating the ninth grade. He had been tutored, had been in remedial-reading classes and had had psychiatric therapy. When he came to the institutes, he was reading at seventh-grade level with difficulty.

After six months of treatment, Ken's parents report that he has started reading for pleasure for the first time in his life. Fiction. They would be happier if he were as much interested in his lessons, but any reading is good.

Has Ken noticed any change in himself? No, Sir, he replies, politely but unenthusiastically. He has developed a liking for stories about undersea adventures, things like that. But he doesn't care much for the crawling-creeping bit, or reading with a patch over his eye. It's awful childish.

Delacato looks at the papers. "Well, here's your reading test. Do you know that you've made a big gain? Your reading comprehension has jumped to tenth grade—ahead of your class. Look, boy, you've got it made. Now all you need to do is to concentrate on speed. But that's mechanical. You could solve your own problem now, even if we never did another thing to you."

The boy relaxes. His tight, polite smile becomes a grin.

Before the next patient, whom we'll call Steven, comes in, Delacato says, "He is one of our failures. A nice, friendly kid, but we can't seem to improve his reading significantly. A tragedy. It makes you want to weep."

Steven proves to be a gentle, loose-jointed boy of nine, wearing big glasses and a dreamy smile, as though he were in a secret world of his own. He is in the third grade and has been coming to the institutes for more than a year, but he still is reading and writing at first-grade level. He never developed clear-cut sidedness; his eyes "stuttered," but seem under control now.

Delacato tells Steven's mother, "I just don't know—his coordination is better, so are his eyes, but not his reading. Either we're not doing the right thing, or not enough."

The mother says, "But doctor, he's learned to ride a bicycle, he's better at games, he gets along better with others."

"But in this world things are tough for a non-reader." says Delacato. He calls the boy over and says, "Steven, old boy, we're going to have to start pounding on you. No more goofing off. We're going to give you a tough program for two months, lots more crawling, creeping and eye exercises. You can do a lot better. Are you man enough to do it?"

Steven's mouth turns down and his eyes fill with tears. "No deal," he says defiantly.

"He'll do it," assures the mother.

As they go out, Delacato says, "That's the first time I ever got through to that kid. Maybe he *will* do better now."

Later, in the wide-open spaces north of Dallas, near the little town of Plano—Spanish for "plain"—I visited the institution which bravely calls itself the University of Plano. The school is a new departure, any way you look at it. The administration building stands out like a pagoda in a cotton field, which is exactly the case, as it was the Malaysian building at the New York World's Fair, bought at a bargain and moved here. There is no stadium, but there is a building especially designed for crawling and creeping. Here students in the College of Developmental Education must spend at least an hour a day on the floor patterning themselves under the supervision of instructors.

"It's a real gas, seeing big guys crawling around on that floor," said one student. "Some of them chewing cigars. You have to see it to believe it."

Robert Swift, of Dallas, is one of the "big guys." He is now 24, and for the first 22 years of his life he was virtually word-blind. He couldn't even read a road sign. He also stuttered badly.

"You can't even begin to imagine what something like that does to your life," he told me.

I asked Swift how words and sentences had appeared to him. He explained that he knew his letters and figures all right: he could write them one at a time. But when they were combined, their image was never constant. "One time I would see a 19 and if I looked again it might be a 91. I couldn't pin down the simplest words long enough for them to mean anything."

Swift's father is an inspector in an aircraft plant and his mother is a commercial artist. They began to realize, soon after Robert started elementary school, that he had a reading problem. He seemed bright enough and he did fairly well in all subjects except reading. He even seemed to limp along in reading for a while, but actually he was memorizing the lessons that he heard other children reading, and could repeat them word for word. He left school at sixth grade, studied for a time with tutors, then took a job servicing vending machines.

In the spring of 1965 Swift's mother read that an experimental school using Doman-Delacato methods was being established in Dallas, and she took Robert to enroll in it. This was the pilot project which preceded the establishment of the University of Plano. When Swift was tested, he proved to be left-handed, right-eyed, and right-footed. His eyes didn't work together properly at reading distance.

The young man crawled and crept for two months. Then one weekend, on a trip, he picked up a menu in a restaurant and discovered he could read it. "Before this, I had bluffed at reading menus—but there it was: 'hamburger steak.' I went right on to veal cutlets, fried chicken, and so on. For the first time, my eyes weren't reversing things."

Swift now is enrolled in the College of Developmental Education at the University of Plano, taking basic courses, such as English, history and mathematics as well as reading, to make up for lost years. This isn't easy. He now reads at about sixth-grade level and is proud that he can understand most of what he sees in newspapers. He no longer stutters.

The University of Plano is the brainchild of Dr. Robert Morris, a chunky, square-faced man, who in times past has been in headlines for his right-wing political views. Originally from New Jersey, he has been a teacher, a lawyer, chief counsel of the U.S. Senate Internal Security Subcommittee, a municipal judge. After running, unsuccessfully, for the Republican nomination for the U.S. Senate in New Jersey in 1960, he became president of Dallas University.

The Morrises have seven children, and because of the problems of the fifth—Willie, now seven years old—they became acquainted with the Doman-Delacato Institutes. Willie's birth was difficult, and he had to be given oxygen, but he seemed to develop normally in his first year. However, by the time he was 18 months old, his parents began to wonder if he wasn't *too* good. Mainly he sat in a bouncing chair and beamed happily.

When Willie reached three, the Morrises knew they had to do something. He was walking, but not well. He still wasn't talking. They also noticed that his eyes seemed "set differently," not tracking together, giving him an out-of-focus look. They took Willie to the Institutes for Achievement of Human Potential. The evaluation indicated that the boy had suffered brain damage. The prescription, of course, was crawling and creeping.

"We literally crawled him," Morris said. "He couldn't do it by himself." In six weeks, Morris recalls, Willie was saying words; in six months he was putting them together in sentences. His eyes began to focus properly.

I later ran into Willie Morris by accident at the Plano Academy, operated in conjunction with the university, a development school for elementary and junior-high-school children. The seven-year-old boy was finishing his daily exercises on the floor, and he came up and shook hands with me. The fact that he had a poor start certainly doesn't show now. He is a bright-eyed, active youngster, whose schoolwork is about average.

Willie's recovery made a crusader of Morris. As an educator he had seen hundreds of students who seemingly couldn't absorb knowledge from books.

Yet they were not being helped to overcome this handicap; they were culled out as misfits. He decided to create a new kind of university, one that first would diagnose and solve students' learning problems, if they were solvable, and then provide a bridge over which such students could advance into a regular liberal-arts education. He talked the plan over with Glenn Doman and Carl Delacato and found them enthusiastic. He also enlisted some friends in Dallas.

Plano University opened in the fall of 1965 with only 65 students, most of them academic shipwrecks from other campuses. Last semester it had 170. Not all of its students are flunk-outs; some of those with reading problems were getting by in college but realized that a reading disability was hampering their learning; they came to Plano in hope of finding a remedy.

As the Doman-Delacato system has spread around the country, the scientific feud it has touched off has become a sort of two-story battle. On the less polite, more emotional, bushwacking level, some Doman-Delacato advocates see a medical conspiracy to disparage and destroy the theory of neurological organization because it is the basis for a relatively simple, if arduous, do-it-yourself therapy.

Some anti-Doman-Delacato neurologists told me that any large amount of personal attention given to backward children is likely to yield some improvement; also, some slow-developing children do "grow out" of their difficulties. Still other medics expressed resentment because, they said, the Doman-Delacato forces continually stressed the successes of their treatments and the failure of conventional ones. Critics frequently pointed out that neither Glenn Doman nor Carl Delacato is an M.D.—but they omit to mention that the institutes at Philadelphia has a number of M.D.'s on its staff. One

cooperating physician, deeply involved in the work, is Dr. Eugene B. Spitz, a neurologist and pediatric neurosurgeon famous for devising an operation, the "Spitz Shunt," which rescues children with hydrocephalus—commonly called "water on the brain"—by valving excess cerebrospinal fluid into the bloodstream.

Another source of friction, frequently mentioned by critics, is the large amount of publicity the Doman-Delacato system has received in the "lay" or popular press, as compared to the few reports appearing in scientific publications. The institutes' people say they have submitted a number of papers on their work to professional journals, but that these have been rejected, that a blackout has been in effect. It is true that the popular press has been kinder to Doman and Delacato—who have written a number of books and articles—than have such journals as *Neurology*. This publication's review of Delacato's book, *The Diagnosis and Treatment of Speech and Reading Problems,* ended on this note: "It is of some passing interest if viewed as an excursion into the realm of science fiction."

The controversy gets less acrimonious and more significant at higher levels. Certain specialists in rehabilitation don't question that many children treated by stimulating exercises do make progress, but they don't believe that this automatically proves the concept of neurological organization.

Dr. Richard L. Masland, the tall, white-haired, deliberately spoken director of the National Institutes of Neurological Diseases and Blindness, diplomatically expresses "a fundamental concern" over the issue.

"The people at the Institutes for the Achievement of Human Potential have done a favor in focusing attention on the problem," he told me. But he questions "the way in which Doman and Delacato impose one hypothesis on top of another." He lists these as follows:

1. That children who have learning disabilities often exhibit other disabilities in physical function and perception. ("This is an accepted one," Masland commented.)

2. That training can improve motor-perceptual skills. ("Generally accepted, as in learning to play a piano.")

3. That by training a person in one motor-perceptual skill, as creeping, you can improve his functioning in a cognitive area. ("This is a big jump.")

No. 3 is the key item and might be put as a question: Can a child improve his learning ability by patterns of exercise supposed to build up his neurological system?

The National Association for Retarded Children asks much the same question and takes the position that the sooner it is answered, the better it will be for all concerned.

"We aren't either proponents or opponents," said Luther W. Stringham, executive director of N.A.R.C., with offices in New York City. "We have pointed out that the Doman-Delacato theory and methods are either *valid, invalid,* or *partially valid.* We want to find out which of those it is. We have asked the Secretary of Health, Education and Welfare to arrange a suitable large-scale study of this method of treatment. We are eagerly awaiting the kind of testing that needs to be done."

Glenn Doman and Carl Delacato emphatically point out that long before N.A.R.C. entered the picture, the institutes was seeking partners among universities and rehabilitation centers for a large-scale, cooperative study to compare the effectiveness of Doman-Delacato therapy with that of the more conventional treatments. "We have been pounding for six years for such a study," declares Doman. "We believe the scientific truth should be established, whatever it may be."

A long-term large-scale comparative test would be costly and difficult. Starting in 1965, there were negotiations for a test involving the institutes, Johns Hopkins, the University of Pennsylvania, the National Institutes of Neurological Diseases and Blindness and foundation money. But last fall the project bogged down in a brawl over whether to use the basic Doman-Delacato diagnostic tool—the profile of neurological organization—along with others. The institutes are trying now to get the test back on the tracks.

Meanwhile, Pennsylvania's Department of Public Instruction has conducted a "small but complete" controlled study—and the results, within their limits, are extremely promising. Toward the end of the study I watched an experimental group of 14 retarded youngsters crawling and creeping with gusto in a public school in Slatington.

"We have made the conditions quite tough so any results we will get will be more significant," explained John R. Kershner, the psychologist who designed the project for the department.

This experiment, he pointed out, was planned to test the effectiveness, if any, of motor-perceptual training under public-school conditions. The test, arranged in cooperation with Lehigh County's school system, ran only 74 days, a short period in which to expect improvement. The children, all pre-tested, were classified as "trainable retarded children"—trainable for simple tasks, but not capable of being educated. Most had I.Q.'s of less than 50. Each school day the teachers put the experimental group through tightly structured developmental patterns of the Doman-Delacato system.

At the same time in another school in the county, a control group of similarly retarded children, 16 of them, was going through a conventional class routine, but with lots of non-patterned physical activities.

At the end of the experiment, the children in both groups were given a battery of tests. The team administering the tests did not know which of the children were from the experimental group and which were controls. The results, when analyzed, were full of surprises. Both groups had improved significantly in use of muscles, in coordination and balance. But when it came to learning, the control group, taught by conventional methods, actually had lost ground, showing a mean drop of three points in I.Q. The patterned, systematically stimulated experimental group did far better, scoring a mean gain of 12 points; these supposedly hopeless children had shown an ability to learn.

John Kershner, who was plainly delighted, believes that "this is the first experimental research program that has yielded an I.Q. gain with trainable retarded children." He hopes to set up a similar study covering a county and hundreds of retarded children.

Glenn Doman and Carl Delacato take the position that most of the attacks on their methods are more or less knee-jerk reactions of "The Establishment," as they call the organized groups, to anything new and upsetting.

Carl Delacato declares that he doesn't mind critics who "actually are working with youngsters, trying to help them." He issues them an invitation: "Let's get together, compare methods and results and maybe we'll both learn something. Right now, for example, we're putting our cases on computers, taking our results apart to find out which elements are significant in reading disability and which may not be. Is laterality really the most important thing, or is there something that goes with it? What about age? We always assumed that results would be better with younger children, but the computer seems to be telling us there isn't much difference because of age."

It can't be said that the Doman-Delacato search for better answers lacks scope and flair. They have mounted expeditions to study the most primitive tribes that could be found, such as the Xingu in Brazil and the Bushmen in Africa, to find out how these people, who have no written language or near-vision art forms, are organized neurologically. The pair got prodded by Xingu spears when they violated a tribal taboo by putting babies on the ground to see how they crawled. So far, the findings aren't clear-cut. True, most of the tribesmen proved to be mixed in laterality, but in each group a few were quite well organized and one-sided.

The institutes also now has a Chair of Anthropology, endowed by the United Steelworkers, and occupied by a world-famous anthropologist and physician, Dr. Raymond Dart of South Africa, the discoverer of the "missing link" ape-man, *Australopithecus africanus,* which lived almost two million years ago. Dart is studying the relationship of individual development to the evolution of the race.

Hundreds of other dedicated researchers in many areas of medicine and education are seeking better answers too. A number of those with whom I talked say that they would be overjoyed if the theory of neurological organization does point to an answer for our appalling number of retarded children. But these specialists have honest doubts. They are deeply bothered by conflicting evidence, not only on patterning but on other types of rehabilitative therapy as well. They are conscious of the many gaps in scientific knowledge of the function of the brain. At the same time, "the pressure to *do something* is building up," one neurologist told me. "I believe we must have a thorough, impartial study of the fundamental principles involved in the neurological organization concept. It will be difficult and take a long time, but it has to be done."

VIII

troubled adolescents

The view that "the younger generation is going to the dogs" is apparently held by each successive adult generation about those soon to enter adulthood. Conflict between generations is interpreted in many ways: Some hold it to be essential to social development and the taking on of adult roles; others regard it as evidence that the older generation is only partially successful in handing down its ideas, values, and solutions to the problems of life; and still others suggest that it reflects the dissatisfaction of youth with contemporary social life and our social order. Apparently, the young in the United States have always been more willing than the old to reject the *status quo* and to challenge values accepted by the adult community member.

The United States is now confronted with particularly sharp conflicts between adults and adolescents. The extensive conflict between generations is attributed to a number of different characteristics of contemporary social life, including the delayed entry of the younger generation into full adult status because of extended requirements for education and training, an emphasis on permissiveness and freedom of expression for the child in his family life, and increased exposure to pleasuristic values and diversity through the mass media. Moreover, the strong association between personal power, prestige, and economic wherewithal is appreciated by the adolescent, and he realizes more than ever before how it affects his own present social relationships and future life chances. The conflict between generations, while perhaps a necessary ingredient of a rapidly changing social order, does produce casualties. The search for new experiences, the rebellion against family norms and the testing of new ideas take their toll on both youths and their families. The cases in this chapter are of adolescents whose behavior is seen by many as having both immediate and long-run undesirable consequences.

Individual ↓ Individual	Individual ↓ Organization

NOT A CASE HISTORY, NOT A STATISTIC: OUR DAUGHTER

The basic conflicts between the adult and the adolescent often lie buried, and the tensions between the generations surface only in the face of specific events which result in unavoidable, open confrontation. In many instances, the behavior of the adolescent is only interpreted as troublesome and embarrassing for the adult involved, and the real conflicts between the norms, values, and aspirations of the two generations are carefully avoided and remain unresolved. In this account, Maria's mother gains new insight through the shock of discovering her daughter's pregnancy. In retrospect, she can identify incidents in which Maria again and again demonstrated her rejection of adult norms. Neither pregnancy, nor the events that followed, however, seem to have reduced the existing discrepancies in values and norms between Maria and her mother.

REPORT FROM TEENY-BOPPERSVILLE

Some teenagers express their rebellion against the adult world in means which increase their dependence on the adult world. Thus, the pregnant girl or the youth apprehended by the police for a felony is placed in the position of using the services and resources of the adult world that he or she rejects. Other adolescents discover avenues for exercising their hostility which are "safe," that is, they engage in deviant behavior, but they minimize their chances for getting caught. Kirk Sale and Ben Appelbaum describe a setting in which teenagers can gather together to participate in behavior that is unacceptable to most of the adult world. Teeny-Boppersville provides them with anonymity, gives them a great deal of protection from the adult world and allows them to have a defiance of the norms of the adult community.

IN RE GAULT

In the eyes of the adolescent, the world is organized and operated by adults, for adults. Young people often feel powerless either to participate in the shaping of their environment or in instigating the changes they feel would bring it closer to the way they believe things ought to be. Not only are they often ignored as participants in the community, but in many ways they are not accorded the same individual rights as other citizens. Gerald Gault's experience in court as a juvenile delinquent, the later appeals on his behalf to the state court, and the verdict in his favor illustrate how the legal system has discriminated against the juvenile. Rights which are carefully protected by legal statute for adults have not been considered equally important for adolescents in the United States.

THE GANG IN ACTION

Aggressive behavior in adolescents has been attributed to many sources, sometimes to difficulty in communicating with adult individuals who are most responsible for leading them to maturity, or to open rejection by individual adolescents of the values of the community, or to the failure of the community to respect the rights of young people. Yet, some of the trouble for adolescents results from conflicts within their own ranks. Lewis Yablonsky describes two organized groups of teenagers and the relationships between them that led to violence. The case portrays a series of social interactions that served to bind members closely to a gang during a daring escapade, and that generated a conflict with another gang which the groups sought to resolve by highly aggressive action.

not a case history, not a statistic: our daughter

JUDITH MARCH

As Maria lay in the hospital bed, in the far sleep of anesthesia, barely stirring, safely rescued from a pregnancy nobody could tolerate, she was someone I hardly knew—all warmth, all animal spirits drained beneath a white, white skin. She stirred with a small moan, the first sign that misery was filling the vacuum of postoperative non-being.

Dan, my husband, sat with his chin on his fist, more anxious than contemplative—because he is an easy prey to anxiety and because this child was the quicksilver in the graying areas of his subsurface, middle-aged emotions. She was a child who sang as part of her breathing, who tossed her impulses about as carelessly, yet as artfully, as her great length of chestnut silk hair.

I sat quietly, aware of the ergotrate dropping slowly through the intravenous equipment, down through Maria's arm, which was held rigid on a board, her palm open and vulnerable.

I was still wondering, futilely, if I could have held her back from her physical relationship with Jeff. From becoming pregnant. Even as a young child, Maria had never been willing to learn through precept, only through experience—no matter what the danger, no matter what anger or punishment could follow. How did *she* feel now? How could I know—unless she confided in me? Would I ever see it as she did, for all my mother antennae and woman's memory of my own youth?

Maria at seventeen gives a strong impression of beauty. Her looks are a compound of vitality, radiance, humor, appetite, sexuality—in short, of life and youth. She can be soft and beguiling, all five-feet-eight of her; or hoydenish and ungainly, like an animal in too small a space. She is nature's child: attuned to the morning sun and the full moon, to insects, fish and all things living. She shares her room with a Dalmatian, a Siamese cat, goldfish and two white mice in a cage. She'd keep a horse if she could. She did not develop into a student. But we consoled ourselves: one can't have everything. We were delighted—sometimes snowed—by her charm, her pleasing looks; much less enthralled with her disposition, which ranged from infectious high humor to infuriating ill-temper. I must smile wryly as I recall that a few months before Dan and I were complimenting ourselves that we still had the upper hand.

When Maria reached high school, we were stricter than other families about hours, cars and boys, because of our knowledge that she was headstrong, not willing to accept the simplest "no" without countering; not easily constrained from acting out her wishes—and being "sorry" afterward.

It is understandable, I think, if a parent sees a child as special rather than typical. To both Dan and me, Maria was especially fascinating. By sixteen, she had grown into her final coat of personality, always on the edge of a strong emotion, whether it was compassion for the retarded child down the street, anger at a social injustice that had momentarily caught her attention or an explosive pleasure in being alive, which she would express by hugging the person or animal nearest her. Dan and I were only too conscious that this feelingful child would not be held back, would not hold herself back from sexual experience for long— not in today's setting of provocation and nonprohibition.

We were not the only ones who saw the problem. Our family doctor—no staid, fatherly prototype, but a handsome man in his early fifties with a nice appreciation for women—told me one day: "Maria's grown into a charming young woman. If she were mine, I'd have a talk and give her contraceptives."

As the mother in this matter, I played Hamlet. I could not resolve the question. I was hung up between the totally rational view, which says: "For the new mores, give the new pill," and the deep wells of constraint, within which I had guarded my own impulses and now sought to guard Maria's. I could not look on sex as a casual, mechanistic act. I hoped only to set up fences Maria might break down—at the right time. Contraception, finally, was a go-ahead I could not, did not give her. My deep instincts won out, for once. But not so much in a clear-cut victory as a long, dull draw.

As I look back, it was not *this* decision that brought us to the morning in Maria's hospital room; it was the many decisions made long before and the non-decisions in the critical time after Jeff arrived.

It all began like the usual teen-age romance, and it was some time before I realized that Jeff was no longer just "a" boy. When he first arrived, I was fully occupied in battling the sick onset of hepatitis, the bleak February snowstorms and the arrival of a new Siamese kitten (Maria's, naturally). Only later did I notice that Jeff, whose family lived in our neighborhood, was coming home from college weekend after weekend—to our house.

Maria and Jeff were shiningly new with each other—she entranced with the attention of an "older" man, and he intrigued with the fun and volcanic life-force he had suddenly encountered.

Our privacy at home was much curtailed. Jeff was on the phone, at the door, honking in the driveway. I could be caught in my own kitchen at unexpected hours of the morning or night, my hair up and my guard down. He was underfoot with the persistence and appeal of an eager young puppy. Maria was never ready when he arrived, so while he waited, he would join me in the kitchen or in the den. He talked about sports, weather and small things, but more about life at the fraternity, which seemed to center on drinking.

We sometimes invited him for Sunday supper. But when he was back in school, we still had him at the table by proxy—"Jeff says . . .," "Jeff thinks . . .," Jeff went . . ." became the replacement for Maria's former conversation. At times, she seemed indifferent to my opinion of Jeff; at others, anxious for my approval:

"He's nice, isn't he?" "You do like him, don't you?"

My attitude, only half formed, was one of surprise, not objection. Maria, who could be equally fired by civil rights, folk music, Beethoven and the entire race of boys, who preferred blue jeans to any dress, had chosen a boy who wore shoes and jackets, who cut his hair regularly and who didn't know SNCC from a snack. To me, Jeff was one more humbling lesson in what every mother does not know about her own child. Dan was glad; he thought Jeff was "safer" than boys with the new look.

Soon after meeting Maria, Jeff dropped out of college. He was within blocks of our house; he had a car, a job and parents who exercised no demands, exacted no disciplines. We held the line on "weekends only" for dating and on Maria's keeping sensible hours.

Jeff didn't change our life so much as join it. In the process of going out together, he and Maria did an amazing amount of staying home. I began to take it as a matter of course that I'd find them lounging in the den on a Sunday afternoon along with Dan. Jeff was at home with us. He'd walk the dog at night or drive the Sunday-school car pool with great willingness. But he would not wash a plate, even for Maria, or think of clearing away the apple cores and ashtrays he accumulated around himself. As time went on, I found myself scolding him as though he were our child. In truth, he was our a priori son-in-law.

He and Maria settled down as a steady thing, without any announcement, but with a clear understanding between themselves. Maria would wear Jeff's sweaters, his jackets, his signet ring. She would not go out with other boys— "There's no one else I like." There was an openness in their relationship that many of us do not achieve after years of marriage. No small pretenses and defenses. No locked-up feelings. No holding back of opinions—or demands.

"They're sweet," said the waitress in the coffee shop where they often went for hamburgers and Cokes. "They're adorable together," said Jeff's mother on the telephone. And as I watched them walk down the front path together, take each other's hands, I had to admit the appeal of their youngness, their self-discovery. But there were elements that troubled me: They were not only confiding in and learning about each other, putting into the relationship all the weight and ceremony of a first year of marriage. Wasn't this too early? Too serious? A shadow play without foundations?

On Sundays, Maria would often cook a steak supper. She would serve Jeff the choicest, largest portion; he, in turn, would compliment her on the cooking. They're playing house, I thought. While it looked sentimentally appealing, I knew it was dynamite. It was child's play in which neither one expected, or was prepared, to take on the more boring, burdensome aspects of responsibility — be it familial, economic or sexual.

In this setting, sex could simply become one more aspect of playing house. Where could such closeness go—except to bed? Yet I could not make myself project forward to a physical relationship and possibly pregnancy, let alone to abortion and that eventual room in the hospital. The life style of the young, I reminded myself, had changed since my day.

I could not, did not meet head on with Maria about sex with Jeff. I would have been embarrassed and confused. I was not the mother of a child but of half a child, half a woman; and mother-in-law, before the fact, to a boy-man, sometimes nineteen going on nine. I relied on *understood* standards. I was not permissive, but somehow I permitted what I feared by default.

We felt secure in saying to Maria, at seventeen, that she *must* do her homework, *must* be in at twelve-thirty on a weekend, *must* do her share in the house. But we could not, with sense or sensitivity, order her to end an ostensibly harmless relationship. We had to allow for choice—even when it did not dovetail with our own. We could only hope that she would outgrow it or grow up in it without the heartbreak and scars of a too-early marriage.

During our annual family holiday at the shore, I could hardly look on Jeff as a passing phase. We had no sooner unpacked the bedclothes and the groceries than Jeff arrived—by arrangement with Maria. He took a room nearby only because I said no, he could *not* bring his sleeping bag and use the floor of our living room. But at nine in the morning, he'd arrive, and Maria would serve him fresh orange juice, bacon and eggs, toast and coffee. At midnight, he was still on hand. He integrated into the family scene: helped with the shopping and the driving, took part in Maria's tangles with her sister, Toby, and was polite to Grandma. Before I could catch myself, we were One Happy Family.

What I saw of Jeff and Maria at close range in that two-week period did not put me at ease. The dependency no longer struck me as appealing. Jeff could not let Maria out of his sight. Maria, who always had a deep need for private time, was never alone. I suspect that the many small frictions between *us* at the shore were her escape valve: reaction to loss of privacy. Maria began showing traits we had fought doggedly against for years: she would become short-tempered, unreasonable, downright nasty with Jeff. But in quick compensation, she would turn to him with love, bacon and eggs or

an enthusiastic plan for the day.

Jeff was undoubtedly better-natured than Maria, yet at times I wanted to shake him, to make him stand up for his rights. But he'd tell me, "You don't understand, Mrs. March. I know she doesn't *mean* it," and Maria would say, "You don't understand, Mom. We're not like this when we're alone."

The "alone" was preying on me in unavoidable, insinuating fashion. Jeff and Maria would go down to the beach and spread a blanket far from the rest of us—but not far enough to blot out the sight of their physical closeness, their bodily ease with each other. I had to look the other way.

Then something snapped. Suddenly I found the situation had become totally untenable. I did not know where to turn in my frenzied worry. Dan had been called back to town on business. But even at home he could display a maddeningly detached attitude toward the problem. There were times when his masculine approach leavened my more emotional responses; but at other times, I *knew* he was not facing the possibilities of the situation.

I vacillated, characteristically, between taking Maria and Jeff's visible conduct as a sign that this was the full extent of their physical relationship and the conclusion that they had consummated their togetherness.

The sex aspect was disturbing, but secondary. My overriding fear was that they might run off and get married. Within only a few months, both would have the legal right to sign their names in a marriage registry. Soon Jeff would come into a small legacy from his grandfather, which must have looked to him like security.

I had one oblique talk with Maria while we were still at the seashore. I asked her to walk with me along the hard-packed sand at the water's edge.

With my eyes more on my feet than on her face, I told her I thought their public display of affection was tasteless. I had never tried to create an aura of intimacy between us in sexual matters. She never came to me with questions. I assumed that any child who knew so much about animals, who read Indian love poetry, Harold Robbins and Henry Miller with equal interest must know the sexual facts.

I skipped Biology One. I did not ask her if she was having sexual relations with Jeff. I did not expect her to tell me. But I felt no confusion or constraint in telling her that the association with Jeff was not good for her; that Jeff was immature and that, in a marriage, she would very soon chafe at his dependency; his boyish charm would not wear well. Only at this point did Maria speak up: "Don't you think I know all that?" But she must have repeated every word to Jeff. The term "public affection" became a light joke. The humor insulated us, kept us safe with one another. But it did not stave off the outcome.

I was glad to have school start again and the rule of weekends only invoked once more. Even back in the autumn schedule, however, the more they went together, the more freedom they assumed. It grew impossible to know where they were at all times, and it was niggling and uncomfortable for me to ask their whereabouts. They'd go off on a Sunday afternoon—"downtown," "over to the duck pond," "to Jeff's house." Jeff's parents made a fuss over Maria. They'd invite her to informal Sunday-evening suppers. "Too bad they're not five years older," commented Jeff's mother. I kept my opinion to myself.

I was equally guarded with my friends and would smile when they asked, "Is Maria still going with Jeff?" I even managed an unperturbed exterior when a busybody on Jeff's street asked, "Isn't that *your* daughter I see so much at Jeff Kohler's house? I saw her there just yesterday."

Yesterday, they'd said they'd been bowling. It had to mean what I suspected: that Jeff and Maria were often at the Kohler house when his parents were not home—in outright violation of one of our strictest, oft-stated rules. I could not be a policeman if I wanted to. How could I accuse? How could I handle what was not out in the open?

But as I look back, the signals were clear. Maria was in foul humor; she would snap at any of us, would sit morosely at the dinner table, would hardly respond when spoken to. I would find her in front of the television set after school, although it was agreed-upon homework time. She seemed to be talking more than ever on the telephone. Then I began to find her asleep after school. She'd always been such a hypochondriac that I did not pay attention to her "tiredness" until it became impossible to ignore. I set up, almost as a routine, an appointment with the family doctor for a checkup. Maria protested with a vehemence that aroused my fears.

The next afternoon, Bessie—who's been "doing" our house on Wednesday for years — said, "Something wrong with Maria, Mrs. March. I think it's serious trouble. I'd talk to her if I were you."

My stomach turned over. I was sick with dread. I realized that Bessie was trying to be helpful without violating the confidence Maria had placed in her. I did not press Bessie further

When Dan came home, I called him aside.

"I'll ask Maria," he said, with masculine directness.

"Absolutely not," Maria told him. "I'm not pregnant."

The reassurance lasted ten minutes. It might have lasted a few days, even a week, if our younger daughter had not come into my room. She'd heard the quarreling over going to the doctor—as Toby always seemed to hear everything. "I don't know whether I should tell you," she began hesitantly, "but I think I know what's wrong with Maria. I heard her talking to Mrs. Dunnock. Maria's pregnant."

Mrs. Dunnock! A woman I hardly knew, but whose name will always be inseparable from that night and from the aura of uneasiness and uncertainty that still remains. Mrs. Dunnock was a school counselor in our community, avowedly prejudiced in favor of children—a friend to every sensitive, rebellious child with a problem. She had known Jeff and his family for many years. She had recently met and taken a fancy to Maria. It was not the important matter at that moment, but I felt a twinge. Mrs. Dunnock knew. We did not.

"Call Mrs. Dunnock," said Dan, "and ask her."

Ask if *our daughter* was pregnant! I was aware of my pride, even while I knew it was inappropriate to have pride in these circumstances. I felt and heard the pulses pounding in my body.

Mrs. Dunnock had something of Bessie's loyalty to Maria and to Jeff, as well. "Maria has a problem" was all she would say at first. She knew little of me as a parent. She was testing: "What would you do—if it *were* so?" I was being challenged to come up with the right answers, so that I might deserve to know the truth. I must have said what was expected of me. Frankly, I cannot remember. Mrs. Dunnock decided· "I'll call Maria and call you back."

It was insane. I could not go directly to my own child, talk to her—even accost her, if necessary. In the midst of these delicate negotiations, I had to put away my hurt that someone else was closer to my child than I was.

Maria came into my room. "I have to see Mrs. Dunnock for five minutes. May I take the car?" It was, under normal conditions, a wild time for visiting: ten o'clock on a Wednesday night. But nothing was normal. The house had the dread expectancy that comes with crisis or deathly illness. While we waited, Dan and I played a mindless game of backgammon. We had to focus, had to make small, nervous moves.

At eleven-thirty, Mrs. Dunnock telephoned. "Maria wants *you* to come over." She was speaking to me, not to Dan. "The kids want to tell you themselves."

Why me? Why not both of us? If I had been in possession of myself, I should never have agreed to go alone. It was frightening. And odd. We were both her parents, and we would act together, no matter what differing emotional signals we might give off in the process. But in the turmoil of that moment, I think I was so relieved to be included that I did not stop to take a stand.

I threw a coat over my pajamas and drove the few blocks to Mrs. Dunnock's with my hands rigid on the wheel. What was I to say? What was I to do? My own attitudes, training, reading were in a jumble.

Jeff opened the door for me, and as I started up the stairs to Mrs. Dunnock's study, he said to my back, "We have something to tell you. Maria is pregnant."

There it was.

I walked into the room, and there was Maria, beaten down, sitting slumped over her knees on a small couch, old and new tears mingling on her face. I found tears in my own eyes—the first—with relief at knowing what we had to know. I held her, more numbed and drained than warm and motherly.

"Oh, Mommy, I'm sorry. I'm sorry," said Maria, over and over.

I said repeatedly, equally compulsively, "We love you. You belong to us. We love you."

In truth, I had not a single small impulse to scold, moralize or say, "I told you so." We sat on the couch together, and Maria leaned on my shoulder. I held her hand tightly in one of mine; with the other, patted her on the back—she might have been a tearful two-year-old.

Jeff sat, stunned, in a chair across the room. Mrs. Dunnock hopped around like a solicitous bird. She offered me coffee, which I accepted, although a tranquilizer would have been more to the point. I wanted to be alone with Maria, to take her home, where she belonged. But they were talking. It was a review for my benefit—and their own. Jeff and Maria had apparently been going from one "doctor" to another, trying to make certain that Maria was pregnant, trying to arrange for an abortion. I thanked God that they had located neither the "doctor" nor the money for a back-room abortion. There was not, never had been, any question of having the baby—only of finding a way out.

No one mentioned marriage except Mrs. Dunnock: "They're very much in love, you know. They plan to get married one day." Maria, tucked into my arms, still said nothing but "I'm so sorry, Mommy." Mrs. Dunnock reassured her: "There are lots of kids like you and Jeff. We can't say it's wrong. We can't say that any communication between two people is wrong."

How could I, at that moment, if I had found my own thoughts and words, have taken a less generous attitude? No, it did not behoove me to debate the ethics or philosophy of the situation with Mrs. Dunnock that evening. It was to be months before I could know even part of the meaning for myself.

We now had the problem of what to do: Let the child be born—disrupt Maria's life for a life that was not wanted? Force them to marry? The implications of the first troubled me deeply. But as for the second, I would far rather that Maria have an abortion than enter into a marriage which, under more favorable auguries, would still be a bad bet. Dan and I were the grown-ups, with resources, but we did not know the way out any more than the children had.

The need for action called forth all Dan's adrenalin and reflexes. He thought systematically of the doctors among our acquaintances who might give us some guidance and came up with Dr. Bailey, an obstetrician who often lectured on sex education to young adults. Dan planned to see Dr. Bailey the following morning.

Meanwhile, Maria came up with an important fact learned from a girl friend: A *legal* abortion could be performed if one had a psychiatrist's letter advising it.

I called Dr. Asch, a woman psychiatrist who had seen Maria a few times during grade school when she'd been giving us a rough time. Yes, Dr. Asch told us, it was true; most hospitals require one or two consent letters from psychiatrists before permitting an abortion. Dr. Asch was instantly alerted to our problem and was willing to write such a letter once she talked to Maria.

Dan called to report that Dr. Bailey would perform the abortion if we had Dr. Asch's letter, but Maria would also have to see a psychiatrist on the hospital staff, whose approval—or disapproval—would be the final hurdle.

The following day, by appointment, Maria and I went to Dr. Bailey's office, which was filled with young women patients at every stage of pregnancy. There were a few middle-aged mother-types, to make me feel less conspicuous.

I was more nervous, more self-conscious than Maria. I turned the pages of a high-fashion magazine, seeing little. Maria sat quietly, her hands in repose, until Dr. Bailey called us in.

He addressed himself chiefly to Maria. "We are not here to make a moral judgment, but to help you, Maria. We are concerned with your well-being, your peace of mind." He turned to matters of fact: When did she have her last period? When did she think she might have conceived?

Maria did not blush, she did not hesitate for words. If she was embarrassed, she gave not one inkling.

"But first, let's be sure you *are* pregnant," Dr. Bailey said.

When he'd examined her, he was almost positive she was pregnant, but took the usual tests, to verify his judgment. With Christmas holidays coming in ten days, we thought it best for Maria to continue at school, to enter the hospital —if approval was forthcoming—on the last day of school and return after New Year's Day. "In the meanwhile, we want to make you as comfortable as possible," Dr. Bailey told Maria, as I would guess he tells every newly pregnant woman who goes to him.

In the intervening week, we did everything to support Maria. We did not avoid the subject at the dinner table. We talked about the plans with Maria. I handled the matter more casually, more offhandedly than I would have thought possible. I was still under the influence of Mrs. Dunnock and of Dan, who said, "Remember, we were young once. I think."

Maria, who can be astonishingly open as well as devious, said, "I never realized how much I wanted to stay in school until this happened. Maybe something good will come of it, after all!" Another time, she told me, "Well, at least I know I can have babies."

I allowed myself one pronouncement, out of deep feeling: "It's sad, darling,

that your first pregnancy should have to end like this. It should be one of the thrilling moments of your life."

Maria listened. She said nothing. But sometimes as she was putting bread into the toaster or backing the car out of the driveway, she would turn to me. "You're wonderful, Mom! I love you so much!" I recognized relief. I recognized gratitude. Yet the cynic within me whispered that both are among our most ephemeral emotions.

We waited a long week for word from the hospital. During that time, Maria confessed, "I was beginning to think about having it!"

Finally, approval came. We could now pass the problem on to professional hands, much as Maria and Jeff had passed it on to us. For the time being, I said only, "We are doing everything we can to help you. There is one thing *you* must do. You must see Doctor Asch, the psychiatrist, when you come home from the hospital." Although I would not force her, for the moment, to come to honest terms with us, I could not let her escape coming to terms with herself. Whether it had been rebellion, hostility, impulse—or some of all three—she had to know it, even though we might never be clear. I took Maria's silence for agreement. . . .

I was calmer before than after the surgery (known on the records as an "interrupted pregnancy")—a classic case of reaction. In the hospital room, I felt a frightening separateness from Maria and the medical details of the abortion. I was as anesthetized, in my own way, as Maria.

Alerted to her slightest pain, she was a demanding patient, quick to ring for a nurse, frank about all the anatomical details. For Dan, who is squeamish, it was punishing.

As she was fighting her way back from anesthesia, I could hardly believe it was Christmas Eve. The hospital was even more remote from life than usual; the floor was emptied of all but the most acute cases, the nurses did not bustle about.

Our house had something of the same dull emptiness. I missed Maria and her delight in the small habits and surprises of our usual Christmas. After opening our presents on Christmas morning, we had our special breakfast of steak, blueberry pancakes and fresh strawberries. But we could not pretend to even the most spurious cheer. Maria's chair was overbearingly present in her absence.

Grim as the day was, we were lucky that the holidays had always been a close, private affair among the four of us. In a widespread family celebration, we would have had the task of covering up for Maria—for we took an uncompromisingly traditional stand: to keep the whole episode as quiet as possible.

In spite of us, the news undoubtedly spread. I told one close friend because, as I explained to Maria, "*I have to* tell someone." Jeff's parents knew, because he had told them. (This is a point on which I cannot dwell comfortably: They knew when we did not know, yet they neither told us nor made any effort to resolve the situation. The responsibility in this situation has not been modernized, but remains squarely with the girl and/or her parents.) Maria, in her early panic and indiscretion, had confided in two girl friends; one of them, she later learned, had told *her* girl friend. Maria reported this angrily; but here was the hard pragmatism of the young: she was resentful of their thinking her "the fool who got caught."

Before I could carry up Maria's first lunch tray when she came home, Jeff arrived. Throughout, he had been simpler than Maria: visibly shaken, openly guilty and abashed, eager as a child to make amends. "I'll pay the bills. Let me pay the bills"—his way of salving his dignity once we had taken over the reins. We had

not permitted him to visit Maria in the hospital; this would have been more casualness than I could tolerate, although I had seemingly tolerated so much else.

Jeff was back on our doorstep: faithful, thoughtful and attentive. "I prayed while Maria was in the hospital," he told me. Even while I was preparing dinner in the kitchen, he would drive out for hamburgers and pizza, because "that's what Maria wants."

Why didn't we forbid him to come to the house afterward? Because we remained the enlightened parents. Dan and I agreed that outright opposition now, as earlier, would only bind them closer. We later learned from Mrs. Dunnock—who, like Toby, always seemed to know what we should have known— that they were both amazed and grateful when we did not play the heavies. Actually, we were hoping that this "incident" might cause the relationship to fall of its own weight. To the contrary, it seemed stronger than ever, and we had to face Jeff's comings and goings once more.

How does one feel, how does one act toward a boy who has been having sexual relations with your unmarried daughter and who has made her pregnant? I had no guidelines for how to behave. It would have been impossible for Jeff to win. If he'd neglected Maria, I'd have said angrily, "See?" But his reappearance in our house, with an assumption of old privileges, enraged me equally.

I realized that Dan, whose innermost feelings were perhaps even more complex than mine, was putting off the task of talking to Jeff. Something *had* to be said. But Dan was unexpectedly called to California on business, and it became my task.

I sat facing Jeff in the den. I told him that he must know I was angry, that I could not accept or welcome him in our house in the same way, that I felt duped by his pleasant manners, his seeming acquiescence to our ground rules. I felt pompous, doling out judgment. I could not escape from myself, from a lifetime habit of trying to be objective, to be fair to young people, to adjust to the cold war between the generations. Suddenly I was *counseling* him: "You know Maria must talk with the psychiatrist when she's recovered. But it wouldn't hurt you to go, too—to find out how you could let this happen if, as you say, you love Maria."

He's young and vulnerable, I thought, remembering that it was he who said to Maria, "You should be grateful," took her to task when she fussed over her boredom, her slow recovery. But when he said, "I know I've caused a great upset, but I cannot feel there's anything dirty or wrong about loving each other," I shrugged angrily at the cliché, at the naïveté, the ego of youth—totally unmindful of anyone, anything other than their own momentary emotions. Yet I do think he behaved more admirably under pressure than at any time in the year we'd known him. He was right when he said, "I've grown up a lot."

It was Maria who troubled me. Following that first night at Mrs. Dunnock's house, she had given no sign of remorse, of awareness that there had been anything wrong on her part. She continued to concentrate at home, as in the hospital, on her bodily well-being, her own comfort and amusement.

We did come, finally, to one moment of angry, distorted truth telling. It began casually. Maria came into my room for some small thing—an aspirin, I believe. I dismissed her brusquely: "When I finish on the phone!" I was out of patience with the Camille role. Maria stormed out, and I hung up quickly, regretting my lack of control.

I found Maria on her bed, sobbing and screaming, "*You* hate me! *Daddy* hates me! You *all* hate me!" I was terrorized by the outburst of such passion after so much control.

Jeff walked onto the scene with the usual bag of hamburgers. I stood by, paralyzed, while he sat on the bed and tried to stop Maria's wild sobs. Within, I was as uncontrolled as Maria. I was racked with guilt. Suddenly I was the villain. How had that happened?

I sent Dan up. I recognized that it was our place, not Jeff's, even though I was numb. Dan talked with Maria for an hour. He didn't say much when he came out, just "Maria wants to see you."

"I'm sorry, Mom," she said. A comically polite ending for that storm of naked anger and emotion. When I stopped shaking, I was relieved. For a moment, the playacting had stopped.

"Maria, I don't know your feelings about this," I said. "You never told me." Her response, immediate, without pretense or defense, was "I don't know." We talked, then, about Jeff and sex; about her feeling that Mrs. Dunnock was right, that sex was a "communication between two human beings." Maria did not feel it was wrong. She said, contemplatively, "I've never had a close relationship with a boy before."

I was nonplused when she told me that "Dr. Bailey says if I have to continue in this relationship, I should come to him for contraceptive pills." What could I say? "You can't," "You shouldn't," which I wanted to say, but was constrained by inadequacy, ineptitude? The new morality was being spelled out for me in my living room. Maria said openly: "I won't say I won't do it again." Weakly, I moved from sexual relations to the dangers of promiscuity. (I did not even *think* of the possibility of another unwanted pregnancy until later.)

"I'm not going to get into bed with every boy!" she protested, as though I were unknowledgeably young and she the woman of the world. I felt a mixture of embarrassment and admiration at her candor. But even more, I felt deep regret that it could not be otherwise.

The episode is past now. Maria has been going to Dr. Asch once a week, refers to her as "Edna-baby" and discusses everything freely with us except the pregnancy. Even as I write, the relationship with Jeff has deteriorated to quarreling, bickering and short, non-lasting reconciliations. "You're smothering me" is Jeff's complaint; and Maria cries in her bed at night because "I don't understand. I've been so honest with him!" Sad echoes of any marriage on its way out. But for Maria, being Maria, there are sounds of new boys in the air—Rusty, Dave, Richard—on the telephone, at the door.

Our family doctor, when I saw him last, said, "You handled it well." I wonder. We did not drive Maria into a rash, unpromising marriage; we did not compel her to accept the life of an unwanted child; on the surface, we did not estrange her from home and family.

The story, in its telling, must arouse different reactions in different parents. Some, enmeshed in a situation like ours, may think we did "the best we could"; others, that we were fools at a dozen different points: for letting Jeff make himself at home; for letting Maria take advantage of, while we gave her the benefit of, our open-ended doubt; for being the parents that we are —indecisive, anxious to understand, afraid to trust reputedly outdated instincts and impulses.

Still others, I hope, will recognize that love makes fools of us all.

Throughout this account, I sense that I have been struggling to tell myself what I have learned, what I really believe and feel. It may be a long while before I see fully who and what we were during this critical time, how it will affect our future lives. We behaved in the spirit of the children's generation. Practicalists meeting immediate dictates without thought of deeper sanctions or morality.

But have we, in the process, created a philosophic Frankenstein's monster—a generation with the non-need to face responsibility, with a super, self-centered arrogance that precludes any *obligation* on their part, any *rights* on ours? Can we, in truth, give them the privileges and the freedoms of adults? Can we say, "Go ahead and express your sex freely," providing them with contraceptives as both caution and precept?

In this era of multiple meanings and interior analysis, it would be foolhardy to cling, for security's sake, to the once-simple, clearly understood directives we were taught. How can we, as one writer has wryly asked, put the genie back in the bottle? We have learned, through our intellect, that our animality is natural, our impulses and drives costly if contradicted. Can we then ask our children to do what is unnatural and inhibitory? Because we are not clear in our minds, we are not convincing when we say or imply "no." We have built fences and left the gates wide open.

I ask myself: Where would I draw the line? I may not be able to prevent a premature sexual acting out of the young (although I frankly admit I wish I could!)—but I can cease to sponsor it. It strikes me that in allowing our children to make their sexual practices so public, we are not resigning ourselves to their independence but fostering dependency. When our daughters and sons behave so openly, it is more than the characteristic self-centeredness of the young. It is anger. They are chafing, showing us, because our hold is so strong, so hard to break. If they were truly independent, they would go about their business, not involving us, not forcing us to react to their hostility, to their defiance.

I no longer wish to denigrate my own "square" belief that there are values that outweigh momentary desire. I no longer believe that responsibility will be the spontaneous result of a child-oriented home, as we once romantically hoped. I believe that responsibility has to be taught, painstakingly, like the habit of brushing one's teeth. I wish I had given houseroom to the antique notion of "what our children owe us"—if only to give them practice in living with others. I wish I had reminded myself of what I knew all along: that freedom is the most difficult human privilege to use and enjoy.

But above all, I wish I had allowed myself an honest moment of anger and bitterness as ugly, open and honest as Maria's moment of truth. I love Maria enough to be angry with her and to withstand the anger I might have stirred in her. We might have avoided the small, nasty resentments that crop up now in the wrong place, with wrong emphasis. The past will not release the present from tentacles of memory and guilt.

Sadly, I feel that Maria and I are not closer, but one step more removed from each other than before—perhaps because each of us has abandoned a part of her traditional role.

Maria is a woman in her sensuality; in her relations to us, she is still the child. How do we resolve the dilemma—by ignoring the child or ignoring the woman? Everything within our culture abets her (as we did) in playing a woman's role with a child's responsibility, while it seduces us into parental confusion and inaction.

When I was the mother of young children, I worried about my ability to love a child with a perfect love. But now

it is equally hard; it is imperative that I find my way through attitudes old and new toward the wisdom to be a mother to a young girl, barefoot, in blue jeans—who, in turn, must find the wisdom to be wife, mother and her own woman.

report from teeny-boppersville

J. KIRK SALE AND BEN APFELBAUM

The miniskirt is the current thing, uh-ha;
Teeny-bopper is our new-born king, uh-ha.*

—Sonny and Cher.

There is no urgency. They move slowly, languidly, along the crowded sidewalks. Brightcolored bell-bottoms, miniskirts, long hair falling straight down the back, a sagging pocketbook swung lazily by its straps, pastel sandals shuffling. Paisley shirts with puffed sleeves and open to the third button, tight cuffless trousers flaring slightly at the ankles, long sideburns flowing into carefully coiffed hair brushing gently on the collar, boots clicking in long, loping strides. Milling and ambling, like a rush-hour crowd in in slow motion, they absorb the sights and sounds of the street. From a garishly painted basement cage, the heavy, shivering, electronic pulse of a band sets an imperceptible rhythm.

"Free admission, come on in, join our

*From "The Beat Goes On," by Sonny Bono. Copyright 1967, Cotillion Music, Inc., and Chris-Marc Music.

show, just starting .... Yeah, Dylan's dead, I'm hip .... My hair isn't short, that's just school rules, look at this .... Oh, yeah, she wears her face that she keeps in the jar by the door.... Hey, baby, so what's happening?"

A piece of pizza at the corner, eaten slowly and carefully, back against the counter, casually appraising the scene. In the window of the Rienzi, boys in full plumage assessing their reflections, a comb from nowhere patting the bobs in place. Strolling past Googie's and the Tin Angel, then, leisurely, drifting up to the park. Eventually back to the crowded heart, outside the Cafe Wha? and the Cock-'n'-Bull, an orange drink at the newsstand, some new faces gossip, moving back as the cops push wearily through, then leaning easily, knee bent, against the wall, humming softly with the rhythm of the bands, and the crowds, and the lauhgter, lots of laughter.

Down in the basement of the Wha? on Macdougal Street, a long and narrow, low-ceilinged cavern, the Raves are into their last set, stark on the blazingly lighted stage, surrounded by huge amplifiers, speakers, microphones and wires. The noise is infectious: both young guitarists on the stage are dancing, shuffling, smiling broadly, and just below them the regulars at the center booths are singing along, yelling to the drummer, pulling on the wires, swaying in their seats, while in the back, against the far wall, two girls, a vinyl miniskirt and a plaid pants suit, are dancing, easily, relaxed, absorbed. The music is satisfying and exhilarating, everyone in the room from ticket-taker to tourist is caught up in it, in the good time the band is having, loose, untroubled, free, and when the last electronic chord fades there is a laughing cheer and a sad, sated, little audible sigh that fills the room.

This is a warm spring Saturday night in the center of New York's Greenwich Village, which in the last two years has become the magnet for the newest, and liveliest, subdivision of New York's teen-age world: the teeny-bopper. Along these special eight blocks teeny-boppers from the entire metropolitan area find a world apart, a world dedicated to them and their pleasures, and every evening, every weekend, they fill it; when they can't make the Village scene they dream of it, or wait for the time, or pretend they are *there*. There are teeny-bopper scenes, of course, all across the country – in Chicago's Old-town, on West Hollywood's Sunset Strip, even Denver and Philadelphia and Toronto, for the teeny-boppers have sprung up wherever the young congregate and electronic bands pulsate. But the Village is special.

"I feel free to do whatever I want down here. I mean, where I live there's nothing to do, no excitement. Here you can do what you want." That, the statement of a young boy from Queens, is the teeny-bopper testimonial to the Village. "I wanted to be a teacher," says a miniskirted girl from the Bronx, "but I changed my mind. Since I came down here, I have no time for school, I want to come here all the time. I want to live here .... I love it down here, it's my kind of people. I'm so comfortable."

"I was a teeny-bopper and I used to come down once a year," said one Village regular, "and then every weekend, and soon you like it so much that you don't want to leave at all." The Village magnet is powerful – and the pull is self-perpetuating. One highschool senior, a boy very close to the teeny-bopper world, talks about its attraction to the girls he knows:

"They take a friend and they come crawling into the Village from Forest Hills and Canarsie, dress the way they see in pictures, talk the way they've learned to, and go and sit in the Cock-'n'-Bull with other kids who are exactly like them in every way. And then they all go home and feel proud that they 'hung out in the Village.' They think it's great, and they say to their friends, 'I hung out in the Village – can you top that?' After all, the Village is famous all over the world. I mean, could you go to Paris and say, 'I hung out in Borough Park?' "

Barbara, a 16-year-old from the Bronx and a student at Evander Childs High School, is a regular at the Cafe Wha? Like most, she makes the standard disclaimer, afraid of being put down, hating the imprisonment of the press's label: "Me? I'm not a teeny-bopper; that's that kid over there." We asked her what she does on Saturday morning.

"I get ready to come down here to the Village at night," She laughed embarrassed.

"And what do you do?"

"Well, first I do all my homework, I do all the things I have to around the house. Then I call my friends and we talk about what we're going to wear – and then we come down the Wha?" ("Down the Wha?," incidentally, is a signal part of the teeny-bopper lexicon.)

"What time do you get here?"

"It starts at 7:30, and we get here at 8:30. We don't want to be the first ones; we have to make our entrance, you know." She laughs at her own frankness. "Then we walk down the aisle, and sometimes if you're lucky you get a wave, you know, from the guys in the group. And then when the set is over, they come down. Then we sit and watch them and wave, and yell, and all that.

"And then we watch the whole show, and after it's over we go out in the lobby. And like last night we were talking with some other kids, and you get to know about them, what they think about the Wha?, you know, and then how old they are, and what *we* think about it. You get to exchange ideas.

"And then at the end, we come back in, the band does its last set, the crazy set, and we're there in the back, singing and joking, and they yell at us to shut up. We sit all the way in the back next to the wall; we can dance there, and crack up and everything." She sighs and smiles and squirms a little.

No easy definition of "teeny-bopper" is possible, for the perimeters of the word change as fast as the Top 10, and as the general press picks it up it is used to describe practically anyone who is not senile. (The word "bopper" itself comes from the old Negro argot "bebopper" of the forties, the bebop jazz enthusiast who dressed oddly and dug the then far-out music.)

But, roughly, the teeny-boppers range from 10 to 19, though the majority are of high-school age, between 14 and 17. They are caught up in the simple fact of being young, scorn the pretense of "acting grownup" or trying to be an adult, and audaciously, aggressively, parade their youthfulness. They are intellectually as well as emotionally set against their parents' standards on sex, drugs, music, clothes, behavior, hair and politics. The word "teeny-bopper" at first seemed to refer to girls, but no special term has been coined for the male of the species, so "teeny-bopper" now applies to both sexes.

They are the kids who deliberately involve themselves in more than just a radio-listening way with the current pop-music world, who spend their weekends and summer vacations religiously visiting the cafes where the bands play, who are friendly, or try to be, with the musicians (who are generally of, or close to, their own age), who can tell gossip from truth in the teen magazines and, in fact, make rock'n'roll the focus of their interest and energy, the theme of their conversations and dreams.

Even in the larger cities, where the

teeny-boppers become identifiable as a group, they probably represent no more than a minority of the teen-age population, though a very distinct, involved and articulate minority. Not just any teen-ager with longish hair and a pair of boots is a teeny-bopper. Coexisting with them are the *hippies* — the descendants of the beats, usually the older teens, somewhat scornful of the youthful musicians, more involved with drugs, usually living away from home and perhaps working at odd jobs, tolerant of the teenies but living in a more adult, though thoroughly anti-Establishment, world; tthe *screamies*— younger children, usually girls, from 9 to 12, who are only beginning to awaken to the world around and have not yet developed any cool about themselves, screaming and fainting at the few big-name concerts they are allowed to go to; and the *squares* — the straitlaced, short-haired, penny-loafer, crew-cut set, football players and A-students.

In a way, the teeny-boppers partake of all these worlds and may have square characteristics along with their hip ones; they may be reading "Silas Marner" and the East Village Other, looking up to both Longfellow and Leary, gossiping about the senior prom as well as last night's party. For teeny-bopperism is a stage, part of a loose evolutionary process of adolescence that connects with other stages. Thus, it is possible for a screamie to become a bopper, or a bopper a hippie — this last is fairly frequent in the Village, where the two worlds overlap — for the categories are loose, and the entries easy.

Although the teeny-boppers resemble earlier teen-age groups in some ways — rebellious, self-centered, questioning — there is a difference of degree so great as to be a difference of kind between them and the flappers of the twenties, the bobby-soxers of the forties

or the Presleyites of the fifties. For one thing, they are more obvious, more aggressive, less inhibited, continually play-acting their youthful roles in public, "goofing on" (putting-on-putting-down) the squares and the adults: panhandling the tourists in the Village streets and reveling in their embarrassment, gaily yelling, "Let's go shoot up" in front of policemen and grownups just for the effect, making fun of the blank unsmiling faces in the subways.

But the music they create and listen to tells most about them. The lyrics of today have come a long way from Patti Page's "How Much Is That Doggie in the Window?" Listen to this rather blunt but accurate sentiment from 15-year-old Janis Ian:

If you think I'm hating grownups, you've
    got me all wrong.
They're very nice people when they stay
    where they belong.
But I'm the younger generation
And your rules are giving me fixations.
I've got those younger generation,
    regurgitating blues.*

And another:

Her mother plays on the golf course ev'ry
    day
And her Daddy sits at home and plays
    with the maid
They've found the perfect alibi:
Stay together for the sake of the child,
Divorce don't fit
And they're too young to split.
Think they're martyrs but they're killing
    the kid.*

It's not unusual for the teeny-boppers' music to be written and played by their contemporaries. A group called the Raves, for example, who are very big with the teeny-bop set at the Cafe Wha? and

*From "Younger Generation Blues," and "Janey's Blues," copyright 1966, Dialogue Music, Inc.

who recently cut a record of their own composition that is moving up on the charts, are led by Michael Jimenez, all of 19, and his brother David, 17. These contemporaries are touchable and talkable to—on the street after their show, in the coffeehouse down the street, at the party on Saturday. It is the everyday quality of these idols that differentiates this generation from those past. Peter Tork of the Monkees, mooned over by girls across the country and probably worth half a million dollars, is right there walking along Macdougal Street and will even stop to talk; Brian Jones of the Rolling Stones, a group nearly as successful and rich as the Beatles, can be seen in the Village restaurants.

John Emelin, a tall, serious young singer of 21, who is a member of a popular new band called Lothar and the Hand People (Lothar is the nickname they have given their theremin, an electronic instrument played by moving the hands along a tubular electrode, hence the "hand people") sums up the attitude of a special group of his generation:

"The difference between 1940 and now is amazing. We don't have a major war, but we have a lot of very strange little ones. We have the memory of an assassination which is still getting fantastic publicity. We have a tremendous race scene that is getting a tremendous amount of publicity. We have a fantastic drug scene that's getting a lot of attention. We have an amazing music scene which was just not happening in the forties the way it's happening now. We have an amazing science scene—fantastic! In the forties they were discovering nylon, or something. We're about to embark for the moon."

What sets the teeny-bopper apart is a special awareness of, and dissatisfaction with, the adult world, and a deliberate attempt to create a separate free-and-easy world through a rough hedonism of music, companionship, emotionalism, sex, drugs and, as the teeny-boppers say, "anything that turns you on, makes you happy."

At the Rienzi, a coffeehouse where boppers and post-boppers mingle, we asked a boy named David, 17, neatly dressed and with well-groomed hair curling under his ears, about his parents. He snorted, "My father wants me to be rich," and made a face. "My father wants me to grow up to be exactly like him. He's a champion bridge player and he goes down to the bridge club all night. And I say, 'I'm going down to Macdougal Street,' and he says, 'You're just hanging around down there.' So I say, 'I'm just going to be with my friends. *You* go to the bridge club: what do you go *there* for? Every—night he goes to the bridge club!'" And a young girl echoes: "You rarely find a girl who can talk to her parents. Her parents are always putting her down."

Iris, a pretty high-school senior who has made the Village scene for some years, argues that the big problem is that the teeny-boppers have to lead double lives because they can't get through to their parents. "They say, 'Oh, Mom, I'm going to hang around at the corner,' and they come down here and smoke [that's not tobacco] and have sex and it's all very teeny. And they go home and they're Miss Goody-Goody again, and comes Friday night, it's 'I'm going to the corner of the park' again. Because they can't say to their parents, 'This is what I am and what I want to do.' So a lot of them lead a kind of double life. How can you go home and when your mother says, 'What did you do tonight, dear?' say, 'Ma, tonight I smoked grass?' "

This generational gap showed itself one night recently in the Village when a big Lincoln pulled up in front of the Cafe

Wha? and a large matron stormed out, went up to the doorman and screamed: "Where's my daughter? Get her up here, you bum! Get her out of this evil place!" She then marched inside and found her daughter talking to a long-haired youth of perhaps 15: "You spend all your time with these disgusting queers?" The daughter took one look and ran off down Macdougal Street. Her mother went tearing after her at a remarkable speed and in a few minutes reappeared, dragging the girl, in tears, back to the car.

An hour later, much to the amusement of the regulars on the street, the daughter was back, strolling casually. She explained: "I ran into the subway and lost the—bitch."

In reaction to the world of their parents which they think they understand and don't want to be a part of, the teeny-boppers run away into a world of their own where they can be young and revel in their childish enthusiasms without anybody tsk-tsking over their shoulders. They want to be left alone in an arena where they can maintain their own mores and values, however flimsy, which they regard as no worse than their parents'. They ask very little from the outside — except money from home and passing grades from school, both usually given easily — and certainly not meaning or guidance or companionship. These they get from their contemporary heroes in the bands and on the streets, from group experience of emotional music shared at fever pitch, and from being a part of a scene that's "happening." amplified twang of an electronic guitar: rock'n'roll is the lingua franca, musical involvement the passport. Frank Zappa, a member of a new group of talented musicians called the Mothers of Invention, whose wild black curls and black anklelength coat have made him a Mac-

dougal Street standout, sees a kind of patriotism in this involvement. "The only real loyalty that exists in the American teen-ager today is to his music. He doesn't give an actual damn about his country or his religion. He has more actual patriotism in terms of how he feels about his music than in anything else. And this just has never happened before."

Part of the exhilaration, of course, comes from the incredible noise level at which the music is played, thanks to the complicated electronic gadgetry that has turned a guitar from a sweet accompanying instrument into a blaring siren and a weak teen-age tenor into an echo-chamber scream. John Emelin, whose own group's theremin is one of the loudest electronic creations of them all, argues that "it's a lot of noise only in the same way that Indian music is a lot of noise sometimes, or symphonies are a lot of noise. It makes you peak out emotionally." hearing the singers and memorizing the songs — it means buying the records ($250-million worth a year), reading the teen magazines (50 million copies a year), and above all talking, talking about the world of the rock'n'roll stars. On the streets, in the cafes, over the sausage sandwiches, the conversations are heavily rock-centered: "Hey, d'you see that that Russian guy—what's it? Yevtushenko?—made the Monkees concert in Hawaii?" Or: "You know the Animals where they say, 'Have you ever been so hungry that you had no pride?' Like that's where I'm at now about Eric Clapton, I told you I saw him at the Tin Angel the other night: he's so beautiful." Even gossip and put-downs are couched in these terms: "Oh, no, man, let's stay away from that chick. You know her bag? Like she sits around and watches the Beatles on Ed Sullivan, she just sits there and screams, or sometimes like she'll take pictures of the screen just to have pictures of *them*. She's got this picture of Paul McCartney, it's all distorted, with no focus, and she'll say, 'This is a picture of Paul.' You know, what kind of —?"

Naturally enough, through this process the culture heroes for the teeny-boppers are in large measure the rock'n'roll musicians of any stripe — not just the locals who have made good like Lothar and the Hand People and the Mothers of Invention or the famous ones who make the scene like the Rolling Stones and the Animals, but also — and especially — Bob Dylan and, still, the Beatles. Even today when a Beatles song comes on in a Village diner, there is a modified hush, everyone listening with one ear. And Dylan, who was the first to turn many of these kids on to some serious ideas and a glimpse of poetry, represents for many a kind of supreme figure, a kid who dropped out of the parental world, made good, got rich, scored whenever he wanted to, and then dropped out again, a mysterious, beautiful figure proving to the teeny-boppers that they must be on to something great.

In the same way the professional dropouts around the Village, seeable and knowable, are culture heroes: Allen Ginsberg especially ("Oh, what a beautiful life, I mean beautiful"), Timothy Leary and Andy Warhol: There is something about the way they are "goofing on" the square world and yet making a go of it that embodies all the teeny-bop ideals. This "grooving with" the hip dropout spills over to such groups as homosexuals and Negroes who while they are not themselves teeny-boppers—the Village scene has no more than a handful of Negro teeny-boppers, largely because Negro youths apparently don't need such a scene to declare their freedom from and hostility to the Establishment power structure—represent the kind of

sentiment the boppers feel they are into.

If there is hedonism in the music, there is also hedonism in the life that surrounds it. The sights and sounds of rock'n'roll are enough for most of the teeny-boppers, but there is no question but that the twin revolutions of the adult world in sex and drugs have also filtered down to become a part of their world as well.

We talked to one girl of 18 who had been coming to the Village regularly for four years — she was pretty, shy, and except for her unusual dress could have been any suburban girl — and asked her about sex.

"Well, I'd meet boys, and like, you know I'd . . . I'd *love* them, not just like them. So I stayed with them. And then the summertime, I stayed down here I smoked a lot, and . . . I didn't just go to *anybody*; I really liked these boys. But they used me. Like I'd tell them I liked them and wanted to be with them, and they'd use me and then say, 'Goodby now, that's it.' And I was very hurt . . . ."

"How do you feel about all that now?"

"I don't know. I think it was a good experience. I mean, I'm better now, I learned. I don't think everything I did was right, but I don't feel guilty. I mean it's just a misfortune that it went wrong. I learned about things and how to handle them.

"But even now, I meet boys and the first thing they say is, 'Come on, let's go to bed.' And I want to show the boy that I like him, but now . . . I don't know what to do."

The confusion is natural enough. "My mother knows I wouldn't go with anybody," one girl told us. "Though sometimes I feel that I would. But I know that when it really comes down to things, I'd be scared witless. I feel that if I . . . went with somebody, I couldn't look them in the face afterward, I really couldn't." In addition to the simple fear of the unknowns of sex, most of the teeny-boppers seem to be aware of the other difficulties – the possibilities of pregnancy, venereal disease, emotional turmoil and "a bad reputation." "This may be old-fashioned," says 16-year-old Barbara, "but I think a boy respects you better if the first time you meet him you don't say, 'How about it?,' you know?" She laughs at the exaggeration. "I think it's not good, that you should know what you're doing better, when you're 20 or so."

There are enough sad stories of girls who have slept around to indicate that sex is a real – if troublesome – part of the liberality of this world (but whether it is more so than in the corn belt no one knows). "I know this one girl," admits a young teeny, "she was going with this guy in a band, and she went to bed with him. And after that he wouldn't talk to her, and she felt funny. So then pretty soon everybody in the group had her. She's walking around now like she's lost."

The fact is that with the sexual mores of the teeny-boppers the possibilities, and the pitfalls, are much more open than in the past.

Marijuana, too, is more or less routine, though of course it is not confined to the teeny-boppers ("I can get more grass in East Orange than I can down here," said one girl in the Village). By the time they are 16 probably most of the teenies have experimented with marijuana, and quite a number may smoke regularly – "They don't think marijuana is a drug, they think it's normal," one teenie says – and a sizable minority is "into the acid scene," i.e., taking LSD occasionally. But it appears that very few go on to amphetamines – "Stay away from A, man," one boy warns – and almost none to heroin.

Marijuana is obviously a convenient release for some of the teeny-bopper set, most of whom are too young to get a drink legally (their hangouts are all liquor-free and the only thing stronger than Coke is the music) and many of whom profess to be rather repulsed by what they have seen of adult use of alcohol, anyway. ("I came home about 2:30 in the morning when my mother was having a party," one boy told us, "and I saw all these disgusting middle-aged people, all drunk and doing all these foolish disgusting things.") Marijuana is a way, they say, of getting high without being either sloppy or particularly noticeable (losing cool); it is simple and inexpensive; and it serves to heighten rather than diminish the sights and sounds of the scene.

Though marijuana is considered normal enough, the teeny-boppers are keenly aware that possession of it is against the law. "Like, I *know*, man, you can get busted for smoking and sometimes I get up tight when I see these plainclothes guys come with their badges. But I've read all the stuff; I know it can't hurt you – pot, that is – and all that about how it can lead to stronger stuff – well, no one believes that anymore except maybe in Indiana." And they also know the dangers of the stronger drugs -- like music, this is a subject on which they seem well-informed – and pretty religiously steer away from them. For though there is indeed a dangerous drug scene in the Village (as elsewhere) and a few of the teenies do get sucked into it – either through some older teen-ager who is pushing drugs for a living or just as a result of youthful experimentation – there is also a powerful built-in correction in the Village: the wasted, empty men you can see around in the darkened doorways who have been hooked. The teeny-boppers can know, perhaps better than their suburban friends, just how evil the addiction scene is.

And so what, in the end, is to be made of this strange new world? What will become of it?

It is really too early to tell. Some of the teeny-boppers will probably simply fade from the scene as they reach 17 and 18 — maybe bored, or choosing to go away to college, or settling into a job and its square responsibilities. Some will surely go into the hippie life, find a pad in the East Village, try to live along the Village fringes as long as they can. But whatever happens, it is unlikely that the years of bopperhood will have failed to make their mark.

There is no question about what today's teeny-boppers and those around them believe: "We're on to something new, and wonderful." The singer John Emelin says, "A whole return to a simple philosophy is what's happening. A whole group of kids is now rediscovering the concept of love — and not a romantic love, it's like *agape* or whatever. It's like Christian love without any of the hang-ups of the church scene."

Or, in the words of a 16-year-old boy: "There's one thing the adult generation in this country doesn't dig, man: we are the future generation." "Yeah, I can see our next President with long hair and a beard," said one youngster. Another added, "Look at us. The society has changed so much since we were 6 years old. Some day you'll see a long-haired cat sitting in Congress saying, 'Fourscore,' right?"

Phil Leone, a 19-year-old drummer with the Raves and very much a part of the subculture of the new generation, says: "Let's put it this way. The teeny-boppers now are going to be the future leaders of the world. And like if they're still thinking the way they are

now it's going to be a beautiful place to live in."

in re gault

THE PRESIDENT'S COMMISSION

ON LAW ENFORCEMENT AND

ADMINISTRATION OF JUSTICE

Mr. Justice Fortas delivered the opinion of the Court.

This is an appeal under 28 U.S.C. § 1257(2) from a judgment of the Supreme Court of Arizona affirming the dismissal of a petition for a writ of habeas corpus. 99 Ariz. 181, 407 P.2d 760 (1965). The petition sought the release of Gerald Francis Gault, petitioners' 15-year-old son, who had been committed as a juvenile delinquent to the State Industrial School by the Juvenile Court of Gila County, Arizona. The Supreme Court of Arizona affirmed dismissal of the writ against various agruments which included an attack upon the constitutionality of the Arizona Juvenile Code because of its alleged denial of procedural due process rights to juveniles charged with being "delinquents." The court agreed that the constitutional guarantee of the due process of law is applicable in such proceedings. It held that Arizona's Juvenile Code is to be

Reprinted from The President's Commission on Law Enforcement and Administration of Justice: Task Force Reports: Juvenile Delinquency and Youth Crime, Appendix A, In re-Gault, pp. 57-76. Footnotes have been deleted.

read as "impliedly" implementing the "due process concept." It then proceeded to identify and describe "the particular elements which constitute the due process in a juvenile hearing." It concluded that the proceedings ending in commitment of Gerald Gault did not offend those requirements. We do not agree, and we reverse. We begin with a statement of the facts.

I.

On Monday, June 8, 1964, at about 10 a.m., Gerald Francis Gault and a friend, Ronald Lewis, were taken into custody by the Sheriff of Gila County. Gerald was then still subject to a six months' probation order which had been entered on February 25, 1964, as a result of his having been in the company of another boy who had stolen a wallet from a lady's purse. The police action on June 8 was taken as the result of a verbal complaint by a neighbor of the boys, Mrs. Cook, about a telephone call made to her in which the caller or callers made lewd or indecent remarks. It will suffice for purposes of this opinion to say that the remarks or questions put to her were of the irritatingly offensive, adolescent, sex variety.

At the time Gerald was picked up, his mother and father were both at work. No notice that Gerald was being taken into custody was left at the home. No other steps were taken to advise them that their son had, in effect, been arrested. Gerald was taken to the Children's Detention Home. When his mother arrived home at about 6 o'clock, Gerald was not there. Gerald's older brother was sent to look for him at the trailer home of the Lewis family. He apparently learned then that Gerald was in custody. He so informed his mother. The two of them went to the Detention Home. The deputy probation officer, Flagg, who was also superintendent of the Detention Home, told Mrs. Gault "why Jerry was there" and said that a hearing would be held in Juvenile Court at 3 o'clock the following day, June 9.

Officer Flagg filed a petition with the Court on the hearing day, June 9, 1964. It was not served on the Gaults. Indeed, none of them saw this petition until the habeas corpus hearing on August 17, 1964. The petition was entirely formal. It made no reference to any factual basis for the judicial action which it initiated. It recited only that "said minor is under the age of 18 years and in need of the protection of this Honorable Court [and that] said minor is a delinquent minor." It prayed for a hearing and an order regarding "the care and custody of said minor." Officer Flagg executed a formal affidavit in support of the petition.

On June 9, Gerald, his mother, his older brother, and Probation Officers Flagg and Henderson appeared before the Juvenile Judge in chambers. Gerald's father was not there. He was at work out of the city. Mrs. Cook, the complainant, was not there. No one was sworn at this hearing. No transcript or recording was made. No memorandum or record of the substance of the proceedings was prepared. Our information about the proceedings and the subsequent hearing on June 15, derives entirely from the testimony of the Juvenile Court Judge, Mr. And Mrs. Gault and Officer Flagg at the habeas corpus proceeding conducted two months later. From this, it appears that at the July 9 hearing Gerald was questioned by the judge about the telephone call. There was conflict as to what he said. His mother recalled that Gerald said he only dialed Mrs. Cook's number and handed the telephone to his friend, Ronald. Officer Flagg recalled that Gerald had admitted making the lewd remarks.

Judge McGhee testified that Gerald "admitted making one of these [lewd] statements." At the conclusion of the hearing, the judge said he would "think about it." Gerald was taken back to the Detention Home. He was not sent to his own home with his parents. On June 11 or 12, after having been detained since June 8, Gerald was released and driven home. There is no explanation in the record as to why he was kept in the Detention Home or why he was released. At 5 p.m. on the day of Gerald's release, Mrs. Gault received a note signed by Officer Flagg. It was on plain paper, not letterhead. Its entire text was as follows:

"Mrs. Gault:
    "Judge McGHEE has set Monday June 15, 1964 at 11:00 A.M. as the date and time for further Hearings on Gerald's delinquency
                                    /s/Flagg"

At the appointed time on Monday, June 15, Gerald, his father and mother, Ronald Lewis and his father, and Officers Flagg and Henderson were present before Judge McGhee. Witnesses at the habeus corpus proceeding differed in their recollections of Gerald's testimony at the June 15 hearing. Mr. and Mrs. Gault recalled that Gerald again testified that he had only dialed the number and that the other boy had made the remarks. Officer Flagg agreed that at this hearing Gerald did not admit making the lewd remarks. But Judge McGhee recalled that "there was some admission again of some of the lewd statements. He—he didn't admit any of the more serious lewd statements." Again, the complainant, Mrs. Cook, was not present. Mrs. Gault asked that Mrs. Cook be present "so she could see which boy had done the talking, the dirty talking over the phone." The Juvenile Judge said "she didn't have to be present at that hearing." The judge did not speak to Mrs. Cook or communicate with her at

any time. Probation Officer Flagg had talked to her once—over the telephone on June 9.

At this June 15 hearing a "referral report" made by the probation officers was filed with the court, although not disclosed to Gerald or his parents. This listed the charge as "Lewd Phone Calls." At the conclusion of the hearing, the judge committed Gerald as a juvenile delinquent to the State Industrial School "for the period of his minority [that is, until 21], unless sooner discharged by due process of law." An order to that effect was entered. It recites that "after a full hearing and due deliberation the Court finds that said minor is a delinquent child, and that said minor is of the age of 15 years."

No appeal is permitted by Arizona law in juvenile cases. On August 3, 1964, a petition for a writ of habeas corpus was filed with the Supreme Court of Arizona and referred by it to the Superior Court for hearing.

At the habeas corpus hearing on August 17, Judge McGhee was vigorously cross-examined as to the basis for his actions. He testified that he had taken into account the fact that Gerald was on probation. He was asked "under what section of . . . the code you found the boy delinquent?"

His answer is set forth in the margin. In substance, he concluded that Gerald came within ARS § 8–201–6(a), which specifies that a "delinquent child" includes one "who has violated a law of the state or an ordinance or regulation of a political subdivision thereof." The law which Gerald was found to have violated is ARS § 13–377. This section of the Arizona Criminal Code provides that a person who "in the presence of or hearing of any woman or child . . . uses vulgar, abusive or obscene language, is guilty of a misdemeanor. . . ." The penalty specified in the Criminal Code, which would apply to an adult, is $5 to $50, or imprisonment for not more than two months. The judge also testified that he acted under ARS § 8–201–6(d) which includes in the definition of a "delinquent child" one who, as the judge phrased it, is "habitually involved in immoral matters."

Asked about the basis for his conclusion that Gerald was "habitually involved in immoral matters," the judge testified, somewhat vaguely, that two years earlier, on July 2, 1962, a "referral" was made concerning Gerald, "where the boy had stolen a baseball glove from another boy and lied to the Police Department about it." The judge said there was "no hearing," and "no accusation" relating to this incident, "because of lack of material foundation." But it seems to have remained in his mind as a relevant factor. The judge also testified that Gerald had admitted making other nuisance phone calls in the past which, as the judge recalled the boy's testimony, were "silly calls, or funny calls, or something like that."

The Superior Court dismissed the writ, and appellants sought review in the Arizona Supreme Court. That court stated that it considered appellants' assignments of error as urging (1) that the Juvenile Code, ARS § 8–201 to § 8–239, is unconstitutional because it does not require that parents and children be apprised of the specific charges, does not require proper notice of a hearing, and does not provide for an appeal; and (2) that the proceedings and order relating to Gerald constituted a denial of due process of law because of the absence of adequate notice of the charge and the hearing; failure to notify appellants of certain constitutional rights including the rights to counsel and to confrontation, and the privilege against self-incrimination; the use of unsworn hearsay testimony; and the failure to make a record of the proceedings. Appellants further asserted that it was error for the Juvenile Court to remove Gerald from the custody of his parents without a showing and finding of their unsuitability, and alleged a miscellany of other errors under state law.

The Supreme Court handed down an elaborate and wide-ranging opinion affirming dismissal of the writ and stating the court's conclusions as to the issues raised by appellants and other aspects of the juvenile process. In their jurisdictional statement and brief in this Court, appellants do not urge upon us all of the points passed upon by the Supreme Court of Arizona. They urge that we hold the Juvenile Code of Arizona invalid on its face or as applied in this case because, contrary to the Due Process Clause of the Fourteenth Amendment, the juvenile is taken from the custody of his parents and committed to a state institution pursuant to proceedings in which the Juvenile Court has virtually unlimited discretion, and in which the following basic rights are denied:

1. Notice of the charges;
2. Right to counsel;
3. Right to confrontation and cross-examination;
4. Privilege against self-incrimination;
5. Right to a transcript of the proceedings; and
6. Right to appellate review.

We shall not consider other issues which were passed upon by the Supreme Court of Arizona. We emphasize that we indicate no opinion as to whether the decision of that court with respect to such other issues does or does not conflict with requirements of the Federal Constitution.

II.

The Supreme Court of Arizona held that due process of law is requisite to the constitutional validity of proceedings in which a court reaches the conclusion that a juvenile has been at fault, has engaged in conduct prohibited by law, or has otherwise misbehaved with the consequence that he is committed to an institution in which his freedom is curtailed. This conclusion is in accord with the decisions of a number of courts under both federal and state constitutions.

This Court has not heretofore decided the precise question. In *Kent* v. *United States,* 383 U.S. 541 (1966), we considered the requirements for a valid waiver of the "exclusive" jurisdiction of the Juvenile Court of the District of Columbia so that a juvenile could be tried in the adult criminal court of the District. Although our decision turned upon the language of the statute, we emphasized the necessity that "the basic requirements of due process and fairness" be satisfied in such proceedings. *Haley* v. *Ohio,* 332 U.S. 596 (1948), involved the admissibility, in a state criminal court of general jurisdiction, of a confession by a 15-year-old boy. The Court held that the Fourteenth Amendment applied to prohibit the use of the coerced confession. Mr. Justice Douglas said, "Neither man nor child can be allowed to stand condemned by methods which flout constitutional requirements of due process of law." To the same effect is *Gallegos* v. *Colorado,* 370 U.S. 49 (1962). Accordingly, while these cases relate only to restricted aspects of the subject, they unmistakably indicate that, whatever may be their precise impact, neither the Fourteenth Amendment nor the Bill of Rights is for adults alone.

We do not in this opinion consider the impact of these constitutional provisions upon the totality of the relationship of the juvenile and the state. We do not even consider the entire process relating to juvenile "delinquents." For example, we are not here concerned with the procedures or constitutional rights applicable to the pre-judicial stages of the juvenile process, nor do we direct our attention to the post-adjudicative or dispositional process. See note 48, *infra.* We consider only the problems presented to us by this case. These relate to the proceedings by which a determination is made as to whether a juvenile is a "delinquent" as a result of alleged misconduct on his part, with the consequence that he may be committed to a state institution. As to these proceedings there appears to be little current dissent from the proposition that the Due Process Clause has a role to play. The problem is to ascertain the precise impact of the due process requirement upon such proceedings.

From the inception of the juvenile court system, wide differences have been tolerated—indeed insisted upon—between the procedural rights accorded to adults and those of juveniles. In practically all jurisdictions, there are rights granted to adults which are withheld from juveniles. In addition to the specific problems involved in the present case, for example, it has been held that the juvenile is not entitled to bail, to indictment by grand jury, to a public trial or to trial by jury. It is frequent practice that rules governing the arrest and interrogation of adults by the police are not observed in the case of juveniles.

The history and theory underlying this development are well-known, but a recapitulation is necessary for purposes of this opinion. The juvenile court movement began in this country at the end of the last century. From the juvenile court statute adopted in Illinois in 1899, the system has spread to every

State in the Union, the District of Columbia, and Puerto Rico. The constitutionality of juvenile court laws has been sustained in over 40 jurisdictions against a variety of attacks.

The early reformers were appalled by adult procedures and penalties, and by the fact that children could be given long prison sentences and mixed in jails with hardened criminals. They were profoundly convinced that society's duty to the child could not be confined by the concept of justice alone. They believed that society's role was not to ascertain whether the child was "guilty" or "innocent," but "What is he, how has he become what he is, and what had best be done in his interest and in the interest of the state to save him from a downward career." The child—essentially good, as they saw it—was to be made "to feel that he is the object of [the State's] care and solicitude," not that he was under arrest or on trial. The rules of criminal procedure were therefore altogether inapplicable. The apparent rigidities, technicalities, and harshness which they observed in both substantive and procedural criminal law were therefore to be discarded. The idea of crime and punishment was to be abandoned. The child was to be "treated" and "rehabilitated" and the procedures, from apprehension through institutionalization, were to be "clinical" rather than punitive.

These results were to be achieved, without coming to conceptual and constitutional grief, by insisting that the proceedings were not adversary, but that the State was proceeding as *parens patriae*. The Latin phrase proved to be a great help to those who sought to rationalize the exclusion of juveniles from the constitutional scheme; but its meaning is murky and its historic credentials are of dubious relevance. The phrase was taken from chancery practice, where, however it was used to describe the power of the State to act in *loco parentis* for the purpose of protecting the property interests and the person of the child. But there is no trace of the doctrine in the history of criminal jurisprudence. At common law, children under seven were considered incapable of possessing criminal intent. Beyond that age, they were subjected to arrest, trial, and in theory to punishment like adult offenders. In these old days, the State was not deemed to have authority to accord them fewer procedural rights than adults.

The right of the State, as *parens patriae*, to deny to the child procedural rights available to his elders was elaborated by the assertion that a child, unlike an adult, has a right "not to liberty but to custody." He can be made to attorn to his parents, to go to school, etc. If his parents default in effectively performing their custodial functions—that is, if the child is "delinquent"—the state may intervene. In doing so, it does not deprive the child of any rights, because he has none. It merely provides the "custody" to which the child is entitled. On this basis, proceedings involving juveniles were described as "civil" not "criminal" and therefore not subject to the requirements which restrict the state when it seeks to deprive a person of his liberty.

Accordingly, the highest motives and most enlightened impulses led to a peculiar system for juveniles, unknown to our law in any comparable context. The constitutional and theoretical basis for this peculiar system is—to say the least—debatable. And in practice, as we remarked in the *Kent* case, *supra,* the results have not been entirely satisfactory. Juvenile court history has again demonstrated that unbridled discretion, however benevolently motivated, is frequently a poor substitute for principle and procedure. In 1937, Dean Pound wrote: "The powers of the Star Chamber were a trifle in comparison with those of our juvenile courts. . . ." The absence of substantive standards has not necessarily meant that children receive careful, compassionate, individualized treatment. The absence of procedural rules based upon constitutional principle has not always produced fair, efficient, and effective procedures. Departures from established principles of due process have frequently resulted not in enlightened procedure, but in arbitrariness. The Chairman of the Pennsylvania Council of Juvenile Court Judges has recently observed: "Unfortunately, loose procedures, high-handed methods and crowded court calendars, either singly or in combination, all too often, have resulted in depriving some juveniles of fundamental rights that have resulted in a denial of due process."

Failure to observe the fundamental requirements of due process has resulted in instances, which might have been avoided, of unfairness to individuals and inadequate or inaccurate findings of fact and unfortunate prescriptions of remedy. Due process of law is the primary and indispensable foundation of individual freedom. It is the basic and essential term in the social compact which defines the rights of the individual and delimits the powers which the State may exercise. As Mr. Justice Frankfurter has said: "The history of American freedom is, in no small measure, the history of procedure." But in addition, the procedural rules which have been fashioned from the generality of due process are our best instruments for the distillation and evaluation of essential facts from the conflicting welter of data that life and our adversary methods present. It is these instruments of due process which enhance the possibility that truth will emerge from the confrontation of opposing versions and conflicting data. "Procedure is to law what 'scientific method' is to science."

It is claimed that juveniles obtain benefits from the special procedures applicable to them which more than offset the disadvantages of denial of the substance of normal due process. As we shall discuss, the observance of due process standards, intelligently and not ruthlessly administered, will not compel the States to abandon or displace any of the substantive benefits of the juvenile process. But it is important, we think, that the claimed benefits of the juvenile process should be candidly appraised. Neither sentiment nor folklore should cause us to shut our eyes, for example, to such startling findings as that reported in an exceptionally reliable study of repeaters or recidivism conducted by the Stanford Research Institute for the President's Commission on Crime in the District of Columbia. This Commission's Report states:

"In fiscal 1966 approximately 66 percent of the 16- and 17-year-old juveniles referred to the court by the Youth Aid Division had been before the court previously. In 1965, 56 percent of those in the Receiving Home were repeaters. The SRI study revealed that 61 percent of the sample Juvenile Court referrals in 1965 had been previously referred at least once and that 42 percent had been referred at least twice before." *Id.*, at 773.

Certainly, these figures and the high crime rates among juveniles to which we have referred (*supra*, note 26), could not lead us to conclude that the absence of constitutional protections reduces crime, or that the juvenile system, functioning free of constitutional inhibitions as it has largely done, is effective to reduce crime or rehabilitate offenders. We do not mean by this to denigrate the juvenile court process or to suggest that there are not aspects of the juvenile system relating to offenders which are valuable. But the features of the juvenile system which its proponents have asserted are of unique benefit will not be impaired by constitutional domestication. For example, the commendable principles relating to the processing and treatment of juveniles separately from adults are in no way involved or affected by the procedural issues under discussion. Further, we are told that one of the important benefits of the special juvenile court procedures is that they avoid classifying the juvenile as a "criminal." The juvenile offender is now classed as a "delinquent." There is, of course, no reason why this should not continue. It is disconcerting, however, that this term has come to involve only slightly less stigma than the term "criminal" applied to adults. It is also emphasized that in practically all jurisdictions, statutes provide that an adjudication of the child as a delinquent shall not operate as a civil disability or disqualify him for civil service appointment. There is no reason why the application of due process requirements should interfere with such provisions.

Beyond this, it is frequently said that juveniles are protected by the process from disclosure of their deviational behavior. As the Supreme Court of Arizona phrased it in the present case, the summary procedures of juvenile courts are sometimes defended by a statement that it is the law's policy "to hide youthful errors from the full gaze of the public and bury them in the graveyard of the forgotten past." This claim of secrecy, however, is more rhetoric than reality. Disclosure of court records is discretionary with the judge in most jurisdictions. Statutory restrictions almost invariably apply only to the court records, and even as to those the evidence is that many courts routinely furnish information to the FBI and the military, and on request to government agencies and even to private employers. Of more importance are police records. In most States the police keep a complete file of juvenile "police contacts" and have complete discretion as to disclosure of juvenile records. Police departments receive requests for information from the FBI and other law-enforcement agencies, the Armed Forces, and social service agencies, and most of them generally comply. Private employers word their application forms to produce information concerning juvenile arrests and court proceedings, and in some jurisdictions information concerning juvenile police contacts is furnished private employers as well as government agencies.

In any event, there is no reason why, consistently with due process, a State cannot continue, if it deems it appropriate, to provide and to improve provision for the confidentiality of records of police contacts and court action relating to juveniles. It is interesting to note, however, that the Arizona Supreme Court used the confidentiality argument as a justification for the type of notice which is here attacked as inadequate for due process purposes. The parents were given merely general notice that their child was charged with "delinquency." No facts were specified. The Arizona court held, however, as we shall discuss, that in addition to this general "notice" the child and his parents must be advised "of the facts involved in the case" no later than the initial hearing by the judge. Obviously, this does not "bury" the word about the child's transgressions. It merely defers the time of disclosure to a point when it is of limited use to the child or his parents in preparing his defense or explanation.

Further, it is urged that the juvenile

benefits from informal proceedings in the court. The early conception of the juvenile court proceeding was one in which a fatherly judge touched the heart and conscience of the erring youth by talking over his problems, by paternal advice and admonition, and in which, in extreme situations, benevolent and wise instutitons of the State provided guidance and help "to save him from a downward career." Then, as now, goodwill and compassion were admirably prevalent. But recent studies have, with surprising unanimity, entered sharp dissent as to the validity of this gentle conception. They suggest that the appearance as well as the actuality of fairness, impartiality and orderliness—in short, the essentials of due process may be a more impressive and more therapeutic attitude so far as the juvenile is concerned. For example, in a recent study, the sociologists Wheeler and Cottrell observe that when the procedural laxness of the *"Parens patriae"* attitude is followed by stern disciplining, the contrast may have an adverse effect upon the child, who feels that he has been deceived or enticed. They conclude as follows: "Unless appropriate due process of law is followed, even the juvenile who has violated the law may not feel that he is being fairly treated and may therefore resist the rehabilitative efforts of court personnel." Of course, it is not suggested that juvenile court judges should fail appropriately to take account, in their demeanor and conduct, of the emotional and psychological attitude of the juveniles with whom they are confronted. While due process requirements will, in some instances, introduce a degree of order and regularity to juvenile court proceedings to determine delinquency, and in contested cases will introduce some elements of the adversary system, nothing will require that the conception of the kindly juvenile judge be replaced by its opposite, nor do we here rule upon the question whether ordinary due process requirements must be observed with respect to hearings to determine the disposition of the delinquent child.

Ultimately, however, we confront the reality of that portion of the juvenile court process with which we deal in this case. A boy is charged with misconduct. The boy is committed to an institution where he may be restrained of liberty for years. It is of no constitutional consequence—and of limited practical meaning—that the institution to which he is committed is called an Industrial School. The fact of the matter is that, however euphemistic the title, a "receiving home" or an "industrial school" for juveniles is an institution of confinement in which the child is incarcerated for a greater or lesser time. His world becomes "a building with white-washed walls, regimented routine and institutional laws. . . ." Instead of mother and father and sisters and brothers and friends and classmates, his world is peopled by guards, custodians, state employees, and "delinquents" confined with him for anything from waywardness to rape and homicide.

In view of this, it would be extraordinary if our Constitution did not require the procedural regularity and the exercise of care implied in the phrase "due process." Under our Constitution, the condition of being a boy does not justify a kangaroo court. The traditional ideas of juvenile court procedure, indeed, contemplated that time would be available and care would be used to establish precisely what the juvenile did and why he did it—was it a prank of adolescence or a brutal act threatening serious consequences to himself or society unless corrected? Under traditional notions, one would assume that in a case like that of Gerald Gault, where the juvenile appears to have a home, a working mother and father, and an older brother, the Juvenile Judge would have made a careful inquiry and judgment as to the possibility that the boy could be disciplined and dealt with at home, despite his previous transgressions. Indeed, so far as appears in the record before us, except for some conversation with Gerald about his school work and his "wanting to go to . . . Grand Canyon with his father," the points to which the judge directed his attention were little different from those that would be involved in determining any charge of violation of a penal statute. The essential difference between Gerald's case and a normal criminal case is that safeguards available to adults were discarded in Gerald's case. The summary procedure as well as the long commitment were possible because Gerald was 15 years of age instead of over 18.

If Gerald had been over 18, he would not have been subject to Juvenile Court proceedings. For the particular offense immediately involved, the maximum punishment would have been a fine of $5 to $50, or imprisonment in jail for not more than two months. Instead, he was committed to custody for a maximum of six years. If he had been over 18 and had committed an offense to which such a sentence might apply, he would have been entitled to substantial rights under the Constitution of the United States as well as under Arizona's laws and constitution. The United States Constitution would guarantee him rights and protections with respect to arrest, search and seizure, and pretrial interrogation. It would assure him of specific notice of the charges and adequate time to prepare his defense. He would be entitled to clear advice that he could be represented by counsel, and at least if a felony were involved, the State would be required to provide counsel if his parents were unable to afford it. If the court acted on the basis of

his confession, careful procedures would be required to assure its voluntariness. If the case went to trial, confrontation and opportunity for cross-examination would be guaranteed. So wide a gulf between the State's treatment of the adult and of the child requires a bridge sturdier than mere verbiage, and reasons more persuasive than cliché can provide. As Wheeler and Cottrell have put it, "The rhetoric of the juvenile court movement has developed without any necessarily close correspondence to the realities of court and institutional routines."

In *Kent* v. *United States, supra*, we stated that the Juvenile Court Judge's exercise of the power of the State as *parens patriae* was not unlimited. We said that "the admonition to function in a 'parental' relationship is not an invitation to procedural arbitrariness." With respect to the waiver by the juvenile court to the adult of jurisdiction over an offense committed by a youth, we said that "there is no place in our system of law for reaching a result of such tremendous consequences without ceremony—without hearing, without effective assistance of counsel, without a statement of reasons." We announced with respect to such waiver proceedings that while "We do not mean . . . to indicate that the hearing to be held must conform with all of the requirements of a criminal trial or even of the usual administrative hearing; but we do hold that the hearing must measure up to the essentials of due process and fair treatment." We reiterate this view, here in connection with a juvenile court adjudication of "delinquency," as a requirement which is part of the Due Process Clause of the Fourteenth Amendment of our Constitution.

We now turn to the specific issues which are presented to us in the present case.

III.

Notice of Charges.

Appellants allege that the Arizona Juvenile Code is unconstitutional or alternatively that the proceedings before the Juvenile Court were constitutionally defective because of failure to provide adequate notice of the hearings. No notice was given to Gerald's parents when he was taken into custody on Monday, June 8. On that night, when Mrs. Gault went to the Detention Home, she was orally informed that there would be a hearing the next afternoon and was told the reason why Gerald was in custody. The only written notice Gerald's parents received at any time was a note on plain paper from Officer Flagg delivered on Thursday or Friday, June 11 or 12, to the effect that the judge had set Monday, June 15, "for further hearings on Gerald's delinquency."

A "petition" was filed with the court on June 9 by Officer Flagg, reciting only that he was informed and believed that "said minor is a delinquent minor and that it is necessary that some order be made by the Honorable Court for said minor's welfare." The applicable Arizona statute provides for a petition to be filed in Juvenile Court, alleging in general terms that the child is "neglected, dependent, or delinquent." The statute explicitly states that such a general allegation is sufficient, "without alleging the facts." There is no requirement that the petition be served and it was not served upon, given, or shown to Gerald or his parents.

The Supreme Court of Arizona rejected appellants' claim that due process was denied because of inadequate notice. It stated that "Mrs. Gault knew the exact nature of the charge against Gerald from the day he was taken to the detention home." The court also pointed out that the Gaults appeared at the two hearings "without objection." The court held that because "the policy of the juvenile law is to hide youthful errors from the full gaze of the public and bury them in the graveyard of the forgotten past," advance notice of the specific charges or basis for taking the juvenile into custody and for the hearing is not necessary. It held that the appropriate rule is that "the infant and his parent or guardian will receive a petition only reciting a conclusion of delinquency. But no later than the initial hearing by the judge, they must be advised of the facts involved in the case. If the charges are denied they must be given a reasonable period of time to prepare."

We cannot agree with the court's conclusion that adequate notice was given in this case. Notice, to comply with due process requirements, must be given sufficiently in advance of scheduled court proceedings so that reasonable opportunity to prepare will be afforded, and it must "set forth the alleged misconduct with particularity." It is obvious, as we have discussed above, that no purpose of shielding the child from the public stigma of knowledge of his having been taken into custody and scheduled for hearing is served by the procedure approved by the court below. The "initial hearing" in the present case was a hearing on the merits. Notice at that time is not timely; and even if there were a conceivable purpose served by the deferral proposed by the court below, it would have to yield to the requirements that the child and his parents or guardian be notified in writing, of the specific charge or factual allegations to be considered at the hearing, and that such written notice be given at the earliest practicable time, and in any event sufficiently in advance of the hearing to permit preparation. Due process of law requires notice of the sort we have described—that is, notice which would be deemed constitutionally adequate in a civil or criminal proceeding. It does not allow a hearing to be held in which a youth's freedom and his parents' right to his custody are at stake without giving them timely notice, in advance of the hearing, of the specific issues that they must meet. Nor, in the circumstances of this case, can it reasonably be said that the requirement of notice was waived.

IV.

Right to Counsel.

Appellants charge that the Juvenile Court proceedings were fatally defective because the court did not advise Gerald or his parents of their right to counsel, and proceeded with the hearing, the adjudication of delinquency and the order of commitment in the absence of counsel for the child and his parents or an express waiver of the right thereto. The Supreme Court of Arizona pointed out that "there is disagreement [among the various jurisdictions] as to whether the court must advise the infant that he has a right to counsel." It noted its own decision in *State Dept. of Public Welfare* v. *Barlow*, 80 Ariz. 249, 296 P. 2d 298 (1956), to the effect that *the parents* of an infant in a juvenile proceeding cannot be denied representation by counsel of their choosing." (Emphasis added.) It referred to a provision of the Juvenile Code which it characterized as requiring "that the probation officer shall look after the interests of neglected, delinquent and dependent children," including representing their interests in court. The court argued that "The parent and the probation officer may be relied upon to protect the infant's interests." Accordingly it rejected the proposition that "due process requires that an infant have a right to counsel." It said that

juvenile courts have the discretion, but not the duty to allow such representation; it referred specifically to the situation in which the Juvenile Court discerns conflict between the child and his parents as an instance in which this discretion might be exercised. We do not agree. Probation officers, in the Arizona scheme, are also arresting officers. They initiate proceedings and file petitions which they verify, as here, alleging the delinquency of the child; and they testify, as here, against the child. And here the probation officer was also superintendent of the Detention Home. The probation officer cannot act as counsel for the child. His role in the adjudicatory hearing, by statute and in fact, is as arresting officer and witness against the child. Nor can the judge represent the child. There is no material difference in this respect between adult and juvenile proceedings of the sort here involved. In adult proceedings, this contention has been foreclosed by decisions of this Court. A proceeding where the issue is whether the child will be found to be "delinquent" and subjected to the loss of his liberty for years is comparable in seriousness to a felony prosecution. The juvenile needs the assistance of counsel to cope with problems of law, to make skilled inquiry into the facts, to insist upon regularity of the proceedings, and to ascertain whether he has a defense and to prepare and submit it. The child "requires the guiding hand of counsel at every step in the proceedings against him." Just as in *Kent* v. *United States, supra*, at 561-562, we indicated our agreement with the United States Court of Appeals for the District of Columbia Circuit that the assistance of counsel is essential for purposes of waiver proceedings, so we hold now that it is equally essential for the determination of delinquency, carrying with it the awesome prospect of incarceration in a state institution until the juvenile reaches the age of 21.

During the last decade, court decisions, experts, and legislatures have demonstrated increasing recognition of this view. In at least one-third of the States, statutes now provide for the right of representation by retained counsel in juvenile delinquency proceedings, notice of the right, or assignment of counsel, or a combination of these. In other States, court rules have similar provisions.

The Presidents Crime Commission has recently recommended that in order to assure "procedural justice for the child," it is necessary that "Counsel . . . be appointed as a matter of course wherever coercive action is a possibility, without requiring any affirmative choice by child or parent." As stated by the authoritative "Standards for Juvenile and Family Courts," published by the Children's Bureau of the United States Department of Health, Education, and Welfare:

"As a component part of a fair hearing required by due process guaranteed under the 14th Amendment, notice of the right to counsel should be required at all hearings and counsel provided upon request when the family is financially unable to employ counsel." Standards, at p. 57.

This statement was "reviewed" by the National Council of Juvenile Court Judges at its 1965 Convention and they "found no fault" with it. The New York Family Court Act contains the following statement:

"This act declares that minors have a right to the assistance of counsel of their own choosing or of law guardians in neglect proceedings under article three and in proceedings to determine juvenile delinquency and whether a person is in need of supervision under article seven.

This declaration is based on a finding that counsel is often indispensable to a practical realization of due process of law and may be helpful in making reasoned determinations of fact and proper orders of disposition."

The Act provides that "At the commencement of any hearing" under the delinquency article of the statute, the juvenile and his parent shall be advised of the juvenile's "right to be represented by counsel chosen by him or his parent. . .or by a law guardian assigned by the court . . . ." The California Act (1961) also requires appointment of counsel.

We conclude that the Due Process Clause of the Fourteenth Amendment requires that in respect of proceedings to determine delinquency which may result in commitment to an institution in which the juvenile's freedom is curtailed, the child and his parent must be notified of the child's right to be represented by counsel retained by them, or if they are unable to afford counsel, that counsel will be appointed to represent the child.

At the habeas corpus proceeding, Mrs. Gault testified that she knew that she could have appeared with counsel at the juvenile hearing. This knowledge is not a waiver of the right to counsel which she and her juvenile son had, as we have defined it. They had a right expressly to be advised that they might retain counsel and to be confronted with the need for specific consideration of whether they did or did not choose to waive the right. If they were unable to afford to employ counsel, they were entitled in view of the seriousness of the charge and the potential commitment, to appointed counsel, unless they chose waiver. Mrs. Gault's knowledge that she could employ counsel is not an "intentional relinquishment or abandonment of a fully known right.

V.

Confrontation, Self-Incrimination, Cross-Examination.

Appellants urge that the writ of habeas corpus should have been granted because of the denial of the rights of confrontation and cross-examination in the Juvenile Court hearings, and because the privilege against self-incrimination was not observed. The Juvenile Court Judge testified at the habeas corpus hearing that he had proceeded on the basis of Gerald's admissions at the two hearings. Appellants attack this on the ground that the admissions were obtained in disregard of the privilege against self-incrimination. If the confession is disregarded, appellants argue that the delinquency conclusion, since it was fundamentally based on a finding that Gerald had made lewd remarks during the phone call to Mrs. Cook, is fatally defective for failure to accord the rights of confrontation and cross-examination which the Due Process Clause of the Fourteenth Amendment of the Federal Constitution guarantees in state proceedings generally.

Our first question, then, is whether Gerald's admission was improperly obtained and relied on as the basis of decision, in conflict with the Federal Constitution. For this purpose, it is necessary briefly to recall the relevant facts.

Mrs. Cook, the complainant, and the recipient of the alleged telephone call, was not called as a witness. Gerald's mother asked the Juvenile Court Judge why Mrs. Cook was not present and the judge replied that "she didn't have to be present." So far as appears, Mrs. Cook was spoken to only once, by Officer Flagg, and this was by telephone. The judge did not speak with her on any occasion. Gerald had been questioned by the probation officer after having been taken into custody. The exact circumstances of this questioning do not appear but any admissions Gerald may have made at this time do not appear in the record. Gerald was also questioned by the Juvenile Court Judge at each of the two hearings. The judge testified in the habeas corpus proceeding that Gerald admitted making "some of the lewd statements . . . [but not] any of the more serious lewd statements." There was conflict and uncertainty among the witnesses at the habeas corpus proceeding—the Juvenile Court Judge, Mr. and Mrs. Gault, and the probation officer— as to what Gerald did or did not admit.

We shall assume that Gerald made admissions of the sort described by the Juvenile Court Judge, as quoted above. Neither Gerald nor his parents was advised that he did not have to testify or make a statement, or that an incriminating statement might result in his commitment as a "delinquent."

The Arizona Supreme Court rejected appellant's contention that Gerald had a right to be advised that he need not incriminate himself. It said: "We think the necessary flexibility for individualized treatment will be enhanced by a rule which does not require the judge to advise the infant of a privilege against self-incrimination."

In reviewing this conclusion of Arizona's Supreme Court, we emphasize again that we are here concerned only with proceedings to determine whether a minor is a "delinquent" and which may result in commitment to a state institution. Specifically, the question is whether, in such a proceeding, an admission by the juvenile may be used against him in the absence of clear and unequivocal evidence that the admission was made with knowledge that he was not obliged to speak and would not be penalized for remaining silent. In light of *Miranda* v. *Arizona*, 384 U.S. 436 (1966), we must also consider whether, if the privilege against self-incrimination is available, it can effectively be waived unless counsel is present or the right to counsel has been waived.

It has long been recognized that the eliciting and use of confessions or admissions require careful scrutiny. Dean Wigmore states:

"The ground of distrust of confessions made in certain situations is, in a rough and indefinite way, judicial experience. There has been no careful collection of statistics of untrue confessions, nor has any great number of instances been even loosely reported ... but enough have been verified to fortify the conclusion, based on ordinary observation of human conduct, that under certain stresses a person, especially one of defective mentality or peculiar temperament, may falsely acknowledge guilt. This possibility arises wherever the innocent person is placed in such a situation that the untrue acknowledgement of guilt is at the time the more promising of two alternatives between which he is obliged to choose; that is, he chooses any risk that may be in falsely acknowledging guilt, in preference to some worse alternative associated with silence.

"The principle, then, upon which a confession may be excluded is that it is, under certain conditions, *testimonially untrustworthy* .... [T]he essential feature is that the principle of exclusion is a testimonial one, analogous to the other principles which exclude narrations as untrustworthy...."

This Court has emphasized that admissions and confessions of juveniles require special caution. In *Haley* v. *Ohio, supra*, where this Court reversed the conviction of a 15-year-old boy for murder, Mr. Justice Douglas said:

"What transpired would make us pause for careful inquiry if a mature man were involved. And when, as here, a mere child—an easy victim of the law—is before us, special care in scrutinizing the record must be used. Age 15 is a tender and difficult age for a boy of any race. He cannot be judged by the more exacting standards of maturity. That which would leave a man cold and unimpressed can overawe and overwhelm a lad in his early teens. This is the period of great instability which the crisis of adolescence produces. A 15-year-old lad, questioned through the dead of night by relays of police, is a ready victim of the inquisition. Mature men possibly might stand the ordeal from midnight to 5 a.m. But we cannot believe that a lad of tender years is a match for the police in such a contest. He needs counsel and support if he is not to become the victim first of fear, then of panic. He needs someone on whom to lean lest the overpowering presence of the law, as he knows it, crush him. No friend stood at the side of this 15-year-old boy as the police, working in relays, questioned him hour after hour, from midnight until dawn. No lawyer stood guard to make sure that the police went so far and no farther, to see to it that they stopped short of the point where he became the victim of co-ercion. No counsel or friend was called during the critical hours of questioning."

In *Haley*, as we have discussed, the boy was convicted in adult court, and not a juvenile court. In notable decisions, the New York Court of Appeals and the Supreme Court of New Jersey have recently considered decisions of juvenile courts in which boys have been adjudged "delinquent" on the basis of confessions obtained in circumstances comparable to those in *Haley*. In both instances, the State contended before its highest tribunal that constitutional requirements governing inculpatory statements applicable in adult courts do not apply to juvenile proceedings. In each case, the State's contention was rejected, and the juvenile court's determination of delinquency was set aside on the grounds of inadmissibility of the confession. *In the Matters of Gregory W. and Gerald S.*, 19 N.Y. 2d 55, – N.E. 2d – (1966) (opinion by Keating, J.), and *In the Interests of Carlo and Stasilowicz*, 48 N.J. 224, 225 A. 2d 110 (1966) (opinion by Proctor, J.).

The privilege against self-incrimination is, of course, related to the question of the safeguards necessary to assure that admissions or confessions are reasonably trustworthy, that they are not the mere fruits of fear or coercion, but are reliable expressions of the truth. The roots of the privilege are, however, far deeper. They tap the basic stream of religious and political principle because the privilege reflects the limits of the individual's attornment to the state and—in a philosophical sense—insists upon the equality of the individual and the State. In other words, the privilege has a broader and deeper thrust than the rule which prevents the use of confessions which are the product of coercion because coercion is thought to carry with it the danger of unreliability. One of its purposes is to prevent the State, whether by force or by psychological domination, from overcoming the mind and will of the person under investigation and depriving him of the freedom to decide whether to assist the State in securing his conviction.

It would indeed be surprising if the privilege against self-incrimination were available to hardened criminals but not to children. The language of the Fifth Amendment, applicable to the States by operation of the Fourteenth Amendment, is unequivocal and without exception. And the scope of the privilege is comprehensive. As Mr. Justice White, concurring, stated in *Murphy* v. *Waterfront Commission*, 378, U.S. 52 (1964), at 94:

"The privilege can be claimed in *any proceeding*, be it criminal or civil, administrative or judicial, investigatory or adjudicatory . . . it protects *any disclosures* which the witness may reasonably apprehend *could be used in a criminal prosecution or which could lead to other evidence that might be so used.*" (Emphasis supplied.)

With respect to juveniles, both common observation and expert opinion emphasize that the "distrust of confessions made in certain situations" to which Dean Wigmore referred in the passage quoted above is imperative in the case of children from an early age through adolescence. In New York, for example, the recently enacted Family Court Act provides that the juvenile and his parents must be advised at the start of the hearing of his right to remain silent. The New York statute also provides that the police must attempt to communicate with the juvenile's parents before questioning him, and that a confession may not be obtained from a child prior to notifying his parents or relatives and releasing the child either to them or to the Family Court. In *In the Matters of Gregory W. and Gerald S.*, referred to above, the New York Court of Appeals held that the privilege against self-incrimination applies in juvenile delinquency cases and requires the exclusion of involuntary confessions, and that *People* v. *Lewis*, 260 N.Y. 171 (1932), holding the contrary, had been specifically overruled by statute.

The authoritative "Standards for Juvenile and Family Courts" concludes that, "Whether or not transfer to the criminal court is a possibility, certain procedures should always be followed. Before being interviewed [by the police] the child and his parents should be informed of his right to have legal counsel present and to refuse to answer questions or be fingerprinted if he should so decide."

Against the application to juveniles of the right to silence, it is argued that juvenile proceedings are "civil" and not "criminal," and therefore the privilege should not apply. It is true that the statement of the privilege in the Fifth Amendment, which is applicable to the States by reason of the Fourteenth Amendment, is that no person "shall be compelled in any *criminal case* to be a witness against himself." However, it is also clear that the availability of the privilege does not turn upon the type of proceeding in which its protection is invoked, but upon the nature of the statement or admission and the exposure which it invites. The privilege may, for example, be claimed in a civil or administrative proceeding if the statement is or may be inculpatory.

It would be entirely unrealistic to carve out of the Fifth Amendment all statements by juveniles on the ground that these cannot lead to "criminal" involvement. In the first place, juvenile proceedings to determine "delinquency," which may lead to commitment to a state institution, must be regarded as "criminal" for purposes of the privilege against self-incrimination. To hold otherwise would be to disregard substance because of the feeble enticement of the "civil" label-of-convenience which has been attached to juvenile proceedings. Indeed, in over half of the States, there is not even assurance that the juvenile will be kept in separate institutions, apart from adult "criminals." In those States juveniles may be placed in or transferred to adult penal institutions after having been found "delinquent" by a juvenile court. For this purpose, at least, commitment is a deprivation of liberty. It is incarceration against one's will, whether it is

called "criminal" or "civil." And our Constitution guarantees that no person shall be "compelled" to be a witness against himself when he is threatened with deprivation of his liberty—a command which this Court has broadly applied and generously implemented in accordance with the teaching of the history of the privilege and its great office in mankind's battle for freedom.

In addition, apart from the equivalence for this purpose of exposure to commitment as a juvenile delinquent and exposure to imprisonment as an adult offender, the fact of the matter is that there is little or no assurance in Arizona, as in most if not all of the States, that a juvenile apprehended and interrogated by the police or even by the juvenile court itself will remain outside the reach of adult courts as a consequence of the offense for which he has been taken into custody. In Arizona, as in other States, provision is made for juvenile courts to relinquish or waive jurisdiction to the ordinary criminal courts. In the present case, when Gerald Gault was interrogated concerning violation of a section of the Arizona Criminal Code, it could not be certain that the Juvenile Court Judge would decide to "suspend" criminal prosecution in court for adults by proceeding to an adjudication in Juvenile Court.

It is also urged, as the Supreme Court of Arizona here asserted, that the juvenile and presumably his parents should not be adivsed of the juvenile's right to silence because confession is good for the child as the commencement of the assumed therapy of the juvenile court process, and he should be encouraged to assume an attitude of trust and confidence toward the officials of the juvenile process. This proposition has been subjected to widespread challenge on the basis of current reappraisals of the rhetoric and realities of the handling of juvenile offenders.

In fact, evidence is accumulating that confessions by juveniles do not aid in "individualized treatment," as the court below put it, and that compelling the child to answer questions, without warning or advice as to his right to remain silent, does not serve this or any other good purpose. In light of the observations of Wheeler and Cottrell, and others, it seems probable that where children are induced to confess by "paternal" urgings on the part of officials and the confession is then followed by disciplinary action, the child's reaction is likely to be hostile and adverse—the child may well feel that he has been led or tricked into confession and that despite his confession, he is being punished.

Further, authoritative opinion has cast formidable doubt upon the reliability and trustworthiness of "confessions" by children. This Court's observations in *Haley* v. *United States,* are set forth above. The recent decision of the New York Court of Appeals referred to above, *In the Matters of Gregory W. and Gerald S.,* deals with a dramatic and, it is to be hoped, extreme example. Two 12-year-old Negro boys were taken into custody for the brutal assault and rape of two aged domestics, one of whom died as the result of the attack. One of the boys was schizophrenic and had been locked in the security ward of a mental institution at the time of the attacks. By a process that may best be described as bizarre, his confession was obtained by the police. A psychiatrist testified that the boy would admit "whatever he thought was expected so that he could get out of the immediate situation." The other 12-year-old also confessed." Both confessions were in specific detail, albeit they contained various inconsistencies. The Court of Appeals, in an opinion by Keating, J.,

concluded that the confessions were products of the will of the police instead of the boys. The confessions were therefore held involuntary and the order of the Appellate Division affirming the order of the Family Court adjudging the defendants to be juvenile delinquents was reversed.

A similar and equally instructive case has recently been decided by the Supreme Court of New Jersey. *In the Interests of Carlo and Stasilowicz, supra.* The body of a 10-year-old girl was found. She had been strangled. Neighborhood boys who knew the girl were questioned. The two appellants, aged 13 and 15, confessed to the police, with vivid detail and some inconsistencies. At the Juvenile Court hearing, both denied any complicity in the killing. They testified that their confessions were the product of fear and fatigue due to extensive police grilling. The Juvenile Court Judge found that the confessions were voluntary and admissible. On appeal, in an extensive opinion by Proctor, J., the Supreme Court of New Jersey reversed. It rejected the State's argument that the constitutional safeguard of voluntariness governing the use of confessions does not apply in proceedings before the juvenile court. It pointed out that under New Jersey court rules, juveniles under the age of 16 accused of committing a homicide are tried in a proceeding which "has all of the appurtenances of a criminal trial," including participation by the county prosecutor, and requirements that the juvenile be provided with counsel, that a stenographic record be made, etc. It also pointed out that under New Jersey law, the confinement of the boys after reaching age 21 could be extended until they had served the maximum sentence which could have been imposed on an adult for such a homicide, here found to be second degree murder carrying up to 30 years' imprisonment. The court concluded that the confessions were involuntary, stressing that the boys, contrary to statute, were placed in the police station and there interrogated; that the parents of both boys were not allowed to see them while they were being interrogated; that inconsistencies appeared among the various statements of the boys and with the objective evidence of the crime; and that there were protracted periods of questioning. The court noted the State's contention that both boys were advised of their constitutional rights before they made their statements, but it held that this should not be given "significant weight in our determination of voluntariness." Accordingly, the judgment of the Juvenile Court was reversed.

In a recent case before the Juvenile Court of the District of Columbia, Judge Ketcham rejected the proffer of evidence as to oral statements made at police headquarters by four juveniles who had been taken into custody for alleged involvement in an assault and attempted robbery. *In the Matter of Four Youths*, Nos. 28–776–J, 28–778–J, 28–783–J, 28–859–J, Juvenile Court of the District of Columbia, April 7, 1961. The court explicitly stated that it did not rest its decision on a showing that the statements were involuntary, but because they were untrustworthy. Judge Ketcham said:

"Simply stated, the Court's decision in this case rests upon the considered opinion—after nearly four busy years on the Juvenile Court bench during which the testimony of thousands of such juveniles has been heard—that the statements of adolescents under 18 years of age who are arrested and charged with violations of law are frequently untrustworthy and often distort the truth."

We conclude that the constitutional privilege against self-incrimination is applicable in the case of juveniles as it is with respect to adults. We appreciate that special problems may arise with respect to waiver of the privilege by or on behalf of children, and that there may well be some differences in technique—but not in principle—depending upon the age of the child and the presence and competence of parents. The participation of counsel will, of course, assist the police, juvenile courts and appellate tribunals in administering the privilege. If counsel is not present for some permissible reason when an admission is obtained, the greatest care must be taken to assure that the admission was voluntary, in the sense not only that it has not been coerced or suggested, but also that it is not the product of ignorance of rights or of adolescent fantasy, fright or despair.

The "confession" of Gerald Gault was first obtained by Officer Flagg, out of the presence of Gerald's parents, without counsel and without advising him of his right to silence, as far as appears. The judgment of the Juvenile Court was stated by the judge to be based on Gerald's admission in court. Neither "admission" was reduced to writing, and, to say the least, the process by which the "admissions" were obtained and received must be characterized as lacking the certainty and order which are required of proceedings of such formidable consequences. Apart from the "admission," there was nothing upon which a judgment or finding might be based. There was no sworn testimony. Mrs. Cook, the complainant, was not present. The Arizona Supreme Court held that "sworn testimony must be required of all witnesses including police officers, probation officers and others who are part of or officially related to the juvenile court structure." We hold that this is not enough. No reason is suggested or appears for a different rule in respect of sworn testimony in juvenile courts than in adult tribunals. Absent a valid confession adequate to support the determination of the Juvenile Court, confrontation and sworn testimony by witnesses available for cross-examination were essential for a finding of "delinquency" and an order committing Gerald to a state institution for a maximum of six years.

The recommendations in the Children's Bureau's "Standards for Juvenile and Family Courts" are in general accord with our conclusions. They state that testimony should be under oath and that only competent material and relevant evidence under rules applicable to civil cases should be admitted in evidence. The New York Family Court Act contains a similar provision.

As we said in *Kent* v. *United States*, 383, U.S. 541, 554 (1966), with respect to waiver proceedings, "there is no place in our system of law for reaching a result of such tremendous consequences without ceremony. . . ." We now hold that, absent a valid confession, a determination of delinquency and an order of commitment to a state institution cannot be sustained in the absence of sworn testimony subjected to the opportunity for cross-examination in accordance with our law and constitutional requirements.

VI.

Appellate Review and Transcript of Proceedings

Appellants urge that the Arizona statute is unconstitutional under the Due Process Clause because, as construed by its Supreme Court, "there is no right of appeal from a juvenile court order. . . ." The court held that there is no right to a transcript because there is no right to appeal and because the proceedings are confidential and any record must be destroyed after a prescribed period of time. Whether a transcript or other recording is made, it held, is a matter for the discretion of the juvenile court.

This Court has not held that a State is required by the Federal Constitution "to provide appellate courts or a right to appellate review at all." In view of the fact that we must reverse the Supreme Court of Arizona's affirmance of the dismissal of the writ of habeas corpus for other reasons, we need not rule on this question in the present case or upon the failure to provide a transcript or recording of the hearings—or, indeed, the failure of the juvenile court judge to state the grounds for his conclusion. Cf. *Kent* v. *United States, supra*, at 561, where we said, in the context of a decision of the juvenile court waiving jurisdiction to the adult court, which by local law, was applicable: ". . . it is incumbent upon the Juvenile Court to accompany its waiver order with a statement of the reasons or considerations therefor." As the present case illustrates, the consequences of failure to provide an appeal, to record the proceedings, or to make findings or state the grounds for the juvenile court's conclusion may be to throw a burden upon the machinery for habeas corpus, to saddle the reviewing process with the burden of attempting to reconstruct a record, and to impose upon the juvenile judge the unseemly duty of testifying under cross-examination as to the events that transpired in the hearings before him.

For the reasons stated, the judgment of the Supreme Court of Arizona is reversed and the cause remanded for further proceedings not inconsistent with this opinion.

It is so ordered.

Mr. Justice Black, concurring.

The juvenile court laws of Arizona and other States, as the Court points out, are the result of plans promoted by humane and forward-looking people to provide a system of courts, procedures, and sanctions deemed to be less harmful and more lenient to children than to adults. For this reason such state laws generally provide less formal and less public methods for the trial of children. In line with this policy, both courts and legislators have shrunk back from labeling these laws as "criminal" and have preferred to call them "civil." This, in part, was to prevent the full application to juvenile court cases of the Bill of Rights safeguards, including notice as provided in the Sixth Amendment, the right to counsel guaranteed by the Sixth, the right against self-incrimination guaranteed by the Fifth, and the right to confrontation guaranteed by the Sixth. The Court here holds, however, that these four Bill of Rights safeguards apply to protect a juvenile accused in a juvenile court on a charge under which he can be imprisoned for a term of years. This holding strikes a well-nigh fatal blow to much that is unique about the juvenile courts in the Nation. For this reason, there is much to be said for the position of my Brother Stewart that we should not pass on all these issues until they are more squarely presented. But since the majority of the Court chooses to decide all of these questions, in this situation I must either do the same or leave my views unexpressed on the important issues determined. In these circumstances, I feel impelled to express my views.

The juvenile court planners envisaged a system that would practically immunize juveniles from "punishment" for "crimes" in an effort to save them from youthful indiscretions and stigmas due to criminal charges or convictions. I agree with the Court, however, that this exalted ideal has failed of achievement since the beginning of the system. Indeed, the state laws from the first one on contained provisions, written in emphatic terms, for arresting and charging juveniles with violations of state criminal laws, as well as for taking juveniles by force of law away from their parents and turning them over to different individuals or groups or for confinement within some state school or institution for a number of years. The latter occurred in this case. Young Gault was arrested and detained on a charge of violating an Arizona penal law by using vile and offensive language to a lady on the telephone. If an adult, he could only have been fined or imprisoned for two months for his conduct. As a juvenile, however, he was put through a more or less secret, informal hearing by the court, after which he was ordered, or more realistically "sentenced," to confinement in Arizona's Industrial School until he reaches 21 years of age. Thus, in a juvenile system designed to lighten or avoid punishment for criminality, he was ordered by the State to six years' confinement in what is in all but name a penitentiary or jail.

Where a person, infant or adult, can be seized by the State, charged, and convicted for violating a state criminal law, and then ordered by the State to be confined for six years, I think the Constitution requires that he be tried in accordance with all the guarantees of all the Bill of Rights made applicable to the States by the Fourteenth Amendment. Undoubtedly this would be true of an adult defendant, and it would be a plain denial of equal protection of the law—an invidious discrimination—to hold that others subject to heavier punishments could, because they are children, be denied these same constitutional safeguards. I consequently agree with the Court that the Arizona law as applied here denied to the parents and their son the right of notice, right to counsel, right against self-incrimination, and right to confront the witnesses against young Gault. Appellants are entitled to these rights, not because "fairness, impartiality and orderliness—in short, the essentials of due process" require them and not because they are "the procedural rules which have been fashioned from the generality of due process," but because they are specifically and unequivocally granted by provisions of the Fifth and Sixth Amendments which the Fourteenth Amendment makes applicable to the States.

A few words should be added because of the opinion of my Brother Harlan who rests his concurrence and dissent on the Due Process Clause alone. He reads that clause alone as allowing this Court "to determine what forms of procedural protection are necessary to guarantee the fundamental fairness of juvenile proceedings" "in a fashion consistent with the 'traditions and conscience of our people.'" Cf. *Rochin* v. *California*, 342 U.S. 165. He believes that the Due Process Clause gives this Court the power, upon weighing a "compelling public interest," to impose on the States only those specific constitutional rights which the Court deems "imperative" and "necessary" to comport with the Court's notions of "fundamental fairness."

I cannot subscribe to any such interpretation of the Due Process Clause. Nothing in its words or its history permits it, and "fair distillations of relevant judicial history" are no substitute for the words and history of the clause itself. The phrase "due process of law" has through the years evolved as the successor in purpose and meaning to the words "law of the land" in Magna Charta which more plainly intended to call for a trial according to the existing law of the land in effect at the time an alleged offense had been committed. That provision in Magna Charta was designed to prevent defendants from being tried according to criminal laws or proclamations specifically promulgated to fit particular cases or to attach new consequences to old conduct. Nothing done since Magna Charta can be pointed to as intimating that the Due Process Clause gives courts power to fashion laws in order to meet new conditions, to fit the "decencies" of changed conditions, or to keep their consciences from being shocked by legislation, state or federal.

And, of course, the existence of such awesome judicial power cannot be buttressed or created by relying on the word "procedural." Whether labeled as "procedural" or "substantive," the Bill of Rights safeguards, far from being mere "tools with which" other unspecified "rights could be fully vindicated," are the very vitals of a sound constitutional legal system designed to protect and safeguard the most cherished liberties of a free people. These safeguards were written into our Constitution not by judges but by Constitution makers. Freedom in this Nation will be far less secure the very moment that it is decided that judges can determine which of these safeguards "should" or "should not be imposed" according to their notions of what constitutional provisions are consistent with the "traditions and conscience of our people." Judges with such power, even though they profess to "proceed with restraint," will be above the Constitution, with power to write it, not merely to interpret it, which I believe to be the only power constitutionally committed to judges.

There is one ominous sentence, if not more, in my Brother Harlan's opinion which bodes ill, in my judgment, both for legislative programs and constitutional commands. Speaking of procedural safeguards in the Bill of Rights, he says:

"These factors in combination suggest that legislatures may properly expect only a cautious deference for their procedural judgments but that conversely, courts must exercise their special responsibility for procedural guarantees with care to permit ample scope for achieving the purposes of legislative programs . . . . [T]he court should necessarily proceed with restraint."

It is to be noted here that this case concerns Bill of Rights Amendments; that the "procedure" power my Brother Harlan claims for the Court here relates solely to Bill of Rights safeguards; and that he is here claiming for the Court a supreme power to fashion new Bill of Rights safeguards according to the Court's notions of what fits tradition and conscience. I do not believe that the Constitution vests any such power in judges, either in the Due Process Clause or anywhere else. Consequently, I do not vote to invalidate this Arizona law on the ground that it is "unfair" but solely on the ground that it violates the Fifth and Sixth Amendments made obligatory on the States by the Fourteenth Amendment. Cf. *Pointer* v. *Texas,* 380 U.S. 400, 412 (Goldberg, J., concurring). It is enough for me that the Arizona law as here applied collides head-on with the Fifth and Sixth Amendments in the four respects mentioned. The only relevance to me of the Due Process Clause is that it would, of course, violate due process or the "law of the land" to enforce a law that collides with the Bill of Rights.

Mr. Justice White, concurring.

I join the Court's opinion except for Part V. I also agree that the privilege against compelled self-incrimination applies at the adjudicatory stage of juvenile court proceedings. I do not, however, find an adequate basis in the record for determining whether that privilege was violated in this case. The Fifth Amendment protects a person from being "compelled" in any criminal proceeding to be a witness against himself. Compulsion is essential to a violation. It may be that when a judge, armed with the authority he has or which people think he has, asks questions of a party or a witness in an adjudicatory hearing, that person, especially if a minor, would feel compelled to answer, absent a warning to the contrary or similar information from some other source. The difficulty is that the record made at the habeas corpus hearing, which is the only information we have concerning the proceedings in the juvenile court, does not directly inform us whether petitioner or his parents were told of petitioner's right to remain silent; nor does it reveal whether the parties were aware of the privilege from some other source, just as they were already aware that they had the right to have the help of counsel and to have witnesses on their behalf. The petition for habeas corpus did not raise the Fifth Amendment issue nor did any of the witnesses focus on it.

I have previously recorded my views with respect to what I have deemed unsound applications of the Fifth Amendment. See, for example, *Miranda* v. *Arizona,* 384 U.S. 436, 526, and *Malloy* v. *Hogan,* 378 U.S. 1, 33, dissenting opinions. These views, of course, have not prevailed. But I do hope that the Court will proceed with some care in extending the privilege, with all its vigor, to proceedings in juvenile court, particularly nonadjudicatory stages of those proceedings.

In any event, I would not reach the Fifth Amendment issue here. I think the Court is clearly ill-advised to review this case on the basis of *Miranda* v. *Arizona,* since the adjudication of delinquency took place in 1964, long before the *Miranda* decision. See *Johnson* v. *New Jersey* 384 U.S. 719. Under these circumstances, this case is a poor vehicle for resolving a difficult problem. Moreover, no prejudice to appellants is at stake in this regard. The judgment below must be reversed on other grounds and in the event further proceedings are to be had, petitioner will have counsel available to advise him.

For somewhat similar reasons, I would not reach the questions of confrontation and cross-examination which are also dealt with in Part V of the opinion.

Mr. Justice Harlan, concurring in part and dissenting in part.

Each of the 50 States has created a system of juvenile or family courts, in which distinctive rules are employed and special consequences imposed. The jurisdiction of these courts commonly extends both to cases which the States have withdrawn from the ordinary processes of criminal justice, and to cases which involve acts that, if performed by an adult, would not be penalized as criminal. Such courts are denominated civil, not criminal, and are characteristically said not to administer criminal penalties. One consequence of these systems, at least as Arizona construes its own, is that certain of the rights guaranteed to criminal defendants by the Constitution are withheld from juveniles. This case brings before this Court for the first time the question of what limitations the Constitution places upon the operation of such tribunals. For reasons which follow, I have concluded that the Court has gone too far in some respects, and fallen short in others, in assessing the procedural requirements demanded by the Fourteenth Amendment.

I.

I must first acknowledge that I am unable to determine with any certainty by what standards the Court decides that Arizona's juvenile courts do not satisfy the obligations of due process. The Court's premise, itself the product of reasoning which is not described, is that the "constitutional and theoretical basis" of state systems of juvenile and family courts is "debatable"; it buttresses these doubts by marshaling a body of opinion which suggests that the accomplishments of these courts have often fallen short of expectations. The Court does not indicate at what points or for what purposes such views, held either by it or by other observers, might be pertinent to the present issues. Its failure to provide any discernible standard for the measurement of due process in relation to juvenile proceedings unfortunately might be understood to mean that the Court is concerned principally with the wisdom of having such courts at all.

If this is the source of the Court's dissatisfaction, I cannot share it. I should have supposed that the constitutionality of juvenile courts was beyond proper question under the standards now employed to assess the substantive validity of state legislation under the Due Process Clause of the Fourteenth Amendment. It can scarcely be doubted that it is within the State's competence to adopt measures reasonably calculated to meet more effectively the persistent problems of juvenile delinquency; as the opinion for the Court makes abundantly plain, these are among the most vexing and ominous of the concerns which now face communities throughout the country.

The proper issue here is, however, not whether the State may constitutionally treat juvenile offenders through a system of specialized courts, but whether the proceedings in Arizona's juvenile courts include procedural guarantees which satisfy the requirements of the Fourteenth Amendment. Among the first premises of our constitutional system is the obligation to conduct any proceeding in which an individual may be deprived of liberty or property in a fashion consistent with the "traditions and conscience of our people," *Snyder* v. *Massachusetts* 291 U.S. 97, 105. The importance of these procedural guarantees is doubly intensified here. First, many of the problems with which Arizona is concerned are among those traditionally confined to the processes of criminal justice; their disposition necessarily affects in the most direct and substantial manner the liberty of individual citizens. Quite obviously, systems of specialized penal justice might permit erosion, or even evasion, of the limitations placed by the Constitution upon state criminal proceedings. Second, we must recognize that the character and consequences of many juvenile court proceedings have in fact closely resembled those of ordinary criminal trials. Nothing before us suggests that juvenile courts were intended as a device to escape constitutional constraints, but I entirely agree with the Court that we are nonetheless obliged to examine with circumspection the procedural guarantees the State has provided.

The central issue here, and the principal one upon which I am divided from the Court, is the method by which the procedural requirements of due process should be measured. It must at the outset be emphasized that the protections necessary here cannot be determined by resort to any classification of juvenile proceedings either as criminal or as civil, whether made by the State or by this Court. Both formulae are simply too imprecise to permit reasoned analysis of these difficult constitutional issues. The Court should instead measure the requirements of due process by reference both to the problems which confront the State and to the actual character of the procedural system which the State has created. The Court has for such purposes chiefly examined three connected sources: first, the "settled usages and modes of proceeding," *Murray's Lessee* v. *Hoboken Land & Improvement Co.*, 18 How. 272, 277; second, the "fundamental principles of liberty and justice which lie at the base of all our civil and political institutions," *Hebert* v. *Louisiana,* 272 U.S. 312, 316; and third, the character and requirements of the circumstances presented in each situation. *FCC* v. *WJR,* 337 U.S. 265, 177; *Yakus* v. *United States,* 321 U.S. 414. See, further, my dissenting opinion in *Poe* v. *Ullman,* 367 U.S. 497, 522, and compare my opinion concurring in the result in *Pointer* v. *Texas,* 380 U.S. 400, 408. Each of these factors is relevant to the issues here, but it is the last which demands particular examination.

The Court has repeatedly emphasized that determination of the constitutionally required procedural safeguards in any situation requires recognition both of the "interests affected" and of the "circumstances involved." *FCC* v. *WJR, supra,* at 277. In particular, a "compelling public interest" must, under our cases, be taken fully into account in assessing the validity under the due process clauses of state or federal legislation and its application. See, *e.g., Yakus* v. *United States, supra,* at 442; *Bowles* v. *Willingham,* 321 U.S. 503, 520; *Miller* v. *Schoene,* 276 U.S. 273, 279. Such interests would never warrant arbitrariness or the diminution of any specifically assured constitutional right, *Home Bldg. & Loan Assn.* v. *Blaisdell,* 290 U.S. 398, 426, but they are an essential element of the context through which the legislation and proceedings under it must be read and evaluated.

No more evidence of the importance of the public interests at stake here is required than that furnished by the opinion of the Court; it indicates that "some 601,000 children under 18, or 2% of the total population of that age, came before juvenile courts" in 1965, and that "about one-fifth of all arrests for serious crimes" in 1965 were of juveniles. The

Court adds that the rate of juvenile crime is steadily rising. All this, as the Court suggests, indicates the importance of these due process issues, but it mirrors no less vividly that state authorities are confronted by formidable and immediate problems involving the most fundamental social values. The state legislatures have determined that the most hopeful solution for these problems is to be found in specialized courts, organized under their own rules and imposing distinctive consequences. The terms and limitations of these systems are not identical, nor are the procedural arrangements which they include, but the States are uniform in their insistence that the ordinary processes of criminal justice are inappropriate, and that relatively informal proceedings, dedicated to premises and purposes only imperfectly reflected in the criminal law, are instead necessary.

It is well settled that the Court must give the widest deference to legislative judgments that concern the character and urgency of the problems with which the State is confronted. Legislatures are, as this Court has often acknowledged, the "main guardian" of the public interest, and, within their constitutional competence, their understanding of that interest must be accepted as "well-nigh" conclusive. *Berman* v. *Parker*, 348 U.S. 26, 32. This principle does not, however, reach all the questions essential to the resolution of this case. The legislative judgments at issue here embrace assessments of the necessity and wisdom of procedural guarantees; these are questions which the Constitution has entrusted at least in part to courts, and upon which courts have been understood to possess particular competence. The fundamental issue here is, therefore, in what measure and fashion the Court must defer to legislative determinations which encompass constitu-

tional issues of procedural protection.

It suffices for present purposes to summarize the factors which I believe to be pertinent. It must first be emphasized that the deference given to legislators upon substantive issues must realistically extend in part to ancillary procedural questions. Procedure at once reflects and creates substantive rights, and every effort of courts since the beginnings of the common law to separate the two has proved essentially futile. The distinction between them is particularly inadequate here, where the legislature's substantive preferences directly and unavoidably require judgments about procedural issues. The procedural framework is here a principal element of the substantive legislative system; meaningful deference to the latter must include a portion of deference to the former. The substantive-procedural dichotomy is nonetheless, an indispensable tool of analysis, for it stems from fundamental limitations upon judicial authority under the Constitution. Its premise is ultimately that courts may not substitute for the judgments of legislators their own understanding of the public welfare, but must instead concern themselves with the validity under the Constitution of the methods which the legislature has selected. See, *e.g., McLean* v. *Arkansas,* 211 U.S. 539, 547; *Olsen* v. *Nebraska,* 313 U.S. 236, 246-247. The Constitution has in this manner created for courts and legislators areas of primary responsibility which are essentially congruent to their areas of special competence. Courts are thus obliged both by constitutional command and by their distinctive functions to bear particular responsibility for the measurement of procedural due process. These factors in combination suggest that legislatures may properly expect only a cautious deference for their procedural judgments, but that, conversely, courts must exercise their special responsibility for procedural guarantees with care to permit ample scope for achieving the purposes of legislative programs. Plainly, courts can exercise such care only if they have in each case first studied thoroughly the objectives and implementation of the program at stake; if, upon completion of those studies, the effect of extensive procedural restrictions upon valid legislative purposes cannot be assessed with reasonable certainty, the court should necessarily proceed with restraint.

The foregoing considerations, which I believe to be fair distillations of relevant judicial history, suggest three criteria by which the procedural requirements of due process should be measured here: first, no more restrictions should be imposed than are imperative to assure the proceedings' fundamental fairness; second, the restrictions which are imposed should be those which preserve, so far as possible, the essential elements of the State's purpose; and finally, restrictions should be chosen which will later permit the orderly selection of any additional protections which may ultimately prove necessary. In this way, the Court may guarantee the fundamental fairness of the proceeding, and yet permit the State to continue development of an effective response to the problems of juvenile crime.

II.

Measured by these criteria, only three procedural requirements should, in my opinion, now be deemed required of state juvenile courts by the Due Process Clause of the Fourteenth Amendment: first, timely notice must be provided to parents and children of the nature and terms of any juvenile court proceeding in which a determination affecting their rights or interests may be made; second, unequivocal and timely notice must be given that counsel may appear in any such proceeding in behalf of the child and its parents, and that in cases in which the child may be confined in an institution, counsel may, in circumstances of indigency, be appointed for them; and third, the court must maintain a written record, or its equivalent, adequate to permit effective review on appeal or in collateral proceedings. These requirements would guarantee to juveniles the tools with which their rights could be fully vindicated, and yet permit the States to pursue without unnecessary hindrance the purposes which they believe imperative in this field. Further, their imposition now would later permit more intelligent assessment of the necessity under the Fourteenth Amendment of additional requirements, by creating suitable records from which the character and deficiencies of juvenile proceedings could be accurately judged. I turn to consider each of these three requirements.

The Court has consistently made plain that adequate and timely notice is the fulcrum of due process, whatever the purposes of the proceeding. See, *e.g.*, *Roller* v. *Holly*, 176 U.S. 398, 409; *Coe* v. *Armour Fertilizer Works*, 237 U.S. 413, 424. Notice is ordinarily the prerequisite to effective assertion of any constitutional or other rights; without it, vindication of those rights must be essentially fortuitous. So fundamental a protection can neither be spared here nor left to the "favor or grace" of state authorities. *Central of Georgia Ry*, v. *Wright*, 207 U.S. 127, 138; *Coe* v. *Armour Fertilizer Works, supra*, at 425.

Provision of counsel and of a record, like adequate notice, would permit the juvenile to assert very much more effectively his rights and defenses, both in the juvenile proceedings and upon direct or collateral review. The Court has frequently emphasized their importance in proceedings in which an individual may be deprived of his liberty, see *Gideon* v. *Wainwright*, 372 U.S. 335, and *Griffin* v. *Illinois*, 351 U.S. 12; this reasoning must include with special force those who are commonly inexperienced and immature. See *Powell* v. *Alabama*, 287 U.S. 45. The facts of this case illustrate poignantly the difficulties of review without either an adequate record or the participation of counsel in the proceeding's initial stages. At the same time, these requirements should not cause any substantial modification in the character of juvenile court proceedings: counsel, although now present in only a small percentage of juvenile cases, have apparently already appeared without incident in virtually all juvenile courts; and the maintenance of a record should not appreciably alter the conduct of these proceedings.

The question remains whether certain additional requirements, among them the privilege against self-incrimination, confrontation, and cross-examination, must now, as the Court holds, also be imposed. I share in part the views expressed in my Brother White's concurring opinion, but believe that there are other, and more deep-seated reasons to defer, at least for the present, the imposition of such requirements.

Initially, I must vouchsafe that I cannot determine with certainty the reasoning by which the Court concludes that these further requirements are now imperative. The Court begins from the premise, to which it gives force at several points, that these courts need not satisfy "all of the requirements of a criminal trial." It therefore scarcely suffices to explain the selection of these particular procedural requirements for the Court to declare that juvenile court proceedings are essentially criminal, and thereupon to recall that these are requisites for a criminal trial. Nor does the Court's voucher of "authoritative opinion," which consists of four extraordinary juvenile cases, contribute materially to the solution of these issues. The Court has, even under its own premises, asked the wrong questions: the problem here is to determine what forms of procedural protection are necessary to guarantee the fundamental fairness of juvenile proceedings, and not which of the procedures now employed in criminal trials should be transplanted intact to proceedings in these specialized courts.

In my view, the Court should approach this question in terms of the criteria, described above, which emerge from the history of due process adjudication. Measured by them, there are compelling reasons at least to defer imposition of these additional requirements. First, quite unlike notice, counsel, and a record, these requirements might radically alter the character of juvenile court proceedings. The evidence from which the Court reasons that they would not is inconclusive, and other available evidence suggests that they very likely would. At the least, it is plain that these additional requirements would contribute materially to the creation in these proceedings of the atmosphere of an ordinary criminal trial, and would, even if they do no more, thereby largely frustrate a central purpose of these specialized courts. Further, these are restrictions intended to conform to the demands of an intensely adversary system of criminal justice; the broad purposes which they represent might be served in juvenile courts with equal effectiveness by procedural devices more consistent with the premises of proceedings in those courts. As the Court apparently acknowledges, the hazards of self-accusations, for example, might be avoided in juvenile proceedings without the imposition of all the requirements and limitations which surround the privilege against self-incrimination. The guarantee of adequate notice, counsel, and a record would create conditions in which suitable alternative procedures could be devised; but, unfortunately, the Court's haste to impose restrictions taken intact from criminal procedure may well seriously hamper the development of such alternatives. Surely this illustrates that prudence and the principles of the Fourteenth Amendment alike require that the Court should now impose no more procedural restrictions than are imperative to assure fundamental fairness, and that the States should instead be permitted additional opportunities to develop without unnecessary hindrance their systems of juvenile courts.

I find confirmation for these views in two ancillary considerations. First, it is clear that an uncertain, but very substantial number of the cases brought to juvenile courts involve children who are not in any sense guilty of criminal misconduct. Many of these children have simply the misfortune to be in some manner distressed; others have engaged in conduct, such as truancy, which is plainly not criminal. Efforts are now being made to develop effective, and entirely noncriminal, methods of treatment for these children. In such cases, the state authorities are in the most literal sense acting *in loco parentis*; they are, by any standard, concerned with the child's protection, and not with his punishment. I do not question that the methods employed in such cases must be consistent with the constitutional obligation to act in accordance with due process, but certainly the Fourteenth Amendment does not demand that they be constricted by the procedural guarantees devised for ordinary criminal prosecutions. Cf. *Minnesota ex. rel. Pearson* v. *Probate Court*, 309 U.S. 270. It must be remembered that the various classifications of juvenile court proceedings are, as the vagaries of the available statistics illustrate, often ar-

bitrary or ambiguous; it would therefore be imprudent, at the least, to build upon these classifications rigid systems of procedural requirements which would be applicable or not in accordance with the descriptive label given to the particular proceeding. It is better, it seems to me, to begin by now requiring the essential elements of fundamental fairness in juvenile courts, whatever the label given by the State to the proceeding; in this way the Court could avoid imposing unnecessarily rigid restrictions, and yet escape dependence upon classifications which may often prove to be illusory. Further, the provision of notice, counsel, and a record would permit orderly efforts to determine later whether more satisfactory classifications can be devised, and if they can, whether additional procedural requirements are necessary for them under the Fourteenth Amendment.

Second, it should not be forgotten that juvenile crime and juvenile courts are both now under earnest study throughout the country. I very much fear that this Court, by imposing these rigid procedural requirements, may inadvertently have served to discourage these efforts to find more satisfactory solutions for the problems of juvenile crime, and may thus now hamper enlightened development of the systems of juvenile courts. It is appropriate to recall that the Fourteenth Amendment does not compel the law to remain passive in the midst of change; to demand otherwise denies "every quality of the law but its age." *Hurtado* v. *California*, 110 U.S. 516, 529

III.

Finally, I turn to assess the validity of this juvenile court proceeding under the criteria discussed in this opinion. Measured by them, the judgment below must, in my opinion, fall. Gerald Gault and his parents were not provided adequate notice of the terms and purposes of the proceedings in which he was adjudged delinquent; they were not advised of their rights to be represented by counsel; and no record in any form was maintained of the proceedings. It follows, for the reasons given in this opinion, that Gerald Gault was deprived of his liberty without due process of law, and I therefore concur in the judgment of the Court.

Mr. Justice Stewart, dissenting.

The Court today uses an obscure Arizona case as a vehicle to impose upon thousands of juvenile courts throughout the Nation restrictions that the Constitution made applicable to adversary criminal trials. I believe the Court's decision is wholly unsound as a matter of constitutional law, and sadly unwise as a matter of judicial policy.

Juvenile proceedings are not criminal trials. They are not civil trials. They are simply not adversary proceedings. Whether treating with a delinquent child, a neglected child, a defective child, or a dependent child, a juvenile proceeding's whole purpose and mission is the very opposite of the mission and purpose of a prosecution in a criminal court. The object of the one is correction of a condition. The object of the other is conviction and punishment for a criminal act.

In the last 70 years many dedicated men and women have devoted their professional lives to the enlightened task of bringing us out of the dark world of Charles Dickens in meeting our responsibilities to the child in our society. The result has been the creation in this century of a system of juvenile and family courts in each of the 50 States. There can be no denying that in many areas the performance of these agencies has fallen disappointingly short of the hopes and dreams of the courageous pioneers who first conceived them. For a variety of reasons, the reality has sometimes not even approached the ideal, and much remains to be accomplished in the administration of public juvenile and family agencies—in personnel, in planning, in financing, perhaps in the formulation of wholly new approaches.

I possess neither the specialized experience nor the expert knowledge to predict with any certainty where may lie the brightest hope for progress in dealing with the serious problems of juvenile delinquency. But I am certain that the answer does not lie in the Court's opinion in this case, which serves to convert a juvenile proceeding into a criminal prosecution.

The inflexible restrictions that the Constitution so wisely made applicable to adversary criminal trials have no inevitable place in the proceedings of those public social agencies known as juvenile or family courts. And to impose the Court's long catalog of requirements upon juvenile proceedings in every area of the country is to invite a long step backwards into the Nineteenth Century. In that era there were no juvenile proceedings, and a child was tried in a conventional criminal court with all the restrictions of a conventional criminal trial. So it was that a 12-year-old boy named James Guild was tried in New Jersey for killing Catherine Beakes. A jury found him guilty of murder, and he was sentenced to death by hanging. The sentence was executed. It was all very constitutional.

A state in all its dealings must, of course, accord every person due process of law. And due process may require that some of the same restrictions which the Constitution has placed upon criminal trials must be imposed upon juvenile proceedings. For example, I suppose that all would agree that a brutally coerced confession could not constitutionally be considered in a juvenile court hearing. But it surely does not follow that the testimonial privilege against self-incrimination is applicable in all juvenile proceedings. Similarly, due process clearly requires timely notice of the purpose and scope of any proceedings affecting the relationship of parent and child. *Armstrong* v. *Manzo,* 380 U.S. 545. But it certainly does not follow that notice of a juvenile hearing must be framed with all the technical niceties of a criminal indictment. See *Russel* v. *United States*, 369 U.S. 749.

In any event, there is no reason to deal with issues such as these in the present case. The Supreme Court of Arizona found that the parents of Gerald Gault "knew of their right to counsel, to subpoena and cross examine witnesses, of the right to confront the witnesses against Gerald and the possible consequences of a finding of delinquency." 99 Ariz. 181, 185, 407 P. 2d 760, 763. It further found that "Mrs. Gault knew the exact nature of the charge against Gerald from the day he was taken to the detention home." 99 Ariz., at 193, 407 P. 2d, at 768. And, as Mr. Justice White correctly points out, p. —, *ante*, no issue of compulsory self-incrimination is presented by this case.

I would dismiss the appeal.

the gang
in action

LEWIS YABLONSKY

On the night of July 30, 1957, a fifteen-year-old boy partially crippled by polio was beaten and stabbed to death in a New York City park. His best friend was critically injured by stab wounds inflicted with a bread knife in the same attack.

The motives for this crime fit no simple category. No money was taken. No direct personal revenge was involved. According to all reports the victims did not personally know their assailants, nor did the youths who committed the homicide know their victims.

It was a hot summer night. A casual observer of the boys huddled in discussion in a tenement hallway near the corner of 135th Street and Broadway would detect nothing unusual about this gathering. In New York City youths often congregate like this when there is no place to go, but this group had a destination.

They talked excitedly, calling each other by nicknames. Magician, Little King, Louie, Big Man were familiar names. One youth clutched a long brown paper bag in his hand. It contained a machete. Another had a razor-point five-inch-long knife tucked away in his clothes. Still another held a harmless-appearing chain—used normally to hold a dog on a leash; the chain had a heavy metal sinker on the end.

Part of the discussion revolved around the previous evening. "I think we scared the shit out of them—they'll show up." "They better or I'll get the bastards myself," claimed another. "Anybody who doesn't swing out will have to tangle with me when we get back." They were not talking about enemy gang members; they were referring to their "own boys":

See, because we say before, if anybody don't beat up somebody, when we get back, he's gonna get beat up. So I say, "OK." They got special guys, you know, to keep their eyes on the boys. Anyone who don't swing out is gonna get it when we come back. They got to pass through

Reprinted with permission of the publisher from Lewis Yablonsky, The Violent Gang *(New York: The Macmillan Company, 1962), pp. 9-25.*

a line; they got about fifteen boys over here, and fifteen boys over there, and you know, in a straight line, like that. They got to pass through there and they all got belts in their hand.[1]

On the previous night, July 29th, two boys had been subjected to this "kangaroo court." They were found "guilty," had to pass through the line, and were lacerated with garrison belts. The boys did not really take this "courtroom procedure" seriously. In some ways they were producing what was to them a caricature of adult justice. One of the "judges" later commented, "Oh, man, we just jive around with that stuff—but they better show anyway."

Discussion about "who would show" was important, but a side issue to the central theme of the violent discussion. "They think they can get away with chasing us out of the pool—they're crazy." Another boy described how they had called him a "Spick":

They kept on callin' me a Spick. They kept on saying, "You dirty Spick, get out of this block." Every time I go in the pool, they said the same thing to me. I don't bother them, cause, you know, I don't want to get into no trouble with them, but one day they beat me up. You know, there was about five of them, and they wouldn't leave me alone. They beat me up, and I had to take a chance to get the boys so we could beat them up.

This boy was Puerto Rican. The Kings, however, had a mixed background. Although dominantly Puerto Rican and Negro, a number of gang members came from Italian and Irish origins. One boy was from the Dominican Republic. They were generally representative of the neighborhood population. Some boys used racial or ethnic discrimination as a reason for "calling on the rumble" with the Jesters. However, the main overt complaint of the group in the scarred-up

tenement hallway at 602 West 135th Street was that the Jesters had barred them from swimming in the pool at Highbridge Park.

Egyptian King version:

They came behind the pool. One guy, the president, he's a Negro, he said, "I'm gonna burn you." So he pulled out a gun; it looked like a .45, but we weren't too sure. So he put it behind my back; and the rest of the guys' backs, and one pulled out a sawed-off rifle, and pointed it at us. Everyone said, "Run to the water," you know, so I ran. I dived into the water, they were waiting outside, you know around the pool, we seen them, so we told some little kids to go down and get some of the fellas, so we could get out of the pool. So they went down, and three of them came to the pool, in front of the gate, and told us it was all right to come out now, cause we had the fellas around.

Jester version:

There was about fifteen of them in the pool, and a few of us walked behind there, and we looked in, and we seen them, and they started hollerin' things out, like, you know, names and you're gonna be blasted, and all this, so we told them they weren't going home then, and we went back around the block, and we thought they were gonna come around the block for a fight. And this boy was walkin' in the park, and he isn't on a team, or anything like that, just walkin' through the park lookin' at the pool, and about thirty-five guys from the Kings come out and they smacked him on the head with a bat. And he got eight stitches. . . .

Both versions distort an incident that occurred two weeks before the gang killing. There were many versions, and in a sense they are all true—at least to each gang observer. Whatever the variations, the overt theme was conflict over the use of a public pool. So-called "turf"

[1] This statement and those to follow in this section are verbatim comments taken from some ten hours of taped interviews with gang members.

(gang territory) rights were at stake.

The Jesters were the uptown gang with whom the Egyptian Kings were feuding. According to one spokesman for the Jesters, they were a "defensive fighting team":

We're mostly a defensive fighting team, you know, but they're offensive. You know, they . . . they start the trouble. Then we just . . . you know, we're just protectin' ourselves. Now, like they . . . they come up here on raidin' parties then we'll fight, you know, but if they don't come up, we don't fight. There's never been a time when we've invaded them when they haven't come up here first.

The Egyptian Kings and Dragons in the hallway were the core of an offensive or fighting gang. Their origins went back several years to two gangs then known as the Scorpions and the Villains. They joined forces to become the West Side Dragons. The Dragons about a month prior to this evening had developed a brother gang association with the Egyptian Kings. The Kings and Dragons "controlled" gang turf from 125th Street to 155th Street. The Dragons came from the southern part of this territory, primarily from 135th Street and below. The Kings came from the northern section; their main hangout was a candy store at 152nd Street and Broadway.

The hallway discussion became more intense and violent. It had some characteristics of the violent rituals engaged in by the Hollywood version of warlike Indian tribes about to go on the warpath. This core part of the gang moved out of the 602 hallway at about 7:00 P.M., bound north for the candy store at the corner of 152nd Street and Broadway.

This was the rendezvous point for the now consolidated Dragons and Egyptian Kings. The administrator of this consoli-

dation was a "man," or at least he was twenty-six years old. Frankie Cruz was better known to the gang boys in this area of the upper West Side as Frankie Loco. Loco was a standard "professional" teen-age gangster. He was always giving advice on gang organization, telling gang boys when and with whom to fight. Most of the time he was discussing nonexistent enemies conjured up in his wild fantasy world:

GANG BOY: Oh, Frankie Loco, he's from the East Side Dragons. Like he would tell us what to do. He got us [the Dragons] together with the Kings. Yeah, sometimes he acts crazy—always talkin', talkin', talkin' . . . .

Loco traveled up and down the West Side "talkin', talkin', talkin' " and stirring up gang trouble. Loco at one time was under psychiatric observation at Bellevue. Short in stature, he had a scar across the top of his head—the result of a childhood battle. Loco's favorite topic was blood. He had a job cleaning up the blood in an operating room at a city hospital. He liked his work. In one taped interview he mentioned the word blood over thirty times.

Loco had provoked the gang action. At the Egyptian King court trial he was mentioned by almost all the defendants, on trial for first-degree murder, as their adviser; yet the night of this homicide he was nowhere around. He was primarily a "consultant," and was not with the group swaggering up Broadway from 135th Street to 152nd Street.

The walk up this part of Broadway passes pool halls, a kosher delicatessen, and *bodegas*—Spanish grocery stores. It is a neighborhood in transition.

One pool hall is a hangout for "junkies" (drug addicts). Some former gang boys may have smiled as they detected this entourage—obviously going to fight a gang war. They smiled because, as they put it, "We don't fool with this punk gang stuff any more." They had found another way out of this world. For many gang youths drug addiction is a next step—when gang kicks become for them "kid stuff."

On the way up Broadway the gang leader with the machete under his arm met an "old friend" on his way to a movie:

GANG BOY: I was walkin' uptown with a couple of friends, and we run into Magician and them there. They asked us if we wanted to go to a fight, and we said "Yes." When they asked me if I wanted to go to a fight, I couldn't say, "No." I mean I could say, "No," but for old-time's sake, I said, "Yes."

This boy later took an active role in striking down Michael Farmer. "He got up and I knocked him down again."

The candy store at 152nd Street and Broadway is a standard part of New York's scenery. It stands cluttered with forceful advertising: "Be sociable," "They said it couldn't be done," "The pause that refreshes." Steps lead down into the candy store, which was heavily congested that evening.

When the group arrived at the store they were greeted by a number of other gang youths who had heard about the evening's expedition through the rumor mill. There was a shifting group of seventy or eighty boys present around the candy store that night, all ready for action.

"Some of the gang drank sodas, played the jukebox, and joked around." About 8:30 P.M. one King leader, Louis Alvarez, phoned a candy-store hangout on Jackson Avenue in the Bronx. He spoke to a then famous gang leader called Michael "Pee Wee" Ramos. Pee Wee was supposed to command a brotherhood Dragon division. He was another Loco-type gang leader. At

the Egyptian King trial he gave the following testimony describing his end of the phone conversation:

I answered the phone and then he told me he was Louis from the Dragons, from the West Side. So he told me that Frankie Loco says when he gets in trouble, give me a ring, to call me up. So I told him Frankie Loco was my boy, he was with me in the old Dragons. I told him, what the trouble was? Then he told me he got some trouble with the Irish boys up on the West Side.
Did he ask you for anything?
He told me—you know, the rifle.
What else did he say, if anything?
Make it, up there with my boys, up to the West Side. Yes, I told him I make it up there, ten o'clock I make it up there. Told him I'd come down with some weapons, you know, some guns in a car, some rifles and a car.
Did you tell him you would come down right away, or that there would be a delay?
I told him I had some trouble of my own. After I finished that I may get down there.

Later that night there had been another telephone conversation. It was the same voice on the telephone, Pee Wee said:

I said—he said, what happens, why can't I make it up there? I told him I still got my own troubles up here and that I can't make it up there. He said, then he told me, "You got experience," you know. So I said, "Yes, that is where I got it from." That is where, you know, I got it from, you know, experience from. So I told him like this, in the old Dragons, you know, we used to bop, we used to hit, you know, and talk later. So go right up there and whip it on them.
Now, have you ever met Louis Alvarez in your life?
Never.

(On April 27th, 1959, Pee Wee's

gang-leader activities were curtailed. A boy named Raymond Serra, another gang leader, confronted Ramos in a candy store. According to Serra, Ramos gave him a "bad look." Serra, who was holding a shotgun, blew away most of Pee Wee's head.)

At 9:00 P.M. several core members of the gang left the candy store and walked down to the park along Riverside Drive. They carried with them, in addition to their weapons, a few bottles of cheap liquor. They "talked about plans and joked around." They were accompanied by some girl friends, who were also around the candy store that night:

We went down to the park and we sat around for a while. Then we started drinking and we drank whisky and wine and we was drunk. Then we started talkin' about girls. We started sayin' to the girls that if they get us to bring us some roses an' all that—that if we get caught to write to us and all this.

After bolstering their courage they walked back up the block to the candy store. The collection of some eighty boys inside, in front of the candy store, and on the concrete "island" in the center of Broadway was a mixed group. Some had no intention of participating in gang action. Some were worried and had doubts:

I didn't wanna go at first, but they said come on. So then all the big guys forced me to go. I was scared. I was worried. I realized like I was doing I'd probably get in trouble.

Central leaders of the gang did not know what the excursion north to Highbridge Park would bring, but they

had no doubts about making the trip. They were ready to go in any direction.

Judge Irwin Davidson, the trial judge, summarized his reflections on the gang's mood that night prior to the homicide, based on court testimony:

There had been up to seventy-five boys gathered around the island at one time or another during the evening, all ready to take off and go up to battle the Jesters. They had been assured by Alvarez that reinforcements were arriving from other parts of the city, riding in cars, bringing guns. During the long—and, as it turned out, fruitless—wait [at the candy store] for the allies, the boys had begun to drift away. Some had to go home because they had been adjured by their mothers and fathers to return at certain times. Others simply had lost interest in the rumble and wandered off, indicating that they originally had been more interested in the prospect of excitement and violence than in coming to terms with the Jesters; they probably would have been just willing to go along, in order to pass the time, if Alvarez, Lago and the rest of the leaders had proposed an expedition down to fight one of the Italian kid gangs in Greenwich Village. . . .

The seventy-five-odd boys on the island had dwindled to eighteen. I wondered again where the police had been. Surely there had been patrol cars in the neighborhood. The boys had sticks, knives, and a machete wrapped in paper. Any passer-by could have seen that they were there for no good reason.[2]

A police station was one block away. Citizens in cars and on foot passed this gang build-up for almost two hours. Gang activity blends well into some New York City neighborhoods. At about 10:00 P.M. eighteen members of the gang collected

[2] Judge Irwin D. Davidson, *The Jury Is Still Out* (New York: Harper & Brothers, 1959), pp. 56-57. This volume gives an analysis of the Egyptian King trial as seen by the judge.

and headed north toward Highbridge Park. In one hour Michael Farmer would be dead.

The walk from 152nd Street and Broadway to Highbridge Park is about twenty New York City blocks. The route passes slum tenements, modern apartment buildings, and old residential homes abandoned to deterioration. A police station is on the way. More than halfway to the Park, on Edgecomb Avenue in the Bronx, a dusty view encompasses the East Side Highway, the soon-to-be obsolete Polo Grounds, and thriving Yankee Stadium. That night thousands of fans were engrossed in watching the Yanks beat the Red Sox 8 to 5. The Bronx County Courthouse looms in the background.

What were the thoughts of the boys making this journey? We can only speculate from later comments: "Nobody's gonna steal my rep." "I felt kinda cold inside." "They'll get me later if I don't swing out at somebody." "I'm going to kill some mother fucker."

Of more than seventy boys, eighteen made the final trip, traveling in twos and threes to avoid detection. They reconvened at 10:15 P.M. in Stitt Park, a small park that faces Stitt School about seven blocks from Highbridge Pool. The boys discussed a plan of action, then sent out scouts to patrol the neighborhood "to see how many Jesters were around." There is some evidence of other boys hanging around in the park; however, they were not necessarily Jesters. To the "scouts" all youths looked like Jesters by this time:

E. KING: We walked around the block to see how strong the club was we was gonna fight. To see if they had lots of guys and whatnot. What we saw, they had lots of big guys. I'd say about nineteen, twenty, or eighteen, like that. And we figured it out so we kept on walking around the block.

Gang boys under these extreme emotional conditions often perceive all youths in a neighborhood as potential enemies. By this time they were ready to "swing out" at anyone.

Highbridge Pool is rather large, roughly half a city block in size. An American flag waves high over the pool; nearby is the tall old water tower. In a city like New York, with its few available recreation opportunities, it is a treasured spot for cooling off in the hot summer. On a hill overlooking the East River, it provides a welcome breeze for people sitting on benches around the pool.

The Kings and Dragons entered the bushy area surrounding the pool in twos and threes to avoid attention. Staked out around the pool, at this time they were, in their own words, "ready to jump anyone who came along."

Michael Farmer and a friend, Roger McShane, were at this time in the Farmer apartment about a block from the park, listening to rock 'n' roll records.

MRS. FARMER: They stayed in his room playin' these new records that they had bought and Michael came out to the kitchen, just as I asked my husband what time it was, to set the clock. It was then five after ten. He asked for a glass of milk and as he walked from the kitchen, he asked, "I'm going to walk Roger home." (Sighs) That was the last time I saw him.

Youngsters in the area were warned to stay out of the park at night when the pool was closed but not drained. However, it was usual for some of the local boys to slip through a break in the gate entrance and sneak an evening swim.

The slightly curved footpath that enters the part at Amsterdam Avenue and 174th Street is about a one-minute walk to the high concrete stairway entrance to Highbridge Pool. It was Michael Farmer's last walk:

McSHANE: It was 10:30 when we entered the park; we saw couples on the benches, in the back of the pool, and they all stared at us, and I guess they must 'ave saw the gang there—I don't think they were fifty or sixty feet away. When we reached the front of the stairs, we looked up and there was two of their gang members on top of the stairs. They were two smaller ones, and they had garrison belts wrapped around their hands. They didn't say nothin' to us, they looked kind of scared.

FIRST E. KING: I was scared. I knew they were gonna jump them, 'an everythin' and I was scared. When they were comin' up, they all were separatin' and everything like that.

McSHANE: I saw the main body of the gang slowly walk out of the bushes, on my right. I turned around fast, to see what Michael was going to do, and this kid came runnin' at me with the belts. Then I ran, myself, and told Michael to run.

SECOND E. KING: He couldn't run anyway, cause we were all around him. So then I said, "You're a Jester," and he said, "Yeah," and I punched him in the face. And then somebody hit him with a bat over the head. And then I kept punchin' him. Some of them were too scared to do anything. They were just standin' there, lookin'.

THIRD E. KING: I was watchin' him. I didn't wanna hit him, at first. Then I kicked him twice. He was layin' on the ground, lookin' up at us. I kicked him on the jaw, or some place; then I kicked him in the stomach. That was the least I could do, was kick 'im.

FOURTH E. KING: I was aimin' to hit him, but didn't get a chance to hit him. There were so many guys on him—I got scared when I saw the knife go into the guy, and I ran right there. After everybody ran, this guy stayed,

and started hittin' him with a macnete.

FIRST E. KING: Somebody yelled out, "Grab him. He's a Jester." So then they grabbed him. Magician grabbed him, he turned around and stabbed him in the back. I was . . . I was stunned. I couldn't do nothin'. And then Magician—he went like that and he pulled . . . he had a switch blade and he said, "You're gonna hit him with that bat or I'll stab you." So I just hit him lightly with the bat.

SECOND E. KING: Magician stabbed him and the guy he . . . like hunched over. He's standin' up and I knock him down. Then he was down on the ground, everybody was kickin' him, stompin' him, punchin' him, stabbin' him so he tried to get back up and I knock him down again. Then the guy stabbed him in the back with a bread knife.

THIRD E. KING: I just went like that, and I stabbed him with the bread knife. You know, I was drunk, so I just stabbed him. *(Laughs)* He was screamin' like a dog. He was screamin' there. And then I took the knife out and I told the other guys to run. So I ran and then the rest of the guys ran with me. They wanted to stay there and keep on doin' it.

FOURTH E. KING: The guy that stabbed him in the back with the bread knife, he told me that when he took the knife out o' his back, he said, "Thank you."

McSHANE: They got up fast right after they stabbed me. And I just lay there on my stomach and there was five of them as they walked away. And as they walked away they . . . this other big kid came down with a machete or some large knife of some sort, and he wanted to stab me too with it. And they told him, "No, come on. We got him. We messed him up already. Come on." And they took off up the hill and they all walked up the hill and right after that they all of 'em turned their heads and looked back at me. I got up and staggered into the street to get a cab. And I got in a taxi and I asked him to take me to the Medical Center and get my friend and I blacked out.

The coroner's report reveals the intensity of the violence:

"I found a fifteen-year-old white boy, five feet and a half inches in length, scale weight 138 pounds, the face showing an ecchymosis . . . [a] hemorrhage beneath the skin . . . you would compare it to a black-and-blue mark.

There was an ecchymosis of the outer aspect of the right eye, with a superimposed superficial abrasion. . . . There was an incised wound . . . one made with a very sharp implement . . . situated over the bridge of the nose and [extending] . . . over the right eyebrow."

He had found wounds and abrasions on the knuckles and hands of the body, the doctor said, which seemed to indicate that Michael Farmer had raised his hands to defend himself against the torrential blows being inflicted upon him. He had also found an incised wound beneath the left armpit, but that one had not penetrated deeper than the epidermis. A wound on the right thigh had been deeper: "It measured one and a half inches in length with a gap that was slightly less than three-quarters of an inch . . . a gaping wound with sharp edges. . . ."

On the left side was another penetrating stab wound, lower and more deadly. This one "went through the entire back into the pleural cavity," and "severed a vein and a nerve." This wound, four inches deep, had caused Farmer's death.

AFTERMATH

Roger McShane was on the critical list at the Presbyterian Medical Center.

Michael Farmer's parents were notified the same evening of his death.

MR. FARMER: The sergeant from the 34th Precinct called us, and asked who I was, and was I the father of Michael Farmer. I said I was, and he said, "Well, your boy is in Mother Cabrini Hospital, in serious condition." I identified myself further, as a fireman in this area, and he said, "Oh, I'll come right down and give you a lift down to the hospital." So this sergeant drove us down to the hospital; as we walked in, the officer who was on duty there called the sergeant, and he said the boy had died fifteen minutes earlier.

MRS. FARMER: And the sister there in the hospital took us downstairs to identify the body. He had an expression as though he was just calling for help.

After the stabbing the gang scattered and fled. The gang members reported their postkilling reactions in various ways. One boy went home, had a glass of milk, went to bed, but couldn't sleep.

GANG MEMBER: I couldn't sleep that night or nuthin' 'cause I used to fall asleep for about half an hour. Wake up again during the middle of the night. My mother said, "What was the matter with you? Looks like something was wrong." I said, "Nothin'."

ANOTHER GANG MEMBER: First I went to the river to throw my knife away and then I went home. An' then I couldn't sleep. I was in bed. My mother kept on askin' me where was I and I . . . I told her, you know, that I was in the movies. I was worried about them two boys. If they would die . . . I knew I was gonna get caught.

This boy was more concerned with getting caught and locked up than remorseful over his violent act. In a later interview with him in a reformatory I asked him:

QUESTION: Well, how do you feel about this all now? Are you sorry about the killing?

ANSWER: Of course, I'm sorry. I'm locked up, ain't I?

The banner headlines of the homicide shocked many residents of New York City on their way to work the following morning. A large number of detectives worked through the night to piece the crime together. By dawn they began to round up the gang.

At 6:30 A.M. one gang member heard a knock on the door of his apartment in a housing project on 125th Street:

I hear this knockin' on the door. I didn't think it was the police, you know. 'Cause, you know, I thought I wasn't gonna get caught, so I was layin' in bed and told my mother, "Mommie, I think that's the milkman knockin' on the door or somebody." She said, "Why don't you answer it?" and I said, "No, I'm in my underwear." So she says, "OK, I'll go." She opened the door and my mother comes over, "You get in any trouble last night?" And I says, "No, Mommie, I didn't get in no trouble last night." And then she says, "Well, there's a policeman over here, wants to see you." And I says, "What for?" and he says, "Somethin' that happened last night," and I says, "OK," then I started thinkin' of my clothes and acted innocent, you know. He said to me, "you know what happened last night?" I say, "No, no. I don't know a thing that happened last night. I was in the car from ten on." He says, "Oh, if that's the truth, you have nothin' to worry about. You like to come down to the police station with us?" And I said, "OK."

Another gang member spent the following morning in Children's Court, pleading innocent to a robbery committed two weeks earlier. He was released, pending a hearing. When he returned home, police were waiting to question him about the murder of Michael Farmer. This was the boy who used a bread knife in the assault at Highbridge Park. During my later hour-long interview with him, he was quite calm in relating the killing and his role in it. He became excited only once:

Well, when we was goin' to the . . . to the paddy wagon, the detective, he kept wipin' his feet on my suit. So I told him to cut it out, and he still won't cut it out. So then, then the sergeant says, "Cut it out," so then he said, "Why don't you mind your business?" and he kept on doin' it. He kept on wipin' his feet on my suit, and I just got the suit out of the cleaners', that's all. I told him, "I just got the suit out of the cleaner's," and he says to me, "That's just too bad. That suit belongs in the garbage can." So he kept on wipin' his feet on my suit, and he kept on sayin' "You murderer" and all this. They kept on sayin', "You're gonna get the electric chair, you're gonna get the electric chair, you murderer, you murderer, you're gonna get the electric chair." He kept on sayin' that to me; he made me mad. If I had a gun, I would have shot them all.

This same boy later told a police officer, "I always wanted to see how it would feel to stick a knife through human bone."

Another youth felt "all right with the fellas" after he was arrested:

I was crackin' up 'cause I wanted them to hurry up and come and get me and get it over with, so when I got picked up, I felt safe then. We went in the car and then they threatened me. I mean, not exactly a threat, but they told me what was goin' to happen: I'd get beat up if I didn't talk. So I told them, "Tell me, who was the guy that squealed?" They told me, "Who do you think you are, Dillinger or somebody—ya gonna get even with the guy?" I said, "No, I just wanted to know." They said, "No." So they took me to the precinct; it made me laugh to see all the guys sitting there in the . . . in the . . . when I walked in, everybody said,

"Ha,ha," and started laughin' so I felt all right with the fellas.

In court Mr. Farmer made an observation about the Kings as he watched them arraigned:

They are monsters—in my mind I classify them as savage animals. That's all. I don't think that they have any civilization in them. I think they're just two-legged animals. They haven't any concept of living with other people, outside of to show that they can do something worse than the other or to claim any sort of notoriety. These boys didn't even hang their heads, most of them, when they came to court. They stood erect and looked around the court for their relatives. And so forth. One of them had a small smirk when they looked in our direction. They should be put away, and kept away. Or if the penalty is death, to be executed. Certainly they set themselves up in the form of a judge, jury and execution squad in the case of my son. All in the matter of minutes. This is pure jungle activity.

A killing of this kind also has a profound impact on many people not directly related either to the offenders or to the victims. A typical reaction of the general public to this act was shock, at its seeming senselessness and irrationality. One might expect that people close to these youths could have foreseen or expected this behavior. The gang boys' parents also reacted with shock and disbelief:

MOTHER: I had absolutely no problems with him. Everyone in the neighborhood can vouch for that. When I walked out there this morning all my storekeepers and everythin' just can't believe that my son is mixed up in anything like this. I have no idea what I can do for him right now. I doubt if there is anything we can do for him right now. I can't let him down now. Even though he was wrong. I still can't just turn my back on him.

Shame was another characteristic response:

GANG BOY: My mother said she was ashamed of me, and everything, and I told her that it wasn't my fault and I couldn't help it. My father wanted to kill me at first, and after I explained to him what happened he was still ... he was still like ... felt bad about it, ashamed to walk the streets.

Shock was expressed in several forms:

GANG BOY: My father understood. He didn't actually understand, but you know, he didn't take it as hard as my mother. My mother ... it came out in the newspapers, she had a heart attack. It's a lucky thing she's alive today.

One mother described her guilt:

He has lived with my mother all his life from birth. I lived there up to two, three years ago. It seems like since I left my child everything has happened. Not that I just walked out on him, but when I planned to get married I spoke to him. He said, "Well, go ahead, you have to have some happiness: you can't just stay with me all the time." So I said, "Will you be willing to come with me?" He said, "No, I don't want to leave my grandparents." *Do you think that it would have been important if he had stayed with you?* I think it would have been important had I stayed with him and not left him at the age of fifteen.

One mother gave covert approval to the act. This even shocked the tough gang members who related the incident:

When she sees him she says to him, "How did it feel when you did that to Farmer? It was good, eh?" You know, jokin' around with the kid. So we told her, "You know what your son did?" I says, "He stabbed him in the back." She says, she just went like that, shrugged her, you know, shoulders. Then we didn't pay any attention to her, because ya know, you don't like to see a mother actin' like that with a kid.

The legal forces of society moved swiftly in this case. Within twenty-four hours the eighteen youths involved in the crime were apprehended and arraigned. The eleven younger members of the gang, age fifteen or under, were quickly tried in Children's Court and committed to various state reformatories for indeterminate sentences.

The older group of seven, ranging in age from fifteen to eighteen, were indicted and tried for first-degree murder in an unprecedented trial lasting ninety-three days and involving twenty-seven trial lawyers for the defense. An all-male, blue-ribbon jury rendered the following verdict:

CHIEF JUROR: Louis Alvarez and Charles Horton guilty of murder in the second degree. Lencio de Leon and Leroy Birch guilty of manslaughter in the second degree. Richard Hills and George Melendez not guilty because we believe these boys were forced to go along with the gang the night of the murder. John McCarthy not guilty because we were convinced, beyond a reasonable doubt, that this boy was mentally sick and didn't know what was going on at any time.

Three of these boys were released immediately. Two were sentenced to twenty years to life imprisonment. One was sentenced to seven-and-one-half years and the other was sentenced to five to fifteen years.

IX

the
self-abusers

One function of society is to protect the self-interests of its members. Not only does the state protect the individual from other members of society, but it also places barriers before individuals who would abuse, injure, or destroy themselves. For example, social control mechanisms are employed when there is clear-cut evidence of the self-destructive character of individual or group actions. This is the case with suicide: The community or individuals stand in the person's way if he decides to destroy himself even if circumstances of excessive pain or confirmed feelings of futility characterize his life. In other instances, laws and norms are imposed because certain behaviors are contradictory to dominant moral values and seem to threaten long-standing social patterns for conduct, such as certain sexual behaviors. In still other instances, certain activities of community members are held to be undesirable because of myths or the lack of experience with the consequences of the actions involved. For example, scientific evidence does not support the view that marijuana is habituating or that it calls forth bizarre or undesirable behavior to any greater extent than other substances which are freely available in the community. Its use, however, remains illegal, for it is defined as harmful to the individual.

Condemnation of certain behaviors often runs counter to the value of the right of individuals to make their own decisions with respect to personal behavior. Groups in society often regard methods of control as an invasion of individual freedom and privacy. Controversies recur in many areas because of the incompatibility of the values of the right of the community to regulate individual behavior and the right of the individual to act as a free agent. The four cases presented here vary in the extent of self-abuse inflicted as well as the degree of community consensus on the impropriety of the behavior involved.

Individual	Individual
↓	↓
Individual	Organization

SUICIDE

Death is a part of life, and unless the party involved is an intimate, the event is usually treated in a rather routine fashion. Physicians particularly are often bland in the face of death because they are constantly confronted by it. However, the moral imperatives against taking one's own life are strong in the western world, and such a death has a different effect. "Suicide" is a personal account by a physician who attended another doctor, a close friend, during his last hours of life after a suicide attempt. The case portrays the ultimate act of self-abuse and the hostility and guilt felt by one who attended in both a professional and a personal role. The reader must decide for himself who is the protagonist and who the victim in this account.

THE FANTASTIC LODGE

Heroin addiction is viewed with great alarm in American society, perhaps because of the difficulty in reversing the habit once it is formed. Few community members feel that the individual should have the option to elect a life of drug use for himself. Consequently, a variety of methods exist to limit the access that individuals have to drugs, and a range of therapeutic regimens are applied to addicts in spite of the slim chance for cure. The confirmed drug addict can be seen as a protagonist of the social order who breaks the rules and opposes the attitudes of the community. The selection here is part of an edited account of a young girl drug addict and her rejection of a number of community norms in the face of coping with her "monkey."

Organization

↓

Individual

Organization

↓

Organization

TWILIGHT OF THE WCTU

Community members often mobilize individuals into a structured organization in order to focus on and control what they regard as self-abusive activities of individuals. Alcohol, at least in moderation, is regarded by many as an appropriate substance that inspires conviviality and relaxation. But there are also those who hold that *any* use of alcohol is self-destructive and that it should not be available to the individual. Although the WCTU today is an anemic organization compared to ts once powerful status, it still operates to harass the consumer and purveyor of alcohol. Kloman's report of the activities of the WCTU demonstrates how the organization impinges on the lives of individuals in an area of activity that a minority regards as self-abusive.

INSIDE THE HIPPIE REVOLUTION

Flower people may not represent an enduring collectivity on the American scene. Few social groups so small in numbers and so unusual in behavior undertake cooperative and group actions with so minimal a formal structure. Hedgepeth describes the hippie organization *vis-à-vis* the larger community. He points out that the hippies provide an organizational setting in which the rules for behavior in society can be flaunted. They conform to viable alternative norms in their abhorrence for violence, sexual expression, living arrangements, personal goals, and use of drugs. The community, however, sees such behavior as self-abuse for, by rejecting accepted social arrangements for carrying on life, they seriously limit the opportunities available to them in the future. Thus, the community supposedly acts to protect them.

suicide

HOWARD M. FEINSTEIN, M.D.

November 2–, 195–
4:30 p.m.

"Dr. B– – –was found unconscious at about 3:30 p.m. He had lacerations of both wrists and neck which were self-inflicted with broken window glass. He lost an undetermined amount of blood. Efforts to maintain blood pressure with fluids failed. Respirations ceased at about 4:05 and he was pronounced dead."

The high-pitched screech of the telephone operator rasped against my drums. "They need you here in a hurry doctor—it's urgent—an emergency!" I mumbled something about it being a hell of a way to spend Thanksgiving and charged out of the door into gray deserted streets. I tried to keep the meaning of "emergency" hidden from myself, but I couldn't. In our hospital it most often meant suicide. I stopped for a light. The dull red brick hospital came into view as I turned the corner. It stood solid, complacent and ugly. There were lights in most of the windows but no faces I pulled up to the entrance between two "No Parking" signs and stopped the car.

The powder-caked face of the operator looked even whiter and more masklike than usual. "They're in the operating room!" she yelled, but I didn't need to hear. I was off following a thin trail of blood spattered over the freshly waxed asphalt tile floor.

He was stretched out limply on the table. The resident in shirt sleeves bent over a flaccid arm, tensely probing for a vein. "Lost lot of blood . . . broken window . . .wrists . . .neck." I looked at the ashen face. He was a handsome young man with blonde hair still neatly combed. Ice-blue eyes stared vacantly at the ceiling. A jagged necklace of clotted blood and torn flesh hung about his throat.

"Give me a stethoscope and blood pressure cuff," I demanded, trying to force down the revulsion that mounted within me. The nurse searched the room fruitlessly, looked up as if to excuse herself, and ran off to the ward. His pulse beat faintly but regularly against my cold fingers. He breathed shallow sighs. "Maybe I can do something . . . I'm supposed to be able to do something!" I reached for things once known. The infusion dripped briskly. I looked at the lemon-yellow face and knew that would never be enough. We had no blood bank. He needed extensive surgical repair. "Better call an ambulance and warn the General that he's coming." The male attendant pushed his horn-rimmed glasses up on the bridge of his nose and disappeared.

I looked around the prison-gray tile room noticing the others drawn by the blood of a near-headless man. A crew-cut medical student hovered over the end of

Reprinted with permission of the author and the publisher from COMMUNITY MENTAL HEALTH JOURNAL, *III,3 (Fall 1967), pp. 259-61.*

the table pecking away at a cold ankle with a needle trying to start another infusion. I wondered at his calm and then remembered the comfortable feeling of learning in a situation where someone else was responsible. He missed a third time and droplets of sweat joined us together. The young nurse with tight black curls ran through the door waving the cuff and stethoscope triumphantly, as if they really mattered.

There was no measurable blood pressure. I moved the black bell onto his chest, dutifully searching for parts of the body that might still be alive. The sallow chest shuddered and a hand pushed the bell away. I looked toward the head of the table. The eyes pleaded. Parched lips formed voiceless words: "Let . . . me . . . be."

I turned away so that he could not sense my rage. I fought the urge to raise my fist and bring it smashing down on his face, then pushed the helpless hand out of my way and pressed the black thorn into the flesh.

The male attendant peered over the glasses which had once again slipped down his nose. In a respectful, apologetic whisper he told me that the police had sent a squad car by mistake. They just left to get an ambulance. They would come back in a hurry. Both infusions were running now. The chest still rose and fell mechanically with the tide of unwanted air. I put some gauze pads in place to hide his wounds.

A cop, stuffed in a soiled uniform with tarnished brass buttons, entered. His cap was shoved back on his head. As he looked over the resident's shoulder, the tough professional veneer peeled away revealing horror and fright. He wrinkled his nose at the sweet smell of fresh-cut meat. I asked for the stretcher, and he turned to the three others that had filed in behind him. There was none. He ran out. He came back carrying a gray canvas stretcher. They each held one corner and moved alongside the table. The blonde head turned slowly and glared at the buttons. We grabbed hold to move him to the waiting stretcher. He shrugged loose. I asked for a sheet and we spread it out to wrap around him. He bellowed like a trapped animal and sat up. The resident grabbed one bloody wrist and I took hold of the other. Another raucous, outraged bellow filled the room. He pulled and tugged to break free. His head balanced precariously like a ping-pong ball on a pencil. Blood ejaculated from his wounds. He began to laugh. Then he sagged back onto the table. He clutched his throat.

"Give me the tracheotomy set," I demanded. The nurse with tight curls ran to the instrument cabinet. It was locked. She fled to get the nursing supervisor.

She came back nervously fingering a jingling mass of unfamiliar keys. As she tried them one by one, the supervisor commented in an oily smooth voice, "We don't use this room very often, you know." The nurse brought over the jar with scalpel blades resting on the bottom. She couldn't find a forceps so I reached into the viscous preservative and fished out a blade.

By now the young man lay motionless. None of us wanted to put the knife to his throat. I offered the instrument to the resident. He turned away. The student said that he had never done a tracheotomy. Instead of extending the minutes of his life, it felt like one of us would finish with steel what he had started with jagged glass. I fingered the bare cartilage of his neck and shoved the blade down with a twist. The student pushed in on the chest to breathe for him, but it was useless. Again I pressed the ball against him, but this time there was no sound. He was dead.

We turned from the body to ourselves. A gray-headed attendant with a thick Irish brogue told how worried she had been. After the resident put him in seclusion, she had checked on him frequently. Surely there was nothing more she could have done. "Why I spoke with him at three-fifteen ... No, I remember now it was three-twenty."

The charge nurse, an old hand, confirmed this and grumbled, "I told his doctor two days ago that he was sick. But did he listen to me? Oh no. The trouble with these young residents is they're too wrapped up with talk. What he needed was shock treatment."

The resident and I bent over the sink washing our hands. He had spent half an hour talking with Dr. B— — — when he made rounds in the afternoon. He had seemed okay then. "He gave me his word that he would let me know if he felt the urge to harm himself."

I listened but I was intent on what I was doing. I soaped my hands for the third time and scrubbed vigorously. The preservative had fixed brown flecks of blood on my fingers. They wouldn't wash off.

There were forms to fill out and procedures to follow. They fell in place easily, like grains of sand erasing his path. With this finished, I made a note in the chart as I had been trained to do.

AFTERMATH

This is the context in which the word "suicide" became meaningful to me. Dr. B— — —'s suicide touched us all. In the many group meetings that were held with residents, patients, and staff to discuss our dismay at his death, there was never any discussion of the nature of professional responsibility vis-à-vis a man intent on taking his own life. The upset of the hospital was treated as a pain that needed amelioration—like a boil that wants lancing rather than an ethical dilemma to be thought through. I suspect this was no accident or peculiarity of a

particular hospital. Rather, it was to be expected in the medical training setting. Unfortunately, psychiatrists still begin their specialty training hobbled by the medical materialism of earlier training more suitable for the internist or the surgeon. Our education begins with death as an event that has significance primarily as a cause, the effect of which is to produce dissection material. By the time the smell of formaldehyde has given way to the nameless odors of the hospital corridor, the psychiatrist-to-be has also been taught that suicide is the act of a diseased machine that he is responsible for labeling and impounding before it runs off a cliff. We undertake to stamp out suicide like one would stamp out poliomyelitis. A problem that involves human choice is misunderstood with the mental equipment more suitable to the solution of physicochemical problems.

With the image of Dr. B— — —'s suicide fresh in mind, I would like to make a distinction that seems obvious to me now but was not then. The word "suicide" can refer to a medical emergency and also to an existential problem. One needs to understand that the assumptions and actions of a physician acting to restore physiological integrity are quite different (or should be) from those of a psychotherapist working with someone contemplating suicide. I have no quarrel with medical training that places the physician reflexly on the side of perpetuating the body in an emergency—even that of a man who has tried to end his own life. A man who attempts to kill himself should expect that a doctor called to the scene would attend to his circulation. In so doing, the doctor is acting on behalf of the professional ethic of physicians, which places him uncritically on the side of prolonging bodily function.

The psychotherapist is in a quite different situation. But because he has had training experiences like the one described here, the differences may be obscured. A man contemplating suicide is a human being weighing the choice of life or death. Dr. B— — — decided that his life was no longer worth living, and he might have been right. As a physician I pushed this question out of sight. As a psychotherapist, I find it is a central concern. Weighing the value and meaning of one's life is not a question of physiology. A psychotherapist has, I believe, a contractual commitment to help that man in his attempt at self-understanding and self-mastery. Talk of suicide is an invitation to inquiry, not a reason for intrusive action.

To withhold intrusive action is not the same as being disinterested in the outcome. This too is a distinction that it is hard for the physician psychotherapist to make. Action on behalf of the preservation of life is the doctor's function. Such action may conflict with the work of the psychotherapist. He cares about the outcome but insists that he cannot perform his function as a therapist when the possibility is ever present that he may act to interfere with another's action if the patient's decision does not coincide with his own. The therapist cannot help another examine his life if he sits in judgment. His concern shows itself in a respect for another's powers to manage his own life or his own death. Though he may choose life, the therapist can see that for some death may be more desirable and he acknowledges their right to choose.

As I think back over Dr. B— — —'s death, I am troubled that so many of us were ready to force him onto a stretcher but none even thought of taking his hand.

the

fantastic

lodge

HELEN MacGILL HUGHES

They had to send me down to see how much bread I had. Well, when I first went down there, she looked at me and she said, "Two dollars." "Two dollars!" I said.

"Well, you've got a three-dollar book."

I said, "Well, cash it in." And that's what she did, thank God, which gave me five whole wonderful dollars!

I didn't realize just how much it meant to me to leave the place, and how much tension I had been under during the time that I had been there, until I started to get into the station wagon that was to drive me to town, and I was lifting my suitcase. All of a sudden, my legs started shaking uncontrollably—I had heels on. I was all dressed up. It felt marvelous to be dressed up again. And I couldn't stop them from shaking. I just lost all control. I got into the station wagon and started to light a cigarette, and it's the same thing: I had to hold both hands to get the cigarette up to my mouth and then, just as we were driving out the gate, I started crying. I didn't know why it should have been so tremendous, but it was.

Reprinted by permission of the publisher from Helen MacGill Hughes, The Fantastic Lodge, *(Boston: Houghton Mifflin Company, 1961), Chapter Eleven, pp. 229-44.* © *1961 by the Chicago Area Project.*

Meanwhile, I was thinking fast. I knew I couldn't take a train home: I didn't have enough bread. Also, I knew I had to get out of town. About eight hours, I think they give you, after you sign your AMA papers, or else you'll be picked up.

There wasn't a train until eight or eleven, or something fantastic like that, that night. There was a bus, and so I decided to take a bus as far as I had bread for. I got to the bus station, said good-by to the cab, and walked in feeling like, you know, everyone knew what kind of a station wagon I had gotten out of and where I came from. I couldn't get used to looking at the people in the station, and they'd look at me and I'd think they were staring at me. I finally had to get up and go in the washroom and sit there for a while, while I calmed myself down and talked myself out of all these jitters.

I bought a ticket and bought some candy. I hadn't had anything to eat all day. And a pack of cigarettes – ah, they tasted good! And got on the bus and went.

I had the strangest feeling all that day until I got back home. I had been used to whatever existence Lexington had meant to me. I'd just begun to get used to the routine – and yet, it had been so foreign to me that I had hardly gotten over the newness. And then, to be confronted suddenly with all these strange towns, just nowhere, with no money, and no real means of getting anywhere for sure. Yet I enjoyed it, perversely, in some fashion. I felt: "Well, here I am. I don't have any money. I can't get any junk for at least twelve hours. I'll be a normal person for that long, anyway." Incidentally, since I got on the bus I *knew* that I would be making it as soon as I got back into town. In fact, I felt that that would be the first thing I would do.

Now, when I got as far as I could, to this strange city, I tried to call Bob, collect. And there was no answer, at first. I hadn't thought of that. And I was hungry, and I was down to a couple of pennies. It was really very bad. So, finally, I went to Travelers' Aid and laid this story on them, and asked them what they suggested, and they said call Bob back. And this time he was in. When I heard his voice, I burst into tears again. And he, or course, he asked me how I would like to have the money sent. Well, there was a Western Union strike on, but in spite of the strike, the service was supposedly still on.

So I sent a telegram, and I was to wait. A hard old bench. Nothing was happening. Nothing was happening. And four hours had gone by. My mother had, supposedly, wired the money to me, and it still hadn't come. I was sounding the chick every five minutes now. I made another frantic phone call to Bob. The last quick bus that would take me home in a reasonable amount of time was due to leave in another hour and a half, and I *still* hadn't gotten the money. So then Bob's people were going to run frantically down to Travelers' Aid there and leave some more bread, and do it that way. Finally, just at the last possible minute – the way those things always work out – the wire came through. And they stopped the other money coming from Travelers' Aid. And I thanked everybody and I trotted off on the bus.

I hadn't had any sleep now for over thirty hours. I hadn't had anything to eat outside of one sandwich for twenty-four hours. I was feeling all the effects of kicking the habit, right all over again. And I couldn't sleep, I was so worked up emotionally.

It was all so unreal, driving through all these strange towns. Bus travel is crazy, even if it is tiring and sweaty and everything else. At nights, there's nothing like it. And I was plenty sick, but I still enjoyed it.

Bob met me at the bus station. And then we went over to my mother's house. And already it had begun. Why had I done this? Actually, why had I? I came out without any money, made a big scene out of it, so that his parents were aware, my mother was aware I was a complete failure, in all of their eyes. Even Bob was disappointed with me, I knew. I was disappointed with myself. We had no place to stay. We'd given up our pad. It was all just very ridiculous and very typical of me. And on top of that, I was trying to cope with the feelings that I got from Lexington. Must've been from Lexington, because that was the only experience I've had. It changed me.

I had the idea, then, when I first got out of the treatment center, for the first time in my life that I was an incurable junkie. For the first time, I could see myself. Always before, I had thought of myself as, well, someday, someday, somehow, I'll kick this. But I felt beaten. "Why am I fighting it and spending money, and hanging up and going two flips, and why don't I just accept it and do the best I can? Because that's the way it is. I'll never change." Well, of course, this feeling nearly broke my heart. It's not an easy thing, I mean, to accept that. It would be like accepting cancer, I guess.

And because I just accepted it and had no urge to fight it, or anything else, I felt terrible, as far as Bob was concerned. We went through quite an emotional scene. I wanted him to leave me, because I felt more and more an awareness of how I was dragging him down. And that when I came back each time from some sort of an escapade it would be *me* that was really the instigator, as far as getting back on again was concerned.

I couldn't actually go so far as to say that I hated him, didn't want any part of him, or anything. And that's all he wanted to know . . . was how I felt about

him. So for two days I didn't take anything. But it was just tooth and nail, every minute of the day. I felt very weak, physically, which didn't help. But I just felt there was no reason at all to be doing this, that I was with my own kind down there, and I saw how things were with them, and that's what I would be in another fifteen or twenty years. And time in joints across the nation, being locked up for years, didn't seem to make any difference to them. Why should I expect that it would make any difference with me? I stayed in bed most of the time and cried, and felt miserable. So naturally, I made it again.

Then we got a pad, furnished place, and went into there, and started making it pretty regularly. The rent was expensive, the fact that we were making it again meant Bob would become dependent on his parents again for money. Ah, the same routine! Into it just like it was an old fairy tale we both knew our parts in completely well, you know. And everybody just sort of fell into line, you know. I mean, his people, and my mother, they all seemed the same role to me. Well, of course, with them, that's the role they *want* to play. With us, it's sort of half-and-half; we do and we don't. We do, and we can't seem to be strong enough to get out of it.

I don't even like to think about those days. We moved out into a hotel for a week. still downhill. Then we got a sixth-story monstrosity in a tenement. I had plans. I was thinking about getting furniture and straightening it up and then, once I had straightened up, of doing something about all this.

We had begun scoring at the Hill Hotel, and since it was much too hot to have Bob over there, I was doing most of the trips. We were scoring from a spade cat, who had a fay chick who was his old lady, and he was pimping for her, and they were constantly hitting on me:

either go to work for Bob through the connection, or do some free-lance work or something. It was silly — all this money to be run down; I was a white girl; I was attractive; if I had to have it, I might as well be realistic about it and face it. The world at the Hill Hotel, I mean, it's a world of small pimps and whores and small-time dope-peddlers and petty thieves and boosters. It's just a little section of the underworld, the dirty end of the underworld, the small-time rackets. We were frantic for money, naturally, to score with, and here was all this money to be made, and I thought, This is what I'm going to be eventually, anyway. And these are eventually my people. And for what am I holding back? But, of course, this made me so terribly unhappy at the same time. I think it was all an urge on my part to really just wallow in it. I was going to play this game and play it the whole way, instead of messing around and playing it halfway and still trying to pretend that I was different. Or that I was a sensitive person or something — anything that would distinguish me, you know, from the run of junkies.

I even tried to talk Bob into letting me hustle,* and I was serious about it, and of course, this nearly broke his heart. And I think I, inside, must have enjoyed hurting him as much as I was hurting myself. That's only one aspect of our relationship, anyway, that's been forged in neurotic fires. And at the same time, I had become so despondent. We weren't getting good junk. We didn't have the *bad* habit, but I had thrown myself so completely into the mechanisms of being hooked — of waking up feeling horrible, of having to have the first fix, of copping frantically, you know — the pace and the misery that go with real addiction. It was more the externals than the internals, really, but

nonetheless, just as big and just as high. And we were so high up — six floors.

I thought, one day when I was sitting out on the fire escape, of how easy it would be just to stop everything. I was in so much pain, and I was putting Bob in so much pain. At the same time, I was being pressed very definitely by Zimpert to come to a decision. And Bob and I seemed to grow farther and farther apart, because of all our arguments and so forth and so on. We had some terrible fights during this period, I mean, regular physical fights. Once he chased me down the street, then knocked me down on the ground. There were some people there — they were on his side. And he was on my side, telling me he wasn't a gentleman, and what was he doing this thing for? And I grew very angry at them for interfering and we marched off together.

And I did think about taking my life then. Bob fought me one night when I tried. And another night, while he was gone out to work I went out and sat on the fire escape and I was smoking a cigarette and I threw it down, and I watched. You know, when you watch little objects. And I thought how I would feel if I were going down. And I thought that wouldn't be so hard. It was almost as though I were hypnotized by the ground and by hitting. I could feel myself hitting it. But I waited.

And then came the night that started all of the events of the last bust. Bob and I had had another big fight that evening, and I threw a glass of water at him and threw a shoe at him that missed him and went through the glass door of the apartment and broke it. I think the thing that started it, if I remember correctly, was that he thought we shouldn't score. And I was saying, in effect, "Why try? Why try to do anything?" And so he said,

*Be a prostitute

"All right! *You* can go to the Hill Hotel, and get the junk." And he took the money and he cut out.

I waited for a while, and he didn't come back. I waited for a little while longer and he still didn't come back. I knew the trip should take him an hour at the outside. And he still hadn't come back. So I went down to the drugstore to make the phone call. I phoned the police, thinking that maybe Bob had gotten picked up. No, he wasn't down there. I couldn't figure that out. Where would he be? So then I called the connection's house, but he never got there. So then I was *really* puzzled. I thought maybe Bob had come in while I was gone, so I decided to go back upstairs. I was walking up the narrow stairs in the hall and I happened to look down the stairs. I thought I heard my name. I thought, God, I'm hearing things.

And I looked down, and there was my mother coming up the stairs. I thought, Now, what in Christ's name is she doing on the scene? Then I started to say hello to her. And then I saw two cats coming up behind her. And I thought, Uhh-oh, what is this? They were right behind me. I was cut off. So I just kept going up the stairs, past our floor, which was the top floor, and went across the narrow boarding that was up at what would have been the seventh floor and was out on the roof. And hung there, and watched them go into my pad, the two cats and my mother.

I tried to hear what they were saying, got my head next to the door, and I thought I heard one of the cats say, "I'm a police officer. I'm only a police officer," or something. And I was so right! But I didn't know at the time. And Phil Schaefer, meantime, was just coming up the stairs, from the drugstore. So I yelled down the elevator shaft: I said, "Phil! get out!" And he didn't need any further word. He went — like that! So

then I met him downstairs, and we went and called the police station, thinking I might be able to find out if Bob had been picked up, and maybe they just weren't telling me, or something.

I don't think I would have gone back if I had known where Bob was. I still went cautiously. I went up the fire escape and hung outside the window. And then I became aware of the fact that she was alone in the pad. Now she was in the kitchen doing the dishes. So I came in the window. I said, "What's going on? Who were these two cats?" And so forth and so on. And she gave me a story a yard long: "Well, oh, they just had a flashlight. I couldn't find your apartment. And they gave me the flashlight, and they were showing me upstairs."

"Well, what were they doing in the apartment, talking?"

"Well, I broke down when I got up here, and saw the broken glass and the door, and I didn't know what happened. I thought you may have committed suicide, Janet. I was so upset! And I started crying and they were very sympathetic. And then they left." She said, "And I'm sorry to be so emotional. I was just a mother."

And she lied beautifully — superbly — I must say not so much in what she did as how she said it. My mother's never been good at lying to me.

And then I said, "Well, have you heard from Bob?"

She said, "Well, yes, yes, yes. He called our house. He's going to meet you at my place. You come home with me now. To my place." And I said, "Uuh-uuh. I'll wait here for him. But I will go downstairs and we'll call your house, and see if he's there."

All right. So we went downstairs together and she called. She was talking on the phone, when this cat came up behind me. And just stood there for a couple of minutes first. He didn't really look like the man, frankly. He was a tall, thin, dark-haired cat; almost looked more like a junkie then he did the man. And then I realized what the score was, all right.

"Come on. You're under arrest."

And I said, What? On what grounds?" You know, I really gave him a good argument, at this point, still believing in our Bill of Rights. And he said, "Why? Because you're a drug addict."

I said, "Because I'm a drug addict?" I said, "Even saying that I was, and I'm not saying that I am, there's no law that says you can't be a drug addict in this state or in this city."

And he told me, "Yes, there is!" And then he starts reading off the number – and I know the number; that's the law putting narcotics addicts in jail.

And I said, "Well, that's nothing. A little two-hundred-bond state disorderly-loitering narcotics-addict op." I said, "You can't even take me in for that, because you're arresting me in my own home. I'm minding my own business. There's nothing you can do." he said, "Well, your mother has signed a complaint against you." And I turned around, and I said, "Why, you dirty bitch!" And I lunged at her, you know. And then he grabbed me.

And she says, "Oh, I know you feel this way, Janet." She's standing there. She says, "But this is all for the best. I'm doing it for you, Janet." And the tears are pouring out of her eyes.

I said, "You fucking bitch! You lousy cocker!" I'm screaming at her, and the neighbors were coming out, meantime – "Oh, look at the cops! Look at the junkie! Look at the mother!" You know.

And I said, "Well, let's talk outside. I don't want to make a scene." And we cut outside, and then there was this little pause. What's the proper decorum in this

sort of situation? She pulls out a cigarette and lights it. And I remember at that time, I thought: This is not going to happen to me again! I am not going through this. And I saw all the implications, you know. There's no feeling worse than the point when you're just arrested. I knew I had to go through it. I knew how sick I was going to be. I knew the Main Station deal.

And so I waited until he relaxed, and I was off, down the street, as fast as I could go. I had the idea that he would take out a gun and try to shoot me, you know, the way they do in the movies. And I just thought, Well, at least, then, they'll take me to a hospital. That's the only thing I can remember running through my mind. I took him completely off guard, so I had a good head-start. But he was young and a pretty fast runner. And the other cat tried to run, too; but he gave up. In fact, if he'd been there by himself (he was a little fat bastard), he never would make it in a million years. As he said, "I wouldn't have run after you. It'd wear me out."

So I was doing pretty good, you know, keeping a couple of yards between us. And I was making it toward these buildings, where I figured I could dodge in and out of the doors and throw him off, and then cut through an alley. And that's when I made that fatal little stumble over a piece of glass, and went down and couldn't get up on my ankle. And he was on top of me. But I still wouldn't go of my own volition. They had to bring cops and drag me to the car, and everything. And then I found out they had another cat stationed at my mother's house. It had all been very complete.

At the station started the usual pseudo questioning. First, the young cat, the thin one, the one who caught me, started giving this little routine about "Give us your man, and I won't kick you." This is the man-to-man talk, as distinguished from the man-to-rat talk you get from some of 'em. And he says, "We know you been going to the Hill Hotel. And we know a lot about you. Now, you know and I know that if you talk, we'll protect you, and we can get the man behind this, we can drive our own car."

I let him talk and agreed with him and everything, and then when he got to the end, I looked at him. I said, "Well, you know I won't do that. Call it honor among thieves, if you will," I said, "but I have certain amount of ethics. I simply couldn't. It would be against everything that I believe in. So let's not talk about it any more."

"Well, I'm disappointed, Janet," he says, "I knew you wouldn't."

Then they started filling out the sheet. They got a new sheet they're using around at all the stations. Very funny. It's junkie sheet. Like, "Why did you first use dope?" When he asked me that, I had to laugh. What could you possibly say? I looked at him for a couple of minutes and I said, "Sure got me." That was the only thing I could think of.

So we went through that. And my mother very kindly and magnanimously—the victor, you know—sends in a hamburger and a cup of coffee.

It's a little like a class. You all sit around and they say, "Janet, you're a good-looking girl." The young one: "You look like my wife." "I do?" "Yes, you do. Why, but what you need is carnies and beer. Go to a tavern. Have a drink. Meet a nice boy. Stay away from these musicians. They're no good, no good at all. They got to have stuff to beat those instruments the way they do." And the cat says, "Eat steaks. Buy yourself clothes. And love your mother."

Love your mother! All mothers are good. All these cats have mother complexes. I have heard this from every mother-fucking cop, practically, that I have ever talked to. You know, when they're scratching their heads and figuring "Now what the hell can you tell this kid to do? What's gonna save her?" This is the obvious answer.

And naturally, all I wanted to do was just get in a room with my mother for two minutes. Man! It was like a piece of iron inside me, hard and warped. Every time they just mentioned the word "mother," I wanted to regurgitate. But I mean, I played it cool.

"Now, my mother, after she died," he says, "I thought of the things that she did for me. Things that nobody else would do. Mothers take everything." So, anyway, he said he'd buy me a steak when I got out.

I waited for the wagon to come. And it was all sort of incongruous – I was right in my own neighborhood there. There was a street – a very familiar street. There was the movie. I could be over there in that movie! I was thinking of all kinds of things like that. I felt like trying to make another break for it, but I knew I wouldn't get anywhere.

Soon as I get to the Main Station and they're fingerprinting me, there's a broad in the cell right even with the little place where they sign in. It's four thirty in the morning, and here was this broad, standing up there, quacking in a storm. This is my first introduction to the opera singer. She was an older-looking Polack, or something, about forty-five years old and husky. Then she started singing operatic arias, and partiotic American songs, and Polish and oh, my God, what she didn't sing! That woman could sing anything.

They took me way down to the end and locked me up. And that's where I met another girl who was going to be with me for some time, Muriel Lane, an older junkie. And, later on, a young pickpocket, shoplifter, who used to use junk. So we talked, with slight interruptions for Muriel and I to be sick.

And there we were – hung up. What can you say about that, except that it happened? I was supposed to be booked and processed Wednesday and go to court Thursday. Every time they'd come down and take somebody to the Narcotics Unit and processed them that day, I'd say, "Me? Now, me?" I was afraid I was just going to be hung up there a couple of days.

And the opera singer was singing all this time, all day and all night and all day and all night. They finally took her out. We had four blissful hours in the afternoon of utter silence, except for our quacking. And then they bring in the grande dame. She was worse. She'd say, "I don't know why I'm in here. I know the Monsignor. My brother-in-law owns a furniture company. I'm a voting citizen! I don't know why they brought me down here. I'm just here as a witness for the FBI." And then all these gloomy stories. There was constantly that voice in your ear. It was enough to drive you mad. And then she'd cry. When she cried, she didn't cry silently; she bawled.

Everyone in the cell started yelling, "Shut up, bitch!" You know, all these hard bitches off Madison Street called her everything. And the grande dame: "Oh, oh, Mother of God," she said, "Oh, Jesus Christ! That they should be talkin' this way! These common scum, these bums, these low women!" And then, "Speak to me! What's the matter?" And then someone would say, "Up you, sister." And she'd say, "Oh, oh, my God, did you hear that? Did you hear that? Mary, Mother of God, did you hear that?"

This would keep on all day and all night. Well, she finally slipped completely before I left the joint. That was the worst yet. It was on my last day. I'll never forget that as long as I live. She'd been quiet for two hours. We should have known something was happening.

It was absolutely quiet – no sound – everybody was sleeping. All of a sudden, she lets out the most horrible scream. Nobody paid any attention to her. By this time, the matron and everybody figures, you know, that she is completely cracked. She said, "They're in here! They're in here! They're in the cell! Matron! Matron! My God! They're in the cell! Oh Mary, Mother of God!" You know she was praying – getting up and down and screaming.

I said, "Muriel, can't you do something? What's she yelling about?" Muriel said, "I don't know. Something's in the cell." Then the grande dame said, "There like a little mesh screen on the bars. Watch the screen! There it is, ther it is! I'm watching!" There on in, for about eight hours, this is all we heard. Like she was a pilot talking on an intercom system to somebody else. "I'm watching! I'm watching!" Muriel said she moved her mouth like she was talking through a microphone. "There he is! There we are! There it is, on the screen! I'm watching! They're coming from the left, the left, the left. . . ." She'd say nothing but "the left," for instance, for five minutes. "It's dark, it's dark on the bottom of the screen. There they are! There they are! I'm watching them!" She kept that up until we left the next day. We swore we'd kill her, but of course we never got a chance.

At any rate, I was booked that night, after I'd been processed. I went to the Narcotics Unit. It was a mere nothing. The usual, even less than last time.

I made the phone call to Roy. And Roy said he didn't have the bread to bail me out. Could I wait, since it was just a couple of hours to court? And I thought, Sure! It's only a couple of hours and I'll be out! I was so sure that there would be no hang-ups in court and that everything would go cool and that I would be free.

twilight of

the wctu

WILLIAM KLOMAN

Shortly before last Christmas a brisk matronly shopper stopped in front of a display of candied fruits arranged in small plastic tubs in the S. S. Kresge store in Evanston, Illinois, and paid twenty-nine cents for a jar of brandy sauce which was being sold for use on holiday puddings. The sale would have been routine in another town or to another customer, but Evanston is the home of the Woman's Christian Temperance Union and the customer was Mrs. Fred J. Tooze, its president.

Mrs. Tooze returned with her purchase to her office where she fired off indignant letters to the mayor and chief of police of Evanston and to the Illinois Liquor Control Commission in Chicago, charging that minors were buying the brandy sauce "for beverage purposes" and demanding "criminal prosecution of these selling activities by this store." The Liquor Control chairman, accustomed to such correspondence from Chicago's nearest northern suburb, telephoned the Kresge store manager, Dwain Tubbs, and told him to remove the item from sale.

Old S.S. Kresge himself, who was a ranking member of the tough-minded Anti–Saloon League, would have understood perfectly well what was happening but the manager of his Evanston branch reacted as if he had been hit by a sniper. "I wouldn't know the lady if I seen her," he said later. "She bought the stuff and did everything under the cloak of anonymous." The sauce itself, he claimed, was harmless enough. "We just bought it for fruitcake."

Tubbs isn't the only Evanston merchant to run afoul of the WCTU in recent years. Two years ago, also at Christmas time, Mrs. Tooze, accompanied by a local Baptist minister, made a small but successful raid on a Walgreen's drug store which had attracted her attention by offering for sale a battery-powered contrivance called the Charley Weaver Bartender Toy.

Mrs. Tooze recalled the incident recently. "It was a cute little gadget, really. There was this little old guy sat there at the bar shaking a cocktail, putting it in a glass, and drinking it down. Now we went after the Walgreen's to get it out of there because they had put it out where the kids could get to it and get the idea of shaking the cocktail and so on. Well, when we went in to remonstrate with them about it, the manager, he said, 'Well, that isn't for children. That's a gadget for adults.' But you see, that's why we went in there. Because it was a toy that had been produced for children, in order to build up a ... what? ... a *brainwashing* or psychological something

Reprinted by permission of CURTIS BROWN, LTD. from William Kloman, "Can the Forces of Virtue Defeat John Barleycorn?" Saturday Evening Post, *March 11, 1967, pp. 85-89. Copyright © 1967 THE CURTIS PUBLISHING COMPANY, INC.*

in their minds about how this thing can be shaken up and so on. So the pastor said to the manager, 'Well, then. What have you put it down *here* for? There, look at the kids—they're the ones that are looking at it. The adults aren't paying any attention to it.' And you see, the manager went over and grabbed the thing off the shelf, and we never saw it in Walgreen's any more." Before the bartender toy incident, it was cooking sherry in the Kroger store.

Evanston, Illinois, is one of the last strongholds of a crusade for total abstinence from alcoholic beverages that began in the nineteenth century and which by the end of the First World War had succeeded in getting its legislative demands written into the Constitution of the United States. Although the Prohibition Amendment was repealed in 1933, Evanston remains bone-dry and the WCTU means to keep it that way, not only in fact, but also in spirit.

Evanston's dry laws, which antedate national prohibition by more than half a century, are a classic case of what might be called legislative Overkill. The town was born dry since the state-enforced Charter of Northwestern University, written twelve years before Evanston was incorporated, includes a permanent injunction against the sale of alcohol beverages within four miles of the campus — roughly the distance of the town's perimeter. There is also a city ordinance against selling beverage alcohol, backed up, in turn, by a state law making it a crime to sell beer or whiskey where local law forbids it.

As an added guaranty of permanent sobriety the original University trustees, who held title to most of the land that later became Evanston, planted clauses in their property deeds automatically invalidating the documents should future

owners countenance trade in spirits. As one local lawyer put it, "If the town fathers had been able to arrange for a Doomsday Machine to activate itself the day the first highball was sold in Evanston, they probably would have done it."

The Woman's Christian Temperance Union, which continues to exercise surveillance over the morals of Evanston under a self-imposed mandate which it calls "home protection" is a national organization which was born in a spontaneous flurry of energy and indignation on Christmas Eve, 1783, in Hillsboro, Ohio. That morning seventy-five of the leading ladies of the community marched on the local saloons and, with much singing and praying and a smattering of modest civil disobedience, extracted promises from the proprietors that they would give up their trafficking in liquor and beer. These first raids were remarkably successful, and the distilleries in nearby Cincinnati quickly sent in reinforcements to buy up the available licenses and thus salvage some of their previously profitable trade.

The target of the first protests were immigrant saloon-keepers who insisted on selling beer from immigrant-owned breweries to their immigrant customers. In the nineteenth century teetotaling was the mark of the solid native middle-class respectables. And much of the impetus behind national prohibition, when it came, was the determination of the white, rural, Protestant, Anglo-Saxon majority to enshrine their personal values in the Constitution for all time. Come what may in the way of foreign scum to swell the urban proletariat, the newcomers would be forced to recognize as sacred writ the prevailing customs of the sturdy yeoman farmer who made the country what it is, etc., etc. It is not accidental that Prohibition was finally passed in 1918 and that the temperance propaganda of the time made good use of the anti-German sentiments aroused by the World War.

The original motto of the WCTU was "For God and Home and Native Land," and the organization remained a parochial cabal of small-town do-gooders until it was taken in hand by its second president, Frances E. Willard, an authentic organizational genius who was raised on a Wisconsin farm where applications of freshwater were considered a proper specific for all ailments from sore throats to broken legs. Before Miss Willard took over the WCTU in 1879, she had been a teacher in the Evanston College for Ladies, which later merged with Northwestern in a daring experiment in co-education. Miss Willard stayed on as dean of women in the university and taught a course in aesthetics (which was thought rather too avant-garde by her dowdy male superiors) but soon left teaching to devote all of her time to the Movement. Once in office, she set about streamlining its jumbled structure, expanding its membership rolls, and broadening its perspective to include women's suffrage, minimum wage legislation, and laws against white slavery.

She also founded the World WCTU. Returning to her hotel room after a tour of San Francisco's Chinatown, Miss Willard came to a conclusion notable for both its social and its geographic insight: "But for the intervention of the sea," she said, "the shores of China and the Far East would be part and parcel of our fair land. We are one world of tempted humanity." The motto of the WCTU was then changed to "For God and Home and Every Land," and the already receding values of rural America were made available on a global scale.

* * *

The WCTU is organized in every state in the Union, and while policies and activities—down to what is discussed in local meetings each month—are set in Evanston, the organizational pattern roughly follows a federal scheme. Each state has its own president (California and Washington for some reason each have two) and each county has a district president. The smallest unit, usually consisting of about thirty members, is the local "union."

The organization is technically non-sectarian, but the bulk of the members belong to Protestant churches of the funadmentalist variety. As one national officer put it, "We're a Christian organization right down the line. Of course we do have a few Catholic members as well."

In four states—Maryland, North Carolina, Tennessee, and Oklahoma—there are parallel groups for Negroes, who, in those states, elect their own officers and send their own delegates to national conventions. These groups are called Sojourner Truth unions, in honor of Sojourner Truth, an escaped female slave who had the distinction of being the first Negro to win a slander suit against a white man in an American court of law. Sojourner Truth died in 1883. One of her favorite phrases—she was, from all reports, a fiery platform-speaker—was "Chillun, I talk to God and God talks to me," which is approximately the same feeling Frances Willard had about her own work among the upper-middle-class whites of her day. Alabama had a Sojourner Truth group, but it died out a few years ago. Kentucky's has recently been incorporated into the regular WCTU, a step which the ladies at national headquarters believe to be indicative of social progress.

Mrs. Herman Stanley, a deep-bosomed, regal, and completely dedicated WCTU lady who serves as promotional secretary, is in charge of keeping track of the local unions and, if possible, attracting new members. She told me that she had no idea how many local unions there were, although she is in the process of creating an organizational chart by which she hopes to keep better track of things in the future. She estimates that there are perhaps five or six thousand local organizations, ranging in size from seven or eight members to five hundred. Each member pays a dollar a year to belong to the WCTU, of which ten cents is forwarded to national headquarters. The rest remains in the state, most of it going to finance state newspapers. There are also more honorific forms of membership, such as the Rock of Ages member, whose dues are "a penny a day and a prayer."

The WCTU national officers are decisive and outspoken on practically every topic except the number of members the organization has. Mrs. Stanley didn't know. Some of the ladies put the estimate as high as half a million, she said, but "I think that's overdoing it a bit." Mrs. Tooze said a quarter of a million, "in round figures." The round figures include the children, but as to how many children and how many adult ladies they involved, she said, "I can't tell you that right now. I don't even know really. It's a shame. We're trying to get that straightened out this year so we can . . . right now I can't break that down for you. We just say in round figures a quarter of a million. Total."

A district president in a Western state was more direct. "Membership?" she said. "That is information I have been instructed never to give. At national headquarters they feel that information on membership has been misused in the past." How misused? "Just misused." Also referring to the national officers, another member told me, "They're cagey about those numbers. They'll never tell."

The reason for the caginess can be found tucked away in the annual Treasurer's Report presented to the national convention. According to "income from dues" figures in these reports, the WCTU currently has 164,184 members. This is not a paltry number for a national protest organization, but a year-by-year comparison for the past five years shows that the movement has been going down, and the decline has been sharp. For the past five years, the WCTU has been losing members at a rate of 8420 a year, a trend which would totally deplete the membership of the group within twenty years.

Not all states are losing members. When there are net gains—usually in the South and Midwest—they are conspicuously and joyfully marked with an asterisk in the convention minutes each year. The incentives to the local unions also tell the story: Holdfast Unions (granted a certificate recognizing them as such) are those which retain all their living resident members on the rolls. Steadfast Unions (same reward) are those which have as many members this year as last—in other words, those which replace deceased members with new living ones. Fruitful Unions are those which show a net gain of one or more, and Life-line Unions—the significance of the honorary title is not lost on the ladies—are those which gain new members and contribute to the various fund-raising projects set up by national headquarters. "We had almost four hundred Life-line Unions last year," Mrs. Stanley told me. "We were very, very proud of them."

The Evanston union is one of about one hundred-fifty Iota Sigma chapters in the country, which means that it is designed especially for professional women and working girls. The WCTU has long believed that women "out in the world" face especially fierce temptations, so in 1934 it was decided that their specific needs could best be met by separate organizations. Iota Sigma means "To Prevail with a Sane Mind."

The professional women who comprise Evanston Iota Sigma are the thirty-two officers and staff members of the national headquarters, and they meet in Rest Cottage at noon on the second Tuesday of each month. Each lady brings her own sandwich, but dessert and coffee are provided by the Dessert Committee. After lunch comes a business session and business is followed by an educational program appropriate to a specific monthly theme. I was invited to sit in on a recent meeting. The theme was Character Building.

At Rest Cottage I was taken in hand by Mrs. Stanley, the promotion secretary, who acts as sort of an information officer for the WCTU and handles their usually unsatisfactory relations with the press. She asked me if I had brought my lunch along. I had not, and word was passed back to the kitchen, from which a roast-beef sandwich done up in Saran-Wrap was presently brought.

The ladies were seating themselves at folding card-tables, in foursomes, and I was asked to sit at a table which had already acquired two occupants—the only other men in the room. "I'll just sit over here with the boys," Mrs. Stanley explained to no one in particular. "The boys" turned out to be Mrs. Stanley's husband, Herman, who works around the headquarters building (locking up at night and delivering packages and the like) and Mr. Paul Wright, who has worked in the headquarters mail-room for the past fifteen years.

"I can remember when William McKinley was elected," Mr. Wright said. "How about that?" Mr. Stanley, a mild-mannered man, somwhat shorter than his wife, said that he remembered the day McKinley was assassinated but that the election was before his time. Mrs.

Stanley smiled and said that it was time to stand for grace-before-meals. Grace, which was sung, was led by a large woman who wore orthopedic shoes and kept time with both arms. The singing was loud and spirited.

During lunch Mr. Stanley told me of a recent trip to Washington, D.C., which he and his wife had taken. Inside the Capitol there had been a large mural of the Battle of Lake Erie which he had wanted to photograph. A Capitol policeman, however, told him that taking pictures inside the building was against regulations. "It was the right thing for the policeman to have done," Mrs. Stanley told her husband. "Some people will distort pictures to make them show things which aren't there." Stanley said that he had meant no harm.

"Our national shrines should be sacred," Mrs. Stanley told us. "And we should have a Sacred Patriotism where out nation's traditions are concerned, too." She was warming to her topic. "You take the Supreme Court. They're supposed to preserve the Constitution and yet they change it around to mean things it's not supposed to mean. They interpret and distort and . . . and . . . why, the first thing you know it doesn't mean *anything* any more." Mr. Stanley sat very straight, listening, while Mr. Wright ate his lunch and ignored the conversation. "The churches do it too," Mrs. Stanley said, "change our documents and water them down until we have nothing left to hold on to."

Mr. Stanley recalled that in a recent *National Geographic* he had read that Andrew Johnson had asked to be buried with his head resting on a copy of the Constitution. "Ach," said Mrs. Stanley. "Buried with the Constitution. Sentimentality. That's not what I'm talking about. Not at all."

Mr. Wright interrupted his lunch to ask what she *was* talking about and Mrs.

Stanley told him that she had hoped to see the cherry blossoms in Washington, but that the city had been too crowded. "There were people all over the place," she said.

Just then a heavy-set Negro wearing a dark blue suit and black tie entered the room. He was about forty-five, and was accompanied by a slightly younger woman in a tan suit and light blue coat. Her skin was lighter than her companion's and she wore a furry pill-box hat which matched her coat. Miss Allen, the Narcotics Education lady, crossed the room to meet them and showed them to two seats at a table near the door which had been left vacant. Several of the ladies present apparently knew the newcomers and nodded greetings, which were returned. The gentleman was later introduced as the Reverend King L. Mock, a graduate of the WCTU narcotics Education course in Chautauqua, New York, and today's guest speaker. The woman was his wife, Charlotte.

As coffee was poured and the Dessert Committee served slices of Sara Lee cheesecake a woman announced that everybody should look at the underside of his teaspoon. One spoon at each table was marked with a strip of tape and the person with the marked spoon was to be allowed to keep the cloth flower which had served as the center-piece for each table. No one at our table had a marked spoon and Mrs. Stanley suggested that Mr. Wright take the flower on our table home to his wife, who had been visiting her sister in South Bend and therefore had missed the meeting. "Don't want to," he replied. "You take the thing. You're the woman." Mrs. Stanley thanked him, and with everyone's assent pinned the flower to her dress and ate her dessert.

When Mr. Wright had finished eating he folded up the table leg on his right and held the table in place with his hand until the rest of us were done and the remaining dishes had been cleared away. Then Mr. and Mrs. Stanley and I each folded a table-leg and Mrs. Stanley carried the table away. The chairs were then placed in a semi-circle two or three chairs deep; Mrs. Tooze took a seat in the back row (she does not hold office in the local chapter). A bust of Frances Willard on a pedestal behind Mrs. Tooze's chair peered over her shoulder and looked as if it were in attendance at the meeting. The monthly meeting of the Evanston WCTU was then called to order.

The business part of the meeting took twelve minutes. The treasurer reported a balance of $82.93 in the kitty and announced that "almost ten dollars" had been spent on books for the Haven Junior High School, the health director of which was reported to be delighted by the gift of anti-alcohol propaganda. The acquisition of seven new card tables (the ones we had used at lunch) and thirty-six new folding chairs (on which we were sitting) was announced. The tables and chairs had been purchased with green stamps the chapter members had accumulated.

It was announced that serveral White Ribbon Recruits were ready to be presented to the chapter but that their induction ceremony would be postponed until the national convention so that they could be shown to the delegates. White Ribbon Recruits are children under the age of six dedicated to total abstinence and purity by their mothers. A white ribbon is tied around their wrists to symbolize their dedication, and it is expected that at the age of six the Recruits will join the Loyal Temperance Legion and sign the pledge for themselves.

Under new business it was moved that any remaining premium stamps be used to get a portable ice chest to prevent the candy bars which are sold in the headquarters building to raise money for

Iota Sigma from "going limpy" during the summer. The measure aroused some controversy: one lady thought that hard candy or gumdrops would answer the problem more economically, but was informed that some of the members preferred Hershey Bars, even in the summer. Another member suggested keeping the candy in the basement during hot spells, but her proposal was met by general derision. "You don't expect us to go traipsing all the way down the basement just to buy a candy bar?" One lady said. The original motion was re-stated and passed unanimously.

After the business meeting was adjourned the lady in the orthopedic shoes who had earlier led the singing rose to deliver an inspirational message on the theme of Mother. She cited several Biblical mothers and grandmothers as evidence of God's particular interest in motherhood, and went on to generalize her theme to apply to women in general. "You don't have to bear the child to be a mother," she said, "or to share in the special grace which God has showered upon the holy estate of motherhood. For God has raised up Woman to have, I shall not say a sixth sense, but to have a heart of compassion and love not only for this child which may be her own, but for all of mankind." Several of the ladies nodded vigorously. "Amen," one of them said.

It was Hannah Whitall Smith, a prominent Philadelphia Quaker and the mother-in-law of both Bertrand Russell and Bernard Berenson, who called the WCTU Organized Mother-Love. Frances Willard herself, of course, was not a mother, and neither is the present WCTU national president, which perhaps suggests that Mother-Love is most potent when it is vicarious. Miss Willard, as a result of her association with the WCTU, became known as the Uncrowned Queen of American Womanhood.

Now, in Evanston, Charlotte Mock, as a representative of Woman, was asked to make a few remarks in advance of her husband's address. "I'd rather let my husband do the talking," Mrs. Mock said. "He's the one you want to hear." "Ladies first," said one of the ladies, and the rest laughed lightly as Mrs. Mock rose to speak.

"Well," she said. "I should like to thank you ladies for inviting us up here this afternoon to share some of our experiences with you." She looked around the room at the ladies, who were smiling in anticipation, and smiled back at them. "I am reminded of my home in Kansas," she told them. "I grew up in a house much like this one, a lovely Victorian cottage with gingerbread on the eaves and lovely shade trees in the front yard and grass. I couldn't help but think on the way up here that Evanston and Rest Cottage are a long way, not only in miles, from the concrete and steel which is the basic design of the South Side of Chicago. My home now is in a high-rise and the problems of the families who live in those places are different from the problems we knew as children. My husband and I are seeking answers to those problems and that is why we have turned to you. We heard that you offered a course in narcotics education, and that's what we needed—narcotics education. Those who try to do something about narcotics on the South Side find that nobody is willing to teach them."

She drew a short breath; she had been talking rapidly. "There is also an alcohol problem on the South Side and it is not limited to adults. There are children who drink and children who take dope and we are looking for the answer to problems like these. We know of children, even those whose families can afford to give them money for lunch at school, who rather than buy that lunch will kitty up their money and buy liquor. The teachers tell me they can spot the ones who do. They droop in class. They droop and sleep because they have gotten liquor or had older children get it for them and have been drinking that liquor even before the school day has begun."

Several of the ladies exchanged wide-eyed glances. Some shook their heads.

"We have found a strange thing, "Mrs. Mock continued. "We have found, or teachers have found and told us, that there are many bright children among their pupils. Children who will work and in many cases over-excel, but only until they get to the fourth grade. That seems to be the cut-off point and even the bright ones seem to give up by the time they're in the fourth grade. Now we don't know what causes this but we have our suspicions, and it all has to do with the way these children and their families live.

"It is said that the poor you will always have with you," Mrs. Mock said. Several of the ladies smiled appreciatively, nodding their heads. "And we have found this to be true. Even when you work to instill pride in these people—for pride is the secret ingredient—and your work is crowned with success, why, the next thing you know the people become middle-class and move out of the high-rise and others move in to fill their places and it's with them that you have to start all over again." Mrs. Mock stopped abruptly. "But please," she said, "here I am running on. My husband is the one who knows this thing first-hand. He must tell you. Thank you for your kind attention."

The ladies applauded and nodded vigorously to Mrs. Mock, who smiled and sat down.

King Mock, a powerfully built and serious man with deep lines in his full face, is a graduate of the Chicago Baptist Institute and an ordained minister in the Baptist church. Until 1958 Mr. Mock had been pastor of the Beersheba Baptist Church, on the South Side, but resigned his pastorate and took a job as a high-rise apartment house supervisor. "To get closer to people's lives," he says.

He now stood before the Evanston WCTU holding a packet of six large filing cards, a bulging manila envelope, a small worn brown paper bag, and a rolled-up square of black fabric. Without acknowledging the applause, which had trailed off after his wife sat down and which was now reviving for him, he opened the square of cloth and draped it over a small table which stood in the front of the room. Then he laid the file-cards flat on the cloth to form a U.

"These cards represent our high-rise complexes on the South Side," he said. "They have laundries and playgrounds and every other thing you can think of. Even some grass is beginning to grow in some cases." The ladies were amused by this comment and the atmosphere of the room grew more relaxed. Mr. Mock opened his manila envelope and peered inside. He turned it upside-down over the high-rise cards and several hundred pennies clattered onto the table. The pennies formed a mound which spilled over the cards, partly obscuring them. "These pennies represent people and how they spill over," he said.

The ladies looked intently at the pennies. Mr. Mock opened his paper bag and emptied twenty or so hypodermic syringes and several small pharmacy vials on top of the pennies. There was now heavy breathing in the room and some audible gasps. Several of the women shifted uneasily in their folding chairs. Mr. Mock continued. "And this is what happens to the people when they spill over. Each of these syringes I have personally taken away from a narcotics addict in the neighborhood where I live. I have scared some of them into turning them over; some I have taken from small children whose older brothers or sisters have led me to them hoping I could do some good before it was too late."

He surveyed his audience. "Those of you who have not been exposed to this problem, I can't say that you're blessed because it gives you a feeling of humanness and compassion for a fellow human being to know such things and to enter into them, and we have a while ago heard some very fine sentiments expressed concerning compassion and the instincts of love which God has put into mothers." Attention shifted briefly to the lady in the Dr. Scholl's shoes, who smiled brightly.

"But you *are* blessed because your nerves are not torn apart by some kid who has gotten to you and kept you awake at night wondering *why*?" Mr. Mock had shouted the question. His voice now became gentle and conversational. "You and I have been brought up to respect the gray hair and to have reverence for the woman." There was a general nodding of heads. "Uh-huh," said Mr. Stanley, nodding. "You and I have been taught to think of dope pushers as hardened male criminals." Quizzical looks were exchanged. "But I am here to tell you that there are some women who will lead children astray. Many of those who sell the dope to the young people in the South Side of Chicago are women, and some of them are not young women." "No," said one of the ladies, "no." "Tsk," said another.

"So the question arises, what to do? And the fact is that there are no simple answers to this question. How many of you have read *The Ugly American*?" Mr. Mock asked. "I read part of it," one lady volunteered. "I read a review," said another. "Well, from studying the story of that American diplomat, faced every day with situations nobody had ever faced before and for which his training had not prepared him, we see that I cannot take solutions from one area over into the next one. Instead of being so ready with our cut-and-dried answers, we must look deeply into the causes of things, and in coming to understand the causes—what causes people to lose their pride in the first place, for instance—there comes a great frustration.

"There is a great incursion of rural people into the cities. You go down any day to the Illinois Central railroad and see them coming in from the South." "Mmm, yes," someone said. "There are not sufficient jobs for these people. We don't even have enough jobs for the people already *here*. And the government won't let them work for their relief checks. There's work enough to be done, but they have to take the relief money like a hand-out and that's part of what kills people's pride in themselves. I say put them to work cleaning vacant lots, cleaning up alleys or fixing up the parks. Anything, so they can say they earned that money they get from the government. But here you run up against the labor unions and they want to protect themselves and what they've got, so they want their people to get whatever jobs there are. And if there isn't enough money to pay union wages they would rather see the job not done at all.

"Then there is the entire attitude of the housing people. I have been working for eight years trying to get them to take the name project out of the housing. Think of living in a 'project.' A project is something experimental. Something not completed. These are our *homes,* so leave the name project out of it. If you call us project people then we must be here for manipulation and experiment. And I say to the housing people, if you have something else in mind for us, let's hear it. Otherwise don't call it a project."

Mr. Wright, who had taken a front seat, was now asleep.

"There was a day," Mr. Mock continued, "and you all remember it, when the family dwelling was passed down from one generation to the next. Grandfather or Grandmother was there to advise the young ones as they came up, and the father was the head of the family. We are in a new age, groping our way. And we are fast arriving at a situation where there is a head of nothing.

"Adults greedy for money are waiting to lead our children astray. And it isn't just the little old woman who's pushing the stuff. Take her away and three like her are waiting to take her place. It's a business. There is no dope grown in America. It all has to be imported, so it comes on somebody's ship or in somebody's plane. That's business. The government spends millions every year to keep it out, but someone's making millions on it and they have the money to protect their investment. I don't know where it comes from and I don't *want* to know. People who know get killed. But it comes all the same.

"Like I say, I don't have the answers. I just want to tell you what the problem is like. Maybe you have the answers. I don't." Mr. Mock turned to gather up his illustrative materials. He picked up a small bottle from among the syringes and read its label. "Looks like someone robbed Saul's Pharmacy," he said.

The ladies clapped vigorously and nodded to one another. Miss Allen smiled broadly and formed a silent "thank you" for Mr. and Mrs. Mock. A woman in the back of the room tapped her cane on the carpet and asked if a question were in order, and as the speaker gathered his file card housing development together the woman with the cane delivered a brief speech in which she pointed out that she had learned, while doing volunteer work in the Welfare Office, that people on relief were lazy and unappreciative and that they lacked self-respect. She said that they didn't really want to work so long as the government was feeding them. Mr. Mock answered that his experience had been different and that maybe we shouldn't draw firm conclusions from only a few cases.

A second woman suggested that Mr. Mock go to speak with the labor leaders in Chicago and convince them "to open their doors more freely to Negroes." Mr. Mock thanked her for her suggestion.

A third lady, perhaps recalling the story of Miss West and the thousand opium pipes, wanted to know if Mr. Mock had reformed all of the drug addicts whose syringes he had brought with him. Mock looked blankly at his questioner for a moment, then looked at his wife, who smiled gently and lowered her eyes. "Ma'am, perhaps we'd better explain something to you," he began.

Several days later I asked Mrs. Tooze her impression of Mr. Mock's talk. "I thought that maybe he would have something there he would leave us. Some literature or something," she said. She seemed disappointed, a little puzzled. "But he didn't seem to have any literature."

It was late afternoon and Mrs. Tooze had put in a hard day struggling against the rich and crafty legions of King Alcohol. This dope addiction business—it seemed to keep cropping up. Was it meant to lure the ladies into dividing their forces? If so, it wouldn't work. Organized Mother-Love would not be diverted from its purpose. "There's nothing that the liquor people would like to see us do any better than to go off on a tangent," she said firmly. "Our main line is alcohol. We were organized to fight the liquor traffic, and that's where we'll stay."

inside the hippie revolution

WILLIAM HEDGEPETH

Heeeere, Jake. Lovely thing. La, la, la, lee. Come to sissy, beautiful, gorgeous red love. Oh star in heaven. La, la, dee, dee, dee, dee."

It was all wispy and faint at first, and I couldn't tell where the oddly liberated little singsong voice was coming from until I had groped through the thick vines and greenery nearly all the way down into the small secluded glen, almost to the edge of the tiny, lily-padded lake. There, over near the trees at one end of the lake—with her head almost hidden by the low-hanging branches and her legs mostly covered by patches of high grass and tall yellow flowers—a brightly-beaded, long-haired, Ophelia-like girl of about 19 or 20 knelt in an orange-and-blue robe knotting a 15-foot-long chain of flower blossoms and reeling off detached, mindless little utterances in a soft, girlish, psychedelic voice. The only other sound was the dim, slow wail of a harmonica from the far end of the glen where a lone boy with shoulder-length hair sat on a rock improvising a Southern Negro-style blues tune.

I was fairly near the girl now, but as I got closer, I realized she was skimming farther and farther away in her drug-stretched mind. "Oh, loo, loo, blue, blue, Jakejakejakejake," she sang, with her deranged eyes still fixed on the lengthening flower chain in her hands. Suddenly, out of a thick clump of bushes, bounded a huge Irish setter—Jake, apparently—who was just far enough away so that I was able to claw my way wildly back up the bank and out of the valley before he had a chance to pounce on me.

Earlier that morning, I had strolled into San Francisco's huge Golden Gate Park—which borders the Haight-Ashbury district — with a barefoot, blanketed veteran hippie from Minneapolis named MacGregor, who claimed a major portion of his waking hours were usually spent wandering through the foliage or rolling down the park's grassy slopes. "Man, just smell all the flowers and all the dope," he smiled as soon as we passed between the stone pillars at the Haight St. entrance. The morning fog had cleared, and scores of other hippies were walking about to the soft accompaniment of their jangling ankle bells or sunning themselves on the ground or gathered in tiny groups under the bushes smoking "grass" (marijuana) or clustered in larger numbers around the endless, hypnotic beating of bongo drums, with each one lost in the swirl of his own private planetary orbit.

MacGregor and I walked through the clearing into a woodsy area and up hills and over fences until we came upon what seemed an infinity of huge bushes bursting with pink and white rhodo-dendrons and blue hyacinths and vivid explosions of yellows and reds and purples. Almost as if on cue, though without thinking, we separated and faded wordlessly into the flowers to become lost in the thick maze of colors, making absentminded figure eight's and lazy circles. I drifted out later on to a wooded path and was maneuvering back to the park entrance when I saw coming toward me two girls in sandals and somber, full-length gowns. They would have looked like women from India if it had not been for the large clanging cowbells around their necks and the drug-induced lumpy litheness of their walk. As we passed, one of them glanced up at me with a benign smile and warm, dazed-looking eyes, and without breaking stride, cooed, "I love you," and floated away without waiting for a reply—which saved me some embarrassment, since my initial, stunned, stupid reaction was to mutter, "Well. . .uh. . .thank you," in a lame, small voice. At that point, I had been living in Haight-Ashbury only two days, and in spite of my beads and long hair and short beard, I was still a blatant amateur as hippies go.

Two days earlier, it had been even worse. Less than an hour and a half after flying in from New York and dressing for the part, I bounced out of a cab at Haight and Ashbury Streets, and the best I had been able to do was ogle openmouthed at the wild, shaggy parade of hip characters sitting or milling and dancing up and down Haight, the major avenue of the largest hippie ghetto in the world. ("Haight is love," said signs everywhere.) After a few minutes, a hairy fellow with a ring in his nose and red designs painted on his cheeks stopped and asked me for some help in raising his rent money. In return, he directed me to the free store where he said I could get some food and a place to "crash" that night.

The free store is exactly that: Anything in the place is yours if you need it—second- and third hand clothing of any description, old magazines and books and whatever food may be lying around. The store is run by the Diggers, a sort of hippie civic association whose members spend their time scrounging about for clothes and other goods they can give away.

Since it was chilly, I had bought a blanket in town, and now I took a straw hat and an old suit coat several sizes too large. I was hungry and was about to ask where one could get something to eat when a ragged, dumpy-looking, straggle-haired girl with wire-rim glasses and feathers in her headband loped into the store carrying a sack. She plopped it in the middle of the room and, with an air of shy authority as she started back out the door, said, "Food." Then she disappeared down the street as everyone in the store leaped to the bagful of cookies and peanut butter and radishes.

After wolfing down the groceries I could get hold of, I asked a tall, intense-looking hippie beside me if he knew of a place to sleep. At once, his eyes widened as he leaned toward me conspiratorially and asked in a low voice, "Have you ever done any writing?" I said yes, I had, and before I could say anything more, we were halfway down the street on the way to his pad. He told me his name was Dunbar, and thanks to this meeting, I not only now had a nice piece of messy floor to sleep on, with about eight other semi-permanent hippie tenants, but also a job as a writer for *Fusion* magazine, an underground hip publication for which he was assembling enough material to put out a first issue. The total contents at this point consisted of 30 terrible poems, a maudlin story about a coyote and an incomprehensible essay. But Danbar had just acquired a tiny portable typewriter, and so things seemed to him to be looking up, journalistically speaking.

The next morning, I set out to find some good material for *Fusion*. But before leaving the pad, I made the mistake of asking the time from a hippie who had just washed his beard and was strolling around aimlessly thumping a tambourine. He looked astonished and said, "Naw, man, we never know what time it is." As I came to learn, time is one of the many things that mean nothing here. The days blur namelessly into one another without regard to date or hour or light or darkness.

It *was* worth the effort, however, to find out when Sundays rolled around because of the all-day "happenings" that were staged in the Panhandle, a narrow strip of land extending from the park. Hundreds of hippies would gravitate to the Panhandle each Sunday and huddle around a large truck that served as the stage for one or more local rock groups. Rock music – referred to here as "love-rock" or "acid-rock" – is a vital ingredient in this whole way of life.

In its ideal form—fast and almost too loud for the normal ear to withstand—it blanks the mind, stuns the senses and forcibly reaches out and commandeers all the nerve fibers and viscera of the body, so that you find yourself leaping and twitching to the contagious drum-thump-twang rhythm with total and unconscious abandon.

This Sunday's program featured a nondescript group of males with hair shagging well past their shoulder blades. Without a word of warning, they ripped out their electrically amplified guitar-drum-bass beat through a solid phalanx of five-foot-tall speaker systems, powered by a portable generator chugging away behind the truck bed. As the pelvic pulsing began to soak into the audience, a narcotized girl in Levis, wearing only a loose poncho with nothing underneath, and a grassy-eyed rail of a boy dangling a single unfired flashbulb on a cord around his neck began writhing in a trancelike rhythmic rite around an old bicycle tire lying on the ground. Other dancers began at once to flap and jump and gyrate in stuporous ecstasy and dead seriousness

with eyes half-closed, oblivious to everyone, including their own partners.

The rock group geared up and poured themselves into a long, improvised, semimelodic stream of notes held together only by the steady, flagrantly sensual reverberating beat of the drums. Propelled by sheer atavistic instinct, everyone danced or shook or rolled uncontrollably on the ground. It was an infectious Indian ritual in which all – momentarily – were warriors. A grandmother type twitched her shoulders like a Ziegfeld Follies flapper. An elderly work-a-daddy in a wide-brimmed hat and a 1940's-style suit, who had just stopped to watch, began waving his arms at the sky like a Hallelujah shouter at a Baptist camp meeting. Everything became a part of this expanding megabeat momentum that built up and up and on and on until, at last, the day cooled and darkened and the frenzy calmed and the music quieted and those of the crowd who were still able to walk inched their way back to Haight St.

I walked back with Rick, a small, wiry artist wearing circular earrings, and Kathy, his pregnant, unofficial wife. Kathy had admired the colorful Indian-design blanket I had around me, which established, as far as we three were concerned, a lifelong bond of affection. Although it didn't seem to bother them, they had less than a dollar between them and were going to be evicted from their pad the next day, along with about 30 others, for nonpayment of rent. When I heard this, I gave them half of the $20 in my wallet. Thinking I was homeless, they responded by inviting me to spend the night at their place. (I later learned they used part of my $10 to buy food and drugs and then gave the rest to people they thought were destitute.)

Unlike Dunbar's pad, full of sober, utopian-minded idealists ("Let's abolish money; let's set up pilot communities of love all over the country," etc.), Rick and Kathy's place was a filthy, litter-strewn, swarming dope fortress that was a great deal less savory and sanitary than a sewer, since people attempted to live in it. Along the hallway when we walked in there were at least a half-dozen hippies lying in various stages of drug stupor. And in the darkened bedrooms, blank-faced males and females sat stupefied on the floors as rock music howled full volume from radios and hundreds of flies churned through the layers of sweet-smelling marijuana smoke. A pasty face in a coonskin cap rolled a fresh "joint" of grass and passed it around for all to smoke, except for two in the corner who were shooting their arm veins full of "speed," or Methedrine, a super-powerful pep drug.

About one that morning, "The Bat" drifted into the pad, accompanied by two Negro hip types, one of whom, I was told, had been a "nark" (narcotics agent) until he became turned on to the glories of "acid" (LSD) and other glories of the inner universe. The Bat wore an ankle-length black cape with a little red collar poking up into thick, kinky black hair that poofed out about eight inches on each side of his head. The Bat was so stoned when he arrived that he was talking in a whiny, scary falsetto voice — yet whatever he had been taking still wasn't enough. Around five a.m., I woke up briefly to catch sight of him sitting in the hall, wrapped in his cape, talking in an even higher falsetto than before and shooting sugared water into the veins of his neck, since he had run out of real drugs as well as available places to stick the needle. Each time he injected himself, he would moan, "Oooooohhh, oooohhh, this is my thing...this is my thing," and would "freak out" by rolling around the floor, thrashing and flopping and hooting like an owl.

By the time everyone came to and cleared out the next morning, the pad had been rented by a burly hippie named Ed, who made good money hanging pennants for used-car lots. Rick, Kathy and I had met Ed the night before, and now we were asked to be the nucleus of a new communal "family" under the condition that we would keep our rooms clean and not allow any friends in the pad who happened to be "speed freaks." Taking too much Methedrine over a time can cause bizarre mental effects or blow people's minds so that they end up walking around like wild, freaky vegetables. Speed is not a hallucinatory drug and is avoided not only by most hippies but even by the strangely nonviolent variety of Hell's Angels who wander around the "Hashbury."

With these ground rules, our new communal family took shape. One of the earlier residents, a genial dealer in grass and acid named Janice, asked if she could live in the hall closet where she could close herself in and not bother with people when she was coming off a drug high. Frank, a soft-spoken Venezuelan, also asked to stay, though he was not particular about his sleeping arrangements. It turned out that he rarely slept anyway. He spent his days panhandling on Haight St. and his evenings slumped in the front hall hopped up on one chemical or another, endlessly drawing pictures of Jesus in pencil or adding to some interminable prose work he was writing in Spanish—while a radio pumped constant rock music into his ears.

Rabbit, a Bostonian with a voice like Bullwinkel the moose, and Linda, his chick, moved in a few days later. When I first saw them, they were both so stoned and giggly on acid that they seemed lost and helpless. Good-hearted Rabbit remained helpless. First, he tried selling hippie papers on Haight St., and then he became a full-time panhandler; but no matter what he did, at the end of each day, he would almost always wind up giving away the money he had collected. Then he would come home and mope hungrily until someone gave him some food.

Somehow, our pad soon became an all-night civic center for itinerant speed freaks. When Kathy, who was pregnant, became a steady speed user, I gave her a bottle of vitamins I had brought to ward off creeping malnutrition. I don't know if I looked underfed — actually, I had been eating huge quantities of rice as well as some cans of chicken-flavored cat food that wasn't bad at all. And if that weren't enough, I could go to the Panhandle around four every day to fight my way to the day-old bread and free pots of food left over from restaurants, all of which the Diggers collected and served up to hungry hippies and to any brooding, groggy, middle-aged winos who happened to be standing around. Nevertheless, Rick became concerned about my health and offered to suggest a drug to suit my mood. "Man," he said, "you know, I feel everyone's my better half. Like we're all part of the same side-show. I mean, there may be some who'd call you and me freaks, and maybe we are. But by whose standards? LBJ and his boys? I think what you need is some smack, some scag. Groovy stuff. If you're feelin' up-tight, it makes you loose and fills in all the blank spaces." I asked him if scag was like acid, and he said, "No, man, no. It's smack, you know, smack—*heroin*, man!"

I declined, but Rick didn't mind since he was feeling pepped up and philosophical. As he looked around his and Kathy's room, with its religious symbols and drawings all over the walls, he changed pace and said, "Hell, this isn't what we want—to live like this. This isn't our whole trip. We're out to bust up the concrete, man—to let the flowers grow. What we're really looking for is a new beginning.

He winced and shook his head. "Everything's too *sterile*. Man's creative spirit is being destroyed. He's become so unnatural that he's freaked out the order of the universe, and now the universe is trying to restore itself. A radical change is taking place in this generation. Middle-aged people just can't accept that their children are prophesying to them. The proof is that there's no communication between the generations." Rick was prancing fiercely around his room, and a candle on the floor cast his shadow huge against the wall. "Back to the land!" he shouted as he and his shadow gestured wildly. "I'll groove with the elements." He paused and said more quietly, "We're a threat to the world, you know. But it's God's plan. There are more people 25 and under now than there are of 'Them.' "

The dark reference to "Them" means the "straight" people, the nonhip, tuned-out guardians of the Establishment and the status quo—in other words just about everyone else. Straight society is seen here as an irrelevant, cruel, sneaky, dehumanizing, soul-devouring fraud. The hippies' attitude toward it is not one of rebellion but of rejection. "The Establishment's falling apart. Why fool with it?" my friend MacGregor had said. To take its place, hippies are working toward an open, loving, tension-free, nature-oriented world of their own. On an individual basis, each hippie simply seeks to "do his thing"—to lead the private, personalized way of life that grooves him and turns him on. Out of respect for this, hippie philosophy cautions that "you don't try to force your 'thing' on anyone else." On this basis, a few hippie zealots have been persuaded, at least for the moment, to abandon their idea of polluting San Francisco's water system with enough LSD to turn the whole straight city on.

But the straight people are not similarly content to leave the Hashbury in peace. Every day—and unbearably so on Sundays—Haight St. is choked with automobiles stuffed with sight-seers who snap photos of the hippies from behind locked car doors and window glass rolled up as tighly as if this were a tour through the reptile house at the zoo. Little children peer wide-eyed from the back seat; white-haired grannies stare in near shock with mouths agape; Mr. and Mrs. So-and-so in the front seat point and smirk nervously in their voyeurism—and then they talk of returning next week.

Of course, there are a number of would-be hippies and mixed-up teeny-boppers who dress outlandishly on the weekends and drive over to the Hashbury so they can parade around gaudily and feed the public's "image" appetite. But these types usually don't know what's going on any more than the tourists. They may have even nodded approvingly with the "respectable" citizenry when a local politician, described by the press as a "smiling 48-year-old Republican," announced his candidacy for mayor and "came out four-square against hippies."

That the generation gap yawns widest here was proved further when the transit company announced in June that certain bus lines were to be rerouted to avoid "the Sodom of the Haight-Ashbury." This fearful and distorted public view of the whole scene came home to me very pointedly when a writer on contract to a confession magazine picked me as a candidate for an interview, and then went on to ask questions too sexual and bizarre to repeat here. Within the limits of decency and accuracy and fantasy, I "confessed" to everything she suggested and everything I could think of—except that I was with LOOK—until she left, satisfied and smacking her lips.

Besides the nameless strangers who would be found each morning sleeping all over the floors, our family took in some new members. The first was Don, a sophisticated East Coast hippie who was a large-scale dealer in drugs. Morton, a practicing Buddhist from Chicago, served to help the rest of us get high each night by leading us in The Great Mantra, a slow, hypnotic Buddhist chant. Eileen was an 18-year-old who sewed any kind of cloth she could get her hands on. And finally, there was a second Kathy, who wore glasses. This Kathy With Glasses was a mystical sort of borderline paranoid who—when she was not immersed in her comic books—spouted dark intuitive revelations. A suspicious, paranoid style of thinking is really very common here, partly because hippies are so passive in almost all that they do. When they are on "trips," the drugs are the agents in control; in their normal states, their emotions are allowed to direct their actions. The Establishment is seen as controlling the country as a whole; and on the local level, police and narks snoop everywhere. In addition, the hippies' almost-unanimous faith in astrology and fatalism further convinces them they are powerless to cope with anything that might happen.

Kathy With Glasses, among others, claimed to have a vision predicting that the President was going to declare war sometime this summer, at which time the hippies—as vocal pacifists—would be branded as traitors and herded into concentration camps. She also foresaw a colossal earthquake that would send part of the State of California sliding into the Pacific Ocean. No one really minded the earthquake idea especially, but the concentration-camp business was a source of genuine fear within the community.

In spite of these omens, the hippies all share the confident belief that they are the right astrological track and that their gentle, anarchistic mode of life is in line with the universal plan. In the life-style they are evolving, in which the goal is not to hoard but to contribute, survival is no problem and money is of no special value. Happiness, to them, is not just the old material goal of "three hots and a place to flop," it is a matter of what you can create and give to other people.

"But what do you *do*?" I heard visitors on the street asking hippies over and over again. Actually, as far as regular jobs are concerned, a great many work for the Post Office Department. Otherwise, they may play in rock bands, sell papers to tourists, get unemployment checks, receive money from home, deal in drugs, or panhandle on the street. There is a Hip Job Co-op that acts as a low-key employment service. But the general motto in all things is "Don't do it if it doesn't groove ya."

What the hippies say they are "doing" in the more important sense is living creatively, experimenting with new styles of living and generally appreciating the wonder and changeability of human life. They have consciously "dropped out," or detached themselves, from what they consider the regimented, stultifying, dog-eat-dog "games" of the straight world, and have redefined "progress" and "success" in purely human terms. No boundaries are drawn between art and life. Everyone is creative and can realize his own full creative potential in everything he does, whether it is sandal-making or song-writing. Hippie paintings and music are created not for public display but for the supreme private job of spontaneous artistic creation in itself.

To a large extent, this road to hippiness may be a one-way avenue: To some who have made the trip, the straight life may seem totally artificial, biologically unsound and suitable only for dropping out of. Straight life, in the eyes of most hippies, is a long, stifling process

designed to thwart and hem in all that is natural and spontaneous in humans. They believe that social conditioning, mass taste-making and indoctrination steadily stunt and narrow the individual human potential, with the result that society itself has become fragmented, specialized and narrow—and thereby tense, alienated and lonely. By contrast, as Rick put it, "Hippies don't separate and pigeonhole and categorize. All in one. All in love. And love is where it's at."

If life to the hippies has any "purpose" in the ordinary context of the word, that purpose is religious discovery. For religion is not only consciousness-expanding but it offers a further sense of identification and common understanding among those who have "seen the light." To the hippies, LSD is a sort of sacrament, which, as one 35-trip veteran said, "turns the keys to the inner doors." It's impossible to say what each individual finds behind his own door—that's "his thing" or "his trip." But basically, an acid voyage breaks down the ego and, as Court, an on-and-off padmate put it, "lifts the veil of illusion to show the holiness and oneness of the universe."

Most others claim the psychedelic experience reveals a unity with God, an effusion of joy and a feeling of love, compassion and identity with everything. Darlene said: "It's like seeing the world again through a child's eyes—a transcendental glory. A wonder. Everything's all at once. Oh, beautiful." (I met Darlene in the faint early grayness of the morning as she sifted through sand crystals in the park with her senses soaring far out in space on a magic carpet of acid.)

The common denominator is the psychedelic experience, whether achieved through hallucinatory drugs or grass or religious chanting or sex—with sex as the most accessible of psychedelics among the hippies. Psychedelic drugs are used by some as on immediate plunge into the sensation of personal divinity and fusion with the universe, as sought by Eastern religions—a sort of instant Buddhist *satori*, available at last through the chemical fruits of American technology. To others, acid is an avenue to primitive Christianity. In the park, I fell in with about 40 hippies all sitting on the ground rhythmically pounding the concrete sidewalk with rocks and tin cans to the chant: "Let's all be Jesus till it starts to hurt." Two nuns stopped and smiled and swished slightly in their black robes as they patted their feet to the tin-can beat before passing on. "I mean, some guy dies for you, it can't help but turn you on emotionally, man," one of the pounders said to me.

Allen Cohen, the editor of the hippie *Oracle*, has been in the Hashbury almost from the start of the movement. He calls this a "prophetic community." The Victorian — era houses in this lower-middle-class run-down neighborhood were large enough and cheap enough to be rented by family-style groups of young people who soon learned to live and think and trust each other and act communally. More and more of the young were attracted until they realized that this new common unity they were developing was a "different style of life than the whole culture had."

When LSD came on the scene about 1963, its power to "decondition the mind" to old social values of separatism and individualism, he said, led its users to a greater personal trust in the deep feelings and desires of men that had been smothered in straight society. Also, LSD "taps and releases the collective unconscious. If you feel, on your trip, the Indian or the peasant or Christ within yourself, you can don the robes and see how it feels to be that person and to discover his inner meaning for use in your own life."

The hippies' belief in the spiritual oneness of all men makes any kind of violence or aggressiveness appear as a monstrous biological crime. In the same way, property ownership and the financial arrangements of society lead to a sense of separation and tension among people. As Cohen insisted, "Human beings must be ready to give away the property they think they own but which no one really owns except God."

The whole Hashbury scene is one of rapid, constant, fluid change. The evolution of the movement thus far has led hundreds to apply their sense of unity with themselves and with nature by setting up communal farms. Even further evolutionary developments are the Indian-style "tribes" of hippies now springing up in remote rural areas—"an instinctive response by the human organism to a society that's become unnatural," as one tribesman called it.

For Haight-Ashbury to remain the same next year would signal a failure of this whole hippie experiment in gentle anarchy. Even while I was there, the "short-hairs," the college kids on vacation and the teeny-boppers with braces on their teeth and brand-new beads around their necks, were showering in by the thousands, looking for excitement or all that loose sex they'd heard about or a place to hide from the draft board. The important upshot of this is that the gurus and older hippies are steadily moving elsewhere, making new converts and turning new people on. For unlike the nihilistic "Beat Generation" of the 1950's, this is a proselytizing, revolutionary kind of soft-sell Mass Movement. What it offers, the hippies say, are new depths of sensitivity and feeling between people and new styles of perception. But along with the abstract ideas of this crusade, there are the casualties. Cases of hepatitis and syphilis are nearly keeping pace with the hippie population growth; immature minds are sometimes permanently derailed almost every day by powerful chemicals their users neither understand nor often can even pronounce; and in many cases, the Hashbury becomes simply a sanctuary for the shiftless.

Still, there is an enormous "spill over" of hippie art and music and language into the otherwise straight world. Amid the swirling colored lights of San Francisco's Fillmore Auditorium, surrounded by hippies with their long hair flopping up and down and their beads and amulets jangling, ad men and bank-teller types dance to the visceral, biologic rock beat of groups like The Grateful Dead or Moby Grape.

"The hippies are more honest with themselves than anyone else is," said the cabdriver who carried me, in hippie attire, from the Hashbury for the last time. "Most people spend all their time working and then enjoy life only as a sideline. With the hippies, life comes first, and work is the sideline."

The driver had picked me up at one of the sandal shops on Haight St., where I was saying good-bye to some of my friends and padmates. "I'll tell you what we'll do," one of them wearing a cape and a long blond beard said to me as we walked outside. "I'll send you something in the mail in a few weeks. There may not be anything in the envelope, but be sure to lick the stamp. I'll put some acid on it, and I guarantee it'll turn you on. Don't forget."

The cab started down Haight St. I looked back to see my hippie friend, growing smaller in the distance, with his hands cupped to his mouth, yelling the reminder: "LICK . . . THE . . . STAMP . . . TURN . . . on . . ."

X

the
marks
of crime

It is impossible to remain unaware of the pervasiveness of crime today. Many parts of our cities are literally out of bounds in daytime as well as at night, unless one is willing to risk life, serious injury, or, at the very least, economic loss. Thefts of household property and of automobiles are so commonplace that the police, insurance companies, and even the victims regard them with relative unconcern and are apathetic that anything can be done about the situation. Moreover, as community members are aware, in the course of the routine of daily life, much of the business of the community is conducted on an extra-legal basis. Crimes that involve bodily harm or weapons are perhaps the only ones that consistently raise the wrath of community members, and result in calls for increased measures of prevention and detection. Other violations of the legal norms, such as petty thefts, are tolerated, and certain illegal behavior, such as gambling, affronts but a small proportion of the population and is often allowed to prosper openly.

While most Americans subscribe in the abstract to the principles of law and order, they are often uncommitted to these principles in their own behavior, allow many types of illegal acts to continue as long as they are unaffected by them or benefiting from them, and fail to vigorously support the police and the courts in their efforts to control and prevent illegal activities. One result of this state of affairs is a weak, sometimes corrupt, legal system with our police, prison, and court officials behaving as criminally as those they are supposed to apprehend, punish, and rehabilitate. The cases here indicate some of the dimensions of a problem currently occupying considerable attention at both a federal and local level.

Individual	Individual
↓	↓
Individual	Organization

WE BURNED A BUM FRIDAY NIGHT

Taking the life of another community member is the gravest of all offenses, yet under certain circumstances, it is possible to understand that it could happen. For example, revenge, jealousy , self-defense, or even rage during a personal interchange are generally regarded as mitigating motives for murder. The most difficult of all crimes to understand, however, is that of senseless murder. Some lives are taken for no apparent reason and seem to result from a desire to destroy, rather than from a conflict between the killer and his victim. The story of Leonard Benton, Jr.'s death is one of cruelty. It is particularly difficult to understand because of the youth of the perpetrators and the helplessness of the victim.

FRANKIE CARLIN, THE BOOKIE

Some laws seem to exist primarily as an expression of an unrealistic moralism or as attempts of virtuous men to save lesser men from sin and vice. These laws are usually enforced because of the demands of a few, rather than "because of a widespread community feeling that the conduct involved is improper and ought to be suppressed. Gambling is illegal in most communities, but many otherwise relatively obedient citizens participate in it. The majority of community members are simply unconcerned and undisturbed about gambling as a crime. Frankie Carlin, the bookie, is a man whose occupation is to help others gamble; his customers are more than willing "victims." His occupation offends but a virtuous few in the community, and it is very much a part of ordinary life.

A WOMAN'S STORY OF JAIL

Various punishments have been devised to promote law-abiding behavior and to keep in check those who violate our legal code. Threat of confinement is a major ploy in the United States to discourage illegal behavior. Some argue that the modern prisons should not only be a place to punish misdeeds, but also should serve as a setting where criminals can be rehabilitated. The success of most prisons as rehabilitation centers is highly questionable. In fact, it seems that prison communities are places where illegal behavior is taught and encouraged. Moreover, some of those responsible for our prisons and jails are as corrupt and ruthless as the inmates in their charge. This account of a woman's experience in jail indicates how an organization that is supposed to correct the behavior of an individual may have the opposite effect.

WINCANTON: THE POLITICS OF CORRUPTION

Beyond causing grief for victims, crime can make great demands on the economic resources of the community. A murder, for example, involves not only loss of a life; in addition, the community must bear the cost of apprehending, adjudicating and finally caring for the offender. Yet the costs of such crimes actually may be negligible in comparison with those incurred through corruption of the community's civic and political structures. When the offices of the community are subtly subverted to plunder its coffers or victimize its citizens, the loss often is too great and far reaching to calculate. Wincanton is a community which was victimized by its own municipal organization, and the account of organized crime gives penetrating insights into some of the intricacies of such corruption.

we burned a bum friday night

NICHOLAS PILEGGI

It was dark outside when the bar-and-grill's owner looked up and saw "a yellow ball of fire" reflected in his plate-glass window. He remembered seeing some children run past the bar and suddenly he realized that the ball of fire was bounding across Mercer Street and that it was a man. The man appeared to be suspended for a moment; as though caught in the middle of a brilliant leap, and then, and then, touching the ground, he began to scream. The man threw himself onto the street and, as he rolled about, an arm, a leg, the back of his head would become visible for an instant and then, again, would be lost in the flames. Seconds later the figure of another man was silhouetted against the light and then a blanket fell over the flames. A fireman, who had been on duty a hundred fifty feet away, fell upon the blanket and tried to halt the spastic jerks of the figure beneath him. Other firemen raced toward the pair with wet sheets and more blankets and they all began to strip the man of his burning clothes. The man's screams soon turned to moans and, though the flames he inhaled had burned the inside of his throat and part of his windpipe, he managed to rasp:

"Some kids set me on fire."

Leonard Benton, Jr. was from eastern Kentucky, an ordained Protestant minister and a fifty-one-year-old Bowery derelict. He had sustained second- and third-degree burns over forty percent of his body and the skin of his face, neck, back, chest, stomach and buttocks was completely charred. "His hair, lashes, lids and ears seemed to be gone," one fireman later recalled. "He was burned so badly that it was impossible to tell whether he was a white man or colored," another added. Benton lived six painful days after his burning—long enough to describe to the police his own immolation and the boys who set him on fire.

Benton had come to the Bowery in 1953. He usually paid $1.10 a night to sleep on a narrow cot in a sunless cubicle at the Sunshine Hotel, at 241 Bowery. He earned what little money he needed for lodgings and wine by collecting wastepaper in a pushcart supplied by a lower East Side waste dealer. It is common practice among local rag and paper dealers to lend pushcarts to derelicts they know to be "regulars." In addition, Benton earned a few cents from sympathetic motorists by wiping automobile windshields at the corner of Houston and Lafayette Streets. When drinking his thirty-three-cents-a-pint Linda Lee muscatel, Benton would sometimes forego his hotel room and spend a night or two, during the warm weather, sleeping outdoors. He would find a doorway in a deserted loft and warehouse district near the Bowery, a part of what the Fire Department calls "Hell's Hundred Acres." The area, which separates the Bowery from the southern tip of Greenwich Village, has long been used by many of the Bowery's thousands of homeless men as a "doorway flop." The largely uninhabited district is thought by derelicts to be comparatively safe from the Bowery "hawks" who strip them of their clothing and shoes while they sleep.

The three or four nights before his burning, Benton had been drinking heavily and he did not have enough money for the Sunshine Hotel. The weather was still warm and the pressure to sleep indoors had not yet struck the Bowery. During cold spells in New York, the city's morgue van routinely visits the street each morning to haul away the bodies of derelicts frozen to death the night before. At approximately six o'clock Monday night, September 19, 1966, Benton sat down on some collapsed cardboard cartons in the doorway of a loft building at 147 Mercer Street, seven blocks west of the Bowery. He had with him a day-old newspaper with which he intended to read himself to sleep.

Benton was a very private man and what it was that took him from Eastern State Teachers College and Grayson Christian College—both in Kentucky—to the doorway on Mercer Street no one knows. According to Benton's father, a retired conductor with fifty years on the Louisville & Nashville Railroad, he had no idea what his son did in New York. He did say, to The New York *Times,* that Benton, an ordained minister in the Christian Churches (Disciples of Christ), a predominantly Southern denomination of nearly two million members, had peached in some small churches in eastern Kentucky before World War II. During the war, the elder Benton recalled, his son joined the Merchant Marine and became a meatcutter, an electrician and a painter, but not a chaplain. He said that Benton had been married, but did not know what had happened to his son's wife.

"He got in with the wrong crowd and got to drinking. We haven't heard from him in a long time."

Benton was the second derelict in three days to be set on fire by a fourteen-year-old blond boy and his thin twelve-year-old companion. Both boys were residents of the small Italian tenement neighborhood on the southern tip of the Village. Their first victim was burned after the boys had finished classes at St. Anthony's of Padua parochial school. This earlier burning, however, was not brought to the attention of the police because doctors at St. Vincent's Hospital assumed the man was just another wine-fogged derelict who had set himself on fire. They performed an emergency tracheotomy on the street and when they transferred the man to the hospital they refused detectives permission to talk to him. They said it would be too painful to talk to anyone in that condition.

"There was no way of knowing it was kids that first time," one of the detectives explained later. "Even though we didn't talk to the guy until after Benton was burned, we did smell his clothes and there was no gasoline smell on any of them. On that first night the idea that neighborhood kids had found themselves a new hobby was the least likely of many possibilities."

The boys, however, were not pleased by the lack of attention they received as a result of their first victim, a sixty-seven-year-old ex-sandhog named Frank Cassidy. They had burned him on Friday after school by pouring gasoline from a Coke bottle onto his head and setting him on fire. All day Saturday and Sunday, the boys, especially the blond boy, whispered to friends what they had done. At school all day Monday, while nuns and brothers taught classes, knots of children gathered in corners around the blond boy.

"We burned a bum Friday night," the blond boy calmly told every kid who would listen. "We burned a bum Friday night and we're going to burn another one tonight," he boasted.

The boy's claims were greeted, for the most part, with derisive hoots, not because of the horror of his boast, police later learned, but because the children thought he was a liar. His schoolmates later told police that they doubted his story of burning the man because they did not hear it on the radio news or see it on television. At one point during the day a nun saw a little girl giggling in class. She called the girl to the front of the room and demanded to know what was so funny. The girl told her that she had heard some of the boys talking about burning bums. The nun took the girl to the parish priest, but apparently no further action was taken that day. Both the police and the church refuse to discuss what steps were taken as a result of the girl's revelation. The police did say, however, that as the day progressed the blond boy became more and more frustrated by the fact that none of his friends seemed to take his boast seriously and at one point he told three or four local boys, "Yeah, well come with us tonight, smart guys, and watch us burn another bum. You'll find out."

Even before the first burning,

incidents of derelict harassment had been reported to the police. Youngsters from the neighborhood would go into the warehouse district and throw rocks at derelicts. Sometimes they would creep up on a sleeping man, kick him and run. It seems to have been accepted, if not as a local sport, at least as a way of keeping the derelicts from getting too close to the section in which the children lived. Local youngsters had been seen spilling gasoline and lighter fluid in puddles on the sidewalk of the warehouse district and watching it burn. A variation of the game was to pour gasoline in a stream along the street, light one end of it and watch the flames travel the track of fuel. To some detectives the burning of Cassidy on Friday night was no more than the next step on a regular progression of violent street pranks. They had seen wanton violence before. It was not until the second burning, three nights later, of Benton, that the police became worried and very anxious to capture the children before, as one detective said, "we had an epidemic of bum burnings spread through the whole neighborhood."

The blond boy lived on the top floor of a seven-story walk-up tenement. He had a reputation around the neighborhood for being a bit odd. He was considered somewhat spoiled and willful, and on one occasion, a local story goes, he is supposed to have dangled from the seventh-floor fire escape until his parents capitulated to his wishes. The boy's father was a taxicab driver, and there was enough money in the house for a color television and a set of expensive drums. The furniture in his house was new and his mother had a washing machine in her kitchen. The family was, by the standards of the working-class community, well-off. The boy's mother, who was pleased that he showed an interest in music, insisted that he be considerate of their neighbors and not practice on his drums after six in the evening. He agreed. He was vain about his hair. His mother told police that it often took her son fifteen minutes to arrange his elaborate coiffure. When newly combed, one of the detectives said, the boy's hair looked as though it had been poured on his head by a cake decorator.

His thin twelve-year-old companion, who lived just a few doors away, had difficulty sleeping without a night-light, stuttered slightly and liked to draw. His mother described him to detectives as "sensitive," and pointed out that he had been working "very hard" on a painting of John F. Kennedy on the days of both burnings. She told people that she was pleased that the boy wanted to become an artist, and she said she encouraged him to continue his drawing and painting studies. The boy's father, a longshoreman who lost a leg in a dockside brawl, was less enthusiastic about his son's ways. One of the things which annoyed the father was the fact that his wife had to go to bed with their son before the boy could fall asleep. While the mother attributed this to his "high-strung and sensitive" qualities, his father disapproved but could not stop the practice. As soon as her son fell asleep she would get up and go to her own bed. However, the night-light could not be turned off.

On Monday, after a day of derision at school, the blond boy and his friend met again. This time they were joined by three other boys who would serve as witnesses to the act. The five set out with a distinct intention to burn another man. Detectives established that it was the blond boy who started the group toward a garage. As they were walking it was also the blond boy who, after looking in garbage heaps in vain for a Coke bottle, finally settled on a waxed milk container. The difference in the amounts of gasoline about to be thrown on a man—the Coke's six ounces compared to the milk carton's thirty-two—was the difference between life for Frank Cassidy and death for Leonard Benton. At the garage the blond boy filled the waxed container with the gasoline left in an extra-long truck-service hose. There is always gasoline left in a pump hose, and the youngsters knew that in the truck-length hoses sometimes a quart of gasoline could be found. In the doorway at 147 Mercer Street, two blocks away from the garage, they found Benton asleep on a cardboard mattress. The twelve-year-old took the gasoline from the blond boy and the two of them approached the brown metal doorway as the three witnesses hovered in the rear. They all shouted and whooped in an effort to wake up Benton, and one of them yelled: "Hey, mister, wake up, hey mister, what time is it?"

They all laughed and jumped about, the thin twelve-year-old careful not to spill any of the gasoline. Benton did wake and drowsily told the boys that he did not have a wristwatch and did not know the time. He later told police, "I tried to shoo them away." The twelve-year-old ran some gasoline along the ground to Benton's foot. The blond boy lit a match and the flames moved toward the man's shoe and then went out. It is no longer clear in the minds of the five boys how long the harassment of Benton continued. Memory returns solidly only with the vision of the twelve-year-old boy leaning over Benton and tipping the milk container onto his head. He remembered later how easily the gasoline poured out of the container. He told police that it poured out in a steady stream. It had been more difficult, he recalled, getting the gasoline out of the Coke bottle onto Cassidy's head on Friday night. The blond boy, who was standing next to him, waited until Benton was thoroughly drenched, then took a book of matches from his pocket, struck one and touched it to Benton's hair.

The doorway in which Benton had been sleeping when he suddenly burst into flames showed no sign of having been scorched. Neither did the hand-lettered signs, Jamie Togs Inc. and Peta-Pat Inc., directly over Benton's head. The collapsed cardboard mattress showed no sign of having been burned. It was all too obvious, according to the firemen who first saw the scene, that the center of the fire was Benton himself.

At the hospital, in what detectives came to think of as a heroic effort on Benton's part, he managed to rasp out a few words about what had happened to him. Doctors and nurses, working nearby, moved as quietly as possible, and the detective who listened had his ear close to Benton's mouth. Doctors had performed a tracheotomy on Benton in order that he might breathe more easily, so a nurse had to hold a compress against the breathing hole in his neck in order for him to speak. After four or five words, the nurse would release the compress and Benton would gasp for air through the hole in his neck. It was a long and painful session for Benton, but when it was over the detectives had a clear picture of what had taken place.

"I was reading a paper," Benton stated.
"I got tired of reading.
"I tried to get some sleep.
"Some kids came by.
"They woke me up.
"They asked me for the time.
"One was a big kid.
"One had a lot of blond hair.
"I shooed them away.
"I didn't have a watch.
"Then I felt something wet.
"On my head.
"On my shoulders.
"I saw a milk container.
"I heard a high-pitched voice yell.
"It said, 'Oh my God, Vinnie.'
"I was on fire."

Accompanied by doctors, detectives went to a ward upstairs, and there sixty-seven-year-old Cassidy, having spent a weekend in silence, confirmed that it was a blond boy who had set him on fire and added that he could identify the boy who poured the gasoline.

The morning after Benton's burning there was no one in that small, closely knit community who did not know that a man, perhaps two men, had been critically burned by neighborhood children. With the description of the youngsters—especially the blond boy—detectives had started moving about the tenements, explaining, cajoling, lying, tempting, even vaguely threatening, doing, in other words, everything detectives do when they want information. The nature of detective work is not the following of a circuitous though rational route through threats, clues and hints that leads finally to one neat, tidy suspect who is simply taken away and "booked." At its most subtle it has to do with making as many people as possible feel they personally have something to gain by turning stool pigeon. A detective involved in the investigation said he knew it would be difficult. He described the neighborhood as filled with "hard-working, suspicious, religious and close-mouthed people. It is strictly an interfamily neighborhood," he went on. "They settle their own problems with the help of their church. The police are considered strangers and are not trusted. The people are basically law-abiding, but they kind of follow their own rigid morality. That entire neighborhood knew the whole story about the burnings, but no one would call the police."

One of the detectives who was of Italian descent, like most of the people in the neighborhood, tried to explain the insularity of the community:

"Do you know, for instance, that the apartments in the neighborhood are handed down from family to family? In some buildings you have three and four generations of the same family. It's a neighborhood they know. They feel safe in it. There are no locks on any of the doors. When one man's son gets married to a neighbor's daughter, the whole neighborhood starts looking for someplace for the couple to live. They're protective toward each other and toward each other's children. No matter how horrible they might think the burning of those men was, you've got to remember, it would be a very, very difficult thing for them to turn in someone else's son."

The first reaction detectives met among most of the neighborhood residents was one of horror at the deed, but at the same time anger at their questioners.

"Why are you asking us?"

"How do you know the kids didn't come from somewhere else?"

"We've been having a lot of trouble with the coloreds."

To Lieutenant Albert Dandridge, who is colored, they said, "We've been having a lot of trouble with the Puerto Ricans." It is a neighborhood that clings to its own heritage and the people who live there identify all other people by either racial, national or religious stamps. In such a situation the tip of an outsider is often all the detectives can hope for.

By noon Tuesday, less than twelve hours after detectives began expressing interest in the blond boy, the telephone call for which they all had been waiting came through. The call was from "a friend" of one of the detectives. The caller said, "The kid you're looking for lives at—Sullivan Street." When Lieutenant Dandridge and two other detectives got to the Sullivan Street building they asked people downstairs where the blond boy lived. They climbed the six flights and knocked on the door. The blond boy's mother answered. The detectives identified themselves. The apartment was clean, neat and well-organized. There was a full set of drums in the living room, and seated at the kitchen table doing arithmetic homework was the blond boy, bent over a loose-leaf binder. The boy's father

was not home, but a roast was in the oven.

"We know that last night a fellow was burned at Mercer and Prince Streets and we're looking for help," Dandridge said. "Have you heard anything from any boys you know?"

"Oh no!" the blond boy's mother answered immediately. "Oh no! They're all good boys."

"Do you know a boy named Vinnie?" Dandridge asked, using the name Benton had mentioned.

The blond boy shuffled about, detectives recalled, and then said, "Yeah."

"Where is he?"

"I don't know. Sometimes he goes to Staten Island."

"Where does he live?"

"Down the block."

"Do you know anything you can tell us about the burning?"

The blond boy simply shrugged.

"Anything at all?" the detectives asked.

"Nah. I haven't heard anything about it in the neighborhood. Just what I heard on the radio."

This is what detectives call "the wedge." There had been no news broadcasts about the burning at that time.

"Who was with you when you heard it on the radio? Maybe they can help us."

"I don't know. I don't remember. Just some of the guys."

"Well, when did you hear it. Maybe that'll make you remember who you were with."

"I guess it was around nine o'clock."

(One of the detectives remarked later that in questioning children in front of their parents there is always a period of uncertainty when the parent doesn't know what the child is going to say next. The parent's facial expressions and unaccustomed attention to the exact wording of the child's reply always reveal his own uneasiness and apprehension.)

"Where were you when you were listening to the radio?"

"I don't remember."

"Well, who was with you at nine o'clock last night?"

Here the blond listed the names of several boys, including Vinnie. The detectives walked into the hallway and when they returned they asked the blond boy's mother if she and her son would mind accompanying them to the station house for further questioning.

"Well, I don't see why," was her first answer. "He's told you all he knows. He's only a boy. But if you think it will help any, we will."

At that point, all the detectives agreed, the mother had no idea that her son was guilty. In fact, as they were on their way to the station house, she kept trying to help him remember where he was when he might have heard the news on the radio. He continued to rattle off the names of friends, but detectives noted that Vinnie and a name which turned out to be that of the twelve-year-old boy were repeated most frequently.

Within a few hours all five boys and their parents were in the Beach Street station house being apprised of their rights. The boys sat beneath a row of the F.B.I.'s Ten-Most-Wanted posters in Dandridge's office. The room is painted a municipal green, has heavy wooden furniture and screened windows. The parents, for the most part stood around their children as if to shelter them from any harm. The arrests of their sons had surprised the parents; the men arrived in their work clothes and the women wore the cotton housedresses in which they had been cooking the evening meal. The lack of formality seemed to give the parents courage—as though they understood that nothing really very bad can happen to you when you are wearing everyday clothes. It was at the court appearance the next day when the men wore dark suits and the women dark crepe dresses and no makeup that the parents first seemed to recognize fully the import and deadliness of what their sons had done. At the police station, however, there were many tears that evening, not necessarily for the burned men.

"Gee, he's only twelve years old," the mother of the boy who poured gasoline on both men pleaded. "What do you want to pick on him for?"

"His voice," she kept repeating. "His voice. My son has the best singing voice in his school."

The boy's father, the one-legged longshoreman, was the only parent who attempted to strike his son during the questioning. A detective standing next to him said the man went through an elaborate ritual of unstrapping his belt and shouting threats about whipping the boy within an inch of his life. He was, of course, restrained.

The boy's mother, meanwhile, paid very little attention to her husband's rage.

"How could he do this?" she kept asking. "He wouldn't step on a bug."

It was after the threat of his father's strap that the twelve-year-old made his first admission:

"I guess we shouldn't have done it," he said. "We just got nothing to do." And then, brightly, he asked, "Will I be able to go to school tomorrow?"

Outside Dandridge's office the blond boy's mother told a reporter: "I don't know why in the name of God the boys did a thing like this. I always told my boy I'd give him anything in my power and I asked only one thing from him. I asked him never to disgrace me. I wonder now if he knows what he has done to me."

She told the reporter that she had shopping to do, but was "too ashamed" to be seen in the streets. She said she would have to go home and stay home. She had a dental appointment the next day, but she would not keep it because she could not face her neighbors.

The mother of one of the boys who acted as a witness was outraged. "They were only bums," she kept insisting. "Everybody talks about how bad the bums are and how we should get rid of them; the children did something about it. But it was just a stupid mistake—nothing wrong. Why did the cops have to pick on these children and put their names in the record? Because the cops wanted a fast arrest and a solution to the crime so they could get a promotion, that's why," she said.

"I feel bad about the bums who were burned," she admitted, "but what about my son's life? That's the important thing to me and now he's marked."

At the end of the night all of the youngsters had admitted either to witnessing or taking part in the burning. Statements were taken by the District Attorney and a stenographer. The boys were all charged with "juvenile delinquency," with the specification in parentheses, "Felonious Assault." In New York, cases involving children under sixteen are tried in Children's Court and no public record is permitted of the hearings, nor is the Court's disposition of the case revealed. The case of Cassidy's and Benton's burning, in fact, would have been handled in just this manner except that on Sunday afternoon, six days after he was burned, Benton died. This altered the city's position in the case entirely and the prosecution of the five boys was turned over to the Corporation Counsel by the District Attorney's office. The police department rearrested the boys—who had been allowed to go home with their parents after their first arraignment—and the specific charge against them was changed to homicide.

Joseph Halpern, who acted as the prosecutor for the city, said he was convinced the youngsters were not impressed at all by what they had done. Halpern insists they were neither contrite nor remorseful when they walked into the court charged with homicide. For whatever reasons, Halpern said, the lawyers for the children had apparently convinced the parents that they would be able to take their children home after the homicide hearing. Now the lawyers pleaded with the judge that keeping the boys in jail until the formal trial date would make them miss two weeks of school. Halpern objected strenuously and the judge ordered the children to remain in jail.

It was then that the twelve-year-old's mother fainted and the other mothers began to cry and wail. It was also then, according to Halpern, that the children began for the first time to show some concern.

"They were evidently able to comprehend the seriousness of their actions only through the distress of their mothers, and the mothers seemed to regard the action of their sons as serious only to the extent that their sons were being kept from them."

Children's Court is on the second floor of a midtown municipal office building. Every attempt is made to keep the youngsters who appear there from freezing at the awesome "dignity" of the court. The judge, for instance, though he wears judicial robes, does not sit on a raised platform, but behind a desk in a room which looks very much like an office. The children, however, are usually unaware of the court decor. A clerk who has watched many of these confrontations says that it is the sight of their parents in "Sunday clothes" during the week—a father standing uncomfortably in a suit—to which the child most often will respond.

"The most heinous crimes in the past few years," Halpern states flatly, "have all been committed by kids."

He pointed specifically to the blond boy and his friend:

"We must remember that they came back. They burned Cassidy on Friday night, they heard his screams, they saw he was on fire, they knew what fire does, they knew what they had done, and they came back again and did it all over again on Monday night to Benton. The whole horror here is that they came back. The blond boy's mother even said that her son had seen a woman in an apartment across the street burned to a crisp in a fire. He knew what fire did. And yet, the two of them came back."

Never, from the very first time Halpern read of the case until its conclusion, was he able to understand why the pair had burned the two men. The boys were never able to give a response to that question which anyone felt was meaningful. Halpern suspects that any youngster in that particular neighborhood could have become involved as a witness to the burning. He insists, however, that the two boys who did pour the gasoline and light the match, especially the blond boy, had to be a very special type of child. He said he was struck during the testimony by how facile the pair were in telling about the steps involved in burning the men. The two boys spoke as though they were not participants, Halpern said, a trait common among persons confessing to a crime. Halpern felt that there should have been some final recognition by the two boys of what they had done, but there never was. The three boys who witnessed the burning were allowed to return home with their parents twenty-two days after Benton died. The blond boy and his friend were given preliminary psychiatric examinations while jailed at Youth House. When the report was returned with the prison psychiatrist's suggestion that the twelve-year-old boy, not the blond, be given a full-scale examination at Bellevue Hospital, the attorneys and detectives connected with the case became suspicious that somehow the

reports had gotten mixed up. When the psychiatrist was questioned about the possibility of an error he became immediately defensive, according to an attorney who spoke to him, and started muttering about privileged communication. He refused to disclose anything about his findings or even to discuss them. The sentence finally imposed on the pair ordered that both boys be remanded to Youth House for an indeterminate period. Their parents returned to the insular safety of their neighborhood and became convinced, more and more each day, that their sons were the victims of police and judicial zeal. Benton's body, after an autopsy, was released by the city and flown to Kentucky at his father's expense. Cassidy, after being treated for three months at St. Vincent's hospital, was finally well enough to leave.

"He just checked out one day and was gone," a detective said. "He probably went back to the Bowery. He didn't have anyone, you know. Usually when someone's injured we get calls from friends, relatives, somebody. With Cassidy a guy by the name of Gallagher called. No first name, just Gallagher. He said he thought maybe he knew Cassidy. He never called back."

frankie carlin, the bookie

JOE FLAHERTY

It was 10:45 Saturday morning and Frankie Carlin was finishing his soft-

Reprinted by permission of the author and publisher from The New York Times, *April 2, 1967.* © *1967 by The New York Times Company.*

boiled eggs and his second cup of Irish home-brewed tea. His squat wife sat in a kitchen chair, dressed in drab wool slippers and a flowered smock, looking like a familiar house plant. He rose and slipped a light tan topcoat over his large frame and with fleshy hands molded his chocolate-brown hat into shape. It was time to go to work.

On the molding of the front door hung a blue plastic holy-water font with a sculptured crucifix. With his right hand he took some water and made the sign of the cross, his protection against evil spirits. Carlin's devils dress in blue. He's a bookmaker.

Recently United States Attorney Robert M. Morgenthau, functioning as the Dow-Jones of the underworld, stated that the annual business of bookmakers in the metropolitan area was $100-million. Recently also, New York State announced that it would run a quarterly series of lotteries based on horse-race results, the idea being to channel some of that money into the state coffers. So, contrary to the tenets of free enterprise, the state has set out to create unemployment in one of the oldest and most skilled trades in the history of man.

Of course this is all laughable to the people inside the trade. The trouble with reformers is that they equate their need for action with that of the general public, and envision themselves as Nick the Greek every time they wager a quarter at a church bazaar. Mark Twain once said the world was made up of turtles and goats, and no matter how much you explained, the turtles would never understand the depravity of the goats. The turtles in the State Assembly passed their Mock Reformation on the theory that a gambler needs action only quarterly. It is the same as saying that if we put everyone in the Yankee Stadium over the Fourth of July weekend for an orgy, the city would remain celibate for the rest of the year.

Carlin (a fictional name) runs his operation in the Prospect Park area of Brooklyn. He walks to work through quiet tree-lined streets. The houses are mostly brownstone and limestone, and the occupants fall in the lower-middle- to middle-class income level.

Bookmaking, like everything else in our graduated society, adheres to economic class levels. The underprivileged bookie, like his clientele, usually hustles the street, taking action on a catch-as-catch-can basis: street corners, playgrounds, hallways. The middle-class bookie (Carlin's level) operates out of a permanent location. And those bookies who cater to the rich give all the advantages to the beautiful people: tell-a-phone credit card action.

Carlin paused outside the window of a bar bearing an Irish name. He stood lighting a cigarette while he casually viewed the interior. The bartender waved a greeting. Carlin nodded. His office was safe, his workday was about to begin.

The bar was one of those classic Irish "made bars" that exist only in Brooklyn and Queens. It was strictly a no-nonsense joint, no frills, no extras, you came here to drink. A long mahogany bar dominated the room. Workmanlike whisky bottles, without pouring spouts, formed a shapeup on the back bar. John Fitzgerald Kennedy's memory was encased on the wall between Irish and American flags. A shuffleboard stood against the side window like a low, sleek schooner in a bottle. The white marble floor gave a regimental click to every footstep. The only feminine-appearing thing in the place was a garishly made-up jukebox, but even that was denied: it was not plugged in.

Carlin draped his coat over a wooden booth. A guy in his 20's wearing a windbreaker, his slick hair sweeping back like jet streams, called down to the end of the bar, "Hey, Frankie, how about an eye-opener?" "Sure, Richie, first today." Faking enthusiasm, Carlin turned to the bartender. "Make it a creme de menthe on the rocks, Lenny." Carlin turned and muttered. "I haven't even digested breakfast—Christ, this slop will kill me." Why take it then, I asked. "Look, if you don't booze with your players, they think you're playing it sober and trying to hustle them."

"Frank, mind if I join you?" The windbreaker was trying to feel out my presence. "Sure, glad to have you—I want to introduce you to a friend of mine." I shook hands with my new acquaintance. Still unsure of my presence, he played it cool. "Frank, let me pay you the 15 I owe you from the other night." Carlin smiled, "It's all right, Richie, you can talk—he's all right." Richie still seemed uncomfortable. "Here's the dog I owe you and give me 20 to win on Advocator." Richie moved back to the bar and began to mingle among the patrons. This was the last time anybody approached Carlin with trepidation all day; the word was out—I was all right.

All operations like Carlin's give their clients the benefit of the "dog" or the "marker," inside names for credit. Carlin explained: "The average working stiff is tapped out by Tuesday or Wednesday so I let them place their action on the cuff. Come Saturday, he has his pay and he straightens out his tab. If they legalize bookmaking is Rockefeller going to let the bettor hand a marker on the state till Saturday?" He frowned slightly, registering his displeasure at the Governor's inhumanity.

It was 12:30 now and the bar began to become more crowded, Saturday is a big day for Carlin and this one in all probability would be bigger than most. At 4:30 every Saturday Channel 5 televises two horse races. This week the action was from Hialeah, and the feature was the Widener Handicap, a mile-and-a-quarter race with the value placed at $125,000 added. Hundred-grand races always stimulate the bankroll of the bettors; they have a mystique about them that is similar to a championship prizefight.

The projected star of the production, the incomparable Buckpasser, was sidelined with an injury on the West Coast. But this was lamentable only to the big-money boys who delight in picking up 20 cents on every $2 wagered—for the average bettor. Buckpasser's payoffs are as exciting as a dividend check on one share of A.T.&T. Carlin's clientele likes action, a quick turnover. So, with Buckpasser's absence, the field was reduced to eight mediocrities, all going off at a decent price. In short, the Widener became a "good betting race."

Carlin was now drinking highballs. He moved among the drinkers like a social butterfly at a cocktail party. But there was a lot more happening than chit-chat. The action was being taken at all times, but even when you were looking for it, it was almost impossible to spot.

His performance was perfected by years of repetition. First he approaches the client and then bellows to the Bartender, "Lenny, give this deadbeat a drink on me." The client feigns anger. "Lord, if you're buying I'd better go to confession; the world must be coming to an end." A great curtain opener.

Scene two: the fabled Irish politician's "personal" touch. "How's Mary, Tim?" "Fine, Frankie, just grand." "The Pope will canonize that woman for living with a scoundrel like you." Some light jabbing and mock scuffling. The action is passed. Carlin gently slides the slip with the bet on it and the money into his pocket.

Find an exit line. "Tim, what are your

Mets going to do this year?" "First division, absolutely." "My God, Carmine, did you hear what this crazy Mick just said?" A young Italian kid seated two stools away smiles and answers, "All Micks are crazy." Carlin booms, "Hell, Lenny, I'll buy a drink to that." What transition! Exit lines lead into new entrances. Right here in a Brooklyn gin mill, techniques Shakespeare couldn't master.

Ethnic joking is a big thing in bars like this. "That crazy clown thinks the Mets will wind up in first division." Carlin places his highball glass on the bar. Tony slides a $10 bill with his bet slip folded inside toward the glass. "Mets, what Mets?" Theatrical outrage. Carlin takes the 10 and slips it into his pocket. Tony adds, "This is the year of the Yankees, with that beautiful Italian kid Joe Pepitone in center field. A new DiMag."

Carlin displays weary frustration. "Pepitone? Why do I bother with you when there's a good squarehead in the bar? Fred, drink up."

An old man drinking whisky with an orange juice chaser delivers a stage imitation of a Swede. "Min-na-sota will win the pen-nant by seven games, by Yim-a-nee." The bar roars with laughter. It's all familiar, it's been in the repertory for years. The drinkers love the safeness of its familiarity. And Carlin moves along the length of the bar majestically. Not a line is missed, the interplay is beautiful. Alfred Lunt playing to revolving Lynn Fontannes.

Carlin now has many slips in his pocket. This is known as his "work" and a good bookie always protects his work. Checking everyone at the bar, he slowly moves to the back of the saloon. The back room is used only on special occasions like bachelor parties or an affair for some local kid going into the service. From it a large mahogany door leads to the cellar. Carlin opens it and disappears.

The cellar is where his "bunk" or "stash" is located. His bunk is where he hides his work.

When Carlin disappeared through the door not a head at the bar would take note of his movement. It was as if Lady Godiva were riding through Coventry; there was a religious dedication to blindness. The bunk is the most important factor in the bookie's business. And for a good bookie there are two unbreakable commandments about his work: (1) Don't let the police seize it. (2) Never destroy it.

In actuality, it is preferable—and less expensive—to let the cops confiscate the work than destroy it. To be caught with wager slips is only a misdemeanor under Section 986 of the New York State Penal Law, but the destruction of one's work could mean grave financial losses. A bookmaker of Carlin's stature takes in up to $1,500 a week and as much as $500 on a given Saturday. If the word gets out that he has been raided and had to destroy his work many of these bets miraculously become winning ones. The client, realizing that the bookmaker has no record of the transactions, claims he wagered on winning horses, winning teams or what have you. The bookmaker, no matter how doubtful of the validity of the claims, must pay off the conjured wager to protect his reputation. When a bookmaker gets the reputation of a deadbeat or a welcher, his action dwindles till he finally has to close shop.

By 3:50 the action started to ebb. Carlin's work for the most part was done for the day. Late stragglers still approached him with bets on the televised races. Carlin kept moving from the bar to the cellar to deposit any new action. He seemed tired.

"Doesn't this get you down day after day?" I asked. He smiled. "I don't get any wearier than a guy working a regular job and I earn a hell of a lot more. Thirty years ago before I got into this I worked as a clerk in a small brokerage house earning three thousand a year. It seemed to me then that my laundry bill for white shirts was about two thousand. Where would I be today with them? Eight-nine thousand a year. Now I put in about five hours a day and I'm good for anywhere from 30 to 40 thousand a year. No, when I think of that I don't tire of it."

"What about the pressure, the aggravation of the business?" He patted his full head of hair. "It may be white but it's still there and I'm nearly 60. Sure you have to be on the lookout for the cops all the time but guys with regular jobs come in here to booze and you swear to God they were the Fugitive the way their bosses hound them. Everybody's got aggravation."

He ordered another highball and raised it to me. "Do you know of anybody who has these working conditions? Besides the cops, what do I really have to worry about? Certainly not a lack of supply and demand. Some clown with a crazy longshot isn't going to break me. I've got enough collateral to cover me and if any action is too big I can always hedge off."

The term "hedge off" means that if a bookmaker is receiving too much money on a certain horse he can call another bookie (usually a wire-room set-up) and place a good part of the bet with a fellow operative. This eliminates the chance of taking a severe financial beating on a particular bet. The "hedge off" system also protects the bookmaker from being the sole target of a "sure thing."

Carlin deals only with flat horse races. He will take action on any flat horse on any track in the country. When a large bet materializes on a horse running at a bush track (a small out-of-town track), it is time to hedge off. Big money appearing on an obscure horse at an obscure track usually means the bettor has information, thus the danger of the "sure thing."

Carlin will handle only horses. "I'm no sportsman," he said. "That's where the big action is today, but I leave that to the big-money boys, the syndicate crowd. I operate alone. Besides, sports are too easy to rig. Who in their right mind would take action on college basketball? Those kids are so hungry they're easy pickings for any sharpie who waves a couple of hundred under their noses for a dump."

"What about the trotters?" I asked. "If the college kids are looking for spending money," he said, "those old men driving the trots must be looking for retirement pensions. I wouldn't touch them. I stick strictly to the flats."

A man no bigger than 5 foot 2, wearing a gray peaked cap, approached Carlin and handed him a slip with $2. Carlin read the slip and laughed. "Big Joe, are you still trying to break me with your crazy longshot parlays?" The little man grinned. "I'll get you yet, you big lug," he said.

As the small man retreated, Carlin motioned for the bartender. "Lenny, send Big Joe down a drink." Carlin turned back to me. "You see that little guy? He's a real sweetheart. He wouldn't bet a horse under 20-to-1. I always like to see him catch a couple of long ones. He's been playing with me now for about 20 years."

Carlin excused himself and disappeared into the cellar again. No matter how small the ticket, he didn't want it on his person. When he returned he laughed and said, "I'm going to have them build an escalator down to that place."

Looking at the clock on the wall, he said, "Four-ten—that should be about it for the day." He looked at my near-empty glass. "Come on—drink up."

"How much does it cost you buying drinks on a day like this?"

"I never count, these people are my friends. I've been operating out of this place nearly 30 years. I saw most of these kids you see here christened. Their fathers played with me, even some of their grandfathers. This very bar, I've been paying the rent in this place as long as I have been using it as a location. There are hundreds of set-ups like this around the boroughs.

"You know, John Q. Public thinks guys like me scoop in all the money and run home and bank it in the sugar bowl. Hell, I love to gamble as much as the next guy; that's how I got into this business in the first place. I always liked the horses. When I was with the brokerage house over 70 per cent of the employees liked to bet on one thing or another. We used to have this runner come around and pick up the action, but he was unreliable. Most days he was late and others he never showed. So I got myself a small bankroll and started to handle the action myself. I was single then and I lived in a small rooming house a couple of blocks from here and in the evening and Saturdays I would come here to drink. The guys at the bar were always talking about betting and how hard it was to find a bookie so I got together with the owner and I set up shop. After about a year things went so well I quit the brokerage house and I've been here ever since."

"Do you still gamble?" I asked. "Hell, I chase the ponies down to Florida a couple of weeks a year and in August, I chase them up to Saratoga. You know what the cops call us? Degenerate gamblers." He snorted. "You know something? They're right! Very few bookies can stay away from the action themselves."

He was completely relaxed now and he began to enjoy the whisky. Sitting back in the booth, he talked of how television with its extensive coverage of sports has aided gambling. "The average guy sits down to watch a football game and he likes to back his rooting interest with a five or a ten." When I asked him what events take the most money today his answer sounded more like Daniel Moynihan than a bookmaker. "The Jews like baseball and basketball, but especially baseball. That's the biggest play today. The big-money boys like the one-to-one situation of the starting pitchers. Guys today follow Koufax and Marichal like guys years ago would follow Man o' War and Dan Patch. The Irish and the Italians like the horses and pro football. The Negroes and the Puerto Ricans, because they don't have the bread, play the numbers—sucker odds at 500-to-1; they get a pipe dream for two bits."

"Have you had much trouble over the years?" I asked. "In any business there is always trouble. I had guys give me bets and welch. About eight years ago a couple of kids I knew since they were babies fleeced me for about $1,700. One of them would drive to Bowie in Maryland and watch the races and wait for a big pay-off. When the pay-off was official he would run out of the track and call his buddy here in Brooklyn with the name of the horse. Then the kid would charge over her and dump $30 to $40 on the sure thing. It's called past posting. Normally I wouldn't touch a ticket like that, but hell, like I said, I knew the kids all their lives. I wasn't going to refuse a bet with a neighborhood kid because he was about four minutes late. They strong me about four times then I got wise."

"What did you do when you caught on?" "What was I going to do? Beat them? Kill them? They took me and that was that. I let everyone here know what they pulled, they never showed their faces here again. I have a lot of friends here, but I wouldn't let anyone lay a hand on them. I don't run that kind of operation, my friend—I'm no mobster."

"The kind of trouble I was really talking about was the cops," I said. Carlin started to laugh. He told of how six years ago the cops began to lean on him. Every day there was a plainclothesman or two dressed as mail carriers or longshoremen standing at the bar. Carlin couldn't move. Then a brilliant idea struck him.

Since he couldn't circulate among the patrons and most certainly the patrons couldn't walk down to the basement to place their slips in his bunk, he decided to have the men's room redecorated. The bathroom is one of those museum pieces with gigantic marble urinals that Toulouse-Lautrec could have used for a shower stall. Carlin decided to replace the old plaster ceiling with a Cello-Tex one. The idea was that he would leave one Cello-Tex square loose and his clients, by mounting the urinal, could stash their action and their cash in the false ceiling. Carlin would remove his work late at night when the bar was no longer under surveillance.

The operation worked great for about three days till the plainclothes men began to wonder if the bar patrons were plagued by kidney disease. Finally, his curiosity aroused, one plainclothes man decided to follow a patron to the men's room. Giving the guy a few minutes headstart, the cop pushed in the door and saw his suspect standing on the urinal with his arms stretched upward. Unable to explain his peculiar form of toilet training, the bettor wound up in cuffs while the cop mounted the urinal and flushed out the evidence. Carlin had tears of laughter running from his eyes at the completion of the story.

"What happened?" I asked. "Let's just say it cost me plenty to get out of that one." Pointing to the end of the bar at a lanky guy in a sports jacket, Carlin said, "That's him. Since then we baptized him 'Johnny Highchair.'" His laughter was rich, and the best kind—self-directed.

"You seem like a contented man," I said.

"I am."

"No regrets?"

"I'll lay you 7 to 5 no one can say that."

I laughed. "No bet."

The television set was now turned on. The voice of Fred Caspella nasally intoned, "It is now post time." George Widener's Ring Twice was an easy winner under a front-running ride by Billy Boland. Carlin was pleased by the results. Most of the big money he had taken in this race was on Advocator, the favorite, who finished down the track. But he wouldn't know how his day came out till he heard all the results from around the country that evening at 6:30 on FM radio. Then he would balance his books. Sunday afternoon at 1:30 after the 12:15 mass at the parish church, he would wait for the winning bettors inside the bar. Their winnings would be in white sealed envelopes with their names on them inside his topcoat pocket. Every bet paid precisely, rounded off to the nearest dollar.

Saturday's results were now turf history. But come Sunday the papers would list the entries for Monday. And come Monday the bettors would be back again. Why? You looked up at the electronic picture and television truly became educational.

There they were in the winner's circle. Ring Twice worth $24.40 to his believers. Seventy-seven-year-old George Widener winning his ancestor's race. Seventy-eight-year-old Wilbert "Bert" Mulholland training the winner. Dynasty! Continuity! Ring Twice, whose sire was Gallant Man, the Belmont Stakes winner, his stock reaching back to mysterious Arabia. Widener, Mulholland, Arabia—permanence, history. Carlin talking of generations of bettors. Man's passage through life. His history, his need to test overwhelming odds. His need for action.

This historic need. Why? One of their own, Nick the Greek, said it as neat as an inside straight. "The next best thing to winning—is losing."

'an absolute hell':

a woman's

story of jail

DONALD JONJACK AND
WILLIAM BRADEN

Cook County Jail has been described as a jungle. But that is the wrong word, according to a North Shore matron who was a prisoner there.

"A jungle is a dark and dangerous place," said Mrs. Jean Macdonald. "That much is true. But it is also a thing of nature, and it can be beautiful. County Jail to me is a hell . . . an absolute hell."

The 57-year-old Evanston woman, mother of nine, told the story of her 1964 confinement this week to The Sun-Times—and to the state's attorney's office. She will testify before a grand jury that is investigating charges of terror and corruption at the jail.

Mrs. Macdonald said she went to jail to defend a principle. She was cited for contempt of court when she refused to allow a bank to assess her home in connection with a complicated inheritance suit dating back to 1938.

If recent stories coming out of jail are accurate, the conditions she describes have not changed since then—except perhaps to become even worse.

Mrs. Macdonald is a widow and a 1931 graduate of the University of Illinois, where she was voted most popular co-ed during her senior year. She owns a games company and with her late husband James she created a card game, based on the U.S. Constitution, that won an award from the Freedoms Foundation.

After routine processing at the jail, she said, she was examined by a doctor.

"I told him I was a heart patient," she said. "But he wouldn't let me keep the prescription medicine I had in my purse. It might be dope, he said. But he assured me the medicine would be checked out, and he said I would be supplied with the drug later."

Mrs. Macdonald said she was taken then to the women's section.

"As I walked through the gates," she said, "I saw female prisoners in this open room, which was a compound. They were walking around without any tops on—nude from the waist up in view of the male guards. I couldn't believe it."

She was greeted, she said, by prisoners who told her immediately that she would be in trouble if she didn't supply them with cigarettes and candy. Said one of the women:

"You had better provide, baby."

Mrs. Macdonald said she was directed next to the "barn boss," a prisoner in charge of that section of the jail.

"She was a very stout Negro woman who was in jail on a murder charge. She seemed nice enough, and she never

Reprinted with permission of the publisher from Donald Jonjack and William Braden, " 'An Absolute Hell': A Woman's Story of Jail," Chicago Sun-Times, XX, No. 264, December 6, 1967.

threatened me. She gave me a pair of smelly shoes and a filthy dress. She also gave me a dirty towel and a cup.

"The barn boss could shift people around, and she was the person who decided where I would stay. She showed me a cell intended for four persons, but there was only one woman in it—a woman named Judy.

"Judy was in jail on a dope-peddling charge. She did a lot to protect me, and I don't know what I would have done without her."

"In the cell, the sheets were practically black and had bed bugs. The toilet didn't work, and the air had a terrible odor. I learned later that the 68 women on my tier had only three workable toilets and the rest of them had been shut off for a long time.

"I wasn't to say anything about this, I was told, or I would be severely punished—and not by the guards.

"The reason was, the empty pipes were used to transport things from the first floor. I was told that candy and narcotics were pulled up by strings through the pipes.

"On the very first day, I noticed many kinds of strange behavior. When I'd ask Judy what was wrong with a person, she'd say: 'Oh, she's high.' Which meant she was on dope.

"Everything was so out in the open there. It was unbelievable. In the compound, women would take off their clothes and climb on top of the table and molest each other. They would touch each other and cry out. They never even bothered to clean the tables when they were finished, and then later they would eat at those same tables."

Mrs. Macdonald said there was a disregard on the part of jail personnel for basic sanitary procedures. It started with the processing physical examination, she said.

Before she was assigned to a tier,

Mrs. Macdonald and six other women were taken into a room where a matron ordered her and the others to remove all their clothing.

"The matron had a vaginal tool," said Mrs. Macdonald. "She said she had to examine us with it to see if we were concealing narcotics.

"Then she started to examine the second girl, without sterilizing the tool. I was shocked. And I protested. The matron looked at me and said: 'just for that, you are going to be last.'

"I was the last one she examined. and the women before me included prostitutes and murderers."

Mrs. Macdonald tried to keep her own cell clean, she said, and that earned her a nickname with the other prisoners. They called her the Wipe Lady.

"There was a catwalk running all around the section," she said. "At night the guards would walk around to make sure everybody was accounted for. But during the day they never walked around, and the prisoners were left to themselves. So you were helpless. Everybody was at the mercy of the strong and violent ones.

"There was nothing to do, nothing to read, and you couldn't go outside—not even in the summer. Dope was the only thing. Dope and perversions.

"You'd hear a woman screaming lewd conversations with men prisoners. I have raised nine children, and I have an idea what life is about. But these people raved and screamed the most ugly, dirty things they would like to do with each other—sadism and masochism—every filthy thing that can be imagined they screamed back and forth, back and forth.

"What really hurt me was hearing about the young boys who were molested. The male prisoners forced them into homosexual acts under threat of stabbing, beatings, starving. The boys were frightened and defenseless. The guards just pretended not to hear, or were not around."

On the second day, said Mrs. Macdonald, the barn boss transferred her to another cell where she was approached by two formidable looking women. They laughed, she said, and one of them told her:

"I'm Queenie from 63d St., and I never had a white woman before. Are we going to have fun with you tonight!"

Said Mrs. Macdonald:

"I never prayed so much in my life. I told them if they would leave me alone I would buy them cigarettes and candy or whatever they wanted. I also mentioned Judy, who apparently was close to the barn boss. And so they did leave me alone, except for insults and threats."

Then there was the shower room at the end of the cell block.

"The entrance is wide enough for only one person," said Mrs. Macdonald. "I went in on my second day to take a shower and I found two women in the middle of a perverted act. Later I learned that the shower room was used only for acts of perversion, and it was a place where new women were often attacked sexually. After my one experience which was a close call, I decided it wasn't worth the risk to be clean."

Mrs. Macdonald did not care for the jail food.

"It was served on trays that were caked with old food," she said. "The potatoes we got were orange. If I had 30 cents a day, I could serve better food."

She told of narcotics addicts going through withdrawal.

"These unfortunate persons had no help, no pity. Sometimes they were preyed upon by other prisoners who would sexually assault them even while they were in their terrible agony. They rolled around on the concrete floor, trying to keep cool during the worst of it. And then afterward they would have a great craving for sugar, which they would steal or fight for."

Mrs. Macdonald said a fellow inmate at that time was Mrs. Irwinna Weinstein, convicted of slaying her husband in a celebrated murder case. (The charge against her was dropped this year after a successful appeal for a new trial.)

"I hardly ever saw her," said Mrs. Macdonald. "I was told she was never in her cell, except at night. Once I did see her, and she looked as if she'd just come from Elizabeth Arden. Her hair had been done—that's something a woman knows and her nails had been manicured. She never talked to anyone, and she kept apart from the other prisoners.

"Her cell was beautiful, filled with satins and silks, and there was even perfume. It was the difference between heaven and hell. I asked the other prisoners how it was possible, and they told me: 'Well, Wipe Lady, money talks; if you've got money, you can get anything.'"

There was another prisoner—named Shirley.

"What happened to her was inhuman," said Mrs. Macdonald. "If it had happened in a jail 500 years ago, somebody would have stopped it."

"Shirley was mentally ill. She thought she had killed her husband after catching him in an affair with her maid.

"There were two women in the next cell. They started to torment her. They yelled things like: 'Hey, honey, show us how you found your husband and the maid,' 'Were your husband and she real close, loving?'

"The woman was reeling, tortured. And the more she reacted, the more they tortured her. She begged. She pleaded with them to stop. She hit her head against the wall. And they said: 'That's good. Do it once more—once for your maid.'

"Finally she put her head in the bowl

of her toilet and tried to drown herself, flushing the toilet over and over again while the animal women screamed and laughed.

"I couldn't stand it any more.

"I'd been warned never to call a guard under any circumstance, unless I wanted a beating. But I called now. I screamed for a guard.

"Nobody came.

"I grabbed a broom and shoved it through the bars. I pushed her away from the toilet. And then I kept pushing with the broom to keep her away.

"Finally somebody came. The guards strapped her to her bed and then left. As soon as they were gone the women started again, redoubling their efforts. Shirley thrashed and cried out. She broke the springs in her bed, and they were cutting her back.

"That day Shirley was given no food. She cried that she would do anything the women wanted—would emulate what the maid had been doing with her husband—if only they would leave her alone. But of course they wouldn't, and didn't. What finally happened to her I don't know.

"I thought I would be punished for calling the guards. But I wasn't. A cart came around once a day, and I was able to buy things for the other prisoners to keep them from attacking me.

"What I couldn't buy was my medicine. I asked for it repeatedly, but I never got it. The doctor didn't keep his promise.

"One day in the compound two women got into a fight, and one of them threw a large container of scalding water. It spilled over me and burned me. But none of the prisoners tried to get any help, and nobody came for 10 minutes. Then they smeared Vaseline on the burns,

and that was all. I never saw a doctor, never once after that first time.

"On the sixth day I was nursed by a woman named Helen, in her 70s, who was in jail for bad checks. She brought me cold towels for relief, and she brought me water. But I couldn't eat, and I couldn't sleep.

"Then my daughter Jeanette came to the jail to visit me, and she begged me to obey the court order. She told me a dear friend of our family had just been killed in an auto accident. And I had become a grandmother again.

"So I obeyed the order, and I left the jail. After seven days.

"I saw what happens there. And I don't see how any person who has the slightest connection with the jail can be ignorant about all the hate, torture and terror there. I don't see how it is possible."

wincanton: the politics of corruption

JOHN A. GARDINER, WITH THE ASSISTANCE OF DAVID J. OLSON

In general, Wincanton represents a city that has toyed with the problem of corruption for many years. No mayor in the history of the city of Wincanton has

From the President's Commission on Law Enforcement and Administration of Justice: Task Force Reports: Organized Crime, Appendix B, John A. Gardiner, with the assistance of David J. Olson, Wincanton: The Politics of Corruption, pp. 61-70, 78-79. Footnotes omitted.

ever succeeded himself in office. Some mayors have been corrupt and have allowed the city to become a wide-open center for gambling and prostitution; Wincanton voters have regularly rejected those corrupt mayors who dared to seek reelection. Some mayors have been scrupulously honest and have closed down all vice operations in the city; these men have been generally disliked for being too straitlaced. Other mayors, fearing one form of resentment or the other, have chosen quietly to retire from public life. The questions of official corruption and policy toward vice and gambling, it seems, have been paramount issues in Wincanton elections since the days of Prohibition. Any mayor who is known to be controlled by the gambling syndicates will lose office, but so will any mayor who tries completely to clean up the city. The people of Wincanton apparently want both easily accessible gambling and freedom from racket domination.

Probably more than most cities in the United States, Wincanton has known a high degree of gambling, vice (sexual immorality, including prostitution), and corruption (official malfeasance, misfeasance and nonfeasance of duties). With the exception of two reform administrations, one in the early 1950's and the one elected in the early 1960's, Wincanton has been wide open since the 1920's. Bookies taking bets on horses took in several millions of dollars each year. With writers at most newsstands, cigar counters, and corner grocery stores, a numbers bank did an annual business in excess of $1,300,000 during some years. Over 200 pinball machines, equipped to pay off like slot machines, bore $250 Federal gambling stamps. A high stakes dice game attracted professional gamblers from more than 100 miles away; $25,000 was found on the table during one Federal raid. For a short period of time in the 1950's (until raided by U.S. Treasury Department agents), a still, capable of manufacturing $1 million in illegal alcohol each year, operated on the banks of the Wincanton River. Finally, prostitution flourished openly in the city, with at least 5 large houses (about 10 girls apiece) and countless smaller houses catering to men from a large portion of the state.

As in all cities in which gambling and vice had flourished openly, these illegal activities were protected by local officials. Mayors, police chiefs, and many lesser officials were on the payroll of the gambling syndicate, while others received periodic "gifts" or aid during political campaigns. A number of Wincanton officials added to their revenue from the syndicate by extorting kickbacks on the sale or purchase of city equipment or by selling licenses, permits, zoning variances, etc. As the city officials made possible the operations of the racketeers, so frequently the racketeers facilitated the corrupt endeavors of officials by providing liaison men to arrange the deals or "enforcers" to insure that the deals were carried out.

The visitor to Wincanton is struck by the beauty of the surrounding countryside and the drabness of a tired, old central city. Looking down on the city from Mount Prospect, the city seems packed in upon itself, with long streets of red brick row houses pushing up against old railroad yards and factories; 93 percent of the housing units were built before 1940.

Wincanton had its largest population in 1930 and has been losing residents slowly ever since. The people who remained—those who didn't move to the suburbs or to the other parts of the United States—are the lower middle class, the less well educated; they seem old and often have an Old World feeling about them. The median age in Wincanton is 37 years (compared with a national median of 29 years). While unemployment is low (2.5 percent of the labor force in April 1965), there are few professional or white collar workers; only 11 percent of the families had incomes over $10,000, and the median family income was $5,453. As is common in many cities with an older, largely working class population, the level of education is low—only 27 percent of the adults have completed high school, and the median number of school years completed is 8.9.

While most migration into Wincanton took place before 1930, the various nationality groups in Wincanton seem to have retained their separate identities. The Germans, the Poles, the Italians, and the Negroes each have their own neighborhoods, stores, restaurants, clubs and politicians. Having immigrated earlier, the Germans are more assimilated into the middle and upper middle classes; the other groups still frequently live in the neighborhoods in which they first settled; and Italian and Polish politicians openly appeal to Old World loyalties. Club life adds to the ethnic groupings by giving a definite neighborhood quality to various parts of the city and their politics; every politician is expected to visit the ethnic association, ward clubs, and voluntary firemen's associations during campaign time—buying a round of drinks for all present and leaving money with the club stewards to hire poll watchers to advertise the candidates and guard the voting booths.

In part, the flight from Wincanton of the young and the more educated can be explained by the character of the local economy. While there have been no serious depressions in Wincanton during the last 30 years, there has been little growth either, and most of the factories in the city were built 30 to 50 years ago and rely primarily upon semiskilled workers. A few textile mills have moved out of the region, to be balanced by the construction in the last 5 years of several electronics assembly plants. No one employer dominates the economy, although seven employed more than 1,000 persons. Major industries today include steel fabrication and heavy machinery, textiles and food products.

With the exception of 2 years (one in the early 1950's the other 12 years later) in which investigations of corruption led to the election of Republican reformers, Wincanton politics have been heavily Democratic in recent years. Registered Democrats in the city outnumber Republicans by a margin of 2 to 1; in Alsace County as a whole, including the heavily Republican middle class suburbs, the Democratic margin is reduced to 3 to 2. Despite this margin of control, or possibly because of it, Democratic politics in Wincanton have always been somewhat chaotic candidates appeal to the ethnic groups, clubs, and neighborhoods, and no machine or organization has been able to dominate the party for very long (although a few men have been able to build a personal following lasting for 10 years or so). Incumbent mayors have been defeated in the primaries by other Democrats, and voting in city council sessions has crossed party lines more often than it has respected them.

To a great extent, party voting in Wincanton follows a business-labor cleavage. Two newspapers (both owned by a group of local businessmen) and the Chamber of Commerce support Republican candidates; the unions usually endorse Democrats. It would be unwise, however, to overestimate either the solidarity or the interest in local politics of Wincanton business and labor groups. Frequently two or more union leaders may be opposing each other in a Democratic primary (the steelworkers frequently endorse liberal or reform candidates, while the retail clerks have been more tied to "organization" men); or ethnic allegiance and hostilities may cause union members to vote for Republicans, or simply sit on their hands. Furthermore, both business and labor leaders express greater interest in State and National issues—taxation, wage and hour laws, collective bargaining policies, etc.—than in local issues. (The attitude of both business and labor toward Wincanton gambling and corruption will be examined in detail later.)

Many people feel that, apart from the perennial issue of corruption, there really are not any issues in Wincanton politics and that personalities are the only things that matter in city elections. Officials assume that the voters are generally opposed to a high level of public services. Houses are tidy, but the city has no public trash collection, or fire protection either, for that matter. While the city buys firetrucks and pays their drivers, firefighting is done solely by volunteers—in a city with more than 75,000 residents. (Fortunately, most of the houses are built of brick or stone.) Urban renewal has been slow, master planning nonexistent, and a major railroad line still crosses the heart of the shopping distruct, bringing traffic to a halt as trains grind past. Some people complain, but no mayor has ever been able to do anything about it. For years, people have been talking about rebuilding City Hall (constructed as a high school 75 years ago), modernizing mass transportation, and ending pollution of the Wincanton River, but nothing much has been done about any of these issues, or even seriously considered. Some people explain this by saying that Wincantonites are interested in everything—up to and including, but not extending beyond, their front porch.

If the voters of Wincanton were to prefer an active rather than passive city government, they would find the municipal structure well equipped to frustrate their desires. Many governmental functions are handled by independent boards and commissions, each able to veto proposals of the mayor and councilmen. Until about 10 years ago, State law required all middle-sized cities to operate under a modification of the commission form of government. (In the early 1960's, Wincanton voters narrowly by a margin of 16 votes out of 30,000 rejected a proposal to set up a council-manager plan.) The city council is composed of five men—a mayor and four councilmen. Every odd-numbered year, two councilmen are elected to 4-year terms. The mayor also has a 4-year term of office, but has a few powers not held by the councilmen; he presides at council sessions but has no veto power over council legislation. State law requires that city affairs be divided among five named departments, each to be headed by a member of the council, but the council members are free to decide among themselves what functions will be handled by which departments (with the proviso that the mayor must control the police department). Thus the city's work can be split equally among five men, or a three-man majority can control all important posts. In a not atypical recent occurrence, one councilman, disliked by his colleagues, found himself supervising only garbage collection and the Main Street comfort station! Each department head (mayor and councilmen) has almost complete control over his own department. Until 1960, when a $2,500 raise became effective, the mayor received an annual salary of $7,000, and each councilman received $6,000. The mayor and city councilmen have traditionally been permitted to hold other jobs while in office.

To understand law enforcement in Wincanton, it is necessary to look at the activities of local, county, State, and Federal agencies. State law requires that each mayor select his police chief and officers "from the force" and "exercise a constant supervision and control over their conduct." Applicants for the police force are chosen on the basis of a civil service examination and have tenure "during good behavior," but promotions and demotions are entirely at the discretion of the mayor and council. Each new administration in Wincanton has made wholesale changes in police ranks—patrolmen have been named chief, and former chiefs have been reduced to walking a beat. (When one period of reform came to an end in the mid-1950's, the incoming mayor summoned the old chief into his office, "You can stay on an officer," the mayor said, "but you'll have to go along with my policies regarding gambling.""Mr. Mayor," the chief said, "I'm going to keep on arresting gamblers no matter where you put me." The mayor assigned the former chief to the position of "Keeper of the Lockup," permanently stationed in the basement of police headquarters.) Promotions must be made from within the department. This policy has continued even though the present reform mayor created the post of police commissioner and brought in an outsider to take command. For cities of its size, Wincanton police salaries have been quite low—the top pay for patrolmen was $4,856—in the lowest quartile of middle-sized cities in the Nation. Since 1964 the commissioner has received $10,200 and patrolmen $5,400 each year.

While the police department is the prime law enforcement agency within Wincanton, it receives help (and occasional embarrassment) from other groups. Three county detectives work under the district attorney, primarily in rural parts of Alsace County, but they are occasionally called upon to assist in city investigations. The State Police, working out of a barracks in surburban Wincanton

Hills, have generally taken a "hands off" or "local option" attitude toward city crime, working only in rural areas unless invited into a city by the mayor, district attorney, or county judge. Reform mayors have welcomed the superior manpower and investigative powers of the State officers; corrupt mayors have usually been able to thumb their noses at State policemen trying to uncover Wincanton gambling. Agents of the State's Alcoholic Beverages Commission suffer from no such limitations and enter Wincanton at will in search of liquor violations. They have seldom been a serious threat to Wincanton corruption, however, since their numbers are quite limited (and thus the agents are dependent upon the local police for information and assistance in making arrests). Their mandate extends to gambling and prostitution only when encountered in the course of a liquor investigation.

Under most circumstances, the operative level of law enforcement in Wincanton has been set by local political decisions, and the local police (acting under instructions from the mayor) have been able to determine whether or not Wincanton should have open gambling and prostitution. The State Police, with their "hands off" policy, have simply reenforced the local decision. From time to time, however, Federal agencies have become interested in conditions in Wincanton and, as will be seen throughout this study, have played as important a role as the local police in cleaning up the city. Internal Revenue Service agents have succeeded in prosecuting Wincanton gamblers for failure to hold gambling occupation stamps, pay the special excise taxes on gambling receipts, or report income. Federal Bureau of Investigation agents have acted against violations of the Federal laws against extortion and interstate gambling. Finally, special attorneys from the Organized Crime and Racketeering Section of the Justice Department were able to convict leading members of the syndicate controlling Wincanton gambling. While Federal prosecutions in Wincanton have often been spectacular, it should also be noted that they have been somewhat sporadic and limited in scope. The Internal Revenue Service, for example, was quite successful in seizing gambling devices and gamblers lacking the Federal gambling occupation stamps, but it was helpless after Wincantonites began to purchase the stamps, since local officials refused to prosecute them for violations of the State antigambling laws.

The court system in Wincanton, as in all cities in the State, still has many of the 18th century features which have been rejected in other States. At the lowest level, elected magistrates (without legal training) hear petty civil and criminal cases in each ward of the city. The magistrates also issue warrants and decide whether persons arrested by the police shall be held for trial. Magistrates are paid only by fees, usually at the expense of convicted defendants. All serious criminal cases, and all contested petty cases, are tried in the county court. The three judges of the Alsace County court are elected (on a partisan ballot) for 10-year terms, and receive an annual salary of $25,000.

GAMBLING AND CORRUPTION: THE INSIDERS

The Stern Empire

The history of Wincanton gambling and corruption since World War II centers around the career of Irving Stern. Stern is an immigrant who came to the United States and settled in Wincanton at the turn of the century. He started as a fruit peddler, but when Prohibition came along, Stern became a bootlegger for Heinz Glickman, then the beer baron of the State. When Glickman was murdered in the waning days of Prohibition, Stern took over Glickman's business and continued to sell untaxed liquor after repeal of Prohibition in 1933. Several times during the 1930's, Stern was convicted in Federal court on liquor charges and spent over a year in Federal prison.

Around 1940, Stern announced to the world that he had reformed and went into his family's wholesale produce business. While Stern was in fact leaving the bootlegging trade, he was also moving into the field of gambling, for even at that time Wincanton had a "wide-open" reputation, and the police were ignoring gamblers. With the technical assistance of his bootlegging friends, Stern started with a numbers bank and soon added horse betting, a dice game, and slot machines to his organization. During World War II, officers from a nearby Army training base insisted that all brothels be closed, but this did not affect Stern. He had already concluded that public hostility and violence, caused by the horses, were, as a side effect, threatening his more profitable gambling operations. Although Irv Stern controlled the lion's share of Wincanton gambling throughout the 1940's, he had to share the slot machine trade with Klaus Braun. Braun, unlike Stern, was a Wincanton native and a Gentile, and thus had easier access to the frequently anti-Semitic club stewards, restaurant owners, and bartenders who decided which machines would be placed in their buildings. Legislative investigations in the early 1950's estimated that Wincanton gambling was an industry with gross receipts of $5 million each year; at that time Stern was receiving $40,000 per week from bookmaking, and Braun took in $75,000 to $100,000 per year from slot machines alone.

Irv Stern's empire in Wincanton collapsed abruptly when legislative investigations brought about the election of a reform Republican administration. Mayor Hal Craig decided to seek what he termed "pearl gray purity" to tolerate isolated prostitutes, bookies, and numbers writers but to drive out all forms of organized crime, all activities lucrative enough to make it worth someone's while to try bribing Craig's police officials. Within 6 weeks after taking office, Craig and District Attorney Henry Weiss had raided enough of Stern's gambling parlors and seized enough of Braun's slot machines to convince both men that business was over for 4 years at least. The Internal Revenue Service was able to convict Braun and Stern's nephew, Dave Feinman, on tax evasion charges; both were sent to jail. From 1952 to 1955 it was still possible to place a bet or find a girl. But you had to know someone to do it, and no one was getting very rich in the process.

By 1955 it was apparent to everyone that reform sentiment was dead and that the Democrats would soon be back in office. In the summer of that year, Stern met with representatives of the east coast syndicates and arranged for the rebuilding of his empire. He decided to change his method of operations in several ways; one way was by centralizing all Wincanton vice and gambling under his control. But he also decided to turn the actual operation of most enterprises over to others. From the mid-1950's until the next wave of reform hit Wincanton after elections in the early 1960's, Irv Stern generally succeeded in reaching these goals.

The financial keystone of Stern's gambling empire was numbers betting. Records seized by the Internal Revenue

Service in the late 1950's and early 1960's indicated that gross receipts from numbers amounted to more than $100,000 each month, or $1.3 million annually. Since the numbers are a poor man's form of gambling (bets range from a penny to a dime or quarter), a large number of men and a high degree of organization are required. The organizational goals are three; have the maximum possible number of men on the streets seeking bettors, be sure that they are reporting honestly, and yet strive so to decentralize the organization that no one, if arrested, will be able to identify many of the others. During the "pearl gray purity" of Hal Craig, numbers writing was completely unorganized, many isolated writers took bets from their friends and frequently had to renege if an unusually popular number came up; no one writer was big enough to guard against such possibilities. When a new mayor took office in the mid-1950's, however, Stern's lieutenants notified each of the small writers that they were now working for Stern or else. Those who objected were "persuaded" by Stern's men, or else arrested by the police, as were any of the others who were suspected of holding out on their receipts. Few objected for very long. After Stern completed the reorganization of the numbers business, its structure was roughly something like this; 11 subbanks reported to Stern's central accounting office. Each subbank employed from 5 to 30 numbers writers. Thirty-five percent of the gross receipts went to the writers. After deducting for winnings and expenses (mostly protection payoffs), Stern divided the net profits equally with the operators of the subbanks. In return for his cut, Stern provided protection from the police and "laid off" the subbanks, covering winnings whenever a popular number "broke" one of the smaller operators.

Stern also shared with out-of-State syndicates in the profits and operation of two enterprises, a large dice game and the largest still found by the Treasury Department since Prohibition. The dice game employed over 50 men drivers to "lug" players into town from as far as 100 miles away, doormen to check players' identities, loan sharks who "faded" the losers, croupiers, food servers, guards, etc. The 1960 payroll for these employees was over $350,000. While no estimate of the gross receipts from the game is available, some indication of its size can be obtained from the fact that $50,000 was found on the tables and in the safe when the FBI raided the game in 1962. Over 100 players were arrested during the raid; one businessman had lost over $75,000 at the tables. Stern received a share of the game's profits plus a $1,000 weekly fee to provide protection from the police.

Stern also provided protection (for a fee) and shared in the profits of a still, erected in an old warehouse on the banks of the Wincanton River and tied into the city's water and sewer systems. Stern arranged for clearance by the city council and provided protection from the local police after the $200,000 worth of equipment was set up. The still was capable of producing $4 million worth of alcohol each year, and served a five-State area, until Treasury agents raided it after it had been in operation for less than 1 year.

The dice game and the still raise questions regarding the relationship of Irv Stern to out-of-State syndicates. Republican politicians in Wincanton frequently claimed that Stern was simply the local agent of the Cosa Nostra. While Stern was regularly sending money to the syndicates, the evidence suggests that Stern was much more than an agent for outsiders. It would be more accurate to regard these payments as profit sharing with coinvestors and as charges for services rendered. The east coasters provided technical services in the operation of the dice game and still and "enforcement" service for the Wincanton gambling operation. When deviants had to be persuaded to accept Stern's domination, Stern called upon outsiders for "muscle" strong-arm men who could not be traced by local police if the victim chose to protest. In the early 1940's, for example, Stern asked for help in destroying a competing dice game; six gunmen came in and held it up, robbing and terrifying the players. While a few murders took place in the struggle for supremacy in the 1930's and 1940's, only a few people were roughed up in the 1950's and no one was killed.

After the mid-1950's, Irv Stern controlled prostitution and several forms of gambling on a "franchise" basis. Stern took no part in the conduct of these businesses and received no share of the profits, but exacted a fee for protection from the police. Several horse books, for example, operated regularly; the largest of these paid Stern $600 per week. While slot machines had permanently disappeared from the Wincanton scene after the legislative investigations of the early 1950's, a number of men began to distribute pinball machines, which paid off players for games won. As was the case with numbers writers, these pinball distributors had been unorganized during The Craig administration. When Democratic Mayor Gene Donnelly succeeded Craig, he immediately announced that all pinball machines were illegal and would be confiscated by the police. A Stern agent then contacted the pinball distributors and notified them that if they employed Dave Feinman (Irv Stern's nephew) as a "public relations consultant," there would be no interference from the police. Several rebellious distributors formed an Alsace

County Amusement Operators Association, only to see Feinman appear with two thugs from New York. After the association president was roughed up, all resistance collapsed, and Feinman collected $2,000 each week to promote the "public relations" of the distributors. (Stern, of course, was able to offer no protection against Federal action. After the Internal Revenue Service began seizing the pinball machines in 1956, the owners were forced to purchase the $250 Federal gambling stamps as well as paying Feinman. Over 200 Wincanton machines bore these stamps in the early 1960's, and thus were secure from Federal as well as local action.) In the 1950's, Irv Stern was able to establish a centralized empire in which he alone determined which rackets would operate and who would operate them (he never, it might be noted, permitted narcotics traffic in the city while he controlled it). What were the bases of his control within the criminal world? Basically, they were three: First, as a business matter, Stern controlled access to several very lucrative operations, and could quickly deprive an uncooperative gambler or numbers writer of his source of income. Second, since he controlled the police department he could arrest any gamblers or bookies who were not paying tribute. (Some of the local gambling and prostitution arrests which took place during the Stern era served another purpose—to placate newspaper demands for a crackdown. As one police chief from this era phrased it, "Hollywood should have given us an Oscar for some of our performances when we had to pull a phony raid to keep the papers happy.") Finally, if the mechanisms of fear of financial loss and fear of police arrest failed to command obedience, Stern was always able to keep alive a fear of physical violence. As we have seen, numbers writers, pinball distributors, and competing gamblers were brought into line after outside enforcers put in an appearance. Stern's regular collection agent, a local tough who had been convicted of murder in the 1940's, was a constant reminder of the virtues of cooperation. Several witnesses who told grand juries or Federal agents of extortion attempts by Stern, received visits from Stern enforcers and tended to "forget" when called to testify against the boss.

Protection. An essential ingredient in Irv Stern's Wincanton operations was protection against law enforcement agencies. While he was never able to arrange freedom from Federal intervention (although, as in the case of purchasing excise stamps for the pinball machines, he was occasionally able to satisfy Federal requirements without disrupting his activities), Stern was able in the 1940's and again from the mid-1950's through the early 1960's to secure freedom from State and local action. The precise extent of Stern's network of proection payments is unknown, but the method of operations can be reconstructed.

Two basic principles were involved in the Wincanton protection system—pay top personnel as much as necessary to keep them happy (and quiet), and pay something to as many others as possible to implicate them in the system and to keep them from talking. The range of payoffs thus went from a weekly salary for some public officials to a Christmas turkey for the patrolman on the beat. Records from the numbers bank listed payments totaling $2,400 each week to some local elected officials, State legislators, the police chief, a captain in charge of detectives, and persons mysteriously labeled "county" and "State." While the list of persons to be paid remained fairly constant, the amounts paid varied according to the gambling activities in operation at the time; pay-off figures dropped sharply when the FBI put the dice game out of business. When the dice game was running, one official was receiving $750 per week, the chief $100, and a few captains, lieutenants, and detectives lesser amounts.

While the number of officials receiving regular "salary" payoffs was quite restricted (only 15 names were on the payroll found at the numbers bank), many other officials were paid off in different ways. (Some men were also silenced without charge—low-ranking policemen, for example, kept quiet after they learned that men who reported gambling or prostitution were ignored or transferred to the midnight shift; they didn't have to be paid.) Stern was a major (if undisclosed) contributor during political campaigns—sometimes giving money to all candidates, not caring who won, sometimes supporting a "regular" to defeat a possible reformer, sometimes paying a candidate not to oppose a preferred man. Since there were few legitimate sources of large contributions for Democratic candidates, Stern's money was frequently regarded as essential for victory, for the costs of buying radio and television time and paying pollwatchers were high. When popular sentiment was running strongly in favor of reform, however, even Stern's contributions could not guarantee victory. Bob Walasek, later to be as corrupt as any Wincanton mayor, ran as a reform candidate in the Democratic primary and defeated Stern-financed incumbent Gene Donnelly. Never a man to bear grudges, Stern financed Walasek in the general election that year and put him on the "payroll" when he took office.

Even when local officials were not on the regular payroll, Stern was careful to remind them of his friendship (and their debts). A legislative investigating committee found that Stern had given mortgage loans to a police lieutenant and the police chief's son. County Court Judge Ralph Vaughan recalled that shortly after being elected (with Stern support), he received a call from Dave Feinman, Stern's nephew, "Congratulations, judge. When do you think you and your wife would like a vacation in Florida?"

"Florida? Why on earth would I want to go there?"

"But all the other judges and the guys in City Hall—Irv takes them all to Florida whenever they want to get away."

"Thanks anyway, but I'm not interested."

"Well, how about a mink coat instead. What size coat does your wife wear?"

In another instance an assistant district attorney told of Feinman's arriving at his front door with a large basket from Stern's supermarket just before Christmas. "My minister suggested a needy family that could use the food," the assistant district attorney recalled, "but I returned the liquor to Feinman. How could I ask a minister if he knew someone that could use three bottles of scotch?"

Campaign contributions, regular payments to higher officials, holiday and birthday gifts—these were the bases of the system by which Irv Stern bought protection from the law. The campaign contributions usually ensured that complacent mayors, councilmen, district attorneys, and judges were elected; payoffs in some instances usually kept their loyalty. In a number of ways, Stern was also able to reward the corrupt officials at no financial cost to himself. Just as the officials, being in control of the instruments of law enforcement, were able to facilitate Stern's gambling enterprises, so Stern, in control of a network of men operating outside the law, was able to facilitate the officials' corrupt enterprises. As will be seen later, many local officials were not satisfied with their legal salaries from the city and their illegal salaries from Stern and decided to demand payments from prostitutes, kickbacks from salesmen, etc. Stern, while seldom receiving any money from these transactions, became a broker; bringing politicians into contact with salesmen, merchants, and lawyers willing to offer bribes to get city business; setting up middlemen who could handle the money without jeopardizing the officials' reputations; and providing enforcers who could bring delinquents into line.

From the corrupt activities of Wincanton officials, Irv Stern received little in contrast to his receipts from his gambling operations. Why then did he get involved in them? The major virtue, from Stern's point of view, of the system of extortion that flourished in Wincanton was that it kept down the officials' demands for payoffs directly from Stern. If a councilman was able to pick up $1,000 on the purchase of city equipment, he would demand a lower payment for the protection of gambling. Furthermore, since Stern knew the facts of extortion in each instance, the officials would be further implicated in the system and less able to back out on the arrangements regarding gambling. Finally, as Stern discovered to his chagrin, it became necessary to supervise official extortion to protect the officials against their own stupidity. Mayor Gene Donnelly was cooperative and remained satisfied with his regular "salary." Bob Walasek, however, was a greedy man, and seized every opportunity to profit from a city contract. Soon Stern found himself supervising many of Walasek's deals to keep the mayor from blowing the whole arrangement wide open. When Walasek tried to double the "take" on a purchase of parking meters, Stern had to step in and set the contract price, pro-vide an untraceable middleman, and see the deal through to completion. "I told Irv," Police Chief Phillips later testified, "that Walasek wanted $12 on each meter instead of the $6 we got on the last meter deal. He became furious. He said, 'Walasek is going to fool around and wind up in jail. You come and see me. I'll tell Walasek what he's going to buy.'"

Protection, it was stated earlier, was an essential ingredient in Irv Stern's gambling empire. In the end, Stern's downfall came not from a flaw in the organization of the gambling enterprises but from public exposure of the corruption of Mayor Walasek and other officials. In the early 1960's Stern was sent to jail for 4 years on tax evasion charges, but the gambling empire continued to operate smoothly in his absence. A year later, however, Chief Phillips was caught perjuring himself in grand jury testimony concerning kickbacks on city towing contracts. Phillips "blew the whistle" on Stern, Walasek, and members of the city council, and a reform administration was swept into office. Irv Stern's gambling empire had been worth several million dollars each year; kickbacks on the towing contracts brought Bob Walasek a paltry $50 to $75 each week.

OFFICIAL CORRUPTION

Textbooks on municipal corporation law speak of at least three varieties of official corruption. The major categories are nonfeasance (failing to perform a required duty at all), malfeasance (the commission of some act which is positively unlawful), and misfeasance (the improper performance of some act which a man may properly do). During the years in which Irv Stern was running his gambling operations, Wincanton officials were guilty of all of these. Some residents say that Bob Walasek came to regard the mayor's office as a brokerage, levying a tariff on every item that came across his desk. Sometimes a request for simple municipal services turned into a game of cat and mouse, with Walasek sitting on the request, waiting to see how much would be offered, and the petitioner waiting to see if he could obtain his rights without having to pay for them. Corruption was not as lucrative an enterprise as gambling, but it offered a tempting supplement to low official salaries.

Nonfeasance

As was detailed earlier, Irv Stern saw to it that Wincanton officials would ignore at least one of their statutory duties, enforcement of the State's gambling laws. Bob Walasek and his cohorts also agreed to overlook other illegal activities. Stern, we noted earlier, preferred not to get directly involved in prostitution; Walasek and Police Chief Dave Phillips tolerated all prostitutes who kept up their protection payments. One madam, controlling more than 20 girls, gave Phillips et al. $500 each week; one woman employing only one girl paid $75 each week that she was in business. Operators of a carnival in rural Alsace County paid a public official $5,000 for the privilege of operating gambling tents for 5 nights each summer. A burlesque theater manager, under attack by high school teachers, was ordered to pay $25 each week for the privilege of keeping his strip show open.

Many other city and county officials must be termed guilty of nonfeasance, although there is no evidence that they received payoffs, and although they could present reasonable excuses for their inaction. Most policemen, as we have noted earlier, began to ignore prostitution and gambling completely after their

reports of offenses were ignored or superior officers told them to mind their own business. State policemen, well informed about city vice and gambling conditions, did nothing unless called upon to act by local officials. Finally, the judges of the Alsace County Court failed to exercise their power to call for State Police investigations. In 1957, following Federal raids on horse bookies, the judges did request an investigation by the State Attorney General, but refused to approve his suggestion that a grand jury be convened to continue the investigation. For each of these instances of inaction, a tenable excuse might be offered—the beat patrolman should not be expected to endure harassment from his superior officers, State police gambling raids in a hostile city might jeopardize State-local cooperation on more serious crimes, and a grand jury probe might easily be turned into a "whitewash" in the hands of a corrupt district attorney. In any event, powers available to these law enforcement agencies for the prevention of gambling and corruption were not utilized.

Malfeasance

In fixing parking and speeding tickets, Wincanton politicians and policemen committed malfeasance, or committed an act they were forbidden to do, by illegally compromising valid civil and criminal actions. Similarly, while State law provides no particular standards by which the mayor is to make promotions within his police department, it was obviously improper for Mayor Walasek to demand a "political contribution" of $10,000 from Dave Phillips before he was appointed chief in 1960.

The term "political contribution" raises a serious legal and analytical problem in classifying the malfeasance of Wincanton officials, and indeed of politicians in many cities. Political campaigns cost money; citizens have a right to support the candidates of their choice; and officials have a right to appoint their backers to noncivil service positions. At some point, however, threats or oppression convert legitimate requests for political contributions into extortion. Shortly after taking office in the mid-1950's, Mayor Gene Donnelly notified city hall employees that they would be expected "voluntarily" to contribute 2 percent of their salary to the Democratic Party. (It might be noted that Donnelly never forwarded any of these "political contributions" to the party treasurer.) A number of salesmen doing business with the city were notified that companies which had supported the party would receive favored treatment; Donnelly notified one salesman that in light of a proposed $31,000 contract for the purchase of fire engines, a "political contribution" of $2,000 might not be inappropriate. While neither the city hall employees nor the salesmen had rights to their positions or their contracts, the "voluntary" quality of their contributions seems questionable.

One final, in the end almost ludicrous, example of malfeasance came with Mayor Donnelly's abortive "War on the Press." Following a series of gambling raids by the Internal Revenue Service, the newspapers began asking why the local police had not participated in the raids. The mayor lost his temper and threw a reporter in jail. Policemen were instructed to harass newspaper delivery trucks, and 73 tickets were written over a 48-hour period for supposed parking and traffic violations. Donnelly soon backed down after national news services picked up the story, since press coverage made him look ridiculous. Charges against the reporter were dropped, and the newspapers continued to expose gambling and corruption.

Misfeasance

Misfeasance in office, says the common law, is the improper performance of some act which a man may properly do. City officials must buy and sell equipment, contract for services, and allocate licenses, privileges, etc. These actions can be improperly performed if either the results are improper (e.g., if a building inspector were to approve a home with defective wiring or a zoning board to authorize a variance which had no justification in terms of land usage) or a result is achieved by improper procedures (e.g., if the city purchased an acceptable automobile in consideration of a bribe paid to the purchasing agent). In the latter case, we can usually assume an improper result as well—while the automobile will be satisfactory, the bribe giver will probably have inflated the sale price to cover the costs of the bribe.

In Wincanton, it was rather easy for city officials to demand kickbacks, for State law frequently does not demand competitive bidding or permits the city to ignore the lowest bid. The city council is not required to advertise or take bids on purchases under $1,000, contracts for maintenance of streets and other public works, personal or professional services, or patented or copyrighted products. Even when bids must be sought, the council is only required to award the contract to the lowest responsible bidder. Given these permissive provisions, it was relatively easy for council members to justify or disguise contracts in fact based upon bribes. The exemption for patented products facilitated bribe taking on the purchase of two emergency trucks for the police department (with a $500 campaign contribution on a $7,500 deal), three fire engines ($2,000 was allegedly paid on an $81,000 contract), and 1,500 parking meters (involving payments of $10,500 plus an $880 clock for Mayor Walasek's home). Similar fees were allegedly exacted in connection with the purchase of a city fire alarm system and police uniforms and firearms. A former mayor and other officials also profited on the sale of city property, allegedly dividing $500 on the sale of a crane and $20,000 for approving the sale, for $22,000, of a piece of land immediately resold for $75,000.

When contracts involved services to the city, the provisions in the State law regarding the lowest responsible bidder and excluding "professional services" from competitive bidding provided convenient loopholes. One internationally known engineering firm refused to agree to kickback in order to secure a contract to design a $15 million sewage disposal plant for the city; a local firm was then appointed, which paid $10,700 of its $225,000 fee to an associate of Irv Stern and Mayor Donnelly as a "finder's fee." Since the State law also excludes public works maintenance contracts from the competitive bidding requirements, many city paving and street repair contracts during the Donnelly-Walasek era were given to a contributor to the Democratic Party. Finally, the franchise for towing illegally parked cars and cars involved in accidents was awarded to two garages which were then required to kickback $1 for each car towed.

The handling of graft on the towing contracts illustrates the way in which minor violence and the "lowest responsible bidder" clause could be used to keep the bribe payers in line. After Federal investigators began to look into Wincanton corruption, the owner of one of the garages with a towing franchise testified before the grand jury. Mayor Walasek immediately withdrew his franchise, citing "health violations" at the garage. The garageman was also "encouraged" not to testify by a series of "accidents"—wheels would fall off towtrucks on the highway, steering cables were cut, and so forth. Newspaper satirization of the "health violations" forced the restoration of the towing franchise, and the "accidents" ceased.

Lest the reader infer that the "lowest responsible bidder" clause was used as an escape valve only for corrupt purposes, one incident might be noted which took place under the present reform administration. In 1964, the Wincanton School Board sought bids for the renovation of an athletic field. The lowest bid came from a construction company owned by Dave Phillips, the corrupt police chief who had served formerly under Mayor Walasek. While the company was presumably competent to carry out the assignment, the board rejected Phillips' bid "because of a question as to his moral responsibility." The board did not specify whether this referred to his poor corruption as chief or his present status as an informer in testifying against Walasek and Stern.

One final area of city power, which was abused by Walasek et al., covered discretionary acts, such as granting permits and allowing zoning variances. On taking office, Walasek took the unusual step of asking that the bureaus of building and plumbing inspection be put under the mayor's control. With this power to approve or deny building permits, Walasek "sat on" applications, waiting until the petitioner contributed $50 or $75, or threatened to sue to get his permit. Some building designs were not approved until a favored architect was retained as a "consultant." (It is not known whether this involved kickbacks to Walasek or simply patronage for a friend.) At least three instances are known in which developers were forced to pay for zoning variances before apartment buildings or supermarkets could be erected. Businessmen who wanted to encourage rapid turnover of the curb space in front of their stores were told to pay a police sergeant to erect "10-minute parking" signs. To repeat a caveat stated earlier, it is impossible to tell whether these kickbacks were demanded to expedite legitimate requests or to approve improper demands, such as a variance that would hurt a neighborhood or a certificate approving improper electrical work.

All of the activities detailed thus far involve fairly clear violations of the law. To complete the picture of the abuse of office by Wincanton officials, we might briefly mention "honest graft." This term was best defined by one of its earlier practitioners, State Senator George Washington Plunkitt who loyally served Tammany Hall at the turn of the century.

There's all the difference in the world between [honest and dishonest graft]. Yes, many of our men have grown rich in politics. I have myself.

I've made a big fortune out of the game, and I'm gettin' richer every day, but I've not gone in for dishonest graft—blackmailin' gamblers, saloonkeepers, disorderly people, etc.—and neither has any of the men who have made big fortunes in politics.

There's an honest graft, and I'm an example of how it works. I might sum up the whole thing by saying': "I seen my opportunities and I took 'em."

Let me explain by examples. My party's in power in the city, and it's goin' to undertake a lot of public improvements. Well, I'm tipped off, say, that they're going to lay out a new park at a certain place.

I see my opportunity and I take it. I go to that place, and I buy up all the land I can in the neighborhood. Then the board of this or that makes its plan public, and there is a rush to get my land, which nobody cared particular for before.

Ain't it perfectly honest to charge a good price and make a profit on my investment and foresight? Of course, it is. Well, that's honest graft.

While there was little in the way of land purchasing—either honest or dishonest—going on in Wincanton during this period, several officials who carried on their own businesses while in office were able to pick up some "honest graft." One city councilman with an accounting office served as bookkeeper for Irv Stern and the major bookies and prostitutes in the city.

Police Chief Phillips' construction firm received a contract to remodel the exterior of the largest brothel in town. Finally one councilman serving in the present reform administration received a contract to construct all gasoline stations built in the city by a major petroleum company; skeptics say that the contract was the quid pro quo for the councilman's vote to give the company the contract to sell gasoline to the city.

How Far Did It Go? This cataloging of acts of nonfeasance, malfeasance, and misfeasance by Wincanton officials raises a danger of confusing variety with universality, of assuming that every employee of the city was either engaged in corrupt activities or was being paid to ignore the corruption of others. On the contrary, both official investigations and private research lead to the conclusion that there is no reason whatsoever to question the honesty of the vast majority of the employees of the city of Wincanton. Certainly no more than 10 of the 155 members of the Wincanton police force were on Irv Stern's payroll (although as many as half of them may have accepted petty Christmas presents—turkeys or liquor.) In each department, there were a few employees who objected actively to the misdeeds of their superiors, and the only charge that can justly be leveled against the mass of employees is that they were unwilling to jeopardize their employment by publicly exposing what was going on. When Federal investigators showed that an honest (and possibly successful) attempt was being made to expose Stern-Walasek corruption, a number of city employees cooperated with the grand jury in aggregating evidence which could be used to convict the corrupt officials.

Before these Federal investigations began, however, it could reasonably appear to an individual employee that the entire machinery of law enforcement in the city was controlled by Stern, Walasek, et al., and that an individual protest would be silenced quickly. This can be illustrated by the momentary crusade conducted by First Assistant District Attorney Phil Roper in the summer of 1962. When the district attorney left for a short vacation, Roper decided to act against the gamblers and madams in the city. With the help of the State Police, Roper raided several large brothels. Apprehending on the street the city's largest distributor of punchboards and lotteries, Roper effected a citizen's arrest and drove him to police headquarters for proper detention and questioning. "I'm sorry, Mr. Roper," said the desk sergeant, "we're under orders not to arrest persons brought in by you." Roper was forced to call upon the State Police for aid in confining the gambler. When the district attorney returned from his vacation, he quickly fired Roper "for introducing politics into the district attorney's office."

If it is incorrect to say that Wincanton corruption extended very far vertically into the rank and file of the various departments of the city—how far did it extend horizontally? How many branches and levels of government were affected? With the exception of the local Congressman and the city treasurer, it seems that a few personnel at each level (city, county, and State) and in most offices in city hall can be identified either with Stern or with some form of free-lance corruption. A number of local judges received campaign finances from Stern, although there is no evidence that they were on his payroll after they were elected. Several State legislators were on Stern's payroll, and one Republican councilman charged that a high-ranking State Democratic official promised Stern first choice of all Alsace County patronage. The county chairman, he claimed, was only to receive the jobs that Stern did not want. While they were later to play an active role in disrupting Wincanton gambling, the district attorney in Hal Craig's reform administration feared that the State Police were on Stern's payroll, and thus refused to use them in city gambling raids.

Within the city administration, the evidence is fairly clear that some mayors and councilmen received regular payments from Stern and divided kickbacks on city purchases and sales. Some key subcouncil personnel frequently shared in payoffs affecting their particular departments—the police chief shared in the gambling and prostitution payoffs and received $300 of the $10,500 kickback on parking meter purchases. A councilman controlling one department, for example, might get a higher percentage of kickbacks than the other councilmen in contracts involving that department.

The Future of Reform in Wincanton

When Wincantonites are asked what kind of law enforcement they want, they are likely to say that it is all right to tolerate petty gambling and prostitution, but that "you've got to keep out racketeers and corrupt politicians." Whenever they come to feel that the city is being controlled by these racketeers, they "throw the rascals out." This policy of "throwing the rascals out," however, illustrates the dilemma facing reformers in Wincanton. Irv Stern, recently released from Federal prison, has probably, in fact, retired from the rackets; he is ill and plans to move to Arizona. Bob Walasek, having been twice convicted on extortion charges, is finished politically. Therefore? Therefore, the people of Wincanton firmly believe that "the problem" has been solved—"the rascals" have been thrown out. When asked, recently, what issues would be important in the next local elections, only 9 of 183 respondents felt that clean government or keeping out vice and gambling might be an issue. (Fifty-five percent had no opinion, 15 percent felt that the ban on bingo might be an issue, and 12 percent cited urban renewal, a subject frequently mentioned in the papers preceding the survey.) Since, under Ed Whitton, the city is being honestly run and is free from gambling and prostitution, there is no problem to worry about.

On balance, it seems far more likely to conclude that gambling and corruption will soon return to Wincanton (although possibly in less blatant forms) for two reasons—first, a significant number of people want to be able to gamble or make improper deals with the city government. (This assumes, of course, that racketeers will be available to provide gambling if a complacent city administration permits it.)

Second, and numerically far more important, most voters think that the problem has been permanently solved, and thus they will not be choosing candidates based on these issues, in future elections.

Throughout this report, a number of specific recommendations have been made to minimize opportunities for wide open gambling and corruption—active State Police intervention in city affairs, modification of the city's contract bidding policies, extending civil service protection to police officers, etc. On balance, we could probably also state that the commission form of government has been a hindrance to progressive government; a "strong mayor" form of government would probably handle the city's affairs more efficiently. Fundamentally, however, all of these suggestions are irrelevant. When the voters have called for clean government, they have gotten it, in spite of loose bidding laws, limited civil service, etc. The critical factor has been voter preference. Until the voters of Wincanton come to believe that illegal gambling produces the corruption they have known, the type of government we have documented will continue. Four-year periods of reform do little to change the habits instilled over 40 years of gambling and corruption.